Introduction to
HOMELAND SECURITY

Daniel Byram, Editor

Taken from:

Emergency Planning and Security Measures I
by Matthew Pope

Terrorism in the Twenty-First Century, Third Edition
by Cindy C. Combs

Current Events in Homeland Security
by Daniel Byram

Terrorism: A Growth Industry and the Intelligence Analyst
by General Richard Wilmot

Anti-Terrorism Risk Assessments: Effective Profiles, Predictions and Prevention
by Marcus Mann

Catastrophic Event Prevention Planning
by Irmak Renda-Tanali and Claire B. Rubin

Catastrophic Event Response Planning
by Matthew Pope with James Biesterfeld

Tactical Communications, Revised Edition
by Dr. Julie Brown

Moving Forward When Others Move Back: Managing Critical Incidents
by Victor Herbert

Custom Publishing

New York   Boston   San Francisco
London   Toronto   Sydney   Tokyo   Singapore   Madrid
Mexico City   Munich   Paris   Cape Town   Hong Kong   Montreal

Pearson
Custom Publishing
is a division of

PEARSON

www.pearsonhighered.com

ISBN 10: 0-536-13276-3
ISBN 13: 978-0-536-13276-5

Copyright Acknowledgments

Grateful acknowledgment is made to the following sources for permission to reprint material copyrighted or controlled by them:

Table of Contents

CHAPTER TWO

The Motivations of Terrorism and Target Selection   39

CHAPTER THREE

Intelligence   97

CHAPTER FOUR

Critical Infrastructure   155

CHAPTER FIVE

Cyber Terrorism   193

CHAPTER SIX

Transportation   223

CHAPTER SEVEN

Public Health   259

CHAPTER EIGHT

National Response Framework (NRF)   287

CHAPTER NINE

Disaster Management   311

CHAPTER TEN

Incident Command System (ICS)   361

CHAPTER ELEVEN

All-Hazards Approach   413

CHAPTER TWELVE

ICS Roles and Procedures   449

CHAPTER THIRTEEN

Ethics & the Art of War   503

CHAPTER **14**

Emergency Communications and Technology   543

Emergency Communications and Technology   543

Careers and the Role of Education   569

Content was taken from the following sources:
Chapter 1: *Emergency Planning and Security Measures 1,* ISBN 0536833648
Chapter 2: *Current Events in Homeland Security,* ISBN 0536822719
Terrorism in the 21st Century, Third Edition by Cindy C. Combs, ISBN 0130975192
Terrorism: A Growth Industry and the Intelligence Analyst, ISBN 0536822794
Chapter 3: *Current Events in Homeland Security,* ISBN 0536822719
Chapter 4: *Current Events in Homeland Security,* ISBN 0536822719
Anti-Terrorism Risk Assessments, ISBN 0536905576
Chapter 5: *Current Events in Homeland Security,* ISBN 0536822719
Terrorism in the 21st Century, Third Edition by Cindy C. Combs, ISBN 0130975192
Chapter 6: *Managing Change through Post-Event Evaluations,* ISBN 0536941564
Chapter 7: *Current Events in Homeland Security,* ISBN 0536822719
Managing Change through Post-Event Evaluations, ISBN 0536941564
Chapter 8: *Catastrophic Event Prevention Planning,* ISBN 0536941556
Chapter 9: *Catastrophic Event Prevention Planning,* ISBN 0536941556
Chapter 10: *Catastrophic Event Response Planning,* ISBN 053695416X
Chapter 11: *Catastrophic Event Prevention Planning,* ISBN 0536941556
Chapter 12: *Moving Forward When Others Move Back: Managing Critical Incidents,* ISBN 0536822743
Chapter 13: *Current Events in Homeland Security,* ISBN 0536822719
Managing Change Through Post-Event Evaluations, ISBN 0536941564
Chapter 14: *Tactical Communications,* ISBN 0536822727

CHAPTER ONE

WHAT IS HOMELAND SECURITY?

Let our advance worrying become advance thinking and planning.
—Winston Churchill

KEY TERMS

Homeland Security
All Hazards Approach
Department of Homeland Security
Homeland Security Strategy
Terrorism
Border Security
Smart Borders
Aviation and Transportation Security Act
Counter Terrorism
Infrastructure
Super Terrorism
USA Patriot Act
NORCOM
NORAD

OBJECTIVES

- Describe how national security policy was viewed and reported prior to 9/11.

- Compare approaches to national security before and after the 9/11 attacks.

- Examine the circumstances leading to the creation of the Department of Homeland Security (DHS).

- Describe the Patriot Act and its impact on national security policy.

DISCUSSION TOPICS

- How would you define homeland security?

- What are the major factors that make securing the country so difficult?

- What strategic goals would you set for developing a security plan for the country?

1

INTRODUCTION

Homeland security may be one of the most subjective terms in the American vernacular. It holds a variety of meanings for different people based on their personal and professional background, their training, and their education. For example, when asked to describe homeland security one might say *terrorism*, *disaster response*, *emergency planning*, *military operations*, and *law enforcement*. Any and all of these terms are elements of homeland security.

Homeland security may be interpreted from an individual perspective and it is critical that we begin a process of thinking about homeland security in a holistic framework. All elements of planning, prevention, and response require an ability to cope with what is called *All Hazards*. This approach of thinking about homeland security enables us to see how the work of the doctor, police officer, emergency planner, business owner, firefighter, and others all must be considered, coordinated, and organized for a response to any type of catastrophe, emergency, or disaster.

Homeland security, not unlike "terrorism," is a concept that is easily recognized but not necessarily universally understood. To some the term refers only to a massive new federal agency within the U.S. government that has pulled together 22 separate smaller agencies responsible for various aspects of domestic security.

To others, "homeland security" is the first truly concerted effort to provide a domestic security screen across the North American continent, using technology, innovation and public/private partnerships to protect the borders, and cities of our national homes. Still others would define "homeland security" as enlisting and coordinating public safety and private security organizations as the first line of defense and response in community protection against terrorism, disaster, and other forms of catastrophic loss.

Homeland security deals with large themes. In many respects, it harkens back to the activist philosophy of "think globally, act locally." To begin your preparation in assuming a role as a homeland security specialist and first responder for community-level disasters, we will spend this first chapter discussing the need, history, and goals of this new millennium concept: homeland security....

HOMELAND SECURITY DEFINED

Resources[1]

- Three and a half million square miles of land
- Over two thousand miles of the longest undefended border in the world
- 290 million people
- Two of the ten largest cities in the world, and nin cities with populations in excess of one million people
- 22 major shipping ports
- 407 long runway airports
- A $10.5 trillion gross domestic product
- A $2 trillion budget
- 104 nuclear power reactors[2]
- Vast deposits of coal, copper, lead, molybdenum, phosphates, uranium, bauxite, gold, iron, mercury, nickel, potash, silver, tungsten, zinc, petroleum, natural gas, timber
- A massive industrial base consisting of leading steel, petroleum, automotive, high technology, entertainment; finance, mining, aerospace, and defense sectors
- Much of the world's wheat, grain, soy, and beef supply

Politically

- The leading provider of financial and military aid to some of the world's most controversial governments and troubled regions including Columbia, Egypt, Saudi Arabia, and Israel
- The world's largest military and economic power with bases and corporate interests spread throughout the globe
- The only nation to have ever used atomic weapons in warfare against civilian populations
- A fundamental tenet of "separation of church and state" which infuriates militant religious movements domestically and abroad
- An open and mobile society with a high expectation of privacy among the citizenry and a premium placed on individual liberties
- A citizenry that makes up less than five percent of the world's population but consumes approximately one-fourth of the Earth's natural resources[3]
- A level of wealth, a standard of living, and a vast global presence that sometimes evokes envy and resentment

The preceding describes the United States of America in the early twenty-first century. Imagine if it was your job to develop a comprehensive security plan for this collection of people, resources, and ideologies. If that thought feels like a daunting prospect then you are beginning to appreciate the challenge of homeland security.

The concept of a federal agency and a coordinated national effort towards the overall security of the domestic homeland had been considered for many years. Unfortunately, it took the deaths of 3,000 people in New York City, Washington, D.C., and Pennsylvania on the morning of September 11, 2001 and the subsequent anthrax-letter attacks for this concept to become a reality.

The creation of the Department of Homeland Security has been the largest reorganization within the United States federal government since the sweeping reforms initiated by Franklin Roosevelt's "New Deal" in the 1930s. Twenty-two federal agencies were consolidated to form this new department, which now consists of approximately 183,000 employees organized into five major directorates, with a yearly budget of $36.2 billion.[4]

The Secret Service; U.S. Citizenship + Immigration Service; Border Patrol; Customs Service; Coast Guard; Transportation Security Administration; Federal Emergency Management Agency; Office of Domestic Preparedness; Federal Protective Agency—and even more obscure entitles such as the Animal and Plant Health Inspection Service and Plum Island Animal Disease Center—are all separate federal agencies that, under the Homeland Security Act of 2002 and amendments to the National Security Act of 1947, were merged into the new massive U.S. Department of Homeland Security. DHS cut across several departments such as Treasury, Justice, Transportation, Health and Human Services and even Agriculture to pull together multiple federal agencies with various responsibilities for providing security and emergency preparedness.[5]

The U.S. Department of Homeland Security is a particularly unique study in the need for, and the logistical reality of, forming such an organization. The federal government of the United States is one of the most sectionalized institutions in the world, consisting of: three separate branches—judicial, legislative, and executive; fourteen distinct departments, each with its own cabinet level secretary; and then, literally hundreds of agencies and offices carrying out separate missions. As a result of this sub-dividing, there are many times when agencies, which should be cooperating, end up either inadvertently competing with one another, or failing to coordinate operations—assuming another agency is addressing important issues when in fact no one is.

The government's approach to homeland security prior to 9/11 was a great example of this phenomenon. There were critical failures in intelligence sharing, cooperation and counter-terrorism coordination. Security was defined many different ways and responsibility was given to many different agencies.

The ability of terrorists to successfully coordinate such a massive attack in the Untied States with such relative ease, and the resultant public outcry, prompted the federal government to address the need for better sharing of intelligence information and streamlining of federal agencies responsible for security. With the passage of the Homeland Security Act of 2002 former Pennsylvania governor Tom Ridge became the Nation's first Secretary of Homeland Security and the agency was tasked with the following critical mission areas.[6]

1) Intelligence and Warning

Terrorism depends on surprise. With it, a terrorist attack has the potential to do massive damage to an unwitting and unprepared target. Without it, the terrorist stand a good chance to being preempted by authorities, and even if they are not, the damage that results from their attacks is likely to be less severe. The United States will take every necessary action to avoid being surprised by another terrorist attack. We must have an intelligence and warning system that can detect terrorist activity before it manifests itself in an attack so that proper pre-emptive, preventive, and protective action can be taken.

The National Strategy for Homeland Security identifies five major initiatives in this area:

- Enhance the analytic capabilities of the FBI;
- Build new capabilities through the Information Analysis and Infrastructure Protection Division of the proposed Department of Homeland Security;
- Implement the Homeland Security Advisory System;
- Utilize dual-use analysis to prevent attacks; and
- Employ "red team" techniques.

2) Border and Transportation Security

America historically has relied heavily on two vast oceans and two friendly neighborhoods for border security, and on the private sector for most forms of domestic transportation security.The increasing mobility and destructive potential of modern terrorism has required the United States to rethink and renovate fundamentally its systems for border and transportation security. Indeed, we must now begin to conceive of border security and transportation security as fully integrated requirements because our domestic transportation systems are inextricably intertwined with the global transport infrastructure. Virtually every community in America is connected to the global transportation network by the seaports, airports, highways, pipelines, railroads, and waterways that move people and good into, within, and out of the Nation. We must therefore promote the efficient and reliable flow of people, goods, and services across borders, while preventing terrorists from using transportation conveyances or systems to deliver implements of destruction.

The National Strategy for Homeland Security identifies six major initiatives in this area:

- Ensure accountability in border and transportation security;
- Create "smart borders;"

- Increase the security of international shipping containers;

- Implement the Aviation and Transportation Security Act of 2001;

- Recapitalize the U.S. Coast Guard; and

- Reform immigration services.

The President proposed to Congress that the principal border and transportation security agencies—the Immigration and Naturalization Service, the U.S. Customs Service, the U.S. Coast Guard, the Animal and Plant Health Inspection Service, and the Transportation Security Agency—be transferred to the new Department of Homeland Security. This organizational reform will greatly assist in the implementation of the above initiatives.

3) Domestic Counter-Terrorism

The attacks of September 11 and the catastrophic loss of life and property that resulted have redefined the mission of federal, state, and local law enforcement authorities. While law enforcement agencies will continue to investigate and

Figure 1.1 U.S. DHS Organization ca. 2003

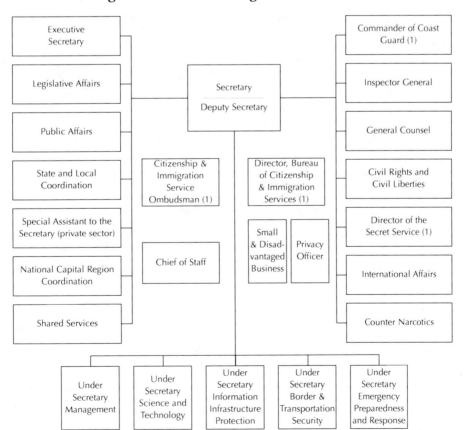

prosecute criminal activity, they should now assign priority to preventing and interdicting terrorist activity within the Untied States. The Nation's state and local law enforcement officers will be critical in this effort. Our Nation will use all legal means—both traditional and nontraditional—to identify, halt, and, where appropriate, prosecute terrorists in the United States. We will pursue not only the individuals directly involved in terrorist activity but also their sources of support: the people and organizations that knowingly fund the terrorists and those that provide them with logistical assistance.

Effectively reorienting law enforcement organizations to focus on counter terrorism objectives requires decisive action in a number of areas. The National Strategy for Homeland Security identifies six major initiatives in this area:

- Improve governmental law enforcement coordination;
- Facilitate apprehension of potential terrorists;
- Continue ongoing investigations and prosecutions;
- Complete FBI restructuring to emphasize prevention of terrorist attacks;
- Target and attack terrorist financing; and
- Track foreign terrorists and bring them to justice.

4) Protection of Critical Infrastructure and Key Assets

Our society and modern way of life are dependent on networks of infrastructure—both physical networks such as our energy and transportation systems and virtual networks such as the Internet. If terrorists attack one or more pieces of our critical infrastructure, they may disrupt entire systems and cause significant damage to the Nation. We must, therefore, improve protection of the individual pieces and interconnecting systems that make up our critical infrastructure. Protecting America's critical infrastructure and key assets will not only make us more secure from terrorist attack, but will also reduce our vulnerability to natural disasters, organized crime, and computer hackers.

America's critical infrastructure encompasses a large number of sectors. The U.S. government will seek to deny terrorists the opportunity to inflict lasting harm to our Nation by protecting the assets, systems, and functions vital to our national security, governance, public health and safety, economy, and national morale.

The National Strategy for Homeland Security identifies eight major initiatives in this are:

- Unify America's infrastructure protection effort in the Department of Homeland Security;
- Build and maintain a complete and accurate assessment of America's critical infrastructure and key assets;
- Enable effective partnership with state and local governments and the private sector;
- Develop a national infrastructure protection plan;

- Secure cyberspace;

- Harness the best analytic and modeling tools to develop effective protection solutions;

- Guard America's critical infrastructure and key assets against "inside" threats; and

- Partner with the international community to protect our transnational infrastructure.

5) Defending Against Catastrophic Threats

The expertise, technology, and material needed to build the most deadly weapons known to mankind—including chemical, biological, radiological, and nuclear weapons—are spreading inexorably. If our enemies acquire these weapons, they are likely to try to use them. The consequences of such an attack could be far more devastating than those we suffered on September 11—a chemical, biological, radiological, or nuclear terrorist attack in the Untied States could cause large numbers of casualties, mass psychological disruption, contamination and significant economic damage, and could overwhelm local medical capabilities.

Currently, chemical, biological, radiological, and nuclear detection capabilities are modest and response capabilities are dispersed throughout the country at every level of government. While current arrangements have proven adequate for a variety of natural disasters and even the September 11 attacks, the threat of terrorist attacks using chemical, biological, radiological, and nuclear weapons requires new approaches, a focused strategy, and a new organization.

The National Strategy for Homeland Security identifies six major initiatives in this area:

- Prevent terrorist use of nuclear weapons through better sensors and procedures;

- Detect chemical and biological materials and attacks;

- Improve chemical sensors and decontamination techniques;

- Develop broad-spectrum vaccines, anti-microbials, and antidotes;

- Harness the scientific knowledge and tools to counter terrorism; and

- Implement the Select Agent Program.

6) Emergency Preparedness and Response

We must prepare to minimize the damage and recover from any future terrorist attacks that may occur despite our best efforts at prevention. An effective response to a major terrorist incident—as well as a natural disaster—depends on being prepared. Therefore, we need a comprehensive national system to bring together and coordinate all necessary response assets quickly and effectively. We must plan, equip, train, and exercise many different response units to mobilize without warning for any emergency.

Many pieces of this national emergency response system are already in place. America's first line of defense in the aftermath of any terrorist attack is its first responder community—police officers, firefighters, emergency medical providers, public works personnel, and emergency management officials. Nearly three million state and local first responders regularly put their lives on the line to save the lives of others and make our country safer.

Yet multiple plans currently govern the federal govern the federal government's support of first responders during an incident of national significance. These plans and the government's overarching policy for counter terrorism are based on an artificial and unnecessary distinction between "crisis management" and "consequence management." Under the President's proposal, the Department of Homeland Security will consolidate federal response plans and build a national system for incident management in cooperation with state and local government. Our federal, state, and local governments would ensure that all response personnel and organizations are properly equipped, trained, and exercised to respond to all terrorist threats and attacks in the United States. Our emergency preparedness and response efforts would also engage the private sector and the American people.

The National Strategy for Homeland Security identifies twelve major initiatives in this area:

- Integrate separate federal response plans into a single all-discipline incident management plan;
- Create a national incident management system;
- Improve tactical counter terrorist capabilities;
- Enable seamless communication among all responders;
- Prepare health care providers for catastrophic terrorism;
- Augment America's pharmaceutical and vaccine stockpiles;
- Prepare for chemical, biological, radiological, and nuclear decontamination;
- Plan for military support to civil authorities;
- Build the Citizen Corps;
- Implement the First Responder Initiative of the Fiscal Year 2003 budget;
- Build a national training and evaluation system; and
- Enhance the victim support system.

The National Strategy for Homeland Security also describes four foundations—unique American strengths that cut across all of the mission areas, across all levels of government, and across all sectors of our society. These foundations—law, science and technology, information sharing and systems, and international cooperation—provide a useful framework for evaluating our homeland security investments across the federal government.

Law

Throughout our Nation's history, we have used laws to promote and safeguard our security and our liberty. The law will both provide mechanisms for the government to act and will define the appropriate limits of action.

The National Strategy for Homeland Security outlines legislative actions that would help enable our country to fight the war on terrorism more effectively. New federal laws should not preempt state law unnecessarily or overly federalize the war on terrorism. We should guard scrupulously against incursions on our freedoms.

The Strategy identifies twelve major initiatives in this area:

Federal level

- Enable critical infrastructure information sharing;
- Streamline information sharing among intelligence and law enforcement agencies;
- Expand existing extradition authorities;
- Review authority for military assistance in domestic security;
- Revive the President's reorganization authority; and
- Provide substantial management flexibility for the Department of Homeland Security.

State level

- Coordinate suggested minimum standards for state driver's licenses;
- Enhance market capacity for terrorism insurance;
- Train for prevention of cyber attacks;
- Suppress money laundering;
- Ensure continuity of the judiciary; and
- Review quarantine authorities.

Science and Technology

The Nation's advantage in science and technology is a key to securing the homeland. New technologies for analysis, information sharing, detection of attacks, and countering chemical, biological, radiological, and nuclear weapons will help prevent and minimize the damage from future terrorist attacks. Just as science has helped us defeat past enemies overseas, so too will it help us defeat the efforts of terrorist to attack our homeland and disrupt our way of life.

The federal government is launching a systematic national effort to harness science and technology in support of homeland security. We will build a national research and development enterprise for homeland security sufficient to mitigate the risk posed by modern terrorism. The Federal government will consolidate most federally funded homeland security research and development under the Department of Homeland Security to ensure strategic direction and avoid duplicative efforts. We will create and implement a long-term research and development plan that includes investment in revolutionary capabilities with high-payoff potential. The federal government will also seek to harness the energy and ingenuity of the private sector to develop and produce the devices and systems needed for homeland security.

The National Strategy for Homeland Security identifies eleven major initiatives in this area:

- Develop chemical, biological, radiological, and nuclear countermeasures;

- Develop systems for detecting hostile intent;

- Apply biometric technology to identification devices;

- Improve the technical capabilities of first responders;

- Coordinate research and development of the homeland security apparatus;

- Establish a national laboratory for homeland security;

- Solicit independent and private analysis for science and technology research;

- Conduct demonstrations and pilot deployments;

- Set standards for homeland security technology; and

- Establish a system for high-risk, high-payoff homeland security research.

Information Sharing and Systems

Information systems contribute to every aspect of homeland security. Although American information technology is the most advanced in the world, our country's information systems have not adequately supported the homeland security missions. Databases used for federal law enforcement, immigration, intelligence, public health surveillance, and emergency management have not been connected in ways that allow us to comprehend where information gaps or redundancies exist. In addition, there are deficiencies in the communications systems used by states and municipalities throughout the country; most state and local first responders do not use compatible communications equipment. To secure the homeland better, we must link the vast amounts to knowledge residing within each government agency while ensuring adequate privacy.

The National Strategy for Homeland Security identifies five major initiatives in this area:

- Integrate information sharing across the federal government;

- Integrate information sharing across state and local governments, private industry, and citizens;

- Adopt common "meta-data" standards for electronic information relevant to homeland security;

- Improve public safety emergency communications; and
- Ensure reliable public health information.

International Cooperation[7]

In a world where the terrorist threat pays no respect to traditional boundaries, our strategy for homeland security cannot stop at our borders. America must pursue a sustained, steadfast, and systematic international agenda to counter the global terrorist threat and improve our homeland security. Our international anti-terrorism campaign has made significant progress since September 11. The full scope of these activities will be further described in the forthcoming National Security Strategy of the United States and the National Strategy for Combating Terrorism. The National Strategy for Homeland Securities identifies nine major initiatives in this area:

- Create "smart borders;"
- Combat fraudulent travel documents;
- Increase the security of international shipping containers;
- Intensify international law enforcement cooperation;
- Help foreign nations fight terrorism;
- Expand protection of transnational critical infrastructure;
- Amplify international cooperation on homeland security science and technology;
- Improve cooperation in response to attacks; and
- Review obligations to international treaties and law.

HOMELAND SECURITY: THE COSTS[8]

The national effort to enhance homeland security will yield tremendous benefits and entail substantial financial and other costs. Benefits include reductions in the risk of attack and their potential consequences. Costs include not only the resources we commit to homeland security but also the delays to commerce and travel. The United States spends roughly $100 billion [$100,000 million] per year on homeland security. This figure includes federal, state, and local law enforcement and emergency services, but excludes most funding for the armed forces.

The responsibility of providing homeland security is shared between federal, state, and local governments, and the private sector. In many cases, sufficient incentives exist in the private market to supple protection. Government should fund only those homeland security activities that are not supplied, or are inadequately supplied, in the market. Cost sharing between different levels of government should reflect the principles of federalism. Many homeland security activities, such as intelligence gathering and border security, are properly accomplished at the federal level. In other circumstances, such as with first responder capabilities, it is more appropriate for state and local governments to handle these responsibilities.

In 2004, Homeland Security was one of very few items in the U.S. Federal Government's budget that received an increase—approximately nine percent or $3.6 billion—for FY05.[9] Even in the difficult economic conditions of 2004, the federal government felt that the need for improved homeland security spending was critical. Where the Department of Homeland Security will go next, and what it may evolve into over time remains to be seen. Whether the new department will endure or be repealed in years to come; whether it will continue to see increases in federal dollars and budget share, or will face cuts; whether the DHS will remain focused on its charter missions or will expand and adapt to take on new roles is a matter now for time and history. Regardless, the Homeland Security Act of 2002; the creation of the federal Department of Homeland Security and even the introduction of the phrase, "homeland security" into the public vernacular reflects a shift of the American mindset not seen for almost half a century—a sign of the times that an age of innocence and a sense of insulation from a hostile world is gone, if not for good, then at least for a foreseeable future.

9/11 was unique as a terrorist attack. The traditional aim of a terrorist is to violently underscore a point about a perceived injustice—often centered on an acute issue such as Israeli settlements in Palestine, the presence of British troops in Northern Ireland, or to reverse laws around abortion or gun ownership. The hijackers and planners of 9/11, however, never issued a statement or specified a cause. American support of Israel; the presence of U.S. troops in Saudi Arabia; American aid to repressive regimes in the Arab world; fear of western influenced globalization were all formative causes to al-Qaeda to be sure; however, the language, writings and doctrine of fanatics involved in the 9/11 plot all seemed murkier than these straightforward, geo-political/sociological motives.

The 9/11 hijackers wrote in personal diaries and last wills about the rewards of martyrdom—promises of an eternity in paradise with a cadre of 72 virgins each—if they should take their own lives while at the same time murdering their "enemies." In the warped theology of al-Qaeda, all Americans were fair game—civilians, women, children, and the elderly. Not only was it permissible to murder any and all Americans (and their collaborators), but God actually demanded it. The motives of the 9/11 hijackers didn't seem to land on practical matters of politics, but rather on dark, apocalyptic visions of a holy war between the forces of God and Satan, with themselves on the side of righteousness and their enemies as the dehumanized incarnations of evil. Thus, while all acts of terrorism are senseless, 9/11 took on a particular note of nihilistic gloom.

9/11 was also unique in the sense that the whole world experienced the attacks together. Terrorists typically rely on media coverage to enhance their ability to intimidate and broadcast their agenda. Most time however, we only see the aftermath with journalists and cameras arriving after the explosion or shooting has taken place. 9/11 was filmed from start to finish. The whole world watched as the first tower burned. Millions were tuned in when United Airlines 175 slammed into the south tower. We saw the Pentagon smoldering; heard the tapes of anguished but resolved voices called loved ones from cell phones sensing their doom; we saw both towers come down. 9/11 was a long, agonizing and traumatic experience for millions, with every second recorded and broadcast repeatedly. The attacks of 9/11 unfolded over a period of hours, letting the enigma and horror of the event bore into the collective consciousness of civilized people everywhere. For sheer effect it is without equal in the annals of terrorism.

9/11 was also a spectacular attack in the original sense of the word—to cause a spectacle. 9/11 was in a strange way original; designed to be more than just a bombing or a hijacking, but also to create a morbid sense of drama. Terrorists seeks to use symbolism in their attacks, but September 11th was designed to create something that would not only kill and injure on a grand scale, but would also create indelible and unsettling visuals. The surreal image of an aluminum jumbo jet's fuselage being swallowed up by the World Trade Center before erupting in a vicious orange ball-of-flame; the notion that commercial airliners and office buildings would suddenly be turned into the scene of life and death struggles; the realization that the Nation's capital city and the central headquarters of the world's most powerful military could be effectively attacked using a civilian jet liner, created a deeply disturbing and unnerving sense. The exploitation of our freedom and mobility, the helplessness and horror we felt, the nagging mystery of who was doing this and why conspired to make an eerie, and outraging point.

Finally, September 11th was unique in its lethality. The death toll surpassed the only other coordinated attack of that magnitude on U.S soil—the Pearl Harbor bombing of December 7, 1941. 9/11 stands alone as the most deadly terror attack in history.

Mass Anxiety and the Terror Formula: "Super-Terrorism"

9/11 was a new form of terrorism, a type of "super-terrorism." Following the Second World War, the United States and the Soviet Union redefined geo-politics by emerging as "super-powers:" nation states characterized by large populations and geographic territories; leadership in several strategic alliances; enormous military, naval and air forces; powerful economies and industrial bases; nuclear arsenals sufficient to obliterate all life on earth many times over; and unquestioned status as the predominant global champions of opposing ideologies (democracy and the free-market economy versus Marxism-Leninism and the command economy). In much the same way, al-Qaeda has used in the super-terrorist organization.

Al-Qaeda operates as a loose-knit yet well coordinated global network, decentralized enough that the myriad of cells which compose the network are able to melt virtually unnoticed into target populations, yet synchronized enough to carry out simultaneous attacks against disparate targets hundreds of miles apart. Al-Qaeda is well financed, with numerous surreptitious revenue streams and money laundering schemes. Recruits are trained at fairly sophisticated bases in third-world nations throughout the globe. Al-Qaeda, at least prior to the U.S.-led attack on Afghanistan commencing October 7, 2001, was the largest terrorist network ever, complete with a command structure and communications network.

More than anything, however, al-Qaeda possesses a certain degree of morbid "vision." Al-Qaeda sends a profound message with every attack. They invest a great deal of time in researching particular targets so as to ensure that their point is plainly understood without the formality of having to issue a statement. Some suggest that al-Qaeda's practice of not issuing a statement reflects the group's intense hatred and pseudo-religious apocalyptic theology letting the bitterness and the horror of the act itself be the only "statement" Other terrorism experts suggest the purpose of not issuing a statement is more practical—to generate a sense of anxiety and insecurity by increasing the mysteriousness of the attack.

The terror formula is simple: "kill 10, terrorized 10,000." As their title implies, the purpose of a terrorist to to terrorize "to fill with terror; to coerce by threat or violence."[10] For terrorism to be truly successful, knowledge of an attack and the resultant fear must reach a much larger audience than merely those present at the scene. Terrorism not only relies upon media coverage, but also in a perverse way, actually courts it. Not unlike celebrity publicists or marketing agencies, terrorist planners invest a great deal of time and energy in determining which attacks will generate maximum interest and impact. Terrorists must study media behavior to decide what sort of attack will seize and capture the media's often fleeting attention span. Sadly, in the United States, where the population is highly acclimated to sensationalist imagery, an attack the size and scale of 9/11 was really the first event to capture long-term media attention, to mobilize civic leaders and ordinary citizens to act, and to advance terrorism as a serious consideration for the public.

Al-Qaeda had been active in operations against the U.S. for eight years prior to 9/11, including the 1993 bombing of the World Trade Center, which was the first attempt to bring the twin towers down. The 1996 Air Force barracks bombing at Khobar towers in Saudi Arabia; the synchronized 1998 bombings of the U.S. embassies in Kenya and Tanzania; and the year 2000 suicide attack on the naval ship U.S.S. Cole in Yemen were all al-Qaeda operations targeted at the United States. In 1998, the chief organizer and spiritual leader of al-Qaeda, Osama bin Laden, issued a "fatwa" (which could be translated as a "religious edict" or "commandment") to his followers to "kill Americans—including civilians— wherever you find them."

Osama bin Laden is the sone of an extremely wealthy Saudi businessman and construction contractor. The Bin Laden Group is a very lucrative construction concern in the Saudi kingdom. According to Saudi law, polygamy (a man having several wives) is legal. Bin Laden's father had nine wives and a total of 52 children. Osama grew up in this rather large and extended family and likely felt rather overlooked competing with fifty-one siblings for his father's attention. In 1979, a younger Osama found a cause to give his heretofore pampered life some sense of significance: the struggle of Islamic rebels in Afghanistan against Soviet troops who were sent to uphold the unpopular communist government of that nation. Bin Laden packed up his share of the millions his father had doled out to his children and left for Afghanistan. There he used his fortunes and ties to his father's construction business to begin funding various humanitarian projects for the people of Afghanistan.

Eventually bin Laden joined the direct fighting and soon he was regarded as a hero of the native Afghani resistance known as the Muhajadeen. Following the 1989 defeat of the Soviets in Afghanistan, international attention on the war torn region wanted and soon bin Laden was without an enemy to distinguish himself against. Afghanistan fell into chaos for several yeas with Muhajadeen elements fracturing into regional-tribal clans where they began battling for control of the nation. From 1989 onward, bin Laden began setting his sites on more global objectives, inculcating and training his followers with an apocalyptical, pseudo-theological campaign against "non-believers" and secular societies. He formed a new network that was given only the vague and ominous name "the base," which in Arabic is translated as "al-Qaeda."

When Saddam Hussein ordered Iraqi forces into the tiny, oil-rich Arab nation of Kuwait in August 1990, the Kingdom of Saudi Arabia feared that they might be invaded next. As home to two of Islam's holiest sites: the cities of Mecca and Medina; bin Laden proposed to the Saudi government, perhaps unrealistically, to raise a legion of Muhajadeen fighters to defend Saudi Arabia against Saddam Hussein. Bin Laden regarding Hussein as a non-believer and a decadent secularist unworthy of leading an Arab nation or even being a "fellow Muslin."[11] The Saudi government declined bin Laden's offer and opted instead to invite the American military in to defend the Saudi kingdom. This infuriated bin Laden who felt the Kingdom of Saudi Arabia and the holy sites of Islam should not be protected by westerners. Bin Laden began preaching against the United States and the Saudi government, a move that eventually resulted in the revocation of his Saudi citizenship. His ire at the U.S., the West and cooperative Arab governments manifested itself as a fiery mix of literal interpretation of Islamic law known as "Wahibbism" and violent militancy.

Al-Qaeda emerged as a functioning terror network when it staged its first concerted operations in 1992 and 1993. On the 29th of December 1992, a bomb detonated at the Gold Mohur Hotel in Aden, Yemen. U.S. military personnel on their way to support the on-going humanitarian mission in Somalia had recently stayed at the hotel. Although the bombing was planned too late to impact the servicemen who had been there, two Australian tourists were killed.

Al-Qaeda ambitiously raised the stakes for international terrorism by conducting its next attack within the United States. On February 26, 1993, operatives drove a truck loaded with a massive bomb into an underground parking garage at the World Trade Center in Manhattan. Six people were killed and almost a thousand were wounded when the bomb exploded. The subsequent investigation and trail of captured suspects revealed that the attacked hoped to cause a structural failure below the south tower, collapsing it in to the north tower—bringing both skyscrapers down.

Al-Qaeda showed up significantly again during American military operations in Somalia in 1993. Although the October 3, 1993 raid on Mogadishu's Bakara market by U.S. Special Forces resulted in the successful capture of several influential Somali figures, resistance fighters using rock-propelled grenades (RPGs) shot down two U.S. Army Blackhawk helicopters. The loss of the helicopters significantly complicated the mission and ultimately resulted in the deaths of 18 American soldiers. Muhajadeen in Afghanistan had developed the tactic of using RPGs as surface-to-air weapons against slow flying helicopters during the Soviet invasion. The ability of the Somalis to do the same thing suggested the presence of al-Qaeda in Mogadishu. Two years later in November 1995, al-Qaeda placed a truck bomb at a Saudi military training facility in Riyadh, killing seven Americans and two Indians.

Bin Laden returned to Afghanistan in 1996 after being banned by the Saudi government. At about that same time the Islamic extremist Taliban movement seized control of the country.[12] Bin Laden was believed to be a chief financier and supporter of the Taliban, who in turn offered him political sanctuary and a base of operations for al-Qaeda.

August 7, 1998, two powerful car bombs exploded almost simultaneously in front of the U.S. Embassies in Dar es Salaam, Tanzania, and Nairobi, Kenya. Two hundred twenty-four people, mostly African citizens working as part of the embassy staff, were murdered and another 5,000 were injured. A few weeks later the U.S. fired a salvo of 70 Tomahawk cruise missiles from navy ships into al-Qaeda facilities and training camps in the Sudan and Afghanistan. Although the attacks missed bin Laden, they did injure and kill several key al-Qaeda operatives and rattled the Taliban government of Afghanistan. Taliban leader Mullah Omar scolded bin Laden in the aftermath of the cruise missile attacks and warned him not to initiate any more threatening actions or statements against the United States from inside the country. Bin Laden said he would comply, but the pledge did not last long.

On October 12, 2000, a Navy destroyer, the U.S.S. Cole, was performing routine refueling operations at a port near Aden, Yemen when a small boat packed with explosives rammed it. Seventeen American sailors were killed.

Then of course, September 11, 2001, the world was changed forever when al-Qaeda carried out the most brazen terror attack in history. There have been subsequent lethal attacks by al-Qaeda in Riyadh, Casablanca, Kabul, Jakarta, Baghdad, Istanbul, Bali, Mombassa, Kerbala, and Madrid. There is an equally long list of failed al-Qaeda attempts and disrupted attacks since 1989. Al-Qaeda has murdered an estimated 4,000 people around the globe and has injured approximately 8,300.

Of course, al-Qaeda is not the only terrorist organization in the world, and the network itself is, in many respects, an amalgam of smaller, affiliated terror groups. Hundreds of terrorist groups ranging from 20 to 2,000 members operate in all corners of the globe and claim to advocate all manner of ideological and political agenda. Other major terrorist groups include the Al-Aqsa Martyr's Brigade in the West Bank and Gaza Strip; Hamas in the occupied territories of Palestine; Islamic Jihad which operates throughout the Middle East; Armed Islamic Group in Algeria; Sendero Luminoso ("Shining Path") in Peru; Revolutionary Armed Forces (FARC) in Colombia; Abu Sayyaf in the Philippines; and the Irish Republic Army in northern Ireland. [The IRA has been in a state of relative dormancy since a cease first accord in July 1997.] This of course is just a small fraction of known terrorist organizations operating in the world.

Although the history of terrorism dates back hundred, if not thousands, of years, the period from the 1960 on has seen a steady rise in the concerted and consistent use of terror as a tool for social, political, and religious change.

The advent of al-Qaeda has created new and very serious phenomena for the homeland security specialist. The super-terrorist group has a global organization with thousands of adherents operating independently and yet with an unified network which includes rather sophisticated technology such as steganography [the hiding of a message in hyper-text transfer protocol image—i.e., a picture on a website—such that it may only be read by browsers who know a specific DOC command to decode the message]; training programs and facilities; a vast recruiting network; surreptitious, lucrative and far reaching financing streams; a particular fondness for large-scale, dramatic attacks; and a willingness to be patient.

In this new millennium, all homeland security specialists—frontline security agents and supervisors, first responders, intelligence operatives and disaster recovery planners—will all have to be familiar with the mindset, tactics and objectives of the super-terrorist organization. Whatever you are assigned to protect and defend or wherever you find yourself in the community, you will always have to be thinking and planning in much the same way a terrorist would, asking yourself the following:

- What vulnerabilities could be exploited?

- What targets are of high symbolic and media interest value?

- What manner of attack would produce the greatest damage with the least risk of the attacker exposing himself beforehand?

- What would seem suspicious, unusual, or out-of-place?

- Are the security measures in place sufficient to stop someone who is intent on killing himself as part of the attack?

- Have I witnessed any activity that would seem consistent with my facility or community being under surveillance?

Use of the Media

The media is a key concern for all security specialists. The media can be a great asset in alerting the general public or calming widespread alarm by managing information. At the same time, if used irresponsibly or ineffectively, the media may contribute to mass panic, or be exploited by terrorists as a tool. As mentioned in a previous section, terrorists often court the media as a means of increasing the reach of their attacks and to generate publicity for their cause. In fact, without public exposure it is doubtful terrorism would retain much value as a practice. Terrorism, in its modern incarnation, is really almost entirely dependent on media coverage. The dramatic practice of hijacking commercial airlines, for example, became very popular only after the advent of satellite television broadcasting when stories could be beamed around the world live-time. There is some speculation that the targets were chosen specifically by the 9/11 hijackers top underscore a point about America's vulnerability.

In 1974, the scholar Brian Jenkins stated, "terrorism is theater,"[13] and he was correct. A lethal form of theater to be sure, but as homeland security specialists, it is important for us to understand that the objective of the terrorist is not solely to maim and kill, but also to do it in a manner that will inure the greatest media exposure and message proliferation. The creation of panic and fear' to instill a sense of chaos and disorder; and to discredit a government and ideology—these are the goals of the terrorist. The media obviously can be an unwitting accomplice in the achievement of these goals. 9/11 is a paramount example. Many of us remember the first broadcasts of World Trade Center One, the north tower, burning after a low-flying airplane struck it. In their frenzy to break and carry this dramatic story, scores of news agencies were broadcasting, and millions of viewers tuned in when the second plane hit the south tower. We collectively shared the moment. Many of those who were watching the second strike live shared the same experience of confusion, not realizing for a few moments what had happened, and the slow dread of understanding that this could not possibly be an accident.

News agencies are often aware that they are being exploited, especially dyring live broadcasts when it is impossible to predict and edit events. The pressure to generate subscriber-ship and ratings usually compels media organizations to carry the story because that is ultimately how they succeed. Terrorists are aware of this media tendency and use it to further their aims. Like good advertisers, terrorists typically plot and plan their attacks based on what will generate maximum interest and attention. Panic and hysteria become "force multipliers" to their attacks, especially when the media reports only partial facts about the terrorist attack, leaving the public imagination to fill in the rest.

In 1995, when the Aum Shinrikyo cult released deadly Sarin gas in the Tokyo subway system, twelve people were killed and just over 1,000 were admitted into hospitals and treated for illness related to Sarin poisoning. Altogether, however, 5,500 people showed up in various Tokyo hospital emergency rooms. The majority of them falsely believed they had been poisoned. The panic caused by early media images of chaos and death in the subways resulted in an additional 4,000 people developing psychosomatic symptoms and needing to be rushed to the hospital.[14] These imaginary symptoms caused very real problems as you might imagine, as overworked hospital staff now had the additional headache and burden of having to triage and diagnoses actual illness from hysterical illness.

Following the anthrax letter attacks of October of 2001, a panic ensued in the U.S. Although only 23 people were actually sickened by anthrax and there were five fatalities, there were millions of "psychological causalities" throughout the country, with thousands of calls to 911 to report on mysterious white powders and unsolicited mailings that the public would normally just ignore.[15]

The scars of terrorism are not found only at the scene of the attack, but also in the post-traumatic stress, the sleep disorders, the anxiety, depression and malaise found throughout the affected public. Studies conducted by the National Organization for Research at the University of Chicago found that while, by in large, Americans responded quite resiliently to the 9/11 attacks, a full eight percent of people of the U.S. and fifteen percent of the people living in New York exhibited significant symptomology of Post Traumatic Stress Disorder (PTSD), a serious psychological condition affecting persons exposed to a profound or sustained crisis (i.e., combat veterans, disaster survivors, victims of violent crimes, etc.). Far beyond the immediate tragic loss of 9/11, millions more became, in effect, psychological casualties. For many of these casualties the trauma of the event was experienced only through the exhaustive media coverage.

The media may also be an effective tool in combating terrorism. In the same way that broadcast coverage of attacks can multiply the residual anxiety of terrorism, the media may also allow government agencies the ability to disseminate messages of reassurance and guidance to the general public. During the Second World War, U.S. President Franklin Roosevelt would have regular "fireside chats" broadcast via radio to millions of Americans. The mental image conjured up of the wise and grandfatherly Roosevelt sitting in a cozy salon next to a crackling fire was very comforting to a nation at war and recovering from economic depression. One of the factors that psychologists believe contributed to the resiliency of Americans in coping with September 11th, even in New York and Washington, DDC, was the public celebration of the heroism around 9/11 as well. Although the continuous broadcasting of the horror of the attacks likely contributed to the mass trauma, the almost equally continuous media coverage of emergency workers' heroism, the unity of Americans and people around the world waving flags and holding candlelight vigils, prayer services, and images such as a united Congress singing "God Bless America" likely accelerated the healing process as well.

Media broadcasting may also be effective in deterring terrorist attacks. Terrorists by definition enjoy the element of surprise. Thorough news coverage of terror warnings, especially when accompanied by instructions for simple things the public can do to protect themselves and their communities create a heightened awareness, may be disquieting to terrorist planners. Terrorists seem to be sensitive to feeling that they are being watched or scrutinized beforehand. Capture and incarceration before carrying out an operation is an inglorious result for someone intent on achieving esteem through martyrdom or successful terror attack. Increased media attention to terror threats or use of the media to alert the general public to be more vigilant may cause terrorists to abort mission. Finally, a better-informed public may be more likely to report suspicious activity and objects such as backpacks left unattended or persons.

LEGISLATIVE CHANGES: USA PATRIOT ACT

After September 11th, as well as the subsequent anthrax letter attacks, American's denial regarding terrorism quickly shifted to a state of near hysteria. Suddenly the fear of terrorism was everywhere and all manner of funds and ideas were being advanced to combat the threat. Among the changes that came quickly on the heels of 9/11 was the enactment of sweeping new security legislation. On October 24, 2001—six weeks after the attacks in New York, Washington DC, and Pennsylvania, and in the midst of the anthrax letter attacks—House Resolution 3162, the USA Patriot Act (Uniting and Strengthening America by providing Appropriate Tools Required to Intercept and Obstruct Terrorism) was overwhelmingly passed in Congress and was signed into law the next day by the President. Soon after its passing, the Act began generating controversy. Some felt the Patriot Act was an overdue expansion of resources needed by law enforcement to investigate and prosecute terrorists—an expansion that could have helped prevent the 9/11 terrorist attacks. Others feared that the Act represented an encroachment on basic civil liberties that was hastily passed during a time of great anxiety; and, that it was a dangerous over-reaction that served more as a impediment to the U.S. Constitution than to future acts of terrorism.

Since its enactment, there have been a lot of misconceptions about the Patriot Act. Within the 342-page legislation, the Patriot Act addresses a broad range of concerns related to combating terrorism. This chapter will conduct an in-depth examination of the provisions of the Act, but to begin with, it is important that we separate fact from fiction regarding the more controversial aspects of the Patriot Act.

What the USA Patriot Act Does

1. Instructs and facilitates means for the Federal Bureau of Investigation (FBI) and Central Intelligence Agency (CIA) to share information related to terrorist activity;

2. Enables the FBI to directly access federal judges on the highly secretive Foreign Intelligence Service Act (FISA) court, and to secure FISA court orders for businesses to hand over records that the FBI suspects may be related to terrorism;

3. Greatly eases the definition of "probable cause" for searches and surveillance. Under the Patriot Act federal agents need to only articulate that the business records sought are "related to a terrorism investigation or intelligence probe."

4. Codifies the "delayed notification" of searches. Delayed notifications have been used in the past for the investigation of organized crime. The Patriot Act however, makes delayed notification a written federal law instead of a general, unwritten rule-of-thumb used on a limited, case-by-case basis. This allows prosecutors to request a "reasonable delay period" from judges in notifying people that federal agents have searched their homes or businesses. If a probe is terminated because the subject is found not to be involved in terrorism or an effective case cannot be proven, the subject may never be notified, meaning that he or she will never know that their home or business has been searched.

5. Allow agents to secure "roving wiretaps," which involves tapping various electronic devices the subject uses.

What the USA Patriot Act Does NOT Do

1. After 9/11, thousands of people in the United States, mostly of Middle Eastern descent, were detained under a special authority given to the U.S. Department of Justice (DoJ). Because of the prolonged nature of this detention without subjects necessarily having the opportunity to appear before a

judge, and the ambiguity of some of the reasons given for detaining suspects, this action has raised concerns that public anxiety over terrorism could erode the concept of Due Process as articulated in the Sixth Amendment of the Bill of Rights. This detention power was afforded to the DoJ by immigration law and not the USA Patriot Act.

2. The Patriot Act did not grant the President the authority to detain 650 Taliban and al-Qaeda combatants captured in Afghanistan. The authority to hold enemy combatants until the cessation of hostilities is an interpretation of executive war powers as articulated in the Constitution.

3. Similarly, two enemy combatants have also been detained in a U.S. Navy brig without having charges levied against them or access to attorneys. This is also an application of executive war powers, although it is currently being challenged in the U.S. Supreme Court.

4. The Patriot Act contains no provisions regarding military tribunals being called to adjudicate terrorism charges against non-citizens being held by the U.S. This power is granted to the U.S Department of Defense (DoD).

5. The U.S. Attorney General did alter rules for investigators post-9/11 to enter houses of worship and attend rallies while conducting terrorism probes. This was done internally at the DoJ and is not written into the Patriot Act.

The USA Patriot Act is a far-reaching piece of legislation, which addresses many disparate pieces of counter terrorism concepts and attempts to codify them into one sweeping law. The Patriot Act does deal extensively with technology-based investigations and in many ways serves as an excellent benchmark for the types of questions and challenges facing investigators in a technology environment.

More than creating a lot of new laws, the USA Patriot Act amended a great deal of existing legislation. Included in the U.S. law, specifically amended by the Patriot Act, are the following:

- Electronic Communications Privacy Act

- Computer Fraud and Abuse Act

- Foreign Intelligence Surveillance Act

- Family Education Rights and Privacy Act

- Pen Register and Trap and Trace Statute

- Money Laundering Act

- Immigration and Nationality Act

- Bank Secrecy Act

- Right to Financial Privacy Act

- Fair Credit Reporting Act

- Title III of the Federal Wiretap Statute

Chronology of the US "War on Terror"

September 29, 2001	The President proposes a new Office of Homeland Security.
October 7, 2001	The President announces Operation Enduring Freedom to dismantle the Taliban regime in Afghanistan, which is harboring al-Qaeda
October 8, 2001	The President establishes the Office of Homeland Security in the Executive Office of the President and appoints Pennsylvania Governor Tom Ridge as Director.
November 19, 2001	The President signs the Aviation and Transportation Security Act, creating the Transportation Security Administration.
October 4, 2002	Six suspected members of the al-Qaeda terrorist network operating near Buffalo are indicted.
November 24, 2002	President Bush signs the Homeland Security Act of 2002, establishing the Department of Homeland Security
January 17, 2003	Congress creates the Select Committee on Homeland Security with authorizing and oversight responsibility for the new Department of Homeland Security.
January 24, 2003	President Bush swears in Tom Ridge as the first Secretary of the Department of Homeland Security.
March 1, 2003	Khalid Sheikh Mohammed, the alleged architect of the September 11 attacks is captured in Pakistan.
March 17, 2003	Homeland Security Department commences Operation Liberty Shield, an increase in protective measures to defense the homeland.
May 1, 2003	The Terrorist Threat Integration Center begins operation.
May 12, 2003	Homeland Security Department launches Top Off II, a week-long national training exercise for emergency preparedness and response.
June 8, 2003	Acting on a tip from U.S. authorities, Thai policy arrest Narong Penanam, who tried to sell cesium-137 to make a "dirty bomb."
June 19, 2003	Lyman Faris, the Ohio truck driver who plotted with Osama bin Laden to cut the cables on the Brooklyn Bridge, pleads guilty.
June 24, 2003	House passes the first even Homeland Security Appropriations bill, approving $29.4 billion to bolster homeland security, bringing funding for First Responders to more than $20 billion since 9/11.

July 16, 2003	House passage of Project Bioshield to help prevent and inoculate for bio-terror attack.
August 12, 2003	Arrest in Newark of Hemant Lakhani, London arms dealer who tried to smuggle surface-to-air missiles.
September 2, 2003	Secretary Ridge announces the "One Face at the Border" initiative to unify the border inspection process.
September 23, 2003	Authorities arrest Rusman Gunawan, the brother of al-Qaeda operative Riduan Isamuddin, in Pakistan and 14 students who were with him were also arrested on charges of suspected terrorism.
October 1, 2003	President Bush signs the first Homeland Security Appropriations bill into law.
October 30, 2003	HR 2886, the Department of Homeland Security Financial Accountability Act is reported favorably out of the Homeland Security Committee.
November 20, 2003	The Homeland Security Department released final rules to allow the customs and border protection directorate to collect information necessary to identify high-risk cargo shipments bound for the United States.
November 26, 2003	Mohammed Hambi al-Ahdal, a top al-Qaeda leader in Yemen, is captured. Al-Ahdal was one of the top 20 al-Qaeda members at large, and is suspected of planning the bombing of the USS Cole in 2000.
February 24, 2004	The Department of Homeland Security releases their strategic plan, "Securing Our Homeland."
March 1, 2004	The one-year anniversary of the creation of Department of Homeland Security.
March 11, 2004	Terrorist bombing on commuter trains in Madrid, Spain take hundreds of lives in the deadliest terrorist attack on a European target since World War II.
March 14, 2004	In Spain, Jose Luis Rodriguez Zapatero of the Socialist Party is elected Prime Minister, ousting the ruling Popular Party. The result, it is said, reflects voter backlash against Prime Minister Jose Aznar's strong support for the action in Iraq.

Stock Market/Economic Impact

Given the immeasurable cost in human suffering, it may seem distasteful to put the 9/11 attacks in the context of money. As security specialists though, we must look at terrorism, or any type of loss and disruption, in terms of the total impact, including economic. 9/11 shut down the New York Stock Exchange for four business days—an unprecedented event. Of the two airlines directly affected by the attacks one had to declare chapter eleven, bankruptcy protection and the other was pressed to cut four billion dollars in operating costs to stay financially solvent. The federal government issued a $15 billion bailout of the airline industry and almost one year later the industry as a whole was still operating at a loss of almost $3.6 billion. Hospitality and entertainment industries were hurt badly as people shied away from travel. The loss to New York City alone was totaled in the billions in missing tourism and travel revenues, and of course the enormous property, rental and retail loss of the World Trade Center facilities. Factor in healthcare, worker's compensation, insurance, productivity losses, increases in public and private security, and clean up and the total costs related to the 9/11 terrorist attacks are nothing short of astronomical.

The vitality of a national economy is largely driven by the psychological comfort of the general population. When people feel confident and optimistic they will tend to spend more, incur debt and invest. When the public feels insecure and unsure about the future, people are more likely to save up and hold their money close. Many economists estimated that the U.S. economy began a recession in March of 2001. There is a general sense that the unsettling events of 9/11, and subsequent corporate scandals, profoundly exaggerated the depth and length of the recession, exacerbating anxiety from the "dot-com" burst and the natural cooling of the 1990s stock market, prolonging sluggish economic conditions and staving off recovery for a longer than necessary period.

Being the son of a billionaire businessman and himself a financier and millionaire, Osama bin Laden was no stranger to stock market forces and the movement of wealth. The selection of the World Trade Center in Manhattan's financial district as a target suggests that al-Qaeda was deliberately seeking to make a point about the vulnerability of the American economic might. Economic disruption is an important goal of al-Qaeda. One of the purposes of the 9/11 attacks was not solely to cause loss of life and damage, but to negatively impact the financial vitality of a free-market nation like the United States.

The following is an except from an October 2001 report on the economy by the Board of the of Governors for the United States Federal Reserve:

Retail sales followed much the same pattern throughout the country. In the week following the attack, consumer spending dropped sharply for all items except those that were likely purchased in preparation for possible additional attacks. Sales of groceries, security devices, and bottled water increased; purchases of insurance also rose. One to two weeks later, consumer buying picked up somewhat, although in must Districts it was weaker than in early September. Contacts in the Chicago District note that the weakness is the result of fundamental economic causes prevailing before the attack, higher unemployment, and falling stock prices, rather than the attack itself.

The grounding of aircraft caused some very short-run effects. For example, the transport of fresh vegetables from the West Coast to the East Coast was disrupted somewhat. The supply chain of parts to manufacturers also was interrupted but appeared to recover quickly for dislocations in air transportation, as air cargo was promptly rerouted through ground networks.

All Districts except Boston and Kansas City report sharp declines in the hotel, airline, and tourism industries. In many Districts, demand dropped sharply immediately following the attack but later rebounded partially. Some cancelled conventions have been rescheduled. In Manhattan, Broadway theaters have noted some pickup in attendance after a sharp drop-off in mid-September. However, large layoffs in the airline industry may be the result of previously observed weakness in the industry, which was then amplified by the attack. Manhattan lost roughly 7 percent of its office space in the September 11 attack, but an estimated four percent will be repaired in upcoming months. Despite the damage, however, office availability increased slightly on balance in September.

The attack is likely to have a longer-term effect on manufacturing. Aircraft orders are down sharply, causing layoffs in the aircraft and aircraft parts industries in the Boston, Kansas City, and San Francisco regions. There has been an increase in demand for security products and data storage devices produced in the Cleveland and San Francisco Districts. Boston reports a large rise in insurance demand, while Atlanta, Dallas, and San Francisco report an increase in insurance premiums. The Atlanta and Chicago Districts report a fall in business productivity due to increased security precautions.

Consumer Spending

Retail sales softened in September and early October in all Districts except St. Louis, where sales were flat, and Minneapolis, where sales were considered normal, and Richmond, where sales returned to pre-attack levels. In the New York District, recent sales were well below levels of a year ago. Almost all regions reported that discount chains were doing much better than specialty stores, and luxury items did poorly. The softer sales tempered the retail sector's forecasts for the holiday season. Most Districts report sales expectations that are both more uncertain and lower then they had been in August.

Automobile sales were much weaker during the first weeks of September, but all Districts, except Boston and New York, report a rebound in sales because of zero-percent financing options that are being offered. In most cases, sales were back to normal, except in the San Francisco and Atlanta Districts, where they were weaker than normal. Atlanta and Chicago also mention that sales of trucks were down.

Manufacturing

Industrial activity was generally weak throughout the country in September and early October. The only exceptions were New York, which reports some pickup in activity, and Richmond, which reports steady activity. Most Districts mention that shipments and orders are weaker than the year before, and, indeed, than in early September. The continued weakness in manufacturing has contributed to pessimism about when orders will improve, as many Districts report that they do not exp3ect a turnaround until 2002.

The weakness is broadly based. The industries affected by lower shipments and orders include high-tech industries, such as semi-conductors in the Boston, Dallas, and San Francisco regions, as well as the more traditional heavy industries such as steel in the Chicago and Cleveland regions. In spite of robust auto sales, the auto parts industries in the Boston, Cleveland, Dallas, and St. Louis Districts all reported difficult times. The resource-based industries such as lumber reported mill closures in the regions of Atlanta, Dallas, and San Francisco. A few industries are doing well. Cement in the Dallas region, some textiles in the Richmond region, and luxury goods in Cleveland report some gains.

Real Estate and Construction

Construction generally slowed during September and early October, although there were exceptions in some locations and in some types of construction. Commercial construction weakened in the Atlanta, Boston, Cleveland, Kansas City, and San Francisco regions and in the western Kentucky portion of the St. Louis region. Some commercial and industrial projects were put on hold in the Chicago, Dallas, Minneapolis, Richmond, and San Francisco Districts. Office builders were less active than in the past in the Atlanta, Cleveland, and Richmond regions, as well as in the city of St. Louis. Commercial vacancies rose in the Atlanta, Chicago, Kansas City, and San Francisco Districts. New York, in spite of the attack, still experienced a slight up-tick in vacancies. Office building held stead in the Cleveland District.

Residential construction rose only in Philadelphia and some areas of the St. Louis region. It held steady in the Cleveland and Minneapolis Districts and fell in the Atlanta, Boston, Chicago, Dallas, Kansas City, New York, Richmond and San Francisco Districts and some portions of the St. Louis region. In Boston, the decline followed a strong summer, so that on a year-over-year basis, construction activity was still up. In the Richmond and New York regions, the decline was seen in the construction of luxury homes. New York also reports a sharp decline in rents in Manhattan.

Agriculture and Natural Resources

Most of the year's crops have not been harvested. Corn and soybean harvests were good in Richmond and St. Louis regions and in the southern part of the Cleveland region, but were below normal in the Chicago and Kansas City regions and in the northern part of the Cleveland region. Prices for cattle and jogs are low. Kansas City reports that the winter wheat crop is in the ground ahead of schedule. Atlanta reports a poor cotton harvest. Minneapolis and Dallas report weather-related poor crop yields, but San Francisco notes that West Coast harvests have generally been good.

Decreases in oil and natural gas prices have led to a decline of drilling activity in the Dallas and Kansas City Districts. Decreases in steel production have caused several iron ore mines to close in the Minneapolis District.

Financial Services and Credit

Banks experienced greater mortgage refinancing activity in response to lower interest rates across District. New mortgage lending was also reported to have increased in all but four Districts: Kansas City and San Francisco, where load activity generally decreased in most categories, and Boston and Dallas. Atlanta, Cleveland, New York, Philadelphia, and St. Louis report consumer loans were down. Cleveland, Philadelphia, and St. Louis report increases in commercial lending, and Chicago, New York, Richmond, and St. Louis report decreases in these loans.

The Chicago, Cleveland, New York, and San Francisco Districts report that loan delinquencies were up, and credit standards were reportedly higher in the Atlanta, Kansas City, and New York Districts. Non-performing loans were higher in the Philadelphia and St. Louis Districts.

Employment

Many Districts report layoffs in a wide variety of jobs. Large manufacturing lay-offs are reported in the Boston, Dallas, Kansas City, Chicago, Philadelphia, San Francisco, and St. Louis regions. In the service sector, hotel, tourism, and airline industries laid off people throughout the country. In addition, the Dallas, Richmond, and Philadelphia Districts saw cutbacks in the retail sector, and New York reports layoffs in the financial services industry. The West Coast's media and advertising industry also experienced large layoffs.

Wages and Prices

Most Districts report little or no change in wages. Manufacturers were reducing salaries in the Boston District, and wages were down in parts of the San Francisco District. Steady wages or no wage pressure are reported in the Chicago, Kansas City, New York, and Richmond regions, as well as among temporary workers in the Minneapolis region. The Atlanta, Cleveland, and Dallas Districts report that wage pressures had subsided or were subdued. Dallas and San Francisco also report an increase in healthcare costs.

Most Districts report steady or declining consumer prices. Districts reporting steady retail prices included Kansas City and Richmond. San Francisco reports steady prices except for declining prices in apparel. Districts reporting lower retail prices included Atlanta, Boston, Chicago, and Dallas. The prices for manufactured goods also fell in the Chicago, Dallas, and New York regions, while they were steady in Atlanta, Kansas City, and San Francisco.

THE ORGANIZATION OF NORTH AMERICAN HOMELAND SECURITY APPARATUS

Security is often a simple matter of "extending the perimeter." The large perimeter of defending the North American homeland is protected by a number of civilian, law enforcement and military agencies throughout Canada and the United States.

U.S. Department of Homeland Security[16]

The National Strategy for Homeland Security and Homeland Security Act of 2002 served to mobilize and organize our nation to secure the homeland from terrorist attacks. This exceedingly complex mission requires a focused effort from our entire society if we are to be successful. To this end, one primary reason for the establishment of the Department of Homeland Security was to provide the unifying core for the vast national network of organizations and institutions involved in efforts to secure our nation. In order to do this better and to provide guidance

Figure 1.2 Members and Regions of North American Aerospace Defense

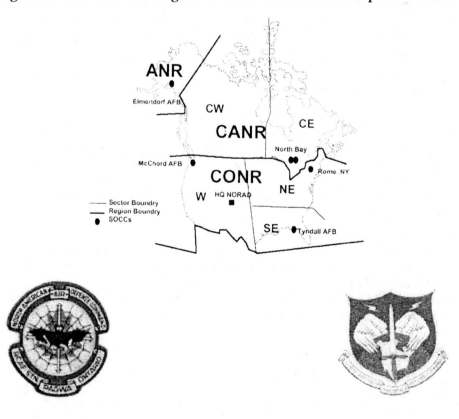

to the 180,000 DHS men and women who work every day on this important task, the Department developed its own high-level strategic plan. The vision and mission statements, strategic goals and objectives provide the framework guiding the actions that make up the daily operations of the department.

Vision

Preserving our freedoms, protecting American ... we secure our homeland.

Mission

We will lead the unified national effort to secure America. We will prevent and deter terrorist attacks and protect against and respond to threats and hazards to the nation. We will ensure safe and secure borders, welcome lawful immigrants and visitors, and promote the free-flow of commerce.

Strategic Goals

Awareness—Identify and understand threats, assess vulnerabilities, determine potential impacts and disseminate timely information to our homeland security partners and the American public.

Prevention—Detect, deter and mitigate threats to our homeland.

Protection—Safeguard our people and their freedoms, critical infrastructure, property and the economy of our Nation from acts of terrorism, natural disasters, or other emergencies.

Response—Lead, manage and coordinate the national response to acts of terrorism, natural disasters, and other emergencies.

Recovery—Lead national, state, local and private sector efforts to restore services and rebuild communities after acts of terrorism, natural disasters, or other emergencies.

Service—Serve the public effectively by facilitating lawful trade, travel and immigration.

Organizational Excellence—Value our most important resource, our people. Create a culture that promotes a common identity, innovation, mutual respect, accountability and teamwork to achieve efficiencies, effectiveness, and operational synergies.

U.S. Northern Command (NORCOM)

The Department of Defense established U.S. Northern Command in 2002 to consolidate under a single unified command existing missions that were previously executed by other military organizations.

The command's mission is homeland defense and civil support, specifically:

Command operations to deter, prevent, and defeat threats and aggression aimed at the United States, its territories, and interests within the assigned area of responsibility; and

As directed by the President or Secretary of Defense, provide military assistance to civil authorities including consequence management operations.

U.S. Northern Command plans, organizes, and executes homeland defense and civil support missions, but has few permanently assigned forces. The command will be assigned forces whenever necessary to execute missions as ordered by the President.

Approximately 500 civil service employees and uniformed personnel representing all service branches provide this essential unity of command.

North American Air Defense Command (NORAD)

There are three regions, two countries, one team responsible for protecting the airspace of two vast countries. North American Aerospace Defense Command's area of responsibility stretches from Clear, Alaska, to the Florida Keys, and from St. John's Newfoundland to San Diego, California. Thousands of U.S. and Canadian military members have worked side-by-side in both countries for more than 40 years to protect North America against an aerospace attack. Aerospace warning and control are the cornerstones of the NORAD mission.

To perform its twin missions of aerospace warning and aerospace control, NORAD consists of three regions: Alaskan NORAD Region (ANR), Canadian NORAD Region (CANR), and the Continental U.S. NORAD Region (CONR).

CONR is further broken into three sectors: Western Air Defense Sector at McChord AFB, Washington; Northeast Air Defense Sector at Rome, New York; and Southeast Air Defense Sector at Tyndall AFB, Florida, which is also the headquarters for CONR.

CANR's headquarters is in Winnipeg, Manitoba, and the Canadian Air Defense Sector is located in North Bay, Ontario. ANR's headquarters is located at Elmendorf ARB, Alaska, adjacent to Anchorage.

The Department of Public Safety & Emergency Preparedness: Canada

On December 12, 2003, Prime Minister Paul Martin announced restructuring changes to government on Securing Canada's Public Health and Safety. While globalization offers enhanced opportunities for Canada, it also brings new risks, including new threats of disease, international criminal activity and terrorism.

The Government of Canada must play a fundamental role in securing the public health and safety of Canadians, while ensuring that all Canadians continue to enjoy the benefits of an open society. The government will achieve these goals by making the following changes to integrate federal activities under strong leadership, maximize the effectiveness of interagency cooperation, and increase accountability to all Canadians.

1. Creating a new Minister of Public Safety and Emergency Preparedness, to integrate into a single portfolio the core activities of the existing Solicitor

General portfolio that secure the safety of Canadians and other activities required to protect against and respond to natural disasters and security emergencies;

2. Integrating the Office of Critical Infrastructure Protection and Emergency Preparedness (currently in the Department of National Defence) into the Public Safety and Emergency Preparedness portfolio to maximize emergency preparedness and responses to natural disaster and security emergencies, as well as improving connections to provincial and territorial emergency preparedness networks, and by adding the National Crime Prevention Centre to actively support crime prevention activities;

3. Increasing National Defence Reserves available for civil preparedness, including capacity to deal with natural disasters and local emergencies;

4. Creating a Canada Border Services Agency to build on the Smart Border Initiative and the important progress that has been made in expediting trade and travel while enhancing security with respect to high risk arrivals, and continue to work in close collaboration with business, labour, immigrant and refugee groups, and other important stakeholders in pursuing these changes.

5. Protecting the interests of immigrants and refugees remains the responsibility of Citizenship and Immigration, which will continue to be present at all major airports and land crossings to issue immigration benefits, to greet new Canadians and to make immigration determinations that will be based on existing criteria. There will be consultations with stakeholders to fully define this presence;

6. Reforming the refugee determination process to create a more predictable and streamlined system, including a reformed appointment process to ensure the quality and effectiveness of the Immigration and Refugee Board;

7. Creating an independent arm's length review mechanism for the RCMP's activities with respect to national security. The mechanism will be designed in a way that respects the important principle of the independence of the police in relation to law enforcement and criminal investigations;

8. Creating a new position of National Security Advisor to the Prime Minister in the Privy Council Office, to be responsible for intelligence and threat assessment integration and interagency cooperation, and to assist the Minister of Public Safety and Emergency Preparedness in the development and overall implementation of an integrated policy for national security and emergencies, to be referred to the appropriate House Standing Committee;

9. Creating a new Canada Public Health Agency, under the Minister of Health, Intergovernmental Affairs, and Minister responsible for Official Languages, following consultations with provincial and territorial governments, to address public health risks and coordinate a national response to health crises, assisted by the Minister of State (Public Health);

10. Establishing a new Cabinet Committee on Security, Public Health, and Emergencies, chaired by the Minister of Public Safety and Emergency Preparedness, to manage national security and intelligence issues and activities and coordinate government-wide responses to all emergencies, including public health, natural disasters and security;

11. Proposing a National Security Standing Committee in the House of Commons whose members would be sworn-in as Privy Councilors so that they could be briefed on national security issues; and

12. Rationalizing responsibility for marine safety and security policy under the Minister of Transport to consolidate responsibility for security in all transportation sectors and creating the Coast Guard as a special operating agency in the Fisheries and Oceans department.

Study: The North Atlantic Treaty Organizations (NATO) Article Five: "An Attack Against One is an Attack Against All"—invoked for the first time on September 12, 2001

What is NATO?[17]

The North Atlantic Treaty Organization (NATO) is an alliance of 26 countries from North America and Europe committed to fulfilling the goals of the North Atlantic Treaty signed on 4 April 1949. In accordance with the Treaty, the fundamental role of NATO is to safeguard the freedom and security of its member countries by political and military means. NATO is playing an increasingly important role in crisis management and peacekeeping.

What is Article 5?[18]

Article Five of the North Atlantic Treaty Organization—Signed in Washington, D.C., on April 4, 1949.

"The Parties agree that an armed attack against one or more of them in Europe or North America shall be considered an attack against them all and consequently they agree that, if such an armed attack occurs, each of them, in exercise of the right of individual or collective self-defence recognised by Article 51 of the Charter of the United Nations, will assist the Party or Parties so attacked by taking forthwith, individually and in concert with the other Parties, such action as it deems necessary, including the use of armed force, to "restore and maintain the security of the North Atlantic area."

The decision:

On 12 September, NATO decided that, if it is determined that the attack against the United States was directed from abroad, it shall be regarded as an action covered by Article 5 of the Washington Treaty.

This is the first time in the Alliance's history that Article 5 has been invoked.

Article 5 of the Washington Treaty:

The Parties agree that an armed attack against one or more of them in Europe of North America shall be considered an attack against them all and consequently they agree that, if such an armed attack occurs, each of them, in exercise of the right of individual or collective self-defense recognized by Article 51 of the Charter of the United Nations, will assist the Party or Parties so attacked by taking forthwith, individually and in concert with the other Parties, such action as it deems necessary, including the use of armed force, to restore and maintain the security of the North Atlantic area.

Any such armed attack and all measures taken as a result thereof shall immediately be reported to the Security Council. Such measures shall be terminated when the Security Council has taken the measures necessary to restore and maintain international peace and security.

NATO's Strategic Concept recognizes the risks to the Alliance posed by terrorism.

What does Article 5 mean?

Article 5 is at the basis of a fundamental principle of the North Atlantic Treaty Organization. It provides that if a NATO ally is the victim of an armed attack, each and every member of the Alliance will consider this act of violence as an armed attack against all members and will take the actions it deems necessary to assist the Ally attacked.

This is the principle of collective defence.

Article 5 and the case of the terrorist attacks against the United States:

The United States has been the object of brutal terrorist attacks. It immediately consulted with the other members of the Alliance. The Alliance determined that the U.S. had been the object of an armed attack. The Alliance therefore agreed that if it was determined that this attack was directed from abroad, it would be regarded as covered by Article 5. NATO Secretary General, Lord Robertson, subsequently informed the Secretary-General of the United Nations of the Alliance's decision.

Article 5 has thus been invoked, but not determination has yet been made whether the attack against the United States was directed from abroad. If such a determination is made, each Ally will then consider what assistance it should provide. In practice, there will be consultations among the Allies. Any collective action by NATO will be decided by the North Atlantic Council. The United States can also carry out independent actions, consistent with its rights and obligations under the UN Charter.

Allies can provide any form of assistance they deem necessary to respond to the situation. This assistance is not necessarily military and depends on the material resources of each country. Each individual member determines how it will contribute and will consult with other members, bearing in mind that the ultimate aim is to "restore and maintain the security of the North Atlantic area."

By invoking Article 5, NATO members have shown their solidarity toward the United States and condemned, in the strongest possible way, the terrorist attacks against the United States on 11 September.

If the conditions are met for the application of Article 5, NATO allies will decide how to assist the United States (many allies have clearly offered emergency assistance). Each Ally is obliged to assist the United States by taking forward, individually and in concert with other Allies, such action it deems necessary. This is an individual obligation on each Ally and each Ally is responsible for determining what it deems necessary in these particular circumstances.

No collective action will be taken by NATO until further consultations are held and further decisions are made by the North Atlantic Council.

Reprinted from http://www.nato.int/issues/faq, April 23, 2004, North Atlantic Treaty Organisation.

SUMMARY

The all-hazards approach provides architecture of organization, and an opportunity to use imagination and creativity in the process of best applying resources to coping with the potential threats we face, whether caused by man or nature.

By assessing the risks, evaluating resources, and planning for all contingencies, individuals, businesses, and government can better prepare to avoid or mitigate a crisis.

ADDITIONAL DISCUSSION TOPICS

- How would you compare and contrast the psychological impact on the American psyche versus the physical damage to life and property of the terrorist attacks against US targets?

- How do you balance freedoms guaranteed by the U.S. Constitution in contrast to restrictions of freedom required by the need for security?

Endnotes

[1] "United States of America," *Central Intelligence Agency—The World Fact Book 2003*, 2003.

[2] US Nuclear Regulatory Commission.

[3] Denny, Charlotte, Paul Brown, and Tim Radford. "The Shackles of Poverty," *The Guardian*, August 2002. Posted on www.sierraclub.org/population/consumption (the website of the Sierra Club).

[4] "DHS Budget in Brief," U.S. Department of Homeland Security; February 2003; www.dhs.gov/dhspublic

[5] "DHS Organization," U.S. Department of Homeland Security; 2003; www.dhs.gov/dhspublic

[6] The National Strategy for Homeland Security; The White House," U.S. Government Printing Office, 2003.

[7] Ibid.

[8] Ibid.

[9] "Department of Homeland Security," *Budget of the United States Government: Fiscal Year 2005*, United States Office of Budget and Management, 2004.

[10] *The Merriam-Webster Dictionary*, Pocket Books, NY, NY.

[11] Douglas Jehl, "Ex-Saudi Chief of Intelligence Casts Doubt on Iraq-Qaeda Tie," *The New York Times* Service, November 22, 2001.

[12] Kasra Naji, Reuters, "Taliban Wants Bin Laden to Stop Making Anti-U.S. Threats," Cable News Network, August 24, 1998.

[13] Council on Foreign Relations, "Terrorism and the Media," *Terrorism Q&A*, 2004.

[14] Robyn Pangi, "After the Attack: The Psychological Impact of Terrorism," Executive Session of Domestic Preparedness, John F. Kennedy School of Government, Harvard University, August, 2002.

[15] Ibid.

[16] *National Strategy for the Protection of Critical Infrastructures and Key Assets.*

[17] North Atlantic Treaty Organisation Official Homepage, http://www.nato.int/issues/faq, April 23, 2004.

[18] Ibid.

CHAPTER TWO

THE MOTIVATIONS OF TERRORISM AND TARGET SELECTION

If inciting people to do that [9/11] is terrorism, and if killing those who kill our sons is terrorism, then let history be witness that we are terrorists.
—Osama bin Laden, interview, October 2001

I was called a terrorist yesterday, but when I came out of jail, many people embraced me, including my enemies, and that is what I normally tell other people who say those who are struggling for liberation in their country are terrorists. I tell them that I was also a terrorist yesterday, but, today, I am admired by the very people who said I was one.
—Nelson Mandela, on *Larry King Live*, May 16, 2000

We do not create terrorism by fighting the terrorists. We invite terrorism by ignoring them.
—George W. Bush, speech, December 18, 2005

KEY TERMS

Terrorism
Anti Terrorism
Counter Terrorism
High Value Asset
Hit and Run Tactic
Cellular Structure

OBJECTIVES

■ Describe common definitions of terrorism.

■ Describe the historical perspective of terrorism.

■ Identify common components associated with terrorism.

■ List the types and tactics of terrorism.

■ Describe the difference between anti-terrorism efforts and counterterrorism tactics.

DISCUSSION TOPICS

■ Why is it so difficult to develop a widely accepted definition of terrorism?

■ How do terrorists use the media as a weapon?

■ In what ways do guerillas, whether nationalist, ideological etc, differ from terrorists?

■ Why do terrorist groups have to use hit-and-run tactics? Is this a strength or weakness?

■ Why are mines, bombs, and other explosive devices so especially suitable for terrorist use?

2

INTRODUCTION

Terrorism is much in the news these days, but the widely varying definitions of terrorism make discussion of the topic difficult. By developing a better understanding of terrorist goals and tactics students will come closer to deriving their own working definitions of terrorism, and gain a better perspective from which both counter terrorist and anti terrorist activities can be evaluated. In this chapter we'll be exploring many facets of terrorism, and the responses to terrorism. From sources of funding and equipment, to the cellular structure used by the most professional and successful groups, to the strategies terrorists use to choose the targets they will attack, students will have a basic understanding of this ancient form of asymmetrical warfare. Terrorism is not a new tactic, and it cannot be expected to go out of favor any time soon.

FBI's DEFINITION OF TERRORISM[1]

There is no single, universally accepted definition of terrorism. Terrorism is defined in the *Code of Federal Regulations* as "...the unlawful use of force and violence against persons or property to intimidate or coerce a government, the civilian population, or any segment thereof, in furtherance of political or social objectives." (28 C.F.R. Section 0.85)

The FBI further describes terrorism as either domestic or international, depending on the origin, base, and objectives of the terrorist organization. For the purpose of this report, the FBI uses the following definitions of terrorism:

- Domestic terrorism refers to activities that involve acts dangerous to human life that are a violation of the criminal laws of the United States or of any state; appear to be intended to intimidate or coerce a civilian population; to influence the policy of a government by mass destruction, assassination, or kidnapping; and occur primarily within the territorial jurisdiction of the United States. [18 U.S.C. § 2331(5)]

- International terrorism involves violent acts or acts dangerous to human life that are a violation of the criminal laws of the United States or any state, or that would be a criminal violation if committed within the jurisdiction of the United States or any state. These acts appear to be intended to intimidate or coerce a civilian population; influence the policy of a government by intimidation or coercion; or affect the conduct of a government by mass destruction, assassination or kidnapping and occur primarily outside the territorial jurisdiction of the United States or transcend national boundaries in terms of the means by which they are accomplished, the persons they appear intended to intimidate or coerce, or the locale in which their perpetrators operate or seek asylum. [18 U.S.C. § 2331(1)]

The FBI divides terrorist-related activity into two categories:

- A terrorist *incident* is a violent act or an act dangerous to human life, in violation of the criminal laws of the United States, or of any state, to intimidate or coerce a government, the civilian population, or any segment thereof, in furtherance of political or social objectives.

- A terrorism *prevention* is a documented instance in which a violent act by a known or suspected terrorist group or individual with the means and a proven propensity for violence is successfully interdicted through investigative activity.

NOTE: The FBI investigates terrorism-related matters without regard to race, religion, national origin, or gender. Reference to individual members of any political, ethnic, or religious group in this report is not meant to imply that all members of that group are terrorists. Terrorists represent a small criminal minority in any larger social context.

TERRORISM AND OUR PROTECTIVE MEASURE

There are two elements in the response to terrorism: anti-terrorism and counter terrorism. The former represents *target-hardening* (or defensive measures) and recovery-the latter outlines an offensive strategy attacking either pre-emptively or punitively.

Security specialists, in most cases, will focus on the concept of anti-terrorism. This requires knowledge of the terror groups and an ability to plan accordingly to the latest intelligence and professional security standards.

However, there is a new horizon with which the criminal justice system, security profession, and the military must cope: the overlap in responsibilities and jurisdiction in terror prevention and response.

The criminal element is the subject of the first article in this chapter. A race-based prison gang terrorizes the heartland with crime and intimidation. Are they true terrorists in the sense of the FBI or Department of Homeland Security definitions? Perhaps, but they also present a clear threat to the community in terms of safety and economy.

Case Study: Prison Gang Built Network of Violence and Intimidation[2]

The woman had been ripped off on a drug sale she made, but she knew exactly what to do about it.

She got hold of her incarcerated son, a member of the 211 Crew prison gang, and told him to have the guy who didn't pay her for the methamphetamine she'd sold him taken care of.

With an elaborate network of gang members inside and outside prison, that could easily be done.

But instead of a gang member, undercover Denver police Detective Aaron Lopez called her.

Lopez, who spent months infiltrating the gang and went by the name of "Salvage," offered his services to her.

"I'm going to beat ... and rob him for everything he's got," he told the woman, who seemed pleased by his enthusiasm.

Several days later, another undercover agent met with her. He showed her items she believed were taken during the beating and robbery: $460, a watch and a ring.

The woman's son was so happy he wrote Salvage a letter.

"I ... wanted to send you my sickest respect your way," the letter said. "If ever I can do anything for you let me know and it's done!!"

The undercover work by Lopez and others was extremely important in bringing down the gang, authorities said.

Last week, top leaders and associates of the 211 Crew organization were indicted for racketeering, accused of making money by selling guns and drugs and using violence inside and outside of prison to collect debts, rectify imagined slights and go after former members who had deserted the organization.

The group is a prison-based gang of white supremacists with an estimated 300 members. In all, 24 were indicted.

Lopez called the 18 months investigating the 211 Crew the worst of his life.

During part of that time, Lopez posed as a gang member to stop one of the many hits directed by gang members in prison to their compatriots on the outside.

They showed undercover agents how to properly kill someone, by putting a gun in someone's mouth in just the right position to blow his brains out.

Many times, the lives of the undercover officers were at stake.

"Those kinds of high-risk people create a high-risk environment," said Jim Welton, commander of the Safe Streets Metro Gang Task Force, who led the investigation. "If the officer is detected or they discover the identity, you can reasonably anticipate that they are going to respond in a violent way as they have done on so many other occasions."

Codes Were the Key

What gave Lopez and others key insight into the gang was their ability to decipher coded phone calls and letters between gang members.

By doing so, Lopez was able to communicate with them and insinuate himself into the gang. He'd say he was getting paroled from a prison in Buena Vista soon, and when he got out, he'd be available for any retaliation or drug sales the gang needed.

Thousands of documents were examined, including communication records, phone calls and letters, and put into a logical sequence and pattern, allowing investigators to decode the hidden messages.

Lopez said that the codes were intricate.

"We deciphered one where it looked like a normal letter but within it you'd take the first word, the second word, something like that, and within that, there magically would be a sentence," Lopez said.

In some letters, only every third word had significance and compiling them would form a message. Other letters had numbers with special symbolism.

Welton said the 211 Crew is different from any other prison-based gang he has seen in his 31 years in law enforcement.

In most prison gangs, you are free to leave the gang when your prison sentence is over, Welton said. But not the 211.

Either you did what they wanted or you were dealt with, sometimes costing a gang member his life.

"The expectation of this gang was clearly once you affiliated with this organization you would remain affiliated, and our information clearly indicated that breaking from them could result in retaliatory violence," Welton said.

Five members of the group were indicted for murdering Arkansas Valley Correctional Facility inmate Donald Mayfield, allegedly for no other reason than to let inmate Brad Simpson, 26, "earn his stripes" so he could become a 211 Crew member.

Gang's Roots in Racism

The gang had its roots at the Arkansas Correctional Facility in Crowley County in the early 1990s when a black inmate beat a white inmate, said Lt. Dan Foster, an intelligence officer at the Colorado State Penitentiary in Cañon City, the state's highest-security prison.

Inmate Benjamin Davis vowed he wouldn't allow that to happen again. Davis, of Irish descent, often etched 211 in shamrocks on tattoos and correspondence. The gang was first intended to provide protection for white inmates.

And to make it the meanest, toughest prison gang in Colorado, the gang recruited the most violent of offenders.

"That's what they really like. They want to recruit killers and people like that because someone with a life sentence inside has nothing to lose," Lopez said. "They want to recruit people who create fear in other inmates."

But the 211 leaders in prison also wanted short-termers who could go out and sell drugs and weapons and send money back into the prison to make life comfortable for gang leaders and also to funnel money to compatriots on the outside, Lopez said.

Welton said that for 211 members with shorter sentences, there was a certain allure to being a member. In prison, they had status and credibility, and when they left they had access to narcotics and drug trafficking to provide a money-making source upon release.

Jay Kirby, the Colorado Department of Corrections' intelligence coordinator, said the prison gang evolved from a protection organization with a white-supremacist ideology to an active criminal enterprise specializing in the drug trade. Targets for violence tended mostly to be the gang's own members who failed to carry out orders to deal drugs or who violated the gang's loose race code.

Even after Davis was sent to the Colorado State Penitentiary, where inmates are isolated in single-occupant cells 23 hours a day, he allegedly managed to hold court and deal out punishment as the crew's top leader. He got his message out by screaming at crew members during his one-hour exercise periods and by writing encrypted letters.

Among the two most prominent figures indicted for racketeering are Davis, 29, leader of the 211 Crew, and Dan Shea, 29, a member of 211's "inner circle."

Shea was indicted for, among other things, having the cat of his former girlfriend kidnapped because he was afraid she was about to testify.

Lopez believes the indictments will have an impact on the 211 Crew.

"I think people are going to realize that we are going after the upper echelon people of the group," he said. "It is groups like this who I believe corrupt the whole system."

Ethical Considerations...

You are a supervisor in a special operations unit. You have captured a terrorist who is clearly involved in an imminent plot to attack the United States. You have captured him in a workshop and a power drill is nearby. He is refusing to answer questions. Americans may die. What, if anything, would you do?

THE ONGOING THREAT FROM WITHIN

Criminal enterprises do not present the only threat to the homeland. There is the existence of dangerous extremist groups that also create an additional category of threat to the United States. In this article, the Section Chief for Domestic Terrorism addresses a group known as ALF (the Animal Liberation Front), and other groups in a statement before the House Resources Committee.

Case Study: "The Threat of Eco-Terrorism"[3]

Good morning Chairman McInnis, Vice-Chairman Peterson, Congressman Inslee and Members of the Subcommittee. I am pleased to have the opportunity to appear before you and discuss the threat posed by eco-terrorism, as well as the measures being taken by the FBI and our law enforcement partners to address this threat.

The FBI divides the terrorist threat facing the United States into two broad categories, international and domestic. International terrorism involves violent acts or acts dangerous to human life that are a violation of the criminal laws of the United States or any state, or that would be a criminal violation if committed within the jurisdiction of the United States or any state. Acts of international terrorism are intended to intimidate or coerce a civilian population, influence the policy of a government, or affect the conduct of a government. These acts transcend national boundaries in terms of the means by which they are accomplished, the persons they appear intended to intimidate, or the locale in which perpetrators operate.

Domestic terrorism is the unlawful use, or threatened use, of violence by a group or individual based and operating entirely within the United States (or its territories) without foreign direction, committed against persons or property to intimidate or coerce a government, the civilian population, or any segment thereof, in furtherance of political or social objectives.

During the past decade we have witnessed dramatic changes in the nature of the terrorist threat. In the 1990s, right-wing extremism overtook left-wing terrorism as the most dangerous domestic terrorist threat to the country. During the past several years, special interest extremism, as characterized by the Animal Liberation Front (ALF) and the Earth Liberation Front (ELF), has emerged as a serious terrorist threat. Generally, extremist groups engage in much activity that is protected by constitutional guarantees of free speech and assembly. Law enforcement becomes involved when the volatile talk of these groups transgresses into unlawful action. The FBI estimates that the ALF/ELF have committed more than 600 criminal acts in the United States since 1996, resulting in damages in excess of 43 million dollars.

Special interest terrorism differs from traditional right-wing and left-wing terrorism in that extremist special interest groups seek to resolve specific issues, rather than effect widespread political change. Special interest extremists continue to conduct acts of politically motivated violence to force segments of society, including the general public, to change attitudes about issues considered important to their causes. These groups occupy the extreme fringes of animal rights, pro-life, environmental, anti-nuclear, and other movements. Some special interest extremists — most notably within the animal rights and environmental movements — have turned increasingly toward vandalism and terrorist activity in attempts to further their causes.

Since 1977, when disaffected members of the ecological preservation group Greenpeace formed the Sea Shepherd Conservation Society and attacked commercial fishing operations by cutting drift nets, acts of "eco-terrorism" have occurred around the globe. The FBI defines eco-terrorism as the use or threatened use of violence of a criminal nature against innocent victims or property by an environmentally oriented, subnational group for environmental-political reasons, or aimed at an audience beyond the target, often of a symbolic nature.

In recent years, the Animal Liberation Front (ALF) has become one of the most active extremist elements in the United States. Despite the destructive aspects of ALF's operations, its operational philosophy discourages acts that harm "any animal, human and nonhuman." Animal rights groups in the United States, including the ALF, have generally adhered to this mandate. The ALF, established in Great Britain in the mid-1970s, is a loosely organized movement committed to ending the abuse and exploitation of animals. The American branch of the ALF began its operations in the late 1970s. Individuals become members of the ALF not by filing paperwork or paying dues, but simply by engaging in "direct action" against companies or individuals who utilize animals for research or economic gain. "Direct action" generally occurs in the form of criminal activity to cause economic loss or to destroy the victims' company operations. The ALF activists have engaged in a steadily growing campaign of illegal activity against fur companies, mink farms, restaurants, and animal research laboratories.

Estimates of damage and destruction in the United States claimed by the ALF during the past ten years, as compiled by national organizations such as the Fur Commission and the National Association for Biomedical Research (NABR), put the fur industry and medical research losses at more than 45 million dollars. The ALF is considered a terrorist group, whose purpose is to bring about social and political change through the use of force and violence.

Disaffected environmentalists, in 1980, formed a radical group called "Earth First!" and engaged in a series of protests and civil disobedience events. In 1984, however, members introduced "tree spiking" (insertion of metal or ceramic spikes in trees in an effort to damage saws) as a tactic to thwart logging. In 1992, the ELF was founded in Brighton, England, by Earth First! members who refused to abandon criminal acts as a tactic when others wished to mainstream Earth First!. In 1993, the ELF was listed for the first time along with the ALF in a communique declaring solidarity in actions between the two groups. This unity continues today with a crossover of leadership and membership. It is not uncommon for the ALF and the ELF to post joint declarations of responsibility for criminal actions on their web-sites. In 1994, founders of the San Francisco branch of Earth First! published in The Earth First! Journal a recommendation that Earth First! mainstream itself in the United States, leaving criminal acts other than unlawful protests to the ELF.

The ELF advocates "monkeywrenching," a euphemism for acts of sabotage and property destruction against industries and other entities perceived to be damaging to the natural environment. "Monkeywrenching" includes tree spiking, arson, sabotage of logging or construction equipment, and other types of property destruction. Speeches given by Jonathan Paul and Craig Rosebraugh at the 1998 National Animal Rights Conference held at the University of Oregon, promoted the unity of both the ELF and the ALF movements. The ELF posted information on the ALF website until it began its own website in January 2001, and is listed in the same underground activist publications as the ALF.

The most destructive practice of the ALF/ELF is arson. The ALF/ELF members consistently use improvised incendiary devices equipped with crude but effective timing mechanisms. These incendiary devices are often constructed based upon instructions found on the ALF/ELF websites. The ALF/ELF criminal incidents often involve pre-activity surveillance and well-planned operations. Members are believed to engage in significant intelligence gathering against potential targets, including the review of industry/trade publications, photographic/video surveillance of potential targets, and posting details about potential targets on the Internet.

The ALF and the ELF have jointly claimed credit for several raids including a November 1997 attack of the Bureau of Land Management wild horse corrals near Burns, Oregon, where arson destroyed the entire complex resulting in damages in excess of four hundred and fifty thousand dollars and the June 1998 arson attack of a U.S. Department of Agriculture Animal Damage Control Building near Olympia, Washington, in which damages exceeded two million dollars. The ELF claimed sole credit for the October 1998, arson of a Vail, Colorado, ski facility in which four ski lifts, a restaurant, a picnic facility and a utility building were destroyed. Damage exceeded $12 million. On 12/27/1998, the ELF claimed responsibility for the arson at the U.S. Forest Industries Office in Medford, Oregon, where damages exceeded five hundred thousand dollars. Other arsons in Oregon, New York, Washington, Michigan, and Indiana have been claimed by the ELF. Recently, the ELF has also claimed attacks on genetically engineered crops and trees. The ELF claims these attacks have totaled close to $40 million in damages.

The name of a group called the Coalition to Save the Preserves (CSP), surfaced in relation to a series of arsons that occurred in the Phoenix, Arizona, area. These arsons targeted several new homes under construction near the North Phoenix Mountain Preserves. No direct connection was established between the CSP and ALF/ELF. However, the stated goal of CSP to stop development of previously undeveloped lands, is similar to that of the ELF. The property damage associated with the arsons has been estimated to be in excess of $5 million.

The FBI has developed a strong response to the threats posed by domestic and international terrorism. Between fiscal years 1993 and 2003, the number of Special Agents dedicated to the FBI's counterterrorism programs grew by approximately 224 percent to 1,669 — nearly 16 percent of all FBI Special Agents. In recent years, the FBI has strengthened its counterterrorism program to enhance its abilities to carry out these objectives.

Cooperation among law enforcement agencies at all levels represents an important component of a comprehensive response to terrorism. This cooperation assumes its most tangible operational form in the Joint Terrorism Task Forces (JTTFs) that are established in 44 cities across the nation. These task forces are particularly well suited to responding to terrorism because they combine the national and international investigative resources of the FBI with the street-level expertise of local law enforcement agencies. Given the success of the JTTF concept, the FBI has established 15 new JTTFs since the end of 1999. By the end of 2003 the FBI plans to have established JTTFs in each of its 56 field offices. By integrating the investigative abilities of the FBI and local law enforcement agencies, these task forces represent an effective response to the threats posed to U.S. communities by domestic and international terrorists.

The FBI and our law enforcement partners have made a number of arrests of individuals alleged to have perpetrated acts of eco-terrorism. Several of these individuals have been successfully prosecuted. Following the investigation of the Phoenix, Arizona, arsons noted earlier, Mark Warren Sands was indicted and arrested on 6/14/2001. On 11/07/2001, Sands pleaded guilty to ten counts of extortion and using fire in the commission of a federal felony.

In February 2001, teenagers Jared McIntyre, Matthew Rammelkamp, and George Mashkow all pleaded guilty, as adults, to title 18 U.S.C. 844(i), Arson, and 844(n), Arson Conspiracy. These charges pertain to a series of arsons and attempted arsons of new home construction sites in Long Island, New York. An adult, Connor Cash, was also arrested on February 15, 2001, and charged under the same federal statutes. Jared McIntrye stated that these acts were committed in sympathy of the ELF movement. The New York Joint Terrorism Task Force played a significant role in the arrest and prosecution of these individuals.

On 1/23/2001, Frank Ambrose was arrested by officers of the Department of Natural Resources with assistance from the Indianapolis JTTF, on a local warrant out of Monroe County Circuit Court, Bloomington, Indiana, charging Ambrose with timber spiking. Ambrose is suspected of involvement in the spiking of approximately 150 trees in Indiana state forests. The ELF claimed responsibility for these incidents.

On September 16, 1998, a federal grand jury in the Western District of Wisconsin indicted Peter Young and Justin Samuel for Hobbs Act violations as well as for animal enterprise terrorism. Samuel was apprehended in Belgium, and was subsequently extradited to the United States. On August 30, 2000, Samuel pleaded guilty to two counts of animal enterprise terrorism and was sentenced on November 3, 2000, to two years in prison, two years probation, and ordered to pay $364,106 in restitution. Samuel's prosecution arose out of his involvement in mink releases in Wisconsin in 1997. This incident was claimed by the ALF. The investigation and arrest of Justin Samuel were the result of a joint effort by federal, state, and local agencies.

On April 20, 1997, Douglas Joshua Ellerman turned himself in and admitted on videotape to purchasing, constructing, and transporting five pipe bombs to the scene of the March 11, 1997, arson at the Fur Breeders Agricultural co-op in Sandy, Utah. Ellerman also admitted setting fire to the facility. Ellerman was indicted on June 19, 1997 on 16 counts, and eventually pleaded guilty to three. He was sentenced to seven years in prison and restitution of approximately $750,000. Though this incident was not officially claimed by ALF, Ellerman indicated during an interview subsequent to his arrest that he was a member of ALF. This incident was investigated jointly by the FBI and the Bureau of Alcohol, Tobacco, and Firearms (ATF).

Rodney Adam Coronado was convicted for his role in the February 2, 1992, arson at an animal research laboratory on the campus of Michigan State University. Damage estimates, according to public sources, approached $200,000 and included the destruction of research records. On July 3, 1995, Coronado pled guilty for his role in the arson and was sentenced to 57 months in federal prison, three years probation, and restitution of more than $2 million. This incident was claimed by ALF. The FBI, ATF, and the Michigan State University police played a significant role in the investigation, arrest, and prosecution.

Marc Leslie Davis, Margaret Katherine Millet, Marc Andre Baker, and Ilse Washington Asplund were all members of the self-proclaimed "Evan Mecham Eco-Terrorist International Conspiracy" (EMETIC). EMETIC was formed to engage in eco-terrorism against nuclear power plants and ski resorts in the southwestern United States. In November 1987, the group claimed responsibility for damage to a chairlift at the Fairfield Snow Bowl Ski Resort near Flagstaff, Arizona. Davis, Millet, and Baker were arrested in May 1989 on charges relating to the Fairfield Snow Bowl incident and planned incidents at the Central Arizona Project and Palo Verde nuclear generating stations in Arizona; the Diablo Canyon Nuclear Facility in California; and the Rocky Flats Nuclear Facility in Colorado. All pleaded guilty and were sentenced in September 1991. Davis was sentenced to six years in federal prison, and restitution to the Fairfield Snow Bowl Ski Resort in the amount of $19,821. Millet was sentenced to three years in federal prison, and restitution to Fairfield in the amount of $19,821. Baker was sentenced to one year in federal prison, five months probation, a $5,000 fine, and 100 hours of community service. Asplund was also charged and was sentenced to one year in federal prison, five years probation, a $2,000 fine, and 100 hours of community service.

Currently, more than 26 FBI field offices have pending investigations associated with ALF/ELF activities. Despite all of our efforts (increased resources allocated, JTTFs, successful arrests and prosecutions), law enforcement has a long way to go to adequately address the problem of eco-terrorism. Groups such as the ALF and the ELF present unique challenges. There is little if any hierarchal structure to such entities. Eco-terrorists are unlike traditional criminal enterprises, which are often structured and organized. The difficulty investigating such groups is demonstrated by the fact that law enforcement has thus far been unable to effect the arrests of anyone for some recent criminal activity directed at federal land managers or their offices. However, there are several ongoing investigations regarding such acts. Current investigations include the 10/14/2001 arson at the Bureau of Land Management Wild Horse and Burro Corral in Litchfield, California, the 7/20/2000 destruction of trees and damage to vehicles at the U.S. Forestry Science Laboratory in Rhinelander, Wisconsin, and the 11/29/1997 arson at the Bureau of Land Management Corral in Burns, Oregon.

Before closing, I would like to acknowledge the cooperation and assistance rendered by the U.S. Forest Service in investigating incidents of eco-terrorism. Specifically, I would like to recognize the assistance that the Forest Service is providing with regard to the ongoing investigation of the 7/20/2000 incident of vandalism and destruction that occurred at the U.S. Forestry Science Laboratory in Rhinelander, Wisconsin.

The FBI and all of our federal, state, and local law enforcement partners will continue to strive to address the difficult and unique challenges posed by eco-terrorists. Despite the recent focus on international terrorism, we remain fully cognizant of the full range of threats that confront the United States.

Chairman McInnis and Members of the Subcommittee, this concludes my prepared remarks. I would like to express appreciation for your concentration on the issue of eco-terrorism and I look forward to responding to any questions.

The FBI and local law enforcement are aggressively pursuing terror leads and making criminal cases against terrorists across the country and abroad. There is much controversy about the effectiveness of these efforts. The next article in this chapter addresses the statistics involved in the war on terror and the accuracy of the concerns about the return on investment (ROI) in time and resources.

A SPECIAL TRAC REPORT: CRIMINAL ENFORCEMENT AGAINST TERRORISTS[4]

A Word about the Data

In the last few years, the federal effort to prevent terrorism and punish terrorists has become one of the government's most important jobs. By its very nature, however, the scope and effectiveness of this effort is hard for the public to understand, partly because of the necessary secrecy that shrouds aspects of the struggle.

Three weeks ago, after an aggressive FOIA campaign, TRAC obtained under court order 131 computer tapes with data that off the American people the most up-to-date and complete view ever available about how the government is enforcing the law against international and domestic terrorists.

The date—the most recent of which cover the first nine months of the Bush administration—have been collected routinely by federal prosecutors for many years. Following long-established rules, assistant U.S. Attorneys all over the country are required to record information about every individual matter that the government's many investigative agencies bring to them for prosecution.

Presented here are selected findings about the 1,338 referrals from October 1, 1996 through September 30, 2001 that were classified by federal prosecutors as involving "domestic terrorism" or "international terrorism." How many of the matters did the assistant U.S. Attorneys decline to prosecute? Why were they declined? Which went forward to court? How many defendants were found guilty? How many not guilty? What were the sentences? Which investigative groups were identified as the "lead agency?" What districts around the country had the most referrals? Related information drawn from other sources is available on such subjects as the anti-terrorism spending by the FBI and the special warrants granted by the Foreign Intelligence Surveillance Court.

For further details, the referral-by-referral files can be directly queried on TRAC's subscription services. The subscription services also provide comprehensive data on all other types of criminal matters from immigration to official corruption, civil rights to weapons offenses, civil suits by and against the government, tax enforcement, the staffing of most executive branch agencies and federal spending.

Many Investigations But Few Referred for Prosecution

The FBI now reports conducting more than 10,000 terrorism investigations a year. (See Table 2.1.) By contrast, just released Justice Department data show that in the fiscal year ending September 30, 2001 that all the criminal investigative agencies of the government asked federal prosecutors to bring criminal charges against 463 individuals who the assistant U.S. Attorneys had identified as being involved in either international or domestic terrorism.

TABLE 2.1　FBI EFFORTS IN COMBATTING TERRORISM

Fiscal Year	Terrorism Investigations	Terrorism Funding (millions)
1997	7,125	n/a
1998	9,046	$450.5
1999	10,151	$432.9
2000	10,538	$443
2001 (approved)	n/a	$527
2002 (requested)	n/a	$565.5

n/a　not available

Source: Compiled by TRAC from FBI budget reports, budget submissions and Congressional Research Service reports.

- The gap between the reported investigations and referrals for prosecution would appear to document a major challenge facing law enforcement in its attempts to prevent terrorism and punish terrorists.

Referrals for Prosecution Up Sharply Even Before September 11

The Justice Department's internal administrative data — unlike the information reported by the FBI — distinguish between international and domestic terrorism. Investigative requests for prosecution increased substantially in FY 2001 — particularly for international terrorism — but still represented only a tiny fraction of all federal criminal matters:

- In FY 1997 there were 48 referrals for prosecution involving *international terrorism*. For the next three years, the numbers remained relatively steady— 33 in 1998, 60 in 1999, and 40 in 2000. They jumped to 204 in 2001 — 124 out of the 204 occurred before September 11. (See graph and table.)

- There were somewhat more referrals against those suspected of *domestic terrorism* during the same period: 147 in 1997, 166 in 1998, 187 in 1999, 194 in 2000 and 259 in 2001. A total of 214 out of the 259 occurred before September 11. (See Table 2.2 and Figure 2.1.)

But Federal Prosecutors Usually Decline To Bring Charges

The data also show that federal prosecutors declined to bring charges against more than two out of three of the criminal suspects who they themselves had classified as being involved in domestic or international terrorism. (See Figure 2.2.) Most of the suspects were referred to the prosecutors by the FBI.

Such matters made up only a very small part of the 681,000 criminal referrals of all kinds that the prosecutors said they had received from the investigative agencies during the five- year period. (See Figure 2.3.) But the events of September 11 — and before that the bombings in Oklahoma City, Nairobi and Aden — have made the processing of them a subject of major public concern.

The prosecutors cited many reasons for rejecting the recommendations of the investigators during the five-year period ending on September 30, among them Justice Department policy, the death of the defendant, and jurisdictional or venue problems. But the prosecutors said they had declined more than one third of the matters presented to them because the referrals lacked evidence of criminal intent, were of minimal federal interest, were backed up by weak or insufficient admissible evidence, or did not involve a federal offense. (See Tables 2.4 and 2.5 for reasons.)

Curiously, sharp changes appear to have occurred in regard to the bringing of formal criminal charges against terrorist suspects during the last five years. Whether these changes are the result of new investigative practices, different prosecutorial procedures, modifications of the law or simply the mix of types of cases handled is not clear. Whatever the reason, while the proportion of domestic terrorism referrals that were declined was going up, the declination rate for international terrorism referrals was going down. (See Figure 2.4.)

TABLE 2.2   INTERNATIONAL TERRORISM REFERRALS FOR CRIMINAL PROSECUTION

Investigative Agency Recommending Prosecution	Fiscal Year					Total	Percent
	1997	1998	1999	2000	2001		
Total	48	33	60	40	204	385	100.0
Major Investigative Agencies: Federal Bureau of Investigation	47	31	45	31	180	334	86.8
Other Investigatory Agencies: Alcohol Tobacco and Firearms	—	—	3	—	—	3	0.8
Army	—	—	1	1	—	2	0.5
Bureau of Prisons	—	—	—	—	1	1	0.3
Customs Service	—	—	—	3	6	9	2.3
Export/Import Bank of the U.S.	—	—	—	—	1	1	0.3
Forest Service	—	—	—	1	—	1	0.3
Immigration and Naturalization	1	—	—	2	1	4	1.0
Internal Revenue Service	—	—	1	1	5	7	1.8
Joint ATF/State or Local Task Force	—	—	5	—	—	5	1.3
Joint FBI/State or Local Task Force	—	—	1	—	3	4	1.0
National Aeronautics and Space Admin.	—	—	1	—	—	1	0.3
Other Justice Department	—	—	—	—	1	1	0.3
Other State Department	—	—	2	—	1	3	0.8
Secret Service	—	1	—	1	4	6	1.6
U.S. Information Agency	—	1	—	—	—	1	0.3
U.S. Marshal Service	—	—	1	—	1	2	0.5

One perspective on the substantial number of terrorism referrals being turned down by federal prosecutors can be gained by considering the "declination rate" for other groupings. Under law and custom federal prosecutions have always declined to prosecute a portion of the matters brought to them by the agencies. The Justice Department data show, for example, that during the last five years one out of three referrals were declined by prosecutors. (See Table 2.6.) Accordingly, the odds of declination for terrorism cases was twice as high since more than two out of three of these referrals were turned down by federal prosecutors during the same period. It must be assumed that collecting solid evidence about a terrorist is harder than for drug, immigration and white-collar criminals.

TABLE 2.3   DOMESTIC TERRORISM REFERRALS FOR CRIMINAL PROSECUTION

Investigative Agency Recommending Prosecution	Fiscal Year					Total	Percent
	1997	1998	1999	2000	2001		
Total	147	166	187	194	259	953	100.0
Major Investigative Agencies: Federal Bureau of Investigation	105	118	136	135	169	663	69.6
Secret Service	8	23	19	27	53	130	13.6
Alcohol Tobacco and Firearms	14	11	13	10	15	63	6.6
Other Investigatory Agencies: Air Force	1	1	—	1	—	3	0.3
All Other Independent Agencies	—	—	1	—	2	3	0.3
Army	—	—	—	—	1	1	0.1
Customs Service	1	4	—	1	—	6	0.6
General Services Administration	1	—	—	—	1	2	0.2
Immigration and Naturalization	—	1	—	3	—	4	0.4
Indian Affairs Bureau	—	1	—	—	—	1	0.1
Internal Revenue Service	8	—	1	—	2	11	1.2
Joint ATF/State or Local Task Force	—	—	—	7	—	7	0.7
Joint FBI/State or Local Task Force	—	—	2	—	1	3	0.3
Joint Secret Service/State or Local Task	—	—	—	1	—	1	0.1
Land Management Bureau	—	—	1	—	—	1	0.1
Massachusetts	—	—	—	1	—	1	0.1
Navy	—	—	1	1	1	3	0.3
Other Commerce	—	—	1	—	—	1	0.1
Other Defense	—	—	4	—	—	4	0.4
Other Justice	—	—	—	2	4	6	0.6
Other Treasury	1	6	1	—	3	11	1.2
State/County/ Municipal Authorities	5	—	1	—	2	8	0.8
Tennessee Valley Authority Commission	—	—	—	1	—	1	0.1
U.S. Marine Corps	1	—	—	—	—	1	0.1
U.S. Marshal Service	2	1	1	2	2	8	0.8
U.S. Postal Service	—	—	4	2	3	9	0.9
Veterans Administration	—	—	1	—	—	1	0.1

Figure 2.1

Referrals for Terrorism
1997–2001

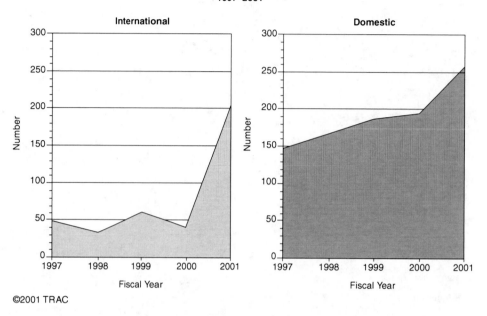

©2001 TRAC

Figure 2.2

Domestic and International Terrorism
Prosecutions and Declinations
1997–2001

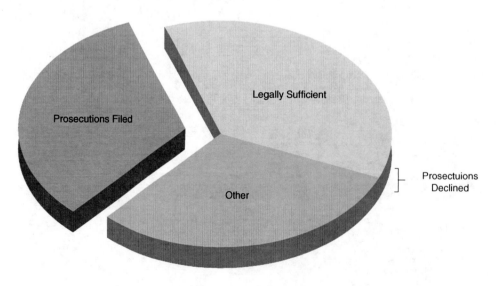

©TRAC 2001

Figure 2.3

Volume of Referrals for Prosecution
Years 1997–2001

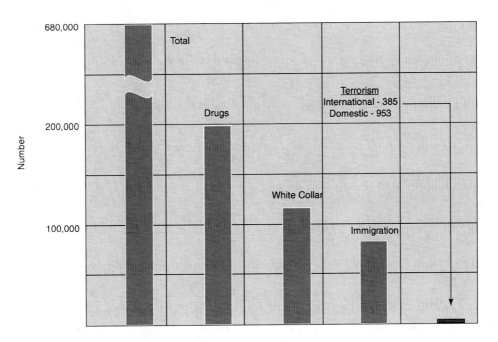

©TRAC 2001

TABLE 2.4   DOMESTIC TERRORISM REFERRALS FOR PROSECUTION DECLINED BY REASON

	Fiscal Year					
	1997	1998	1999	2000	2001	Total
Prosecutions Filed	47	37	41	48	38	211
Prosecutions Declined	52	85	108	147	160	552
Percent Prosecutions Declined	53%	70%	72%	75%	81%	72%
Reason Prosecution Declined: Lack of evidence of criminal intent	8	21	29	27	27	112
Weak or insufficient admissible evidence	10	18	18	25	27	98
Agency request	6	10	14	20	20	70
No known suspect	1	3	18	16	19	57

(continued)

**TABLE 2.4   DOMESTIC TERRORISM REFERRALS FOR PROSECUTION
DECLINED BY REASON (*continued*)**

	Fiscal Year					
	1997	1998	1999	2000	2001	Total
No federal offense evident	7	8	8	7	4	54
Suspect to be prosecuted by other authorities	9	7	5	10	15	46
Minimal federal interest or no deterrent value	1	4	4	6	19	34
Other reasons given: All work completed	—	—	—	—	1	1
By action of the grand jury	—	—	—	—	1	1
Civil, admin. or other disciplinary alternatives	—	1	1	1	2	5
Declined per instructions from DOJ	—	—	—	—	1	1
Department policy	—	1	—	—	1	2
Jurisdiction or venue problems	1	2	1	—	—	4
Juvenile suspect	—	2	—	1	3	6
Lack of investigative resources	—	1	—	1	1	3
Lack of prosecutive resources	—	—	3	—	2	5
Offenders age, health, prior record, or personal matter	1	1	1	7	1	11
Office policy	1	1	1	3	—	6
Petite policy	1	1	—	—	—	2
Pretrial diversion completed	1	—	1	—	—	2
Rule 20 (Magistrate Court)	1	—	—	—	—	1
Rule 40	2	—	—	—	—	2
Staleness	—	—	1	2	—	3
Suspect a fugitive	—	—	—	1	—	1
Suspect being prosecuted on other charges (e.g., UFAPs)	1	1	—	8	1	11
Suspect deceased	—	—	1	1	2	4
Suspect serving sentence	—	—	2	—	1	3
Suspects cooperation	1	1	—	—	1	3
Witness problems	—	2	—	1	1	4

TABLE 2.5   INTERNATIONAL TERRORISM REFERRALS FOR PROSECUTION DECLINED BY REASON

	Fiscal Year					
	1997	1998	1999	2000	2001	Total
Prosecutions filed	8	7	29	14	57	115
Prosecutions declined	33	11	29	22	33	128
Percent prosecutions declined	80%	61%	50%	61%	37%	53%
Reason prosecution declined: Lack of evidence of criminal intent	6	5	16	1	4	32
Weak or insufficient admissible evidence	4	2	3	7	8	24
Suspect to be prosecuted by other authorities	5	—	3	3	5	16
No federal offense evident	2	1	2	1	3	9
Suspect deceased	9	—	—	—	—	9
No known suspect	1	—	1	3	2	7
Minimal federal interest or no deterrent value	—	—	1	4	—	5
Office policy	—	—	1	1	3	5
Other reasons given: Agency request	1	—	1	1	1	4
All work completed	—	—	—	—	2	2
Declined per instructions from DOJ	2	1	—	—	—	3
Jurisdiction or venue problems	—	—	1	—	2	3
Juvenile suspect	—	1	—	—	—	1
Lack of investigative resources	—	1	—	1	—	2
Lack of prosecutive resources	—	—	—	—	1	1
Rule 40	1	—	—	—	1	2
Suspect a fugitive	—	—	—	—	1	1
Suspect being prosecuted on other charges (e.g., UFAPs)	1	—	—	—	—	1
Suspect serving sentence	1	—	—	—	—	1

Figure 2.4

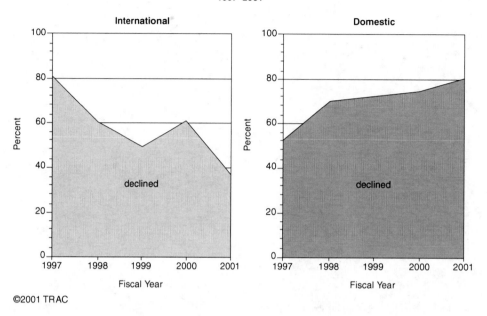

Percent of Terrorism Referrals Declined
1997–2001

©2001 TRAC

TABLE 2.6	HANDLING TERRORISM VS. OTHER CRIMINAL REFERRALS FOR PROSECUTION			
	Terrorism Referrals		**All Criminal Referrals**	
	Number	**Percent**	**Number**	**Percent**
Referrals where Prosecution Decision Made	1006	100%	645,709	100%
Prosecution Filed	326	32%	423,218	66%
Prosecution Declined	680	68%	222,491	34%
All Reasons Prosecution Declined	680	68%	222,491	34%
Legally Insufficient*	368	37%	103,014	16%
Other Reasons	312	31%	119,477	18.5%

* Legally insufficient includes: lack of criminal intent, weak or insufficient admissible evidence, no federal offense evidence, minimal federal interest or no deterrent value.

Actual Federal Indictments Are Relatively Few

The number of actual indictments are dwarfed by the numbers of investigations and referrals for prosecution. This is because so few investigations result in actual referrals and because so few referrals then end up being accepted for prosecution by U.S. Attorneys. While small in number, trends for prosecutions of *international terrorists* were also sharply up last year: 8 indictments in 1997, 7 in 1998, 29 in 1999, 14 in 2000 and 57 in 2001. (See Table 2.7.) Indictments for *domestic terrorism* in sharp contrast did not increase despite the rise in referrals. Domestic terrorism prosecutions were: 47 in 1997, 37 in 1998, 41 in 1999, 48 in 2000, 38 in 2001. (See Table 2.8.)

Actual convictions are smaller than the number of prosecutions since about one third of indictments do not result in a conviction. This occurs for a variety of reasons, including the dismissal of the case or a not guilty verdict. (See Figure 2.5.)

TABLE 2.7   INTERNATIONAL TERRORISM LEAD CHARGE ON PROSECUTIONS FILED

	Fiscal Year					Total	Percent
	1997	1998	1999	2000	2001		
Total	8	7	29	14	57	115	100.0
Lead Charge (US Code Title and Section) 16 USC 0551—Protection of national forests, rules and regs	—	—	—	1	—	1	0.9
18 USC 0032—Destruction of aircraft or aircraft facilities	—	—	1	1	—	2	1.7
18 USC 0113—Assaults in maritime and territorial jurisdictions	—	1	—	—	—	1	0.9
18 USC 0371—Conspiracy to commit offense or to defraud US	—	1	—	—	—	1	0.9
18 USC 0471—Obligations or securities of United States	—	—	—	—	1	1	0.9
18 USC 0844—Explosives— Importation and storage of explosives	—	—	1	1	—	2	1.7
18 USC 0878—Threats/extortion against foreign officials, etc.	—	1	—	—	—	1	0.9
18 USC 0922—Firearms, Unlawful acts	—	—	—	2	—	2	1.7
18 USC 0951—Agents of foreign governments	—	2	12	—	—	14	12.2

(continued)

**TABLE 2.7   INTERNATIONAL TERRORISM LEAD CHARGE ON PROSECUTIONS
FILED (*continued*)**

	Fiscal Year						
	1997	**1998**	**1999**	**2000**	**2001**	**Total**	**Percent**
18 USC 1001—Fraud/false statements generally	—	—	—	3	2	5	4.3
18 USC 1028—Fraud and related activity—ID documents	—	—	—	—	1	1	0.9
18 USC 1119—Foreign murder of U.S. nationals	—	—	—	—	14	14	12.2
18 USC 1201—Kidnapping	—	—	—	1	—	1	0.9
18 USC 1203—Kidnapping—Hostage taking	—	—	12	—	10	22	19.1
18 USC 1343—Fraud by wire, radio, or television	—	—	—	—	1	1	0.9
18 USC 1426—Reproduction of naturalization	—	—	—	—	1	1	0.9
18 USC 1542—False statement in application and use of passport	—	—	1	1	—	2	1.7
18 USC 1546—Fraud and misuse of visas, permits, and use of passport	—	1	—	—	4	5	4.3
18 USC 1656—Conversion or surrender of vessel to pirate	—	—	—	—	8	8	7.0
18 USC 2155—Destruction of National-defense materials, etc.	1	—	—	—	—	1	0.9
18 USC 2320—Trafficking in counterfeit goods or services	5	—	—	—	—	5	4.3
18 USC 2331—Terrorism—Definitions	—	—	—	1	—	1	0.9
18 USC 2332—Terrorism—Criminal penalties	1	—	2	3	2	8	7.0
18 USC 2339—Providing material support to terrorists	—	—	—	—	9	9	7.8
49 USC 46501-7—Threats/interference/weapons—aircraft	1	1	—	—	2	4	3.5
Withheld by govt. from TRAC (FOIA challenge pending)	—	—	—	—	2	2	1.7

TABLE 2.8   DOMESTIC TERRORISM LEAD CHARGE ON PROSECUTIONS FILED

| | Fiscal Year | | | | | | |
	1997	1998	1999	2000	2001	Total	Percent
Total	47	37	41	48	38	211	100.0
Lead Charge (US Code Title and Section)							
08 USC 1324—Bringing in and harboring certain aliens	—	—	—	1	—	1	0.5
18 :842a—Dealing in explosives without a permit	5	—	—	—	—	5	2.4
18 :894—Fraudulent Credit Cards	—	—	1	—	—	1	0.5
18 USC 0003—Accessory after the fact	3	1	—	—	—	4	1.9
18 USC 0013—Laws of States Adopted in Federal jurisdiction	—	—	—	—	1	1	0.5
18 USC 0035—Imparting or conveying false information	—	—	1	—	—	1	0.5
18 USC 0113—Assaults in maritime and territorial jurisdictions	—	—	1	—	—	1	0.5
18 USC 0115—Threats against a federal official's family member	—	1	1	2	3	7	3.3
18 USC 0175—Prohibitions with respect to biological weapons	1	—	1	—	—	2	0.9
18 USC 0371—Conspiracy to commit offense or to defraud US	5	—	—	2	—	7	3.3
18 USC 0542—Entry of goods by means of false statements	1	—	—	—	—	1	0.5
18 USC 0842—Explosives—Importation, manufacture, etc.	—	5	—	—	—	5	2.4
18 USC 0844—Explosives—Importation and storage of explosives	10	9	5	17	8	49	23.2
18 USC 0871—Threats against President and successors	1	6	9	4	3	23	10.9
18 USC 0875—Extortion/threats—Interstate communications	—	—	1	4	5	10	4.7
18 USC 0876—Mailing threatening communications	6	—	5	4	1	16	7.6

(continued)

TABLE 2.8   DOMESTIC TERRORISM LEAD CHARGE ON PROSECUTIONS FILED (*continued*)

	Fiscal Year						
	1997	1998	1999	2000	2001	Total	Percent
18 USC 0877—Mailing threatening communications from foreign country	—	1	—	—	—	1	0.5
18 USC 0922—Firearms, Unlawful acts	1	1	—	1	—	3	1.4
18 USC 0930—Possession of firearms/dangerous weapons in federal	—	—	—	—	1	1	0.5
18 USC 1001—Fraud/false statements generally	—	—	—	—	1	1	0.5
18 USC 1113—Attempt to commit murder or manslaughter	1	—	—	—	—	1	0.5
18 USC 1201—Kidnapping	—	2	—	1	—	3	1.4
18 USC 1203—Kidnapping—Hostage taking	—	—	3	5	1	9	4.3
18 USC 1344—Bank fraud	—	1	—	—	—	1	0.5
18 USC 1361—Malicious mischief—govt. property or contracts	—	—	—	1	—	1	0.5
18 USC 1363—Malicious mischief—special jurisdictions	—	1	—	—	—	1	0.5
18 USC 1366—Destruction of an energy facility	1	—	—	—	—	1	0.5
18 USC 1382—Entering military, naval, or Coast Guard property	—	—	—	—	2	2	0.9
18 USC 1503—Influencing or injuring officer or juror generally	—	—	—	1	—	1	0.5
18 USC 1512—Tampering with a witness, victim, or an informant	1	—	—	—	—	1	0.5
18 USC 1716—Injurious articles as nonmailable	—	—	—	—	2	2	0.9
18 USC 1951—Hobbs Act	4	4	—	—	1	9	4.3
18 USC 1952—Racketeering—interstate/foreigntravel/transport	—	—	—	—	1	1	0.5
18 USC 2119—Carjacking	—	—	1	—	—	1	0.5

(continued)

TABLE 2.8   DOMESTIC TERRORISM LEAD CHARGE ON PROSECUTIONS FILED (*continued*)

	Fiscal Year						
	1997	1998	1999	2000	2001	Total	Percent
18 USC 2332—Terrorism—Criminal penalties	—	3	3	4	2	12	5.7
18 USC 2339—Providing material support to terrorists	1	—	—	1	—	2	0.9
22 USC 2778—Control of arms exports and imports	—	—	4	—	—	4	1.9
26 USC 5841—Registration of firearms	—	—	1	—	—	1	0.5
26 USC 5861—Tax on making firearms—Prohibited acts	6	2	2	—	2	12	5.7
49 USC 46501-7—Threats/interference/weapons—aircraft	—	—	1	—	2	3	1.4
Withheld by govt. from TRAC (FOIA challenge pending)	—	—	1	—	2	3	1.4

Figure 2.5

**Domestic and International Terrorism
Matters Disposed of 1997–2001**

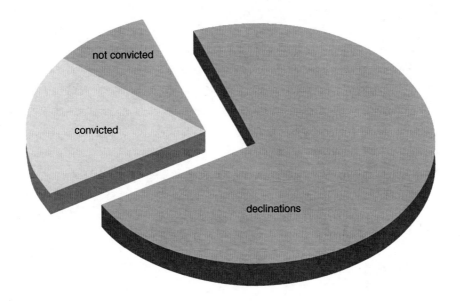

©TRAC 2001

Which Communities Most Active?

Government referrals for *international terrorism* have been made to U.S. Attorneys all over the country. But six federal judicial districts stood out. From 1997 to 2001, the U.S. Attorney in the District of Columbia reported 67 referrals. Right next door, the U.S. Attorney in Eastern Virginia counted 29. Given the location of the government these counts are hardly surprising. New York South (Manhattan) reported 40. The last three standout districts were California Central (Los Angeles), Michigan East (Detroit) and Florida South (Miami). In Virginia East and Michigan East virtually all of the referrals came in 2001. (See Table 2.9.)

TABLE 2.9   INTERNATIONAL TERRORISM REFERRALS FOR PROSECUTION BY FEDERAL DISTRICT

	Fiscal Year					
	1997	1998	1999	2000	2001	Total
Total	48	33	60	40	204	385
Federal Judicial District						
Ala, N	—	—	—	—	1	1
Ala, S	—	—	—	—	2	2
Alaska	—	—	—	—	1	1
Arizona	—	—	—	—	1	1
Ark, E	—	—	—	—	2	2
Cal, C	2	2	6	1	15	26
Cal, N	—	—	3	2	4	9
Cal, S	—	—	—	1	—	1
Conn	—	—	—	—	1	1
D. C.	17	3	8	9	30	67
Delaware	—	—	—	—	1	1
Fla, M	—	—	—	—	8	8
Fla, N	—	—	—	—	1	1
Fla, S	—	10	5	—	6	21
Ga, M	—	1	—	—	—	1
Guam	—	—	—	1	8	9

(continued)

TABLE 2.9 INTERNATIONAL TERRORISM REFERRALS FOR PROSECUTION BY FEDERAL DISTRICT (*continued*)

	Fiscal Year					
	1997	1998	1999	2000	2001	Total
Federal Judicial District						
Idaho	—	1	—	2	—	3
Ill, N	1	1	4	3	—	9
Ind, N	—	—	—	—	4	4
Ind, S	—	—	1	—	1	2
Iowa, S	—	—	—	—	2	2
Kansas	—	1	—	—	—	1
Ken, W	2	—	1	1	—	4
Maryland	—	—	1	1	3	5
Mich, E	—	—	3	—	20	23
Mich, W	—	—	—	—	1	1
Minnesota	—	—	2	1	1	4
Miss, S	—	—	—	—	3	3
Mo, E	—	—	—	—	1	1
Mo, W	—	1	—	—	1	2
N Car, E	—	—	—	—	1	1
N Car, M	—	—	—	—	4	4
N Car, W	—	—	—	—	1	1
N Mar Is	—	—	11	—	—	11
N Mexico	—	—	—	—	2	2
N. J.	—	1	2	2	2	7
N.Y., E	—	5	—	1	8	14
N.Y., N	—	—	—	—	2	2
N.Y., S	19	2	8	4	7	40
N.Y., W	—	—	—	—	2	2
Nevada	—	—	—	—	1	1

(*continued*)

TABLE 2.9   INTERNATIONAL TERRORISM REFERRALS FOR PROSECUTION BY FEDERAL DISTRICT (*continued*)

	Fiscal Year					
	1997	1998	1999	2000	2001	Total
Federal Judicial District						
New Hamp	—	—	—	—	1	1
Ohio, S	—	1	—	—	3	4
Oregon	—	—	—	—	3	3
Penn, E	—	2	1	3	3	9
Penn, M	—	—	—	—	1	1
Penn, W	1	—	—	—	2	3
S Car	1	—	—	—	1	2
S Dakota	—	—	—	—	1	1
Tenn, E	—	—	—	—	1	1
Tenn, W	—	—	—	—	1	1
Texas, E	—	—	—	—	5	5
Texas, N	1	—	2	3	1	7
Texas, S	—	—	—	1	2	3
Texas, W	—	2	—	1	—	3
Utah	—	—	—	1	—	1
Virg, E	1	—	1	—	27	29
Wash, W	1	—	—	2	1	4
Wisc, E	2	—	1	—	1	4
Wisc, W	—	—	—	—	2	2

The line-up of districts showing the most referrals for *domestic terrorism* for the same period looked strikingly different. California North (San Francisco) leads the list with 80 referrals, followed by Georgia North (Atlanta) with 51. Three other districts also had more than 40 referrals each: Tennessee Middle (Nashville), Texas North (Fort Worth) and Florida Middle (Tampa) (See Table 2.10. For federal district boundaries, see Figure 2.6.)

TABLE 2.10   DOMESTIC TERRORISM REFERRALS FOR PROSECUTION BY FEDERAL DISTRICT (*continued*)

	Fiscal Year					
	1997	1998	1999	2000	2001	Total
Total	147	166	187	194	259	953
Federal Judicial District						
Ala, M	—	6	—	1	1	8
Ala, N	—	1	—	—	2	3
Alaska	—	4	1	—	2	7
Arizona	—	—	—	1	3	4
Ark, E	1	2	4	7	10	24
Cal, C	—	1	6	2	5	14
Cal, E	—	1	—	—	—	1
Cal, N	4	3	20	10	43	80
Cal, S	—	2	1	1	—	4
Colorado	1	2	—	—	—	3
Conn	—	—	1	—	5	6
D. C.	—	—	1	—	1	2
Delaware	—	—	—	1	1	2
Fla, M	17	9	5	8	5	44
Fla, N	2	—	1	—	—	3
Fla, S	1	2	5	5	1	14
Ga, M	1	—	2	—	4	7
Ga, N	11	6	4	11	19	51
Ga, S	1	1	—	—	—	2
Guam	—	—	—	2	—	2
Hawaii	—	3	1	6	2	12
Idaho	10	1	13	2	5	31
Ill, C	—	2	1	3	2	8
Ill, N	—	—	—	—	2	2

(*continued*)

TABLE 2.10   DOMESTIC TERRORISM REFERRALS FOR PROSECUTION BY FEDERAL DISTRICT (*continued*)

	Fiscal Year					
	1997	1998	1999	2000	2001	Total
Federal Judicial District						
Ill, S	2	6	8	—	—	16
Ind, N	—	1	—	—	1	2
Ind, S	—	—	3	4	—	7
Iowa, S	—	—	—	1	—	1
Kansas	6	4	3	1	—	14
Ken, E	—	1	—	2	2	5
Ken, W	—	—	—	—	5	5
La, W	1	2	2	—	2	7
Maine	—	—	—	—	2	2
Maryland	—	—	—	3	—	3
Mass	—	1	—	3	2	6
Mich, E	—	1	—	2	2	5
Mich, W	—	4	4	13	4	25
Minnesota	—	—	1	—	—	1
Miss, S	—	—	3	1	1	5
Mo, E	2	1	1	1	2	7
Mo, W	2	2	2	2	1	9
Montana	6	4	—	1	2	13
N Car, E	2	3	2	1	1	9
N Dakota	—	—	—	—	1	1
N Mexico	2	—	6	—	2	10
N. J.	—	—	1	—	—	1
N.Y., E	3	6	1	2	3	15
N.Y., N	—	—	1	1	—	2
N.Y., S	—	—	—	7	1	8

(continued)

TABLE 2.10   DOMESTIC TERRORISM REFERRALS FOR PROSECUTION BY FEDERAL DISTRICT (*continued*)

| | Fiscal Year | | | | | |
	1997	1998	1999	2000	2001	Total
Federal Judicial District						
N.Y., W	4	4	4	5	11	28
Nebraska	—	·	—	—	1	1
Nevada	4	5	3	8	1	21
New Hamp	3	—	4	2	1	10
Wisc, E	1	2	2	2	5	12
Wisc, W	4	4	1	5	1	15
Wyoming	—	—	1	—	3	4

Figure 2.6

Federal Judicial District Boundaries

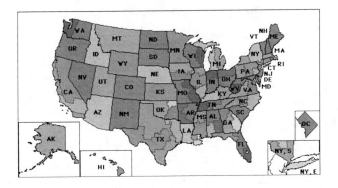

International Terrorists Receive Light Sentences

News reports about high-profile cases leave the impression that extremely long sentences usually are imposed on all convicted terrorists. Justice Department data focusing only on international terrorists, however, suggest otherwise. Eleven of the 19 convicted terrorist where sentencing information was available, for example, received no prison time or one year or less. The median sentence — half got more, half got less — was ten months. The average time was much higher — 65 months — because a few people received very long sentences.

TABLE 2.11   LENGTH OF PRISON SENTENCES: FISCAL YEARS 1997—2001

Department of Justice	Receive Little Prison Time		Prison Time (months)	
Program Area	None	One Year or Less (includes none)	Median*	Average**
International Terrorism	37%	58%	10	65
Domestic Terrorism	10%	23%	37	79
Narcotics/Drugs	8%	21%	45	69
Weapons	9%	17%	48	84

* half get more, half get less.

** Average prison sentences run higher because a small proportion of these offenders receive very long sentences. For example, two convicted domestic terrorists received life sentences.

Domestic terrorists do receive heavier sentences. Only one in ten convicted domestic terrorists receive no prison time. The median sentence — half got more, half got less — was 37 months. But this is still less than the median sentence for drug offenses (45 months) or general weapons crimes (48 months). Average prison sentences run higher — 79 months (domestic terrorism), 69 months (drug crimes), 84 months (weapons crimes) — because a small proportion of these offenders receive very long sentences. (See Table 2.11.)

Dozens of Agencies Lead Terrorism Investigations

Federal prosecutors identified a surprisingly wide range of investigative groups as the "lead agency" in a terrorism investigation during the past five years — from the U.S. Postal Service to the Commerce Department, from the Export-Import Bank of the United States to the Forest Service. But the Justice Department credits the FBI as being the lead agency in most:

■ The FBI was the lead agency in almost 9 out of 10 of the 385 matters classified as involving *international terrorism* from 1997 to 2001. (See Table 2.2.)

■ In regard to *domestic terrorism,* the FBI was cited as the lead in seven out of ten of the 953 matters in the same period. (See Table 2.3.)

The Secret Service and the Bureau of Alcohol, Tobacco and Firearms were the lead agencies in most of the balance of domestic terrorism cases.

What Constitutes Terrorism Offenses?

The agencies of the federal government appear to define terrorism in several different ways. This lack of consistency may raise difficult legal questions when the government — as is now planned — starts investigating and processing terrorist suspects under different legal procedures than it applies to other suspects. The Justice Department's Executive Office for United States Attorneys (EOUSA) defines domestic terrorism as involving matters where individuals or groups seek to further political goals wholly or in part through activities that involve force or the threat of force. The EOUSA defines international terrorism in an even more circular way: a federal offense relating to international terrorism which impact on United States interests.[5] In 1999, the EOUSA said 59 domestic or international terrorists were convicted in federal court. The FBI, in its annual budget submission to Congress, claimed 103 terrorist convictions. It is assumed that the different counts for terrorism convictions may be explained by differences in what is being counted. The FBI, however, has not responded to a November 5 inquiry from TRAC requesting information on this question.

Federal prosecutors listed more than 40 specific statutes as the "lead charge" in *domestic terrorism* prosecutions. The largest grouping — about one third of the total — involved explosives and weapons. Another group centering on threats against the president and members of a federal official's family came to 14 percent of the total. The lead charge against three individuals concerned threats, interference and firearms on board aircraft. Two people were charged with violating certain prohibitions with respect to biological weapons. (See Table 2.8.) A smaller number of lead charges were reported in connection with *international terrorism* cases. Here, 20 percent were charged with kidnapping or hostage taking, 12 percent with murdering U.S. nationals, 12 percent with being foreign agents, 8 percent with providing material support of terrorists and 4 percent with fraud and misuses of visas, etc. (See Table 2.7.)

Other Indicators

The changing number of referrals, indictments and convictions provides the public a narrow but imperfect way to measure the intensity of the government's overall effort to contain domestic and international terrorism. But there are several other indicators.

One such indicator is the annual number of special warrants the government obtains to conduct electronic and physical searches under the Foreign Intelligence Surveillance Act (FISA). According to a brief report that the Attorney General is required by law to submit to Congress each year, the number of FISA warrants granted in calendar year 2000 was 1,012. This total — the latest available — compared with 886 warrants in 1999, 796 in 1998, 748 in 1997 and 839 in 1996. The work under FISA is thought to be carried out mostly by the FBI. (See Figure 2.7.)

Another measure involves FBI funding earmarked for fighting terrorism. According to a July report by the Congressional Research Service, the bureau's actual funding devoted to this purpose was $450.5 million in fiscal year 1998, $432.9 million in 1999, and $443 million in 2000. Funds approved by Congress for fiscal year 2001 were $527 million. The Research Service said in its July report that $565.5 million had been requested for fiscal year 2002. (See Table. 2.1)

An annual count of the FBI's terrorist investigations — submitted in recent years to Congress — provides another activity gauge. There were 7,125 such investigations reported in FY 1997, 9,046 in FY 1998, 10,151 in FY 1999, and 10,538 in FY 2000. (See Table 2.1.)

Figure 2.7

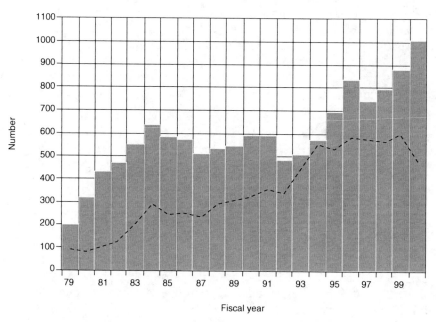

Foreign Intelligence Surveillance Act (FISA) Warrants
Exceed All Wiretaps Against Traditional Criminals

©TRAC 2001

- Foreign Intelligence Surveillance Act warrants aimed at spies and terrorists (mostly executed by the FBI)
- - - All electronic surveillance warrants aimed at traditional criminals (executed by all federal agencies)

Note (6/02): The Justice Department has revised some referral dates in the files originally furnished TRAC. This affected the breakdown of referral counts before and after September 11, 2001. The text has been revised to reflect these DOJ updates.

Were the 1990s truly a decade of violence? Perhaps. But it was clearly less violent than those decades during which the world experience the trauma of global war. There was certainly less loss of life than during the years in which the Indochina conflict raged. Fewer lives were claimed by political violence during the 1990s than by traffic accidents on U.S. highways annually.

So why is so much attention directed toward developing policies to cope with terrorist violence in recent years? It has, as experts like Walter Laqueur note, attracted what could be considered an inordinate amount of attention, compared to other major problems of our times, such as global debt and world hunger. Terrorism has been the subject of countless speeches by political leaders throughout the world and the impetus for numerous initiatives and conference s by foreign policy experts. The drama of terrorist-directed events attracts enormous attention in the press and on television worldwide. Terror-violence did, in many respects, become an accepted method of warfare during the latter part of the twentieth century.

Moreover, in the wake of events of September 2001, a global "war on terrorism" has begun to be waged, led by the United States and sanctioned by the United Nations. While the initial context of the "war" took place in Afghanistan, it is unlikely that either the toppling of the Taliban leadership or the destruction of the al Qaeda network in Afghanistan will suffice to "win" this new war. Terrorism is an ancient "enemy" with roots in many cultures and followers in many creeds. A "war" against such an enemy is unlikely to be quickly brought to a successful conclusion.

Certainly terrorism has been waged by a variety of individuals and groups. It has been a favorite tactic of national and religious groups, by groups on both the left and the right of the political spectrum, by nationalist and internationalist movements. It has been used as an instrument of state policy. It has been directed against autocratic as well as democratic regimes, although political democracies have been the most frequent target. At times, it has been an instrument of last resort for movements of national liberation whose political attempts to change the system has failed; and at other times, it has been deliberately chosen by such movements *before* other such political options have been attempted.

States have sponsored terrorism outside their own frontiers and have used terrorism as a weapon against their own citizens. Terrorism has become, paradoxically, both an instrument designed to force radical social and political changes and an instrument of oppression in seeking to prevent such changes.

Even with the increased use of terrorist violence, or perhaps because of its proliferation, there remains a great deal of confusion as to what the term terrorism really encompasses. Many definitions of terrorism are, in fact, encoded political statements. Too often the term is used in a pejorative sense, attached as a label to those groups whose political objectives one finds objectionable. To study this phenomenon, we must first establish a workable and useful definition – workable in that it has sufficient precision to allow us to identify the phenomenon when it occurs and useful in that it is acceptable to a fairly broad range of political persuasions. For terrorism is a politicized term, just as terrorism is a political crime. Its definition must therefore be politically acceptable.

MODERN DEFINITIONS OF AN OLD CONCEPT

Terrorism is a phenomenon that is becoming a pervasive, often dominant influence in our lives. It affects the manner in which governments conduct their foreign policy and the way corporations transact their business. It causes alterations in the role and even the structure of our security forces. It forces us to spend huge amounts of time and money to protect our public figures, vital installations, citizens, and even our system of government. It influences the way we travel and the places we travel to see. It even affects the manner in which we live our daily lives. Our newspapers, radios, and televisions inundate our every waking moment with vivid details of terrorist spectaculars from all corners of the globe.

But what is terrorism—this "it" to which we attribute so much influence today? Before we can assess just how great a threat "it" poses and exactly whom "it" threatens, we need to determine what "terrorism" is. And it is precisely those problems of definition that has caused political, legal, and military leaders to throw up their hands, metaphorically, in discouragement and dismay.

Because terrorism is a political as well as a legal and a military issue, its definition in modern terms has been slow to evolve. Not that there are not numerous definitions available—there are hundreds. But few of them are of sufficient legal scholarship to be useful in international law, and most of those that are legally useful lack the necessary ambiguity for political acceptance.

Thus, the problem of defining terrorism is not insuperable, but it must be handled with caution in order for subsequent use of the term to have meaning. To say that the number of terrorist incidents is rising annually would have little clear meaning unless it is clear precisely what such an incident *is* and *is not*.

Moreover, it helps to put the term into an historical perspective. Terrorism is not a modern phenomenon. The admixture of religion and politics fomenting terrorism in many areas today has a counterpart in the Hashashin of the Middle Ages. Incidents such as the *Achille Lauro* hijacking have precedents dating back many centuries. The statement that "one man's terrorist is another man's patriot" illustrates the historical continuum of conflict under which terrorism is operationally defined.

Ideology has always had an ambiguous relationship with terrorism—at one point justifying and at another condemning the same act. Theorists (and practitioners) of both the left and the right have advocated the use of what has been termed "terrorist" violence. Understanding the context of the ideological debate helps to deal with the justifications offered in contemporary times for terrorist acts.

It also helps to assess the ideological commitment of the perpetrators of terrorism. Profiling modern terrorists is one way of assessing what terrorism is committed for today. An understanding of the impact of group dynamics is also useful in critiquing the rationale behind such acts. Patterns in the type of recruiting done among groups committing terrorist acts lends substance to these profiles of modern terrorists.

But terrorism is not strictly a phenomenon committed by individuals or groups. In fact, *terrorism* as a political term derived from state terror. So analysis of ways in which states use terrorism as an instrument of foreign and domestic policy offers interesting insights.

Some states are even involved in the network emerging among individuals and groups involved in the commission of terrorist acts. Opinions differ as to the extent, cohesiveness, and ideological commitment of this network, but evidence of its existence is beyond reasonable dispute. Nations such as Libya, Syria, and Iran have repeatedly been accused of involvement in state-sponsored terrorism. The linkage between these states and terrorism will be explored in depth later, focusing on such questions as: How is terrorism financed? What are its targets? These and other fascinating questions offer opportunities to plumb the murky depths of the terrorist network.

Understanding of why and who leads to questions of how. Profiles of terrorist events offer thumbnail sketches and interesting insights into the how of terrorism. The depth of media involvement in the making of a terrorist spectacular, for instance, can provide useful clues to understanding why this is so sensitive an area of democratic policy making. Analysis of potential targets and weapons raises crucial and frightening questions for democratic systems.

The responses of the systems—legal, military, and political—to the threat and reality of terrorism is, of course, crucial to any understanding of the problem of terrorism today. The willingness as well as the capacity of the international community, and of an individual nation, to respond to this form of "warfare" is critical to any assessment of the role of terrorism in shaping our world. The difference between the responses to domestic, as opposed to international, terrorism may also be critical as democratic nations seek ways to respond to terrorism without sacrificing fundamental principles of democracy.

Democracies, throughout history, have been the effective targets of terrorist attacks, because democratic systems must "play by the rules" and thus cannot respond in comparable fashion to terrorist attacks. Autocracies and totalitarian systems are able to respond more easily to terrorist acts with terrorist acts, which sometimes services as an effective deterrent, but democracies cannot make such responses. A quick look at terrorism in a democratic system such as the United States offers insights into the patterns of terrorism and response characteristic of many democracies today.

Ultimately, the question may not be how nations can eliminate terrorism—if it is indeed a centuries-old practice and well entrenched as a useful tool in warfare—but rather how much terrorism a state can tolerate. New laws and new technology are changing the face of terrorism, but since it is not vanishing, then new thresholds for "acceptable" violence may well be emerging. With the development of effective and accessible chemical and biological as well as nuclear weapons, these thresholds may determine the survival of humanity.

This discussion in no sense covers all that could be said about terrorism. This is a contemporary review of current acts of terrorism. Definitions of terrorism, like the act itself, continue to undergo changes. The definition suggested in the following section highlights certain important facets of the issue, answering some questions while raising a multitude of others. Such a study can only provide a frame of reference from which it should be possible to analyze this phenomenon—the instrument and the nemesis of rulers, governments, and citizens.

CRUCIAL COMPONENTS OF TERRORISM

While it has not been possible, yet, to create a universally acceptable definition of terrorism, it is both possible and necessary to specify certain features common to the phenomenon. This in turn makes it feasible to create an operational definition of this term. Acts possessing all of these attributes could then be identified as terrorist acts with some consistency. Without falling into the political quagmire of attempting to label individuals or groups as terrorist, certain types of actions could be identified as terrorism, regardless of who commits them, for however noble a cause.

Let us consider a loose definition of contemporary terrorism. It must of necessity be loose, because its elements tend to form a variety of compounds, which today fall within the rubric of terrorism. For the purposes of this investigation, terrorism will be defined as a synthesis of war and theater, a dramatization of the most proscribed kind of violence—that which is perpetrated on innocent victims—played before an audience in the hope of creating a mood of fear, for political purposes.

This description of terrorism has a number of crucial components. Terrorism, by this definition, involves an act of violence, an audience, the creation of a mood of fear, innocent victims, and political motives or goals. Each of these elements deserves some clarification for us to formulate a clear set of parameters for this frequently misunderstood and misused term.

Violence, Audience, and a Mood of Fear

First, note that terrorism is fundamentally a violent act. Sit-ins, picket line, walkouts, and other similar forms of protest, no matter how disruptive, are not terrorist acts. Violence-the threat of violence where the capacity and the willingness to commit violence are displayed-is endemic to terrorism. The violence need not be fully perpetrated-that is, the bomb need not be detonated or all of the passengers aboard an airliner killed-for it to be considered a terrorist act. Buy the capacity and the willingness to commit a violent act must be present.

This means, then, that it is the perception of the audience of that violent potential that is crucial to classifying an act as terrorism. Terrorism is, essentially, theater, an act played before an audience, designed to call the attention of millions, even hundreds of millions, to an often unrelated situation through shock-producing situations of outrage and horror, doing the unthinkable without apology or remorse. Unlike similar acts of murder or warfare, acts of terrorism are neither ends themselves nor often more than tangentially related to the ends sought, they are simply crafted to create a mood of fear or terror in that audience.

This mood is not the result, moreover, of the numbers of casualties caused by the act of violence. Automobile accidents cause great numbers of injuries and deaths each year in the United States, without necessarily invoking a mood of terror among other drivers (or pedestrians). Nor is it the deliberate nature of the death inflicted that causes the audience response. Individuals are murdered in nonpolitical, nonterrorist acts throughout the world each year, without provoking widespread fear.

Victims: The Right Place, But the Wrong Time

Instead, the creation of this mood of intense anxiety seems to be specifically linked to the nature of the victim of terrorist acts. As on scholar notes:

> To qualify as an appropriate victim of a terrorist today, we need not be tyrants or their sympathizers; we need not be connected in any way with the evils the terrorist perceives; we need not belong to a particular group. We need not only be in the wrong place at the wrong time.

Terrorism is thus distinguished from guerilla warfare by deliberate attacks on innocent persons and the separation of its victims from the ultimate goal-the "playing to an audience" aspect of a terrorist act. Terrorism can be distinguished from legal acts of warfare and ordinary crimes of murder. As David Fromkin points out:

> Unlike the soldier, the guerilla fighter, or the revolutionist, the terrorist... is always in the paradoxical position of undertaking actions the immediate physical consequences of which are not particularly desired by him. An ordinary murderer will kill someone because he wants the person to be dead, but a terrorist will shoot somebody even though it is a mater of complete indifference to him whether that person lives or dies.

Put more simply, the difference between a terrorist act and a similar crime or war activity is that terrorist acts are perpetrated deliberately on innocent third parities in an effort to coerce the opposing party pr persons into some desired personal course of action. Victims are thus chosen, not primarily because of their personal guilt (in terms of membership in an opposing military or governmental group), but because their deaths or injuries will so shock the opposition that concession can be forced to prevent a recurrence of the incident or will focus attention on a particular political cause. Terrorist acts, in other words, are constructed to deliberately "make war" on innocent persons.

This distinction between terrorist act and a legitimate act of guerilla warfare is not always clear. General George Grivas, founder and head of the Cypriot EOKA, asserted in his memoirs: "We did not strike, like a bomber, at random. We shot only British servicemen who would have killed us if they could have fired first, and civilians who were traitors or intelligence agents." The French Resistance, the Polish Underground, and the Greek Guerillas were called terrorists by the Nazi Occupation; yet they, like the EOKA, attacked primarily military personnel, government officials, and local collaborators.

During World War II, the Polish-Jewish Underground planted explosives at the Café Cyganeria in Krakow, a meeting place for Nazi officers, which no doubt resulted in injury to Polish waiters as well as to the desired military targets. The point here is that the terrorist deliberately chooses to invoke injury on the innocent in an effort to shock the "guilty" political or military audience. Injury to the innocent thus is not an undesirable accident or by-product, but the carefully sought consequence of a terrorist act.

A terrorist act is committed, not against a military target necessarily—as the individual or group perpetrating the act does not seek to overthrow by military force—nor against the person in direct opposition to the perpetrators, as the ultimate goal is not usually the death of one leader. Unlike the terrorism practiced by nineteenth-century anarchists, twentieth-century terrorist acts are deliberately aimed against noncombatants, unarmed third parties whose loss of well being can be expected to evoke a desired response from the opposition or from the audience watching the event throughout the world.

Until recently it appeared that, although most of the victims of terrorism were innocent of any crime, they were also relatively few in number. In those terrorist incidents recorded in the 1950s and 1960s, the actual number of casualties was relatively small. It has been speculated that perhaps the terrorists felt a need to avoid alienating certain groups of people or portions of society. Perhaps it was also true that terrorists "... want a lot of people watching, not a lot of people dead."

But the recent attacks in New York and Washington, using fully loaded passenger airplanes to crash into crowded centers of commerce and government, would appear to herald a loosening of the threads that have constrained terrorists in their search for victims. As the craving for a worldwide audience increases among groups utilizing terrorism, the increasing tolerance of that audience for violence may actually be pushing terrorists to widen their target range, to create a more spectacular event for their audience.

Thus, as the violence becomes more randomized, it is being directed against a wider range of innocent persons. Children are becoming targets, as the massacres at the Rome and Vienna airports demonstrated. Ironically, this increase in innocent targets may well be a direct result of a viewing audience that is no longer as interested in attacks on military attaches or political figures.

Political Quicksand

Terrorism, then, this an act of violence, perpetrated on an innocent person to evoke fear in an audience. One further component, however, is necessary to this definition. As it stands such a definition could reasonably be applied to actions taken by professional athletes on the playing field!

The addition of a "political purpose" to the concept of terrorism continues to create enormous legal problems. Although establishing parameters for this concept of political purpose is crucial, particularly in light of the fact that political crimes and criminal have enjoyed special statues under international law from centuries, the concept remains largely undefined.

Much of the confusion today results from a misperception that the presence of political motivations sufficient to establish the political character of an action. A recent extradition case clearly stated that: "An offense is not of a political character simply because it was politically motivated." The prevailing Anglo-American rule of law has been derived from in re Castroni, in which two basic criteria were given for determining the political quality of an action: (1) The act at issue must have occurred during a political revolt or disturbance; and (2) the act at issue must have been incidental to and have formed part of that same revolution or disturbance.

A political motive thus may be termed necessary but is not sufficient to earn for an action al "political offense" status under international law. Nicholas Kittrie has suggested that a "pure political offense" would consist of acts "which challenge the State but affect no private rights of innocent parties." By this definition, a political revolution or disturbance is an essential ingredient, in which the political offense plays only a part. Moreover, the offense must bring harm only to the State, while protecting innocent parties from harm through reasonable precautions. This has the effect of narrowing the classes of acceptable victims and eliminating random acts of lone assassins.

Political assassination by committed revolutionaries careful to cause as little harm as possible to innocent persons remains thus protected to some extent within the political offense provisions of international law. Hence, the assassination of the Grand Duke Sergius might qualify for political offense status, whereas the mob violence of the Paris Commune would certainly not.

Obviously, the political element of an act terrorism adds considerable confusion, both in the legal and the political realm. Although it is a necessary component to a definition of terrorism, it is so ambiguous a concept that it is often a two-edged sword, offering insights into the causes of an act while providing gaping loopholes in the law through which perpetrators of heinous acts continue to slither.

One legal expert has described the problem in this manner:

> In order to maintain a proper balance between human rights and world order, it is imperative that the world community in rejecting the proposition that all forms of violence are justified if supported by political goals, avoid the trap of supporting the other extreme, that violent opposition to an established regime is never permissible by international standards. Consequently, the principles of self-defense and the requirement of proportionality need to be re-examined, refined and injected more vigorously into this area.

What distinguishes terrorism, then, from purely political actions may be the illegality of the violence employed, primarily in terms of the victims of the offenses. As noted earlier, many activities, including some sports and many movies, have as a goal the instilling of fear in an audience or opponent. What distinguishes the terrorist of today from the football player, the political assassin, and the revolutionary engaged in regular or irregular warfare may be the lack of legitimacy that his actions enjoy under international norms. By its very nature, terrorism involves the deliberate disruption of norms, the violation of generally accepted standards of decency, including the laws of war as they apply to the innocent and helpless.

Because this area of the definition of terrorism is very confusing and contradictory, it is useful to review the issue once more. What is it, then, that distinguishes the terrorist act from other acts of was, as well as from other political or common crimes? Few would argue that wars, whether between or within states, could or should occur without violence, but as nations we have recognized its inevitability and accorded it a limited legitimacy.

International rules have been created and accepted that govern the acceptable types of violence, even in war. The international community does not forbid the use of all violence; it does, however, suggest basic rules for the use of violence. Many of these rules are directed toward the protection of innocent persons. Even in the life-and-death struggles between nations, these laws focus on the minimizing of danger of injury or death to noncombatants, civilians with neither military nor political rank or involvement in the conflict.

Political motivation, then, is not a lever by which acts of terrorism can be justified under international law. On the contrary, international law makes it clear that, regardless of the motive, some acts of political violence are never acceptable.

TYPOLOGIES OF TERRORISM: USEFUL TOOLS

At this point let us look at some typologies of terror that may serve to help us distinguish between the types of terrorism as they pertain to revolutionary and guerilla movements. Feliks Gross, a leading authority on revolutionary terror, has suggested that at least five types of terror-violence exist:

- **Mass terror** is terror by a state, where the regime coerces the opposition in the population, whether organized or unorganized, sometimes in an institutionalized manner.

- **Dynastic assassination** is an attack on a head of state or a ruling elite, precisely the kind of terrorism that the international community tried to criminalize in the mid-nineteenth century.

- **Random terror** involves the placing of explosives where people gather (such as post offices, railroads, and cafes) to destroy whoever happens to be there. "Algerian revolutionaries left bombs in public places," one scholar notes, "in Paris, apparently convinced that one Frenchman blown to buts was pretty much like any other."

- **Focused random terror** restricts the placing of explosives, for example, to where significant agents of oppression are likely to gather (as in the aforementioned case of the Polish-Jewish Underground).

- **Tactical terror** is directed solely against the ruling government as a part of a "broad revolutionary strategic plan."

Such a typology leaves some guerrilla activity enmeshed in the terrorist label. Although similar difficulties afflict other such typologies, several points of importance can be derived concerning the phenomenon of terrorism by examining some of them. J. Bowyer Bell's excellent study of terrorist types yields many insights into the kings of terrorism prevalent today, thus contributing to an understanding of what is encompassed by the modern meaning of the term.

In addition to psychotic and criminal terror, which Bell links to air piracy and kidnapping, four other categories are suggested: endemic, authorized, vigilant, and revolutionary. Endemic terror in terms of societal anarchy offers an interesting insight into the internal chaos that has characterized Uganda under Idi Amin, for example. Authorized terror is used by the state to intimidate internal enemies or hostile governments, whereas vigilante terror is carried out by nonstate actors with the tacit permission of the state, and revolutionary terror is, like Gross's tactical terror, "purely political."

Unlike Gross, Bell suggests that this final category could be subdivided into at least six types of terror: organized, allegiance, functional, provocative, manipulative, and symbolic. These subdivisions, however, rather overlap with the types of terrorism in general discussed by Gross, particularly the focused random type. Bell's typology adds, in effect, diversification as to the specific targets and audiences of focused random terror and broadens the spectrum of types of state terror.

Although numerous other typologies of terrorism have been offered by various scholars, review of them in detail would not significantly contribute to the development of a workable definition of contemporary terrorism. However, a few important points of interest can be made about these typologies. First, virtually every major typology developed today includes some form of state terrorism as well as individual and group terrorism. What Gross terms "mass" terrorism and Bell calls "authorized" or even "endemic" terror, is described by U.S. State Department analyst Thomas Thornton as "enforcement" terror and by political scientist Paul Wilkinson as "repressive" terror. Whatever the label applied to this particular type of terror, it is obvious that some consensus exists on the propriety of including some repressive state tactics in the classification of terrorist acts.

The typologies also suggest that a wide variety of acts have been encompassed under the rubric of terrorism, including many engaged in by revolutionary groups, and composed of both internal activities and activities that cross state lines, but all of which are politically motivated and directed toward some end other than the immediate act of violence. These observations serve both to fortify the conclusions already drawn concerning the distinctive nature of terrorist acts and to highlight certain points of dissention that may cloud our understanding of this term.

Table 2.12 summarizes some of the types of terrorism in use today. Although not all of the possible categories of terrorism are included, it is useful to compare the tactics, targets, and perpetrators of such types of terrorism.

TACTICS AND LABELS

Before summarizing the conclusions concerning a working definition of terrorism, one further point needs to be emphasized. Both the typologies of terrorism and the working definition of terrorism being offered treat terrorism as a tactic, not as a goal. This is important to remember if the term terrorism is not to be used or misused by governments unsympathetic to a group's cause. To describe a particular action as a terrorist action does not, and should not, in any sense define either the group or the cause for which it uses that tactic as terrorist.

It is true that if an individual, group, or government chooses to use this particular tactic repeatedly, there is every chance that those observing the actions will associate the tactic with those individuals. Continued or prolonged use of such a tactic by any group or government contributes to the perception of that group/government as terrorist by the audience for whom the crime is committed. This is not necessarily accurate, nor is it inaccurate: It is simply a natural phenomenon. A congressman who repeatedly supports war efforts and defense buildups may well expect to be labeled a "hawk" both by those who agree with his position and by those who disagree with it. It is simply a recognition of his patterns of action.

The same point is true to some extent of groups that repeatedly engage in terrorist acts. The frequency with which they engage in such actions, and to some degree the openness with which they do so, will certainly have an effect on

Table 2.12 Types of Terrorism

Type	Committed by...	Target	Tactics
Mass terror ■ Endemic ■ Authorized ■ Enforcement ■ Repressive	Political leaders (e.g., Idi Amin's rule in Uganda)	General population	Coercion, organized or unorganized
Dynastic assassination	Individuals or groups (e.g., Russian anarchists)	Head of state or ruling elite	Very selective violence
Random terror	Individuals or groups (e.g., airline attacks on the World Trade Center in New York	Anyone in "the wrong place at the wrong time"	Bombs in cafes, markets, and similar places
Focused random terror	Individual or groups (e.g., PIRA and UDF bombings in Northern Ireland)	Members of the opposition	Bombs in *specific* cafes and markets
Tactical terror (revolutionary)	Revolutionary movements (e.g., M-19's attacks on Columbian justices)	The government	Attacks on politically attractive targets

whether their audience news them as being terrorists. This does not mean that the ends toward which they strive are bad, somehow tainted with the opprobrium of terrorism. It simply means that the audience for whom the terrorist acts are generally staged have associated in their minds the actors with the actions taken in pursuit of that cause.

This is, of course, a very narrow line of reasoning, one not clearly understood by the general public, which is often the audience for terrorist events. That same public frequently attaches a terrorist label to individuals and even to groups who engage on a fairly regular basis in terrorist acts. But in terms acceptable in the legal and political community, it is only the act that can accurately be labeled as terrorist, not the individual or the group, and certainly not the cause for which the tactic is employed.

Members of a group cannot engage in questionable or even blatantly illegal actions on a regular basis and not be tainted with the negative labels associated with such actions. Members of Mafia families, although they may themselves be several steps removed from the actual commission of organized crimes, are nevertheless viewed by both the general public and by law enforcement agencies as being linked to, and a part of, those deplorable actions.

So it is with terrorism. Those who commit it, and those whose groups or governments have chosen to use it as a tactic, cannot escape the label of terrorist given them, not by governments, but by the very audience toward which such acts are directed. The justice of a cause rarely is sufficient, in that audience's view, to excuse the use of such a tactic. Although politicians and ideologies may accept the rationale, covertly or openly, that the ends for which they struggle justify the means that they choose to employ, most of the civilized world remains unwilling to accept this rationale. Certain acts can be described by definition as terrorist acts whether they are carried out by democratic governments in pursuit of reasonable policy goals or by armed revolutionaries fighting for freedom against tyranny.

THE ELEMENTS OF POWER OF TERRORIST ORGANIZATIONS[6]

There is Power in Leverage

As mentioned earlier, terrorism is an ancient art and it works even in modern times. It works because it never picks a fight that it will lose. It emphasizes the "Pile on Method" of aggressive action. In other words, its tactics involve a clear use of overpowering force against a single target. The terrorist focuses on one mission at a time and goes after relatively small, asymmetrical, isolated, high-value assets.

Terrorists do not take a hill, or hold ground, or defend a position. They do not establish a front line. They do not attack military positions with the idea of dominating the objective and driving the enemy force so that they can control the newly gained area.

They pick a weak target and develop the best possible plan to attack it. They also generate an escape plan that allows them to quickly exit the scene. They hit and run. They make the event significant enough so that it will be publicized and they promise to repeat the attack somewhere else. They are in the business of spreading fear and terror as a means of gaining their objectives.

Terrorists come in all forms. The bully terrorist attacks the weakest kid in school and turns him into a high value target by demanding that the victim give up his lunch money every day.

The killer terrorist plans to attack a bus full of civilians going to work, school, or shopping. He appears to be a normal commuter and gets on a bus with a bomb strapped across his chest. The terrorist detonates the bomb killing himself and twenty-nine innocent people on the bus. Since the terrorist dies in this scenario, no escape plan is needed.

There are technological terrorists who use gadgets to enhance their chances of success. The terrorists who bombed the Madrid, Spain, railroad station in March 2004 were technological terrorists. The bomb killed 190 people and injured hundreds more. They used duffel bags full of explosives that were remotely detonated by cell phones. The terrorists made their exit before they activated the bombs.

Good police work led to the arrest of several suspects within a few days of the event. Just three weeks later a bomb was found on the tracks used by a high-speed train between Madrid and Seville. Again it was to be remotely detonated. But the terrorist installing the bomb along its tracts was frightened off and the police disarmed the weapon before it was detonated thus avoiding damage and injury.

The smart and elusive terrorist owns every advantage. The terrorist group or the individual terrorist picks the target and no one knows what the target is, or where it is located.

The terrorist picks the time to attack the target and he takes advantage of the time factor—for example he might pick "rush hour" the time of maximum activity when the target is rich and maximum effect can be gained. If he is going to blow up a hotel, he might choose a time after midnight when the occupants are more likely to be sleeping in their rooms.

He chooses the method of attack—assault the target with a team, plant and remotely detonate a bomb, hijack a convoy and kill a VIP, derail a fast moving train, hijack and airplane and use it as a bomb to attack a ground target.

He decides on the weapons to be used, such as bombs, poisonous gas, and assassination by rifle or other lethal devices.

He looks for and engages weak but high-value targets so that he can get the biggest bang for his investment.

He uses terrorist attackers who will martyr themselves, making his task complete with the detonation. He doesn't even need to plan an escape.

He appeals to the media and identifies himself to assure that he has international media coverage. This activity is designed to create fear.

The terrorists we are engaged with today clearly have every advantage and this is one of the prime elements of terrorist power. They have leveraged the power of terrorism and they are very difficult to detect before the event is to take place.

The Individual Terrorist

A terrorist organization can be a very small group of individual terrorists or a huge international organization with state support and a broad range of human assets with varying talents, expertise and capability. Human assets are the very core and therefore a major part of the elements of its power.

The number of terrorists populating the organization is a measure of the power base of the group. If the members are highly trained they are even more valuable to the organization and increase the significance of this power factor. The talent, training level and zeal of these humans establishes the significance and possibly the level of danger of the particular organization. Terrorist groups are also resilient. The more they are punished through counter-action the more they seem to grow in strength. They have a zeal for their cause and it is deeply ingrained and makes them unusually dangerous.

Training Centers

The training centers are part of their infrastructure and their power base. These centers can be located in remote areas miles from any town and secure from public scrutiny. Such centers can be primitive in nature. Or they can be modern complexes where the terrorists learn the latest methods and tactics of terrorism.

Modern complexes might include villages for combat training in "built up areas." Vehicles might be available to be used in ambush training and kidnapping. Reconnaissance, intelligence collection techniques and operational planning are also taught.

Afghanistan became a hot bed for training centers in the late 1990s and early into the new millennium. Dozens of remote camps and training sites were created. Huge numbers of adherents went through a variety of training courses encompassing the full range of tactics of terrorists.

In keeping with their fleeting nature, it is not uncommon for a terrorist organization to abandon a training area after only one training session. Terrorists travel often and they travel light; this process is part of their power. While they do not like to establish lasting infrastructures in the final analysis, training centers are a necessary part of the power base of terrorist units.

Mobile and Cellular Terrorists

The terrorist organization is a fleeting entity. It gains its strength and its mystique by its nomadic activities. But more significant is the fact that its ability to move quickly offers an operational security measure that is very effective.

Terrorist organizations are also cellular in make-up. Cells are hidden and inactive till directed to action. They can live in and among their victims without being detected.

When the terrorist completes a mission those cell members will submerged into their bogus life with a job and a home and a normal schedule. At the same time the leadership often disappears to begin planning for the next operation. All of this below-the-surface activity is a power factor for the terrorists and a major problem for the opposing force.

Equipment

Terrorists need certain equipment to efficiently conduct operations and these items are also part of their power. They need weapons, ammunition and material to build bombs and other equipment. If they are planning a major operation, the terrorists may require secure storage facilities to hide their equipment. One option available is to hide the equipment within the local community with the help of trusted agents and friends.

This implies the unthinkable for the American public. It suggest that terrorist cells exist and that weapons can, and are, being stored with the help of supporters all in the local neighborhood.

Allies

Friends, supporters, and trusted agents of terrorist groups are also and important part of the organization. They help to sustain and hide the terrorist group members. They are not as dedicated and zealous about the mission of the terrorist element they support, as are the full-fledged members. If they were, they would be full-time members also. They are, however, important assets to the organization and true supporters.

These allies can provide a variety of services. A very significant example is they can provide early warning of impending danger. On administrative and convenience levels they can also provide legitimate postal addresses and drop boxes. They can handle money and store supplies and equipment. They can also provide housing and food.

Funding and National Sponsorship

The terrorists need money so they can buy equipment, send people around the world on missions, set up training camps and meet numerous other operational expenses. In recent times certain groups have been well-funded, bringing in millions of dollars each year to carry on their activities.

In most of these cases where heavy funding takes place, nations are involved in the support of terrorist groups. Not only do they provide huge sums of money but they also provide military instructors and training areas. Sponsoring nations have also provided sophisticated military equipment to terrorist groups. In the past they have provided a wide variety of items. Such items as land minds, surface to air missiles, shoulder-fired ground to ground missiles, specialized sniped weapons and sights, the latest in high-powered rifles, night sights, high-powered ammunition and other modern technology to make the terrorist very dangerous and effective.

There has been speculation about Saudi Arabia funding the Al Qaeda terrorist group over the past few years. If this turns out to be true it will confirm and offer insight into how a nation supports, encourages, and fund terrorism to the detriment of other nations. It will also put a significant strain on the relationship between the USA and Saudi Arabia.

How do nations fund terrorist groups? So far it has been discovered that finding can be accomplished by using standard international banking procedures. Banks transfer billions of dollar equivalents in a variety of currencies everyday, and terrorists' financing simply flows along transfer channels with legitimate money. It is hidden in the normal daily transactions of legitimate business.

Bank accounts are established by terrorist organizations under bogus names and/or shell companies and many of them are/were "not-for-profit corporations." Money flows through international banking channels to these shell companies as part of the daily transfer of billions of dollars moving in the commercial world. It is hidden because there is so much active and legitimate exchange going on that the relatively small amount of terrorist funding is lost in the traffic.

This is a very convenient method of financing terrorist organizations. However, after the World Trade Center attack, many of these accounts have been exposed and frozen by the international banking and law enforcement community. Law enforcement agencies searched out these accounts, cut them off and dried up the flow of funds. The flow and the availability of money to terrorist organizations is vital. It is also a vulnerability to the life of the terrorist element. If the flow can be cut off, the terrorist organization's effectiveness will be greatly reduced.

With law enforcement putting the squeeze on funding, the terrorist will now become more clever in establishing such accounts or will transfer money person-to-person without the use of banks. They will attempt to find new loopholes and new ways of transferring money. You, as a future analyst, will be devising new methods of determining how money is moving to terrorist organizations and how to stop the flow.

In any event, funds on hand are part of the power base of terrorist organizations. Money is also a necessary commodity in order to do business. Be assured that the terrorists of the world will find clever and surreptitious methods of transferring currency to keep their organizations going. At the same time the opponents of terrorism will be searching out ways and means of stopping the flow of money.

Other Suppliers

The world of the gunrunner is a dark place where terrorists and criminals can find almost any military hardware that has ever been produced. International gunrunners have been involved in selling military equipment to terrorists. Everything from sophisticated communication systems to the latest weapons can be found in the illegitimate marketplace of the gunrunner. Well-connected, reliable gunrunner affiliations are vital to terrorist operations and such contacts are an element of terrorist power.

Gunrunners are an active force of people and they are usually without affiliation. In other words, they will work for anyone and are not concerned about loyalties or affiliations, except for the almighty dollar. They can be very important to terrorists. There have been numerous rumors and reports concerning gunrunners trying to obtain weapons of mass destruction to sell to terrorists. The reports suggest that with the fall of the USSR, numerous weapons are available and on the market from the former Soviet Union arsenal. This must be watched very closely.

Motivation

Many elements of power in a terrorist organization are soft. The terrorist organization needs a motive, a reason for its existence. For example, let's try hate! Assume that the terrorist organization hates America and Americans. This hatred becomes an element of power.

Hate can motivate the terrorist, but it must be relevant to him. To tell the terrorist that he should hate American's because each of them owns a TV probably will not work. But to hate Americans because they come from the same breed that attacked the Muslim world during the crusades hundreds of years ago will work.

To emphasize that the Americans continue to attack the Muslim world—economically, physically, or simply by disrespecting Muslims—will ignite them to terrorist action.

Look again at the motivation. It is based first on history and second by events today, all ignited with a burning passion a powerful hatred. This is but one example to demonstrate to the reader that the people of the Middle East and of Muslim persuasion think much differently than do Westerners. They are passionate about events from history that they find offensive. They are concerned about their history, heritage, image, their honor, and the respect that they demand.

Infrastructure

There are other elements of power that make a terrorist group viable. For example, a terrorist group needs an infrastructure. It must have a leadership element. That element contains people who develop plans, handle money, purchase weapons and ammunition, explosives and other materials used in terrorist activity. These people keep records, use computers, cell phones, fax machines, reproduction equipment and all of the latest technological "widgets" available.

This means that at least some terrorists, probably the leadership, operated from fixed sites. The fixed site might be a cave. Or it might be someone's home and in rare cases it might be an office building.

Remember, however, that security is one of the main advantages to a well-organized and clever terrorist group. The individual terrorist is only given a small look at the group—and it is generally a policy that the entire organization is never revealed to the individual soldier. Cells are formed, and each person in a cell is familiar only with what his cell is doing. This measure promotes security.

The Strategic View

Terrorists have a long-term agenda, and for some that agenda is to take out the world's single superpower. Are they capable of doing it? At issue is, do they have the strategic view and global vision to take down America? Strategic vision and global view is an element of power. It takes sophisticated people to think, scheme and activate missions that are strategic in nature.

Consider the strategic blow they struck in Spain in 2004. The Spanish government had dispatched a contingent of troops to Iraq, thereby aligning itself with the United States and President Bush's efforts in the Middle East. Polls showed the people of Spain were opposed to the deployment of Spanish troops to the Middle East.

Spain was heading for a general election in March 2004. The incumbent party was ahead in the polls by about five percentage points. However, just before the general election a group of terrorists placed several bombs in the Madrid railroad station (the killing zone) and by remote detonation killed hundreds of Spanish commuters.

Just hours later the voters of Spain voted a new party in, including a new president, and turned out the old. Later the terrorists told the Spanish government they would not continue to terrorize the country of Spain if the Spanish government would withdraw its troops from Iraq.

This action requires a strategic view of the relationship between the United States and Spain. It demands and understanding of Spanish politics, voting issues, emotional questions and the efforts of international blackmail. This was a brilliant strategic move designed to isolate the United States.

Those involved are not just a few guys who got lucky blowing up a train station in Madrid, just to disrupt the peace. The leaders of the organization responsible for this tragic attack are smart, informed, dedicated, and aware of world events. They are cognizant of how the international balance can be affected by terrorism and possess a versatile array of power elements.

This terrorist action has caused the loss of a European ally in Iraq. It represents a major setback for the Bush administration. We can expect that every one of our allies with look at their situation vis-à-vis the United States and its involvement in the Middle East, Iraq in particular.

Near the end of March 2004, a bomb attack on a factory occurred in Uzbekistan. The apparent reason was to put pressure on the government of Uzbekistan. Why? Because the government supports the USA by providing landing and flyover rights of its country in support of counter-terrorist operations in Afghanistan.

Another phenomenon of modern day terrorism is the use of splinter terrorist groups that now seem willing to coalesce and work for a larger group on special missions in foreign countries. It is apparently somewhat like the Mafia contract system. If, for example, the leadership of al-Qaeda wants to attack a facility in a country like Uzbekistan, where they have few if any personnel, they will arrange for a local terrorist element to conduct the operation. This gives the organized terrorist groups of the world a broader reach and a more strategic look. It also magnifies their power in the eyes of the victims and those in fear of attack. It promotes dispersion, deception, and security for the entire terrorist movement. At the same time it becomes evident that no region and no country is safe. All are vulnerable and fall within the strategic view of the terrorist.

On review, it is apparent that one of the key elements for power in certain terrorist organizations is having a strategic plan. And now we see the implementation of that strategic plan in powerful and convincing ways.

So What Does All of This Add Up To?

The elements of power of a terrorist organization are totally different from that of the United States or any industrialized nation. The terrorist power elements are characterized by the following list.

- Terrorists used specialized tactics that accomplish a limited mission and spread fear.
- The terrorist has every advantage.

- He picks a weak but significant and manageable target.
- He chooses the best weapons for the job at hand.
- He knows the target to be attacked.
- He knows the time of the attack.
- He focuses on the target and piles on it, using surprise and powerful weapons.
- He does not stay and fight.
- He escapes quickly and usually gets publicity for the attack.
- Terrorist organizations can be strong or weak based on one of the human assets that populate the group. If they have well-trained soldiers their effectiveness goes up and they are more of a threat.
- Terrorists use training centers, but for security reasons they are often abandoned after one or two training sessions. The ability to keep moving and change locations is a powerful tool that promotes security for the terrorist.
- Terrorists are fleeting, nomad-like organizations that disappear into the population.
- Terrorists need equipment and also need storage areas.
- Terrorists have allies in the community.
- Terrorists need funds and are funded by donations or are sponsored by other nations.
- They have bank accounts and transfer monies through banking channels or they move cash from hand to hand.
- Terrorists use gunrunners to buy supplies and equipment
- Terrorists are motivated and the leadership must keep them motivated in order to succeed.
- Terrorists require at least a limited infrastructure.
- Terrorists of today have a strategic view which is very dangerous to world peace.

In the Final Analysis

- Terrorists are not easily detected.
- Terrorists can be well trained.
- Terrorists know how to collect information and create intelligence.
- Terrorists can be very good planners.

- Terrorists can be flexible.

- Terrorists hit and run.

- Terrorists choose the time and place of attack.

- Terrorists avoid conventional forces.

- Terrorists use blackmail.

- Terrorists know how to exploit the civilian population to meet their own needs.

- Terrorists are difficult to identify and hard to stop.

- Terrorists have a limited infrastructure that has little value to anyone other than the terrorist group.

- Since they have a limited infrastructure they are highly mobile.

- Terrorists have limited vulnerabilities.

- Terrorists believe they can defeat a superpower.

- Terrorists and the entire concept of terrorism are very dangerous.

SUMMARY

Based on the information from this chapter, you should have a fairly clear idea of what constitutes terrorism, but the question to be answered is "who are the terrorists?" A thorough knowledge of the laws of terrorism may help define what terrorism is, but that knowledge must be partnered with a knowledge of current events, intelligence, networking in the counter-terror community, and a knowledge base of risks and vulnerabilities. Knowing terrorism definitions is only effective if executed against other factors to develop predictive capabilities in order to counter an attack.

Terrorism, then, is an act comprised of at least four crucial elements: (1) It is an act of violence; (2) it has a political motive or goal; (3) it is perpetrated against innocent persons; and (4) it is staged to be played before an audience whose reaction of fear and terror is the desired result. This definition eliminates football players, lunatics on a killing spree, and the assassin who tries to kill a bad ruler, from the label of terrorist. All acts of violence are not terrorist acts, however heinous the acts may be.

The line between acceptable types of violence and unacceptable types is, unfortunately, not always clear. Violence by revolutionaries and by the state is sometimes difficult to categorize clearly as terrorist, even given the working definition evolved here. Further study of the history, ideology, and individuals involved in terrorist acts may increase our understanding of this important but confusing term.

ADDITIONAL DISCUSSION TOPICS

- Does the threat of Islamic terrorism create a vacuum in the response to the threat presented by domestic terror groups?

- Can the Department of Justice and the FBI be more effective in defending the United States? How? What can they do?

- What danger do organized-criminal street gangs present and do they constitute terror groups?

RESOURCES
Directives & Executive Orders

Directives (http://library.nps.navy.mil/home/terrorism.htm#archives)

(most are courtesy of the National Security Archives at George Washington University).

Managing Terrorist Incidents

NSDD 30 [National Security Decision Directive] April 30, 1982.

Combating Terrorism

NSDD 138 [National Security Decision Directive] [Extract] April 1984.

Task Force on Combatting Terrorism

NSDD 179 [National Security Decision Directive] July 19, 1985.

Civilian Aviation Anti-Terrorism Program

NSDD 180 [National Security Decision Directive] July 20, 1985.

Acting Against Libyan Support of International Terrorism

NSDD 205 [National Security Decision Directive] January 8, 1986.

Acting Against Libyan Support of International Terrorism

NSDD 205 Annex [National Security Decision Directive] January 8, 1986.

The National Program for Combatting Terrorism

NSDD 207 [National Security Decision Directive] January 20, 1986.

U.S. Policy on Counterterrorism

PDD 39 [Presidential Decision Directive] June 21, 1995

Addressing the Threat of Emerging Infectious Diseases

NTSC 7 [Presidential Decision Directive] factsheet, June 12, 1996

Combating Terrorism

PDD 62 [Presidential Decision Directive] factsheet, May 22, 1998

Critical Infrastructure Protection

PDD 63 [Presidential Decision Directive], May 22, 1998

Organization and Operation of the Homeland Security Council

HSPD 1 [Homeland Security Presidential Directive], October 29, 2001

Combating Terrorism Through Immigration Policies

HSPD 2 [Homeland Security Presidential Directive], October 30, 2001

Homeland Security Advisory System

HSPD 3 [Homeland Security Presidential Directive], March 12, 2002

National Strategy to Combat Weapons of Mass Destruction [unclassified version] (Federation of American Scientists)

HSPD 4 [Homeland Security Presidential Directive], December, 2002

Management of Domestic Incidents

HSPD 5 [Homeland Security Presidential Directive], February 28, 2003

Integration and Use of Screening Information

HSPD 6 [Homeland Security Presidential Directive], September 16, 2003

Critical Infrastructure Identification, Prioritization, and Protection

HSPD 7 [Homeland Security Presidential Directive], December 17, 2003

National Preparedness

HSPD 8 [Homeland Security Presidential Directive], December 17, 2003

Defense of United States Agriculture and Food

HSPD 9 [Homeland Security Presidential Directive], January 30, 2004

Biodefense for the 21st Century (Federation of American Scientists)

HSPD 10 [Homeland Security Presidential Directive], April 28, 2004

Comprehensive Terrorist-Related Screening Procedures

HSPD 11 [Homeland Security Presidential Directive], August 27, 2004

Policy for a Common Identification Standard for Federal Employees and Contractors

HSPD 12 [Homeland Security Presidential Directive], August 27, 2004

Web Link

U.S. Department of Justice, Office of Justice Programs, Partnerships for Safer Communities: http://www.ojp.usdoj.gov/terrorism/whats_new.htm

Endnotes

[1] Federal Bureau of Investigation website http://www.fbi.gov

[2] Source: *Denver Post*, January 9, 2005 by staff writer Howard Pankratz and Kirk Mitchell.

[3] Source: Testimony of James F. Jarboe, Domestic Terrorism Section Chief, Counterterrorism Division, FBI. Before the House Resources Committee, Subcommittee on Forests and Forest Health, February 12, 2002.

[4] Source: Transactional Records Access Clearinghouse. A Special TRAC Report: Criminal Enforcement Against Terrorists, found at http://trac.syr.edu/tracreports/terrorism/report011203.html

[5] Source: Department of Justice internal database Users' Manual.

[6] The following section is from 0-536-26458-9, Terrorism: A Growth Industry..., pp 37-45.

CHAPTER THREE

INTELLIGENCE[1]

It is a capital mistake to theorize before one has data. Insensibly one begins to twist facts to suit theories, instead of theories to suit facts.
—*The Adventures of Sherlock Holmes*, 1892, "A Scandal in Bohemia"

Pluralitas non est ponenda sine neccesitate [given multiple theories to explain a set of observations, the simplest explanation is to be preferred].
—Principle from William of Occam, Logician and Franciscan Friar, (c. 1285-1350 or 1280-1349)

KEY TERMS

Intelligence Cycle
Actionable intelligence
Intelligence community
Collection
Dissemination
Open source intelligence
Vulnerability
Critical infrastructure
Intelligence
Critical thinking
Logic fallacy

OBJECTIVES

- Differentiate between intelligence and information.

- Differentiate between strategic, operational, and tactical intelligence.

- Compare how the law enforcement community and the intelligence community define and use intelligence.

- Describe the purpose and steps of the intelligence cycle.

- Describe the types and phases of intelligence briefings.

- Analyze intelligence for reporting in an intelligence brief.

DISCUSSION TOPICS

- What is intelligence?

- What is the Intelligence Cycle?

- Explain the concepts of information, investigation and intelligence.

- How does the business-continuity cycle relate to conducting an analysis of current events?

- What would you consider to be the basic successes and failures of Tom Ridge's tenure as Secretary of Homeland Security?

3

INTRODUCTION

Our way of gathering information and sorting it has evolved as a result of two great changes in history: The Information Age brought about by the development of computers and the Internet, and the Security Age brought about by the war on terrorism. These two eras of change have developed access to intelligence and analytical software that give the individual the power to collect and analyze intelligence, which once was the sole domain of great nation states.

This chapter will address the mechanics of intelligence and the role intelligence plays in the business and political world.

An Insider's Point of View...

Your author served as a police intelligence unit agent and commander in the 1980s and 1990s. Thinking back just those few years, the technical standard for intelligence files was collections of punch cards and index cards. Data was analyzed much the same way but storage and retrieval was a mystery to all but the holder of the files. Literally, if the analyst who managed our file system died, we would have had to start from scratch.

Now we can find out as much from a web-search about a financial history, personal history, or criminal history in five minutes as a month of investigation would produce 20 years ago. And almost anyone can do it.

The purpose of sharing this anecdote is not to reminisce about the good old days, but to point out that critical elements of the Intelligence Cycle have accelerated to such an extent that the law, perceptions of privacy, and data sorting have created a new environment. This rapid pace of change will only continue and probably will become faster exponentially. Therefore, the security specialist must make every effort to research and stay current on all laws, procedures, technology, and tools of the intelligence field as well as maintaining traditional tradecraft.

This writer was in a meeting with a former CIA official, who is also retired, and we reminisced about the "good old days" of wiretapping analog telephone lines with pliers and a service truck. Now, traditional phones and forms of communication are mobile, wireless, and present an entirely new problem for law enforcement and the intelligence community. New laws, such as the Patriot Act, broaden the ability of law enforcement to respond to the new technology. The point is that old-school management personnel must stay on the cutting-edge to effectively support the field staff.

The following article discusses the CIA's Intelligence Cycle. This is very similar to the type of process used by law enforcement, differing in terminology only.

THE INTELLIGENCE CYCLE[2]

The Intelligence Cycle is the process of developing raw information into finished intelligence for policymakers to use in decision-making and action. There are five steps which constitute the Intelligence Cycle.

Step 1: Planning and Direction

... is management of the entire effort, from identifying the need for data to delivering an intelligence product to a consumer. It is the beginning and the end of the cycle—the beginning because it involves drawing up specific collection requirements and the end because finished intelligence, which supports policy decisions, generates new requirements.

The whole process depends on guidance from public officials. Policymakers—the President, his aides, the National Security Council, and other major departments and agencies of government—initiate requests for intelligence.

Step 2: Collection

... is the gathering of the raw information needed to produce finished intelligence. There are many sources of information, including open sources such as foreign broadcasts, newspapers, periodicals, and books. Open source reporting is integral to CIA's analytical capabilities. There are also secret sources of information. CIA operations officers collect such information from agents abroad and from defectors who provide information obtainable in no other way.

Finally, technical collection—electronics and satellite photography—plays an indispensable role in modern intelligence, such as monitoring arms control agreements and providing direct support to military forces.

Step Three: Processing

... involves converting the vast amount of information collected to a form usable by analysts. This is done through a variety of methods including decryption, language translations, and data reduction.

Step Four: All-Source Analysis and Production

... is the conversion of basic information into finished intelligence. It includes integrating, evaluating, and analyzing all available data—which is often fragmented and even contradictory—and preparing intelligence products. Analysts, who are subject-matter specialists, consider the information's reliability, validity, and relevance. They integrate data into a coherent whole, put the evaluated information in context, and produce finished intelligence that includes assessments of events and judgments about the implications of the information for the United States.

The CIA devotes the bulk of its resources to providing strategic intelligence to policymakers. It performs this important function by monitoring events, warning decision makers about threats to the United States, and forecasting developments. The subjects involved may concern different regions, problems, or personalities in various contexts—political, geographic, economic, military, scientific, or biographic. Current events, capabilities, and future trends are examined.

The CIA produces numerous written reports, which may be brief—one page or less—or lengthy studies. They may involve current intelligence, which is of immediate importance, or long-range assessments. The Agency presents some finished intelligence in oral briefings. The CIA also participates in the drafting and production of National Intelligence Estimates, which reflect the collective judgments of the Intelligence Community.

The IC (intelligence cycle) is a federation of executive branch agencies and organizations that work separately and together to conduct intelligence activities necessary for the conduct of foreign relations and the protection of the national security of the United States. These activities include:

- Collection of information needed by the President, the National Security Council, the Secretaries of State and Defense, and other Executive Branch officials for the performance of their duties and responsibilities;

- Production and dissemination of intelligence;

- Collection of information concerning, and the conduct of activities to protect against, intelligence activities directed against the US, international terrorist and international narcotics activities, and other hostile activities directed against the US by foreign powers, organizations, persons, and their agents;

- Special activities;

- Administrative and support activities within the US and abroad necessary for the performance of authorized activities; and

■ Such other intelligence activities as the President may direct from time to time. Use the links at the right to read legislation, reports, and executive orders that have defined the IC since 1947.Members of the Intelligence Community

Members of the Intelligence Community
Director of National Intelligence
Undersecretary of Defense for Intelligence
Air Force Intelligence
Army Intelligence
Central Intelligence Agency
Coast Guard Intelligence
Defense Intelligence Agency
Department of Energy
Department of Homeland Security
Department of State
Department of the Treasury
Drug Enforcement Administration
Federal Bureau of Investigation
Marine Corps Intelligence
National Geospatial-Intelligence Agency
National Reconnaissance Office
National Security Agency

Step Five: Dissemination

The last step, which logically feeds into the first, is the distribution of the finished intelligence to the consumers, the same policymakers whose needs initiated the intelligence requirements. Finished intelligence is provided daily to the President and key national security advisers. The policymakers, the recipients of finished intelligence, then make decisions based on the information, and these decisions may lead to the levying of more requirements, thus triggering the Intelligence Cycle.

The news media, trade journals, government web sites, and other sources provide a daily overview of the state of the security world. There is generally some value in each piece of information that is available. The security specialist must learn to objectively assess these resources and determine what may be useful in *planning* for emergencies and developing policies to deter threats.

The same critical methodology for understanding and assessment of vast information resources can be used whether you are *planning* security for a nation or one local water plant. Like many problems, security should be approached with a global perspective that is refined with local action.

For example, on a national level, a critical difficulty faced by the first Secretary of Homeland Security, Tom Ridge—in what proved to be the biggest reorganization of government since World War II—was changing the way America thought about or

Figure 3.1 INTELLIGENCE CYCLE

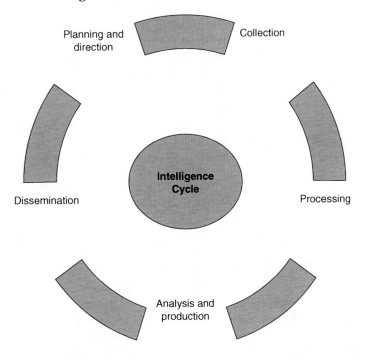

perceived security. The initial steps seemed awkward, and even a little painful (for example, the "duct-tape-and-plastic" press release, or the unpopular color codes); however, the efforts were not in vain. As terms like *vulnerability assessment, critical infrastructure, intelligence,* and *emergency response* became commonplace in the media and in everyday conversations, so the public perception and interest piqued. The concept that Secretary Ridge successfully launched was an awareness, or consciousness, of security as a core piece of any business or government endeavor.

The benefit of monitoring and analyzing current events is obvious to the security specialist or emergency planner. By executing against an existing knowledge base, current events analyses exercises can be leveraged to provide insight into future outcomes. These outcomes can be scheduled from most to least likely to occur, which gives the end-user the ability to effectively conduct business in a rational and effective manner, by pre-planning for potential problems.

The critical elements in the business-continuity cycle are as follows:

- Planning
- Implementing/Preventing
- Responding
- Mitigating
- Recovery
- Analysis

An ability to develop recommendations, policy, and strategic plans based on analyzing current events is a necessary skill set in the modern security environment. Merely being appraised of current happenings around the world is not enough. The security specialist must be able to critically assess happenings and determine the impact on the organization, which the specialist represents. Forward-looking or predictive analysis is a skill that can be developed by not just being aware of issues but determining how to analyze issues effectively in concert with organizational goals, budgets, and security concerns.

Locally, the head of security for a corporate campus, a chemical plant, or local water company will follow the lead of the Department of Homeland Security in developing strategic and tactical plans based on a dynamic information flow during a time of war against terrorism.

Figure 3.2

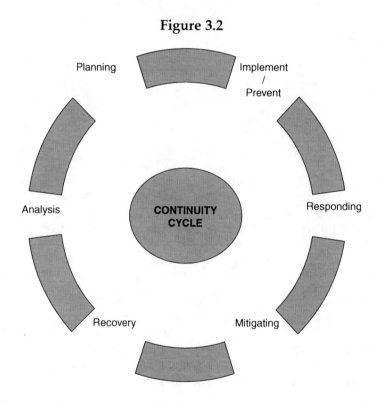

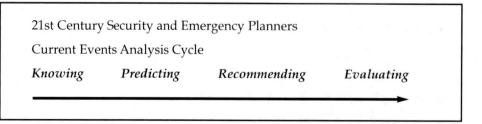

Intelligence.

1. **Definition:** [n] the operation of gathering information about an enemy

2. [n] the ability to comprehend; to understand and profit from experience

3. <u>[n] new information about specific</u> and timely events; "they awaited news of the outcome"

4. [n] secret information about an enemy (or potential enemy); "we sent out planes to gather intelligence on their radar coverage"

5. [n] a unit responsible for gathering and interpreting information about an enemy

SKILL SETS FOR ANALYSIS

Many readings in this text are from media resources. When evaluating media resources, it is critical to take an objective look at the item to be reviewed, and then to apply basic intelligence analyst skills such as evaluating the source and evaluating the information.

Information must be approached critically—that is, the subject matter must be tested for the following factors:

- Objectivity

- Relevance

- Timeliness

- Accuracy

- Credibility

- Verifiability

Critical Thinking

When reviewing *open source* materials, the reader must take steps to logically assess the agenda of the reader, particularly if the source tends to editorialize rather than report objectively. As a homeland security specialist, you will often be asked about current events that have been presented in the news media with a "spin" or biased element. You must be able to assess and evaluate the content to determine what is fact or opinion. In order to effectively assess the materials in point, a list of **logic fallacies** (found below) will be of benefit. Test these on the commentary from television news talk shows for practice in objective analysis.

Ethical Considerations...

Is there an ethical requirement to assessing events critically and objectively? Perhaps for the security specialist in government and the private sector, the ethical standards included in most organizational mission statements presume some sort of responsibility to critically assess events. However the general population has a responsibility to critically assess events as they unfold. During the 2008 presidential campaigns, some books and movies presented as factual actually contained a lot of subjective materials on both candidates that clearly did not pass the "smell" test with most of the public. However, many people allowed themselves to be influenced by the "propaganda" aspects of these products.

In Spain, the government was changed based on the media being manipulated by terrorists following a bomb attack initiated against a train.

Is there an ethical responsibility to actively sort the factual from the fictitious? What, if anything, are the implications for national security in regards to an ethical responsibility to objectively analyze events?

Definition – Open Source Intelligence – Open Source intelligence or OSINT is the body of information available to any member of the public with the means or interest to collect it. This may include media broadcasts, newpapers, Internet blogs, or any other public information resource.

OPEN SOURCE INTELLIGENCE

Open source intelligence or "OSINT" refers to an intelligence gathering discipline based on information collected from open sources, i.e. information available to the general public. This includes newspapers, the internet, books, phone books, scientific journals, radio broadcasts, television, and others. The term is unrelated to open source in the computer software community, which refers to programs whose source code is publicly available. OSINT is also not to be confused with OSIF– anything that is broadcast or distributed is open source information– anything that is tailored to answer a specific question from a specific person or decision-making unit is OSINT.

Collection of information in OSINT is a very different problem from collection in other intelligence disciplines because, by definition, the information sources are publicly available. In other intelligence disciplines, a major difficulty is extracting information from non-cooperative targets. In OSINT, the chief difficulty is identifying relevant, reliable sources from the vast abundance of publicly available information. Obtaining the needed information once a source is identified is a comparatively minor problem.

Master List of Logical Fallacies

The following is a partial list of common **logic fallacies.** For each fallacy an explanation and example is provided.

1. *Ad hominem* or ATTACKING THE PERSON. Attacking the arguer rather than his/her argument. Example: *His objections to capital punishment carry no weight because he is a convicted felon.* Note: Saying something negative about someone is not necessarily *ad hominem.* If a person (politician for example) *is the issue*, then it is not a fallacy to criticize him/her.

2. *Ad ignorantium* or APPEAL TO IGNORANCE. Arguing on the basis of what is not known and cannot be proven. (Sometimes called the "burden of proof" fallacy). If you cannot prove that something is true then it must be false (and vice versa). Example: *You can't prove there isn't a Loch Ness Monster, so there must be one.*

3. *Ad verecundiam* or APPEAL TO AUTHORITY. A deliberate attempt to convince the listener by appealing to the reputation of a famous or respected person. Often manifested by an authority in one field speaking out of his or her field of expertise. Example: *Sports stars endorsing investment firms. Or, a TV commercial by an actor who claims, "I'm not a doctor, but I play one on TV."*

4. AFFIRMING THE CONSEQUENT. An invalid form of the conditional argument. In this case, the second premise affirms the consequent of the first premise and the conclusion affirms the antecedent. Example: *If he wants to get that job, then he must know Spanish. He knows Spanish, so the job is his.*

5. AMPHIBOLY. Syntactical ambiguity involving the position of words in a sentence or the juxtaposition of two sentences that leads to communication of a erroneous idea. This fallacy is like equivocation except that the ambiguity does not result from a shift in meaning of a single word or phrase, but is created by word placement. Example: *Jim said he saw Jenny walk her dog through the window. Ow! She should be reported for animal abuse. [This was supposed to relate Jim's sighting of Jenny through the window, not Jenny's passing bodily through the window.]*

6. APPEAL TO EMOTION. Deliberate introduction of emotional devices in place of logical assertions to persuade the listener. The fallacy can appeal to various emotions including pride, pity, fear, hate, vanity, or sympathy. Generally, the issue is oversimplified to the advantage of the arguer. Example: *In 1972, there was a widespread advertisement printed by the Foulke Fur Co., in response to the frequent protests against the killing of Alaskan seals for highly priced furs. According to the advertisement, clubbing the seals was one of the great conservation stories of our history, a mere exercise in wildlife management, because "biologists believe a controlled colony would be a healthier colony."*

7. ARGUMENT FROM ANALOGY or FALSE ANALOGY. An unsound form of inductive argument in which an argument relies heavily on a weak or irrelevant analogy to prove its point. Example: *This must be a great car, for, like the finest watches in the world, it was made in Switzerland.*

8. BEGGING THE QUESTION. An argument in which the conclusion is implied or already assumed in the premise. Also said to be a circular argument. Example: *Of course the Bible is the word of God. Why...? Because it says so in the Bible.*

9. SLIPPERY SLOPE. A line of reasoning that argues against taking a step because it assumes that if you take the first step, you will *inevitably* follow through to the last. This fallacy uses the valid form of hypothetical syllogism, but uses guesswork for the premises. Example: *We can't allow students any voice in decision-making on campus; if we do, it won't be long before they are in total control.*

10. COMMON BELIEF (Sometimes called the "bandwagon" fallacy or "appeal to popularity"). Assertion of a statement to be true on the evidence that many other people allegedly believe it. Being widely believed is not proof or evidence of the truth. Example: *Of course Nixon was guilty in Watergate. Everybody knows that!*

11. PAST BELIEF. A form of the COMMON BELIEF fallacy. The same error in reasoning is committed except the claim is for belief or support in the past. Example: *Women must obey their husbands. After all, marriage vows contained those words for centuries.*

12. CONTRARY TO FACT HYPOTHESIS. Assertion of an idea based on an unjustified or unsubstantiated degree of certainty that a hypothetical consequence would have resulted. Example: *If President Bush had not gone into the Persian Gulf with military force when he did, Saddam Hussein would have overtaken control of Saudi Arabia and controlled the world's oil today.*

13. DENYING THE ANTECEDENT. An invalid form of the conditional argument. In this one, the second premise denies the antecedent of the first premise, and the conclusion denies the consequent. Often mistaken for *modus tollens*. Example: *If she qualifies for a promotion, she must speak English. She doesn't qualify for the promotion, so she must not know how to speak English.*

14. DIVISION. Conclusion that any part of a particular whole must have a characteristic because the whole has that characteristic. Example: *I am sure that Karen plays the piano well, since her family is so musical.*

15. COMPOSITION. Conclusion that a whole must have a characteristic because some part of it has that characteristic. Example: *The Dawson clan must be rolling in money, since Fred Dawson makes a lot from his practice.*

16. FALSE DILEMMA (often called the either/or fallacy or false dichotomy). Assertion that we must choose one of two alternatives instead of allowing for other possibilities; a false form of *disjunctive syllogism*. Example: *"America, love it or leave it." (The implication is, since you don't love it the only option is to leave it).*

17. EQUIVOCATION. A form of semantic ambiguity. The arguer uses the ambiguous nature of a word or phrase to shift the meaning in such a way as to make the reason offered appear more convincing. Example: *We realize that workers are idle during the period of layoffs. But the government should never subsidize idleness, which has often been condemned as a vice. Therefore, payments to laid off workers are wrong.*

18. HASTY GENERALIZATION. A generalization accepted on the support of a sample that is too small or biased to warrant it. Example: *All men are rats! Just look at the louse that I married.*

19. POST HOC, ERGO PROPTER HOC. ("After this, therefore caused by this.") A form of the false cause fallacy in which it is inferred that because one event followed another it is necessarily caused by that event. Example: *Mary joined our class and the next week we all did poorly on the quiz. It must be her fault.*

20. INCONSISTENCY. A discourse is inconsistent or self-contradicting if it contains, explicitly or implicitly, two assertions that are logically incompatible with each other. Inconsistency can also occur between words and actions. Example: *A woman who represents herself as a feminist, yet doesn't believe women should run for Congress.*

21. NON SEQUITUR. ("It does not follow.") Assertion of premises that have no direct relationship to the conclusion. This fallacy appears in political speeches and advertising with great frequency. Example: *Even visual devices such as a waterfall in the background and a beautiful girl in the foreground in an automobile advertisement. [These of course have nothing to do with the automobile's performance.]*

22. QUESTIONABLE CAUSE. (In Latin: *non causa pro causa*, "not the cause of that"). This form of the false cause fallacy occurs when the cause for an occurrence is identified on insufficient evidence. Example: *I expect that it will rain tomorrow because I washed the car.*

23. RED HERRING. Introduction of an irrelevant issue into a discussion as a smokescreen. It is a tactic designed to divert attention from the issue at hand. Example: *Many people say that engineers need more practice in writing, but I would like to remind them how difficult it is to master all the math and drawing skills that an engineer requires.*

24. SLANTING. A form of misrepresentation in which a true statement is made, but made in such a way as to suggest that something is not true or to give a false description through the manipulation of connotation. Example: *I can't believe how much money is being poured into the space program [Use of the word "poured" suggests heedless and unnecessary spending].*

25. STRAW MAN. Misrepresentation or recasting of an opponent's position to make it more vulnerable. Usually this is done by distorting the issue to a ridiculous extreme. This can also take the form of attacking only the weak premises in an opposing argument while ignoring the strong ones. Example: *Those who favor gun-control legislation just want to take all guns away from responsible citizens and put them into the hands of the criminals.*

26. TWO WRONGS MAKE A RIGHT. An attempt to justify an apparently wrong action by charges of a similar wrong. The underlying assumption is that if they do it, then we can do it too and are somehow justified. Example: *Supporters of apartheid are often guilty of this error in reasoning. They point to U.S. practices of slavery to justify their system.*

In looking at the current events resources used for open source intelligence, the security specialist will find quite a few articles and news stories that may utilize logic fallacy techniques when stating their cases.

Point to Remember...

Just because an article contains some of the logic fallacies, it can still have value as an insight into the writer's point of view. Sometimes what someone says isn't as important as who said it, or who the audience is.

Types of Intelligence

Strategic intelligence is best described as the "big picture" approach to intelligence. It is knowledge gained from analysis, which creates an overall assessment of an organization, threat, or geographic area.

Operational intelligence is evaluated information amassed by ongoing analytical support. Said to be the bridge between strategic and tactical, operational intelligence is focused on active or potential targets of law enforcement investigations, or military activity or other activities the elements of which, combined, lead to the strategic level.

Tactical intelligence is actionable information that supports short-term, offensive campaigns against known targets and target organizations. It supports arrests, seizures, and interdictions in active investigations or provides a counter-terrorist operative the means to interdict or deflect a terrorist mission, or provides a military unit commander details of an enemy strong point he must assault

Critical Thinking and Open Source Intelligence

Read this opinion concerning the value of **open source** intelligence posted on the Central Intelligence Agency website. Many critical thinking issues are cited and some logic fallacies seem to creep into what is overall a very well written essay. Review and assess the material and identify what is fact and what is opinio

A Venerable Source in a New Era

VOL. 48, NO. 3, 2004

The Center welcomes inquiries about its programs from intelligence professionals and scholars. The Center can be reached by writing to:

Paul M. Johnson
Director
Center for the Study of Intelligence
Central Intelligence Agency
Washington, D. C. 20505

Sailing the Sea of OSINT in the Information Age

Stephen C. Mercado

"The world today abounds in open information to an extent unimaginable to intelligence officers of the Cold War."

Our age's increasingly voluminous open-source intelligence (OSINT) sheds light on issues of the day for all-source analysts, covert collectors, and policymakers, but have we done enough to exploit its potential? My short answer is "No," and here's why I think so.

Collecting **intelligence** these days is at times less a matter of stealing through dark alleys in a foreign land to meet some secret agent than one of surfing the Internet under the fluorescent lights of an office cubicle to find some **open source**. The world is changing with the advance of commerce and technology. Mouse clicks and online dictionaries today often prove more useful than stylish cloaks and shiny daggers in gathering intelligence required to help analysts and officials understand the world. Combined with stolen secrets, diplomatic reports, and technical collection, **open sources** constitute what one former deputy director of intelligence termed the "intricate mosaic" of **intelligence**.[1]

Today's commercial and technical advances are only the latest developments in a collection discipline whose pioneers began developing the field in the late 1930s. Building on early work at Princeton University to monitor foreign short-wave radio, the Foreign Broadcast Intelligence Service (FBIS) in 1941 began to turn radio into a primary intelligence source during World War II.[2] The government did not neglect the printed word either. The Interdepartmental Committee for the Acquisition of Foreign Periodicals (IDC) gathered Axis publications through a global collection network.

The men and women who labored in the OSINT fields of the day produced products that compared well in quantity and quality to those of other agencies that stamped their documents "SECRET." Dr. Charles B. Fah, writing in mid-1942 as chief of the Far Eastern Section, Office of Strategic Services (OSS), praised the output of FBIS as "indispensable in our work" and "the most extensive single source available" on developments in Japan and occupied Asia. The OSS itself fared less well, failing to establish an agent network in Japan and reporting the fabrications of an Italian "con man" in Rome as its most valuable source on developments in Tokyo.

Publications also held up well against classified reports. John King Fairbank, the Harvard sinologist who led his field in the postwar era, recounted how, after reading an inaccurate and "unintelligent" British report on Japanese shipbuilding, advised Col. William Donovan that better intelligence on the issue would be found in "scrutinizing the Japanese press." The OSS director evidently found Dr. Fairbank's brief compelling, for he sent the young academic, literate in Chinese and Japanese, to China to help organize a publications procurement program.[3]

Navigating Cold War Waters

After the guns of the Second World War fell silent, intelligence officers expert in **open source**s continued to help analysts and officials navigate the murky waters of the Cold War. For example, analysts in FBIS, whose acronym by then stood for the Foreign Broadcast *Information Service*, and the Foreign Document Division (FDD) led the CIA in detecting the developing estrangement between Moscow and Beijing. FBIS and FDD officers began discerning signs of the Sino-Soviet split from their readings of propaganda material in the early 1950s. In contrast, some CIA officers from the covert side of the house erred, along with many observers elsewhere, in dismissing as disinformation the open evidence well into the next decade.[4]

Throughout the Cold War, in fact, OSINT constituted a major part of all intelligence on the Soviet Union, China, and other adversaries. OSINT on the Soviet Union, for example, grew from modest beginnings to become the leading source. In the closing years of World War II, intelligence officers searched German, Japanese, and Russian documents in the Army's Special Documents Section and the joint Army-Navy Washington Document Center for clues to Soviet technical capabilities. By the late 1950s, the CIA and Air Force had discovered a "wealth of information" in the increasing flow of books and periodicals from the Soviet Union.[5] By the early 1960s, one insider wrote that "In aggregate, **open source**s probably furnish the greater part of all information used in the production of military intelligence on the Soviet Union."[6] By the decade's end, another wrote of the "tidal wave of publicly printed paper" that both supported and threatened "to swamp" the Intelligence Community. He also offered an example of OSINT's value: "Intense scrutiny of the North Vietnamese press and radio has been an essential intelligence element in support of [the] US effort" in the Indochina conflict.[7]

It is worth noting in passing that all powers exploited OSINT during World War II and the Cold War. Indeed, our adversaries used technical information from **open source**s in the United States and other advanced industrial nations to monitor foreign developments and to save time and money on their own projects. The US aerospace publication *Aviation Week*, dubbed "Aviation Leak" for its scoops, was a perennial favorite. The journal was among the US technical periodicals that East German intelligence, among others, translated to monitor current developments in aerospace.[8]

By the Cold War's end, commercial and technical changes had made evident the value of OSINT. Radio, the cutting edge in the 1930s, remained a key source in the Second World War and the years thereafter. When Soviet tanks rolled into Budapest in 1956, for example, intelligence officers in Washington kept current through radio reports. One veteran of the CIA's Directorate of Operations (DO), referring to Moscow's suppression of the Hungarian uprising, wrote: "It is a well-known phenomenon in the field of intelligence that there often comes a time when public political activity proceeds at such a rapid and fulminating pace that secret intelligence, the work of agents, is overtaken by events publicly recorded."[9] Some 30 years later, intelligence officers at Langley and government leaders across the Potomac watched, glued to their television sets, as CNN broadcast the fall of the Berlin Wall.[10]

The world today abounds in open information to an extent unimaginable to intelligence officers of the Cold War. When the Soviet Union sent the first man into space in 1961, secretive officials revealed little and lied even about the location of the launch site. In contrast, television reports, Internet sites, and newspaper articles heralded China's first manned flight into orbit last year. Even intelligence services have emerged from the shadows to some extent. Two journalists caused a stir in 1964 by writing a landmark book on the US Intelligence Community. Today, former case officers recount their clandestine careers.[11]

OSINT, OSINT Everywhere...

The revolution in information technology, commerce, and politics since the Cold War's end is only making **open source**s more accessible, ubiquitous, and valuable. Simply put, one can gather more open intelligence with greater ease and at less cost than ever before. The explosion in OSINT is transforming the intelligence world with the emergence of open versions of the covert arts of human intelligence (HUMINT), overhead imagery (IMINT), and signals intelligence (SIGINT).

The Intelligence Community has seen **open source**s grow increasingly easier and cheaper to acquire in recent years. The Internet's development and commercial innovation has given us Web sites, 'amazon.com,' and countless other vendors. During the Second World War, Dr. Fairbank traveled far and at great expense to gather Japanese publications in China and send them to Washington. Today, anyone, anywhere, can order Japanese media with a click of the mouse from amazon.co.jp or other online merchants and receive the orders by express air shipment. In the "old days," not so long ago, academics and analysts made the pilgrimage to Maryland to browse the shelves of Victor Kamkin's unmatched store for Soviet publications. In the present, one can go on line from the comfort of home to www.kamkin.com to buy from the half million Russian titles in stock or to place a custom order.

Moreover, the IT revolution extends beyond the printed word. More and more local radio and television broadcasts, for example, are found on the World Wide Web. Monitors no longer need to sit close to the broadcast source. Nor do they always need an expensive infrastructure of antennas and other equipment to listen to radio or watch television.

Beyond the usual public media, OSINT is expanding into the areas of HUMINT, IMINT, and SIGINT. In the words of one advocate with experience in both the government and private sector, "OSINT now pervades all of the collection disciplines." He notes that one can gather intelligence today by overtly tasking collectors to elicit information, ordering commercial satellite imagery, and using software to conduct traffic analysis.[12]

IMINT, for example, is becoming such a commercial commodity as to be in danger, in the view of one intelligence expert, of ceasing to be an "INT." Japan offers a fine demonstration of media exploitation of commercial IMINT. A major magazine known for its focus on North Korea, for example, prominently and frequently displays commercial imagery of such sites as the nuclear facilities at Yongbyon and the alleged residences of leader Kim Chong-il. Journalists combine the IMINT with published defector information, leaks, and other sources to analyze issues. As an example of open IMINT closer to home, the Federation of American Scientists (FAS) used Space Imaging photographs of a DPRK missile site to argue in 2000 that P'yongyang's missile threat was far less than Washington had claimed. Whatever the merits of the FAS argument, the case underscores the opening of the covert INTs.[13]

Even so, OSINT is no replacement for covert collection. Rather, **open sources** increasingly enhance secret collection programs. The CIA, NGA, NSA, and other actors on the classified side all benefit from the growing volume of open data serving them as collateral information. Too, OSINT allows covert collectors to marshal limited resources for the most intractable problems. Digital Globe and Space Imaging will never replace NGA, for example, but government acquisition of their commercial imagery for basic requirements can relieve NGA of mundane tasks and permit it focus on higher priorities.

In addition to their influence on collection disciplines, **open sources** have long played a major role in covert action. Imperial Japan, for example, employed the German, Alexander von Siebold, to influence foreign opinion in Tokyo's favor. The agent launched the journal *Ostasien* (East Asia) in 1899 with Japanese backing, contributed favorable articles to the European media, and otherwise worked to shape views on Japan. He also monitored the media, submitting his "Baron von Siebold's Report on the Press" to inform the Japanese of foreign developments and opinion.[14] In the Cold War, covert organs of the major powers disseminated news and views through front organizations to win hearts and minds. **Open sources** still constitute the core of political covert action today, except that overt organizations are often conducting the campaigns.[15]

...Surrounding Targets Hard and Soft...

Not only are **open sources** increasingly accessible, ubiquitous, and valuable, but they can shine in particular against the hardest of hard targets. OSINT is at times the "INT" of first resort, last resort, and every resort in between.

To some, this assertion may represent an overselling of OSINT. Arthur Hulnick, a former CIA officer who went on to teach at Boston University has written about OSINT's importance: "Neither glamorous nor adventurous, **open sources** are nonetheless the basic building block for secret intelligence." He has also noted how OSINT, whether conveyed via FBIS or CNN, provides early warning. He has even estimated that **open sources** may account for "as much as 80 percent" of the intelligence database in general. Nevertheless, Hulnick has suggested that OSINT would probably be far less useful against such tough cases as North Korea.[16]

However, **open sources** may often be more useful in penetrating closed borders than open societies. Because OSINT is intelligence derived from **open sources**, fewer sources mean greater coverage is possible with a limited number of monitors. Take the two Koreas, for example. The Democratic People's Republic of Korea (DPRK), with perhaps the world's most authoritarian government, is a relatively easy OSINT target. North Korea has only two major daily newspapers: *Nodong Sinmun* and *Minju Choson*, the newspapers of the ruling party and the government, respectively. There is no opposition newspaper in the capital and no lively provincial media to offer competing opinions or expose wrongdoing. The Republic of Korea (ROK), on the other hand, has a boisterous press, comprising over a dozen newspapers centered in Seoul, with views spanning the full spectrum of political opinion. Each day brings a flood of government statements, corporate press releases, editorials, scoops, and scandals. In relative terms, monitoring P'yongyang's media is like sipping through a straw; following Seoul's **open sources** is like drinking from a fire hose.

P'yongyang media, while controlled, constitute a valuable resource to anyone seeking to understand the DPRK. More than mere propaganda, as Dr. Wayne Kiyosaki, an expert literate in Korean and well-versed in the media, argued in his study of DPRK foreign relations, P'yongyang's communications are a tool of mass indoctrination. As such, they provide "a barometer of priorities."[17] Dr. Adrian Buzo, a former Australian diplomat with the rare experience of residing in P'yongyang, has seconded the value of DPRK media as a "continuing record of the regime's priorities, of its ideological concerns, and of key personnel changes." Warning readers against the common trap in the West of dismissing the media "out of hand," he has advised that "Sustained exposure to the DPRK media is an essential requirement for the would-be analyst, both in itself and as an essential check on the reportage of the DPRK's adversaries."[18]

Finally, continuing with the DPRK as an example, US analysts and policymakers often have little beyond OSINT upon which to base their judgments. The State Department has no embassy in P'yongyang. Few foreigners reside in the capital; even fewer live in the provinces. Opportunities to make contact with the rare North Koreans who reside or travel abroad have been poor. Only the trusted few may make an international telephone call, send a fax, exchange e-mails, or surf the Internet. Such restrictions reduce covert collection opportunities. The open record for HUMINT is telling. Ambassador Donald Gregg, an "Asia hand" whose DO career included a stint in Seoul, has described the DPRK as "one of the longest-running intelligence failures in the history of US espionage."[19]

Other nations fare no better. One would expect the Japanese, former colonial over-lords of Korea for more than 30 years, to accomplish more covert collection against their neighbors than their writings suggest. Tsukamoto Katsuichi, a retired army general with experience as defense attaché in Seoul, has confessed: "No country is as opaque as the DPRK (North Korea). Almost no information leaks out of there. Therefore, we have no choice but to make our judgments based on the little announced in the official newspaper (*Nodong Sinmun*) and radio broadcasts (Korea Central News Agency), as well as a limited number of visitor accounts."[20] A former officer of the Public Security Intelligence Agency (PSIA), Japan's equivalent to the FBI, has also written that analysis of "published materials" is "central" to analyzing the DPRK, given the absence of nearly all else. Such OSINT, he has written, is "more important and indispensable than is generally imagined."[21]

...But Few To Sail the Sea

> Today, open source has expanded well beyond "frosting" and comprises a large part of the cake itself. It has become indispensable to the production of authoritative analysis.
>
> —John Gannon, former Chairman,
> National Intelligence Council[22]

With **open sources** so accessible, ubiquitous, and valuable, one would expect to see OSINT occupying a commensurately large space within the Intelligence Community. This is not the case. Too many people still reject OSINT as intelligence. Worse, too few are able to gather and exploit **open sources**. Worst of all, the Intelligence Community assigns only a handful of those capable people to the task.

Too many people still mistake secrets for intelligence. The enduring popularity of the fictional James Bond bears much of the blame, perhaps, for the misperception outside of the Intelligence Community that a tuxedo, pistol, and charm are the main tools of intelligence gathering. Even some insiders err in believing intelligence to be identical with covert sources and methods. The following opinion of a retired DO officer is typical: "Despite frequent references to '**open source** intelligence,' within the CIA this term is somewhat of an oxymoron. By definition, intelligence is clandestinely acquired information—stolen, to put it bluntly. Information from a magazine, a television broadcast, or someone's newsletter may be valuable, but it is not intelligence."[23]

More than 40 years after Sherman Kent, the CIA's father of intelligence analysis, persuasively argued that intelligence is knowledge, some still confuse the method with the product. Sadly, such confusion is widespread. As one DPRK watcher noted: "Much of the best political intelligence comes from careful culling of public sources, like reading reports in the North Korean media, but within the intelligence community this source is not considered as reliable as more esoteric technical means, like satellite photography and communications intercepts, or spies."[24] However, as a staff director of the House Permanent Select Committee on Intelligence (HPSCI) once explained to a deputy director of operations, "We don't give you brownie points for collecting intelligence by the hardest means possible."[25]

A few examples should suffice to support Kent's definition of intelligence:

- An intelligence officer would likely have received high marks for stealing a map of the Khabarovsk area of the Soviet Far East in 1988. Drawn at a scale of 1:10,000 and running to 80 pages, the map of the General Staff's Military Topographic Headquarters would have taken a classified stamp and stayed within a secure vault, available only to those with a need to know. The map, published in 1998 and advertised as the first of this scale declassified in Russia, is for sale today.[26]

- Stanislav Levchenko, a KGB officer working under cover as a reporter in Japan, defected to the United States in 1979. In 1983, a Japanese journalist conducted more than 20 hours of interviews with him, during which the former operative named agents and discussed tradecraft. The resulting book and Levchenko's press conferences were, according to a US intelligence officer, more revealing than his CIA debriefing.[27]

- On 7 June 1942, the day after the US "miracle" at Midway due to the top-secret breaking of Japanese communications, the *Chicago Tribune* trumpeted on its front page that the US Navy had known of Japanese plans "several days before the battle began." A Japanese officer reading that newspaper probably would have grasped that the naval codes were insecure.[28]

Information openly acquired, whether open from the start (say, a telephone book), declassified, or leaked, is intelligence when assessed and disseminated appropriately.[29] History abounds with examples of OSINT collection by intelligence officers:

- Military attachés have long attached magazine photographs of aircraft, ships, and tanks to their classified reports.

- Japan's Kempeitai in wartime Shanghai gathered the writings of Agnes Smedley and Edgar Snow in the course of collecting intelligence on the Chinese Communist Party.[30]

- Various services culled intelligence from the pages of the Soviet military daily *Krasnaya Zvezda* (Red Star), including the wartime Imperial Japanese Army's Harbin Special Services Agency and the postwar US Intelligence Community.[31]

Beyond the persistent dismissal of **open source**s as intelligence, the US Intelligence Community suffers from America's general indifference to foreign languages and ideas. Any intelligence agency reflects the society from which it comes. Americans, living in a vast country and speaking a language that has become the world's *lingua franca*, show little interest in learning other languages or, indeed, knowing what those outside their borders think. The result is an Intelligence Community recruiting officers from among a relatively small pool of Americans who, through immigration or education, possess the expertise in foreign languages and area studies required for collecting **open source**s.

Knowing foreign languages is the key to exploiting OSINT. An account with LexisNexis and a subscription to the *Wall Street Journal* are hardly sufficient. English is declining from the world's dominant language to merely "first among equals."[32] Even the Internet fails the monolingual American. Chinese is slated to surpass English as the Internet's leading language in the near future.[33] Domain names, once issued only in English or other languages with Roman letters, increasingly appear in Arabic, Chinese, Farsi, Korean, and other non-alphabet languages. Put simply, English is best for monitoring nations where English is used. But what intelligence challenges confront the United States in Australia, Britain, Canada, Ireland, or New Zealand? On the contrary, languages with which Americans are least familiar are precisely those of countries of greatest concern: Arabic (Iraq), Chinese (China), Farsi (Iran), Korean (DPRK), and Pashto (Afghanistan), to name only some examples.

Although facing such challenges, the United States lacks the education base upon which to develop tomorrow's intelligence officers. Relatively few Americans pursue a foreign language from secondary school through the university level. Worse, most university language students still study the Romance tongues or German in courses designed chiefly to produce professors of literature. The Intelligence Community must then compete with the private sector for the handful of competent linguists graduating from university. The bleak alternative is to start adults on crash courses at the Defense Language Institute (DLI) or elsewhere on some of the world's most difficult languages.

On a related issue, an indifference to foreign languages and even foreign sources in translation diminishes the OSINT value of the US mass media. American journalists on the whole have been ignorant of the countries on which they have reported. Most who have covered the nuclear dispute between P'yongyang and Washington, for example, cannot read a Korean restaurant menu, let alone the pages of *Nodong Sinmun*. Worse, as one observer noted of an earlier period of crisis: "Reporters did not routinely read translations of the North Korean news by the Foreign Broadcast Information Service. Nor did they avail themselves of information circulating among outside experts by e-mail and fax."[34] The resulting level of reporting has been so poor that one prominent academic who can read Korean wrote recently of having to turn to P'yongyang's "tightly controlled press" for information on Washington-P'yongyang relations.[35]

The reluctance of US publishers to introduce foreign books in translation further lessens the flow of **open source**s available to Americans. For example, ROK movie star Ch'oe Un-hui and her former husband, the director Sin Sang-ok, gained extraordinary access to Kim Chong-il after he kidnapped them in 1978 in a bid to upgrade P'yongyang's film industry; they worked for him until their escape in 1986. Their account of the Dear Leader, complete with photographs, appeared in 1988 in Seoul and Tokyo. They were for years the only outsiders who had known Kim and written of their experience, but no American publisher saw fit to issue the book in translation. The same is true of numerous books in recent years from other insiders, including the architect of DPRK ideology and Kim's private sushi chef.[36]

An example closer to home is that of Dr. Emmanuel Todd's *After the Empire: The Breakdown of the American Order*. Published originally in 2003 in French, the book appeared the same year in various languages, including German, Italian, Japanese, Korean, and Spanish. The belated appearance a year later of the American edition of a book regarding what a prominent academic—who had forecast in 1976 the eventual fall of the Soviet Union—sees as Washington's futile struggle to maintain a global hegemony stands as an indictment of the US publishing industry.[37]

Compounding the problem of insufficient foreign information reaching the United States, the decline of area studies since the Cold War's end has reduced the pool of able applicants prepared to exploit foreign information in the vernacular. Russian studies, for example, have suffered grievously in funding and enrollment. Many graduates have found that US businesses prefer to send monolingual accountants to Moscow to teaching a Russian expert accounting. Area experts seeking university tenure find positions going to political scientists churning out papers on "rational choice" regarding countries they know hardly at all. Students attending courses of area studies today are more often seeking their ethnic roots than preparing to join the Intelligence Community. For example, a German professor teaching Korean political economy at a time of high military tension between Washington and P'yongyang found that around three quarters of his students at Columbia University were Asians or Asian-Americans. He wrote, "I was astonished by the relative lack of interest in Korea among American students, especially in such a tense situation as at present, when only deep knowledge about modern Korea can help prevent potentially disastrous policy decisions."[38]

All of this would be bad enough, but even worse is the fact that only a handful of capable officers with language and area skills are casting their nets into the global sea of **open source**s for intelligence. The results have been catastrophic. In the words of one former DO officer who has argued that "covert collectors should not be blamed" for missing Usama Bin Laden: "It is virtually impossible to penetrate a revolutionary terrorist organization, particularly one structured and manned the way al-Qa'ida is. The responsibility falls on the intelligence community's overt collectors and analysts." He suggests that the information was out there, but that analysts were simply not reading the relevant foreign media. The same lack of OSINT exploitation, he asserts, was also behind Washington's failure to comprehend the rise to power of Ayatollah Khomeini in Iran a quarter century ago.[39] Two senior CIA officers warn that things are likely to grow worse. They note how "knowledge of culture, history, and language will be even more critical as the amount of open-source material increases." They also admit that, "Inadequate American foreign language skills are a mismatch for the exponential growth in foreign language materials."[40]

Building a New "Craft" of Intelligence

> "The collection of foreign intelligence is accomplished in a variety of ways, not all of them either mysterious or secret. This is particularly true of overt intelligence, which is information derived from newspapers, books, learned and technical publications, official reports of government proceedings, radio and television. Even a novel or play may contain useful information about the state of a nation."
> —Allen Dulles, *The Craft of Intelligence*[41]

The words of the former director of central intelligence (DCI) seem even more true today than when he published them over 40 years ago, but the Intelligence Community needs to build a better ship to sail the sea of **open sources**. FBIS, the largest and best equipped of the disorganized collection of offices engaged in OSINT, is too small a craft with too few hands to navigate the waters and harvest the catch. Analysts, by and large, lack the knowledge of foreign languages, media expertise, and time to do their own fishing.

What Is To Be Done?

First, the DCI should increase the number of language officers at FBIS. Officers with knowledge of foreign languages, countries, and media are necessary to gather and analyze **open sources**, as photo interpreters are required to make sense of satellite imagery. The sea of **open sources** is arguably as large as that of covert communications, so one could argue that there should be as many **open source** officers surfing the Web as there are signals intelligence officers breaking secure communications. Required are college scholarships for students literate in Chinese and other innovative means of enlarging the pool of future OSINT officers.

Second, the Intelligence Community should take steps to turn the motley group of OSINT units into an organized fleet, with FBIS as the flagship. At a minimum, the Intelligence Community would do well to designate FBIS as the coordinator for OSINT. An enhanced FBIS could build on its expertise, its databases, and its longstanding role of serving the entire Intelligence Community by coordinating the output from the various embassy press translation units, military gray literature collectors, and such. An alternate, and more ambitious, plan would be to build a central agency for open intelligence based on FBIS. The new organization would be for OSINT what the DO is for HUMINT, National Reconnaissance Office is for IMINT, and the National Security Agency is for SIGINT.[42]

Third, the Intelligence Community must organize its own technical resources and tap those of the private sector to exploit the latest information technology for OSINT collection, analysis, production, and dissemination. OSINT collectors, all-source analysts, and others would benefit from smarter search engines, enhanced machine-assisted translation software, and better tools for incorporating audio and video streams into intelligence reports.

Above all, the Intelligence Community requires a sustained approach to **open sources**. As with other collection disciplines, one cannot conjure OSINT programs out of thin air. Assembling a substantial number of officers competent in Arabic, Chinese, Farsi, Korean, and other languages and expert in fishing in the OSINT seas, then giving them the sources and methods to do their work, would be no small feat.

Footnotes

1. Russell Jack Smith, *The Unknown CIA: My Three Decades with the Agency* (Washington, DC: Pergamon-Brassey's, 1989), 195.

2. Information on the Princeton Listening Center, launched in 1939, is available at http://libweb.princeton.edu:2003/libraries/firestone/rbsc/finding_aide/plc.html. For a history of FBIS during the Second World War, see Stephen C. Mercado, "FBIS Against the Axis, 1941-1945," *Studies in Intelligence*, Unclassified Edition no. 11 (Fall-Winter 2001): 33-43.

3. For Dr. Fah's comment, see Mercado, 41. On the Italian "confidence trickster" who fooled James Jesus Angleton and other OSS officers, see David Alvarez, *Spies in the Vatican: Espionage and Intrigue from Napoleon to the Holocaust* (Lawrence: University Press of Kansas, 2002), 248-53. Regarding Dr. Fairbank's role in OSS, see John King Fairbank, Chinabound: *A Fifty-Year Memoir* (New York: Harper Colophon, 1983), 174-75.

4. The downgrading of the "I" in FBIS from "Intelligence" to "Information" reflects the mistaken notion that only stolen secrets count as intelligence. CIA counterintelligence officers, under the leadership of James Jesus Angleton, were among those in Washington who continued to dismiss the growing evidence of the Sino-Soviet split well into the 1960s. On how OSINT officers led the way in understanding the breakup of "monolithic communism," see Harold P. Ford, "Calling the Sino-Soviet Split," Studies in Intelligence, Winter 1998-99, Unclassified Edition: 57-71. On Angleton, see also Harold P. Ford, "Why CIA Analysts Were So Doubtful About Vietnam," *Studies in Intelligence*, Unclassified Edition No.

5. J. J. Bagnall, "The Exploitation of Russian Scientific Literature for Intelligence Purposes," Studies in Intelligence (Summer 1958): 45-49. Declassified article.

6. Davis W. Moore, "Open Sources on Soviet Military Affairs," Studies in Intelligence (Summer 1963-declassified article): 101.

7. Herman L. Croom, "The Exploitation of Foreign Open Sources," *Studies in Intelligence* (Summer 1969-declassified article): 129-30.

8. Joseph Becker, "Comparative Survey of Soviet and US Access to Published Information," *Studies in Intelligence* (Fall 1957-declassified article): 43; John O. Koehler, *Stasi: The Untold Story of the East German Secret Police* (Boulder, CO: Westview Press, 1999), 110. Becker's article includes a reference to Soviet reading of *Aviation Week*.

9. Peer de Silva, *Sub Rosa: The CIA and the Uses of Intelligence* (New York: Times Books, 1978), 120.

10. Antonio J. Mendez, with Malcolm McConnell, *The Master of Disguise: My Secret Life in the CIA* (New York: William Morrow & Co., 1999), 337. On the monitoring of television in the Cold War, see Maureen Cote, "Veni, Vidi, Vid-Int," *Studies in Intelligence*, Fall 1990. Unclassified.

11. See David Wise and Thomas B. Ross, *The Invisible Government* (New York: Random House, 1964). Notable insider accounts of recent years include Duane "Dewey" Clarridge, *A Spy for All Seasons* (New York: Simon & Schuster, 1997) and Robert Baer, *See No Evil* (New York: Crown publishers, 2002).

12. Mark M. Lowenthal, "OSINT: The State of the Art, the Artless State," *Studies in Intelligence* 45, no. 3 (2001): 62.

13. On IMINT ceasing to be an "INT," see Gregory F. Treverton, *Reshaping National Intelligence for an Age of Information* (New York: Cambridge University Press, 2001), 87. A Japanese magazine notable for its prominent use of commercial IMINT on DPRK pol-mil issues is SAPIO, which advertises itself as an "international intelligence magazine." See *SAPIO*, 8 January 2003, for example, for use of Digital Globe imagery of alleged residences of Kim Chong-il. Regarding the FAS dispute, see *New York Times*, 11 January 2000.

14. Foreign Ministry Diplomatic Records Office and Nihon Gaikoshi Jiten Editorial Committee, eds., *Nihon Gaikoshi Jiten* [Dictionary of Japanese Diplomatic History] (Tokyo: Yamakawa Shuppansha, 1992), 361. A British historian of Japanese diplomatic history has also written of "indications" that Von Siebold went beyond OSINT for the Japanese Foreign Ministry and Army. Ian Nish, "Japanese Intelligence and the Approach of the Russo-Japanese War," in Christopher Andrew and David Dilks, eds., *The Missing Dimension: Governments and Intelligence Communities in the Twentieth Century* (Urbana: University of Illinois Press, 1984), 19.

15. Frederick L. Wettering, "(C)overt Action: The Disappearing 'C,'" *International Journal of Intelligence and CounterIntelligence* (Winter 2003-2004), 566-67.

16. Arthur S. Hulnick, *Fixing the Spy Machine: Preparing American Intelligence for the Twenty-First Century* (Westport, CT: Praeger, 1999), 8, 40-41.

17. Wayne S. Kiyosaki, *North Korea's Foreign Relations: The Politics of Accommodation, 1945-75* (New York, Praeger, 1976), x-xi. Dr. Kiyosaki, a graduate in Korean of the Defense Language Institute who later honed his media insights at FBIS, knew of what he wrote.

18. Adrian Buzo, *The Guerrilla Dynasty: Politics and Leadership in North Korea* (Boulder, CO: Westview Press, 1999), 284-85. On the value of DPRK media in charting personnel changes in P'yongyang, it is worth noting that the standard reference works, such as the annual *North Korea Directory* of Japan's impressive Radiopress and the online biographic compilations of the ROK's National Intelligence Service (www.nis.go.kr) are based on media monitoring. For one journalist's recognition of the value of following P'yongyang's media, see Gordon Fairclough, "To See North Korea, Keep Your Eyes Peeled On the Official Press," *Wall Street Journal*, 19 February 2004: 1.

19. Donald P. Gregg, "A Long Road to P'yongyang," *The Korea Society Quarterly*, Spring 2002: 7.

20. Tsukamoto Katsuichi, "Kitachosen josei to Higashi Ajia no anzen hosho" *Securitarian*, July 1995: 22. General Tsukamoto, who began his career as a commissioned officer of the Imperial Japanese Army and finished it as commander of the Ground Self-Defense Force's Western Army, has written several books on Korean security issues.

21. Noda Hironari (pseud.), *CIA supai kenshu: Aru Koan Chosakan no taikenki* [CIA Spy Training: One PSIA Officer's Account] (Tokyo: Gendai Shokan, 2000): 169-170. It is interesting to note that PSIA changed its English name, but not its acronym, in 2003, replacing "Investigation" with "Intelligence."

22. John Gannon, "The Strategic Use of Open-Source Information," *Studies in Intelligence* 45, no. 3 (2001): 67.

23. Thomas Patrick Carroll, "The Case Against Intelligence Openness," *International Journal of Intelligence and CounterIntelligence* (Winter 2001-2002): 561.

24. Leon V. Sigal, *Disarming Strangers: Nuclear Diplomacy With North Korea* (Princeton, NJ: Princeton University Press, 1998), 234.

25. Sherman Kent, *Strategic Intelligence for American World Policy* (Princeton, NJ: Princeton University Press, 1949). There is no more succinct definition of intelligence than the title of Part I: "Intelligence Is Knowledge." For the HPSCI staff director's remark, see Mark M. Lowenthal, "Open Source Intelligence: New Myths, New Realities," *Defense Daily Online*, reprinted in The Intelligencer (Winter 1999): 7.

26. This and many other declassified Russian maps have been advertised on line at East View Information Services of Minneapolis, MN (www.eastview.com).

27. Levchenko's interviews, which appeared in abbreviated form in a series running in the Japanese weekly magazine *Shukan Bunshun* over five weeks in mid-1983, were issued later that year as a book. Shukan Bunshun, ed. *Refuchenko wa shogen suru* [Levchenko Testifies] (Tokyo: Bungei Shunju, 1983). Haruna Mikio, a former Washington bureau chief of Japan's Kyodo News Agency with extensive contacts in the US Intelligence Community, wrote that an unidentified CIA officer was "surprised" at how much more detailed he found Levchenko's public revelations. See Haruna Mikio, *Himitsu no fairu: CIA no tainichi kosaku* [Secret Files: The CIA's Operations Against Japan] (Tokyo: Shinchosha Bunko, 2003), volume 2, 483. Whatever the accuracy of Haruna's purported source, Levchenko's Japanese book is more revealing than the one he published in the United States: *On the Wrong Side: My Life in the KGB* (Washington: Pergamon-Brassey's, 1988).

28. "Navy Had Word of Jap Plan To Strike at Sea," *Chicago Tribune*, 7 June 1942. On the "miraculous" character of the victory, see Gordon Prange *et al., Miracle at Midway* (New York: McGraw-Hill, 1982).

29. Intelligence officers have long worried about the damage done through the leaks of classified intelligence and even the gathering of published information by adversaries. Leaks are an old problem. See, for example, Allen Dulles, *The Craft of Intelligence* (New York: Harper&Row, 1963), 241-43. On leaks today, see James B. Bruce, The Consequences of Permissive Neglect," *Studies in Intelligence* 47, no. 3 (2003, Unclassified). Becker, "Comparative Survey," 35, noted in 1957 Soviet exploitation of US open sources and the repeated failures of the US Government from the 1940s to find a solution to the problem.

30. Tsukamoto Makoto, *Aru joho shoko no shuki* [Memoirs of an Intelligence Officer] (Tokyo: Chuo Bunko, 1998), 195. Agnes Smedley (*China's Red Army Marches*, 1934) and Edgar Snow (*Red Star Over China*, 1938) were prolific American writers with extraordinary access to Chinese communists.

31. Nakano Koyukai, ed., *Rikugun Nakano Gakko* [Army Nakano School] (Tokyo: Nakano Koyukai, 1978), 176, and Moore, "Open Sources," 104.

32. David Graddol, "The Future of Language," *Science* 303 (27 February 2004): 1329-31.

33. The prediction on Chinese Internet was made at a conference of the World Intellectual Property Organization, according to the *Financial Times,* 7 December 2001.

34. Sigal, *Disarming Strangers,* 221.

35. Bruce Cumings, *North Korea: Another Country* (New York: New Press, 2004), 47-48.

36. The architect of North Korea's Chuch'e philosophy, Hwang Chang-yop, has written a number of books, including *Na nun yoksa ui chilli rul poatta: Hwang Chang-yop hoegorok* [I Saw the Truth of History: Memoirs of Hwang Chang-yop] (Seoul: Hanul, 1999). A Japanese sushi chef in Kim's service, publishing under the pseudonym Kenji Fuji-moto, wrote *Kin Seinichi no ryorinin* (Tokyo: Shinchosha, 2003). These are two of many insider accounts likely never to see the light of day in the United States.

37. Emmanuel Todd, *After the Empire: The Breakdown of the American Order* (New York: Columbia University Press, 2004), *Après l'empire: Essai sur la décomposition du système américain* (Paris: Gallimard, 2003) and *La Chute finale: Essai sur la décomposition de la sphère sovietique* (Paris: Robert Laffont, 1976).

38. Constantine Pleshakov, "Russian Studies: A Sinking Academic Atlantis," *Japan Times,* 15 March 1995: 17. Dr. Ruediger Frank of Humboldt-Universität zu Berlin noted the general lack of interest in "An Interview with a Visiting Lecturer," *Annual Report 2002-2003,* Weatherhead East Asian Institute, Columbia University, 21.

39. Robert D. Chapman, "The Muslim Crusade," *International Journal of Intelligence and CounterIntelligence* (Winter 2002-2003): 613-14.

40. Aris A. Pappas and James M. Simon, Jr., "The Intelligence Community: 2001-2015," *Studies in Intelligence* 46, no. 1 (2002): 45. For a view of how deficiencies in foreign languages hurt covert collection, see Matthew M. Aid, "All Glory Is Fleeting: SIGINT and the Fight Against International Terrorism," *Intelligence and National Security* 18, no. 4 (Winter 2003): 100-102.

41. Allen Dulles, *The Craft of Intelligence* (New York: Harper&Row, 1963), 55. For a similar view, see Robert D. Steele, *The New Craft of Intelligence: Personal, Public, Political* (Oakton, VA: OSS International Press, 2002). For those interested in a concrete example of literature serving as a guide to intelligence, see how poems in the DPRK literary journal *Choson Munhak* [Korean Literature] signaled the preparation of Kim Chong-il to succeed his father. Morgan E. Clippinger, "Kim Chong-il in the North Korean Mass Media: A Study of Semi-Esoteric Communication," *Asian Survey* (March 1981): 291.

42. Creating a central OSINT agency is far from a novel idea. The proposal surfaced, for example, in *Studies in Intelligence* in 1969. See Croom, "Exploitation," 135.

Stephen Mercado is an analyst in the Directorate of Science and Technology.

Fight or Flight

The next article looks at more of a historical perspective of intelligence and how it has evolved, which will give the reader a solid foundation for future discussions in intelligence's evolution and change. This article, written in 2003, takes a look at the FBI intelligence system under Director Herbert Hoover. Although this is not a "current event" *per se,* it does provide insight into the discussions and research of the current state of affairs in the intelligence community.

UNCLASSIFIED

STUDIES IN INTELLIGENCE

Journal of the American Intelligence Professional

VOL. 48, NO. 1, 2004

UNCLASSIFIED EDITION

New Insights into J. Edgar Hoover's Role[3]

G. Gregg Webb

The events of 11 September 2001 and the threat from global terrorism have put the structure and composition of the US Intelligence Community under intense scrutiny. An important question in this debate over the organization of US intelligence resources is what role, if any, the Federal Bureau of Investigation should play in meeting the intelligence requirements of the US government in the 21st century. Many wonder whether an organization built to investigate breaches of law can rework itself into an organization capable of predicting and preventing acts of terrorism.

With the FBI's future status in the Intelligence Community uncertain, this seems an especially appropriate moment to review the Bureau's role in the earliest development of US intelligence capabilities. One of the most interesting, but least documented, chapters in the history of the FBI is the experience of its Special Intelligence Service (SIS) during World War II. Established in 1940, the FBI's SIS was the first foreign-intelligence bureaucracy in US history, created years before the Central Intelligence Agency and even before the Agency's forerunner, William "Wild Bill" Donovan's Office of Strategic Services (OSS).

The SIS was responsible for intelligence and counterintelligence activities in the entire Western Hemisphere. Although it was part of J. Edgar Hoover's FBI and the Department of Justice, the SIS worked at the behest of the State Department, collecting political, economic, financial, and industrial intelligence throughout Central and South America.[1] Through the work of an extensive and diligent network of undercover FBI special agents and later legal attaches officially attached to US legations, the Service excelled in its responsibilities.

Limited Research

Highly effective in its execution and pioneering in its mission, the SIS nonetheless has received little scholarly attention compared to its Eastern Hemisphere counterpart, Donovan's OSS. The chief reason for this imbalance rests in where the fighting took place: Donovan and his team operated in the theaters of active combat, while Hoover and his group labored to secure the American homeland in the relative peace of the Western Hemisphere. Although fears of invasion were widespread and tensions from the threat of Axis sabotage high, the focus of history has been, perhaps inevitably, on Donovan's commandos and not Hoover's investigators.

Additionally, the highly sensitive nature of SIS work—specifically, its investigations into the governments of Washington's supposed "good neighbors" in Latin America—kept most SIS records hidden from public view for many years after the war's end. Early on, official chroniclers of the World War II period—including Thomas Troy with the CIA, and Don Whitehead with the FBI—provided glimpses into SIS activities; however, for reasons of space in the former's account and security in the latter's, neither narrative delves more deeply into the SIS's experience than its birth and a few of its most successful operations.[2]

During the mid-1980s, Leslie Rout, Jr., and John Bratzel sought to fill the gap in SIS scholarship with their extensively researched account of German espionage and US counterespionage activities in Latin America during World War II. Their work remains the definitive volume in the historical narrative on the SIS, even though it largely ignores the Service's efforts against Japanese intelligence operatives during the war.[3] The most recent contribution to SIS scholarship came last year with a doctoral dissertation by Raymond Batvinis on the development of the FBI's counterintelligence program.[4] Batvinis's treatment highlights some previously unconsidered documents concerning the management of the SIS, but his discussion of the organization remains incidental to his larger purpose and, thus, only cursory.

The central argument of this article is that historians have misjudged J. Edgar Hoover's attitude toward the SIS during its formative years from 1940 to 1942, attributing to him a more aggressive interest in expanding his purview overseas than the record supports. This conclusion has been developed from a comprehensive study of the administrative files of the SIS, housed at the National Archives at College Park, Maryland.

At the Creation

President Franklin D. Roosevelt officially vested the FBI with responsibility for foreign-intelligence work in the Western Hemisphere on 24 June 1940. Within days, FBI Director J. Edgar Hoover had established the administrative skeleton for a foreign-intelligence entity within the FBI and had named it the FBI Special Intelligence Service.

The SIS story begins, however, a full year earlier. On 26 June 1939, Roosevelt signed a Presidential Directive stating:

> It is my desire that the investigation of all espionage, counter-espionage, and sabotage matters be controlled and handled by the Federal Bureau of Investigation of the Department of Justice, the Military Intelligence Division [MID] of the War Department, and the Office of Naval Intelligence[ONI] of the Navy Department. The Directors of these three agencies are to function as a committee to coordinate their activities.[5]

The President's directive was in response to a wave of espionage that had erupted inside the United States during the previous year.[6] In 1938 alone, the FBI had investigated 634 cases of espionage compared to a previous annual average of just 35 such cases.[7] This upsurge was a direct result of Hitler's ascension to power in Germany and a corresponding redoubling of intelligence collection efforts by German, Japanese, and Italian agents stationed in the United States.[8] By consolidating responsibility for "espionage, counter-espionage, and sabotage matters" in the hands of the FBI and the service intelligence organizations, Roosevelt hoped to bring order to the chaos that had thus far marked the US government's response to internal espionage threats.[9]

After narrowing the field of investigating agencies, the next most important stipulation of the 26 June directive was its call for an interdepartmental committee to "coordinate" the US counterintelligence effort. This body became known as the Interdepartmental Intelligence Committee (IIC) and included the heads of the FBI, MID, and ONI, along with a senior official from the State Department, although representation on the Committee was not always at that level.

The IIC got off to a slow start. Its members were wary of sharing information and resources with each other lest they lose control over their existing influence in the counterintelligence field. Indeed, the heads of the three agencies had stopped coming to IIC meetings by the time that world affairs forced them back to the table in the spring of 1940.[10]

In May 1940, Hitler launched his assault against British and French forces in Western Europe.[11] The heads of the three IIC organizations—Hoover with the FBI, Brig. Gen. Sherman Miles of MID, and Rear Adm. Walter Anderson of ONI—expected increases in espionage activity within the United States as a result of the German successes in Europe.[12]

Gen. Miles felt that, with the heightened tensions, there should be a clearer division of counterintelligence responsibilities among the members of the IIC.[13] In subsequent discussions, IIC members agreed that the civilian FBI was best suited to handle investigations involving espionage and sabotage by civilians in the United States. Similarly, it was agreed that MID and ONI were best equipped to deal with such cases involving threats to military and naval personnel, equipment, and installations both in the United States and its territories.[14]

The major point of jurisdictional conflict between the members of the IIC concerned the conduct of espionage, counter-espionage, and counter-sabotage activities in foreign countries.[15] Neither of the service intelligence organizations wanted responsibility for covert operations because they feared such activities might compromise the diplomatic status that their attachés enjoyed abroad.[16] The FBI lacked a compelling excuse. Thus, a consensus emerged in favor of the FBI taking responsibility for covert foreign-intelligence and counterintelligence work.

MEMORANDUM PREPARED BY ASSISTANT SECRETARY OF STATE BERLE JUNE 24, 1940,
AND APPROVED BY THE PRESIDENT:

        In the presence of General Sherman Miles, I telephoned the
President. Referring to the conversations we have had with Mr. Welles,
I said that the Inter-Departmental Committee charged with coordinating
intelligence work wished his direction as to the formation of a unit for
foreign intelligence work (in addition, of course, to the intelligence
work now being carried on by the Army and the Navy).

        The choice lay between the Federal Bureau of Investigation, the
Military Intelligence Division of the Army, and the Office of Naval Intelligence.

        The President said that he wished that the field should be di-
vided. The FBI should be responsible for foreign intelligence work in
the Western Hemisphere, on the request of the State Department. The existing Military Intelligence and Naval Intelligence branches should cover
the rest of the world, as and when necessity arises.

It was understood that the proposed additional foreign intelligence work
should not supersede any existing work now being done; and that the FBI
might be called in by the State Department for special assignments outside the American Hemisphere, under special circumstances. Aside from
this, intelligence outside the American Hemisphere is to be left to the
officers of the Army and Navy.

But the committee could not agree on who should authorize such activities.[17] The service agencies and the State Department feared FBI encroachment on their domains, while the FBI loathed the thought of working under the other three—in essence, gaining the responsibility for foreign-intelligence work without the authority to control its direction. To resolve this and related concerns regarding foreign-intelligence responsibilities, the IIC established a subcommittee at its 3 June 1940 meeting "to prepare a study of a proposed set-up for a Special Intelligence Service."[18]

The subcommittee's report was discussed at the IIC's next meeting on 11 June. The report emphasized the need for a covert foreign-intelligence capability within the US government, stating that such an organization "is not only desirable but essential at the present time."[19] The subcommittee's specific recommendations for structuring this "Special Intelligence Service" included a "Chief of the Service" based in New York City who would run the new agency with intelligence management support from a "Technical Committee" of intelligence professionals.[20] During the 11 June meeting, the members approved the subcommittee's proposal and agreed that personnel decisions and other administrative considerations would be resolved after the State Department's representative, Assistant Secretary of State Adolf Berle, had gained presidential approval of the plan.[21]

Roosevelt Throws a Curve

On 24 June 1940, Assistant Secretary Berle called President Roosevelt to receive authorization for the IIC's proposal. Instead, Roosevelt decided on a drastically different plan from the IIC's vision of an independent and interdepartmental foreign-intelligence organization. In his telephone directive, Roosevelt stated that "he wished that the field [of foreign-intelligence work] should be divided."[22] He ordered that "The FBI should be responsible for foreign-intelligence work in the Western Hemisphere, on the request of the State Department," while "The existing Military Intelligence and Naval Intelligence branches should cover the rest of the world, as and when necessity arises."[23] President Roosevelt concluded his directive by observing how "It was understood that the proposed additional intelligence work should not supersede any existing work now being done...."[24] Always the astute politician, Roosevelt probably included this condition to calm the fears of the armed forces that the FBI's new mandate might encroach on the intelligence collection efforts of existing military and naval attachés in Latin America.

President Roosevelt's exercise of executive discretion in veering from the IIC's recommendations left the FBI with an unexpected responsibility for foreign-intelligence work in the entire Western Hemisphere. Roosevelt's willingness to diverge from the counsel of his advisers and forge his own division of intelligence responsibility was characteristic of his presidential style, especially on matters of intelligence where he thought his long interest in the subject gave him special insight and authority.[25] In describing Roosevelt's prewar foreign policy-making, historian Christopher Andrew observes how, "Instead of relying on an orderly system of assessment, he preferred to base his judgments on impressions drawn from a wide range of official and unofficial sources."[26] What Roosevelt's specific reasons might have been for dividing foreign-intelligence responsibility as he did in 1940 remain unclear, but his behavior in this instance was certainly not out of the ordinary for him.

Thus, on 1 July 1940, FBI Director Hoover baptized a "Special Intelligence Service" in the FBI and immediately began constructing the administrative framework for his new section, appointing his assistant director, Percy "Sam" Foxworth, as the first SIS chief.[27]

Bureaucratic Challenges

Despite the IIC's agreement to finance the fledgling SIS per Roosevelt's mandate, the FBI's placement at the head of foreign-intelligence and counterintelligence work in the Western Hemisphere did not go unchallenged.[28] Less than a month after the President's decision, MID's Gen. Miles wrote a memorandum to Hoover in which he complained that the FBI was incorrect in maintaining that its intelligence collection mandate was "encyclopedic in scope."[29] Miles "suggested" to Hoover that the work of his new agency might properly "be limited...to subversive activities in foreign countries," because, as Miles observed, "the need for a S.I.S. was envisaged, primarily to supplement by under-cover information the data which our accredited agents in foreign countries [*i.e.* , military and naval attachés] could obtain."[30]

Although sensitive to the FBI's total inexperience in foreign-intelligence work, Hoover refused to allow his bureaucratic mandate to be blurred. His tactful, but pointed, response a week later to Miles's inquiry merely asked the head of MID to either agree or disagree with Hoover's own understanding that "the Conference [IIC] with your concurrence...agreed that no restrictions should be placed on the scope of the S.I.S."[31] Hoover noted, however, that the SIS would place its emphasis on countering the threat from subversive groups in Latin America.[32] Miles, in a letter four days later, was forced to concede the argument to Hoover; the IIC's interpretation of Roosevelt's telephone directive had been clear in giving the SIS free rein over foreign-intelligence work in the Western Hemisphere.[33] The jurisdictional debate between Hoover and Miles was far from over, but the resolution of this early exchange gave Hoover's SIS full institutional recognition for its new mandate.

Institutional recognition within the US government, however, did not constitute full legal authorization. Hoover and his subordinates had their hands full during the next year and a half training new SIS agents and managing the operations of those already abroad, but they conducted all of this work entirely on the authority of President Roosevelt's unofficial telephone directive of 24 June 1940.

With the coming of war in December 1941, Hoover immediately sought official recognition of the informal arrangement under which the SIS had been operating.[34] As an astute bureaucrat, he probably feared that the surprise onset of war would activate currents of reform and expansion within the service intelligence organizations, and he sought to shelter himself and his young SIS from such an onslaught. Hoover got what he requested. On 16 January 1942, Roosevelt signed a presidential directive that officially recognized the FBI's Special Intelligence Service and renewed its mandate as the chief government purveyor of clandestine foreign intelligence in the Western Hemisphere.[35]

Since their first tense exchange over the scope of SIS responsibilities during the summer of 1940, Hoover and Miles had fought a running battle over the nature of the SIS's mission.[36] Hoover sought both to protect his sole authority to administer the SIS and to preserve the SIS's original mandate as the only agency charged with clandestine foreign-intelligence work in the Western Hemisphere. Miles feared that such sweeping authority would cause the SIS to overshadow and impede the efforts of his attachés to collect military intelligence in the region.

The tension between the two persisted until Maj. Gen. George Strong replaced Miles as head of MID. Following this change of command, the two service intelligence organizations and the FBI finally signed a detailed agreement on 14 October 1942 delineating their separate intelligence responsibilities in the Western Hemisphere but emphasizing the need for cooperation.[37] This agreement elaborated on the general division of labor that had previously existed between the FBI, MID, and ONI, with the service intelligence organizations responsible for information and investigations pertaining to their respective fields and the FBI in charge of all other foreign-intelligence and counterintelligence activities in the Americas. The agreement marked the end of skirmishing between the FBI and MID over intelligence work in the Western Hemisphere.

The Historical Record

That J. Edgar Hoover was a master of bureaucratic infighting hardly deserves explicit mention here. His more than half a century as Director of the FBI speaks for itself. Hoover's behavior towards the other members of the IIC, especially Gen. Miles, possessed many hallmarks of a classic Hoover power grab, including private, preemptive visits to the president to pitch his personal agenda and stubborn resistance to efforts to amend his SIS mandate.[38] Indeed, by February 1941, Hoover's recalcitrant behavior in defending his SIS responsibilities from MID had so inflamed both his direct superior, Attorney General Robert Jackson, and Gen. Miles's superior, Secretary of War Henry Stimson, that the two secretaries actually met about the conflict on 13 February 1941. During their meeting, the two agreed to "make another effort to establish a proper collaboration and cooperation" between their subordinates.[39] During the course of this initial struggle between the FBI and MID, Stimson had called one of Hoover's letters of complaint against MID "a very childish, petulant statement" and Attorney General Jackson had been forced to agree that Hoover was "a difficult person" to get along with.[40]

The bulk of historical literature concerning Hoover and the early experience of the SIS casts Hoover in a power-hungry and competitive light. In their seminal work on the subject, Rout and Bratzel refer to the way in which Hoover "vanquished" Gen. Miles "in his bid for hemispheric control."[41] They go on to describe how Hoover emitted "screams of foul play" in response to a similar challenge from the President's Coordinator of Information (COI), Col. Donovan, later in the war.[42] Likewise, Batvinis's narrative cites Hoover's "aggressive attempts to wrest control of intelligence and counterintelligence policy away from the State Department" at the beginning of the negotiations from which the SIS emerged.[43] Thus, according to previous accounts, Hoover's attitude and behavior in establishing the SIS were motivated by his well-documented bureaucratic greed and self-interest.

A New Interpretation

Examination of the official correspondence between Hoover and the other actors in the SIS debate, including his FBI subordinates, his counterparts in the intelligence field, and his cabinet-level superiors, paints a very different picture of the FBI Director's attitude toward the SIS and its foreign-intelligence responsibilities. During the formative period—from the SIS's inception on 1 July 1940 to the signing of the final delimitation agreement between the FBI, MID, and ONI on 14 October 1942—*Hoover tried to rid himself and his agency of the SIS and its foreign-intelligence liabilities three times*. The documents concerning these efforts to transfer the SIS's duties out of the FBI reflect Hoover's trepidation toward building a foreign espionage and counter-espionage organization. In the event, he accepted this assignment with resolve and characteristic ability, but his administrative competence and bureaucratic scheming belied what were clearly his deep reservations concerning management of the SIS's work in Latin America.

The administrative files of the SIS shed light on Hoover's motivations for battling to preserve in the SIS all authority for non-military foreign-intelligence work in Latin America. Commentators both then and since have dismissed Hoover's actions as petty protectionism. Actually, Hoover was a capable bureaucrat and, as such, loathed the thought of interagency power-sharing or nebulous divisions of responsibility.[44] Hoover wanted either all the authority to administer a given task or none of it. Analysis of the three major instances when his authority over the SIS was tested indicate that Hoover was much more interested in preserving the sanctity of the SIS mission than in retaining its accompanying powers and influence for himself. This fact is evinced by his willingness in all three cases to concede FBI control over SIS operations in a given country, and even throughout Latin America, rather than face a division or duplication of SIS responsibilities across multiple agencies.

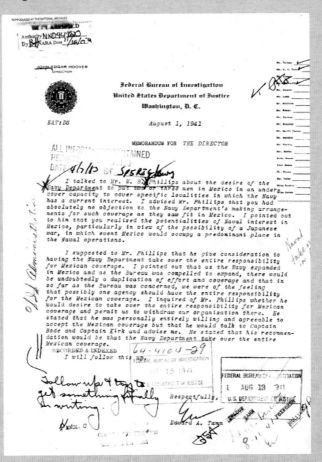

Hoover's first effort to pass off his SIS burden lasted through the spring and summer of 1941 and was directed at the Office of Naval Intelligence. On 15 March 1941, Hoover sent a memorandum to his superior, Attorney General Jackson, in which he "recommended that the Special Intelligence Service be transferred to either the Office of Naval Intelligence or the Military Intelligence Division."[45] In a follow-up memorandum on 4 April, Hoover repeated his call for the reassignment of the SIS to either ONI or MID. He explained that "the Bureau is marking time in so far as any extension of its coverage in the Latin Americas is concerned."[46] Thus, even in April 1941, almost a year after the SIS's inception, Hoover was so hopeful that he could get the SIS reassigned that he hesitated to pump any more FBI time and money into it than was absolutely necessary.

When ONI, represented by W. B. Phillips, approached one of Hoover's chief deputies at the FBI, Edward Tamm, on 1 August 1941 with a proposal to expand ONI's clandestine operations in Mexico, Hoover not only authorized Tamm to accept the Navy's proposal, but also pushed him to offer ONI "the entire responsibility for the Mexican coverage."[47] In a private FBI memorandum, Hoover agreed with Tamm's analysis that if ONI could be made to take over foreign-intelligence work in Mexico, "we will have the services of at least a half dozen Agents who can be well used on other work and possibly by this means we may over a period of time get rid of most of the work in the SIS field."[48]

In their meeting, Tamm used a pragmatic argument to sell Phillips on the idea stating:

> ...as the Navy expanded in Mexico and as the Bureau was compelled to expand, there would be undoubtedly a duplication of effort and coverage and that in so far as the Bureau was concerned, we were of the feeling that possibly one agency should have the entire responsibility for the Mexican [intelligence] coverage.[49]

Hoover's notation at the bottom of this memorandum from Tamm describing the latter's meeting with Phillips emphasizes Hoover's keen desire to see the SIS go. Next to Tamm's statement that Phillips had told him he would recommend to ONI that it take over all responsibility for espionage and counterintelligence coverage in Mexico, Hoover wrote an order to Tamm to "Follow up and try to get something finally in writing."[50]

This transfer initiative, however, was to die quickly and decisively. At a weekly conference on 6 August 1941, the head of ONI, Capt. Alan Kirk, told Tamm that "he was thoroughly and unalterably opposed to this proposal" on the grounds that "the best interests of the Government would be served if the Bureau continued to operate in Mexico..."[51]

Second Effort to Divest

In contrast to Hoover's first effort to divest himself of his SIS responsibilities, his next two opportunities were not initiated by the FBI. Nonetheless, the FBI's position on whether or not the SIS should be handed over to its new suitor, COI chief Donovan, reflected Hoover's two main concerns on the matter: his anxiety over the FBI's total inexperience in foreign-intelligence work and his conviction that the SIS's foreign-intelligence responsibilities should not be divided between agencies.

Donovan was a relatively late arrival on the intelligence scene. On 11 July 1941, he received a presidential appointment as Coordinator of Information and an ambiguous set of responsibilities, including the "coordination and correlation of defense information."[52] In hammering out his mission, Donovan made two attempts to assume control over the SIS's foreign-intelligence activities in Latin America. The first of these efforts came soon after his appointment. In a 27 August 1941 IIC meeting, the head of ONI, Capt. Kirk, broached the subject of Col. Donovan's taking over "the entire SIS project."[53] Kirk said that he had talked to both his Navy superiors and Donovan himself and that all had been amenable to such an arrangement. Kirk noted how Donovan had emphasized that "his willingness to take this project over depends entirely upon the premise that the three intelligence agencies actually desire" his intervention.[54] Gen. Miles expressed a similar concern over the possibility that such a transfer of the SIS from the FBI to the COI might be construed as an effort by the IIC members to rid themselves of responsibility for foreign-intelligence work.[55]

Following discussion over the proper appearance of any power transfer, Kirk went on to note that Donovan had told him "he would hate to see the FBI drop out of the picture in South and Central America."[56] According to Kirk, Donovan had stated that after the transfer of the SIS to his agency, he hoped the FBI might stay on in Latin America and work on matters affecting the "internal security" of the United States.[57] Tamm, representing Hoover on the IIC, reflected his superior's fears of blurred jurisdiction when he observed:

> ...that the difficulty in connection with any such project as this would be the borderline cases and projects where the delimitation of jurisdiction could not be clearly defined, for which reason there would be extreme difficulty in definitely fixing responsibility concerning a large amount of SIS work.[58]

Tamm got the issue tabled until the next IIC meeting on 3 September 1941 by stating that Hoover had made it clear to him that no action concerning the SIS could be taken without first talking to Assistant Secretary of State Berle.[59] Berle managed the SIS for the State Department, which under President Roosevelt's telephone directive of 24 June 1940 held ultimate authority over SIS activities.

On 2 September 1941, in preparation for the IIC meeting the next day, Hoover sent Tamm to the State Department to update Berle on the move to have Donovan take over the SIS. In describing the facts to Berle, Tamm presented the FBI position as indifferent toward handing responsibility for the SIS to Donovan. Tamm stated that "the Bureau had not taken the initiative in the matter, had not pushed it and had no feeling one way or the other as to whether this transfer should be made."[60] According to Tamm, he had further characterized Hoover's personal "attitude" as being "that you [Hoover] had not sought or solicited the SIS operations and that you would continue to perform them until such time as they were transferred to someone else."[61] In this meeting with Berle, Tamm not only expressed Hoover's indifference toward holding the reins of the SIS, but he also noted Hoover's "feeling" that "it would be a mistake to divide the coverage or the responsibility" of the SIS.[62] These would have been alien "attitudes" and "feelings" for Hoover if he really had fought for the early SIS as the greedy bureaucratic gladiator that figures so prominently in most literature on the subject.

Berle's response to the idea of a Donovan-led SIS was negative. Berle told Tamm that he was against the transfer of the SIS to Donovan because the Service "had done such an excellent job with such great efficiency, completely without friction, in the various countries we were operating [sic] that he would be opposed to having it transferred into untried hands."[63]

Berle's opposition squelched this first Donovan initiative, but by December 1941, the possibility of Donovan taking over the SIS's work in Latin America had reemerged. In a memorandum on 31 December 1941 to Attorney General Francis Biddle, Hoover described his previous contacts with Donovan concerning the SIS and outlined his own position on the subject of how it should be administered. Hoover's statements here corresponded with Tamm's earlier accounting of Hoover's attitude toward SIS control. In describing a conversation with Donovan over the idea of COI and FBI agents working side by side in Latin America, Hoover recounted how he had told Donovan that "it had been my experience...that in a matter of as extreme delicacy as existed in investigations in a foreign country... there should be but one agency responsible for the operations."[64] Hoover was explicit in describing his perception of the danger of joint jurisdiction: "If anything should then go wrong, there would be a perfect opportunity for the so-called 'buck passing' that all too frequently develops."[65]

Even if Hoover's motivations for guarding his authority over the SIS were selfish, as they undoubtedly were, his concern lay in minimizing his liability for the foreign-intelligence responsibilities he already possessed and not in seizing greater influence for himself and the FBI. Indeed, Hoover continued his memorandum to Biddle by emphasizing that "The FBI did not seek the special intelligence work in the Western Hemisphere" and that it was the State Department and the President who had felt such activities should be undertaken by the FBI.[66]

Hoover told Biddle that he "had absolutely no objection to relinquishing it [SIS] to Colonel Donovan or any other organization." He stipulated, however, that:

> I do very strongly feel that the character of the work is of such delicacy and involves so many hazards and complications that the responsibility for the carrying on of it should rest in the hands of one agency.[67]

The FBI chief concluded his argument by stating: "I do strongly recommend that the FBI be relieved of all responsibility for the handling of any special intelligence work in the Western Hemisphere, and that this responsibility be completely and fully placed upon Colonel Donovan's organization."[68] Hoover's words here are hardly those of a man scheming to keep the SIS for himself.

In the event, Biddle met with Donovan and leaders from State, MID, and ONI on 6 January 1942 to resolve the issue of intelligence jurisdictions in Latin America.[69] The agreement hammered out in this two-and-a-half-hour meeting directly contradicted Hoover's expressed desire to divest his agency of all foreign-intelligence responsibility. Instead, it reaffirmed the FBI's hegemony over the SIS and explicitly excluded Donovan from conducting any independent intelligence work in Latin America.[70] Although the specific justifications for keeping the FBI *status quo* at this juncture remain cloudy, the Bureau's effective execution of its SIS duties over the preceding months probably encouraged such an outcome.

Final Challenge

The final challenge to Hoover's control over the SIS came during the summer of 1942. In June, MID began operating the American Intelligence Command (AIC) in Latin America.[71] The AIC was an effort by MID to establish a network of undercover intelligence-gathering organizations run by the military attachés assigned to each diplomatic legation in Latin America. Col. R. Townsend Heard ran the American Intelligence Command for MID.

During the summer of 1942, reports from SIS undercover agents throughout Latin America poured in describing conflicts and confusion between SIS agents and the military attachés. These tensions generally revolved around the recruitment and management of foreign agents in their respective, but often overlap-

lobbied hard but unsuccessfully to recruit a Mr. A. L. Smith, who already happened to be a SIS undercover agent. The military attaché then went to the man's brother, who also resided in Guatemala. The brother, Robert Smith, "being unable to give sufficient reasons for refusal, had to accept" the job of being an AIC undercover agent in the same vicinity where his brother was already a SIS undercover informant.[72] Not surprisingly, such duplication plagued the AIC's efforts to establish a clandestine intelligence collection network in Latin America.

When Hoover found out about the AIC, he immediately complained to both Attorney General Biddle and the new head of MID, Maj. Gen. George Strong. In a 10 September 1942 letter to Strong, he outlined his attitude toward the AIC and its work. Following a by-then well-worn line, Hoover stated:

> *I am most anxious and willing to withdraw entirely and completely from the Latin Americas. As I have indicated, I have no interest in prerogatives nor any desire to extend or expand the Federal Bureau of Investigation into varied and far-flung fields. The Bureau already has a full measure of responsibility within the United States and the territorial possessions which, if it discharges it fully, will more than justify the Bureau's existence and maintenance.[73]*

Hoover's efforts to clear up the overlap between the SIS and the AIC were successful; however, his accompanying labors to get the SIS transferred failed, just as had all his previous attempts.

Latin America Operations

After the summer of 1942, Hoover's attitude toward the SIS and its foreign-intelligence mission began to change markedly. By October 1942, the SIS had 156 special agents throughout Latin America operating under a multitude of clandestine covers.[74] Most of these agents, in turn, ran foreign operatives who collected information that was passed directly to FBI headquarters. In addition to its extensive intelligence-collection network, the SIS's counter-espionage capability continued to expand and improve after 1942. SIS agents were FBI agents, after all, and the FBI was the preeminent investigative agency in the world at the time. SIS personnel excelled in their efforts at hunting down Axis agents, breaking up Axis signals intelligence channels, and identifying laundered Axis funds.[75]

The list of SIS operational exploits is both long and varied.[76] One of the more exotic challenges taken up by the SIS during the war was a highly successful campaign against Axis agents attempting to smuggle platinum out of Colombia and send it back to Germany for use in German military equipment.[77] By 1942, Colombia was the only one of the five platinum-producing countries in the world that was not at war with Nazi Germany. Desperate for platinum, the Germans were willing to pay top prices for Colombian platinum, which was usually smuggled overland into Axis-friendly Argentina and, from there, shipped to Europe. SIS agents countered all such efforts aggressively, hiking through the jungles of Colombia in search of smuggling trails and cultivating local residents as informers. These proactive measures proved highly effective. In fact, between 1942 and July 1944, SIS agents monitoring the production of platinum in Colombia were able to account for all but 2,507 troy ounces of the platinum mined during this period. Though some or all of this unaccounted-for metal might have arrived in German hands, such an amount was inconsequential in light of the estimated 137,500 troy ounces of the metal that the German military needed between 1942 and mid-1944.[78]

The SIS was also highly successful in tracking down the clandestine radio stations that German agents used to send wartime intelligence back to Germany. This information ranged from Allied activities in the major ports and airstrips where trans-Atlantic troop and supply movements took place to the pedestrian political gossip of the agents' "host" countries.[79] SIS personnel seized enemy radio transmitters and arrested their operators in most of the major countries of Latin America, taking down some especially sophisticated operations in Brazil and Chile.[80] Between fiscal years 1941 and 1945, the SIS located 24 clandestine radio stations in Latin America and confiscated 30 transmitters, thereby hamstringing the flow of communication between German agents in the Western Hemisphere and their handlers back in Germany.[81]

Although Hoover himself does not appear to have shown much interest in the florid details of SIS clandestine operations, he did demand final review over all administrative decisions concerning the management and organization of the SIS as a division within the FBI.[82] In this regard, he did not vary from his normal, highly centralized management style.

Postwar Proposal

As SIS successes mounted, so did Hoover's confidence in the field of foreign-intelligence and counterintelligence work. Indeed, by December 1944, Hoover was bold enough to propose a "world-wide intelligence system" for after the war that would be administered by the FBI and organized like the SIS.[83] Even though there is little evidence to suggest that Hoover actually enjoyed the SIS's sensitive foreign-intelligence work, he could recognize a promising institutional model when he saw one and he clearly valued the SIS as a vehicle for expanding both his own power and the postwar influence of the FBI. His proposal marked a clear departure from his early reservations over the SIS and his responsibility for it.

Hoover's newfound optimism shines through in a memorandum he wrote to Attorney General Tom Clark on 29 August 1945 seeking a worldwide intelligence role for the FBI along the lines of its work in Latin America. Hoover began his argument by observing that "the SIS program operated by the Bureau in the Western Hemisphere has been completely successful. The program has produced results which were beyond our hope and expectations when we went into this field..."[84] Hoover soon got to his point saying, "It seems to me, therefore, that...it is most logical that the system which has worked so successfully in the Western Hemisphere should be extended to a world-wide coverage."[85] Here, at last, was the fabled drive for power that commentators on the SIS have been so anxious to assign to Hoover. The wily director concluded his pitch to Clark by innocently suggesting:

> *While I do not seek this responsibility for the Federal Bureau of Investigation,*
> *I do believe that upon the basis of our experience of the last five years we are*
> *well qualified to operate such a [worldwide] service in conjunction with par-*
> *allel operations of the Military and Naval Intelligence....*[86]

Although this last paragraph echoed his indifference to the past, Hoover's remarks here were clearly disingenuous. By 1945, Hoover knew that he did not just want to maintain control over his SIS operation in Latin America but wanted to expand its activities to the rest of the world. Ever the good bureaucrat, Hoover did not attach himself or his interests to the SIS until he was certain that it could be a contender in the larger intelligence community.

Alas, Hoover's ambitions in the field of foreign intelligence were to go unful-filled. His plan was dismissed outright by both Donovan, Hoover's rival and the author of a separate plan for a postwar intelligence structure, and President Harry Truman.[87] The FBI was passed over in the postwar reshuffling of the intel-ligence community. The product of this bureaucratic free-for-all was the new and independent Central Intelligence Group (CIG) that came into being by presiden-tial directive on 22 January 1946. The fledgling agency, under the direction of Rear Adm. Sidney Souers, had global jurisdiction and replaced entirely the FBI's Secret Intelligence Service in Latin America. A transition period ensued, but for all intents and purposes the birth of the CIG marked the death of the SIS— and with it, a role for the FBI in foreign-intelligence activities.

Final Observations

The purpose of this paper has not been to minimize or qualify the contribution made by J. Edgar Hoover in the birth and development of America's first foreign-intelligence agency. Hoover managed the SIS like he did the rest of the FBI: as a personal and much-valued project. His internal leadership of the organization was generally out-front and outstanding. Even as he was trying to rid himself and the FBI of the SIS, Hoover pursued his foreign-intelligence mission aggres-sively and constructed a top-notch organization. That he did so with personal reservations should stand not as a criticism but as a tribute to his resolve.

Similarly, this paper is not meant to soften the hard reality of J. Edgar Hoover as a bureaucrat. He was often mean and rarely conciliatory. He protected his inter-ests and covered his liabilities. A substantial part of Hoover's bureaucratic genius was his insistence on clear lines of responsibility and a realistic conception of what he could effectively manage. Hoover worked hard to avoid taking the SIS helm, but when pressed by the weight of peer and presidential insistence, he was quick and steadfast in demanding hegemony over the SIS's activities. Hoover did his best to be the master of his own institutional destiny, never taking on more than he could handle and in absolute control of his responsibilities.

Historians of the Special Intelligence Service have been too quick to paint Hoover as an aggressor at the beginning of the 1940s. Consequently, their narratives fail to account for the FBI director's personal skepticism and discretion in shepherd-ing the SIS to success. Seen in this light, Hoover's caution—his efforts to preserve the integrity of his SIS mandate and his repeated attempts to divest himself of the organization altogether—appears logical. J. Edgar Hoover may have been famous for his bureaucratic assaults on others, but, as his work with the SIS reveals, his true strength lay in his ability to keep his own institutional position well defended.

Footnotes

1. Memorandum from FBI Director J. Edgar Hoover to Head of MID [Military Intelligence Division] Brig. Gen. Sherman Miles, 3 August 1940; Section 1; File 64-4104; Administrative Records of the SIS; General Records of the FBI, Record Group 65 (RG 65); National Archives at College Park, College Park, MD (henceforward, NACP).

2. Troy wrote the official history of the establishment of the CIA and had access to most of the existing documentation, both classified and declassified, concerning the SIS. His account provides a useful narrative of the events and personalities surrounding the formation of the SIS, but the focus of his work is on Donovan and the OSS. Thomas F. Troy, *Donovan and the CIA: A History of the Establishment of the Central Intelligence Agency* (Center for the Study of Intelligence, Central Intelligence Agency, 1981). Whitehead's unofficial history of the FBI—which was sanctioned by FBI Director J. Edgar Hoover— draws on some of the then-classified records of the FBI concerning the SIS. His account provides a colorful, and predictably favorable, account of SIS activities. Because of security requirements, Whitehead's book is vague on the personalities and events surrounding the SIS's institutional development within the US government. Don Whitehead, *The FBI Story: A Report to the People* (New York, NY: Random House, 1956).

3. Leslie B. Rout, Jr., and John F. Bratzel, *The Shadow War: German Espionage and United States Counterespionage in Latin America during World War II* (Frederick, MD: University Publications of America, 1986).

4. Raymond J. Batvinis, "In the Beginning: An Examination of the Development of the Federal Bureau of Investigation's Counterintelligence Program, 1936-1941" (Ph.D. dissertation, Catholic University, 2001).

5. Presidential Directive of 26 June 1939; Section 2; File 64-4104; Administrative Records of the SIS; RG 65; NACP.

6. Troy, p. 11.

7. *Ibid.*

8. *Ibid.*

9. *Ibid.*, p. 13. Previous counterespionage cases had seen agencies ranging from the State Department to the Treasury Department to the Post Office claiming jurisdiction for investigations.

10. Rout and Bratzel, p. 34.

11. Batvinis, p. 64.

12. Rout and Bratzel, p. 34, and Batvinis, p. 64.

13. Rout and Bratzel, p. 34, and Troy, p. 16.

14. This discussion of jurisdictional demarcations among the members of the IIC is derived from similar discussions in Troy, p. 16, and Batvinis, pp. 64-65.

15. *Ibid.*

16. Troy, p. 17.

17. *Ibid.*

18. Minutes, IIC Meeting, 3 June 1940; no. 9794-186A/3; IIC Notes; MID; RG 165, as cited in Troy, p. 17.

19. Memorandum entitled "Special Intelligence Service," 6 June 1940; pp. 40-42, SIS General Files; RG 38, NACP, as cited in Batvinis, p. 305.

20. Troy, p. 17, and Batvinis, pp. 305-07.

21. Troy, p. 17.

22. Memorandum of President Roosevelt's telephone directive prepared by Berle and approved by the President, 24 June 1940; Section 2; File 64-4104; Administrative Records of the SIS; RG 65; NACP.

23. *Ibid.*

24. *Ibid.*

25. Christopher Andrew, *For the President's Eyes Only* (New York, NY: Harper Collins, 1995), Ch. 3.

26. *Ibid.*, p. 86.

27. Rout and Bratzel, , p. 37, and Troy, p. 17.

28. *Ibid.*

29. Memorandum from Miles to Hoover, "Scope of the SIS," 23 July 1940; Section 1; File 64-4104; Administrative Records of the SIS; RG 65; NACP.

30. *Ibid.*

31. Letter from Hoover to Miles, 3 August 1940; Section 1; File 64-4104; Administrative Records of the SIS; RG 65; NACP, and Troy, pp. 17, 20.

32. *Ibid.*

33. Letter from Miles to Hoover, 7 August 1940; Section 1; File 64-4104; Administrative Records of the SIS; RG 65; NACP.

34. Memorandum for the Attorney General, 31 December 1941; Section 2; File 64-4104; Administrative Records of the SIS; RG 65; NACP.

35. Presidential Directive, signed 16 January 1942; Section 2; File 64-4104; Administrative Records of the SIS; RG 65; NACP.

36. For details concerning the conflict between Hoover and Miles after August 1940, see Rout and Bratzel, pp. 38-39, and Troy, pp. 46-47.

37. Agreement between MID, ONI, and FBI for Coordinating Special Intelligence Operations in the Western Hemisphere, October 14, 1942; Section 5; File 64-4104; Administrative Records of the SIS; RG 65; NACP. There is some doubt as to the effective date of this Delimitation Agreement. The copy of the agreement that the author found in the SIS administrative files was dated 14 October 1942; however, in Section 11 of this same set of documents (File 64-4104), the author found a post-war memorandum that set the signing date of the Delimitation Agreement as 25 November 1942. I could find no reference to either document in any of the secondary source material I reviewed.

38. Troy, pp. 46-47.

39. Henry L. Stimson Diary, 13 February 1941; Henry L. Stimson Papers (Sterling Memorial Library, Yale University, New Haven), as cited in Troy, p. 47.

40. *Ibid.*, and Batvinis, p. 61.

41. Rout and Bratzel, p. 37.

42. *Ibid.*, p. 39.

43. Batvinis, p. 60. It should be noted that later in Batvinis's account of events (pp. 316-317) he does make note of Hoover's efforts "to unload the SIS responsibility onto another IIC service," but he does not discuss in depth Hoover's attitude and efforts on this score.

44. Batvinis, p. 50.

45. This 15 March 1941 memorandum was referenced by Hoover in a Memorandum for the Attorney General, 4 April 1941; Section 1; File 64-4104; Administrative Records of the SIS; RG 65; NACP.

46. *Ibid.*

47. Memorandum from Tamm to Hoover, 26 July 1941; Section 1; File 64-4104; Administrative Files of the SIS; RG 65; NACP, and Memorandum from Tamm to Hoover, 1 August 1941; Section 1; File 64-4104; Administrative File of the SIS; RG 65; NACP.

48. Memorandum from Tamm to Hoover, 26 July 1941.

49. Memorandum from Tamm to Hoover, 1 August 1941; Section 1; File 64-4104; Administrative Files of the SIS; RG 65; NACP.

50. *Ibid.*

51. Memorandum from Tamm to Hoover, 11 August 1941; Section 1, File 64-4104; Administrative Files of the SIS; RG 65; NACP.

52. Troy, p. 69.

53. Informal Minutes of the Interdepartmental Intelligence Conference, 27 August 1941; Section 1; File 64-4104; Administrative Files of the SIS; RG 65; NACP.

54. Informal Minutes of the Interdepartmental Intelligence Conference, 27 August 1941; and Memorandum from Foxworth to Hoover, "Agenda [for] Interdepartmental Intelligence Conference," 2 September 1941; Section 1; File 64-4104; Administrative Files of the SIS; RG 65; NACP.

55. *Ibid.*

56. Informal Minutes of the Interdepartmental Intelligence Conference, 27 August 1941.

57. *Ibid.*

58. *Ibid.*

59. *Ibid.*

60. Memorandum from Tamm to Hoover, 2 September 1941; Section 1; File 64-4104; Administrative Files of the SIS; RG 65; NACP.

61. *Ibid.*

62. *Ibid.*

63. *Ibid.*

64. Memorandum from Hoover to Biddle, 31 December 1941; Section 2; File 64-4104; Administrative Files of the SIS; RG 65; NACP.

65. *Ibid.*

66. *Ibid.*

67. *Ibid.*

68. *Ibid.*

69. Troy, p. 119.

70. *Ibid.*

71. Memorandum from D. M. Ladd to Hoover, 25 September 1942; Section 5; File 64-4104; Administrative Files of the SIS; RG 65; NACP.

72. *Ibid.*

73. Letter from Hoover to Strong, 10 September 1942; Section 4; File 64-4104; Administrative Files of the SIS; RG 65; NACP.

74. Batvinis, p. 323.

75. *Ibid.*

76. By far the most detailed and comprehensive study of SIS operations appears in Rout and Bratzel. Whitehead's book also contains useful discussions of SIS operations in Latin America.

77. This discussion of platinum smuggling extends from a similar discussion in Whitehead, pp. 224-27.

78. This sentence mirrors a statement in Whitehead, p. 227.

79. Whitehead, pp. 223-24.

80. *Ibid.*, Ch. 23, p. 24.

81. Table 1, SIS Statistics, Section 10; File 64-4104; Administrative Files of the SIS; RG 65; NACP.

82. These observations concerning Hoover's involvement in the SIS extend from the nature and content of the documents that I encountered in the Administrative Files of the SIS at the NACP. The SIS Administrative Files are filled with memos covering the details of such topics as the reorganization of SIS file cards, the curriculum of the SIS agent training school, and the SIS liaison with the State Department. Most of these documents bear the blue-ink comments and initials of Hoover himself.

83. "Emergence of the Intelligence Establishment," *Foreign Relations of the United States Series, 1945-1950 (FRUS)*, C. Thomas Thorne, Jr., and David S. Patterson, eds. (Washington, DC: United States Government Printing Office, 1996), p. 4.

84. "Emergence of the Intelligence Establishment," FRUS, pp. 24-25.

85. *Ibid.*, p. 25.

86. *Ibid.*, pp. 25-26.

87. *Ibid.*

The security manager or executive faces a dilemma of how to qualify what is actionable intelligence. For example, the Iraq war was based partly on intelligence that may have been faulty. (The intelligence indicated that the Baathist regime was developing weapons of mass destruction.) Nation state executives rely on the intelligence to make critical decisions, but it is the user who determines what is actionable. The leader may take action or push the intelligence back to the provider or abandon it.

Now we will look at a modern intelligence operation occurring in the Iraq war. This perspective will enable the student to determine not only how domestic intelligence evolved, but it also provides a review of military intelligence systems and how they are applied as well. Keep in mind that in the 2004-2005 overhaul of the intelligence community, the battle lines were drawn between the Secretary of Defense, Donald Rumsfield, and Congress over who would be the intelligence czar and how any changes would affect the on-ground, real-time needs of warriors in combat.

UNCLASSIFIED

VOL. 48, NO. 1, 2004

UNCLASSIFIED EDITION

Keeping Pace with the Revolution in Military Affairs[4]

William Nolte

In Operation Iraqi Freedom, the world witnessed a progress report on the revolution in military affairs (RMA). The performance of US forces in the major combat phase of the operation in Iraq demonstrated the ability of institutions functioning within standard bureaucratic, hierarchical structures to operate beyond those structures. To put it bluntly, US forces in Iraq leapt past jointness into networked operating models. *They became hierarchies emulating networks.* The challenge to the Intelligence Community is to keep pace with the significant flow of change emanating from the Department of Defense.

This article was written and submitted to *Studies in Intelligence* in late summer 2003. Subsequent events support the argument, explicit in the following pages, that a "revolution in intelligence affairs (RIA)"—and even the revolution in military affairs—must take place within a comprehensive renewal of US national security capabilities. Nothing in the events between May 2003 and the end of the year fundamentally alters, in the author's view, the lessons intelligence professionals can derive from the early phases of Operation Iraqi Freedom.

The Breadth of Change

From many perspectives, the dramatic advance in military operations in Iraq is an exciting, even inspiring, event. First of all, the previous major event in US military history—the Gulf War (or Gulf War I) —was a US military victory that validated new modes of warfare. Yet the services (and DOD civilian leadership, to be sure) abandoned much of the successful Desert Storm model for something even more revolutionary. *That alone—a hierarchical bureaucracy transforming after success*—is a rare achievement. As a possible result, some of the most vocal critics of the plan for Iraqi Freedom were not "old soldiers" from Korea or Vietnam, but more recently retired officers who had served with success in Desert Storm or the Balkans, in itself a reflection of the pace in which reform has invalidated expertise. Innovation has produced its own "Doppler effect." Such invalidation or at least disruption of conventional judgment (and expertise) will continue to be a product of the RMA and its extension into other areas of national security affairs.

Secondly, the American military accomplished this feat not after a period of budgetary largesse, but immediately following an extended and relatively deep period of budget cuts. The victory in Iraq was won with relatively few new weapons systems. Rather, the characteristic "development" model of Iraqi Freedom was the enhancement of many of the systems that had proven successful in the Gulf War. Platforms as venerable as the B-52, as well as a host of significantly "middle-aged" systems (the Abrams tank, the F-16), were stretched by new or enhanced applications and systems to the point where, one suspects, participants in the Joint Strike Fighter and F-22 program offices may be entitled to some mixed reactions to the success of Iraqi Freedom. The point remains: while resource restriction can clearly reach a tipping point that destroys capability, public institutions—including security instruments—can sometimes benefit from austerity that promotes innovation and even competition, simulating some of the characteristics that the market provides private sector institutions.

Finally, it should be clear that the victory was only partly a technical or technologic victory. Peter Drucker has long argued that historians of the industrial revolution have placed too much attention on railroads, steam engines, and the like. Drucker, among others, emphasizes that the dominance of the West in and through the industrial revolution was more critically the dominance of administrative, organizational, and (in governmental terms) operational skills, which in turn permitted the intelligent and advantage-gaining deployment of technology. At every step, Operation Iraqi Freedom demonstrated a similar organizational and operational success, enabled by technology. But technology was merely the tool of a broader commitment to such considerations as the centrality of information as a dominant weapon rather than merely a supporting agent of war; jointness exercised up and down the command structure; and arrangements that emphasized, permitted, and even demanded flexibility and agility.

By any number of measures, the impact of the RMA has been, for want of a better word, revolutionary. The US Department of Defense and the military services, the embodiments of hierarchical organization for most of the 20th century—renowned (fairly or not) for "Catch 22," Standard Operating Procedure, "do it in triplicate," and overpriced toilet seats and hammers—demonstrated an extraordinary ability to function in ways that should lead to a significant rethinking of many stereotypes. A dramatic increase in the use of precision munitions, exponential increases in information volume and variety, and a corresponding decrease in sensor-to-shooter decision cycles are among the technical symptoms of the state of the revolution in military affairs. Even more impressively, at important moments (and perhaps in routine moments as well), an enormously complex public policy instrument behaved in ways that maximized the technical advantages available to it. History suggests that this is not automatically the case. In the end, innovative behavior and a willingness to encourage such behavior may have proven a more important factor in the success of Operation Iraqi Freedom than any technical achievement or set of such achievements.

Next Steps in RMA

Every indicator suggests that Operation Iraqi Freedom occurred *in the midst of* the RMA. Closer to the beginning than to the end? That is hard to say. But many of the technical manifestations of the RMA seem at least roughly supportive of the proposition (Moore's Law) that the computing power available at a given cost doubles every 12-15 months. The conventional wisdom in information technology suggests that Moore's Law may not be exhausted for another decade or so. If this supposition is even roughly accurate, and if this continues to provide a pace and duration roughly indicative of the pace and duration of the RMA, the compounded results of decades of transforming technical change will continue to produce striking, even disorienting outcomes.

If, as presumed above, the current revolution in military affairs continues for another decade or so, the challenge to other components of American national security, including intelligence, is evident. Either they must develop apace with the RMA. Or they suffer the risk that intelligence (and diplomacy, to mention another critical component of national security) will be unable to contribute to—or even compete with—defense organizations in the making of national security decisions.

Jim Hoagland of *The Washington Post* spoke to this prospect when he wrote that the cliché long used to describe Washington in the midst of an international crisis—"The lights are burning late tonight in the State Department"—was in danger of becoming an anachronism. "Foggy Bottom [has become] a somnolent, darkened nighttime quarter, while working weekends and cots for sleeping in the office" attest to Pentagon dominance of national security affairs.[1] Even if this is hyperbole or journalistic impressionism, impressions count. And the impression is that the war-making capacity of the United States is proceeding at a revolutionary pace to embrace technical and other change, while the other instruments of security policy, even if they see themselves adapting to a changed environment, do so at a pace slower than that of the RMA. If this impression becomes reality, the non-Defense components of US national security risk failure or irrelevance, with implications reaching far beyond institutional marginalization. They raise the risk that the United States could squander its military advantage by failing to use that advantage more to dissuade potential adversaries than to engage them in combat. Ultimately, they raise the risk of failure of American security policy.

Intelligence, non-defense intelligence that is, might survive such an outcome—bureaucracies being extraordinarily difficult to kill—but only as increasingly irrelevant appendages of the national security instrument. The desire to avoid becoming process-driven mandarins rather than outcome-driven participants in national security affairs should in itself be the stimulation of a revolution in intelligence affairs.

It is important to note here that such a revolution is not only inevitable, but also, in many cases, already underway. A discussion of such a revolution, or the need to step up its pace, should not become an excuse for self-flagellation. Parts of the "progress report" on the RMA must address the important and successful contribution of intelligence to the success of Operation Iraqi Freedom. All the precision-guided munitions used, to such great effect, during the campaign needed accurate, timely, and precise information. And the evidence suggests that they received it.

The issue for the Intelligence Community is whether it chooses to embrace that revolution, retaining control of much of the agenda of intelligence reform, or to cede control of the agenda to the Congress, a commission or two, or some other body that would effectively place American intelligence in receivership. The issue is also one of a focus on changing structures—*i.e.*, reorganization—or changing habits and behavior.

RMA Payoffs

Operation Iraqi Freedom suggests that changing culture and behavior, while neither quick nor foolproof, can have dramatic returns. The RMA has not banned bureaucracy from the Pentagon. It is at least likely that while the 3rd Infantry Division was racing toward Baghdad, supported by precision munitions launched from an awesome (if not shocking) range of air, sea, and land platforms, some poor soul needing flashlight batteries from a supply depot in Crane, Indiana, was being told he or she had not properly completed the appropriate standard form. In triplicate. Nor does the RMA guarantee the retirement of traditional expressions of frustration with military bureaucracy (FUBAR or SNAFU).

The RMA does mean that, at the point of attack, one of the world's largest bureaucracies functioned as an emulated network, harnessing information in volumes and at speeds unprecedented in the history of warfare and encouraging behaviors that took advantage of that information. It means that the American defense establishment, even after a decade of budget cuts, achieved significant transformation, largely employing the platforms of Desert Storm (resulting from development efforts begun in the 1970s and 1980s, if not earlier) integrated with the systems of the cyber revolution of the 1990s. Most of all, it means that a bureaucratic structure that had entered the 1990s with the success of Desert Storm—and its participation in the historic success of the Cold War—*continued to reform after victory*. This is a remarkable testament to the degree to which behaviors supportive of the RMA (a predilection for jointness, an acceptance if not embrace of innovation bordering on heresy) were tolerated, even rewarded, within the military culture.

The revolution in military affairs may not be *about* technology, but it will ride on technology—to a great degree on technical developments in information transmission, storage, and management. This is largely, and not coincidentally, the same technology on which any prospective revolution in intelligence affairs will depend. Technology, in scholastic terms, has been and will be the necessary basis for the RMA. But the real revolution will be in judgment, decisionmaking, and other forms of behavior. The RMA, like the larger information revolution of which it is but one manifestation, is about institutions and organizations. It is a social event, as was the industrial revolution. Like the industrial revolution, moreover, its implications are too important to be entrusted fully to engineers.

Manifestations of the RMA in Operation Iraqi Freedom will be important considerations in lessons-learned studies. Max Boot has noted that American forces in Iraq used 30 times the bandwidth available only a decade earlier in the first Gulf War.2 (This is almost an exact extrapolation, in bandwidth, of Moore's Law.) Similar illustrations of the RMA are certain to emerge in the months to come. How many—or how few—sorties were required in the 2003 campaign to place on target the munitions that would have required many more missions in Desert Storm, let alone in earlier conflicts? To what degree did the increasing precision of American weaponry—tank rounds as well as bombs—reduce the supply of munitions needed and therefore change the nature of logistics support? And so on.

Innovation as Developed Technique

How has the RMA affected behavior? It is a truism that no plan survives first contact with the enemy. The ability to adapt to what is encountered rather than what was planned for has been noted in every major military legend from Caesar to Patton. But, at some point, the ability to adapt makes a qualitative shift and becomes the capacity for intended improvisation.

The evidence suggests that the air campaign in Operation Iraqi Freedom benefited from such a shift. On 27 April 2003, *The Washington Post* published an extraordinary report on the air campaign. The news analysis described how early information available to the air commander suggested two potentially intersecting observations: first, that attack aircraft were finding themselves in the proverbial target rich environment but were inhibited by limits on their loiter time; and, second, that Iraqi resistance, in the form of aircraft or ground-based anti-aircraft weapons, was relatively light, except at low altitudes. The air commander, Lt. Gen. T. Michael Moseley, integrated these bits of information and altered the pre-campaign rules governing how far forward to place tanker aircraft. The attack pilots would benefit from their presence, and the risk to the slower, unarmed tankers seemed acceptably low.

This appears to have been an exceptionally sound command decision. What is more interesting is the command process implied in the *Post's* account. The air commander appears to have made the decision while linked to multiple levels of command authority, which could have used those links to impede the decision process; however, through what appears to be the good judgment and discretion of the participants, they did not do so. On the contrary. Gen. Moseley connected the data he was receiving with the pre-war guidance of US Central Command's Gen. Tommy R. Franks ("make it fast and final"), which Moseley described as "the mark on the wall for his commanders."

So what? The implications of this decision are minimal if they reflect only one bold commander's reaction to one set of circumstances. But what if this is indicative of a pattern of behavior that we may see being institutionalized in the defense establishment? Is this any more than a laudable but isolated (and therefore potentially not repeatable) example of behavior cited and honored throughout military history? The answer to this question has significant consequences: Is this a case of individual achievement or of an organizationally encouraged tendency toward the behavior described above as intended improvisation.

Music provides a useful analogy. Musicians, even in a classical setting with its emphasis on noting every tonal marking to the most calibrated point, may be able to adjust to a loss of beat on the part of the conductor. A baritone may realize that his tenor is experiencing vocal difficulties and increase his volume in a key duet, or even cover for the tenor in a climactic high note. But such adaptability is not the same as the jazz musician's bone-deep understanding that the marks on the sheet music (if he's even looking at sheet music) are not intended to limit improvisation. His or her permission to improvise is not contingent on making the best of a situation in which something has gone wrong. His "permission" is much broader, much more inherent in the intent of his performance. Improvisation in this context is neither intuitive nor fortuitous; *it is developed technique.*

On the same day that *The Washington Post* published its article on the air campaign, it ran a story on the disintegration of the Iraqi army. Whether or not Operation Iraqi Freedom achieved "shock and awe," as touted, remains an open question. It is very clear, nevertheless, that at many levels it produced confusion and a misperception of American goals and capabilities. Saddam Hussein and his associates may have learned some lessons from the first Gulf War.

In another manifestation of the RMA's Doppler effect—for this purpose, a misperception of American capability based on a misjudgment of the pace of change and innovation within the US military—it is less certain that any of those lessons provided usefully applicable information. The Iraqi leadership may have been comforted, in the war's first weekend, by concerns expressed by US observers about any number of issues: whether the American-led coalition had deployed sufficient troops; whether it had available the right kinds of troops, especially heavy armor; and whether the race to Baghdad had left coalition supply lines vulnerable to interruption. In the end, however, speed and precision, more than mass, rendered these concerns irrelevant to the outcome of the war. Knowing where the 3rd Infantry Division had been 12 or 15 hours in the past proved of little use to the Iraqis as the coalition forces sped toward both the capture of Iraq's capital and the deconstruction of effective resistance.[3]

One Iraqi officer, obviously schooled in denial and deception as taught in the Iraqi armed forces, reported his dismay to an American reporter. Called to a meeting, he had left his unit hidden under trees to avoid detection by US reconnaissance. Using the best information available to him on US capabilities, he attempted to deny those capabilities the opportunity to "see" his troops. When he returned, his unit's vehicles were burning wrecks and many of its personnel were dead or wounded. The officer's explanation? "The Americans must have had spies." Maybe not. In some respects, what this officer knew about US reconnaissance systems may have been as fatal as what he did not know.

One goal of any revolution in warfare should be to confound an adversary in just this way. Saddam may even have attempted to demonstrate his sagacity by encouraging his officers to watch *Black Hawk Down*. Take notes, there'll be a quiz after the movie! Ernest May has conclusively demonstrated that the admonition that we should learn from history works only if we learn the right lessons from the right history.[4] It's easy to get this wrong. Saddam may have believed that *Black Hawk Down* pointed to critical inabilities of the American empire, especially its aversion to casualties.

This may in fact be *a* lesson to be learned from America's experience in Somalia. But history is rarely so didactic. An alternative lesson that might have proven more useful for the Iraqis was that the American troops in Somalia displayed enormous skill, professionalism, and killing power, stripped of all those material advantages that some critics (those of the "Germany-had-better-tanks-but-the-Americans-had-more-factories" school of military history) use to discredit American military achievement. A second lesson Iraq could have taken from Somalia (and Desert Storm) was that the United States was not likely to deploy major forces in the Gulf without air power, while leaving armored support to one or more foreign partners operating under international command.

Looking Ahead

What are the potential implications of another decade of RMA? At its most basic level, we should assume that US personnel deployed in a major effort in 2010 should expect to have 20 times the bandwidth available during Iraqi Freedom (or 800-1000 times the bandwidth available in Desert Storm). We should further assume that other metrics—the definition of "precision;" the speed at which information is collected and processed; even our ability to distinguish collection, processing, and analysis as distinct phases of an information cycle; and the speed of decisions—will continue to change at blinding speed.

Change at this pace will put enormous pressure on planning and perception, resulting in a continued premium on innovation, improvisation, and information. In describing Operation Iraqi Freedom, President George W. Bush observed that we had entered a new phase in industrial warfare. In earlier phases (beginning, he might have noted, with Sherman and Grant), it was necessary to destroy large parts of an enemy's society and economy in order to defeat its warfighting capability. Even in Desert Storm, breaking Iraq's infrastructure was a key strategy. In Iraqi Freedom, the President continued, the United States was able to surgically destroy a regime while leaving social and economic infrastructure intact.

The "New American Way of War," to use Max Boot's phrase, is not without risks. The United States may have underestimated, for example, the degree to which Iraqis, either regime hardliners or simple criminals, would destroy their own infrastructure. We may not have been prepared for the truly revolutionary event in which an invading (and conquering) army needs to be succeeded by an occupation force of equal or even larger size. That alone turns centuries of experience on its head, a point that fairness suggests should be noted in assessments of the US performance in Iraq. It is hard to plan for the unprecedented.

One advantage, though, of American leadership, in both hard and soft forms of national power, should be that of being able to absorb the unprecedented better than many adversaries. To an even greater degree, moreover, we should be able to force both the direction and extent of new precedents. Much has been written over the last decade about the threat to the United States from asymmetric warfare, most of the literature implying, at least, that asymmetry is a condition inflicted upon the United States. How many examples does it take to convince us that: *We are the asymmetric power*. This should not lull us into complacency about the risk of asymmetric attacks against the United States, its allies, or its interests. But the fact remains that our capacity to go asymmetric on our adversaries is part of America's strategic advantage of the 21st century. Ask the "elite" Republican Guards.

Toward a Revolution in Intelligence Affairs

What are the lessons of the revolution in military affairs for intelligence? First of all, it is essential that the RMA take place within a balanced national security strategy, in which all the components of security—the military, diplomacy, intelligence, and the additional components engaged in the homeland security environment created after 11 September 2001—proceed apace. The National Security Act of 1947 implied, if not directed, a balance among security components. The late historian Carroll Quigley once argued for the concept of historical morphology, meaning the balance between the elements of an institution or society. Developments in one element unmatched by at least roughly parallel developments in others could, in the end, prove detrimental to an institution's ability to function effectively.[5]

This is not to suggest that the revolution in military affairs should slow to allow other institutions of security to catch up. That would be a mistake of potentially tragic proportions. US leadership in the world of the early 21st century is significantly tied to American technical leadership, and one clear way to ensure American security is to maximize, in extent and in duration, our technical advantages, including military technology. At some point, of course, these advantages create other organic imbalances, as, for example, may be occurring in the gap between the capabilities of the American military and those of its allies, even in the other industrial democracies. At some point, gaps of this sort render meaningful coalition operations inefficient or even dangerous.

But the more pertinent issue is the need to ensure a balanced morphology in American national security, with security elements outside DOD matching pace with events in DOD. For intelligence, we should assume that the very presence of the majority of US intelligence assets within the Defense community will ensure their participation in the revolution in military affairs. This will only occur, however, if the Defense components see themselves as subject to the demands of the RMA. The recent establishment of the position of Undersecretary of Defense for Intelligence (USDI) presumes this to be the case. Although the creation of the DOD intelligence position guarantees a degree of bureaucratic tension, it is at least possible, in the short- to mid-term, that the USDI and the DCI will perform supportive, complementary roles. Which of the "two parents" of US intelligence takes effective control of the national agencies and their programs is probably less important than that one of them must, in the context of strategic agreement between both.

Implementing an RIA

For all the criticisms one might make about the hardships faced over time by prophets of military reform, and for all the obstacles placed in the path of reform, it is clear that in the current revolution in military affairs, the defense establishment has remained open and receptive—at some level—to its critics. John Boyd's reputation, for example, surely represents both the strengths and pitfalls of becoming a reform cult figure.6 But it can scarcely be doubted that studies on Operation Iraqi Freedom will find his name in the index. How many Marine commanders, in describing the formation of their professional perspectives and skills, will note Boyd's influence? Probably many of them. Admirals William Owens and Arthur Cebrowski will almost certainly draw attention. It is worth noting in that vein that the defense establishment showed confidence and maturity in how it dealt with people like Adm. Cebrowski, many of whose views were at the very least controversial. He was not assigned to some departmental backwater, but to head—and rejuvenate—the Naval War College, now clearly the center of service-school work on information and its applications, including, but not limited to, information warfare. He now plays a significant role in the "Rumsfeld Revolution," a particular iteration of the RMA under the current Secretary of Defense.

The point here is not to suggest a roadmap for how we generate an intelligence reform movement or a revolution in intelligence affairs. The point is to suggest that we undertake a confident study of how the counterpart revolution in defense took shape, an assessment of our strengths and weaknesses in internalizing operational transformation, and a plan to implement the revolution. We need to look at institutions like the National Training Center and the various "after next" studies done by DOD and the services.

We need to be prepared to look at "concept cars" with the courage and stamina shown by the services. The Navy's DD21 program, for example, will never produce a fleet of ships that meet all the specifications of its original design. But what did the Navy learn from this project about how to reduce crew size? Would it not be at least interesting to commission a concept car asking whether an NSA or CIA "after next" could operate more flexibly with a core staff half its current size? Like the first conception of the DD21, we would probably never see those goals achieved. But what could we learn—about the inverse relationship between size and agility, for example—before we simply go off and assume that the future of the intelligence agencies must be a future of personnel growth?

How do we get our schools to become seedbeds for irritating, unconventional, annoying people? How do we link more effectively with service schools and labs (and with organizations such as the Defense Advanced Research Projects Agency and the Office of Net Assessments) with a history of innovative, even counterinstitutional, thinking. How do we link our research and writing on the future of intelligence with analogous efforts in the Departments of State, Justice, and Homeland Security, among others?7

As one lesson learned from the RMA, we need to focus less on structure and more on behavior. This is not to suggest that some organizational changes—the creation of a single national technical intelligence agency, for example—may lack merit. Or should not be discussed. But what cost are we prepared to expend, in money and time, on changing structure? If changes in behavior can produce most if not all of the gain to be achieved by reorganization, with less turmoil, then why put primary emphasis on wiring diagrams? It is not altogether certain, it must be conceded, that changes in behavior can be achieved faster than changes in organization. Goldwater-Nichols made "jointness" a buzzword from the late 1980s.[8] It did not, however, become an operating habit overnight. Many in the Defense establishment, including those at the center of Operation Iraqi Freedom, can no doubt, from an insider's perspective, point to the areas in which jointness, in thinking and doing, is still not "second nature" in the American military. From the outside, however, the results look very impressive.

For better or worse, it is such external metrics that count greatly. To say our individual agencies are performing more effectively or more efficiently than they did a decade or so ago is largely irrelevant. In an environment marked by the rapid appearance and disappearance of issues or targets; by a relatively finite range of target states but virtually infinite set of real or potential target groups; and by extraordinary volatility in our technical environment; the only measure that counts is how well US intelligence aligns itself with the world beyond its walls. One agency head has described his initial experience in that organization in terms of piloting an airplane: "The nose was pointed down and when I looked out the window the houses were getting bigger." Even if we can say that our agencies now have their noses pointed up, with gains in airspeed and altitude, this is not a guarantee that we will clear the peaks outside the windows. And clearing the peaks, the external metric, is all that counts.

Information is the key to our ability to plan, institutionalize, weaponize, and apply American potential as an asymmetric power. And the ability to move and store information needs to be at the center of intelligence reform. "How do we transform NSA?" (or CIA? or NGA?) is not a bad question. "How do we do intelligence for the United States?" in the midst of volatile operational and technical environments is a better question, even if the answer leaves no room for any of the existing agencies to plan their 75th anniversaries.

Ask most Americans to recount the timeline of the national security experience of the United States from 1945 to the present, and the likely answer will be that we moved from the Second World War to the Cold War, which we then proceeded to win. While roughly accurate, this view omits one of the most important periods in American national security, the interval between 1945 and 1947.

President Truman, at the moment of his ascendancy, held a view of the need for "economy and efficiency" in government not unlike the desire for "normalcy" expressed after the First World War by President Harding. Truman's demobilization efforts matched those of previous postwar periods. Remarkably, however, Truman and the men around him shortly recognized that normalcy, in the sense of the prewar world, was not in America's future. Over the course of the next several years, and especially in the National Security Act of 1947 and the Marshall Plan, they set the United States on an unprecedented path as a permanent world power. The structure implied or built in the National Security Act supported American strategy for half a century, balancing military and non-military expressions of American power and providing for a permanent, peacetime intelligence establishment with a focus independent of any individual department.

The national security structure of the 21st century cannot be a replication of that of 1947. The threat of terrorism means we must now defend Kansas not just at the Fulda Gap in Germany or in the Pacific, but at America's points of entry. And in Kansas itself. We will not be able to function with the relatively neat division between foreign and domestic threats, or between intelligence (by which we implicitly mean foreign intelligence) and law enforcement. We must forge a new understanding of national security, and part of that understanding must be a role for intelligence aligned with the diffuse and complex security environment facing the United States and its allies. Identifying that still emerging environment and achieving alignment with it must be the central issues in any revolution in intelligence affairs.

Footnotes

1. Jim Hoagland, "Fusing Force with Diplomacy," *The Washington Post*, 19 June 2003.

2. Max Boot, "The New American Way of War," *Foreign Affairs* (82,4), July/August 2003.

3. Though not the subject of this article, speed becomes an increasingly important factor in rethinking, in intelligence and the other instruments of national security, the whole issue of "security." Denying an adversary the knowledge of a friendly unit's location at a given moment becomes largely immaterial if the unit is moving faster than the adversary can gain, process, or act on information locating it at that location. Information delay, always a part of security planning, may need to become more important, relatively speaking, than information denial.

4. Ernest R. May, *Lessons from the Past: The Use and Misuse of History in American Foreign Policy* (Oxford, UK: Oxford University Press, 1985).

5. Carroll Quigley, *The Evolution of Civilization: An Introduction to Historical Analysis* (New York, NY: Macmillan, 1961).

6. See Robert Coram, Boyd: *The Fighter Pilot Who Changed the Art of War* (Boston, MA: Little, Brown, 2003) for a thorough, if worshipful, account of Boyd's impact.

7. One of the goals we need to establish in linking with service schools and other institutions is a greater willingness to accept the military principle of "train for the way you fight," or operate, in the case of intelligence. We need to take a hard look at the continued value of simulation in military training and education, for example. And we need to confront some significant differences in operational tempo and practices, especially as they involve training groups or units versus individuals. When the 101st Airborne returns from Iraq, after suitable rest, individuals may go off to advanced schooling. But a significant portion of military training is the training of whole units, taking advantage of a deploy/refit operational schedule. It is hard to imagine that the CIA's Directorate of Intelligence could "stand down" its Middle Eastern elements for a month of training, but somehow the Intelligence Community needs to find opportunities to train not just as units within agencies, but across agencies. The first step is to accept as a goal greater emphasis on "training for the way we operate."

8. The Goldwater-Nichols Act of 1986 is widely credited with adding coherence to the Joint Chiefs of Staff structure (a creation of the National Security Act of 1947), which had long been viewed as fragmented and less effective than it should have been in advising the commander-in-chief. See Ronald H. Cole et al., *The Chairmanship of the Joint Chiefs of Staff* (Washington, DC: Office of the Chairman of the Joint Chiefs of Staff [Joint History Office], 1995), pp. 25-38.

William Nolte is the Deputy Assistant Director of Central Intelligence for Analysis and Production.

***Source: http://www.odci.gov/csi/studies/vol48no1/article01.html Operation Iraqi Freedom and the Challenge to Intelligence

SUMMARY

The assessment of **open source** intelligence, and an introduction to critical thinking go hand in hand in developing ability to approach rapidly evolving current events with a rational, and thoughtful assessment process. The potential for over-response, inappropriate response, or ineffective response can only be precluded through a critical analysis coupled with a clear understanding of security principles.

The intelligence function, with respect to the fundamental process of the intelligence cycle, has not changed but everything around it has. The new alliance among private security, law enforcement, the intelligence community, the military, and emergency services has led to a far broader membership for the collections and sharing of intelligence. The scope of who needs to know has evolved into who needs to share. Private and public interests recognize the critical need of accurate intelligence and are accepting the responsibility of being observers and reporters.

Every manager, whether in the private or public sector, needs to understand the intelligence cycle and determine how they fit into a more global network of intelligence.

ADDITIONAL DISCUSSION TOPICS

- What did Sherman Kent (the CIA's father of intelligence analysis) mean when he persuasively argued that intelligence is knowledge? Why do some still confuse the method with the product? Compare and contrast the method and product.

- What is meant by *"OSINT is at times the 'INT' of first resort, last resort, and every resort in between"*?

- The author of the article says that the "New American Way of War," to use Max Boot's phrase, is not without risks. What are the risks? What did he mean by this statement?

- What are the lessons of the revolution in military affairs for intelligence?

RESOURCES

- Critical Thinking: Tools for Taking Charge of Your Learning and Your Life
  Authors: Richard Paul and Linda Elder
  Publisher: Prentice Hall
  Copyright: 2001
  ISBN: 0-13-086972-4

- Bierman, Arthur K. *The Critical Thinking Handbook*. Prentice Hall, 1996.

- Browne, M. Neil and Stuart M. Keeley. *Asking the Right Questions: A Guide to Critical Thinking*. Prentice Hall, 1994 (4th ed, with manual).

- Ennis, Robert H. *Critical Thinking*. Prentice Hall, 1996.

- Fearnside, W. Ward. *About Thinking*. Prentice Hall, 1997 (2nd ed).

- Feldman, Richard. *Reason and Argument*. Prentice Hall, 1993 (2nd ed).

- *Proactive Security Administration: 1/e*
  (c) 2005 | ISBN: 0131421328
  George Curtis
  R. McBride

- J. Edgar Hoover: The Man and the Secrets, Curt Genrty, 2001, ISBN: 0393321282, W.W. Norton and Company

- Wild Bill and the Intrepid: Donovan, Stephenson, and The Origins of the CIA, Thomas Troy, 1996, ISBN:0300065639

- Roosevelt's Secret War: FDR and World War II Espionage, Joseph Presico, 2001, ISBN: 0375501367, Random House.

Web Links

Central Intelligence Agency: http://www.cia.gov

Military Intelligence web site from Loyola University:
http://www.loyola.edu/dept/politics/milintel.html

Fort Huachuca, U.S. Army, web site: http://huachuca-www.army.mil

Endnotes:

[1] This material is from Chapter 3, "Intelligence and Warnings," from *Current Events in Homeland Security*, 0-536-26130-X

[2] Source: Central Intelligence Agency website: http://www.cia.gov

[3] Source: http://www.odci.gov/csi/studies/vol48no1/article05.htmlhe FBI and Foreign Intelligence.

[4] Source: Operation Iraqi Freedom and the Challenge to Intelligence, http://www.odci.gov/csi/studies/vol48no1/article01.html

CHAPTER FOUR

CRITICAL INFRASTRUCTURE

The terrorist enemy that we face is highly determined, patient, and adaptive. In confronting this threat, protecting our critical infrastructures and key assets represents an enormous challenge. We must remain united in our resolve, tenacious in our approach, and harmonious in our actions to overcome this challenge and secure the foundations of our Nation and way of life.
—President George W. Bush

The infrastructure of the U.S. is a long-term suspension of disbelief that such things won't be exploded deliberately by people who don't create anything.
—Dave Winer

KEY TERMS

Critical infrastructure
Telecommunications
Vulnerability
Proprietary information
Total war
NGO
Profiling

OBJECTIVES

- Define the terms critical infrastructure and key resources.

- Explain the relationship between the public and private sectors in the context of homeland security.

- Describe behavioral profiling.

- Describe the applications of proactive terror threat assessment.

- Describe critical infrastructure and key resources from a U.S. historical perspective.

- Describe the rationale for post-incident investigations.

DISCUSSION TOPICS

- Why does the private sector care about the protection of critical infrastructure?

- Is it fair for the government to impose security standards on private companies?

- Should professional organizations and other non-governmental agencies have input to governmental security planning and policy?

- How do terrorist tactics evolve?

- What are some civil rights concerns about the use of behavioral profiling?

4

INTRODUCTION

Infrastructure is like the air we breathe: it is always all around us, but we never think of it. The bridges we cross going into the city for work, the wires and cables that deliver our electricity and information, pipelines carrying fuel or water great distances, all these are vulnerable to attack. The private sector owns most of the infrastructure in the US, and so the private sector takes an active role in its protection, but the question of how much they should influence lawmakers and government policy is still on many people's minds.

The threat we face from terrorism today is unprecedented in US history. Modern communications and weapons technology allows for a small group to have an effect disproportionate to their numbers, and 24 hour news channels can be trusted to spread the fear almost instantly. Even so, techniques for identifying and thwarting attacks and attackers must pass legal muster and concerns about limiting civil liberties must be addressed.

The challenges are great, but the stakes are also high.

TARGET: INFRASTRUCTURE

The tide turned during the American Civil War with the concept of *total war*. Total war was the policy of the Army of the North led by Ulysses S. Grant, and carried out by General Sherman. This policy approved the destruction of civilian assets that could be used to support the efforts of the enemy. This policy led to the destruction of the economy and the will of the South to continue to fight the war. Although not the only factor, this policy change was a key factor to the North's victory.

Our country never experienced such devastation again until September 11th. Attacks by terrorists against civilian, economic, and military targets rocked the American sense of protection from enemy attacks. Attacks directed against our infrastructure were almost unheard of save a few German saboteurs during World War II.

However, in this modern day act of total war, the American will was not bent or broken. The private sector and the government created new partnership efforts to protect critical infrastructure. The shared efforts have thwarted or deterred new attacks on American soil as of this writing.

This resolve is important in view of the unique role of the private sector in owning over 85 percent of the critical infrastructure as opposed to many countries where such functions are carried out by the government.

The Department of Homeland Security (DHS) supports this government and private sector partnership by coordinating a comprehensive national plan for protecting our infrastructure.

Infrastructure* Sectors[1]

- Food
- Water
- Agriculture
- Health systems
- Emergency services
- Energy (electrical, nuclear, gas and oil, dams)
- Transportation (air, road, rail, ports, and waterways)
- Information and telecommunications
- Banking and finance
- Energy transportation
- Chemical
- Defense industry
- Postal and shipping
- National monuments and icons

*Infrastructure — America's critical infrastructure sectors provide the foundation for our national security, governance, economic vitality, and way of life.

DHS will attempt to enhance protection of significant vulnerabilities, particularly targets with catastrophic potential such as nuclear power plants, chemical facilities, pipelines, and ports by creating a standard of protection, protocols, networks, and rapid response plans.

The infrastructure also relies on telecommunications as a support to many essential areas of emergency response. An attack against the telephone systems, the Internet, or other communications systems can disrupt our ability to respond to other crisis situations—including natural disasters.

The communications among agencies responsible for protecting the infrastructure remain in need of improvement. This article, although not terror related, indicates the continuing problems experienced in many of the critical sectors.

Case Study: Officials Say Water Scare Could Have Been Averted[2]

Ginger D. Richardson
The Arizona Republic
Feb. 16, 2005 12:00 AM

Phoenix officials admitted Tuesday that January's water contamination scare could have been avoided and that the incident exposed serious vulnerabilities within the city's emergency response network.

A preliminary city audit has also concluded that there were breakdowns in communications and procedure during the days and hours leading to the Water Services Department's Jan. 25 decision to issue a boil-water advisory to the city's 1.5 million residents.

"Decisions happened in a vacuum," said Randy Spenla, the city's acting city auditor. "We weren't prepared to make decisions in the middle of the night, and we are going to have to be."

The advisory was issued at 2:30 a.m. Jan. 25 without consultation with the City Manager's Office or the Maricopa County health department when it became obvious that the city wouldn't be able to clean the water leaving the Val Vista Water Treatment Plant well enough to meet federal drinking water standards because of high sediment levels, or turbidity.

Tests ultimately proved that Phoenix residents never received water that was unsafe, but questions lingered about how the city handled the incident and whether it is prepared to deal with a full-scale emergency.

An *Arizona Republic* investigation found that the chaos surrounding the water scare was indicative of more pervasive problems that plagued the city's Water Services Department for years. Documents also portrayed an agency that chronically violated state and federal water laws.

On Tuesday, Spenla and others at City Hall said the scare was a wake-up call.

"One word comes to mind, and that is luck," said Councilman Tom Simplot. "It seems like we were awfully lucky this time around."

Before the Alert

The audit concluded that workers isolated themselves from city leaders as they attempted to solve the problem.

Two days before the alert, water services officials discussed dumping plant water, which had high levels of untreatable particles called colloids, back into the Southern Canal, and the fact that other cities were successfully using lime to clean the water.

Dumping water into the canal, which also serves plants operated by Tempe and Chandler, ultimately solved the crisis, the city believes.

"It was like the Titanic in that it went from bad to worse to worse," said City Manager Frank Fairbanks.

Audit Results

City auditors interviewed 66 people and spent 600 hours looking into why the city failed to treat the turbid water and how it notified the public of the problem.

Among the things that went wrong:

- The city's emergency management coordinator, Marcus Aurelius, was not told of the boil-water advisory and didn't know about it until he turned on the morning news. Spenla said the city must do a better job to alert the public of such emergencies.

- Key water department personnel did not have appropriate emergency contact numbers, and therefore couldn't get information to the people they needed to.

- There is no indication that the Water Services Department has ever conducted emergency preparedness or incident training as required by its operating procedures.

Spenla's report seems to back up the city's belief that a confluence of bad luck and unforeseeable circumstances caused the water mess and that no one is to blame.

Despite those factors, the report concludes that it could have been partially or wholly prevented.

The audit identified several critical steps the city should take to prevent future incidents, including:

- Work with Salt River Project officials to prevent the city's 24th Street and Deer Valley water treatment plants from being shut down simultaneously for routine maintenance, which would build more redundancy into the city's water system.

- Add a lime feeding system to the western portion of the Val Vista plant, which is important because the chemical has been proven to help settle sediments in the water. The city ran out of lime at a crucial time in the crisis.

- Build a sewer connection to the facility, which is key because it would have allowed the city to dump the bad water at the plant without worrying about running afoul of federal regulations.

Room for Improvements

Phoenix also is in the process of hiring an engineer to evaluate the Val Vista plant and is looking at what needs to be done to improve both the water department's and the city's emergency response plans.

There is opportunity here for significant change, for significant improvements," Spenla said.

Mayor Phil Gordon said the report shows that the city needs to make changes to better handle the unexpected. "This will not happen again," he said.

"Were we, as a city, lucky that no one was made sick, that no one died?" Gordon asked. "The answer is yes."

Clearly turf issues and a lack of awareness still exist in the ranks of those charged with the protection of our critical assets. The contamination of water is a serious threat from terrorist cells active in the United States. If procedures are developed and followed for terror threats, then the issues that were involved in this case probably could have been prevented.

An Insider's Point of View...

The good thing about protecting infrastructure and building redundant systems is that the planning and preparation work for natural disasters work as well in terror attacks. In the late 1970s, what was called "a hundred-year flood" literally cut the Metropolitan Phoenix area in half. All the east/west highways and roads-except one-were wiped out. A contingency plan to move commuters to the downtown area was initiated and a passenger train line was set up to move downtown workers across the river on the one remaining bridge. I will always remember how the entire community pulled together to make it work. In today's security environment, however, this story might not have been possible.

Today, terrorists see the infrastructure as a legitimate military target. Terrorists are also known to deliver secondary devices to the scene to wipe out first responders. Remember, as a security manager, to plan backups and then plan for those systems to fail as well.

Critical infrastructures. [Defined as] "systems and assets, whether physical or virtual, so vital to the United States that the incapacity or destruction of such systems and assets would have a debilitating impact on security, national economic security, national public health or safety, or any combination of those matters."

—USA Patriot Act

Many professional associations and organizations that deal with infrastructure have proposed standards to address potential crisis situations and work diligently to put these recommendations into place. For example the chemical industry via the American Chemistry Council (ACC) actively lobbies for support of strict standards.

Case Study: Chemical Industry Security: Legislation Needed to Ensure All Chemical Facilities Working to Harden Facilities[3]

Statement From Tom Reilly, President & CEO

Recent media reports have underscored the urgency of securing one of the most critical parts of this country's infrastructure, the chemical sector. While not top of mind for most Americans, chemical products are essential to the American way of life, as they are used to make everything from safe drinking water and computer chips to critical components for fighter aircraft and health-giving pharmaceuticals. Chemical makers employ more than one million people in high-paying manufacturing jobs and export more products than any other industry.

It's logical for Americans to ask, "What's being done to protect these essential products, the men and women who work at chemical facilities, and their neighbors from terrorist attack?" The members of the American Chemistry Council (ACC) – representing about 90% of America's basic industrial chemical production - spent more than $800 million just last year to make their communities, facilities, and products more secure.

Following 9/11, and without waiting for government direction, ACC members imposed on themselves a mandatory, comprehensive security program — ACC's Responsible Care(r) Security Code. As a result, all 2040 ACC member facilities have completed rigorous security vulnerability assessments; the highest priority facilities have completed security enhancements, and all others are on schedule to complete enhancements by year's end. ACC's Security Code has been acknowledged by Secretary Ridge as a benchmark industry security program, and has been recognized in differing ways by the United States Coast Guard, the City of Baltimore and the states of Maryland and New Jersey. And ACC members have partnered with federal and state agencies, law enforcement, and first responders to increase security for this critical sector of our economy.

Even with all this progress, more work lies ahead and security lapses at chemical facilities are unacceptable. ACC believes the U.S. Department of Homeland Security must have the authority to require security plans across the entire sector. Given reports from the Department of Homeland Security (DHS) of heightened concerns about the potential for terrorist attack in the upcoming months, we are proud of the significant progress we have already made to enhance the security of our facilities.

That's why ACC has been pushing the Administration and both parties in Congress to put aside their differences and enact meaningful federal legislation that will require all chemical facilities to address security as rigorously as do our members. We urge them to act quickly before time runs out in this Congress.

The American Chemistry Council (ACC) represents the leading companies engaged in the business of chemistry. ACC members apply the science of chemistry to make innovative products and services that make people's lives better, healthier and safer. ACC is committed to improved environmental, health and safety performance through Responsible Care, common sense advocacy designed to address major public policy issues, and health and environmental research and product testing. The business of chemistry is a $460 billion enterprise and a key element of the nation's economy. It is the nation's largest exporter, accounting for ten cents out of every dollar in U.S. exports. Chemistry companies invest more in research and development than any other business sector. Safety and security have always been primary concerns of ACC members, and they have intensified their efforts, working closely with government agencies to improve security and to defend against any threat to the nation's critical infrastructure.

***Source: http://www.accnewsmedia.com

June 11, 2004

Contact: Kate McGloon (703) 741-5812

Kate_McGloon@americanchemistry.com

1300 Wilson Boulevard, Arlington, VA 22209 Tel 703-741-5000 Fax 703-741-6000
http://www.accnewsmedia.com

The commitment to infrastructure protection is required from all Americans as a matter of national security. The risks are self-evident: A failure of one element of the infrastructure grid can lead to a collapse of all essential services.

This commitment requires a certain mental toughness and determination. The resilience of the American people in the face of terror threats is addressed in the National Strategy for the Physical Protection of Critical Infrastructures and Key Assets.

Ethical Considerations...

You are the director of a chemical plant that competes directly with two other chemical plants in your business sector. You have found that by not implementing industry-standard security protocols, you can cut prices and beat the competition in the marketplace.

What are the ethical implications of this action?

What if you are the owner of a company that buys products from this industry? Would you do business with the company that ignored security measures but delivered a better price?

NATIONAL RESILIENCE: SUSTAINING PROTECTION FOR THE LONG-TERM[4]

Combating terrorism will be a long-term effort. Its dynamic nature means that we must enhance the protection of our critical infrastructures and key assets in an environment of persistent and evolving threats.

Our Nation's critical infrastructures are generally robust and resilient. These attributes result from decades of experience gained from responding to natural disasters, such as hurricanes and floods, and the deliberate acts of malicious individuals.

The critical infrastructure sectors have learned from each disruption and applied those lessons to improve their protection, response, and recovery operations. For example, during the immediate aftermath of the September 11 attacks, the electric system in New York City remained operational for the island of Manhattan outside of the World Trade Center complex—Ground Zero. Furthermore, needed electric service at Ground Zero was quickly and efficiently restored to support rescue and recovery operations. This success is a good example of American ingenuity, as well as a tenacious application of lessons learned from the 1993 World Trade Center bombing and other terrorist events.

Resilience is characteristic of most U.S. communities, and it is reflected in the ways they cope with natural disasters. Over time, residents of communities in areas that are persistently subjected to natural disasters become accustomed to what to expect when one occurs. Institutions and residents in such areas grow to understand the nature of catastrophic events, as well as their roles and responsibilities in managing their aftereffects.

They are also familiar with and rely on trusted community systems and resources that are in place to support protection, response, and recovery efforts. As a result, they have confidence in their communities' abilities to contend with the aftermath of disasters and learn from each event. Institutions and residents nationwide must likewise come to understand the nature of terrorism, its consequences, and the role they play in combating it. Ideally, they will become familiar with and have confidence in.

SCOPE OF THE PROTECTION MISSION

Agriculture and Food

- 1,912,000 farms
- 87,000 food-processing plants

Water

- 1,800 federal reservoirs
- 1,600 municipal waste water facilities

Public Health

- 5,800 registered hospitals

Emergency Services

- 87,000 U.S. localities

Defense Industrial Base

- 250,000 firms in 215 distinct industries

Telecommunications

- 2 billion miles of cable

Energy

- Electricity 2,800 power plants
- Oil and Natural Gas 300,000 producing sites

Transportation

- Aviation 5,000 public airports
- Passenger Rail and Railroads120,000 miles of major railroads
- Highways, Trucking, and Busing 590,000 highway bridges
- Pipelines 2 million miles of pipelines
- Maritime 300 inland/costal ports
- Mass Transit 500 major urban public transit operators

Banking and Finance

- 26,600 FDIC insured institutions

Chemical Industry and Hazardous Materials

- 66,000 chemical plants

Postal and Shipping

- 137 million delivery sites

Key Assets

- National Monuments 5,800 historic buildings and Icons
- Nuclear Power Plants 104 commercial nuclear power plants
- Dams 80,000 dams
- Government Facilities 3,000 government owned/operated facilities
- Commercial Assets 460 skyscrapers

*These are approximate figures.

***Source - http://www.dhs.gov/interweb/assetlibrary/Physical

This segment reproduced here from the national strategy demonstrates that the almost unimaginable scope of the problem can be met head on by a determined and security-conscious population.

TERROR TRENDS, STYLES, AND MODES

While variation is guaranteed when it comes to the international terrorist, there is commonality in their purpose, drive, and habits. The effective public and private security specialist should have a grasp of the basic terror trends, styles, and modes of operation. The professional security practitioner should also maintain a collection of fluid resource and research sources to maintain awareness of the trends and styles of terror as they change. Commonality in terror trends includes exploitation of our security weaknesses, developing technology, use of all media, and exploiting the sympathy of the ill-informed and radical populous, to mention only a few.

The article reprinted below provides a foundation for some of the key issues surrounding the trends, techniques, and methods used by our current foe.

Future Trends in Terrorism[5]

As a conflict method that has survived and evolved through several millennia to flourish in the modern information age, terrorism continues to adapt to meet the challenges of emerging forms of conflict, and exploit developments in technology and society. Terrorism has demonstrated increasing abilities to adapt to counter-terrorism measures and political failure. Terrorists are developing new capabilities of attack and improving the efficiency of existing methods. Additionally, terrorist groups have shown significant progress in escaping from a subordinate role in nation-state conflicts, and becoming prominent as international influences in their own right. They are becoming more integrated with other sub-state entities, such as criminal organizations and legitimately chartered corporations, and are gradually assuming a measure of control and identity with governments.

Adaptive Capabilities of Terror Groups

Terrorists have shown the ability to adapt to the techniques and methods of counter-terror agencies and intelligence organizations over the long term. The decentralization of the network form of organization is an example of this. Adopted to reduce the disruption caused by the loss of key links in a chain of command, a network organization also complicates the tasks of security forces, and reduces predictability of operations.

Terrorists have also been quick to use new technologies, and adapt existing ones to their uses. The debate over privacy of computer data was largely spurred by the specter of terrorists planning and communicating with encrypted data beyond law enforcement's ability to intercept or decode this data. To exchange information, terrorists have exploited disposable cellular phones, over the counter long-distance calling cards, Internet cafes, and other means of anonymous communications. Embedding information in digital pictures and graphics is another innovation employed to enable the clandestine global communication that modern terrorists require.

Terrorists have also demonstrated significant resiliency after disruption by counter-terrorist action. Some groups have redefined themselves after being defeated or being forced into dormancy. The Shining Path of Peru (Sendero Luminosa) lost its leadership cadre and founding leader to counter-terrorism efforts by the Peruvian government in 1993. The immediate result was severe degradation in the operational capabilities of the group. However, the Shining Path has returned to rural operations and organization in order to reconstitute itself. Although not the threat that it was, the group remains in being, and could exploit further unrest or governmental weakness in Peru to continue its renewal.

In Italy, the Red Brigades (Brigate Rossi) gradually lapsed into inactivity due to governmental action and a changing political situation. However, a decade after the supposed demise of the Red Brigades, a new group called the Anti-Capitalist Nuclei emerged exhibiting a continuity of symbols, styles of communiqués, and potentially some personnel from the original Red Brigade organization. This ability to perpetuate ideology and symbolism during a significant period of dormancy, and re-emerge under favorable conditions demonstrates the durability of terrorism as a threat to modern societies.

Increasing Capabilities of Terrorists

Terrorists are improving their sophistication and abilities in virtually all aspects of their operations and support. The aggressive use of modern technology for information management, communication and intelligence has increased the efficiency of these activities. Weapons technology has become more increasingly available, and the purchasing power of terrorist organizations is on the rise. The ready availability of both technology and trained personnel to operate it for any client with sufficient cash allows the well-funded terrorist to equal or exceed the sophistication of governmental counter-measures.

Likewise, due to the increase in information outlets, and competition with increasing numbers of other messages, terrorism now requires a greatly increased amount of violence or novelty to attract the attention it requires. The tendency of major media to compete for ratings and the subsequent revenue realized from increases in their audience size and share produces pressures on terrorists to increase the impact and violence of their actions to take advantage of this sensationalism.

Current Styles and Modes

Many styles or modes of terrorism are complicated with spectacular political hype and extremism. While the patterns and common tactics are clouded with confusion, they remain predictable. The following are some of the top modes of terror operations:

- **Bombings**. Formal and improvised devices are used because they are inexpensive to make, relatively easy to conceal, and have far reaching impacts on both lives and property.

- **Kidnapping and Hostage Taking**. This is an emotional tactic on the part of the terrorist, which creates a negative impact on the populous. It creates and maintains media attention and appears to place the political decision on the secondary victims and the government.

- **Hijackings and Skyjackings.** When terrorists seize people, property, vehicles, and airlines, they also create a hostage situation that carries the same impact mentioned above.

- **Other Styles and Modes.** The terrorist conducts a number of other criminal acts involving cyber-terrorism (computers), extortion, and threats to businesses, and mutilations within their own group as punishment. Cyber-terror creates a negative impact to key businesses, communications, and critical infrastructures. Extortion and threats create a powerful underlying current to the business culture with minimal detection. Assaults within the terror group create a dynamic of motivation through fear and solidify a deviant form of loyalty.

The use of biological and chemical terror is a serious threat but remains rare in the area of events that have actually occurred. This style should be on our list of valid concerns and watched carefully as an emerging trend.

Signatures and Rituals

Signatures and rituals related to criminal activity have been present in our history for many years. It is important for the security specialist to understand both the definition of signatures and rituals and their significance in the life of the terrorist.

The definitions of criminal signatures and rituals vary, depending on the resource used. In understanding the signature and ritual, it is important to compare it to the criminal's M.O (*modus operandi*) or *mode of operation*. The M.O. of any crime is simply the style used by the offender(s) in carrying out the criminal act. The mode of operation involves *physical acts necessary to commit the crime, in the mind of the offender.* Signatures and rituals involve performances that *are not* necessary for the completion of the criminal act. Examples of mode of operation (M.O.) include the following:

- Using a pry tool to gain entry to a structure

- Always unhooking an alarm system prior to the act

- Shooting all victims in the chest

- Creating a diversion prior to the act

- Using a primary and secondary bomb to maximize injury and death

- Always selecting a target near a freeway

- Selling stolen property within 24 hours of its theft

- Entering a safe via a cutting torch
- Approaching the scene via bicycle

Signatures and rituals may be necessary behaviors in the mind of the offender but *signatures and rituals are not necessary to commit the physical crime*. Signatures and rituals involve offender behavior that is specific to the wrongdoer or his group and, again, are not necessary for the completion of the crime. Examples of terror signatures and rituals include actions in the following list:

- Beheading of innocents
- Literature left at the scene by offenders
- Dumping bodies in public places
- Wearing specific clothing when committing the act
- Distribution of video and audio tapes by the offender
- Political hype before and after the offense

It is crucial for any investigator to recognize behaviors that are not necessary for the completion of a physical crime. By noting the difference between M.O. and signature-ritual behavior, we may understand both the approach (M.O.) and the internal frame of mind (signature) of the offender.

Common Criminals and Terrorists vs. Copycats and Crusaders

While much of the attention of this text is dedicated to terrorism, uneasiness should exist relating to copycat criminals and crusaders within the United States. *Copycats* are those who, for a number of reasons, copy the behavior of normally visible cases in carrying out other crimes. Copycats take advantage of the fear and camouflage offered through the commission of crimes by others or those crimes in the process of being committed. Crusaders (often copycats) agree with the cause of highly visible criminals and strike out on a crusade of their own.

Why would we be concerned about a copycat-crusader in addition to our standard criminal terrorist? Let's answer this issue with a series of additional questions:

- Who is more dangerous, serial killer Ted Bundy or someone who copies all the killing behaviors of Bundy?
- Who is more treacherous, the Boston Strangler or a group of individuals who emulate the habits of the strangler?
- Which group is more murderous, those following Osama Bin Laden overseas or those copying his philosophy and habits in the United States?

In considering those three questions, one may conclude that they are all equally dangerous. Consider these three additional questions before you draw conclusions. Are they *equally dangerous*? Are they easier to identify? Are they being tracked and investigated the same as the original group of terrorists or criminal?

Investigators and security specialists often minimize the roles of the copycat and the crusader. There are a number of reasons for this decrease in concern but, despite the rationale, we believe that diminished concern is dangerous. Well-placed crusaders can wreak havoc on the security and well being of a community and overall security. A sloppy copycat may thoroughly destroy lives and property at the same levels as the terrorist.

Below is an article published within days of the September 11 attack that illustrates one aspect of the copycat dilemma. Keep in mind that this is just one community out of thousands impacted by this type of behavior:

Case Study: Crisis Situation Brings Local Copycats Out as Police Report 15 Bomb Scares[6]

If you hadn't thought it after learning of Tuesday's terrorist attacks, you might have gotten the word from the bag lady at an Albuquerque Wienerschnitzel.

"It's the end of the world," she screeched Tuesday to startled patrons at the Menaul Boulevard hot dog stand before Albuquerque police were called in to disperse the doomsayer.

Over at a local Walgreens, employees called police to report someone there muttering threats that University of New Mexico students would be the next to die.

Downtown, police searched for a mysterious package in a tunnel between the City-County Building and the Albuquerque Police Department.

Similar searches were undertaken twice at the Hilton Inn at 1901 University Blvd. N.E. Ditto at a Southeast Heights apartment complex.

In all, at least 15 bomb scares were fielded across the city Tuesday, Albuquerque police Sgt. Brian McCutcheon said.

"That's a lot," he said.

None of them amounted to anything, he added.

All were apparently part of the usual flotsam that follows any devastating occurrence.

"You just have everybody, all the copycats, jumping on the bandwagon when maybe all they want is a chance not to go to work," said Capt. Fowler Johnston, who is in charge of communications for the Police Department. "They say, `Hey, I'll just call in a bomb threat, take advantage of the situation.'"

But if there was anything positive in the aftermath of Tuesday's devastating attacks thousands of miles away, it was that at least here in Albuquerque things remained quiet.

"The 911 calls we've received have been few and far between," said Bud Lake, 911 communications manager for Bernalillo County. "It was interesting to see that when some new detail on the terrorist attacks came on the television, the calls would completely cease."

The shutdown of many major attractions, from two of Albuquerque's three largest shopping centers to the State Fair, may have also accounted for the quiet, McCutcheon said.

"I don't think as many people are out as usual," he said.

Dispatchers also received several calls Tuesday morning from citizens wondering whether Albuquerque was safe, Lake said.

"We just told them we had no reason to believe we weren't safe," Lake said. "But they probably should keep watching television."

Consider the number of public safety resources that were diverted from critical duties to address the copycat crimes in the previous article. Even without the presence of actual bombs, lives were endangered and other public safety matters delayed by this type offense.

The main goal of understanding copycats and crusaders is to recognize their presence and the possibility of their impact and role in terror. Once criminal behavior is recognized as being of the copycat or crusader variety, it should be treated seriously and aggressively. This should include full investigation and prosecution if at all possible.

Case Study: "Dirty Bomb" Plot Uncovered, U.S. Says[7]

The following article was published by the *Washington Post* in 2002 and covered a fairly extensive plot by terror suspect Abdullah al Muhajir. Al Muhajir is currently in custody for numerous terror-related charges after conspiring to detonate a radioactive device in the USA. While the presence of another terrorism suspect is not new, the understanding of intelligence gathering practices in this case are critical. After reviewing the *Washington Post*'s account, we will take a closer look at the information and intelligence gathering approaches in a case similar to this.

U.S. authorities announced yesterday that they had broken up a terrorist plot to detonate a radioactive "dirty bomb" in the United States, saying they had arrested a U.S.-born al Qaeda associate who was allegedly scouting targets after learning how to build such a device in Pakistan and Afghanistan.

Abdullah al Muhajir, 31, a former street gang member born in Brooklyn as Jose Padilla, was transferred late Sunday to a naval brig in South Carolina after President Bush designated him an "enemy combatant," according to Attorney General John D. Ashcroft and other U.S. officials.

Al Muhajir had been under surveillance overseas by the CIA and FBI, and was arrested May 8 at O'Hare International Airport in Chicago after arriving on a flight from Pakistan, U.S. officials said. His sudden move to military jurisdiction came less than two days before he was scheduled to appear at a secret hearing in front of a civilian judge, officials said.

An associate involved in the alleged plot had been apprehended by Pakistani authorities along with al Muhajir. The Pakistanis released al Muhajir to allow U.S. investigators to track him on his way to the United States, sources said.

Bush administration officials characterized the case as the most specific plot disrupted by the U.S. government since Sept. 11, when al Qaeda hijackers crashed jetliners into the World Trade Center, the Pentagon and a Pennsylvania field, killing more than 3,000 people.

Al Muhajir is the third person with a claim of U.S. citizenship detained in connection with alleged terrorist activities. John Walker Lindh is charged with conspiring to kill Americans abroad, and Yaser Esam Hamdi, who was born in Louisiana, is being detained in Norfolk as an enemy combatant.

Al Muhajir's alleged plot marks the only terror plan targeted at the United States to come to light since the December arrest of British national Richard C. Reid. He was restrained by passengers on a transatlantic flight after he allegedly attempted to light explosives contained in his shoes.

Still, many senior U.S. officials took pains yesterday to describe the plan as rudimentary and unformed.

"There was not an actual plan," Deputy Defense Secretary Paul D. Wolfowitz said at a news conference yesterday. "We stopped this man in the initial planning stages."

Wolfowitz said that al Muhajir "indicated some knowledge of the Washington, D.C., area," but Wolfowitz and other officials played down early reports that the District was the intended terrorist target.

A spokesman for Mayor Anthony A. Williams (D) said the city received no evidence from a federal joint terrorism task force that al Muhajir was a threat.

Ashcroft, in a Moscow news conference held during a visit to Russia, said al Muhajir's arrest "disrupted an unfolding terrorist plot to attack the United States by exploding a radioactive dirty bomb."

"We know from multiple, independent and corroborating sources that Abdullah al Muhajir was closely associated with al Qaeda and that, as an al Qaeda operative, he was involved in planning future terrorist attacks on innocent American civilians in the United States," Ashcroft said.

Administration officials have come under considerable criticism in recent weeks for mishandling clues to the Sept. 11 attacks. They stressed yesterday that foiling the alleged plot involved substantial cooperation between the FBI, the CIA and other agencies.

A "dirty bomb" is a device that would combine conventional explosives with radioactive material. Although such devices may do limited damage if detonated, they could cause widespread panic, eventual cancers and other health problems, and a cleanup nightmare for authorities, experts said.

Al Muhajir, who had spent several years overseas, had direct contact with al Qaeda lieutenant Abu Zubaida in 2001, and traveled to the Pakistani cities of Lahore and Karachi for research and debriefings on the plan, officials said. Zubaida, who is in U.S. custody overseas, provided the initial hints that led to the alleged plot, sources said.

Sources said al Muhajir had been held since May 8 under the same material witness statute that has been employed frequently since the Sept. 11 terror attacks. It recently has come under attack in federal court.

A Justice Department official said that al Muhajir can be held indefinitely as an enemy soldier under U.S. law, but that there are no plans to attempt to try him before a military tribunal. Such proceedings are not designed for U.S. citizens.

A former Latin Kings gang member in Chicago, al Muhajir served time in juvenile hall in connection with a gang killing and other incidents in Chicago. During a later stay in a Florida prison as an adult, he converted to a militant form of Islam, law enforcement sources said. Officials said he is married to a Middle Eastern woman, identified by one law enforcement source as an Egyptian.

Ashcroft and other administration officials alleged that while he was in Pakistan, al Muhajir researched radiological weapons and methods for wiring explosives. On several occasions in 2001 he met with senior al Qaeda leaders, they said.

In possession of a valid, and therefore valuable, U.S. passport, al Muhajir was sent back to the United States to conduct reconnaissance for the eventual detonation of a dirty bomb, officials said.

The disclosure of al Muhajir's arrest came after several weeks of warnings from Bush administration officials about possible attacks by followers of Osama bin Laden, including May 21 testimony from Defense Secretary Donald H. Rumsfeld that terrorists will "inevitably" obtain weapons of mass destruction.

"We have a man detained who is a threat to the country and . . . thanks to the vigilance of our intelligence-gathering and law enforcement, he is now off the street, where he should be," Bush said yesterday during a photo session in Washington with visiting Israeli Prime Minister Ariel Sharon.

Wolfowitz, at a Washington news conference with Deputy Attorney General Larry Thompson and FBI Director Robert S. Mueller III, said that "our number one priority is to defend the American people from future attacks. To do that, we must root out those who are planning such attacks. We must find them and we must stop them, and when we have them in our control, we must be able to question them about plans for future attacks."

By transferring al Muhajir to the Naval Consolidated Brig in Charleston, S.C., investigators can continue seeking information from him with relatively little interference from a defense attorney, several officials said.

Zubaida, who has emerged as one of the United States' most important sources of information about possible al Qaeda plots, told interrogators about the alleged dirty bomb plan in general terms and did not name individuals, sources said. Al Muhajir and his associate were not considered part of Zubaida's inner circle, officials said.

"He described this guy only generically, probably in a way he didn't expect would lead us to him," one senior official said. "But based on other information we had developed, we were able to track him down."

The CIA provided the principal information that led law enforcement to al Muhajir, sources said. The information included other interrogations and captured documents, but did not involve electronic intercepts or foreign intelligence services, two sources said.

In Pakistan, authorities recently arrested al Muhajir and one other associate, government sources said. Al Muhajir, who was detained for Pakistani immigration violations, was released and tricked into boarding a plane for the United States, where CIA and FBI operatives were watching his movements, several sources said.

"We were fully aware of his movements from the time he left Pakistan," one Justice Department official said. Another official said: "We had eyes on him the entire time."

Al Muhajir made one stop of undisclosed duration in Switzerland before arriving in Chicago on May 8, officials said. "This guy thought he was getting away," one U.S. official said. "He thought he escaped."

Had al Muhajir been kept in custody in Pakistan, the process of extraditing him would have complicated the investigation significantly, one official suggested. By trailing him, investigators could watch for other associates. Officials declined to say yesterday whether anyone met al Muhajir at O'Hare.

At the airport, al Muhajir was first escorted to an examination area used by the U.S. Customs Service, which discovered $10,526 in undeclared currency, Customs officials said. Al Muhajir was interviewed, arrested and turned over to the FBI, officials said.

Al Muhajir was flown to New York under a material witness warrant and incarcerated at the Metropolitan Correctional Center in southern Manhattan, officials said. Prosecutors planned to have al Muhajir testify before a New York grand jury investigating terrorism.

But al Muhajir refused to cooperate, federal officials said.

Prosecutors scrambled to build a case against al Muhajir. Two foreign witnesses, in addition to Zubaida, had provided independent intelligence to U.S. officials about al Muhajir, but it was unclear whether that evidence would be admissible in a criminal proceeding, sources said.

After concluding that building a case would be difficult, prosecutors believed they were running out of time. They faced a secret hearing Tuesday before a judge, officials said, and turned in recent days to another option: transferring him to military custody.

On Sunday, prosecutors dropped the material witness warrant and withdrew a subpoena ordering al Muhajir to testify before the grand jury. After Bush signed a directive naming him as an enemy combatant, U.S. marshals escorted al Muhajir out of jail and turned him over to the military.

How did the FBI, CIA, and other U.S. officials learn of the criminal habits of Abdullah al Muhajir? What were/are their sources of intelligence and information and how did they "properly" gather the information?

It is imperative to understand the general definition of information and intelligence when related to investigations specific to the security field:

> **Information.** Information is any source of unconfirmed data, reliable or unreliable.

> **Intelligence.** Information that has been subjected to tests of reliability, credibility, and all-source analysis. Intelligence is the end result of properly processed information.

Simply stated, information has not been fully tested, analyzed and cannot be considered wholly true. Intelligence is much different. Intelligence is defensible, tested, confirmed in some fashion, is far more reliable, and can often be acted upon. Raw *information* is not reliable but should be given much attention; *intelligence* is information that has been given the proper attention and investigation.

The security specialists must remember that there are a number of conventional and unconventional sources of information available through both research and human sources. In the Al Muhajir case outlined by the *Washington Post*, several of the sources below were likely used during the surveillance and investigation. Here is a list of some available intelligence sources and information suppliers:

U.S. Government Agency Sources

CIA	(Central Intelligence Agency)
FBI	(Federal Bureau of Investigation)
TREASURY	(Treasury Department Office of Intelligence Support)
NSA	(National Security Agency)
DIA	(Defense Intelligence Agency)
NRO	(National Reconnaissance Office)
NGA	(National Geospatial-Intelligence Agency - formerly NIMA)
AFI	(Air Force Intelligence)
AI	(Army Intelligence)
NI	(Naval Intelligence)
MCI	(Marine Corps Intelligence)
STATE	(Department of State, Bureau of Intelligence and Research)
ENERGY	(Department of Energy)
HOMELAND	(intelligence-related components of the Department of Homeland Security)
COASTGUARD	(U.S. Coast Guard Intelligence)

International Agency Sources

ADIO	(Australian Defense Intelligence Organization)
ADSD	(Australian Defense Signals Directorate)
IGIS	(Australian Inspector-General of Intelligence and Security)
ASIS	(Australian Secret Intelligence Service)
ASIO	(Australian Security Intelligence Organization)
ONA	(Australian Office of National Assessments)
PJCAAD	(Parliamentary Joint Committee on the ASIO, ASIS, and DSD)
BFCO	(British Foreign and Commonwealth Office)
MI-5	(British Security Service)
CCSE	(Canadian Communications Security Establishment)
CFIBA	(Canadian Forces Intelligence Branch Association)
	Canadian Intelligence Resource Centre (unofficial)
CSIC	(Canadian Security and Intelligence Community)
CSIS	(Canadian Security Intelligence Service)
	(CSIS Public Reports)
SIRC	(Canadian Security Intelligence Review Committee)
AIVD	(Dutch General Intelligence and Security Service (Algemene Inlichtingen- en Veiligheidsdienst, formerly BVD)
IS	(Intelligence Stratégique - unofficial site in French)
BfV	(German Bundesamt fuer Verfassungsschutz / Counterintel)
BND	(German Bundesnachrichtendienst)
MAD	(German Militärischer Abschirmdienst)
NSO	(Hungarian National Security Office)
SISD	(Italian Intelligence and Democratic Security Service)
GID	(Jordanian General Intelligence Department)
GCSB	(New Zealand Government Communications Security Bureau)
NZ-SONS	(New Zealand: "Securing Our Nation's Safety" 2000)
AW	(Polish Foreign Intelligence Agency) (also in English)
ABW	(Polish Internal Security Agency)
SIS	(Portuguese Security and Information Service)

AGENTURA	(Russian Language Site on Intelligence; some pages in English)
FSB	(Russian Intelligence)
SVR	(Russian Foreign Intelligence)
ANSP	(South Korean Intelligence — unofficial)
CESID	(Spanish Intelligence)
SISD	(Swedish Intelligence and Security Directorate)
MIT	(Turkish National Intelligence Organization)
NIM	(United Kingdom National Intelligence Machinery)
GCHQ	(United Kingdom Government Communications Headquarters)
CESG	(United Kingdom Communications-Electronics Security Group)

Other Sources

News articles
News interviews
School papers
Police informants (those charged with a crime and those not charged)
Court and hearing documents
Minutes from meetings
Video-taped meetings
Protests
Newspaper articles
Tattle tales
Those with revenge in mind
Reporters
Radical speeches
Business owners
Civic group leaders
Church members
Fellow students
Groups and associations
Ex-wives
Ex-husbands
Ex-boyfriends
Ex-girlfriends
Angry neighbors
Waiters/waitresses
Postal carriers
Any other source

THE BEHAVIORAL CUES ANALYSIS OF TERROR TOOLS AND TECHNIQUES

Terror tools, techniques, and technologies of terror are broad and the intelligence sources and information regarding them number in the thousands. As we examine the issues addressed in this chapter, we must revisit our basic tools. At this point we will filter our conclusions through an exercise using the six concepts of behavioral.

Referring back to the article above that outlined the "dirty bomb plot" involving Abdullah al Muhajir, apply the six concepts in assessing how you could have detected his conspiracy:

Concept 1: *Every assault or attack happens at least twice; once in the mind and again upon its execution.*

What cues were detectable that would have allowed you to predict Abdullah al Muhajir's future behavior? How would you know what was possibly developing in his mind? What indicators pointed toward an attack developing in his mind?

Concept 2: *Energy follows thought.*

Based upon the evidence of Abdullah al Muhajir's thoughts, was his energy (actions) predictable? Why? What physical evidence of his thoughts do you think existed for investigators? What tools and equipment did he need to collect, for his energy to match his thoughts? Where would he have to go to gather this information and the tools needed? Why?

Concept 3: *Every offender must have <u>opportunity</u> and <u>desire</u> to complete an act.*

In applying this concept to Abdullah al Muhajir, consider his opportunity to plant a dirty bomb rather than his desire. What target in your community would be considered for such an act? What opportunity exists that would allow such an act? Why? If Abdullah al Muhajir was "shopping" for a target, why would he select yours?

Concept 4: *Most offenders prefer a cloak of secrecy.*

What likely attempts were used by Abdullah al Muhajir to hide behind a cloak of secrecy as he conspired to commit this act? What created a challenge to his secrecy? Why? What tactics did investigators use to expose his secrecy?

Concept 5: *Know thyself and know thy enemy.*

What weaknesses do you have that would have created barriers in investigating Abdullah al Muhajir? Why? What would prevent you from acknowledging these weaknesses? What would/could you do to overcome these weaknesses?

Concept 6: *Unconventional criminals require unconventional strategies.*

From an investigative standpoint, what is possibly unconventional in the case involving Abdullah al Muhajir? What unconventional strategies could you use in protecting your target from an offender like him?

COMMON CHARACTERISTICS OF A SUCCESSFUL THREAT ASSESSMENT

To understand security best practices and their contrast, the security practitioner should understand the common traits of a quality risk assessment and the supporting policies and behaviors. The common characteristics of a quality threat assessment and the supporting documentation and actions include the following:

- Developing a risk-management team (employees, community, and government)
- Completing a written policy
- Developing a common language of risk and security
- Defining the term "emergency"
- Balancing customer service/profit/security measures
- Developing/implementing a threat assessment format
- Conducting/completing a thorough threat / risk assessment
- Training and testing the policy
- Training and testing the threat risk assessment
- Developing risk reduction actions
- Re-inspection of risk reduction actions
- Periodic safety meetings and assessments
- Rewarding and recognizing best practices
- Quarterly re-assessments and threat analysis (minimal)

HISTORICAL RISK APPLICATIONS THAT FAIL

The most elementary approach to understand how security plans and threat assessments fail is to invert the accounting cited above (i.e., failure to complete a written policy, failure to conduct the assessment, failure to re-inspect, failure to have safety meetings, overemphasis on customer service rather than security, etc.). Another important tactic in examining security failures is to scrutinize present-day cases where security remains a challenge or subject of criticism. The article below, from *USA Today*, addresses a fairly controversial topic in the travel industry—airline cargo screening and security.

After infusing yourself with the best practices listed above, read this article with a critical operational view:

Case Study: TSA Slow to Act on Cargo Security, Some Say[8]

The report reads like a roadmap to terror. Step by step, it plays out "threat scenarios" of how to get a bomb aboard the belly of a jet.

It even outlines how terrorists could target a flight, stand in the terminal and watch it take off before detonating the bomb that they planted.

Titled "Air Cargo Threat Assessment," the confidential report covers cargo placed aboard passenger flights. It was issued by the Federal Aviation Administration just a month after Sept. 11.

Despite the warnings, government sources familiar with cargo security say, the new Transportation Security Administration has failed to address many weaknesses detailed in the report.

> A TSA working group continues to study possible solutions, and agency spokeswoman Mari Eder insists the issue is important. "Everything that has been learned from that report and subsequent reports issued, we're going to be working on," she says.

But a progress report the agency sent to Congress last week offers few specifics. Under the heading "Cargo" in the report, it lists TSA accomplishments as "clarification regarding national policy and threat assessment requirements; working closely to leverage existing expertise; building relationships with private industry to learn about existing measures and procedures specific to cargo security."

Little, if any, cargo placed aboard passenger jets is screened like a traveler's luggage would be. Since Sept. 11, federal officials have instead relied on the honesty of "known shippers" — primarily companies that have track records with the government dating to at least Sept. 1, 1999.

Some of those shippers work directly with airlines. Others work through companies called "indirect air carriers" or "freight forwarders" — companies that buy space from airlines and resell that space to companies that want to ship. Forwarders then consolidate shipments from a number of companies, pack the goods together and deliver them to an airline ready for shipment.

The government simply trusts that the shipments don't contain explosives.

About 4,000 freight forwarders do business nationally, according to The International Air Cargo Association, a trade group that represents forwarders, shippers, airlines and airports. "A lot of them are mom-and-pop, one or two people businesses," says Daniel Fernandez, secretary general of the trade group. "But I don't think anyone knows how many are out there."

The report also raises concerns about who might work for cargo shippers. It warns: "this threat cannot be ignored and in fact may very well represent the greatest threat to air cargo security.'

Even so, a TSA source with knowledge of cargo security says the agency is disregarding the issue by failing to order forwarders to conduct background checks on their employees.

The lack of action by the agency frustrates some security advocates. "They are approaching aviation security the way a layman would — all the focus is on what's visible, and visible is the checkpoint," says Bob Monetti, whose son was killed when a bomb planted by terrorists brought down Pan Am Flight 103 over Scotland in 1988.

Fernandez says the threat from cargo is overstated. "Aren't we putting a lot of emphasis on things that had nothing to do with Sept. 11?" he asks. "We're trying to make things 100% safe. But you can't make it 100% safe without stopping the flow of commerce." But Monetti says few thought terrorists would use jets as missiles. "Like hijacking a plane and flying it into a building, putting a bomb into the cargo system hasn't been done yet. It hasn't reached Congress' attention," he says.

Indeed, the Aviation and Transportation Security Act calls for the TSA to "provide for the screening of all passengers and property, including cargo" that goes aboard a passenger plane. But the act does not give a deadline for such screening.

Rep. John Mica, R-Fla., chairman of the House aviation subcommittee, concedes lawmakers haven't pushed hard on the issue, but that shouldn't stop TSA from acting. "We put authority (in the act) to cover all of the cargo security, but TSA has to pass the rules and put some of these measures in place," he says. "I'm afraid there are still big gaps."[9]

Best Practices for Threat Assessment

When it comes to this story about security measures in mass transportation cargo and many other accounts like it, we know there is no doubt that several of the best practices listed prior to the article are in place. But which of the best practices are in place and which are evolving? Review a recreated list of best-threat assessment practices; check off and discuss those items you believe to be sound practices a) which are in place; and b) which are likely a challenge to the security of this industry?

Cargo-security practices transportation officials have or have not implemented. Why?

- Developed a risk management team (employees, community, and government)
- Completed a written policy
- Developed a common language of risk and security
- Defined the term "emergency"
- Balancing customer service/profit/security measures
- Developed/implemented a threat assessment format
- Conducted/completed a thorough threat/risk assessment

- Trained and tested the policy

- Trained and tested the threat/risk assessment

- Developed risk reduction actions

- Re-inspected risk reduction actions

- Conducted periodic safety meetings and assessments

- Rewarding and recognizing best practices

What did you conclude? Do transportation officials have a plan? Do they inspect and re-inspect? Do they have periodic safety meetings related to the cargo? Do they reward safety? Do they have a working definition for "emergency"? The answers to these questions are likely "yes, transportation officials have implemented these."

But when we ask if they have *tested their risk practices* we may have another answer. And what about *balancing their customer service and profit with security measures?* Once again, we may have to answer this with a difficult truth. The last point, *balancing customer service and profit with security measures*, has become one of the most contentious and hotly debated issues inside transportation security circles. We challenge you to look for potential answers for this apparent contradiction in these terms: Are security and service mutually inclusive? Is transportation operationally safe and profitable? Is it both free of terrorist risk and quick in the loading and unloading of passengers and cargo? Can we have maximum safety and maximum customer service and appropriate profit all within the same world of mass transportation? The discussion will continue as the enemy, threat assessments, and security countermeasures continue to dare our creativity.

MORE ON "OLD, OUTDATED, SECURITY APPLICATIONS"

During the recent history of terrorism there have been many security applications that seemingly failed, but perhaps didn't stop working at all. It is always a possibility that the tactics of the criminal element (terrorists) outgrew the original threat assessment and related security countermeasures. While intelligence remains a debated issue, what many security practitioners knew and practiced at the time of their target's attack was up to date by their standards; yet, their standards had grown outdated by the tactics and creativity of the offender. This becomes one of the more important reasons to stay extremely well connected in the area of terrorism/criminal trends and intelligence and then adjust accordingly. The unconventional and suicidal nature of the terrorist also begs for a more frequent assessment inspection process and continuous updating of countermeasures. Remember our key concept, "unconventional criminals call for unconventional strategies." Increasing the frequency of inspections, training, mock scenarios, and updating the common language are all examples of unconventional security practices.

Many tragic examples point out that threat assessments completed in 1993 may have been inferior for events as they happened in 1994 and 1995. In the year 2000, we were arguably not prepared for some of the tactics used in the terror attacks of 2001. Most, with regard to the USS Cole when she was attacked, wouldn't have considered a piloted suicide-boat driving into the side of a military vessel as having any success. In spite of that, this is exactly what happened. Whether we are considering the tactics used in the Oklahoma City bombing, the bombing of the USS Cole, the delivery of Anthrax via the postal system, or gas poisoning an entire subway system, we must understand the reality that some tactics will potentially advance beyond our current security plans and assessments. We may only reduce this possibility by awareness and constant vigilance to the best practices outlined above....

In an attempt to understand the success of terrorism in its present state, we will look at some of the organizational tactics used by UBL over the past several years. By examining the organizational accomplishments of this criminal enterprise we may better prepare our response. The excerpts below, gleaned from some of the teachings of George Washington University, scrutinize the success of the UBL model.

Case Study: Al-Qaeda as a System: The Five-Ring Model[10]

At least since world war two, military planners have understood the value of describing their enemies as systems (Rinaldi, 1996). The most successful application of such a view occurred in the air campaign of Desert Storm (Reynolds, 1995; Mann, 1995). In designing that campaign, Air Force Colonel John Warden developed a systems model of warfare that is still in vogue among military planners today (Rinaldi, 1996). Figure 4.1 shows the "five-ring model" that Warden maintains can be used to represent any type of organization that operates autonomously, whether it be a human body, a drug cartel, an electrical grid, a terrorist organization, or an enemy nation (Warden, 1995).

The "five-ring model" provides a simplified picture of al-Qaeda as a system. In the first ring, Usama bin Laden is the most widely recognized leader of the al-Qaeda organization (Alexander & Swetnam, 2001; Bergen, 2001). In fact, before the notoriety of the September 11 attacks, al-Qaeda was rarely mentioned in name and referred to simply as "the bin Laden network" (Arquilla, Ronfeldt, & Zanini, 1999). He is supported by a loose command and control structure, which includes a *maijlis al shura* (consultation council) that considers, discusses, and approves major policies and actions (Alexander & Swetnam, 2001). The group also has a military committee that considers and approves terrorist actions; a business committee that oversees al-Qaeda front businesses and financial matters; a *fatwah* or religious committee that deliberates religious rulings; a media committee that prints information and interfaces with foreign news organizations; and even a travel office (DoS, 2001b). Within this defined committee structure, the leadership provides broad policy guidance and allows a high-degree of autonomy to its affiliated sub-organizations. Leadership functions are well-dispersed and key individuals difficult to identify and easily

Figure 4.1 The Enemy as a System (Warden, 1995)

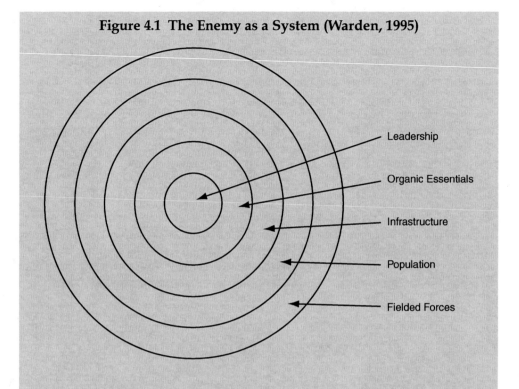

Leadership

Organic Essentials

Infrastructure

Population

Fielded Forces

replaced (Callard, 2001). This flat structure, without rigid command and control, makes al-Qaeda highly resilient to attacks against its leadership (Reeve, 1999; Callard, 2001). Simply removing bin Laden from the organization would likely have little effect on its operational capability (Byman & Pollack, 2001).

Organic essentials (the second ring) include finances, safe haven from state sponsors, and religious support. Al-Qaeda's financial support comes from bin Laden's personal family fortune estimated to be $270-$300 million; an extensive business organization with companies dealing in finance, construction, and agriculture; and contributions from sympathetic Islamic nations, businesses, and charitable organizations (Alexander & Swetnam, 2001, p. 29; DoS, 2001e). Safe haven and other material support are provided by friendly governments in Afghanistan, Somalia, Sudan and other locations (Reeve, 1999). Finally, al-Qaeda and other Islamic terrorist organizations are sustained by ideological support of religious clerics and mullahs, which gives them legitimacy among the population (Stern, 1999).

An amorphous, ill-defined infrastructure (third ring) gives al-Qaeda an adaptive capability (Lesser et al., 1999). Bergen (2001) describes al-Qaeda as a sort of multi-national holding company, headquartered in Afghanistan, under the chairmanship of bin Laden, with subsidiary militant organizations in Egypt, Pakistan, Bangladesh, Algeria, Libya, Yemen, Syria, Kashmir—and links to cells in over 55 countries worldwide (Alexander & Swetnam, 2001). This network provides a high degree of structural autonomy (Burt, 1992) and enhances survivability. The population of the fourth ring consists of thousands of young militant volunteers providing support through recruiting, training, and resources (Bergen, 2001). A blurred line of distinction between the terrorists themselves and the population within which they operate is a unique characteristic of terrorist organizations (Callard, 2001). At al-Qaeda's front lines are the terrorists themselves (fifth ring), well-educated, worldly, clandestine, and willing to die for their cause (Finn, 2001). Among individual terrorists, ad hoc groups can be formed quickly, need no headquarters, and have no recognized leaders; making them more difficult to track and apprehend (Stern, 1999).

While Warden's "five-ring model" provides a useful snapshot of the al-Qaeda organization, it has a number of drawbacks. First, it does not capture the fluid and dynamic structure of the terrorist organization (Callard, 2001). More specifically, it does not address the dynamic interchanges that occur among elements of the system. Second, this model has an inherent bias to hierarchical structures and does not adequately deal with diffused networked systems (Rinaldi, 1996). Finally, Warden's model assumes layered communication between and across various levels of the systems (Rinaldi, 1996). The loosely coupled nature of the various groups in the al-Qaeda conglomerate are not linearly tied to a single command and control structure (Callard, 2001). To address these flaws, a more dynamic model is required to describe al-Qaeda's actions over time.[11]

The five-ring model illustrates some of the reasons Bin Laden and the Al Qaeda movement are successful. Adaptive capabilities, oversight committees, financial infrastructure, a "die-for" cause, and a deviant form of "humanizing one's self" are just some of the success concepts found in his accomplishments. But the organization has flaws and one of the best approaches in examining those flaws includes knowing their approach to success. The competent security specialist will avoid simply looking at the weaknesses of the adversary—a conventional crime prevention approach. We must look at both how they obtain their goals and the weaknesses in their approach.

Weaknesses of UBL's Group Model

It is the opinion of the author that one of the primary weaknesses of UBL is found in his assessment of America as a target. UBL and his leadership team looked primarily at the weaknesses of America and discarded many of our strengths—a serious error in their own tactical planning. UBL exploited many of America's freedoms in carrying out his attacks to include our freedoms of travel, education, immigration, political speech, and communication. By focusing on our weaknesses he apparently failed to examine and respect our own ability to adapt, overcome, pursue, financially support a cause, and make infrastructure corrections. Don't misunderstand this as an editorial on UBL's simplicity as a combat target; this is as far from the truth as the task of minimizing terror is arduous and costly.

UBL has undoubtedly forced unexpected changes to America and her perspective on freedom. He also has mandated the unleashing of a force that was arguably underestimated—the force of her strength, resolve, and character. America's will has become his greatest challenge as he produces plans and videos from the hidden caves of an unknown country. America's tenacity and motivation have historically been underrated until times of crisis and UBL has released this force—probably the utmost strategic error on his part. How do we conclude that he underestimated our response? How do we know that his group model is no longer as valuable? The conclusion is found in his current procedures and through the tactical changes being forced, apparently by the radical response. His group's behavior since September 11, 2001, has been increasingly fragmented, sporadically successful, full of tactical mistakes, and sloppy.

UBL has been forced to make changes within his group that have led to several tactical mistakes on their part. One of the clearest arguments illustrating UBL weakness and vulnerability is found in the fact that despite numerous attempts during the three years after 9/11, he and his operatives have been unsuccessful in further terrorist attacks in the American homeland.

Here are some indicators that the UBL Group Model has weakened:

- Hundreds of arrests have been made in the homeland
- Several Al Qaeda-based operatives have become informants
- Financial centers of terror have been interrupted
- Numerous explosive materials have seized in the homeland
- Attack plans targeting America have been breached
- Recruitment efforts have flowed outside of the Al Qaeda group
- Al Qaeda has tried "twin tower" style attacks in another country and failed
- UBL attempts to manipulate a U.S. election (how does this show weakness?)
- UBL leadership remains in hiding
- Violent reaction to the possibility of a democracy (how does this show weakness?)

These are not the manifestations of a successful group model. The failures and intentional modifications by Bin Laden indicate quite the opposite. Symptoms of a weakening group model are suspected when they are forced to change recruitment tactics, try to continually repeat the same style of attack and fail, get arrested, have individuals turn informant, have plans interrupted, and have to geographically move repeatedly. In simplified terms, what always worked successfully for the Al Qaeda Group Model is no longer so lucrative.

Below is a quote from one of the current leaders within Iraq. Abd-al 'Aziz al-Hakim is leader of the Supreme Council for the Islamic Revolution in Iraq, one of the country's main Shiite parties, founded in 1982. This quote quantifies a public stance of which Al Qaeda forces are very concerned: a stance that indicates yet another force that may further fragment the group model of UBL:

"The security situation indeed remains the prime concern of Iraq and the Iraqi people. The government is attacking this problem by trying to build a new security apparatus on solid bases. From this viewpoint our greatest victory over terrorism has been to have ensured that the transfer of sovereignty took place as envisaged. This sovereignty opens up the prospect of an Iraqi State free to define its own policy. The Prime Minister has also started a tour of neighboring countries to secure their help in border control. The new Iraqi police force is starting to act, and its work is having positive effects. Security will improve because, day by day, the population's awareness is changing, and terrorists are losing support. The Iraqis want stability in order to be able to rebuild their country and their lives."[12]

APPLICATIONS OF A PROACTIVE TERROR THREAT ASSESSMENT

Security specialists may adapt and apply the formal threat assessment from a number of different perspectives. While you may choose one of the options outlined below, we recommend that you balance your effective approach by periodically applying all four approaches. Again, we highly recommend conducting some form of formal threat assessment application every quarter (every three months) as a minimum standard of practice. Clearly, the first series of assessments will be the most critical and often difficult to complete. The main point to remember is that any form of threat/risk assessment is better than the alternative of no threat assessment. The four approaches we will briefly discuss in this section are as follows:

- The Living-Risk Assessment

- The Standard Quarterly Risk Assessment

- The Global Attention Risk Assessment

- The Trend-Based Risk Assessment

The Living-Risk Assessment

The living-risk assessment is similar to any other living document or fluid project. A living risk assessment is growing, evolving, changing, and alive; the living-risk assessment is an attitude as well as a process. When the proficient security practitioner applies the living risk assessment, s/he is approaching the inspection and assessment from a perspective of openness and a willingness to adjust. The contrast of this would be simply repeating the inspection process over and over again without flexibility and attention to change—a fatal and flawed application. When using the "living" approach the assessor is reminded to take in new structural conditions, new employees, adjusted hours of operation, new delivery vendors, new policies, changes in daylight hours, new leaders, and so forth. The living assessment involves using a new, fresh set of eyes during the assessment, possibly a security specialist who has never done the assessment working along side of someone who has. By applying the "living assessment" concept, we may reduce stagnation and avoid mistakes.

The Standard Quarterly Risk Assessment

This assessment, conducted at least every three months, involves all basic infrastructure examinations to include, fire safety, building access, location of rally points for evacuation, trauma care availability, decontamination availability, ventilation issues, access locks, fencing, wear and tear issues, crime prevention technology, and lighting quality. Standard inspections always include a check of assessment telephone numbers to ensure they're still operational, critical and notable cues of danger, flood and other alarms, environmental design concerns, and general employee knowledge. The standard quarterly assessment always involves a meeting with upper management to ensure that they are up to date with the process and concerns.

The Global Attention Risk Assessment

The global risk assessment involves going beyond the structure or item(s) being assessed. Contacting local fire and emergency services, speaking with local police for updates or suggestions, meeting with neighboring businesses to ensure that they know the potential impacts in the event of disaster or disturbance and inviting key stakeholders and emergency workers to tour your target. The global attitude is important for both relations outside of your target and to enhance your own awareness.

The Trend-Based Risk Assessment

The trend-based risk assessment involves taking a critical and in-depth look at the local, regional, national, and worldwide trends of attack or disturbance that have occurred recently. This assessment calls for comparing those incidents with countermeasures in place or countermeasures needed in relation to your target.

Remember: highly publicized incidents of attack or disturbance may affect your target and awareness may be curative. Knowing the trends of attack and disturbance remains an important task for any effective security specialist.

Application of the Four Assessments

The four previous assessment approaches may be applied by a single team of security specialists or split into smaller tasks conducted by a greater number of inspectors. The main thrust of understanding the four assessment approaches is to broaden the perspective of the assessors and to enhance the quality of the risk assessment. If all four are periodically applied, minimizing vulnerability is all but guaranteed.

POST INCIDENT ASSESSMENTS, EVALUATIONS, AND MISSED CUES

A quality security operation would be lax if it did not address one of the most difficult assignments of the competent security practitioner: assessing what happened after an attack or disturbance. This is a step in emergency operations that is easily avoided, dismissed, and/or minimized. It involves a critical look at what went well during the incident, what went wrong, why it went wrong, and what improvements may be addressed in the short-term and long-term. One may easily see why this is overlooked or intentionally avoided; it is painful and rife with the risk of finger pointing. Despite the discomfort of a post incident critique, it the author's opinion that it is not optional. Any holistic emergency and security plan will involve a post-incident evaluation and it is usually the professional security specialist that must pursue its facilitation. Post-incident assessment evaluations are not an addition to our "best practices;" they are part of the completed process.

Post-incident evaluations and assessments are a series of professional and healthy questions that must be addressed. The critique should be conducted as a group and completed behind closed doors. *If public meetings are going to be held to discuss the matter, they should only be facilitated after the private critique has been completed.* The process is most effectively pursued and completed through the examination of four main categories and questions:

Post-Incident Assessment and Critique Dimensions

- **What worked well throughout the attack or disturbance?**
- **What did not work well throughout the attack or disturbance?**
- **What improvements are needed?**
- **What did we learn?**

Applying the behavioral and environmental cues model during this analysis is an effective approach in answering the questions. Some additional questions to ask may include the following:

- What cues did we note and address that improved our reaction and response to this incident?
- What security preparations worked?
- What cues or vulnerabilities did we apparently miss?
- What cues do we now need to look for and integrate into our security awareness plan?
- Did our security plan counter the mental template of our offender(s) in any way? How?

- What did we learn about the mental template of this/these offender(s)?

- Are our physical security elements adequate?

- How did secrecy play into the offender's hands?

- Was this predictable? How? Why?

- How did we respond to the injured?

- Do we need more work with our outside responders?

- What worked well with the outside responders?

- What lessons have we learned?

- Where and how may we improve?

These are just a few questions that may address the four questions in our post-incident assessment. If a post-incident assessment/evaluation is conducted professionally through the use of effective questions one may avoid personal attacks. This is not a time to discuss who was wrong, or who failed to act during the disturbance or attack. Those types of issues should be addressed privately as a personnel matter. It is a time to discuss security principles and behavioral cues and not personalities. If the facilitator stays focused on principles rather than personalities and individual mistakes, success is probable and learning unavoidable. Once again, any post incident evaluation is better than none at all.

SUMMARY

The DHS has identified 17 sections that make up critical infrastructure and key resources (CIKR). They include a variety of essential systems and resources, such as water, energy, transportation systems, and public health.

CIKR must be actively guarded against terrorist attacks, because attacks against these assets can disrupt the whole nation if successfully conducted. Terrorists continuously search for new ways to threaten us and plan attacks. Accordingly, the methods used to deter and prevent their actions also have to be continuously updated and improved. Tools like behavioral profiling must be fairly evaluated and developed to be made effective tools for protecting lives and property from terrorist attacks without sacrificing civil liberties.

ADDITIONAL DISCUSSION TOPICS

- Why would a professional association be motivated to lobby the government for security standards?

- What is the benefit to the US citizen of professional security organizations partnering with the government?

- How is behavioral profiling different than racial profiling? Is it a legitimate tool, or a threat to civil liberties?

- Why do you think that terrorist organizations seem so much more adaptive and flexible than the government security forces fighting them?

- What are the three traits of a failed security assessment?

- What are the dimensions of the "five-ring" group model? What are its strengths and weaknesses?

Endnotes

[1] Source: Compiled from the National Strategy for the Physical Protection of Critical Infrastructures and Key Assets: http://www.dhs.gov/interweb/assetlibrary/Physical_Strategy.pdf

[2] The Arizona Republic (February 16, 2005): http://www.azcentral.com/arizonerepublic/local/articles/0216water16.html

[3] http://www.accnewsmedia.com

[4] Source: http://www.dhs.gov/interweb/assetlibrary/Physical

[5] Compiled through Web-based services, www.Terrorism-Research.com

[6] Compiled from the archives of *Albuquerque Tribune*, New Mexico, 2000. Article by Joline Gutierrez Krueger, *Tribune* reporter.

[7] "'Dirty Bomb' Plot Uncovered, U.S. Says," by Dan Eggen and Susan Schmidt, *Washington Post* (Tuesday, June 11, 2002). Staff writers Steve Fainaru, Barton Gellman and Colum Lynch in New York; Spencer S. Hsu and Bill Miller, research editor Margot Williams and researcher Lynn Davis in Washington contributed to this report.

[8] *USA Today*, Blake Morrison, 2004.

[9] *USA Today*, Blake Morrison, 2004

[10] *Al-Qaeda, A Systems Approach*, Chuck Lutes for George Washington University, 2001.

[11] *Al-Qaeda, A Systems Approach*, Chuck Lutes for George Washington University, 2001

[12] Liberation (www.carebridge.org) translated from French, July 26, 2004.

CHAPTER FIVE

CYBER TERRORISM

Systems are complex, so controlling an attack and achieving a desired level of damage may be harder than using physical weapons.
—Dorothy Denning, U.S. information security researcher and Professor at the Naval Postgraduate School

The Constitution is never tested during times of tranquility; it is during times of tension, turmoil, tragedy, trauma, and terrorism that it is sorely tested.
—Mike Honda, Congressman (D-Ca)

The war we are fighting today against terrorism is a multifaceted fight. We have to use every tool in our toolkit to wage this war —diplomacy, finance, intelligence, law enforcement, and of course, military power—and we are developing new tools as we go along.
—Richard Armitage US Deputy Secretary of State

KEY TERMS

Cyber-terrorism
Cyberspace
Network security
Encryption
Steganography

OBJECTIVES

- Describe ways in which cyber terrorists use technology.

- Discuss the negative consequences of cyber terrorism.

- Identify the tools used by cyber terrorists.

- Describe the difference between cyber crime and cyber terrorism.

- Examine measures to identify and remedy cyber vulnerabilities.

DISCUSSION TOPICS

- How can a useful and innocuous feature like a free Yahoo! email account become a nearly untraceable means of terrorist communication?

- How can cyber-terrorism and physical terrorism be complimentary tactics?

- Where does the line between privacy and security lay? Should that line move as world events change?

- Do you know the information security policies at your school or place of work? How closely do users follow those policies?

5

INTRODUCTION

It is a clichéd phrase that "information is power," but that has never been truer, now that information can travel so quickly and anonymously. This information could be an email that details plans for a physical attack, or those plans could be stored on a stack of disks removed from a garbage can outside an industrial center. Yet, the information does not need to be correct to be powerful—and misinformation covertly added to a network at the right time could cause faulty decision making with terrible consequences, or sent to wrongly convince an automated electrical switching computer that a failure state has been reached and it must shut down.

Technologies have always been two-edged, and misuse is always a potential. The benefits derived from computer technology and widespread networking are too great to abandon. Efforts to secure this resource for proper use and protecting the privacy rights of authorized users, while keeping misuse from occurring, is one of today's greatest security challenges.

THE LAST FRONTIER

The Internet is like the Wild West—full of risks and opportunities, and good guys and bad guys. Protecting and monitoring the Internet is impossible due to the broad expanse of users crossing political and legal boundaries, the volume of communication, and the breakneck speed of technological development.

There are physical security protection risks as well as threats to the software and cyber-elements.

The security specialist must make efforts to educate users to threats and vulnerabilities and to minimize risks, while staying abreast of advances in technology that occur on literally an hourly basis.

The reader will find a plethora of articles about cyber security and terrorism, but the more one learns, the more apparent the vulnerabilities become.

Our first article is a presidential call to action to form a response to the threats to our cyber-tech infrastructure.

CYBERSPACE THREATS AND VULNERABILITIES:[1]
A CASE FOR ACTION

The terrorist attacks against the United States that took place on September 11, 2001, had a profound impact on our Nation. The federal government and society as a whole have been forced to reexamine conceptions of security on our home soil, with many understanding only for the first time the lengths to which self-designated enemies of our country are willing to go to inflict debilitating damage.

We must move forward with the understanding that there are enemies who seek to inflict damage on our way of life. They are ready to attack us on our own soil, and they have shown a willingness to use unconventional means to execute those attacks. While the attacks of September 11 were physical attacks, we are facing increasing threats from hostile adversaries in the realm of cyberspace as well.

A Nation Now Fully Dependent on Cyberspace

For the United States, the information technology revolution quietly changed the way business and government operates. Without a great deal of thought about security, the Nation shifted the control of essential processes in manufacturing, utilities, banking, and communications to networked computers. As a result, the cost of doing business dropped and productivity skyrocketed. The trend toward greater use of networked systems continues.

By 2003, our economy and national security became fully dependent upon information technology and the information infrastructure. A network of networks directly supports the operation of all sectors of our economy—energy (electric power, oil and gas), transportation (rail, air, merchant marine), finance and banking, information and telecommunications, public health, emergency services, water, chemical, defense industrial base, food, agriculture, and postal and shipping. The reach of these computer networks exceeds the bounds of cyberspace. They also control physical objects such as electrical transformers, trains, pipeline pumps, chemical vats, and radars.

Threats in Cyberspace

A spectrum of malicious actors can and do conduct attacks against our critical information infrastructures. Of primary concern is the threat of organized cyber attacks capable of causing debilitating disruption to our Nation's critical infrastructures, economy, or national security. The required technical sophistication to carry out such an attack is high—and partially explains the lack of a debilitating attack to date. We should not, however, be too sanguine. There have been instances where attackers have exploited vulnerabilities that may be indicative of more destructive capabilities.

Uncertainties exist as to the intent and full technical capabilities of several observed attacks. Enhanced cyber threat analysis is needed to address long-term trends related to threats and vulnerabilities. What is known is that the attack tools and methodologies are becoming widely available, and the technical capability and sophistication of users bent on causing havoc or disruption is improving.

As an example, consider the "NIMDA" ("ADMIN" spelled backwards) attack. Despite the fact that NIMDA did not create a catastrophic disruption to the critical infrastructure, it is a good example of the increased technical sophistication showing up in cyber attacks. It demonstrated that the arsenal of weapons available to organized attackers now contains the capability to learn and adapt to its local environment. NIMDA was an automated cyber attack, a blend of a computer worm and a computer virus. It propagated across the Nation with enormous speed and tried several different ways to infect computer systems it invaded until it gained access and destroyed files. It went from nonexistent to nationwide in an hour, lasted for days, and attacked 86,000 computers.

Speed is also increasing. Consider that two months before NIMDA, a cyber attack called Code Red infected 150,000 computer systems in 14 hours.

Because of the increasing sophistication of computer attack tools, an increasing number of actors are capable of launching nationally significant assaults against our infrastructures and cyberspace. In peacetime America's enemies may conduct espionage on our Government, university research centers, and private companies. They may also seek to prepare for cyber strikes during a confrontation by mapping U.S. information systems, identifying key targets, lacing our infrastructure with back doors and other means of access. In wartime or crisis, adversaries may seek to intimidate the nation's political leaders by attacking critical infrastructures and key economic functions or eroding public confidence in information systems.

Cyber attacks on U.S. information networks can have serious consequences such as disrupting critical operations, causing loss of revenue and intellectual property, or loss of life. Countering such attacks requires the development of robust capabilities where they do not exist today if we are to reduce vulnerabilities and deter those with the capabilities and intent to harm our critical infrastructures.

Cyberspace provides a means for organized attack on our infrastructure from a distance. These attacks require only commodity technology, and enable attackers to obfuscate their identities, locations, and paths of entry. Not only does cyberspace provide the ability to exploit weaknesses in our critical infrastructures, but it also provides a fulcrum for leveraging physical attacks by allowing the possibility of disrupting communications, hindering U.S. defensive or offensive response, or delaying emergency responders who would be essential following a physical attack.

In the last century, geographic isolation helped protect the United States from a direct physical invasion. In cyberspace national boundaries have little meaning. Information flows continuously and seamlessly across political, ethnic, and religious divides. Even the infrastructure that makes up cyberspace—software and hardware—is global in its design and development. Because of the global nature of cyberspace, the vulnerabilities that exist are open to the world and available to anyone, anywhere, with sufficient capability to exploit them.

Reduce Vulnerabilities in the Absence of Known Threats

While the Nation's critical infrastructures must, of course, deal with specific threats as they arise, waiting to learn of an imminent attack before addressing important critical infrastructure vulnerabilities is a risky and unacceptable strategy. Cyber attacks can burst onto the Nation's networks with little or no warning and spread so fast that many victims never have a chance to hear the alarms. Even with forewarning, they likely would not have had the time, knowledge, or tools needed to protect themselves. In some cases creating defenses against these attacks would have taken days.

A key lesson derived from these and other such cyber attacks is that organizations that rely on networked computer systems must take proactive steps to identify and remedy their vulnerabilities, rather than waiting for an attacker to be stopped or until alerted of an impending attack. Vulnerability assessment and remediation activities must be ongoing. An information technology security audit conducted by trained professionals to identify infrastructure vulnerabilities can take months. Subsequently, the process of creating a multilayered defense and a resilient network to remedy the most serious vulnerabilities could take several additional months. The process must then be regularly repeated.

Threat and Vulnerability: A Five-Level Problem

Managing threat and reducing vulnerability in cyberspace is a particularly complex challenge because of the number and range of different types of users. Cyberspace security requires action on multiple levels and by a diverse group of actors because literally hundreds of millions of devices are interconnected by a network of networks. The problem of cyberspace security can be best addressed on five levels.

Level 1, the Home User/Small Business

Though not a part of a critical infrastructure the computers of home users can become part of networks of remotely controlled machines that are then used to attack critical infrastructures. Undefended home and small business computers, particularly those using digital subscriber line (DSL) or cable connections, are vulnerable to attackers who can employ the use of those machines without the owner's knowledge. Groups of such "zombie" machines can then be used by third-party actors to launch denial-of-service (DoS) attacks on key Internet nodes and other important enterprises or critical infrastructures.

Level 2, Large Enterprises

Large-scale enterprises (corporations, government agencies, and universities) are common targets for cyber attacks. Many such enterprises are part of critical infrastructures. Enterprises require clearly articulated, active information security policies and programs to audit compliance with cybersecurity best practices. According to the U.S. intelligence community, American networks will be increasingly targeted by malicious actors both for the data and the power they possess.

Level 3, Critical Sectors/Infrastructures

When organizations in sectors of the economy, government, or academia unite to address common cybersecurity problems, they can often reduce the burden on individual enterprises. Such collaboration often produces shared institutions and mechanisms, which, in turn, could have cyber vulnerabilities whose exploitation could directly affect the operations of member enterprises and the sector as a whole. Enterprises can also reduce cyber risks by participating in groups that develop best practices, evaluate technological offerings, certify products and services, and share information.

Several sectors have formed Information Sharing and Analysis Centers (ISACs) to monitor for cyber attacks directed against their respective infrastructures. ISACs are also a vehicle for sharing information about attack trends, vulnerabilities, and best practices.

Level 4, National Issues and Vulnerabilities

Some cybersecurity problems have national implications and cannot be solved by individual enterprises or infrastructure sectors alone. All sectors share the Internet. Accordingly, they are all at risk if its mechanisms (e.g., protocols and routers) are not secure. Weaknesses in widely used software and hardware products can also create problems at the national level, requiring coordinated activities for the research and development of improved technologies.

Additionally, the lack of trained and certified cybersecurity professionals also merits national-level concern.

Level 5, Global

The worldwide web is a planetary information grid of systems. Internationally shared standards enable interoperability among the world's computer systems. This interconnectedness, however, also means that problems on one continent have the potential to affect computers on another [continent]. We therefore rely on international cooperation to share information related to cyber issues and, further, to prosecute cyber criminals. Without such cooperation, our collective ability to detect, deter, and minimize the effects of cyber-based attacks would be greatly diminished.

New Vulnerabilities Requiring Continuous Response

New vulnerabilities are created or discovered regularly. The process of securing networks and systems, therefore, must also be continuous. The Computer Emergency Response Team/Coordination Center (CERT/CC) notes that not only are the numbers of cyber incidents and attacks increasing at an alarming rate, so too are the numbers of vulnerabilities that an attacker could exploit. Identified computer security vulnerabilities—faults in software and hardware that could permit unauthorized network access or allow an attacker to cause network damage—increased significantly from 2000 to 2002, with the number of vulnerabilities going from 1,090 to 4,129.

The mere installation of a network security device is not a substitute for maintaining and updating a network's defenses. Ninety percent of the participants in a recent Computer Security Institute survey reported using antivirus software on their network systems, yet 85 percent of their systems had been damaged by computer viruses. In the same survey, 89 percent of the respondents had installed computer firewalls, and 60 percent had intrusion detection systems. Nevertheless, 90 percent reported that security breaches had taken place, and 40 percent of their systems had been penetrated from outside their network.

The majority of security vulnerabilities can be mitigated through good security practices. As these survey numbers indicate, however, practicing good security includes more than simply installing those devices. It also requires operating them correctly and keeping them current through regular patching and virus updates.

Cybersecurity and Opportunity Cost

For individual companies and the national economy as a whole, improving computer security requires investing attention, time, and money. For fiscal year 2003, President Bush requested that Congress increase funds to secure federal computers by 64 percent. President Bush's investment in securing federal computer networks now will eventually reduce overall expenditures through cost-saving E-Government solutions, modern enterprise management, and by reducing the number of opportunities for waste and fraud.

For the national economy—particularly its information technology industry component—the dearth of trusted, reliable, secure information systems presents a barrier to future growth. Much of the potential for economic growth made possible by the information technology revolution has yet to be realized—deterred in part by cyberspace security risks. Cyberspace vulnerabilities place more than transactions at risk; they jeopardize intellectual property, business operations, infrastructure services, and consumer trust.

Conversely, cybersecurity investments result in more than costly overhead expenditures. They produce a return on investment. Surveys repeatedly show that

- Although the likelihood of suffering a severe cyber attack is difficult to estimate, the costs associated with a successful one are likely to be greater than the investment in a cybersecurity program to prevent it; and

- Designing strong security protocols into the information systems architecture of an enterprise can reduce its overall operational costs by enabling cost-saving processes, such as remote access and customer or supply-chain interactions, which could not occur in networks lacking appropriate security.

Table 5.1 Roles and Responsibilities in Securing Cyberspace

	Priority 1	Priority 2	Priority 3	Priority 4	Priority 5
	National Cyberspace Security Response System	National Cyberspace Security Threat and Vulnerability Reduction System	National Cyberspace Security Awareness and Training Program	Securing Governments' Cyberspace	National Security and International Cyberspace Security Cooperation
Home User/Small Business		X	X		
Large Enterprises	X	X	X	X	X
Critical Sectors/ Infrastructures	X	X	X	X	X
National Issues and Vulnerabilities	X	X	X	X	X
Global					X

These results suggest that, with greater awareness of the issues, companies can benefit from increasing their levels of cybersecurity. Greater awareness and voluntary efforts are critical components of the *National Strategy to Secure Cyberspace*.

Individual and National Risk Management

Until recently overseas terrorist networks had caused limited damage in the United States. On September 11, 2001, that quickly changed. One estimate places the increase in cost to our economy from attacks to U.S. information systems at 400 percent over four years. While those losses remain relatively limited, that too could change abruptly.

Every day in the United States individual companies, and home computer users, suffer damage from cyber attacks that, to the victims, represent significant losses. Conditions likewise exist for relative measures of damage to occur on a national level, affecting the networks and systems on which the Nation depends:

- Potential adversaries have the intent;

- Tools that support malicious activities are broadly available; and,

- Vulnerabilities of the Nation's systems are many and well known.

No single strategy can completely eliminate cyberspace vulnerabilities and their associated threats. Nevertheless, the Nation must act to manage risk responsibly and to enhance its ability to minimize the damage that results from attacks that do occur. Through this statement, we reveal nothing to potential foes that they and others do not already know. In1997 a Presidential Commission identified the risks in a seminal public report. In 2000 the first national plan to address the problem was published. Citing these risks, President Bush issued an Executive Order in 2001, making cybersecurity a priority, and accordingly, increasing funds to secure federal networks. In 2002 the President moved to consolidate and strengthen federal cybersecurity agencies as part of the proposed Department of Homeland Security.

Government Alone Cannot Secure Cyberspace

Despite increased awareness around the importance of cybersecurity and the measures taken thus far to improve our capabilities, cyber risks continue to underlie our national information networks and the critical systems they manage. Reducing that risk requires an unprecedented, active partnership among diverse components of our country and our global partners.

The federal government could not—and, indeed, should not—secure the computer networks of privately owned banks, energy companies, transportation firms, and other parts of the private sector. The federal government should likewise not intrude into homes and small businesses, into universities, or state and local agencies and departments to create secure computer networks. Each American who depends on cyberspace, the network of information networks, must secure the part that they own or for which they are responsible.

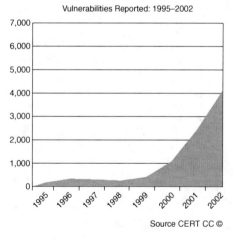

Vulnerabilities Reported: 1995–2002

Source CERT CC ©

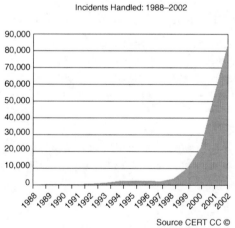

Incidents Handled: 1988–2002

Source CERT CC ©

The president's call to action is a first step in a massive security effort to manage a threat of a scope that is almost impossible to conceptualize. The terrorists not only pose a threat to our security, communications, transportation, and medical assets by attacking the Internet but use the internet as a tool of training and communication to coordinate and launch attacks.

Ethical Considerations...

You are a concerned citizen who monitors the common terror websites to stay up to date on the risks they present. Is it reasonable for the Internet service provider to give the government your name, as well as others who visit those sites?

Should the government have access to the email of persons who visit those sites to make sure they are not terrorists?

THE TERRORIST'S TRICKS AND COUNTER-MEASURES[2]

Tricks

Two terrorists on opposite sides of the globe might agree to open 30 anonymous web-based e-mail accounts with 30 different passwords. On the first of the month the first account is used, on the second of the month the second account is used and so on, until each account is used once.

"It's very difficult to catch, because there is no pattern of use," former U.S. counter-terrorism czar Richard Clarke says. "One-time anonymous accounts are extremely difficult to monitor."

One terrorist drafts a Web-based e-mail and instead of sending it, saves it to the draft folder, accessible online from anywhere in the world. The other terrorist can open the same account, read the message, and delete it. The e-mail has never been sent, and cannot be tracked.

Many e-mails are sent on public computers, for example in libraries or cyber cafés, making them even more difficult to trace.

The language in the e-mails can also be cloaked, says Dale Watson, a 24-year veteran of the FBI who served as the first executive assistant director for counterterrorism. In preparing for the Sept. 11 attacks, suspected hijacker and pilot Mohamed Atta and alleged 9/11 conspirator Ramzi bin al-Shibh pretended to be students as they exchanged e-mails, talking about "architecture" (the World Trade Center), "arts" (the Pentagon), "law" (the Capitol) and "politics" (the White House).

Counter-Measures

If a jihadist site hosted in another country is not taken down by the government in that country, the U.S. needs to hack the site and bring it down, Clarke says.

The U.S. can use active and passive attacks to disrupt terrorists' electronic networks. Active attacks include using computer viruses to infect enemy computers. Passive attacks monitor e-mails and transferred data, and watch traffic patterns.

The viruses used in active attacks wouldn't do damage or send mass mailings, but rather selectively collect data and discreetly send the e-mail back to U.S. intelligence. That could include getting address books, or collecting the "cookies" written to the computer's hard drive when the terrorist visits certain Web sites. There are also ways to monitor keystrokes, even if a terrorist uses encryption. Counterfeit e-mails can also used to confuse or subvert communications.

"They certainly can be very effective," the University of Maryland's Lee Strickland says of active attacks. "To escape, [terrorists] have to be lucky every day. We only have to be lucky once."

Passive attacks aim to monitor the terrorists' information network, not overtly disrupt it. That includes watching electronic banking transactions, for example, and following e-mail traffic patterns and other data exchanges. Doing so may arouse suspicion and force terrorists to use less efficient modes of communication. "The goal is not only to acquire information in the terrorists' possession, but also to force them to use other forms of communication — perhaps slower and less effective, or perhaps someone that may be easier to intercept or that may provide more information upon intercept," Strickland wrote in a 2002 report called "Fighting Terrorism with Information."

As mentioned earlier, the Internet is a frontier with good guys and bad guys. One tool of the good guys is to identify the *modus operandi*, or methods of committing crimes, which may lead to the identity of the suspects in an investigation.

Al Qaida is known for repeating what works. They follow dogma and training manuals to organize terror cells. Watching for clues to the methods used by criminals and terrorists alike may lead to early interdiction into their activities.

TECHNOLOGY AND TERROR: THE NEW MODUS OPERANDI[3]

For all the fear that cyber terrorists will turn the Internet into a weapon of mass disruption, many intelligence experts contend the Web is most effective (or detrimental) as it was designed to be — as a way to communicate and create community. This essay explores how jihadis are using the Web, plus some of the cyber "tricks" used by terrorists to avoid detection and how the authorities can respond.

It was all laid out in a polished, 25-minute training video: how to make an explosive belt to blow yourself up and kill as many people as possible.

This particular video, first posted on a jihadist message board in December 2004, presented the necessary explosives, shrapnel and vest for a suicide bomber. It demonstrated how to assemble the materials and wear the belt. And then the video showed a test of the explosive belt, with a simulated detonation aboard a crowded bus.

As translated on a Web site that tracks Islamic terrorist organizations, the producers analyzed the bomb's impact on the mock victims:

> We notice that the following 2 seats were not directly hit. This is due to the fact that, when the person who will be wearing this explosive vest goes on the bus, and wants to blow himself up, he must be facing the front with his back towards the back. There is a possibility that the 2 seats on his right and his left might not be hit with the shrapnel, however, the explosion will surely kill the passengers in those seats.

Such Web sites and training videos, which are often posted then quickly removed to avoid detection, have multiplied after Sept. 11. In doing so, they opened perhaps the widest front in the war on terror: cyberspace.

In essence, the Internet is the perfect communication tool for terrorists, and it mirrors the framework of their operations: decentralized, anonymous, and offering fast communication to a potentially large audience. The Internet is used to plot and claim responsibility for terrorist acts, to address sympathizers and enemies alike, and to raise money and attract new recruits. It has created a virtual "umma" — Arabic for the larger Muslim community as a whole — and like the actual umma, the cyber umma encompasses both moderate Muslims and Islamic fundamentalists.

For all the fear that cyber terrorists will turn the Internet into a weapon of mass disruption, many intelligence experts contend the Web is most effective (or detrimental) as it was designed to be — as a way to communicate and to create community.

In a keynote speech at a security conference for government agencies in Washington, retired CIA director George Tenet called for tightening security of the Internet, which he said was "a potential Achilles' heel." Tenet acknowledged that it would be "controversial in this age when we still think the Internet is a free and open society," but "ultimately the Wild West must give way to governance and control."

But, as Gabriel Weimann writes in the United States Institute of Peace report "How Modern Terrorism Uses the Internet," the restriction of the Internet under the guise of counterterrorism measures, particularly by authoritarian governments, can infringe on privacy, limit freedom of speech, and impede the free flow of information, in turn placing restrictions on the open society that makes the Western world strong.

"There's just no question that if the Internet wasn't there, the terrorists would have loved to invent it," says Jeffrey Simon, a former terrorism analyst for the RAND Corp., author of *The Terrorist Trap* and a consultant who has studied terrorism for 20 years. "It's always a technological battle with terrorists. The technology is always out there for everyone to take advantage of."

Hosting Terror at Home

Although a number of extremist sites are located abroad, in many cases, terrorists take advantage of the technology inside the U.S.

Recently, more jihadist Web sites in Europe have switched to U.S. computer servers — mostly because they can, says Rita Katz, director of the Washington-based Search for International Terrorist Entities (SITE) Institute. American Web hosting is cheap, easy to access and U.S. servers are technologically among the best in the world. To avoid detection, terrorists frequently change Web addresses and often squat undetected on other Web sites or Internet servers. Katz believes the most hard-core Al Qaeda and jihadist Web sites are hosted in the U.S. because of freedom of speech protections.

Katz points to the August 2004 arrest of Babar Ahmad, a British citizen charged in the U.S. with providing material support to terrorists, conspiring to kill people in a foreign country, and money laundering, because Web sites that he ran from the U.K. were hosted by an Internet service provider in Connecticut. The indictment alleges that through the Web sites and other means, Ahmad provided "expert advice and assistance, communications equipment, military items, lodging, training, false documentation, transportation, funding, personnel and other support designed to assist the Chechen mujahideen, the Taliban and associated groups."

"The Internet today is really 'command central' for all terrorist organizations," says Katz, who wrote a memoir *The Terrorist Hunter* and has tracked international terrorists since the 1990s. "You don't really need to be in Afghanistan anymore. It's all on the Internet."

She keeps edited examples of terrorist training manuals, videos, newsletters and communiqués on the SITE Institute's subscriber-based Web site, including the suicide bomber instructional video. The information on these Web sites can vary from how to set up a safehouse to instructions for using rocket-propelled grenades.

"If you know where to look, [they're] not difficult to find. Not for an Arabic speaker," she says. The Internet is "something we set up for our use to make our life better, but terrorists have hijacked the Internet literally."

Increasing Sophistication

In the summer of 2004, Lee S. Strickland, director of the Center for Information Policy at the University of Maryland and a career senior intelligence officer and computer specialist, oversaw a study that examined terrorists' use of the Internet.

The study found that the terrorist sites tend to be as sophisticated and efficacious as many mainstream Western corporate sites. The researchers used 26 variables of highly effective Web sites including design, content and how often they are updated.

"You're really seeing a growing sophistication of video and the Web," Strickland says.

The study examined a number of terrorist linked sites, ranging from Al Qaeda and Hamas to the Tamil Tigers. When compared with Microsoft.com, Hamas' site, for instance, shared 23 of these 26 highly valuable design features, such as search engines, mission statements, a "what's new" section and a frequently asked questions page. There were even job boards, online applications for recruitment, testimonials, an online store and chat rooms. If the sites aren't directly recruiting, many solicit funds.

Strickland says these sites employ an effective array of interactive games, cartoons, jokes, and even bedtime stories that appeal to children. They recruit young adults ages 14 to 24 with videos and music: For example, in early 2004, a Muslim rapper in Great Britain named Sheik Terra released a video for his song "Dirty Kuffar" (Infidel) in which he carries a copy of the Quran and a pistol and calls for the death of all non-Muslims.

Reconnaissance

With the abundance of information available on the Internet, terrorists also use the Web for reconnaissance, especially with the availability of public information on things like electrical grids and other infrastructure — a problem highlighted by George Tenet.... Terrorists regularly search the Internet for data mining purposes to facilitate financial transactions and crime, according to former counterterrorism czar Richard Clarke.

Clarke says the government should limit what information is available by first examining the content on government Web sites. If they don't, reconnaissance of potential targets by terrorists will continue.

"The Pentagon has done this. It's generally a good idea for any company or government to do," he says. "There's way too much information available."

An Al Qaeda training manual recovered in Afghanistan confirms that the group researched critical infrastructure online. The manual explained that at least 80 percent of the information gathered on the enemy was done through open and legal methods. Whether it's GIS mapping of the electrical and cyberoptic infrastructure of New York City or major dams, much of the information is still openly available, according to Strickland.

"You can get information anonymously, store it in a database and apply data mining tools to it," he says. "And the tools to exploit are commercial tools!"

Avoiding Detection

For years intelligence experts and officials have suspected that some Al Qaeda operatives are technological whizzes who use espionage tools like encryption or the practice of hiding messages within other messages known as steganography.

Encryption works by altering letters or numbers with software. It is illegal to export encryption software to certain countries overseas, but the programs can be easily downloaded.

Arrests of Al Qaeda members and computers captured in U.S. raids have turned up evidence of encrypted e-mails dating to the 1990s, including the 1998 bombings of U.S. embassies in East Africa. Wadih El Hage, an associate of Osama bin Laden who was convicted for his role in the 1998 bombing of U.S. embassies in Kenya and Tanzania, encrypted e-mails while plotting the attacks. Ramzi Yousef, the mastermind behind the 1993 World Trade Center attack, used encryption from his base in the Philippines in the mid-1990s when he plotted to blow up 11 U.S. airplanes over the Pacific.

More recently, U.S. officials believe the Al Qaeda Web site www.alneda.com used encrypted information to link Al Qaeda members to more secure sites, according to Weimann's report.

Steganography dates to ancient Greece and was widely used by Allies and the Axis during World War II. Russ Rogers, a security researcher and CEO of security services company Security Horizon, Inc., says there are more than 100 tools readily available on the Web that can help hide information inside documents such as JPEG image files using algorithms to modify the pixels in a file without altering the visible image. There are even Web sites and programs that can transform a message to make it look like spam e-mail or a play script.

The Virtual Politics of Violence

The Web's use as a propaganda and political tool may be its biggest asset to terrorists.

An intelligence aide to a U.S. senator, who spoke on condition of anonymity says, "The Internet is the poor man's television network. Buy a $300 video camera and a PC and you're in business. You can communicate in a very powerful medium almost instantaneously, almost undetectable and free."

One of the more striking examples of terrorists' political use of the Internet involves a document that argued for an attack against Spanish forces months *before* March 11. Written in early December 2003, the document titled "Jihadi Iraq, Hopes and Dangers" called for attacks in order to influence the parliamentary elections.

A few weeks after the document was published, Brynjar Lia, senior analyst at the Norwegian Defense Research Establishment, found the document on a jihadist Web site while making his usual rounds on the Internet.

"It was interesting to me for two reasons — the document's sophisticated strategic analysis and its specific recommendations," Lia says. "Many of the documents are religious and propagandist in tone and entirely devoted to providing justifications for jihad. If you've read one or two, you've read them all."

But this document was different. It mentioned the Spanish elections, which were four months away, and recommended "painful strikes" in the run-up to the election in order to influence its outcome. The author lays out the argument as for why an attack against Spain would be most effective. There wasn't a specific call for an attack in Europe, Lia says, but rather the terms called for an attack against Spanish forces. As translated by Lia and his colleague Thomas Hegghammer, the document contends:

> We think that the Spanish government could not tolerate more than two, maximum three blows, after which it will have to withdraw as a result of popular pressure. If its troops still remain in Iraq after these blows, then the victory of the Socialist Party is almost secured, and the withdrawal of the Spanish forces will be on its electoral programme.

"Like everyone else, I assumed all the intelligence agencies in the world were monitoring these Web sites and checking them out," Lia says. "I didn't think to alert anyone. It seemed obvious. I thought they must have been read."

Monitoring Web Sites

The U.S. government doesn't actively monitor Web sites, according to Richard Clarke. Some ISPs and Web hosts might, although currently there is no legal obligation to do so.

"You're treading on dangerous ground when you start limiting content, unless the site is clearly linked to a violation of the law," he says.

But while First Amendment concerns exist, it is the sheer volume of Web sites and e-mail traffic that mostly hampers monitoring.

"Unless there is a specific complaint, [Web hosting companies] don't have the wherewithal to monitor the content or the responsibility," says FBI agent Mike Rolince, of the Washington, D.C. field office.

The same issue of resources prohibits the Department of Justice from monitoring Web sites says Department of Justice spokesman Bryan Sierra.

"We don't have the manpower or the desire to sit around and monitor the Web 24-7," Sierra says. "We're not the guys out there trying to determine what is on the Internet. That's not our goal. Our goal is to determine what is illegal."

California-based Yahoo! spokeswoman Mary Osako would not comment on how aggressively Yahoo! monitors the content of the Web sites it hosts, but the company investigates every complaint it receives. She says that the company has the "ability across languages" to scrutinize sites but for the most part Yahoo! relies on its members to report any inappropriate use. Osako would not disclose how many reports the company has received regarding terrorist-related material.

In the end, taking down a Web site isn't going to solve the problem. "The opposition sees that as nothing more than a temporary inconvenience," according to Rolince.

Going forward, Dale Watson, former special agent in charge of counter-terrorism in the Washington bureau of the FBI, expects the bureau to continue to use the e-mail equivalent of telephone wiretaps as a surveillance tool.

Since March 2004, the European Union has discussed imposing requirements on Internet service providers (ISPs) and cell phone companies to keep permanent records accessible to law enforcement. The European Council will vote on the matter in June 2005.

For the Department of Justice, the main obstacle and main challenge will be keeping up with the emerging technologies terrorists use, Sierra says. But the intelligence aide to the U.S. senator believes that the cyber age and "all the cool tools" shouldn't dazzle law enforcement.

"There is an increasing need for old-fashioned, shoe-leather spying, human intelligence and agents who will tell us things about the bad guys," he says. "It's face-to-face where we can really make strides against terrorism."

An Insider's Point of View...

I often am involved in security disagreements with the IT specialists when discussing budgets. I appreciate firewalls, protocols, and access management, but they are only as effective as the physical security elements involved in an organization. Really, what good does it do betting the farm on firewalls and passwords if some moron lets his laptop get stolen off the front seat of his car, or a corrupt employee carries a hard-drive out of his office in his lunchbox, or a terrorist throws a hand grenade into the server room? Always look for balance between the physical security elements and the cyber-security elements at budget time. Conduct some research on lost computers and hard drives and the FBI. You might be surprised.

THE NEW OPERATIONAL BATTLEFIELD

In December 1998 the Department of Defense (DoD) announced that information warfare was being institutionalized as the new operational battlespace (Information Operations Department, School of Information Warfare and Strategy,

National Defense University). The three traditional battlegrounds were land, sea, and air. These elements are now called battlespaces to incorporate the fourth element of information warfare. In essence, cyberspace is formally recognized as permeating all DoD battlespaces.

Battlespaces do not exist in the emergency response world. However, we organize response units in an operations section, with response branches being EMS, fire/rescue, law enforcement, public health, and public works. These critical branches are similar to battlespaces, are dependent on information operations, and are vulnerable to information warfare. Like the DoD, civilian emergency agencies are subject to cyber attack, and must protect this essential battlespace element.

Adapting to Change

As the millennium approached we were constantly reminded that things were changing in the world, that things are different in this century, that new technologies will revolutionize the future. Of course they will. We witnessed miraculous changes over the last 100 yeas and there are no indications that this century will be any different. All of the factors influencing future global social, economic, technologic, information, and political evolution are currently in place or in development. For public safety the concern is not the changes that are occurring, but in which forms they will manifest and whether any potential negatives are associated with them.

For example, we know that information technology will have a profound positive effect on emergency services, yet we also faced the first crisis of the new millennium: the possibility of failure of the information technology platform. The Year 2000 (Y2K) computer problems, also know as the millennium bug, was potentially catastrophic to the national infrastructure of industrial economies. On January 1, 2000, we realized that "apocalypse now" was really "apocalypse not." However, the Y2K nonevent was not an imagined threat. Cyber awareness, preparation, and an intense focus on the information infrastructure saved the say. The transformation to a technology-based society brought not only solutions, but also unanticipated problems. This paradox illustrates that we will always encounter complex future management issues involving critical infrastructure components.

What Is Critical Infrastructure?

The critical infrastructure consists of, in part, information and financial management systems, telecommunications, dispatch centers, cable television, power production, water service, and natural gas and its storage facilities, transportation, and distribution mechanisms. Protecting this infrastructure against physical and electronic attack and ensuring the availability of the infrastructure is a complex issue. In 20002, as a result of a survey conducted by the Computer Security Institute to determine an estimated impact of these attacks, alarming findings were revealed. The highlights of the "2000 Computer Crime and Security Survey" include the following:

- Ninety percent of respondents (primarily large corporations and government agencies) detected computer security breaches within the last twelve months.

- Seventy percent reported a variety of serious computer security breaches other than the most common ones of computer viruses, laptop theft, or employee "net abuse;" for example, theft of proprietary information, financial fraud, system penetration from outsiders, denial of service attacks, and sabotage of data or networks.

- Seventy-four percent acknowledged financial losses due to computer breaches.

- Forty-two percent were willing and/or able to quantify their financial losses. The losses from the 273 respondents totaled $265,589,940 (the average annual total over the last three years was $120,240,180).

The critical infrastructure is currently vulnerable to attack. While this in itself poses a national security threat, the linkage between information systems and traditional critical infrastructures has increased the scope and potential for the use of cyber-terrorism. For economic reasons, increasing deregulation and competition created an increased reliance on information systems to operate, maintain, and monitor critical infrastructure. This, in turn, creates a tunnel of vulnerability previously unrealized in history.[4]

The critical infrastructure of our communities is basically transparent; we cannot function without it, yet we do not see it or realize that it is there. Almost every function without it, yet we do not see it or realize that it is there. Almost every aspect of twenty-first-century life revolves around the efficiency of zeros and ones flowing at near light speed through microchips. Transportation is an example. Air, ground, and water transportation systems depend on computer traffic control. Software, data systems, and communications guide the entire air traffic control system.

The nation's power grid is another example. The system is a complex matrix of generating systems, switching systems, and distribution systems, all computer controlled (sometimes called a system of systems). Major blackouts and brownouts have occurred because of a software failure or the bisection of a fiber-optic cable.

A third example is the world financial system. As reported in a Learning Channel(c) documentary, 90 percent of the world's wealth is digital. Individual and business financial holdings are essentially an account number associated with a fiscal amount in a financial database.

In the previous examples, accidental electronic failures have disrupted the systems. Intentional cyber attacks have likewise caused systems distribution. An information attack can halt air traffic, gridlock a ground transportation system, cause a regional power failure, or cripple a financial system. These events cause multiple deaths and injuries.

Cyber Warfare: Incident and Response

Terrorism, as a tool of the disenfranchised, the disenchanted, and the just plain destructive will undergo fundamental changes during the next decade. Data packets may very likely replace explosives as the favored implement of destruction. TCP/IP (computer protocol) will be preferred over the Kalishnikov (AK-47) and modems rather than suicide bombers will deliver chaos to the world's governments, local communities, and institutional infrastructures. The advent of the cyber warrior is at hand. As just described anove, it is predicted that acts of terrorism will be binary events that couple information and electronic warfare with other activities such as explosives or chemical releases.

The most disconcerting aspect of this threat shift in the nature of terrorism is the magnitude of the destruction that can be inflicted by a single individual with a simple keystroke rather than a detonator. Disruption of the world's financial markets, chaos in the public safety system, reduction in commercial productivity, depletion of health services, and the downing of telecommunication networks will be only the beginning.

Lt. General Kenneth A. Minihan, while director of the U.S. National Security Agency, stated "the threat that is posed by potential by cyber attacks against the U.S. military and computer system networks is now growing beyond the computer hacker stage."[5] He said that groups potentially hostile to the United States are developing, or attempting to develop offensive information warfare capabilities. The Minihan warning is viewed as validating what the prestigious U.S. Defense Science Board has called "a recipe for national disaster." The following illustration is a depiction of local, national, and global information interdependence:

The Rand Corporation was a little more forthcoming. Their report, "Strategic Information Warfare" bluntly states, "Many U.S. allies and coalition partners will be vulnerable to information warfare attacks on their core infrastructure."[6] Lieutenant General Patrick M. Hughes, while he was Director of Defense Intelligence Agency, clarified the threat further in his statement before the Senate Select Committee on Intelligence when he stated, in part:

> Transnational Infrastructure Warfare involves attacking a nation's or sub national entity's key industries and utilities' to include telecommunications, banking and finance, transportation, water, government operations, emergency services, energy and power, and manufacturing. These industries normally have key linkages and interdependencies, which could significantly increase the impact of an attack on a single component. Threats to critical infrastructure include those from nation-states, state-sponsored sub-national groups, international and domestic terrorists, criminal elements, computer hackers, and insiders.[7]

Governments at all levels, have an obligation to secure their information systems and prepare for continuous infrastructure threats; having the will to do so is another matter entirely. Systems security is not a "do it once and you're done" proposition. An effective security plan is similar to an effective response plan. It must evolve and develop as the threat to systems evolves and develops. A firewall that kept the world out yesterday can be Swiss cheese tomorrow.

The lack of geographical, spatial, and political boundaries precludes conventional preventive measures. Attribution is second to information stability and therefore the majority of effort is placed on denying unauthorized access and system manipulation. Information warfare is attractive because it is relatively cheap to wage and offers an asymmetrical return on investment for resource-poor adversaries.

When information systems are under attack, the demand for information will decrease. The law, particularly international law, is ambiguous regarding criminality in, and acts of war on, information infrastructures. This ambiguity, coupled with a lack of clearly designated responsibilities for electronic defense, hinders the development of remedies and limits response options.

The vulnerability of our information systems was painfully demonstrated by the "denial of service" attacks that occurred during a three-day period in February, 2000. A new breed of hacker called a "cracker" prompted this attack. Crackers are sophisticated computer terrorists that attempt to disrupt or totally shut down networks or systems, whereas hackers are satisfied with just breaking into a aystem. According to Knight Ridder, in the 2000 attacks, major providers such as Yahoo!, eBay, Amazon.com, and CNN were shut down.

The real-time use of information assumes the availability of information and information technology. The operational implications of a failure of information and information technology must be addressed in an organized, sequential manner. Redundant capability in command and control capacity must be built into the system. Emergency communications plans must consider the extended system and its processes, and prepare for the eventuality of widespread system failure.

Globalization

Globalization is changing the context in which terrorists operate.[8] A transnational cast of characters that cannot be controlled by governments, either individually or collectively, increasingly affects even so-called domestic terrorism. Information technology has effectively removed the ability of countries to isolate themselves. Information and communication control is difficult, if not impossible to achieve because the information revolution has resulted in democratic access to technology. An important result is that free speech and civil liberty have been given an inexpensive informational medium with which to voice discontent with existing government.

The notional concept of a centrally controlled international terrorist network, previously investigated during the 1960s and 1970s, was deemed to be unlikely due to conflicting ideologies, motivating factors, funding, arming, and training among global practitioners. However, networks are now quite possible with the advent of public access to the Internet, the ability to transfer funds and conduct banking electronically, the international arms market, encrypted digital communication technology, and the emergence of stateless terrorism. An important result is that instant global communication between offensive action cells and their controllers is now possible. Controllers now have global reach and can run multiple independent cells from a single location with no interaction between the cells. They can also contract terrorism services utilizing the local indigenous practitioners in a given target community.

The complexity of weapons acquisition, production, transportation, lethality, and delivery platform has been diminished. Information management technology has also resulted in a reduced requirement for infrastructure, security, and detection avoidance and has resulted in an asymmetry between cause and effect.

The Questioning of Computer Data

Data on a computer screen has a high degree of credibility. Anyone born after 1950 was raised in front of a television screen. Anyone born after 1970 was raised in front of a computer screen along with the television. As a result, data on a screen has a very high degree of believability.

The habit of accepting electronic data without question must change, especially during tactical operations. When data does not agree with reasonable expectations, the data must be questioned, and data corruption suspected. In other words, the data must be "in the ballpark." For example, a chemical database that indicates procedures that appear inaccurate or unsafe should be compared with a printed source or another data system. In another case, if the CAD system suddenly indicates grossly inaccurate unit status, the information should be checked and corruption suspected. Any uses of electronic data by tactical decision makers should observe the following guidelines:

1. Do not blindly trust data screens.

2. Evaluate tactical data as a reality check.

3. Check other sources when data corruption is suspected.

In a terrorism/tactical violence event, consider the possibility of a coordinated information attack. Suspect intentional data manipulation when there is a mysterious communications failure. Maintain low tech information sources (books and paper) as an alternative to vulnerable electronic information.

Data Theft

Recent literature is inundated with articles about sophisticated intrusion methods. Sophisticated hackers (local and international) are able to crack passwords or find a back door route through a security firewall. However, simple theft is still an easy way to use low technology for high technology data corruption.

How easy is it to walk into your agency, remove disks stacked on a desk, and walk out? If the data is removed, altered, and discretely returned, great damage may result. If backup disks are removed, followed by a system attack, provisions for storing the system may be lost. There are several steps that should be taken in any public or private agency to protect vital data from simple theft:

1. *Office design*—no one should be able to freely enter an office area; place a door between the entry lobby and data storage areas.

2. *Entry control*—anyone entering an office or data storage area should encounter a receptionist/secretary or security officer before proceeding.

3. *ID badges*—visitors and guests should sign in and be issued a security badge; employees should wear identification badges; procedures should require that any person without a badge be questioned.

4. *Information storage*—stored data should be locked and never stored on a desktop or in an open area; critical backup data should be stored in a safe at an off-premise location. This is good advice for fire and severe weather protection as well a theft.

5. *Electronic entry*—sensitive areas should be controlled by electronic entry; systems should provide printouts of all names, dates, and times of entries.

Data Protection Standards

Emergency agencies are very familiar with standards. In the fire service there are National Fire Protection Association (NFPA) standards; in EMS there are the NHTSA EMT and paramedic training standards. Law enforcement is governed by Department of Justice standards. The Occupational Safety and Health Administration (OSHA) standards govern most of us. However, there are no present standards for data and information storage/security.

During the Twentieth National Information System Security conference (Baltimore, 1977), Robert T. Marsh (keynote address) stated, "For example, we recommend the National Institute of Standards and Technology (NIST) and the National Security Agency (NSA) jointly set standards and public best practices for information security, and then share these with federal, state, and local governments, as well as private industry.

Most local government response agencies are merely end users of electronic data. They lack the sophistication of federal government agencies and private organizations regarding protection of critical data. Standards and protocols are needed in the following areas:

- Data storage procedures

- Detection of running system attacks (real time)

- System restoration (disaster recovery)

- Physical security protocols

- Training standards for information technology security specialists

In the future we may have standards and protocols on information operations that rival tactical procedures. Presently, no such standards exist. At best, there is an inadequate mix of guidelines borrowed from private industry and federal agencies.

Public Information vs. Data Protection

A major information services issue in state and local government agencies is public disclosure of information. Most state laws are very liberal in their definition of "public information." State legislation usually defines exact types of documents that are confidential; all other documents not specified as confidential are public documents.

In many states, public documents, including electronic data, must be released within the same business day they are requested. Only reasonable charges for copying or duplication are allowed. You may be shocked to discover that the following information is public in your state:

■ Names and addresses of all employees, including elected officials, managers, and emergency response personnel.

■ Standard operating procedures for response agencies and special teams.

■ Locations and descriptions of emergency response units, including equipment inventories.

■ Radio frequencies, codes, and dispatch procedures.

■ Driver's license lists, including social security numbers and pictures.

■ Mutual aid contracts and mutual aid procedures.

■ Incident reports and after-action reports.

■ Building pre-plans and building layout graphics.

Hazardous materials information is a classic example. Federal legislation passed in the 1980s referred to as "The Community Right-to-Know Act" requires that information relating to the storage of hazardous materials be available to any member of the public who seeks the information. In many locales, this information is available at the public library. The data includes storage locations of reportable quantities, layout drawings of the storage sites, transportation routes, materials safety data sheets (MSDS), and descriptions of storage containers.

Right-to-know legislation directly conflicts with information security. The intentional release of industrial hazardous materials provides an effective terrorism/ tactical violence weapon. Because of public records laws and right-to-know legislation, domestic and foreign enemies can use our information to attack us.

Changing the law is admittedly a long and often painful process, but reducing the tactical information available as public record is a worthy goal. As times change and the terrorism/tactical violence threat increases, the naïve twentieth-century public records laws must be altered.

Many emergency response agencies are knowingly releasing sensitive information through the Internet. Agency homepages include links to computer-aided dispatch data screens, tactical response information, and links to communications centers that include real-time audio radio traffic. The motive is usually an attempt to generate positive public relations. Unfortunately, this type of information is very helpful to an adversary. Take another look at your organization's Internet links and homepages, and remove information that may make your system or your people vulnerable.

Infrastructure Protection—A Public/Private Partnership

Most of the critical infrastructure is owned and operated by private business entities or utilities. Private industry shares government's concern about infrastructure protection. The private sector has the advantage of funding, the ability to spend millions on information security problems.

One of the key recommendations of the President's Commission on Critical Infrastructure Protection is a program of public/private partnering (http://www.pccip.gov). The commission's most serious challenge was achieving private sector partnering. For many years, the private sector has conducted research and implemented procedures to protect it from local threats. The federal government has a more national objective; the government must protect the citizens of the United States and all of the country's systems from cyber intrusion or dysfunction. A sharing of information is in the interest of both parties.

In January 2000, President Bill Clinton announced a $2 billion proposal to combat cyber-terrorism. The proposal establishes the Institute for Information Infrastructure Protection. The objective of the institute is to establish a public/private partnership for infrastructure protection research. Other aspects of the president's proposal include increased funding for research and development, and increased computer security.

Local governments have similar information concerns because of ownership of the public safety infrastructure. However, local governments do not have the funds or expertise to conduct research in the information protection arena. Local government must depend on spin-offs from the public/private partnerships at the national level.

Information Security Management

In the future, the director of information security management (ISM) will be a new position in progressive response agencies. Physical security is commonplace; information security will be just as important.

Presently, information security is haphazard at best, and certainly not a prominent unit in public safety organizational charts. In most agencies, security is relegated to someone in the information services (IS) department, who usually has many other duties. In the ideal model, information security should pervade the organization. This means an information security department managed by a professional ISM. This department must be high in the management hierarchy and operate by professional standards and protocols.

An effective ISM department should have the following goals:

1. Develop and maintain systems for real-time detection of running cyber attacks.

2. Conduct ongoing educational awareness programs for all internal agencies.

3. Stay informed regarding national research and development efforts.

4. Maintain the standards and best practices of the information technology industry.

5. Maintain an intelligence system for crisis information about cyber threats.

6. Conduct aggressive investigations on all incidents relating to system attacks or data disruption.

SUMMARY

Internet security is an evolving and exciting field. Every security specialist and public safety executive needs some fundamental understanding of the cyberworld and communications technology. Developing plans and preventing cyber attacks is an effort that must be coordinated through every element of security and is probably the fastest evolving of all "current events."

Information operations, information warfare, and cyber attacks are twenty-first-century concerns. The Department of Defense has added information operations as a fourth battlespace. Information operations is a large part of the nation's critical infrastructure, which consists of our financial systems, transportation systems, utility systems, and communications systems.

The public safety infrastructure includes components that are essential to public safety operations and includes 911, communications, computer-aided dispatch, informational databases, geo-based information systems, and electronic mail. All of these systems are based on software and electronic data systems and must be protected from intrusion and data corruption. The disruption of these systems inhibits emergency response capabilities and causes death and injury.

Electronic data has a high degree of trust. Response agencies must recognize that this trusted data is decision-making material that is vulnerable. Tactical decision makers should be trained to perform reality checks on suspicious data and maintain low technology sources of backup information.

Data theft is a simple method of deleting or corrupting sensitive data. Stored data on disks and tapes should be protected from theft and/or tampering. Office design that prevents unescorted entry, and includes electronic entry control and security badge identification is one method of securing sensitive data.

Presently, there are no national standards for critical data protection and security. There must be national standards, developed by public/private partnerships, that address data storage procedures, real-time detection of running system attacks, system restoration, physical security protocols, and information technology training standards.

Protection of response data and tactical information often conflicts with public records laws. For example, community right-to-know legislation requires that all citizens (including terrorists) have access to information on the storage and transportation of hazardous materials. The public safety community, through the legislative process, must initiate a concentrated effort to protect information that makes the community vulnerable to attack.

ADDITIONAL DISCUSSON TOPICS

- What is the significance of classifying information operations as an operational battlespace?

- Define the national critical infrastructure. List at least four examples of major systems in the critical infrastructure.

- What is the public safety critical infrastructure? Discuss three systems in the public safety infrastructure.

- Why should computer data be questioned? What policies should be implemented to ensure cross-checking of suspicious data?

- List several policies/procedures that should be implemented to reduce data theft.

- Discuss the present data protection standards in the United States. What elements should be included in an ideal standard?

- What are the prevailing issues relating to public records laws versus the need for protection of sensitive data?

- Discuss the concept of information security management in public safety agencies.

RESOURCES

Halting the Hacker: A Practical Guide to Computer Security, 2/E
Donald L. Pipkin, 2003, ISBN: 0-13-046416-3, Prentice Hall PTR.

Security In Distributed Computing: Did You Lock the Door?
Glen Bruce and Rob Dempsey, 1997, ISBN: 0-13-182908-4, Prentice Hall PTR.

Principles and Practice of Information Security, Linda Volonino, Ph.D and Stephen R. Robinson, 2004, ISBN: 0-13-184027-4, Prentice Hall.

Endnotes

[1] Source: http://www.whitehouse.gov/pcpib/case_for_action.pdf

[2] This article was written by Andrew Becker, who is a student at the Graduate School of Journalism at University of California, Berkeley. His articles have appeared in the *Boston Globe*, the *San Francisco Chronicle*, and FRONTLINE. Source: http://www.pbs.org/wgbh/pages/frontline/shows/front/special/techsidebar.html

[3] Source: http://www.pbs.org/wgbh/pages/frontline/shows/front/special/tech.html

[4] INFORMATION WARFARE-DEFENSE, 1996: Defense Science Board Task Force on IW-D, OUSD-A&T.

[5] Lt. General Kenneth Minihan, "Information System Security: National Security Agency," 1998.

[6] R.C. Molander, A.S. Riddle, and P. Wilson, *Strategic Information Warfare: A New Face of War*, Rand Corporation, DocNo: MR-661-OSD, 1996.

[7] Lt. General Patrick M. Hughes, *Global Threats and Challenges: The Decade Ahead, hearing of the Senate Select Committee on Intelligence*, January 28, 1998.

[8] *Strategic Management and Policy-Making, Globalization: What Challenges and Opportunities for Government*, Department of State, 1997.

CHAPTER SIX

TRANSPORTATION

*There can be no doubt that the transportation sector is
the most critical sector of our economy.*
—Robert Brady, U.S. Congressman (D- PA)

*The terrorist attacks in London sadly remind us that the enemies of freedom
do not hesitate to target innocent people simply going about their lives.*
— Cliff Stearns, U.S. Congressman (R-FL)

KEY TERMS

Transportation mode
Initiative

OBJECTIVES

- Identify the principle federal agencies involved in providing security for transportation systems.

- Describe the principle hazards and vulnerabilities faced by the various modes of transportation.

- Identify the local, national, and international interconnections among the various modes of mass transportation.

- Research the initiatives being implemented to improve security for U.S. transportation systems.

DISCUSSION TOPICS

- Why is the transportation sector such an inviting target for terrorist attack?

- How is border security related to transportation security?

- Are transportation security and transportation efficiency incompatible goals?

6

INTRODUCTION

Currently, most of the essential literature on the topic of critical infrastructure is contained in government documents or government-sponsored commission reports. *The National Strategy for the Physical Protection of Critical Infrastructures and Key Assets,* which was released by the White House in February 2003 as part of the President's National Strategy for Homeland Security, defines the critical infrastructure systems, the challenges of protection against terrorist attacks, and strategies in order to overcome those challenges. The following sections are excerpted from that document and describe the challenges associated with each mode of transportation and future strategies to protect them against potential terrorist attacks.

TRANSPORTATION RELATED TOPICS[1]

The transportation sector consists of several key modes: aviation, maritime traffic, rail, pipelines, highways, trucking and busing, and public mass transit. The diversity and size of the transportation sector makes it vital to our economy and national security, including military mobilization and deployment. As a whole, its infrastructure is robust, having been developed over decades of both private and public investment. Together the various transportation modes provide mobility of our population and contribute to our much-cherished individual freedom. The transportation infrastructure is also convenient. Americans rely on its easy access and reliability in their daily lives.

Interdependencies exist between transportation and nearly every other sector of the economy. Consequently, a threat to the transportation sector may impact other industries that rely on it. Threat information affecting transportation modes must be adequately addressed through communication and coordination among multiple parties who use or rely on these systems.

Aviation

The aviation mode is vast, consisting of thousands of entry points. It also has symbolic value, representing the freedom of movement that Americans value so highly as well as the technological and industrial prowess that have made the United States a world power. The

- Nation's aviation system consists of two main parts:

- Airports and the associated assets needed to support their operations, including the aircraft that they serve; and

- Aviation command, control, communications, and information systems needed to support and maintain safe use of our national airspace.

Before September 11, the security of airports and their associated assets was the responsibility of private carriers and state and local airport owners and operators. In the months following the September 11 attacks, Congress passed legislation establishing the Transportation Security Administration as the responsible authority for assuring aviation security.

Aviation Mode Challenges

As the events of September 11 illustrated, [aviation has] vital importance to the U.S. economy and the freedom: it provides our citizens make its protection an important national priority. Aviation faces several unique protection challenges. Its distribution and open access through thousands of entry points at home and abroad make it difficult to secure. Furthermore, components of the aviation infrastructure are not only attractive terrorist targets, but also serve as potential weapons to be exploited. Together, these factors make the U.S. aviation infrastructure a potential target for future terrorist strikes. Additional unique protection challenges for aviation include:

- *Volume:* U.S. air carriers transport millions of passengers every day and at least twice as many bags and other cargo.

- *Limited capabilities and available space:* Current detection equipment and methods are limited in number, capability, and ease of use.

- *Time-sensitive cargo:* "Just-in-time" delivery of valuable cargo is essential for many businesses—any significant time delay in processing and transporting such cargo would negatively affect the U.S. economy.

- *Security versus convenience:* Maintaining security while limiting congestion and delays complicates the task of security and has important financial implications.

- *Accessibility:* Most airports are open to the public; their facilities are close to public roadways for convenience and to streamline access for vehicles delivering passengers to terminals.

Another concern for the aviation industry is the additional cost of increased security during sustained periods of heightened alert. Since September 11, 2001, airports across the country have-in effect-been working at surge capacity to meet the security requirements of the current threat environment. Some cash-strapped operators must now balance providing higher levels of security with staying in business.

Aviation Mode Initiatives

Airport security failures on September 11 have placed the aviation industry under intense public scrutiny. To regain the public's confidence in air travel, public and private organizations have made substantial investments to increase airport security. Much work remains. DHS, as the federal lead department for the transportation sector, will work with DoT, industry, and state and local governments to organize, plan, and implement needed protection activities.

Aviation mode protection initiatives include efforts to:

- *Identify vulnerabilities, interdependencies, and remediation requirements*: DHS and DoT will work with representatives from state and local governments and industry to implement or facilitate risk assessments to identify vulnerabilities, interdependencies, and remediation requirements for operations and coordination-center facilities and systems, such as the need for redundant telecommunications for air traffic command and control centers.

- *Identify potential threats to passengers:* DHS and DoT will work with airline and airport security executives to develop or facilitate new methods for identifying likely human threats while respecting constitutional freedoms and privacy.

- *Improve security at key points of access:* DHS and DoT will work with airline and airport security executives to tighten security or facilitate increased security at restricted access points within airport terminal areas, as well as the perimeter of airports and associated facilities, including operations and coordination centers.

- *Increase cargo screening capabilities:* DHS and DoT will work with airline and airport security officials to identify and implement or facilitate technologies and processes to enhance airport baggage-screening capacities.

- *Identify and improve detection technologies:* DHS and DoT will work with airline and airport security executives to implement or facilitate enhanced technologies for detecting explosives. Such devices will mitigate the impact of increased security on passenger check-in efficiency and convenience, and also provide a more effective and efficient means of assuring vital aviation security.

Passenger Rail and Railroads

During every hour of every day, trains traverse the United States, linking producers of raw materials to manufacturers and retailers. They carry mining, manufacturing, and agriculture products; liquid chemicals and fuels; and consumer goods. Trains carry 40 percent of intercity freight—a much larger portion than is moved by any other single mode of transportation. About 20 percent of that freight is coal, a critical resource for the generation of electricity. More than 20 million intercity travelers use the rail system annually, and 45 million passengers ride trains and subways operated by local transit authorities. Securing railsector assets is critical to protecting U.S. commerce and the safety of travelers.

Rail Mode Challenges

Our Nation's railway system is vast and complex, with multiple points of entry. Differences in design, structure, and purpose of railway stations complicate the sector's overall protection framework. The size and breadth of the sector make it difficult to react to threats effectively or efficiently in all scenarios. This fact complicates protection efforts, but it also offers certain mitigating potential in the event of a terrorist attack. For example, trains are confined to specific routes and are highly controllable. If hijacked, a train can be shunted off the mainline and rendered less of a threat. Similarly, the loss of a bridge or tunnel can impact traffic along major corridors; however, the potential for national-level disruptions is limited.

The greater risk is associated with rail transport of hazardous materials. Freight railways often carry hazardous materials that are essential to other sectors and public services. The decision-making process regarding their transport is complex and requires close coordination between industry and government. A sector-wide information sharing process could help prevent over-reactive security measures, such as restricting the shipment of critical hazardous materials nationwide as a blanket safety measure in response to a localized incident.

Security solutions to the container shipping challenge should recognize that, in many cases, commerce, including essential national security materials, must continue to flow. Stifling commerce to meet security needs simply swaps one consequence of a security threat for another. In the event that a credible threat was to necessitate a shutdown, well-developed continuity of operations procedures can mitigate further unintentional negative consequences. For example, contingency planning can help determine how quickly commerce can be resumed; whether rerouting provides a measure of protection; or what specific shipments should be exempt from a shutdown, such as national defense critical materials.

An additional area of concern is the marking of container cars to indicate the specific type of hazardous materials being transported. During an emergency response, placards on rail cars help to alert first responders to hazardous materials they may encounter. Planners must take care, however, to devise a system of markings that terrorists cannot easily decipher.

Like the aviation sector, the rail industry also faces the additional costs of sustaining increased security during periods of heightened alert. Since the events of September 11, the railroads across the country have—in effect—been working at surge capacity to meet the security requirements of the increased threat environment, which entails assigning overtime and hiring temporary security personnel. Such reservoirs of capacity are costly to maintain. Nevertheless, the rail sector has had to adopt these heightened security levels as the new "normal" state. Some cash-strapped operators now face trade-offs between providing increased levels of security and going out of business.

Railroads have well-developed contingency plans and backups for dispatch, control, and communications equipment that are sufficient for localized or minor disruptions. Developing this type of backup to enable continuation of operations after a cataclysmic event is problematic given the costs associated with extensive structural enhancements.

Rail Mode Initiatives

The rail mode has been working actively with DoT to assess the risk environment. As a result, it has developed a comprehensive modal risk assessment and established a surface transportation ISAC to facilitate the exchange of information related to both cyber and physical threats specific to the railroads.

Since September 11, many rail operators have added investments to their security programs. Additional rail mode protection initiatives include efforts to:

- *Develop improved decision-making criteria regarding the shipment of hazardous materials:* DHS and DoT, coordinating with other federal agencies, state and local governments, and industry will facilitate the development of an improved process to assure informed decision-making with respect to hazardous materials shipment.

- *Develop technologies and procedures to screen intermodal containers and passenger baggage:* DHS and DoT will work with sector counterparts to identify and explore technologies and processes to enable efficient and expeditious screening of rail passengers and baggage, especially at intermodal stations.

- *Improve security of intermodal transportation:* DHS and DoT will work with sector counterparts to identify and facilitate the development of technologies and procedures to secure inter-modal containers and detect threatening content. DHS and DoT will also work with the rail industry to devise or enable a hazardous materials identification system that supports the needs of first responders, yet avoids providing terrorists with easy identification of a potential weapon.

- *Clearly delineate roles and responsibilities regarding surge requirements:* DHS and DoT will work with industry to delineate infrastructure protection roles and responsibilities to enable the rail industry to address surge requirements for resources in the case of catastrophic events.

Costs and resource allocation remains a contentious issue for the rail sector. DHS and DoT will also convene a working group consisting of government and industry representatives to identify options for the implementation of surge capabilities, including access to federal facilities and capabilities in extreme emergencies.

Highways, Trucking, and Busing

The trucking and busing industry is a fundamental component of our national transportation infrastructure. Without the sector's resources, the movement of people, goods, and services around the country would be greatly impeded.

Components of this infrastructure include highways, roads, inter-modal terminals, bridges, tunnels, trucks, buses, maintenance facilities, and roadway border crossings.

Highways, Trucking, and Busing Mode Challenges

Because of its heterogeneity in size and operations and the multitude of owners and operators nationwide, the trucking and busing infrastructure is highly resilient, flexible, and responsive to market demand. For the same reason, the sector is fractionated and regulated by multiple jurisdictions at state, federal, and—sometimes—local levels. The size and pervasive nature of the trucking and busing infrastructure pose significant protection challenges.

Transportation choke points (e.g., bridges and tunnels, inter-modal terminals, border crossings, and highway interchanges) present unique protection challenges. Overall understanding of infrastructure choke points is limited. Common criteria for identifying critical choke points are therefore difficult to establish. We must undertake a comprehensive, systematic effort to identify key assets, particularly those whose destruction or disruption would entail significant public health and safety consequences or significant economic impact.

Although many states have conducted risk assessments of their respective highway infrastructures, no true basis for comparison among them exists to determine relative criticality. Likewise, there is no coordinated mechanism for assessing choke-point vulnerabilities or conducting and evaluating risk mitigation planning. A major reason for this lack of synchronization within the sector is a paucity of funds to promote communication among industry members and facilitate cooperation for joint protection planning efforts. As a result, the sector as a whole has neither a coherent picture of industry-wide risks, nor a set of appropriate security criteria on which to baseline its protection planning efforts, such as what conditions constitute threats for the sector, or standards for infrastructure protection or threat reduction. The sector's diverse and widely distributed constituency complicates this situation.

Given the number of public and private small-business owners and operators in this sector, the cost of infrastructure protection is also a major challenge. Like the rail mode, in addition to the financial concerns associated with new security investments, highway, trucking, and busing organizations also regard the possibility of security-related delays at border crossings as a potential problem of major financial significance.

Another challenge is the way in which sector security incidents are handled across multiple jurisdictions. Because different law enforcement agencies differ in their approaches to crimes like truck theft, law enforcement responses to security incidents in this sector are inconsistent across jurisdictional lines.

Highways, Trucking, and Busing Mode Initiatives

Like the other major transportation modes, the highways, trucking, and busing mode has assessed its own security programs in light of the September 11 attacks. However, the sector's vast, heterogeneous nature requires further expanded coordination among stakeholder organizations to assure a more consistent, integrated national approach. Additionally, a better understanding of the overall system would lead to more adaptable, less intrusive, and more cost-effective security processes. Highways, trucking, and busing protection initiatives include efforts to:

- *Facilitate comprehensive risk, threat, and vulnerability assessments:* DHS, working closely with DoT and other key sector stakeholders, will facilitate comprehensive risk, threat, and vulnerability assessments for this mode.

- *Develop guidelines and standard criteria for identifying and mitigating chokepoints:* DHS, working with DoT and other sector key stakeholders, will develop guidelines and standard criteria for identifying and mitigating choke points, both nationally and regionally.

- *Harden industry infrastructure against terrorism through technology:* DHS will work jointly with industry and state and local governments to explore and identify potential technology solutions and standards that will support analysis and afford better and more cost effective protection against terrorism.

- *Create national transportation operator security education and awareness programs:* DHS and DoT will work with industry to create national operator security education and awareness programs to provide the foundation for greater cooperation and coordination within this highly diverse mode.

Pipelines

The United States has a vast pipeline industry, consisting of many hundreds of thousands of miles of pipelines, many of which are buried underground. These lines move a variety of substances such as crude oil, refined petroleum products, and natural gas.

Pipeline facilities already incorporate a variety of stringent safety precautions that account for the potential effects a disaster could have on surrounding areas. Moreover, most elements of pipeline infrastructures can be quickly repaired or bypassed to mitigate localized disruptions. Destruction of one or even several of its key components would not disrupt the entire system. As a whole, the response and recovery capabilities of the pipeline industry are well proven, and most large control-center operators have established extensive contingency plans and backup protocols.

Pipeline Mode Challenges

Pipelines are not independent entities, but rather integral parts of industrial and public service networks. Loss of a pipeline could impact a wide array of facilities and industrial factories that depend on reliable fuel delivery to operate.

Several hundred thousand miles of pipeline span the country, and it is not realistic to expect total security for all facilities. As such, protection efforts focus on infrastructure components whose impairment would have significant effects on the energy markets and the economy as a whole. For the pipeline industry, determining what to protect and when to protect it is a factor in cost-effective infrastructure protection. During periods of high demand—such as the winter months—pipeline systems typically operate at peak capacity and are more important to the facilities and functions they serve.

The pipeline industry as a whole has an excellent safety record, as well as in-place crisis management protocols to manage disruptions as they occur. Nevertheless, many of the products that pipelines deliver are inherently volatile. Hence, their protection is a significant issue.

Pipelines cross numerous state and local, as well as international jurisdictions. The number and variety of stakeholders create a confusing, and sometimes conflicting, array of regulations and security programs for the industry to manage, especially with respect to the ability of pipeline facilities to recover, reconstitute, and re-establish service quickly after a disruption.

The pipeline industry's increasing interdependencies with the energy and telecommunications sectors necessitate cooperation with other critical infrastructures during protection and response planning. Individually, companies have difficulty assessing the broader implications of an attack on their critical facilities. These interdependencies call for cross-sector coordination for to be truly responsive to national concerns. Additionally, some issues concerning recovery or reconstitution will require at least regional planning within the industry, as well as the sharing of sensitive business information that may run into proprietary concerns.

Pipeline Mode Initiatives

Historically, individual enterprises within this sector have invested in the security of their facilities to protect their ability to deliver oil and gas products. Representatives from major entities within this sector have examined the new terrorist risk environment. As a result, they have developed a plan for action, including industry-wide information sharing. In addition to industry efforts, DoT has developed a methodology for determining pipeline facility criticality and a system of recommended protective measures that are synchronized with the threat levels of the Homeland Security Advisory System. Additional pipeline mode protection initiatives include efforts to:

- *Develop standard reconstitution protocols:* DHS, in collaboration with DoE, DoT, and industry, will initiate a study to identify, clarify, and establish authorities and procedures as needed to reconstitute facilities as quickly as possible after a disruption.

- *Develop standard security assessment and threat deterrent guidelines:* DHS, in collaboration with DoE and DoT, will work with state and local governments and the pipeline industry to develop consensus security guidance on assessing vulnerabilities, improving security plans, implementing specific deterrent and protective actions, and upgrading response and recovery plans for pipelines.

- *Work with other sectors to manage risks resulting from interdependencies:* DHS, in collaboration with DoE and DoT, will convene cross-sector working groups to develop models for integrating protection priorities and emergency response plans.

Maritime

The maritime shipping infrastructure includes ports and their associated assets, ships and passenger transportation systems, costal and inland waterways, locks, dams and canals, and the network of railroads and pipelines that connect these waterborne systems to other transportation networks. There are 361 seaports in the United States, and their operations range widely in size and characteristics.

Most ports have diverse waterside facilities that are owned, operated, and accessed by diverse entities. State and local governments control some port authority facilities, while others are owned and operated by private corporations. Most ships are privately owned and operated. Cargo is stored in terminals at ports and loaded onto ships or other vehicles that pass through on their way to domestic and international destinations. DoD has also designated certain commercial seaports as strategic seaports, which provide facilities and services needed for military deployment.

Maritime Mode Challenges

The size, diversity, and complexity of this infrastructure make the inspection of all vessels and cargo that passes through our ports an extremely difficult undertaking. Current inspection methods—both physical and technological—are limited and costly. As with other modes of transportation that cross international borders, we must manage the tension between efficient processing of cargo and passengers and adequate security.

Major portions of the maritime industry's operations are international in nature and are governed by international agreements and multinational authorities, such as the International Maritime Organization. Negotiation of maritime rules and practices with foreign governments lies within the purview of DoS. Often these international efforts involve extended negotiation timelines.

DoT currently recommends guidelines for passenger vessel and terminal security, including passenger and baggage screening and training of crews. The industry requires R&D for cost-effective technologies for the rapid detection of explosives and other hazardous substances, as well as for new vessel designs to minimize the likelihood of a ship sinking if it were attacked.

Much of the port system represents a significant protection challenge, particularly in the case of high consequence cargo. Physical and operational security guidelines have undergone a comprehensive review, from which DoT and DHS will issue guidance and recommendations for appropriate protective actions. Efforts to increase the security of the maritime industry must also consider infrastructures subject to multi-agency jurisdictions and the international framework in which the industry operates.

Maritime Mode Initiatives

Following the September 11 attacks, initial risk assessments were conducted for all ports. These assessments have helped refine critical infrastructure and key asset designations, assess vulnerabilities, guide the development of mitigation strategies, and illuminate best practices. Most port authorities and private facility owners have also reexamined their security practices. Based on these preliminary risk assessments, DoT increased vessel notification requirements to shift limited resources to maintain positive control of movement of high-risk vessels carrying high-consequence cargoes and large numbers of passengers. DoT and the U.S. Coast Guard have also established a Sea Marshal program and deployable Maritime Safety and Security Teams to implement these activities.

Additionally, DoT has participated in efforts to expedite compliance with existing international standards and to develop additional standards to enhance port, vessel, and facility security. DoT is also working with the U.S. Customs Service to implement the Container Security Initiative to ensure the security of the shipping supply chain. Shippers who do not comply with outlined rules and regulations will be subject to greater scrutiny and delays when entering U.S. ports.

Additional maritime mode protection initiatives include efforts to:

- *Identify vulnerabilities, interdependencies, best practices, and remediation requirements:* DHS and DoT will undertake or facilitate additional security assessments to identify vulnerabilities and interdependencies, enable the sharing [of best practices], and issue guidance or recommendations on appropriate mitigation strategies.

- *Develop a plan for implementing security measures corresponding to varying threat levels:* DHS and DoT will work closely with other appropriate federal departments and agencies, port security committees, and private-sector owners and operators to develop or facilitate the establishment of security plans to minimize security risks to ports, vessels, and other critical maritime facilities.

- *Develop processes to enhance maritime domain awareness and gain international cooperation:* DHS and DoT will work closely with other appropriate federal departments and agencies, port security committees, and port owners and operators, foreign governments, international organizations, and commercial firms to establish a means for identifying potential threats at ports of embarkation and monitor identified vessels, cargo, and passengers en route to the U.S.

- *Develop a template for improving physical and operational port security:* DHS and DoT will collaborate with appropriate federal departments and agencies and port owners and operators to develop a template for improving physical and operational port security. A list of possible guidelines will include workforce identification measures, enhanced port-facility designs, vessel hardening plans, standards for international container seals, guidance for the research and development of noninvasive security and monitoring systems for cargo and ships, real-time and trace-back capability information for containers, prescreening processes for high-risk containers, and recovery plans. Activities will include reviewing the best practices of other countries.

- *Develop security and protection guidelines and technologies for cargo and passenger ships:* DHS and DoT will work with international maritime organizations and industry to study and develop appropriate guidelines and technology requirements for the security of cargo and passenger ships.

- *Improve waterway security:* DHS and DoT, working with state and local government owners and operators, will develop guidelines and identify needed support for improving security of waterways, such as developing electronic monitoring systems for waterway traffic; modeling shipping systems to identify and protect critical components; and identifying requirements and procedures for periodic waterway patrols.

[The U.S. Maritime Strategy[2] released by the U.S. Coast Guard in December 2002, defines the U.S. Coast Guard's role in Homeland Security. The following table summarizes the near-term program initiatives of the Coast Guard in securing maritime assets of the United States.]

Table 6.1 Near-Term Program Initiative of the U.S. Coast Guard

Strategic Elements	Near Term Initiatives
1. Increase Maritime Domain Awareness	<ul><li>Establish Maritime Intelligence Fusion Center at each Area to leverage interagency information sharing .</li><li>Co-chair with Navy a Joint Maritime Surveillance Working Group.</li><li>Install Secret Internet Protocol Router Network at each Captain of the Port and Group.</li><li>Install Global Command and Control System in all command centers.</li><li>Expand sensor capability with RESCUE-21, Ports and Waterways Safety System, Deepwater, and state-of-the-art port surveillance system.</li></ul>
2. Conduct Enhanced Security Operations	<ul><li>Commission Maritime Safety and Security Teams and enhance boarding team capabilities.</li><li>Evaluate arming all HH-60/65s.</li><li>Conduct robust exercise plan to test effectiveness of an expanded layered defense.</li><li>Acquire new small boat fleet.</li><li>Increase acquisition of WPB-87 Coastal Patrol Boat.</li><li>Deploy HC-130J with advanced C2 and sensor systems for increased maritime surveillance capability.</li></ul>
3. Close Port Security Gaps	<ul><li>Conduct and update Port Security Assessments on ports, vessels and facilities using Port Security Risk Assessment Tool methodology.</li><li>Conduct follow-on detailed vulnerability assessments on ports most at risk.</li><li>Plan and conduct port-level counter-terrorism exercises.</li></ul>

	■ Field bio-terrorism response policy.
	■ Establish Port Security Committees in each port with participation from all key stakeholders.
4. Build Critical Security Capabilities and Competencies	■ Expand, train and commission Maritime Safety and Security Teams.
	■ Expand security-training infrastructure to include Operational Intelligence and Maritime Law Enforcement Schools and Fast Boat Center of Excellence.
	■ Modernize via Deepwater upgraded C4ISR capabilities in 37 existing major cutters, all WPBs, selected HC-130s, all HH60Js, all HH65s and 12 command centers, and add new Maritime Patrol Aircrafts and Unmanned Aerial Vehicles.
	■ Develop skill sets in workforce to leverage increased technological capability being fielded.
5. Leverage Partnerships to Mitigate Security Risks	■ Conduct port vulnerability assessments.
	■ Establish and exercise specialized HAZMAT Response Teams and other critical capabilities from existing first responder type organizations.
	■ Pursue efforts to increase cargo security and enhance the security and validity of mariner documentation at international level.
6. Ensure Readiness for Homeland Defense	■ Field Deepwater to increase operational capability and DOD compatibility.
	■ Prepare to conduct operations as a supported and supporting commander to U.S. NORTHCOM.
	■ Prepare, equip, and train forces to conduct both Homeland Security and Homeland Defense operations and to transition smoothly between missions.
	■ Procure "Chemical, Biological, Radiological, Nuclear, and High-Yield Explosives" personal protective equipment for field personnel deemed at risk.
	■ Develop training programs to ensure safety and effectiveness of Coast Guard personnel pursuing Homeland security and Homeland defense missions.

Mass Transit Systems

Each year passengers take approximately 9.5 billion trips on public transit. In fact, mass transit carries more passengers in a single day than air or rail transportation. If the effect on air transportation resulting from the September 11 attacks is an indicator, then a terrorist attack on a major mass transit system could have a significant regional and national economic impact.

Mass transit systems are designed to be publicly accessible. Most are owned and operated by state and local agencies. A city relies on its mass transit system to serve a significant portion of its workforce in addition to being a means of evacuation in case of emergency. Protection of mass transit systems is, therefore, an important requirement.

Mass Transit Mode Challenges

Mass transit is regulated by various agencies. These agencies must communicate and work together effectively to allow transit to work as a system rather than in separate modes. Mass transit is funded and managed at the local level, and operated as a not-for-profit entity. The Federal Transit Authority has limited legislative authority to oversee the security planning and operations of transit systems.

Mass transit systems were designed for openness and ease of public access, which makes monitoring points of entry and exit difficult. Protecting them is also expensive. Transit authorities must have the financial resources to respond to emergencies and maintain adequate security levels to deter attacks over broad geographic areas. The cost of implementing new security requirements could result in significant financial consequences for the industry.

Each city and region has a unique transit system, varying in size and design. No one security program or information sharing mechanism will fit all systems. Despite these differences, as a general rule, basic planning factors are relatively consistent from system to system.

Mass Transit Mode Initiatives

Since transit is localized and varies significantly in size and design from system to system, identifying critical guidelines and standards for planning is key to unifying mass transit security activities. Panels in the Transit Cooperative Research Program have recommended and are overseeing 10 research projects in the areas of prevention, mitigation, preparedness, and response. Their recommendations can provide additional input to the development of these planning areas.

Additional mass transit protection initiatives include efforts to:

■ *Identify critical planning areas and develop appropriate guidelines and standards:* DHS, working closely with DoT and other federal, state, and local mass transit officials, will identify critical planning areas and develop appropriate guidelines and standards to protect mass transit systems. Such critical planning areas and guidelines include design and engineering standards for facilities and rail and bus vehicles; emergency guidance for operations staff; screening methods and training programs for operators; security planning oversight standards; mutual aid policies; and continuity of operations planning.

- *Identify protective impediments and implement security enhancements:* DHS, working closely with DoT and mode representatives, will review legal, legislative, and statutory regimes to develop an overall protective architecture for mass transit systems and to identify impediments to implementing needed security enhancements.

- *Work with other sectors to manage unique risks resulting from interdependencies:* DHS, in collaboration with DoT, will convene cross-sector working groups to develop models for integrating priorities and emergency response plans in the context of interdependencies between mass transit and other critical infrastructures.

AASHTO Study: Highway Transportation Systems

A relatively recent study, conducted under the auspices of the Transportation Security Task Force of the American Association of State Highway and Transportation Officials (AASHTO), by Douglas B. Ham & Stephen Lockwood of Parsons Brinckerhoff (PB) and SAIC, assessed the possible threats and vulnerabilities of the nationwide highway transportation infrastructure and examined countermeasure programs. The three key security planning program areas that the study recommends are:

- Protecting critical mobility assets,

- Enhancing traffic management capabilities, and

- Improving state DOT (Department of Transportation) emergency response capabilities. (p. v)

The SAIC/Parsons Brinckerhoff report identified the key threats to highway transportation infrastructure in terms of targets of attraction and potential methods of attack. It identified critical assets within the highway system based on assumed national level criteria regarding the potential consequences of damage or destruction. Then it assessed the risks to key asset classes, responding principally to the generic vulnerabilities of each asset class. The report specified the deterrent and mitigation countermeasures and estimated costs using current unit costs. Most of the measures proposed in the 2002 report are modest retrofits designed for deterrence and detection with minimal hardening investments. The following sections are excerpted from that report.

THREAT ASSESSMENT[3]

...A countermeasure program must make reasonable assumptions about the nature of threats faced in order to determine an appropriate countermeasures strategy. The definition of the programs assumed for these security programs was built on a series of risk management assumptions: (1) that any particular terrorist target event is essentially a low probability, high consequence event, and as such, risk mitigation strategies should differentiate among priorities, based on target criticality; and (2) that reasonable risk for critical assets must be accepted since mitigation is necessarily incomplete.

Threat Assumptions

Terrorists have a history of attacking transportation assets such as cars and buses. These attacks have normally been associated with violent explosions and/or gunfire. However, the face of terrorism has been changing over the years. Today's international terrorists have been moving from isolated bombings, hijackings, and hostage-taking to the indiscriminate slaughter of innocent men, women, and children. The recent terrorist trend is toward inflicting a high number of civilian casualties, more extensive property damage, and the increasingly devastating effects on economies. [The] 9/11 attack, the Atlanta Olympics and Oklahoma City bombings, and the gassing of the Tokyo subway a few years ago killing 10 and injuring over 5,000, evidence this shift.

However, compared to other transportation modes, physical highway assets are relatively robust and redundant, and the mass casualty potential is lower than other types of targets. Nonetheless, the use of large [weapons of mass destruction (WMD)] has greater potential of destroying and disrupting critical transportation and economic links of the highway network than lesser weapons. At the same time, components of the highway system can play an essential emergency management function. Therefore, while it is appropriate that other assets may receive priority attention for their mass casualty vulnerability, responsible owner-operators should consider the protection of key assets from the point of view of the consequences of loss by direct attack as well as in the context of attacks on other assets.

Key assumptions underlying the threat assessment include:

- Terrorist objectives are presumed to be political, economic, and social disruption inflicted through damage and destruction of physical facilities, large numbers of civilian deaths and injuries, and public demoralization.

- The preferred targets for terrorist attacks continue to be "soft" targets, such as business, tourist sites, and facilities with limited security precautions.

- Transportation assets generally have relatively low attractiveness as terrorist targets because the potential for casualties is fairly modest. Transit and rail systems are regarded by law enforcement to be more likely targets. Highway assets in particular seem less attractive as targets, given their physical robustness, systems redundancy, and relative ease of replacement.

- However, some highway structures, like major bridges and tunnels, play critical roles spanning large natural barriers such as rivers, bays, mountains, and serve unique regional and national transportation and economic roles. Major damage or destruction of these structures could have severe economic and mobility consequences.

- Regarding highway infrastructure, terrorism objectives may focus on destruction/damage to the physical assets as well as the transient use population.

- Open source material indicates that Al-Qaeda-type terrorists also appear to be attracted to targets with high symbolic value. Some bridges and tunnels have high visibility and constitute regional and national symbols.

- Terrorist tactics seem to focus on attacks that are relatively simple, easy to coordinate, and utilize readily available materials, relying on secrecy, surprise, and speed.

- Of those assets under state DOT jurisdiction, major bridges (including interchange bridges) and tunnels are generally assumed to be the most attractive terrorist targets. Headquarters, district, and maintenance facilities appear to be less threatened as probable targets of a terrorist attack; however, disruption of operations in such facilities could significantly impair delivery of public services.

Terrorist threats theoretically include the complete array of WMD—conventional explosives, chemical, biological, and nuclear/radiological weapons. However, bridges and tunnels are not likely to be prime targets for WMD of the chemical, biological, or radiological variety that would normally target civilian population concentrations. This is not to say that a radiological or biochemical attack against a bridge or tunnel is not possible; rather that it is a less probable threat. Limited physical, on-site countermeasures related to bridge and tunnel design or operations with respect to chemical, biological, or radiological threats are included. These are focused on the tunnel ventilation systems. More general deterrence against such WMD attacks with their presumed population targeting is appropriately part of security and law enforcement jurisdiction – not public works entities. Open-source literature indicates that Al-Qaeda-type terrorist attacks seem to be characterized by "high concept/low tech" approaches with a preference for explosive force and martyr risks. Therefore, this analysis focuses on explosive attacks including as threats a range of such weapons as:

- Portable, hand-placed cutting charges placed on or near structures, e.g., 100 pounds of C4;

- Vehicle or boat-borne explosives, e.g., the 4,000 pounds of explosives of fertilizer/oil mix (ANFO) used in the Murrah Center attack; and

- Up to 60,000 pounds of explosives delivered in semi-trailers or boats of various sizes.

These weapons may be maneuvered to locations immediately adjacent to, under, or even inside structures. Remote rocket and missile-borne explosive attacks are theoretically possible, but not likely, and countermeasures within a state DOT's jurisdiction are limited....

The Nation's highway infrastructure is robust. Compared to other transportation assets, the highway infrastructure is relatively invulnerable. Highways and associated facilities are part of networks with a high degree of ubiquity and redundancy. Loss of individual assets could, in some cases, be substantially inconvenient and damage a local economy, but the damage would not be permanent or irreparable. In addition, the physical structures are, by design, relatively resistant to major forces. In some cases, structures are designed to absorb accidents through the use of pier ramming design criteria. It makes sense, therefore, to concentrate protective measures on the segment of the asset inventory where destruction would have the greatest consequences.

Critical Assets and Recognizable Assets

Not all assets are equally important in their function. As a point-of-departure risk management assumption, the most "critical" assets – from a national perspective – are identified from a consequence perspective; that is, critical assets are those major facilities the loss of which would significantly reduce interregional mobility over an extended period and thereby damage the national economy and defense mobility. Such assets include major bridges (including key urban interchange components) and major tunnels on the upper-level highway system in the U.S. that play significant roles in linking important economic activity centers, markets and production centers, urban centers and suburbs, military forts, and ports – across major physical boundaries such as rivers, mountain chains, estuaries, and bays. These may appropriately be classified as "critical". The risk management perspective applied also presumes that even among the most consequence-based "critical" assets, certain assets may be more likely targets, based on the type of thinking that characterizes international terrorists, such as Al-Qaeda. These assets are those that are "recognizable" – highly visible and well-known symbols of a nation or region, the loss of which could demoralize the public as well as be costly or greatly inconvenient. These structures or facilities should be singled out for extra security precautions.

In addition, there are agency assets, such as transportation management centers, the loss of which would significantly handicap emergency response functions. These types of activities are often housed in unprotected commercial buildings. These are also classified as "critical" for the purpose of this analysis.

Critical Bridges

There are over 582,000 bridges in the U.S. over 20 feet in length. As there are no open-source "official" criteria or lists of critical assets, state and authority transportation systems owner-operators will have to make their own determinations as to which structures or facilities to protect and the appropriate level of protection. AASHTO has produced guidance material, and several states are conducting systematic vulnerability analyses and assessing appropriate protective measures.... Critical bridges were defined by functional criteria and presumed to be those deserving of a basic level of protective actions.

The criteria employed to define nationally "critical" include:

> Casualty Risk – Number of users exposed as reflected in:
> - The main span size of the bridge, that is, over 50m/165 feet, and
> - Traffic over 40,000 average daily traffic (ADT).
>
> Economic Disruption – Disruption of the national economy as indicated by:
> - Bridges located on the Interstate Highway System plus the Department of Defense-defined Strategic Highway Network (STRAHNET),
> - Traffic over 40,000 ADT,
> - Main span length over 50 meters/165 feet,
> - Double deck bridges, and
> - Nearest detour distance more than 5 km/3 miles for bridges under 60,000 ADT.

Military Support Function:
- Bridges on STRAHNET and/or on the Military Traffic Management Command (MTMC)-defined "Power Projection Routes" serving forts within 400 miles of port, and
- Main span over 50m/165 feet.

Emergency Relief Function:
- Bridges in 78 major metropolitan areas, and
- On upper level system, i.e., freeways, expressways, and principal arterials.

National Recognition:
- Bridges with symbolic importance.

Collateral Damage Exposure:
- Bridges carrying other utilities, e.g., pipelines and major power and communications lines.

Application of these criteria results in a group of 391 bridges on the 45,376-mile Interstate System and an additional 60 bridges on the 15,668 miles of STRAHNET. This list of 451 includes most of the larger bridges that span the Mississippi and other larger rivers, and major estuaries on all coasts. 142 of the "critical" bridges cross navigable waterways such as major rivers, harbors, and estuaries. The list also includes components of major urban interchanges, i.e., 166 bridges have additional highway service underneath....

Critical and Recognizable Bridges

It may be reasonably assumed that the critical list of 451 bridges identified by the criteria above would include most of the structures that are nationally known by proper name with specific historic or symbolic importance.... It may be reasonably assumed that these are also the largest structures and carry the most traffic....

Critical Tunnels

The "critical" tunnel list was developed based on material in the FHWA report, Development of a Tunnel Management System (TMS) – Phase I Report. This report is not yet complete, but it contains the only listing of most of the major tunnels. The TMS report provides limited physical and jurisdictional characteristics, e.g., size, length, and type, although, unlike the National Bridge Inventory, it does not address use intensity, detour length, or other potentially important factors. Absent additional data, the 54 tunnel facilities over 500m/1640 feet in length were identified as "critical" in light of the physical barriers to quick reconstruction and the detour implications. Eighteen of these facilities are on the Interstate Highway System. Most of these longer tunnels have updated ventilation systems and are also likely to be both staffed and equipped with upto-date fire, incident detection, and safety equipment consistent with National Fire Protection Association (NFPA) 502 standards.

Tunnel ventilation systems represent a point of vulnerability regarding insertion of chemical and/or biological agents targeting tunnel users. While the low density of people at any given time and rate of mechanical and vehicle-induced ventilation reduces potential impacts, some protection of ventilation intakes (often associated with portal buildings) is included.

Among the 54 tunnels, 20 percent were assumed to be critical and recognizable and are singled out for special countermeasures as described in [the next section] below. It may be reasonably assumed that these are also the largest structures and carry the most traffic. However, it should be noted that this study is not designed for disaggregating below the national level and purposely does not identify the "critical" or "recognizable" assets by name or location.

Bridge and Tunnel Vulnerability

Protective measures discussed herein are limited to explosive attacks across the complete range of weapon size delivered as proximity attacks via mechanisms ranging from backpack to semi-trailer truck or boat.

The effect of a blast on a structure depends on several factors:

- The composition, size and shape of the explosive material (the effect of fragments from a vehicle bomb are less damaging than cased military munitions).

- The distance of the explosive from the structure (stand-off distance).

- The material composition and arrangements of the exposed structural element.

Bridges vary widely in their vulnerability depending on structure size, type, design, and setting. In general, explosives in portable quantity applied to the substructure of larger bridges are not considered a serious collapse threat – unless a terrorist demolition expert has the time to carefully place those explosives. However, truck- and boat-borne explosives can cause more damage, including total collapse, depending on proximity, placement, and explosive yield....

Different structure types interact in different ways with the same blast size.... Countermeasures, therefore, focus on minimizing the potential for large explosives at short distances (blast yield/proximity), access to critical locations, and time on target, as well as hardening vulnerable structural elements.

For purposes of estimating countermeasure costs, bridges in the critical class were categorized by three vulnerability-based structure types since proposed countermeasures respond to vulnerability differences. Based on [national bridge inventory] data, the critical bridges include 19 suspension or cable-stayed bridges, 48 through-truss or arch bridges, and 384 "other" types, mostly girder and beam. Forty-four of the longer bridges (over 200m/650 feet total span) have significant above-deck structural components. These bridges present a more direct vulnerability to road-based attacks, just as bridges over navigable water present additional vulnerabilities to attacks on in-water piers.

There is limited open-source material discussing highway facility vulnerability other than that utilized within the Department of Defense (DOD) context. Seismic design experience has some relevance – especially regarding connections that preserve full structural capacity. Current general assumptions regarding bridge vulnerability, based on judgments by USACE (U.S. Army Corps of Engineers),

[Federal Highway Administration], and [Parsons Brinckerhoff] experts, regarding structural vulnerability include:

- Bridges and tunnels cannot be fully protected against significant disruption to roadway decks from even modest explosive quantities.

- Significant damage to the substructure of smaller bridges is to be expected with even modest explosive quantities. However, smaller bridges are not within the criteria used for "critical." Conversely, larger bridges – including double-deck structures – are considered more likely targets.

- Larger bridges are less vulnerable by virtue of member size, spacing, redundancy, and ductility, including cables and hangers. Total collapse of single- or multiple- span bridges is less likely, although significant elements can be destroyed. Hinges and anchorages are special points of vulnerability, although access can be protected....

Bridge and Tunnel Countermeasures and Costs

Current military and engineering judgment indicates that complete protection from destruction of key structural elements is not feasible or cost effective. The countermeasures strategy must therefore include elements that focus on the DOD-based "4-D" approach:

- Deter attacks by the possibility of exposure, capture, or failure due to visible countermeasures.

- Detect potential attacks before they occur and provide the appropriate response force.

- Defend the asset by delaying and distancing the attacker from the asset and protecting the asset from the effects of weapons.

- Design (redesign) the asset to minimize the potential effects of WMD and conventional explosives.

These strategies, while focused in this report on asset protection, also have important life-saving benefits because they reduce the potential of significant damage to structures and facilities, as well as the attractiveness of the targets to threats.

The overall practical objective of the counter-terrorism measures is not to provide full protection of the assets, but to encourage terrorists to look elsewhere for easier targets (displacement) that will most likely involve less critical assets. Countermeasures, therefore, focus on:

- Maximizing standoff distance to key structural members via changes in land-use (relocation of parking, park use, etc.) and installation of various types of barriers at abutments and piers adjacent to above-roadway deck superstructures in through-deck truss and arch bridges.

- Denial of access to locations that would otherwise allow manual placement of explosives at points of structural vulnerability.

- Minimizing time-on-target for terrorists to undertake strategic placement of multiple time-coordinated detonations by using illumination surveillance cameras, real-time intrusion detection devices, and an active security patrol response.

- Selective upgrade of key structural members by strengthening may be feasible within the live- and dead-load limits of the structure. These might include the strengthening of key connections, modifications of hinges, and additions of stiffening elements to key members. Some of the features of earthquake-resistant design (e.g., ductility, connection details, redundancy, load redistribution, carbon fiber reinforced polymer wrapping) are also applicable in blast-resistant design.

- Reduction of access to mechanical systems that introduce threats to personnel, e.g., infiltration of tunnel vents by biological and/or chemical agents and to areas that might compromise bascule or drawbridge operations should be considered.

- Coordination with local law enforcement through the use of automated detection and surveillance equipment, regular patrols and pre-planned routines for intrusion detection, and response to actual incidents....

Countermeasure Programs Suggested (in AASHTO Report)[4]

The principal threat against highway physical assets is explosive attacks on key links such as bridges, interchanges, and tunnels. Facilities most vulnerable to disruptions are those playing important regional and strategic roles, the loss of which would be maximally disruptive and involving greater replacement challenges. On a nationwide basis, approximately 450 bridges and 50 tunnels meet relevant criteria as critical assets. While full asset protection is not feasible, reasonable program objectives include the deterrence of terrorist attacks by (1) adding new and clearly visible security features and reducing vulnerabilities, and (2) minimizing the potential for damage in the event of an attack.

Protecting Critical Mobility Assets

The overall practical objective of the proposed security program is, therefore, not to provide full protection, but to discourage terrorist attack through visible security and reduced vulnerability, as well as to minimize damage in the event of an attack. To protect these assets, the following countermeasures are proposed as retrofits on critical bridge, interchange, and tunnel assets:

- Maximize potential explosives placement standoff distance to key structural members or mechanical systems via various types of barriers.

- Deny access to locations where placement of explosives would affect points of structural integrity and vulnerability for infiltration of mechanical systems through the installation of locks, caging, and various types of fencing.

- Minimize time-on-target for terrorists via installation of real-time intrusion detection and surveillance systems.

- Selectively protect the structural integrity of key members against collapse by strengthening key substructure members and blast shielding.

In addition, these strategies are also assumed to be routinely applied to larger bridges as they undergo their normal reconstruction cycle.

Total costs for this asset protection initiative are estimated at $2.4 billion over the six-year period, including $1.5 billion in capital costs and $880 million for operations and maintenance (O&M). These numbers breakout as follows: (1) bridges: $1.4 billion in capital costs and $880 million for O&M, (2) tunnels: $60 million in capital costs, and (3) transportation management centers: $50 million in capital costs.

Enhancing Traffic Management Capabilities

Many of the nation's larger metropolitan areas are already installing advanced traffic management systems to better manage normal congestion. Expanding deployment of these "intelligent transportation systems" (ITS) is under discussion as a focus of current AASHTO and FHWA (Federal Highway Administration) Reauthorization concepts. Systematic region-wide deployment of such systems could also substantially enhance the ability of metropolitan roadway systems to support terrorism-related evacuation and emergency response. Seventy-eight metropolitan areas with populations over 550,000 are identified for initial implementation. These 78 metro areas collectively encompass 10,500 miles of freeways and expressways and 16,000 miles of signalized principal arterials. In addition, 1,800 miles of connector routes on the Department of Defense Strategic Highway Network (STRAHNET) are included in this initiative because they link to highway-dependent military installations.

The improved evacuation and emergency access capabilities are achieved by the following program:

- Deployment of ITS technologies on the applicable roadways, including (1) automatic vehicle detection, (2) camera surveillance, and (3) variable message signs – together with their integration into existing traffic management centers.

- Establishment of nine new regional security guidance centers capable of issuing real-time, event-responsive routing directives during emergencies based on remote imaging, incident tracking, and dynamic routing technologies.

Total costs for this initiative are estimated at $5.6 billion over the six-year period, including $3.7 billion in capital costs and $1.9 billion for O&M.

Improving State DOT Emergency Response Capabilities

The third program area is focused on upgrading the capabilities of state transportation agencies to conduct their emergency preparation, response, and recovery responsibilities as part of state and local emergency management during and after a terrorist incident. Within existing statewide "all hazard" emergency management planning, there is an opportunity to strengthen the role of state DOTs through capitalizing on their distributed personnel, incident response training, and statewide communications networks. To achieve these objectives, the following state DOT program elements are proposed:

- Strengthen state DOT emergency operations plans and develop specific procedures for various types of terrorist incidents.

- Conduct detailed terrorist incident response training for state DOT personnel, including the staging of interagency emergency response exercises.

- Develop and deploy hardened and interoperable statewide communications networks.

- Prepare network traffic management and surveillance systems for emergency evacuation and access operations.

- Expand and upgrade real-time security operations and coordination, including protection of traffic management centers.

Total costs for this set of countermeasures are estimated at $2.5 billion over the six-year period, including $940 million in capital costs and $1.6 billion for O&M.

EXAMINATION OF BORDER PROTECTION ISSUES POST-9/11

The first National Strategy for Homeland Security issued by President Bush in July 2002 is the most recent official document (as of this writing) that addresses the border protection issues in general post 9/11. This strategy underlines the threat of terrorism within the United States in terms of organizing the domestic efforts of federal, state, local, and private organizations and recommends certain actions to Congress. The strategic objectives of this plan, in order of priority, are "to prevent terrorist attacks within the United States, reduce America's vulnerability to terrorism, and minimize the damage and recover from attacks that do occur (White House, 2002, 2)." The following sections excerpted from the National Strategy for Homeland Security document, describe the post 9/11 border protection issues combined with transportation security issues, and describe the strategic objectives of the Bush Administration in order to deal with those issues.

Border and Transportation Security[5]

The United States shares a 5,525-mile border with Canada and a 1,989 mile border with Mexico. Our maritime border includes 95,000 miles of shoreline and navigable waterways as well as a 3.4 million square mile exclusive economic zone. All people and goods legally entering into the United States must be processed through an air, land, or sea port of entry. Many international airports are dispersed throughout the United States. Each year, more than 500 million people legally enter our country. Some 330 million are non-citizens; more than 85 percent enter via land borders, often as daily commuters. An enormous volume of trade also crosses our borders every day—some $1.35 trillion in imports and $1 trillion in exports were processed in 2001.

America historically has relied heavily on two vast oceans and two friendly neighbors for border security, and on the private sector for most forms of domestic transportation security. The increasing mobility and destructive potential of modern terrorism has required the United States to rethink and rearrange fundamentally its systems for border and transportation security. Indeed, we must now begin to conceive of border security and transportation security as fully integrated requirements because our domestic transportation systems are intertwined inextricably with the global transport infrastructure. Virtually every community in America is connected to the global transportation network by the seaports, airports, highways, pipelines, railroads, and waterways that move people and goods into, within, and out of the Nation. We therefore must promote the efficient and reliable flow of people, goods, and services across borders, while preventing terrorists from using transportation conveyances or systems to deliver implements of destruction.

National Vision

A single entity in the Department of Homeland Security will manage who and what enters our homeland in order to prevent the entry of terrorists and the instruments of terror while facilitating the legal flow of people, goods, and services on which our economy depends. The Department and its partners will conduct border security functions abroad to the extent allowed by technology and international agreements. Federal law enforcement agencies will take swift action against those who introduce contraband or violate terms of entry and pose threats to the American people. The U.S. government will work with the international community and the private sector to secure the transportation systems which link American communities to the world, moving people and goods across our borders and throughout the country within hours.

Major Initiatives

Ensure accountability in border and transportation security. The President has proposed to Congress that the principal border and transportation security agencies—the Immigration and Naturalization Service, U.S. Customs Service, U.S. Coast Guard, Animal and Plant Health Inspection Service, and Transportation Security Agency—be transferred to the new Department of Homeland Security. The new Department also would control the issuance of visas to foreigners through the Department of State and would coordinate the border-control activities of all federal agencies that are not incorporated within the new Department.

Create *"smart borders."* Our future border management system will be radically different from today's which focuses on linear borders. It will create a "border of the future" that will be a continuum framed by land, sea, and air dimensions, where a layered management system enables greater visibility of vehicles, people, and goods coming to and departing from our country. This border of the future will provide greater security through better intelligence, coordinated national efforts, and unprecedented international cooperation against the threats posed by terrorists, the implements of terrorism, international organized crime, illegal drugs, illegal migrants, cyber crime, and the destruction or theft of natural resources. At the same time, the border of the future will be increasingly transparent to the efficient flow of people, goods, and conveyances engaged in legitimate economic and social activities. The federal government will allocate resources in a balanced way to manage risk in our border and transportation security systems while ensuring the expedient flow of goods, services, and people.

Internationally, the United States will seek to screen and verify the security of goods and identities of people before they can harm to the international transportation system and well before they reach our shores or land borders. The Department of Homeland Security would improve information provided to consular officers so that individual applicants can be checked in comprehensive databases and would require visa-issuance procedures to reflect threat assessments. The United States will require visitors to present travel documentation that includes biometric identifiers. The United States will also work with international organizations and the private sector to improve the security of people, goods, conveyances traveling internationally, and the ports that they use. The United States will work with other countries and international organizations to improve the quality of travel documents and their issuance to minimize their misuse by smugglers and terrorist organizations. We will also assist other countries, as appropriate, to improve their border controls and their coordination with us. Finally, we will work closely with Canada and Mexico to increase the security of our shared borders while facilitating commerce within the North American Free Trade Agreement (NAFTA) area.

At our borders, the Department of Homeland Security would verify and process the entry of people in order to prevent the entrance of contraband, unauthorized aliens, and potential terrorists. The Department would increase the information available on inbound goods and passengers so that border management agencies can apply risk-based management tools. The Department would develop and deploy the statutorily required entry-exit system to record the arrival and departure of foreign visitors and guests. It would develop and deploy non-intrusive inspection technologies to ensure rapid and more thorough screening of goods and conveyances. And it would monitor all our borders in order to detect illegal intrusions and intercept and apprehend smuggled goods and people attempting to enter illegally.

The Department of Homeland Security proposed by the President will also build an immigration services organization that administers immigration laws in an efficient, expeditious, fair, and humane manner. The Department would ensure that foreign visitors comply with entry conditions. The Department, in cooperation with colleges and universities, would track and monitor international students and exchange visitors. The Department would enter into national law enforcement databases the names of high-risk aliens who remain in the United States longer than authorized and, when warranted, deport illegal aliens.

Increase the security of international shipping containers. Containers are an indispensable but vulnerable link in the chain of global trade; approximately 90 percent of the world's cargo moves by container. Each year, nearly 50 percent of the value of all U.S. imports arrives via 16 million containers. The core elements of this initiative are to establish security criteria to identify high-risk containers; pre-screen containers before they arrive at U.S. ports; use technology to inspect high-risk containers;

and develop and use smart and secure containers. The United States will place inspectors at foreign seaports to screen U.S.-bound sea containers before they are shipped to America, initially focusing on the top 20 "mega" ports (including Rotterdam, Antwerp, and Le Havre), because roughly 68 percent of the 5.7 million sea containers entering the United States annually arrive from these seaports.

Implement the Aviation and Transportation Security Act of 2001. On November 19, 2001, the President signed into law the Aviation and Transportation Security Act of 2001. The act established a series of challenging but important milestones toward achieving a secure air travel system. More broadly, however, the act fundamentally changed the way transportation security will be performed and managed in the United States. The continued growth of the world economy—and, in particular, commercial transportation and tourism— depends upon effective transportation security measures being efficiently applied. The act recognized the importance of security for all forms of transportation and related infrastructure elements. This cannot be accomplished by the federal government in isolation and requires strengthened partnerships among federal, state, and local government officials and the private sector to reduce vulnerabilities and adopt the best practices available today. Protection of critical transportation assets such as ports, pipelines, rail, and highway bridges, and more than 10,000 FAA facilities is another key requirement established by the act.

Additionally, the Transportation Security Administration will coordinate federal efforts to secure the national airspace—an essential medium for travel, commerce, and recreation. The federal government will work with the private sector to upgrade security in all modes of transportation. Areas of emphasis will include: commercial aviation and other mass transportation systems; intermodal transportation; hazardous and explosive materials; national airspace; shipping container security; traffic-management systems; critical infrastructure; surety of transportation operators and workers; linkages with international transportation systems; and information sharing. We will utilize existing modal relationships and systems to implement unified, national standards for transportation security.

Recapitalize the U.S. Coast Guard. The Budget for Fiscal Year 2003 requested the largest increase in the history of the U.S. Coast Guard. The Budget for Fiscal Year 2004 will continue to support the recapitalization of the U.S. Coast Guard's aging fleet, as well as targeted improvements in the areas of maritime domain awareness, command and control systems, and shore-side facilities. The United States asks much of its U.S. Coast Guard and we will ensure the service has the resources needed to accomplish its multiple missions. We saw the dedication and the versatility of the U.S. Coast Guard in the aftermath of September 11, a performance that vividly demonstrated the U.S. Coast Guard's vital contribution to homeland security. Nevertheless, the U.S. Coast Guard is also responsible for national defense, maritime safety, maritime mobility, and protection of natural resources, and would continue to fulfill these functions in the Department of Homeland Security.

Reform immigration services. The Administration will complete reform of the Immigration and Naturalization Service (INS), separating the agency's enforcement and service functions within, as the President has proposed, the new

Department of Homeland Security. This reform aims to ensure full enforcement of the laws that regulate the admission of aliens to the United States and to improve greatly the administration of immigration benefits to more than 7 million annual applicants. Americans have long cherished our identity as a nation of immigrants. This reform will ensure that every applicant's case is reviewed in a timely and courteous way. Finally, the Department of Homeland Security would implement the Enhanced Border Security and Visa Entry Reform Act, including the requirement that foreign visitors possess travel documents with biometric information.

REFERENCES

Ham, D. B., & Lockwood, S., with Science Applications International Corporation (SAIC). (2002). *National Needs Assessment for Ensuring Transportation Infrastructure Security*. Retrieved from <http://security.transportation.org/sites/security/docs/NatlNeedsAssess.pdf>.

U.S. Coast Guard (USCG). (2002). *Maritime Strategy for Homeland Security* (Dec.) Washington, DC: The United States Coast Guard. Retrieved from <http://www.uscg.mil/news/reportsandbudget/Maritime_strategy/USCG_Maritme_Strategy.pdf>.

White House. (2002). *The National Strategy for Homeland Security* (pp. 21-24). Retrieved from <http://www.dhs.gov/interweb/assetlibrary/nat_strat_hls.pdf>.

White House. (2003). *The National Strategy for the Protection of Critical Infrastructures and Key Assets*. Retrieved from <http://www.whitehouse.gov/pcipb/physical_strategy.pdf>.

... SUPPLEMENTARY READINGS ON TRANSPORTATION INFRASTRUCTURE VULNERABILITY

Hoover Dam[6]

From the standpoint of public officials in Nevada and Arizona, Hoover Dam has been identified as a potential target for terrorists. After decades of planning and years of study, federal and state officials from Nevada and Arizona gathered in October 2002, to mark the start of construction on the Hoover Dam bypass bridge. Preparations to relocate electrical transmission towers from the path of the bridge also in October 2002, on the project officials said will sit alongside Hoover Dam as an engineering marvel and landmark. The bridge will replace U.S. Highway 93's two-lane hairpin route through the volcanic rock of Black Canyon and over the top of the dam as the primary route between Nevada and Arizona. Protection of the dam and Lake Mead, the primary drinking water source for Southern Nevada, has always been one of the project's chief purposes. But officials said the terrorist attacks of Sept. 11, 2001, proved the need is urgent.

The fiscal cost have been high, the ban on big rigs crossing the dam, in place since September 11, 2001, has cost the trucking industry and consumers about $30 million a year, according to some estimates.

The bridge will render the truck ban irrelevant and pave the way for U.S. Highway 93 to become a part of the CANAMEX trade corridor, which stretches from Mexico City to Alberta. The trade route was established under the North American Free Trade Agreement. After crews' finish removing six electrical transmission towers from the path of the bridge and its approach roads, work on the Arizona approach route began in January 2003. Work on the longer and more engineers challenging Nevada portion of the project began in late 2003. The final and most challenging phase of construction will be the 1,900-foot canyon bridge. The bridge, which will combine a concrete arch and steel superstructure, will anchor to the sheer sides of Black Canyon. The project, which is scheduled to be completed by 2007, the total cost of the project should be approximately 108 million dollars.

FBI investigates train derailment[7]

ASSOCIATED PRESS
Oct.11, 1995

HYDER, Ariz.—FBI agents hunting the saboteur who derailed an Amtrak train worked Tuesday to determine whether the Sons of Gestapo is really an anti-government terrorist group or just someone with a grudge against the railroad.

The FBI expanded its painstaking search for evidence to a mile-square area surrounding the gulch where the Sunset Limited lurched off a damaged track and asked the public for help finding the culprit.

The train jumped the tracks at the damaged section early Monday, toppling 30 feet from a bridge, killing a crew member and injuring at least 78 people.

A letter found at the scene mentioned federal raids on right-wing extremists at Waco, Texas, and Ruby Ridge, Idaho. It was signed Sons of Gestapo, raising fears the sabotage was the work of anti-government extremists.

FBI officials had a brief news conference six miles from the scene Tuesday, but offered little insight into the investigation called Operation Splitrail, and refused to comment about the letter.

With about 90 agents on the scene, Larry McCormick, acting special agent in charge of the Phoenix office, said he believed it was the bureau's second-biggest crime scene investigation after the Oklahoma City bombing.

"We are going to pursue every bit of evidence and every lead very thoroughly until we find the person or persons who committed this crime," U.S. Attorney Janet Napolitano said.

Acting on a tip, FBI agents found a derailing device on a set of railroad tracks in downtown Phoenix. Special Agent Al Davidson said the bureau knew nothing to connect the discovery with the derailment.

Derailment devices are not commonly used in railroad operation or maintenance, said Edward Emmett, president of the National Industrial Transportation League.

The case was put under the supervision of Assistant FBI Director Robert Bryant, who runs the bureau's national security division, according to a senior Justice Department official who spoke to the Associated Press in Washington on condition of anonymity. The division handles terrorism cases.

"Bryant's national security division has the case because it has the potential to become a terrorism case, but we have not reached any conclusions yet whether terrorism is the motive or not," the source said.

No group called Sons of Gestapo is known to experts at Klanwatch, which tracks hate groups for the Southern Poverty Law Center in Montgomery, Ala. An extensive search of news archives turned up no reference to the group.

Klaus Haase, a German historian specializing in the Gestapo, said he knows of no German or foreign groups using the name Gestapo.

A veteran federal investigator, speaking on condition of anonymity, told the AP in Washington that a disgruntled Amtrak employee or someone simply bent on mischief might have concocted a note to deflect attention.

"I don't know if this is a disgruntled employee of ours or another railroad, or someone else. Someone did know enough about the railroad to wire this," said Amtrak President Thomas M. Downs at a news conference Sunday.

Downs said the saboteurs removed a 3-foot, 18-pound steel bar that holds sections of rail together, and bridged the gap with a wire to disable an electrical system that gives a red light to warn trains of breaks in the track.

Twenty-nine of the spikes that hold the rail to the wooden crossties on a 19-foot section of track had been removed, according to a source who spoke on condition of anonymity.

The train, carrying 248 passengers and 20 crew members from Miami to Los Angeles, derailed about 1:20 a.m. Monday along an isolated stretch of track 55 miles southwest of Phoenix. Four cars were thrown into a gulch.

The White House said it was too early to be sure terrorism was involved, but President Clinton expressed outrage.

"We will do everything we can within the federal government to catch whoever is responsible," he said. "I am determined that we will make sure in the United States that we will have the tools, the means we need to keep the American people safe."

The investigation—carried out by the FBI, the National Transportation Safety Board and other state and federal agencies—was run from a staging area six miles from the crash site and accessible only by dirt road.

Construction crews began widening and grading a road to the bridge from the staging area. Four cranes stood by to remove the damaged cars.

"Once everyone is satisfied with the information they have, we'll start clearing away the wreckage," NTSB investigator Mike Martino said

Amtrak has stepped up its own security and asked freight railroads whose tracks it uses to do the same, said spokesman Stephen Taubenkibel in Washington. The line is also working with commuter railroads, he said.

"We're asking that everyone be more security conscious," he said.

Gov. Fife Symington said he has read the Sons of Gestapo letter. He wouldn't talk about what it said, except to say he was told there were multiple versions that were comparable in terms of content.

Symington offered a $10,000 reward for information leading to an arrest and conviction and said the Maricopa County Board of Supervisors matched his offer, making the total $20,000.

Oklahoma Gov. Frank Keating sent a letter of condolence to Symington that drew parallels with the April 19 bombing of the federal building there, allegedly by anti-government extremists.

"The people of Oklahoma understand your shock and outrage as few others could," Keating wrote. "May those who are hurting be healed, and may the despicable authors of this act be brought swiftly to justice."

Bridge, tunnel security tightens[8]

One strategy is to check vehicles before, not after, they reach the border crossings

By Gregg Krupa / *The Detroit News*
Oct. 1, 2001

DETROIT—When engineers at the Ambassador Bridge reported for work Sept. 12, they put aside their half-completed designs for expanding operations and immediately began planning for a new reality.

After the terrorist attacks of Sept. 11, any new plans for making the trip to and from Canada would have to address security issues as the top priority. That sense was only magnified the first day of heightened security as columns of trucks waited hours to creep across the bridge, which carries more than 12 million vehicles a year.

The expansion plans now have to account for the possibility of switching the U.S. Customs stops to the Canadian side and the Canadian stops to the U.S. side. While no one has officially proposed such a move, a consensus is emerging around the idea, according to Dan Stamper, the president of the Detroit International Bridge Co., a private concern that owns the bridge. It could apply as well to the Detroit & Windsor Tunnel, he said. Drivers would be checked before crossing.

"Right now, if you are in the tunnel or on the bridge, you are there with others that have not been inspected by anyone, waiting to be inspected," Stamper said.

A complication is that the plan would require U.S. law-enforcement authorities to work on Canadian soil and vice versa. But officials pushing the idea say that emergency legislation in both countries would be sought to allow such an arrangement.

Paul Cellucci, the U.S. Ambassador to Canada, and others are urging that trucks routinely crossing between Michigan and Canada be outfitted with transmitters that would signal officials in both countries about departures from loading docks, approaches to the bridge and arrival at destinations. The information also would include particulars about the load and the driver, as well as helping determine whether the truck made any stops after loading and before crossing.

Meanwhile, advocates of new crossings over and under the Detroit River say the crisis may provide momentum needed for action on their plans. A new bridge and a new tunnel are among the proposals under consideration by a consortium of government agencies in the U.S. and Canada. But officials involved with the proposals confess that not much progress has been made.

"We could very well add substantially more lanes to make things more efficient," said Ross Clarke, of Mich-Can International Bridge Co., which has proposed a new span. "There needs to be a sense of urgency among the governments."

Trucking security still stuck in slow lane[9]

By Sean Kilcarr
Aug 6, 2003 12:00 PM

Efforts to secure the trucking industry and the freight transport infrastructure could be stuck in low gear for some time to come, according to a noted security expert.

"We've made great headway in the areas of research and development and in identifying security problems and solutions when it comes to the freight industry and trucking as a whole," Bob Bevelacqua, executive vp for Reston, VA-based homeland security consulting firm WDC3 Group, told Fleet Owner. "The real issue is the execution and implementation of security efforts – largely because of the size of the trucking industry and the tight profit margins it operates under."

Bevelacqua said the cost of implementing security measures is what's really dissuading the industry both now and in the future.

"Trucking companies will only add security technology if it is mandated by the government or if they can afford to do it," he explained. "Incentives such as freezing or reducing insurance premiums and speeding up border crossings will drive security adoption by the industry."

Bevelacqua warned that the longer the industry and the U.S. as a whole goes without experiencing a terrorist event like 9/11, the less pressure there is to beef up security.

"Right now, homeland security isn't a priority – making money and stabilizing company finances is," he added. "I am afraid that the false sense of security we have that a second Sept. 11-style attack hasn't yet occurred could hurt the industry down the road."

Fact Sheet: Cooperative G-8 Action on Transport Security[10]

"More and more, civilized nations find ourselves on the same side—united by common dangers of terrorist violence and chaos."

President George W. Bush
June 1, 2002

Presidential Action

Today, President Bush secured agreement on a U.S.-driven plan for G-8 Action on transport security.

The G-8 committed to accelerated action on pre-screening people and cargo, increasing security on ships, planes and trucks, and enhancing security in airports and seaports.

The G-8 initiative will enhance transport security through better intelligence, coordinated national efforts, and international cooperation against terrorist threats.

This initiative complements the smart border programs President Bush has launched with Mexico and Canada and advances a vision of security that pushes the perimeter beyond the physical border.

The Challenge: The global transport infrastructure—ships, planes, ports, roads, etc.—is the lifeblood of international commerce. The terrorist attacks on September 11, 2001, illustrated how critical the international transport system is to our economic and national security A key challenge arising from those attacks is to promote the efficient and reliable movement of people and goods across borders, while preventing the tools of transport from becoming tools of terrorism. The challenge is critical: 48 million shipping containers are exported and imported annually, tens of thousands of ships are engaged in trade daily, and more than 14,000 planes are flying in the global fleet of commercial airlines.

G-8 Plan of Action: G-8 countries account for over 50 percent of the world's trade, approximately two-thirds of the world's passenger aircraft fleet, and 13 of the world's 25 busiest international airports. The U.S. proposed in March that the G-8 cooperate in addressing these challenges by advancing key transport security initiatives within G-8 countries, and in multilateral bodies such as the International Civil Aviation Organization, the International Maritime Organization, and the World Customs Organization.

Today, the G-8 agreed on a transport security action plan that will:
Screen people and cargo for security before transit;
Increase security on ships, airplanes, and trucks while en route; and
Enhance security in airports and seaports.

Commitments include:
Collection and transmission of advance passenger information, more secure travel and identity documents, biometrics, and reciprocal bilateral access to departure and transit lounges;
Identification and pre-screening of high-risk containers;

Accelerated implementation by April 2003 of new standards for reinforced cockpit doors and airport security audits;

Accelerated installation of automatic identification systems on certain ships, and development of port and ship security plans; and

Development of new measures related to the transport of hazardous cargoes in trucks.

At the same time, the plan will facilitate the cost-effective and efficient flow of people, cargo, and conveyances engaged in legitimate activities. G-8 countries have agreed to promote policy coherence and coordination in all relevant international organizations, and to review progress every six months.

Other U.S. Efforts: The United States has been working bilaterally and multilaterally to keep the arteries of commerce clear while strengthening security surrounding the world's transportation infrastructure. We have comprehensive smart border initiatives underway with Mexico and Canada that use modern technology to enhance security and expedite legitimate cross-border travel and commerce. We are also working with the ports in Singapore and Rotterdam to create cargo pre-screening programs. Singapore and Rotterdam are, respectively, the second and sixth largest container ports in the world.

SUMMARY

As a mobile society that is accustomed to traveling freely and safely about the country, the citizens of the United States have embraced all forms of transportation for work, leisure, and transportation of goods. As a society of consumers, goods are imported and distributed from all over the world in massive quantities.

ADDITIONAL DISCUSSION TOPICS

- What transportation mode do you feel is most vulnerable to attack and why?

- Discuss the role of the Coast Guard in homeland security. What do you feel is their greatest contribution to security, and why?

- The US has over a half a million bridges. How would you protect the bridges from terrorist attacks?

- Is the massive scope of international and interstate commerce a factor that favors the terrorists or the defenders of the homeland?

- What are the relationships in mission with the border security efforts and the transportation security efforts? Explain.

Endnotes

[1] The section was quoted from the White House. (2003).

[2] U.S. Coast Guard (USCG). (2002).

[3] This section is excerpted from Sections 3.1-3.5 of Ham, D.B., & Lockwood, S., with Science Applications International Corporation (SAIC). (2002).

[4] This section is excerpted from the Executive Summary (pp. v-vii) of Ham, D.B., & Lockwood, S., with Science Applications International Corporation (SAIC). (2002).

[5] This section is excerpted from White House. (2002). pp. 21-23.

[6] For more information, use a search engine and do some background reading... [For more descriptive details see http://www.pbs.org/wgbh/amex/hoover/]

[7] Source: <http://www.mndaily.com/daily/1995/10/11/world_nation/wn2.ap/>.

[8] Source: <http://www.detnews.com/2001/metro/0110/15/a05-318321.htm>.

[9] Source: <http://driversmag.com/ar/fleet_trucking_security_stuck/>.

[10] Source: <http://www.whitehouse.gov/news/releases/2002/06/20020626-9.html>.

CHAPTER SEVEN

PUBLIC HEALTH

The threat of bioterrorism has brought new challenges to our government, to our first responders and to our medical personnel. We are grateful for their services. Not long ago, few of these men and women could have imagined duties like monitoring the air for anthrax, or delivering antibiotics on a massive scale. Yet, this is the world as we find it; this Nation refuses to let our guard down.
—President George W. Bush

Extreme remedies are very appropriate for extreme diseases.
—Hippocrates of Iphicrates

KEY TERMS

Pandemic
Influenza
Vaccine
Medical surveillance
Worried well
Bio-terror
Crisis medicine
DMort

OBJECTIVES

- Define pandemic.

- Identify historical examples of flu pandemics.

- Describe the role of vaccines during a pandemic.

- Examine the use of biological agents as weapons.

- Differentiate between the categories of biological priority agents.

- Examine the role of the Centers for Disease Control and Prevention (CDC).

- Describe future goals for federal public health preparedness.

DISCUSSION TOPICS

- How would emergency and medical services be impacted by an influenza pandemic?

- Would a pandemic be adequate reason for temporary curtailment of civil liberties such as a restriction on travel or involuntary quarantine of the infected?

- How would a covert biological attack first be identified if it occurred in a small, isolated town? How would this differ in a large city?

- Are the CDC's preparations for pandemics conflicting or complimentary to its preparations for a biological terrorist attack?

- How does the CDC use partnerships with non-governmental entities to improve its disease detection and responsive abilities?

- Has the threat of a biological attack impacted how medical professionals respond to individuals?

- Does the public's expectation of medical response capabilities match the medical community's actual level of preparedness?

7

INTRODUCTION

In this chapter we will discuss the impact of disasters on the medical community, including field medics and first responders, and how a disaster may stretch the system to capacity or exceed capacity. The emergency manager and hospital administration roles are addressed. We will also discuss the impact of biological attacks against domestic targets and the impact of pandemics.

WHAT KEEPS EMERGENCY RESPONDERS UP AT NIGHT?

Emergency responders are known for courageously going into situations that others are running from.

What frightens emergency responders? Many will tell you the fear of a biological weapon attack.

In the winter of 2004-2005 there was an unexpected shortage of flu vaccine in the United States. Several events occurred that resulted in this situation:

- In the interests of creating affordable flu shots, then President Clinton put a cap on the price that could be charged for a flu vaccine.

- The industry in the United States could not profitably create flu vaccines and, therefore, quit producing the vaccines.

- The flu vaccines were outsourced to a company outside of the United States.

- The vaccines produced outside the United States were largely contaminated, resulting in the elderly and ill being placed at risk or death from a flu virus due to lack of vaccines.

- The public alarm bordered on panic.

The critical thinker will have to assess whether or not there were other factors that resulted in this situation, or whether this assessment is totally accurate. However, the underlying issue was that there was national alarm concerning a lack of vaccine to fight the common flu virus.

What would happen if a pandemic virus—man-made or naturally developed—were released that was much more dangerous, and with a higher mortality rate?

The last few generations have forgotten about the polio and smallpox outbreaks. Are we mentally prepared to cope with mass casualties as the result of a pandemic or bio-weapon? Currently we can assess the potential scenarios and compare with existing resources to plan a medical response to this type of crisis, but the question of our emotional resolve in the face of the worst case disaster imaginable will only be answered in our actions in the face of disaster. Let's hope we never have to find out.

We have faced anthrax scares in the past, and threats of bird flu pandemic lurk on the horizon. Whether the threat is a natural occurring event or the result of a biological weapon attack is relevant to the medical responders only in terms of the threat of secondary devices attacks at the scene of a release.

A likely scenario of a biological attack or pandemic discovery would be through what is called *medical surveillance*, the identification of unusual symptom patterns communicated by medical professionals to the Centers for Disease Control and Prevention.

In our first article, let's review the impact of the ongoing threat of weaponized anthrax.

Case Study: Anthrax Scare Shuts 11 Washington Postal Buildings[1]

Reuters
Thursday, November 6, 2003; 11:50 PM

WASHINGTON (Reuters) - The U.S. Postal Service shut down 11 postal facilities in the Washington area late on Thursday after preliminary tests indicated possible anthrax at a U.S. Navy mail handling center, officials said.

The Navy closed the automated mail handling operation at its naval air station in Washington on Thursday to run additional tests after sensors detected traces of a substance that could be anthrax, a Navy spokeswoman said.

The substance was identified late on Wednesday by equipment that routinely samples the air in the facility and preliminary tests indicated that it could possibly be anthrax, a deadly bacterial disease, Lt. Corey Schultz said. More definitive testing was underway, she added.

"Almost all the mail that's processed there is irradiated, so it's likely the substance would be inactive," Schultz said. She also noted that it was "very unlikely" that the few people who work in the facility were at risk of exposure, but said that they were being evaluated as a precautionary measure.

As a precaution, the U.S. Postal Service closed 11 facilities that were serviced by the same contractor that transported mail to the Navy center, a spokesman said.

"Out of an abundance of caution we want to make sure we've covered every-thing," spokesman Mark Saunders said. "We learned late Thursday the Navy test was positive and that more samples were being taken at the facility."

Saunders said that the Postal Service would also test its closed facilities. The shutdown affects about 1,500 postal employees. They were being asked to report to their job locations on Friday and would be directed to other centers, Saunders said.

In 2001 a series of anthrax attacks, which spanned the East Coast from Florida to Connecticut, killed at least five people, including two Washington postal workers.

Letters containing anthrax spores were mailed to news media offices in New York and Florida and anthrax-laced letters were sent to the Washington offices of two senators.

Since the anthrax attacks, the Postal Service has spent millions of dollars to test and install equipment to sterilize mail.

Anthrax is a bacteria that causes disease in livestock and in humans who have contact with animals. It is considered the No.1 threat for a biological weapon because it is deadly and the bacteria form spores that are hard to kill.

***Source:** Anthrax Scare Shuts 11 Washington Postal Buildings

Reuters, Thursday, November 6, 2003; 11:50 PM

ARE WE PREPARED?

Contaminating distribution centers, common carriers, and public places multiply the effect of chemical and biological weapons. Using the *Reuters* article as a point of discussion, the reader should reflect on the impact of a biological weapon. Instead of shutting down commerce and placing workers and consumers at risk, a biological attack would likely impact the medical responders from ambulance crews and the hospital workers very early on, if the risk is not clearly identified. That is the primary risk of this type of scenario. In the anthrax case, responders can generally protect themselves and continue to apply protective measures; however, in a hospital environment, the critical responders may be the earliest casualties.

Another aspect of this topic is disaster medicine. In a mass casualty situation, such as a bombing or fire, the medical resources may be stretched to the limits. A more morbid factor to consider is management of the dead who may not be read-ily identifiable or who may be contaminated. A little known branch of FEMA, known as DMORT, responds to mass casualty situations to manage the fatalities. DMORT is trained to handle contaminated casualties, but how prepared is the security and public safety community to manage that type of crisis until DMORT's arrival?

In our next article, we will look at the press release from the CDC during March of 2005 concerning pandemic outbreaks, their history, and the response plan.

Insider's Point of View...

This writer's associate, Dr. Julie Brown, has been a crisis medical responder to numerous aircraft crashes; she was called to New York City during 9/11, as well as other horrific events. Julie is active in FEMA DMORT. Although much of her work is classified, she has shared some comments throughout this chapter that share with us her perspective about the issues surrounding crisis medicine. She is currently practicing medicine in Chicago, Illinois.

"Disaster medicine can be exciting, challenging, exhausting, and heartbreaking - all in the same hour, but the rewards far outweigh all else. I encourage everyone with a medical background to volunteer to get involved in disaster medicine. Planning and preparation for casualties in disasters is a key component so you are ready when disaster strikes unexpectedly."

"The key to working with horribly injured people and children is to remain detached but compassionate. We must remain professional and avoid the temptation to personalize what we see. When we personalize the victims, we are at risk for Critical Incident Stress (CIS). We are human and at great risk for CIS, and if we become disabled by CIS, we cannot help others as effectively, or maybe not at all."

"As a supervisor in high tension medical settings, I always have to remind medical workers to take breaks, rest, drink fluids, and eat. You are no help to the healthcare team if you become a patient/victim, too."

"Healthcare workers should do what YOU do well, and step down and help others do what they can do better than you. Egos do not come before patient's/victim's lives."

"The new bird flu pandemic is making headlines. While it is excellent to prepare for new widespread pandemic diseases, we cannot forget that common diseases like Respiratory Syncytial Virus (RSV), Influenza A and B, and Rotavirus still have high morbidity and mortality rates in certain populations. Nothing replaces good hygiene. Wash your hands often - something as simple as that can help prevent these infections!"

PANDEMIC: A WORLDWIDE OUTBREAK OF INFLUENZA[2]

An influenza pandemic is a global outbreak of disease that occurs when a new influenza A virus appears or "emerges" in the human population, causes serious illness, and then spreads easily from person to person worldwide. Pandemics are different from seasonal outbreaks or "epidemics" of influenza. Seasonal outbreaks are caused by subtypes of influenza viruses that are already in existence among people, whereas pandemic outbreaks are caused by new subtypes or by subtypes that have never circulated among people or that have not circulated among people for a long time. Past influenza pandemics have led to high levels of illness, death, social disruption, and economic loss.

Appearance ("Emergence") of Pandemic Influenza Viruses

There are many different subtypes of Influenza or "flu" viruses. The subtypes differ based upon certain proteins on the surface of the virus (the hemaglutinin or "HA" protein and the neuraminidase or the "NA" protein).

Pandemic viruses appear (or "emerge") as a result of a process called "antigenic shift," which causes an abrupt or sudden, major change in influenza A viruses. These changes are caused by new combinations of the HA and/or NA proteins on the surface of the virus. This change results in a new influenza A virus subtype. The appearance of a new influenza A virus subtype is the first step toward a pandemic, but the new virus subtype also must spread easily from person to person to cause a pandemic. Once a new pandemic influenza virus emerges and spreads, it normally becomes established among people and moves around or "circulates" for many years as seasonal epidemics of influenza. The U.S. Centers for Disease Control and Prevention and the World Health Organization have large surveillance programs to monitor and "detect" influenza activity around the world, including the emergence of possible pandemic strains of influenza virus.

Influenza Pandemics During the 20th Century

During the 20th century, the emergence of new influenza A virus subtypes caused three pandemics, all of which spread around the world within 1 year of being detected.

- **1918-19, "Spanish flu,"** [A (H1N1)], caused the highest number of known influenza deaths: more than 500,000 people died in the United States, and up to 50 million people may have died worldwide. Many people died within the first few days after infection, and others died of complications later. Nearly half of those who died were young, healthy adults. Influenza A (H1N1) viruses still circulate today after being introduced again into the human population in the 1970s.

- **1957-58, "Asian flu,"** [A (H2N2)], caused about 70,000 deaths in the United States. First identified in China in late February 1957, the Asian flu spread to the United States by June 1957.

- **1968-69, " Hong Kong flu,"** [A (H3N2)], caused about 34,000 deaths in the United States. This virus was first detected in Hong Kong in early 1968 and spread to the United States later that year. Influenza A (H3N2) viruses still circulate today.

Both the 1957-58 and 1968-69 pandemics were caused by viruses containing a combination of genes from a human influenza virus and an avian influenza virus. The origin of the 1918-19 pandemic virus is not clear.

Vaccines to Protect Against Pandemic Influenza Viruses

A vaccine probably would not be available in the early stages of a pandemic. When a new vaccine against an influenza virus is being developed, scientists around the world work together to select the virus strain that will offer the best protection against that virus, and then manufacturers use the selected strain to develop a vaccine. Once a potential pandemic strain of influenza virus is identified, it takes several months before a vaccine will be widely available. If a pandemic occurs, it is expected that the U.S. government will work with many partner groups to make recommendations to guide the early use of vaccine.

Antiviral Medications to Prevent and Treat Pandemic Influenza

Four different influenza antiviral medications (amantadine, rimantadine, oseltamivir, and zanamivir) are approved by the U.S. Food and Drug Administration for the treatment and/or prevention of influenza. All four work against influenza A viruses. However, sometimes influenza virus strains can become resistant to one or more of these drugs, and thus the drugs may not always work. For example, the influenza A (H5N1) viruses identified in human patients in Asia in 2004 and 2005 have been resistant to amantadine and rimantadine. Monitoring of avian viruses for resistance to influenza antiviral medications is continuing.

Preparing for the Next Pandemic

Many scientists believe it is only a matter of time until the next influenza pandemic occurs. The severity of the next pandemic cannot be predicted, but modeling studies suggest that its effect in the United States could be severe. In the absence of any control measures (vaccination or drugs), it has been estimated that in the United States a "medium–level" pandemic could cause 89,000 to 207,000 deaths, between 314,000 and 734,000 hospitalizations, 18 to 42 million outpatient visits, and another 20 to 47 million people being sick. Between 15% and 35% of the U.S. population could be affected by an influenza pandemic, and the economic impact could range between $71.3 and $166.5 billion.

Recent examples of avian influenza outbreaks and infections in Hong Kong in 1997, 1998, and 2002 and the ongoing widespread outbreaks of avian influenza among poultry in Asia, show the importance of preparing for a pandemic. It has been 36 years since the last pandemic.

Influenza pandemics are different from many of the threats for which public health and the health-care system are currently planning:

■ The pandemic will last much longer than most other emergency events and may include "waves" of influenza activity separated by months (in 20th century pandemics, a second wave of influenza activity occurred 3 to 12 months after the first wave).

■ The numbers of health-care workers and first responders available to work can be expected to be reduced; they will be at high risk of illness through exposure in the community and in health-care settings, and some may have to miss work to care for ill family members.

■ Resources in many locations could be limited because of how widespread an influenza pandemic would be....

Although a pandemic virus has not yet emerged, the appearance of limited human clusters of H5N1 cases has tested our international surveillance and response capabilities.[3] Should a pandemic emerge, whether from the current H5N1 subtype of concern or from another influenza virus with pandemic potential, the United States is better positioned today to detect an outbreak earlier, to support an international effort to contain the pandemic in its earliest stages, to limit the spread of the pandemic, and to save lives.

The United States has developed protocols and trained personnel to support an international effort to contain the pandemic in its earliest stages. The U.S. Government procured and pre-positioned overseas stockpiles of personal protective equipment, decontamination kits, and antiviral medications to complement global efforts to contain pandemic outbreaks. Today, our Federal and State stockpiles contain enough antiviral medications to treat nearly 50 million people, with up to 6 million courses now reserved for containment efforts. If a pandemic begins outside the United States, and our international containment efforts fail, the U.S. Government is planning to implement border measures during a severe pandemic to slow the entry of a pandemic virus into the United States while allowing the flow of goods and people.

Once an influenza pandemic reaches the United States, the primary focus is safeguarding the health of Americans. The U.S. Government is working to enhance the Nation's ability to detect and respond early and effectively to a pandemic. To better identify the first cases of pandemic influenza in a community, the U.S. Government has provided resources to State and local health departments to increase the number of sentinel providers and improve laboratory detection at public health laboratories. The U.S. Laboratory Response Network (LRN), which includes State public health laboratories, is prepared to conduct initial testing of suspected human infection with H5N1 within 24 hours of receipt. To ensure that suspected cases can be promptly confirmed and treated, the Federal Government is working with industry partners to develop rapid diagnostic tests to quickly discriminate pandemic influenza from seasonal influenza or other illnesses.

The Federal Government is investing in the expansion of vaccine manufacturing capacity, the advanced development of new cell-based vaccines, antigen-sparing technologies to stretch our vaccine supply, and the establishment and maintenance of pre-pandemic vaccine stockpiles. In April 2007, the Federal Government approved the first pre-pandemic vaccine for humans against the H5N1 virus. We currently have enough of this pre-pandemic H5N1 vaccine for approximately 6 million people, with plans to stockpile enough pre-pandemic vaccine for 20 million people. In addition, antiviral medications are an important element of pandemic influenza preparedness. As of June 2007, the Strategic National Stockpile contains more than 35 million regimens of antiviral drugs with an additional 2 million regimens on order. So far, individual States have stockpiled more than 13 million regimens of antiviral drugs. The Government's antiviral strategy includes not only stockpiling existing antiviral drugs, but also developing new antiviral medications to further broaden our capabilities to treat and prevent influenza.

In February 2007, the U.S. Government released groundbreaking Federal guidance for non-pharmaceutical interventions for mitigating the impact of a pandemic. This community mitigation strategy is important because the best protection against pandemic influenza, a matched pandemic vaccine, is not likely to be available at the outset of a pandemic. Recent scientific modeling and historical reviews of the 1918 pandemic suggest that non-pharmaceutical interventions (such as school closures, social distancing, and cancellation of large public gatherings) could be very effective at slowing the spread of disease and mitigating the outbreak, but only if they are implemented early and maintained consistently across communities affected by a pandemic. These interventions, coupled with the use of antiviral medications, could dramatically reduce the number of people who become infected, potentially preventing illness and death in millions of Americans.

The U.S. Government has invested in health system preparedness of hospitals and medical facilities across the country, has produced tools to assist in planning for expansion in hospital capacity during a pandemic, and is stockpiling medical supplies for distribution to individual States in the event of a pandemic.

Each Federal department and agency is developing its own department- or agency-specific pandemic preparedness plan to ensure the continuation of Federal Government essential functions. Over the past year, the Federal Government has produced tools for businesses and other employers to assist them in pandemic planning and has conducted an extensive outreach effort to the private sector. Through these efforts, businesses operating at home and abroad have been provided practical action-oriented information to identify essential functions and critical planning elements, to protect the health of employees, to maintain continuity of business operations, and to sustain community function during a pandemic.

Preparing the Nation for the threat of an influenza pandemic has provided a platform to address issues and concerns common to all types of mass casualty disasters. Promoting a culture of individual, family, and community preparedness is the foundation for all emergency-planning efforts.

Ethical Considerations...

You are on a business trip in another State. You have heard on the radio that there is a flu pandemic that is centered in the area you are in. You are experiencing symptoms that lead you to believe you may have been infected. There is an early flight home. Should you get on it and go home?

There is quarantine on your neighborhood due to a biological weapon attack, but you don't believe you are infected. You know of a way to escape the quarantined area. Should you make an attempt to get to a safe place? What about your family?

You are a security specialist or public safety executive. You are faced with people trying to access public transportation who may be infected, or people trying to escape quarantine? What level of force is acceptable to keep them quarantined?

Even with the emergency medical community discussing the risks of a flu pandemic and planning the response in advance, the predicted outcome is chilling. Homeland security specialists or pubic safety responders must consider their roles, and how they should prepare.

PUBLIC HEALTH IMPLICATIONS AND WEAPONS OF MASS DESTRUCTION (WMDs)[4]

As is true of emerging infectious diseases, early detection and control of biological or chemical attacks depends on a strong and flexible public health system at the local, state, and federal levels. In addition, primary healthcare providers throughout the United States must be vigilant, for they will probably be the first to observe and report unusual illnesses or injuries. The federal Department of Health and Human Services (HHS) has been taking steps since 1999 to prepare for these challenges. In 2001, the anthrax attacks provided a sudden and unanticipated test of these initial steps, and the response benefited from this initial preparedness. Nevertheless, the attacks demonstrated significant gaps in response capabilities and underscored the need to move much more quickly in building a national public health network and strengthening emergency response capacities.

The healthcare industry and traditional healthcare organization must join with public health departments, law enforcement and intelligence, emergency management and defense agencies to address potential national security threats (See Figure 7.1).

Figure 7.1

LINKING RESPONSE SYSTEMS

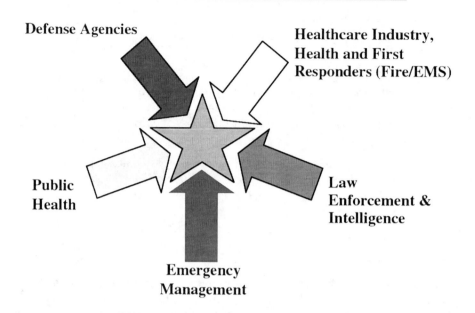

Overt Versus Covert Terrorist Attacks

Terrorist incidents in the United States and elsewhere involving bacterial pathogens (Török, et al., 1997), nerve gas (Okumura, et al., 1998), and a lethal plant toxin (i.e., ricin) (Tucker, 1996), have demonstrated that the United States is vulnerable to biological and chemical threats as well as explosives. Recipes for preparing "homemade" agents are readily available (Uncle Fester, et al., 1997), and reports of arsenals of military bioweapons (Davis, 1999) raise the possibility that terrorists might have access to highly dangerous agents that have been engineered for mass dissemination as small-particle aerosols. Such agents as the variola virus, the causative agent of smallpox, are highly contagious and often fatal. Responding to large-scale outbreaks caused by these agents will require the rapid mobilization of public health workers, emergency responders, and private health-care providers. Large-scale outbreaks will also require rapid procurement and distribution of large quantities of drugs and vaccines, which must be available quickly.

In the past, most planning for emergency response to terrorism has been concerned with overt attacks (e.g., bombings). Chemical terrorism acts usually are overt because the effects of chemical agents absorbed through inhalation or by absorption through the skin or mucous membranes are usually immediate and obvious. Such attacks elicit immediate response from police, fire, and Emergency Medical Services (EMS) personnel.

In contrast, attacks with biological agents are more likely to be covert. They present different challenges and require an additional dimension of emergency planning that involves the public health infrastructure. Because the initial detection of and response to a covert biological or chemical attack probably will occur at the local level, disease surveillance systems at local hospitals, and at state and local health agencies must be capable of detecting unusual patterns of disease or injury, including those caused by unusual or unknown threat agents. Epidemiologists at state and local health agencies must have expertise and resources for responding to reports of clusters of rare, unusual, or unexplained illnesses.

Covert dissemination of a biological agent in a public place will not have an immediate impact because of the delay between exposure and onset of illness (i.e., the incubation period). Consequently, the first casualties of a covert attack will most likely be identified by physicians or other primary healthcare providers. For example, in the event of a covert release of the contagious variola virus, patients will appear in doctors' offices, clinics, and emergency rooms during the first or second week, complaining of fever, back pain, headache, nausea, and other symptoms of what initially might appear to be an ordinary viral infection. As the disease progresses, these persons will develop the papular rash characteristic of early-stage smallpox, a rash that physicians might not recognize immediately. By the time the rash becomes pustular and patients begin to die, the terrorists would be far away and the disease disseminated through the population by person-to-person contact.

Only a short window of opportunity will exist between the time the first cases are identified and a second wave of the population becomes ill. During that brief period, public health officials will need to determine that an attack has occurred, identify the organism, and avoid more casualties through prevention strategies (e.g., mass vaccination in the case of smallpox or prophylactic treatment in the case of anthrax). In the case of smallpox, as person-to-person contact continues successive waves of transmission could carry infection to other worldwide localities similar to what occurred in the emergency SARS virus outbreak in spring 2003. These issues might also be relevant for other person-to-person transmissible etiologic agents (e.g., plague or certain viral hemorrhagic fevers).

Certain chemical agents can also be delivered covertly through contaminated food or water. In 1999, the vulnerability of the food supply was illustrated in Belgium, when chickens were unintentionally exposed to dioxin-contaminated fat used to make animal feed (Ashraf, 1999). Dioxin, a cancer-causing chemical that does not cause immediate symptoms in humans, was probably present in chicken meat and eggs sold in Europe as early as 1999, because the contamination was not discovered for months. This incident underscores the need for prompt diagnoses of unusual or suspicious health problems in animals as well as humans, a lesson that was also demonstrated by the winter 1999 outbreak of mosquito-borne West Nile virus first diagnosed in birds and humans in New York City. The dioxin episode also demonstrated how a covert act of food-borne biological or chemical terrorism could affect commerce and human or animal health.

Focusing Preparedness Activities

Preparedness for terrorist-caused outbreaks and injuries is an essential mission of the U.S. public health system, which is designed to protect the population against any unusual public health event (e.g., influenza pandemics, contaminated municipal water supplies, or intentional dissemination of Yersinia pestis, the causative agent of plague (Janofsky, 1995).

Early detection of and response to biological or chemical terrorism are just as crucial. Without special preparation at the local and state levels, a large-scale attack with variola virus, aerosolized anthrax spores, a nerve gas, or a foodborne biological or chemical agent could overwhelm the local and perhaps national public health infrastructure. Large numbers of patients, including both infected persons and the "worried well,"[5] would seek medical attention, with a corresponding need for medical supplies, diagnostic tests, and hospital beds. Emergency responders, healthcare workers, and public health officials could be at special risk.

The epidemiologic skills, surveillance methods, diagnostic techniques, and physical resources required to detect and investigate unusual or unknown diseases, as well as syndromes or injuries caused by chemical accidents, are similar to those needed to identify and respond to an attack with a biological or chemical agent. However, public health agencies must prepare also for the special features a terrorist attack probably would have (e.g., mass casualties or the use of rare agents).

Terrorists might use combinations of chemical and biological agents, attack in more than one location simultaneously, use new agents, or use organisms that are not on the critical list (e.g., common, drug-resistant, or genetically engineered pathogens). Lists of critical biological and chemical agents will need to be modified as new information becomes available. In addition, each state and locality will need to adapt the lists to local conditions and preparedness needs.

Table 7.1 presents the priority biological agents, and describes the unique characteristics of each category that make them critical elements. Chemical and other agents have been developed for use as weapons, while others are readily found in U.S. society. All agents may cause severe public health risks and require multiagency planning and preparation for an appropriate response. Table 7.2 lists these agents.

Potential biological and chemical agents are numerous, and the public health, hospital and healthcare organization infrastructure must be equipped to quickly resolve crises that would arise from a biological or chemical attack.

Because of the hundreds of new chemicals introduced internationally each month, treating exposed persons by clinical syndrome rather than by specific agent is more useful for public health planning and emergency medical response purposes. Public health agencies and first responders might render the most aggressive, timely, and clinically relevant treatment possible by using treatment modalities based on syndromic categories (e.g., burns and trauma, cardiorespiratory failure, neurologic damage, and shock). These activities must be linked with authorities responsible for environmental sampling and decontamination.

To best protect the public, preparedness efforts must be focused on agents that might have the greatest impact on U.S. health and security, especially agents that are highly contagious or that can be engineered for widespread dissemination via small-particle aerosols (as we are planning now for mass smallpox vaccination of the U.S. population). Preparing the nation to address these dangers is a major challenge to U.S. public health systems and healthcare providers. Early detection

Table 7.1 Priority Biological Agents, by Category[6]

Category A – High Priority Biological Agents	Category B – Second Highest Priority Biological Agents	Category C – 3rd Highest Priority Biological Agents
Pathogens that are rarely seen in the United States and high-priority agents including organisms that pose a risk to national security because they can be easily disseminated or transmitted person-to-person; cause high mortality, with a potential for major public health impact; may cause public panic and social disruption; and require special action for public health preparedness. (CDC, 1998)	Agents that are moderately easy to disseminate; cause moderate morbidity and low mortality; and require specific enhancements of CDC's diagnostic capacity and enhanced disease surveillance. A subset of Category B agents includes pathogens that are food- or waterborne. These pathogens include but are not limited to: Salmonella species, Shigella dysenteriae, Escherichia coli O157:H7, Vibrio cholerae, and Cryptosporidium parvum. (CDC, 1998)	Agents include emerging pathogens that could be engineered for mass dissemination because of availability; ease of production and dissemination; and potential for high morbidity and mortality, with major health impact. Preparedness for Category C agents requires ongoing research to improve disease detection, diagnosis, treatment, and prevention. Prior knowledge of which newly emergent pathogens might be employed by terrorists is not possible; therefore, linking bioterrorism preparedness efforts with ongoing disease surveillance and outbreak response activities as defined in CDC's emerging infectious disease strategy is imperative.* (CDC, 1998)
■ Variola major (smallpox); ■ Bacillus anthracis (anthrax); ■ Yersinia pestis (plague); ■ Clostridium botulinum toxin (Botulism); ■ Francisella tularensis (Tularemia); ■ Filoviruses: ■ Ebola hemorrhagic fever, ■ Marburg hemorrhagic fever ■ Arenaviruses: ■ Lassa (Lassa fever), ■ Junin (Argentine hemorrhagic fever) and related viruses.	■ Coxiella burnetti (Q fever); ■ Brucella species (brucellosis); ■ Burkholderia mallei (glanders); ■ Alphaviruses: ■ Venezuelan encephalomyelitis, ■ Eastern and western equine encephalomyelitis; ■ Ricin toxin from Ricinus communis (castor beans); ■ Epsilon toxin of Clostridium perfringens; ■ Staphylococcus enterotoxin B.	■ Nipah virus, ■ Hantaviruses, ■ Tickborne hemorrhagic fever, ■ Tickborne encephalitis viruses, ■ Yellow fever, ■ Multidrug-resistant tuberculosis.

requires increased biological and chemical terrorism awareness among front-line healthcare providers because they are in the best position to report suspicious illnesses and injuries. Also, early detection will require improved communication systems between those providers and public health officials. State and local healthcare agencies must have enhanced capacity to investigate unusual events and unexplained illnesses and diagnostic laboratories must be equipped to iden-

Table 7.2 Categories of Chemical Agents

CATEGORY OF AGENTS	COMMON AND CHEMICAL NAME
Nerve Agents	■ Tabun (ethyl N, N-dimethylphosphoramidocyanidate), ■ Sarin (isopropyl methylphosphanofluoridate), ■ Soman (pinacolyl methyl phosphonofluoridate), ■ GF (cyclohexylmethylphosphonofluoridate), ■ VX (o-ethyl-[S]-[2-diisopropylaminoethyl]-methylphosphono- Thiolate
Blood Agents	■ Hydrogen cyanide, ■ Yanogen chloride
Blister Agents	■ Lewisite (an aliphatic arsenic compound, 2-chlorovinyldichlor-oarsine), ■ Nitrogen and sulfur mustards, ■ Phosgene oxime
OTHER AGENTS	
Heavy Metals	■ Arsenic ■ Lead ■ Mercury
Volatile Toxins	■ Benzene ■ Chloroform ■ Trihalomethanes
Pulmonary Agents	■ Phosgene ■ Chlorine ■ Vinyl chloride
Incapacitating Agents	■ BZ (3-quinuclidinyl benzilate)
Pesticides	■ Persistent and Nonpersistent
Dioxins, furans, and polychlorinated biphenyls (PCBs);	
Explosive nitro compounds and oxidizers	■ Ammonium nitrate combined with fuel oil ■ flammable industrial gases and liquids, gasoline, propane; ■ Cyanides, Nitriles; and corrosive industrial acids and bases,
Poison industrial gases, liquids, and solids	■ Nitric acid ■ Sulfuric acid.

tify biological and chemical agents that rarely are seen in the United States. Fundamental to these efforts is comprehensive, integrated training designed to ensure core competency in public health preparedness and the highest levels of scientific expertise among local, state, and federal partners.

Table 7.3 and Table 7.4 provide healthcare facility checklists in preparing for chemical and biological exposures from a public health view.

Table 7.3 Healthcare Facility Checklist in Preparing for Chemical Exposures

Enhance awareness of chemical terrorism among EMS personnel, police officers, firefighters, physicians, and nurses.

Enhance inhouse capacity for detecting and responding to chemical attacks.

Ensure education and training of clinical response staff in receiving exposed individuals, including decontamination technique

Establish decontamination location, supplies and equipment to decontaminate those in need

Stockpile appropriate personal protective equipment (PPE) for clinical staff and responders, including training, education and exercises involving their use.

Stockpile chemical antidotes.

Stock and prepare laboratory staff to utilize bioassays for detection and diagnosis of chemical injuries.

Prepare educational materials to inform and reassure the public during and after a chemical attack.

Participate in community-wide disaster exercises involving chemical exposures.

Role of CDC In Preparedness At The Federal Level

The Centers for Disease Control and Prevention (CDC) located in Atlanta, GA is recognized as the lead federal agency for protecting the health and safety of people—at home and abroad, providing credible information to enhance health decisions, and promoting health through strong partnerships. CDC serves as the national focus for developing and applying disease prevention and control, environmental health, and health promotion and education activities designed to improve the health of the people of the United States.

The CDC includes 12 Centers, Institutes and Offices with approximately 8,500 employees in 170 occupations located in CDC facilities in 10 cities, other countries, quarantine offices, and state and local health agencies. (CDC, 2001) CDC has been responding to public health emergencies for decades and has been preparing for bioterrorism since 1998. CDC's bioterrorism plans were activated in Fall 2001, with the first biological attack in the U.S. Outbreaks of anthrax proved that the first line of defense is rapid identification-essential for ensuring a prompt response to a biological or chemical attack so that exposure can be limited and those affected can be treated. To accomplish this, regional and state laboratories have strengthened their capacity to detect different biological and chemical agents and to communicate the results to CDC and others. Along the same lines, CDC's Health Alert Network (HAN) has upgraded the capacity of state and local health agencies to detect and communicate different health threats-including not only bioterrorism but also emerging infectious diseases, chronic diseases, and environmental hazards. We

Table 7.4 Healthcare Facility Checklist in Preparing for Biological Exposures

Enhance awareness of biological terrorism among EMS personnel, police officers, firefighters, physicians, and nurses.

Enhance inhouse capacity for detecting and responding to biological exposures.

Enhance epidemiologic capacity to detect and respond to biological attacks.

Ensure education and training of clinical staff in receiving exposed individuals, including actions to prevent the spread of disease once diagnosed in the facility

Stockpile appropriate personal protective equipment (PPE) for clinical staff and responders, including training, education and exercises involving their use.

Establish supply receipt and exchange program for diagnostic reagents with state or local public health agencies.

Establish inter- and intra-agency communication systems to ensure delivery of accurate information.

Enhance bioterrorism-related education and training for healthcare professionals.

Prepare educational materials that will inform and reassure the public during and after a biological attack.

Stockpile appropriate vaccines and drugs.

Establish laboratory molecular surveillance for microbial strains, including unusual or drug- resistant strains.

Supply appropriate diagnostic tests or have rapid access to them.

Participate in community-wide disaster exercises involving biological exposures.

reap the benefits of these investments every day, for they will serve as useful in all-hazards disaster situations as in a bioterrorist attack.

To further enhance treatment of victims of a bioterrorist attack, CDC has worked with pharmaceutical companies and other partners to create regional stockpiles of the drugs that would be needed quickly to treat man-made outbreaks of anthrax, plague, tularemia, or other diseases. This resource was essential in responding to the terrorist attacks of September 11, 2001, as well as to the ensuing anthrax outbreak in October 2001. Collectively, these measures strengthen the existing public health system while preparing for bioterrorism, infectious disease outbreaks, and other public health threats and emergencies.

CDC has developed and is sustaining many vital partnerships with public and private entities that improve service to the American people. Some of CDC's partners include:

- State and local public health agencies.

- Practicing health professionals, including physicians, dentists, nurses and veterinarians.

- Public health associations.

- Schools and universities.

- Professional, voluntary, and community organizations.

- Philanthropic foundations.

- School systems, churches, and other local institutions.

- Industry and labor.

- CDC Foundation and other foundations.

- International organizations, including the World Health Organization, Pan American Health Organization, and the World Bank.

The CDC strategic plan is based on five focus areas, with each area integrating training and research: preparedness and prevention, detection and surveillance, diagnosis and characterization of biological and chemical agents, response, and communication.[...]

Preparedness and Prevention

- Guidelines, support, and technical assistance to local and State public health agencies

- Self-assessment tools, performance standards, exercises

- MMRS to enhance local public health response to terrorist incidents

Detection, diagnosis, and mitigation of illness and injury caused by biological and chemical terrorism is a complex process that involves numerous partners and activities. Special emergency preparedness in all cities and states is needed to meet this challenge. The Centers for Disease Control and Prevention (CDC) will provide public health guidelines, support, and technical assistance to local and state public health agencies as they develop coordinated preparedness plans and response protocols. The CDC will also provide: self-assessment tools for terror-ism preparedness, including performance standards, attack simulations, and other exercises; will encourage and support applied research to develop innova-tive tools, and will develop strategies to prevent or mitigate illness and injury caused by biological and chemical terrorism.

The Metropolitan Medical Response System (MMRS), created in 1996 and man-aged by the HHS Office of Emergency Response (OER), exists to develop or enhance existing emergency preparedness systems to effectively manage a weapon of mass destruction (WMD) incident. The goal is to coordinate the efforts of local law enforcement, fire, hazardous materials response (hazmat), EMS, hospital, public health and other personnel to improve response capabili-ties in the event of a terrorist attack (see Figure 7.1). Through the development of the local MMRS, HHS has focused on enhancing the local public health and medical capability and capacity to respond to terrorist incidents involving weapons of mass destruction by:

- Developing drop-in surveillance capabilities for special events
- Providing guidance to develop active community surveillance programs
- Improving communication between local, State and Federal public health agencies and the national security community.

Detection and Surveillance

- U.S. disease surveillance system
- Partnerships with state and local health agencies

Early detection is essential for ensuring a prompt response to a biological or chemical attack, including the provision of prophylactic medicines, chemical antidotes, or vaccines. CDC will integrate surveillance for illness and injury resulting from biological and chemical terrorism into the U.S. disease surveillance systems, while developing new mechanisms for detecting, evaluating, and reporting suspicious events that might represent covert terrorist acts. As part of this effort, CDC and state and local health agencies will form partnerships with front-line medical personnel in hospital emergency departments, health care facilities, poison control centers, and other offices to enhance detection and reporting of unexplained injuries and illnesses as part of routine surveillance mechanisms for biological and chemical terrorism.

Diagnosis and Characterization of Biological and Chemical Agents

- Multilevel Laboratory Response Network for Bioterrorism (LRNB)
- In-house Rapid Response and Advanced Technology Laboratory (RRAT)

CDC and its partners will create a multilevel laboratory response network for bioterrorism (LRNB). That network will link clinical labs to public health agencies in all states, districts, territories, and selected cities and counties and to state-of-the-art facilities that can analyze biological agents. As part of this effort, CDC will transfer diagnostic technology to state health laboratories and others who will perform initial testing. CDC will also create an in-house rapid-response and advanced technology (RRAT) laboratory. This laboratory will provide around-the-clock diagnostic confirmatory and reference support for terrorism response teams. This network will include the regional chemical laboratories for diagnosing human exposure to chemical agents and provide links with other related departments such as the U.S. Environmental Protection Agency, which is responsible for environmental sampling.

Response

- Lead agency to plan, prepare for medical emergencies from WME
- National Pharmaceutical Stockpile (NPS)

- Assistance to State and locals

- NDMS and DMATs

- National Medical Response Team-WMD (NMRT-WMD)

In the event of a confirmed terrorist attack, the Office of the Assistant HHS Secretary for Public Health Emergency Preparedness will coordinate with other federal agencies in accord with Presidential Decision Directive (PDD) 39. PDD 39 designates the Federal Bureau of Investigation (FBI) as the lead agency for the crisis plan and charges the Federal Emergency Management Agency (FEMA) with ensuring that the management of the federal response is adequate to address the consequences of terrorism (FEMA 2002).

PDD 62 states, "HHS and the PHS is the lead agency to plan and to prepare for a national response to medical emergencies arising from the terrorist use of weapons of mass destruction."

If requested by a state health agency, HHS will deploy response teams to investigate unexplained or suspicious illnesses or unusual etiologic agents and provide on-site consultation regarding medical management and disease control. HHS, with the support of other Federal agencies will

- provide enhanced local response capabilities through the development of Metropolitan Medical Strike Team systems (now known as Metropolitan Medical Response Systems or MMRS);

- develop and maintain the National Disaster Medical System (NDMS), including the National Medical Response Teams;

- work with Department of Defense (DOD) to ensure deployability of NDMS response teams, supplies and equipment; and

- work with the Department of Veterans Affairs (VA) to will ensure adequate stockpiles of antidotes and other necessary pharmaceuticals nationwide and the training of medical personnel in NDMS hospitals."

National Pharmaceutical Stockpile (NPS)

To ensure the availability, procurement, and delivery of medical supplies, devices, and equipment that might be needed to respond to terrorist-caused illness or injury, the CDC will maintain a National Pharmaceutical Stockpile (NPS). The purpose of the NPS program is to ensure the availability of life-saving pharmaceuticals, vaccines, antidotes, and other medical supplies and equipment necessary to counter the effects of nerve agents, biological pathogens, and chemical agents and augment depleted state and local resources for responding to terrorist attacks and other emergencies. The NPS program stands ready for immediate deployment to any U.S. location in the event of a terrorist attack using a biological, toxin or chemical agent directed against a civilian population. Both 12-Hour Push Packages and Vendor Managed Inventory (VMI) are stored in strategic locations around the U.S. to ensure rapid delivery anywhere in the country. Figure 7.2 summarizes the contents of NPS push packs, while Figure 7.3 compares the immediate and rapid response services of the NPS Program.

Figure 7.2. NPS Contents

NPS Contents

- **Pharmaceuticals:**
  - Antibiotics
  - Mark I kits, diazepam, atropine, praidoxime
- **IV Supplies:**
  - catheters, syringes, fluids, heparin-locks, administration sets
- **Airway Supplies:**
  - ventilators, ambu-bags, ET tubes, laryngoscopes, suction devices, oxygen masks, NG tubes
- **Other Emergency Medications:**
  - for hypotension, anaphylaxis, sedation, pain management
- **Bandages and Dressings**
- **Vaccines**

Figure 7.3. The NPS Program

THE NATIONAL PHARMACEUTICAL STOCKPILE (NPS) PROGRAM

Immediate Response	Rapid Response
12-Hour Push Packages	Vendor Managed Inventory (VMI) Packages
– Ready for deployment to reach designated airfield within 12 hours of federal activation	– To be shipped for arrival within 24-36 hours following request
– Eight packages stored in environmentally controlled and secured facilities	– Packages of pharmaceuticals and supplies delivered from 1 or more VMI sources
– Packaged for rapid identification and ease of content distribution	– "Tailored" to provide specific material depending upon suspected or confirmed agent

A comprehensive medical and public health response to a biological or chemical terrorist event involves epidemiologic investigation, medical treatment, and prophylaxis for affected persons and the initiation of disease prevention or environmental decontamination measures. CDC will assist state and local health agencies in developing resources and expertise for investigating unusual events and unexplained illnesses.

NDMS and DMAT

The National Disaster Medical System (NDMS) is a federally coordinated initiative designed to augment the country's emergency medical response capability in the event of a catastrophic disaster (Figure 7.4). This system is a cooperative program of four federal government agencies: the DOD, DHS, FEMA, and the VA.

NDMS provides an interstate medical mutual aid system linking the federal government, state and local agencies, and private sector institutions to address the medical care needs of catastrophic disasters. The program was designed to supplement the activities of state or local government in a massive civil disaster or to back up the military medical care system in the event of an overseas conventional conflict. NDMS contains a medical response element to bring organized aid to a disaster-affected area, an evacuation system, and a network of pre-committed hospital beds throughout the U.S. Its medical response element includes dozens of volunteer civilian disaster medical assistance teams or DMATs that operate supplemental casualty clearing facilities for triage, stabilization, and holding care for disaster victims, and evacuation facilities for patients in excess of local hospital capacity.

Figure 7.4. NDMS Facts

NDMS Facts

- Over 7,000 participating health professionals.

- 24,000 to 52,000 hospital beds available within 24 hrs.

- 95,000 hospital beds available with 30 days.

- Governance structure:
    - Assistant Secretary of Health (Domestic Emergencies)
    - Assistant Secretary of Defense for Health Affairs (Military Contingency)

- Participating Agencies:
    - DHS provides primary and specialized care (including 4 rapid response WMD-trained) teams.
    - DOD provides victim transportation.
    - DOD and VA provide access to private sector hospital care remote from the disaster site.

Specialized National Medical Response Team-Weapons of Mass Destruction (NMRT-WMD) teams are designed to provide medical care following nuclear, biological, and/or chemical incidents. These teams are capable of providing mass casualty decontamination, medical triage, and primary and secondary medical care to stabilize victims for transportation to tertiary care facilities in a hazardous material environment. There are four NMRTs-WMD geographically dispersed throughout the United States.

Communication Systems

- Develop public health communication infrastructure
- New media issues
- Health Alert Network (HAN)

U.S. preparedness to mitigate the medical and public health consequences of biological and chemical terrorism depends on the coordinated activities of well-trained health-care and public health personnel throughout the United States who have access to up-to-the minute emergency information. Effective communication with the public through the news media will also be essential to limit terrorists' ability to induce public panic and disrupt daily life. During the next 5 years, HHS will work with state and local health agencies to

- develop a state-of-the-art communication system that will support disease surveillance,
- initiate rapid notification and information exchange regarding disease outbreaks that are possibly related to bioterrorism;
- disseminate diagnostic results and emergency health information; and
- coordinate emergency response activities.

Through this network and similar mechanisms, HHS will provide terrorism-related training to epidemiologists and laboratorians, emergency responders, emergency department personnel and other front-line healthcare providers, and health and safety personnel.

FUTURE OF PUBLIC HEALTH PREPAREDNESS

On January 10, 2002, President Bush signed appropriations legislation that provided $2.9 billion for HHS, which was a ten-fold increase in the department's funding for bioterrorism preparedness. The funds have been used to develop comprehensive bioterrorism preparedness plans, upgrade infectious disease surveillance and investigation through the Health Alert Network (HAN), enhance the readiness of hospital systems to deal with large numbers of casualties, expand public health laboratory and communications capacities, and improve connectivity between hospitals, and city, local and state health departments to enhance disease reporting. As the lead federal agency in preparing for the threat of bioterrorism, HHS works closely with states, local government, and the private sector to build the needed new public health infrastructure, and to accelerate research into likely bioterror diseases.

To meet the need for broad-based public health involvement in terrorism preparedness and planning, staff from different agencies in the DHHS participated in developing a strategic WMD plan, including the CDC, Health Resources and Services Administration (HRSA), and Office of Emergency Preparedness (in OBE). The CDC will target state and local programs supporting bioterrorism, infectious diseases, and public health emergency preparedness activities statewide. The HRSA will provide funding, which will be used by states to create regional hospital plans to respond in the event of a bioterrorism attack.

Future goals of Federal public health preparedness efforts include

- Having at least one epidemiologist in each metropolitan area with a population greater than 500,000;

- Developing an education and training plan that will reach health professionals, emergency room physicians and nurses, local public health officials and the public with information relating to bioterrorism, new and emerging diseases, and other infectious agents;

- Targeting bioterrorism research to new vaccines, anti-viral drugs, and new diagnostic tools to better protect against biologics.

Partnerships and Implementation

Implementation of the objectives outlined in HHS's strategic plan will be coordinated through the HHS Office of the Assistant Secretary for Emergency Preparedness and Response. HHS program personnel are charged with

- helping build local and state preparedness,

- developing U.S. medical expertise regarding potential threat agents, and

- coordinating medical response activities during actual bioterrorist events.

Program staffs have established priorities for fiscal year 2004 regarding these focus areas.

SUMMARY

The inability to "do something" in a crisis is probably the most frightening aspect of a crisis for most people. Medical responders are no different in this regard. A major pandemic or biological weapon attack may be a threat that exceeds the capabilities of our resources and technology. Our medical crisis managers are a critical element of our survival, but an ability to do their assigned tasks and to carry on with resolve is critical to their success.

Recent threats and use of biological and chemical agents against civilians have exposed U.S. vulnerability and highlighted the need to enhance our capacity to detect and control terrorist acts. The U.S. must be protected from an extensive range of critical biological and chemical agents, including some that have been developed and stockpiled for military use. Even without threat of war, investment in national defense ensures preparedness and serves as a deterrent against hostile acts. Similarly, investment in the public health and hospital and healthcare systems provides the best civil defense against bioterrorism. Tools developed in response to terrorist threats serve a dual purpose. They help detect rare or unusual disease outbreaks and respond to medical emergencies, including naturally occurring outbreaks or industrial injuries that might resemble terrorist events in their unpredictability and ability to cause mass casualties (e.g., a pandemic influenza outbreak or a large-scale chemical spill). Federal WMD terrorism-preparedness activities, including the development of a public health communication infrastructure, a multilevel network of diagnostic laboratories, an integrated disease surveillance system, and a Metropolitan Medical Response System will improve our ability to investigate rapidly and control public health threats that emerge in the twenty-first century.

ADDITIONAL DISCUSSION TOPICS

- If you were a police executive, how would you plan for your response capability if a third of the police force were ill? How would you protect those who have to respond into the community and continue to be exposed?

- If you are corporate executive how do you protect your workforce? How do you handle "loyal" employees who come to work even though they are sick?

- If you are a medical professional, how do you communicate the discovery of a potential outbreak? How do you find out if there is an emergency?

- Many small towns across America have small medical centers and rural doctor's offices for healthcare. Can contamination reach them? What should they do?

- How could a high-risk virus spread? What can you do in your current role to minimize the impact?

- If you were a county public health director, what sort of clues do you think you might find that would help determine whether an outbreak was a natural epidemic or a covert biological attack?

- What strategies would you recommend to minimize the negative impact of the "worried well" in case of a pandemic or biological attack?

- Describe how an industrial accident might occur which results in epidemic-like effects.

- The CDC's partners in the pharmaceutical industry are dedicated to surging production of vaccines and medications as needed in an emergency. What are the advantages and drawbacks of this production surging strategy as compared to pre-emergency stockpiling?

RESOURCES

America's Achilles' Heel: Nuclear, Biological, and Chemical Terrorism and Covert Attack, Richard A. Falkenrath, Robert D. Newman, and Bradley A. Thayer (BCSIA Studies in International Security),1998, ISBN: 0262561182, The MIT Press.

Toxic Terror: Assessing Terrorist Use of Chemical and Biological Weapons, Jonathan B. Tucker (BCSIA Studies in International Security), 2000, ISBN: 0262700719, The MIT Press.

REFERENCES

Ashraf, H. (1999). European dioxin-contaminated food crisis grows and grows [news]. *Lancet, 353,* 2049.

Centers for Disease Control and Prevention (CDC). (1998). *Preventing emerging infectious diseases: A strategy for the 21st century.* Atlanta, GA: U.S. Department of Health and Human Services.

Centers for Disease Control and Prevention (CDC). (2001). *CDC Fact Book 2000/2001.* Atlanta, GA: U.S. Department of Health and Human Services. Retrieved from <http://www.cdc.gov/maso/factbook/main.html>.

Davis, C. J. (1999). Nuclear blindness: an overview of the biological weapons programs of the former Soviet Union and Iraq. *Emerging Infectious Disease, 5,* 509-512.

Department of Homeland Security. (2003). *National Response Plan: Initial plan (draft).* Retrieved July 2003, from <www.nemaweb.org/docs/National_Response_Plan.pdf>.

Federal Emergency Management Agency (FEMA). (2002). *Federal Response Plan.* Washington, DC: U.S. Government Printing Office. Retrieved January 3, 2003, from <http://www.fema.gov/r-n-r/frp>.

Janofsky, M. (1995, May 28). Looking for motives in plague case. *New York Times,* p. A18.

Okumura, T., Suzuki, K., Fukuda, A., et al. (1998). Tokyo subway sarin attack: Disaster management, Part 1: community emergency response. *Acad Emergency Medicine, 5,* 613-7.

Török, T. J., Tauxe, R. V., Wise, R. P., et al. (1997). Large community outbreak of Salmonellosis caused by intentional contamination of restaurant salad bars. *JAMA, 278,* 389-95.

Tucker, J.B. (1996). Chemical/biological terrorism: coping with a new threat. *Politics and the Life Sciences, 15,* 167-184.

U.S. Department of Homeland Security. (2003). *Homeland Security Presidential Directive (HSPD) -5,* February 28. Retrieved July 2003 from <http://www.whitehouse.gov/news/releases/2003/02/20030228-9.html >.

Uncle Fester, et al. (1997). *Silent death: Forbidden art & science of deadly toxins* (2nd Ed.). Port Townsend, WA: Festering Publications.

Recommended Readings

Dunaway, W. M. (2003). *Strategies for Incident Preparedness: A National Model.* Philadelphia, PA: National Bioterrorism Civilian Medical Response Center (CIMERC) at Drexel University.

Gursky, E., Inglesby, T. V., & O'Toole, T. (2003). Anthrax 2001: Observations on the Medical and Public Health Response. *Biosecurity and Bioterrorism: Biodefense Strategy, Practice and Science, 1(2),* 97-110.

Johns Hopkins Center for Civilian Biodefense, Center for Strategic and International Studies, ANSER, & Memorial Institute for the Prevention of Terrorism. (2001). *Dark Winter: Bioterrorism Exercise; Andrews Air Force Base; June 22-23, 2001.* Final Script.

Noji E, Goodwin T, & Hopmeier M. (2005). Demystifying Bioterrorism: Common myths and Misperceptions. Prehospital and Disaster Medicine, 20(1), 3–6. <http://pdm.medicine.wisc.edu>.

Noji E. (2001). Bioterrorism: A 'New' Environmental Health Threat. *Global Change & Human Health*, 2(1), 46-53.

Noji E. K. (2003). Medical Preparedness and Response to Terrorism Secondary to Weapons of Mass Destruction in the USA. *International Journal of Disaster Medicine, 1,* 1-7.

U.S. General Accounting Office (GAO). (2002, Sept.). *Chemical Weapons: Lessons Learned Program Generally Effective but Could be Improved and Expanded* (GAO-02-890).

Zilinkas, R. A., & Pate, J. (2002). *Responding to Bioterrorism: Assessing California's Preparedness* (CRB 02-2004). Sacramento, CA: California Research Bureau

Endnotes

[1] Source: Reuters, Thursday, November 6, 2003; 11:50 p.m.

[2] Source: http://www.cdc.gov/flu/avian/gen-info/pandemics.htmcomment in August 2004.

[3] Source: The following excerpt is from the White House. National Strategy for Pandemic Influenza Implementation Plan One Year Summary July 17, 2007, found at http://www.whitehouse.gov/homeland/pandemic-influenza-oneyear.html

[4] This excerpt was written by Eric K. Noji, M.D., M.P.H. Special Assistant to the U.S. Surgeon General for Homeland Security and Emergency Preparedness and Response to U.S. Public Health Service, Washington, D.C.

[5] "Worried well" - term used to describe those physically unaffected by an event, yet displaying symptoms more related to psychological stress and concern. No obvious disease or injury - potentially exposed.

[6] Source: Centers for Disease Control (CDC). (1998). *Preventing emerging infectious diseases: a strategy for the 21st century.* Atlanta, GA: U.S. Department of Health and Human Services.

CHAPTER EIGHT

NATIONAL RESPONSE FRAMEWORK (NRF)

We live in the midst of alarms; anxiety beclouds the future;
we expect some new disaster with each newspaper we read.
—Abraham Lincoln

Disasters teach us humility.
—St. Anselm

KEY TERMS

National Response Framework
Emergency Management
Natural Disaster
Technological Disaster
Disaster
Emergency
Response
Non-Governmental Organizations (NGO)
National Incident Management Systems (NIMS)

OBJECTIVES

- Describe the difference between catastrophic events, emergencies, and disasters.

- Identify how catastrophic events are measured.

- Describe how human encroachment upon the natural environment has affected human exposure to natural hazards.

- Describe the difference between technological disasters and natural disasters.

- Describe the impact terrorism has had on the types of threats that emergency managers must confront.

- Explain the factors that have contributed to an increasing salience of emergency management in American society.

DISCUSSION TOPICS

- How should catastrophic events be measured?

- What are "technological disasters"?

- How does the threat of terrorism complicate emergency management?

8

INTRODUCTION

Planning for disaster response has slowly evolved from the intuitive to the finely detailed and orchestrated outline of cooperation and synergy.

Form its origins in NIMS, ICS and other systems, the National Response Framework takes the concept of preparedness for all hazards to a comprehensive level. The National Response Framework is being developed to preclude, or at least mitigate, the pitfalls and failures that can occur at the time of a catastrophic events, whether caused by man or nature

We will review the overview materials and develop content that will allows us to see the direction in which this evolving process is going and how local and national resources will be coordinated.

THE PRACTICE OF EMERGENCY MANAGEMENT[1]

There are many ways to introduce emergency management as it is practiced in the U.S. and to establish the importance of the field of emergency management for study at the higher-education level. It hardly seems necessary to explain the need for a profession and field aimed at saving lives and property. While many people recognize environmental threats and the need for systematic concern with protection, only a few appreciate the magnitude and diversity of the threats. One can introduce the study of emergency management by acknowledging that losers from disasters—in the United States and the world—have been growing over the years, and are likely to continue to grow. Losses may be measured in a variety of ways, with deaths, injuries, and property damage the most common indices. In 1995, the Kobe, Japan earthquake killed more than 6,000 people and left another 30,000 injured. In the previous year, the Northridge, California earthquake resulted in approximately $33 billion in damages. When impacts are accumulated over time, the losses appear even more dramatic. Mileti (1999:5) reports that between 1989 and 1999, the average annual losses in the United States due to natural disasters were $1 billion each week. Furthermore, many costs are not insured—Mileti estimates about 17 percent of losses are insured—and simply must be absorbed by civilians, whether they are individuals, businesses, or governments. One must also remember that these losses from the past pale when compared with potential losses in the future. For example, among the most likely future events are large magnitude earthquakes in the greater Los Angeles area and on the New Madrid fault in the Midwest. Such events would generate thousands of deaths, tens of thousands of injuries, and billions of dollars in economic losses.

The world appears to be plagued by an increasing number and variety of types of disasters. This impression is certainly heightened when we observe what seem to be frequently very large-scale natural disasters—earthquakes, floods, hurricanes, volcanic eruptions, and wildland fires—all over the globe. When we add to these events a wide range of severe storms, mudslides, lightening, tornadoes, and other "small" natural disaster agents, one could conclude that natural disasters are on the increase. Technological agents and processes also initiate events that we call disasters. Hazardous materials are transported via road, rail and air; when containment is breached, death, environmental destruction and dollar loss are all possible consequences. Some technologies—nuclear power generation—pose risks by their very operation, while other even common place technological processes—metal plating operation—use chemical agents that are inherently dangerous. Even the epitome of American technology, the space program, has experienced disaster associated with product failures. Finally, we see terrorists operating on U.S. soil—made highly visible by attacks on the World Trade Centers, September 11, 2001....

Geophysical, meteorological and hydrologic processes are unfolding as they have for millennia, beginning long before humans occupied the earth and continuing to the present. Given the eons-long perspective of the natural environment, it would be very difficult to meaningfully identify changes in event frequency for any given small time window. Event frequency, from an emergency management perspective, is not really the issue. Over the years, the number of people who have been affected by natural disasters and losses is becoming progressively greater. The significant feature driving these observations, however, is the extent of human encroachment upon the natural environment. With increasing population size and density, and changing settlement and land-use patterns, more people are exposed to natural hazards and consequently our accumulated human and economic losses are increasing. Much of this exposure is a matter of choice. Sometimes people choose hazardous places, building houses on picturesque cliffs, on mountain slopes, in floodplains, near beautiful volcanoes, or along earth faults. Sometimes people choose hazardous building materials that don't accommodate environmental extremes—for example masonry block in earthquake vulnerable areas. Some exposure involves less choice: the cheap land or cheap rent in flood plains often attracts the poor. The point is that one need cannot precisely estimate event frequency to understand rising disaster losses in the United States. As Mileti (1999) writes in *Disasters by Design*, the increasing numbers of humans, our settlements patterns, the density with which we pack together, and our choices of location for homes, work and recreation place more of us at risk and, when disasters occur, exact an increasing toll.

The pattern observed among technological disasters is somewhat different. Certainly more people are affected by technological threats simply because there are more people, and we make unfortunate choices (as was the case with natural threats) about our proximity to known technological dangers. The nature of the threat from technological sources also appears to be inherently changing. The potential for human loss from technological sources increases with the growth and change of existing technologies and with the development of new technologies. For example, risks are rising from the increasing quantity and variety of hazardous materials used in industry, and from energy technologies, such as coal and nuclear power plants and liquefied natural gas (LNG) facilities. Such facilities and the processes they use pose a variety of risks for both employees who are in direct contact and more geographically distant members of the public. Furthermore, as technologies develop, it is sometimes found that what was thought not to be hazardous a decade ago does, in fact, have deleterious effects upon health, safety, and/or the environment. Yet, unlike natural events, advancing technology often produces an improved capability to detect, monitor, control, and repair the release of hazardous materials into the environment. Ultimately, of course, because technologies grow, diversify, and become increasingly integrated into human life, the associated risks also grow.

The specter of terrorism represents a recent addition to the types of threats that emergency managers must confront. There appears to be consensus that the outcomes of at least some terrorism can be termed disasters. It also appears that principles of human behavior in disaster conditions generalize in many cases to terrorist events (Perry and Lindell 2003a). However, unlike natural disasters, terrorism is human action; and unlike technology, terrorism is specifically aimed at creating death and destruction. It remains to be seen precisely how terrorism will be fitted into the lexicon of disaster research. Definitions of terrorism vary between the academic community and emergency managers (Buck 1998). Although for emergency managers, at least the consequences of terrorism must be addressed, like other emergencies and disasters. But terrorism is a special challenge that has only recently begun to be systematically examined from an emergency management perspective. There is little system or design to most terrorism that might be penetrated and used to develop a meaningful prediction algorithm. Detection seems to be a prime path for forewarning, but the mechanisms of detection lie in law enforcement and intelligence—outside the traditional purview of emergency managers. Furthermore, terrorism is not a single agent, but humans taking advantage of a variety of destructive agents—biological, chemical, radiological—to do harm. Indeed, even helpful "friendly" technologies—crop dusting airplanes for example—can be turned into destructive agents by terrorists. At this early stage, managerial efforts focus on detection, preparedness, response and recovery. And even these strategies are complicated bec cause it is so difficult to anticipate agents, timing, consequences, and vulnerabilities. Even the skill of terrorists has an impact on the consequences that must be managed. For example, the Aum Shinrikyo attempt to diffuse the nerve agent sarin in the Tokyo subway in 1995 underscored the importance of agent quality and diffusion effectiveness. Cult members carried bags of the liquid form of the agent onto subway cars and cut the containers as a means of initiating the threat. Although sarin is extremely lethal, the attack resulted in only twelve deaths and approximately 1,046 patients being admitted to hospitals (Reader 2000). If the sarin had been effectively aerosolized, the death and injury rates could have been phenomenal. Ultimately, whether terrorism and its consequences are increasing or not seems to be a matter of many factors that defy meaningful measurement at this time.

It is clear that more people, worldwide, are subject to a greater range of disasters arising from natural forces, technology, and terrorism. In fact, the number and types of risks are large and human exposure is constant. Through the joint action of natural phenomena and human agency, American society is subject to risks that have come to be characterized as more or less "acceptable." When faced with a risky environment, coupled with finite time and resources to engage in risk management, decisions must be made about which risks to engage (Lawrance 1976). When individuals, organizations, or political jurisdictions reach consensus that a given risk is unacceptable, resources are marshaled to reduce the risk to some level deemed more acceptable. Such resources can be used to attempt to eliminate the source of the danger, or, alternatively, change the way people relate to the source of danger. For example, building dams or channeling streams can eliminate the risk of seasonal floods (at least for a time). Alternately, people and dwellings can be relocated outside the floodplain, or a warning and evacuation system could be devised to provide protection only in times of an acute flood threat. Emergency management is rooted in this process of identifying unacceptable risks, assessing vulnerabilities, and devising strategies for converting unacceptable risks into more acceptable risks.

[One classic definition of] emergency management is "the discipline and profession of applying science, technology, planning, and management to deal with extreme events that can injure or kill large numbers of people, do extensive damage to property, and disrupt community life" (Drabek 1991a: xvii). Thus, emergency managers identify, anticipate, and respond to the risks of catastrophic events in order to reduce to more acceptable levels the probability of their occurrence or the magnitude and duration of their social impacts. In the United States, emergency management traditionally has been conceptualized as the job (if not the legal responsibility) of government—local, state and federal. Particularly in the second half of the 20th century, private business organizations have taken an active interest in emergency management, largely as it relates to natural and technological threats that bear upon their own business preservation. Certainly as the 21st century begins, emergency management is seen as achieved through alliances of all levels of government and the broader private sector (including profit and non-profit organizations with a wide range of missions).

A variety of factors have contributed to an increasing salience of emergency management in American society.

■ One important factor lies in changes in the principle of sovereign immunity at the state level in the last quarter of the 20th century and the establishment of levels of tort liability for local and state governments (Pine 1991). While some levels of immunity persist, it is important that government liability can be established under state and federal law, particularly in cases where negligence (failure to plan where appropriate) can be contended.

■ Another factor promoting the importance and visibility of emergency management is the professionalization of emergency managers. The recognition of the need for specialized training and development for emergency managers has lead to the establishment of professional associations, the use of training certifications (e.g., technician certificates for hazardous materials and emergency medical expertise, and general certificates in incident management systems), and of professional credentialing processes such as the Association of Emergency Manager program sustained by the International Association of Emergency Managers. These developments have contributed to the growth of an organized body of specialists who understand how to appraise and cope with a range of environmental threats.

- A third factor in a growing sensitivity to hazards on the part of the public at-large that is driven by media attention to periodic catastrophes associated with the forces of nature and technology.

- Finally, private businesses have become increasingly sensitive to the fact that disaster losses can have significant negative consequences on business plans and performance, sometimes forcing bankruptcy, closure, or the loss of significant market share (Lindell and Perry 1998).

With such significant potential consequences, vulnerability assessment, and disaster preparedness have become both imbedded in business planning and thriving businesses in themselves. Collectively, these factors have generated a social environment in which governments' ethical and legal obligations to protect citizens, and private sector responsibility for self-protection, are kept in the forefront demanding explicit attention to emergency management.

EMERGENCIES AND DISASTERS

Emergencies and disasters have been present in human societies much longer than either the practice of emergency management or the beginning of the formal study of disasters. Many terms and definitions are used which refer to negative consequences that accrue from environmental events: accident, emergency, crisis, disaster, catastrophe, tragedy, and calamity, to name a few. Over the years, many of these terms have become embedded in the American vocabulary, often introduced through some mass media or literary usage. As such events become the focus of emergency management and academic study, it is necessary to devise technical—as opposed to vernacular—meanings for them to precisely clarify the referent of the terms and facilitate analytic usage. For the purposes of an introduction to emergency management, it is important to distinguish the meaning of at least three terms: hazards, disasters, and emergencies.

The environment that humans occupy may be conceived as containing natural and man-made components. Each of these components contains elements that pose a variety of risks to the human occupants. These risks include both health and safety dangers for the occupants themselves and dangers to the physical or material culture created by the occupants. The risks are magnified to the extent that the human use system intrudes upon natural and man-made processes. The term *hazard* captures the notion that to the extent that individuals co-exist with risky natural and man-made processes, there is a non-zero probability that the operation of the processes will produce negative consequences for humans (Burton, Kates and White 1993; Cutter 2001). Human danger posed by hazards varies and depends upon the level of human intrusion and the knowledge and technology associated with the hazard (Lindell and Perry 1992). Tsunami (tidal waves or seismic sea waves) hazard is negligible in Ames, Iowa (no ocean or which to intrude), but very significant along coastal Japan. Hazards are inherently probabilistic; they represent processes present in the environment, not an event. Thus, hurricane hazard refers to the presence of the possibility of hurricanes in the environment. A hazardous materials transportation hazard refers to the condition where hazardous materials are transported as an environmental feature. Hurricane hazard does not describe the condition when a hurricane strikes a coastal community causing death, injury, and property destruction. Of course, to achieve long-term survival, humans must adjust to or accommodate both natural and man-made processes in some fashion. The classic definition of hazard adjustment focuses upon the modification of human behavior (broadly speaking, to include even settlement patterns) or the modification of environmental features to enable people to live in a given place (or with a given technology) under prevailing conditions (Lindell and Perry 2003b).

The term disaster is reserved for the events themselves that produce human and property damage. The riverine flood hazard refers to the probability that a flood will impact encroaching humans, while a riverine flood disaster refers to a particular event in time and space where people and/or property were affected by rising water. Samuel Prince's (1920) study of an explosion in Nova Scotia was the first modern piece of disaster research, but it was 12 years later that the first attempt at a formal definition was made by Lowell Carr (1932). Presently, disaster is commonly defined as a nonroutine event in time and space, producing human, property and/or environmental damage, whose remediation requires the use of resources from outside the directly affected community. This definition captures the two features that are minimally (and traditionally) cited as features of disasters: they are out of the ordinary events with consequences substantial enough to require that extra-community resources be marshaled to respond to and recover from the impact (Quarantelli 1984; Perry 1991; Tierney, Lindell and Perry 2001).

There are many different definitions of disaster present in the professional and academic literature. The definitions embrace the above critical dimensions, but them go on to do something else, often specifying in some way the mechanism that generates the event (acts of God, social injustice, acts of nature, aspects of social organization, etc.). There are serious distinctions to be made about disasters and the conduct of emergency management depending upon assumptions about disaster origins (Drabek 1997). Certainly whether one believes God, nature, social injustice or purposeful encroachment produce disasters, does affect the attitude we express toward victims. In the academic community in particular, the details of such distinctions are still being specified and consensus about the accuracy and desirability of different meanings is still developing (Quarantelli 1998). However, in the profession of emergency management, the focus is typically on the assumption that disasters are caused by the overlap of human-use systems with nature and technological processes and the charge is to manage those consequences. At last on this applied level, emergency managers can operate on a concise definition of disasters, while remaining cognizant that the concept can be extended in a variety of ways and it has a myriad of dimensions.

Finally, an *emergency*—like a disaster—refers to an event involving negative consequences for human life or property. But emergencies are usually distinguished as events that are commonly experienced, relatively more predictable, and whose remediation may be accomplished within the resources of a single community, and often a single community response organization. Emergencies are the daily events that we see uniformed responders managing: car crashes, ruptured natural gas pipes, house fires, trauma injuries, or cardiac crises. They are managed via (government or sometimes private) organizations with specially trained, specially equipped personnel. One commonly associates emergencies with fire departments, police departments, ambulance services, and emergency medical services organizations. These events are "routine" in the sense that they are common (frequent) occurrences and over time are similar enough to permit the use of generic response protocols and equipment (Quarantelli 1987). From a irst responder perspective, however, it is important to remember that each emergency situation can present unique elements—there is no such thing as a "routine house first." A mindset that permits one to believe that one first will be like "all the others" is a mindset that produces firefighter deaths and injuries (Brunacini 2002).

NATIONAL RESPONSE FRAMEWORK

The National Response Framework provides emergency responders with architecture for organization rather than fixed procedures. This enables emergency responders the develop a structure for coordination supported with general guidelines which are flexible allowing for the on-scene decision making required at any emergency, disaster, or catastrophe.

While emergencies often share similar characteristics, each incident has its own unique mix of circumstances and the individuals who respond have their own unique capabilities and resources. Flexibility in developing response strategies is essential for the on-scene commander, particularly in the first hours of response. For example, an on scene commander managing response to a tornado in a small mid-western town may face a completely different scenario, set of resources and capabilities that might be available during the response to an earthquake in Los Angeles; however many elements of planning, responding, and recovery may be the same.

As an architectural design, the plan emphasizes the importance of the role-players and stakeholders who are involved with and impacted by the dynamic state of a critical situation.

This introduction to the National Response Framework will provide an overview of this visionary approach to future crisis response.

Overview

The *National Response Framework (NRF)* [or *Framework*] is a guide to how the Nation conducts all-hazards responses. It is built upon *scalable, flexible, and adaptable coordinating structures* to align key roles and responsibilities *across the Nation*. It describes responsible authorities and best practices for managing incidents that range from the serious local occurrences, to large-scale terrorist attacks or catastrophic natural disasters.

The *Framework* explains the common discipline and structures that have been exercised and matured at the local, tribal, State, and national levels over time. It describes key lessons learned from Hurricanes Katrina and Rita and focuses on how the Federal Government is organized to support communities and States in catastrophic incidents. Most importantly, it builds upon the *National Incident Management System (NIMS)*, which provides a consistent template for managing incidents.

The term "response" as used in the *Framework* includes immediate actions to save lives, protect property and the environment, and meet basic human needs. Response also includes the execution of emergency plans and actions to support short-term recovery. The *Framework* is always in effect, and necessary elements can be implemented on a flexible, scalable basis to improve response.

Intended Audience

The *Framework* is written especially for government executives, private sector and nongovernmental organization (NGO) leaders, and emergency management practitioners. First, it is addressed to senior elected and appointed leaders, such as Federal department or agency heads, State Governors, mayors, tribal leaders, and city or county officials – those who have a responsibility to provide for effective response. For the Nation to be prepared for any and all hazards, its leaders must have a baseline familiarity with the concepts and mechanics of the *Framework*.

The *Framework* informs emergency management practitioners about the operating structures and tools used by first responders and emergency managers at all levels of government. For these readers, the *Framework* is augmented with online access to supporting documents, further training, and an evolving resource for exchanging lessons learned.[2]

One of the challenges to effective response is the relatively high turnover and short tenure among elected and appointed officials responsible for response at various levels. Effective response hinges upon well-trained leaders and responders who have invested in response preparedness, developed engaged partnerships, and are able to achieve shared objectives. While the players' bench is constantly changing, a concise and common playbook is needed.

The *Framework* is intended to supply that essential playbook. It is rooted in extensive consultation among practitioners and policymakers at all levels. Operational planning for specific types of incidents has accelerated and improved nationwide since the terrorist attacks of September 11, 2001 (or 9/11). Such plans will continue to evolve in alignment with the *Framework*.

Evolution of the Framework

This document is an outgrowth of previous iterations of Federal planning documents. A brief discussion of its history underscores important elements of the *Framework* and highlights improvements to the previous *National Response Plan* (*NRP*). The *Federal Response Plan* (1992) preceded the current Framework by 15 years and focused largely on Federal roles and responsibilities.

Following the 9/11 attacks, more urgent efforts were made to understand and implement common incident management and response principles and to develop common planning frameworks. The 2004 *NRP* was an early outgrowth of those discussions, replacing the *Federal Response Plan*. It was published one year after creation of the Department of Homeland Security (DHS). The *NRP* broke new ground in integrating all levels of government in a common incident management framework. It incorporated incident coordination roles for Federal agencies[3] as defined by several new laws and Presidential directives. Nine months after Katrina's landfall, a notice of change to the *NRP* was released, incorporating preliminary lessons learned from the 2005 hurricane season.

Stakeholders suggested changes to the *NRP* – *both structural and substantive.* Stakeholders have advised that both the initial *NRP* and its 2006 iteration were bureaucratic and internally repetitive.

Users also suggested the *NRP* was still insufficiently *national* in its focus, which is to say that it should speak more clearly to the roles and responsibilities of all parties involved in response. Moreover, it was evident that the *NRP* and its supporting documents did not constitute a true operational *plan* in the sense understood by emergency managers. Its content was inconsistent with the promise of its title.

In the last several years, operational planning on a national basis for specific types of incidents has matured. Both public and private sectors are making significant homeland security investments to strengthen the Nation's response capability.

By adopting the term "framework" within the title, the document is now more accurately aligned with its intended purpose. Effective response to an incident is a shared responsibility of governments at all levels, the private sector and NGOs, and individual citizens. This *Framework* commits the Federal Government, in partnership with local, tribal, and State governments and the private sector, to complete both strategic and operational plans for the incident scenarios specified in the *National Preparedness Guidelines.*[4] These plans will ultimately improve significantly the Incident Annexes to this *Framework*, which have been carried forward from the *NRP*.

Framework Unpacked

The *Framework* presents the key response principles, participants, roles, and structures that guide the Nation's response operations. The remainder of the *Framework* is organized as follows:

- *Chapter I – Roles and Responsibilities.* This chapter sharpens the focus on *who* is involved with emergency management activities at the local, tribal, State, and Federal levels and with the private sector and NGOs.

- *Chapter II – Response Actions.* This chapter describes *what* we as a Nation collectively do to respond to incidents.

- *Chapter III – Response Organization.* This chapter explains *how* we as a Nation are organized to implement response actions.

- *Chapter IV – Planning: A Critical Element of Effective Response.* This chapter emphasizes the importance of planning and summarizes the elements of national planning structures.

- *Chapter V – Additional Resources.* This final chapter summarizes the content and plan for the online **NRF Resource Center**, a new, actively managed DHS/Federal Emergency Management Agency Web site that will deliver state-of-the- art support for the *Framework* with additional support tools shaped by and addressed to the response community.

How the Framework Is Organized

The *National Response Framework* is comprised of the core document, the Emergency Support Function (ESF), Support, and Incident Annexes, and the Partner Guides. The core document describes the doctrine that guides our national response, roles and responsibilities, response actions, response organizations, and planning requirements to achieve an effective national response to any incident that occurs. The core document of the *National Response Framework* is effective 60 days after publication. The annexes and Partner Guides will be updated periodically and effective 60 days after publication.

Organization of the Framework

The following documents provide more detailed information to assist practitioners in implementing the *Framework*:

- **Emergency Support Function Annexes** group Federal resources and capabilities into functional areas that are most frequently needed in a national response (e.g., Transportation, Firefighting, Mass Care).

- **Support Annexes** describe essential supporting aspects that are common to all incidents (e.g., Financial Management, Volunteer and Donations Management, Private-Sector Coordination).

- **Incident Annexes** address the unique aspects of how we respond to seven broad incident categories (e.g., Biological, Nuclear/Radiological, Cyber, Mass Evacuation).

- **Partner Guides** provide ready references describing key roles and actions for local, tribal, State, Federal, and private sector response partners.

The *National Incident Management System* **(NIMS)** is a companion document that provides standard command and management structures that apply to response activities. This system provides a consistent, nationwide template to enable Federal, State, tribal, and local governments, the private sector, and NGOs to work together to prepare for, prevent, respond to, recover from, and mitigate the effects of incidents regardless of cause, size, location, or complexity. This consistency provides the foundation for utilization of the *NIMS* for all incidents, ranging from daily occurrences to incidents requiring a coordinated Federal response.

These documents are available at the **NRF Resource Center:** http://www.fema.gov/NRF.

Response: The Who

An effective, unified national response requires layered, mutually supporting capabilities. The *Framework* systematically incorporates public-sector agencies, the private sector, and NGOs. It also emphasizes the importance of personal preparedness by individuals and households.

Communities, tribes, States, the Federal Government, NGOs, and the private sector should each understand their respective roles and responsibilities, and complement each other in achieving shared goals. Each governmental level plays a prominent role in developing capabilities needed to respond to incidents. This includes developing plans, conducting assessments and exercises, providing and directing resources and capabilities, and gathering lessons earned. These activities require that involved organizations understand their roles and responsibilities, and how they fit within and are supported by the *Framework*.

It is important that each level of government adapts and applies the general roles outlined in the *Framework*. To do this, organizations should define key leadership and staff functions, adopt capabilities-based planning as the method to build response capabilities, and impose the discipline needed to plan and operate effectively. Partner Guides that summarize core *Framework* concepts and are tailored specifically to leaders at different levels and types of organizations are provided through the online **NRF Resource Center.**

Even when a community is overwhelmed by an incident, there is still a core, sovereign responsibility to be exercised at this local level, with unique response obligations to coordinate with State, Federal, and private-sector support teams. Each organization or level of government therefore has an imperative to fund and execute its own core emergency management responsibilities.

Below is a brief summary of emergency management roles at the local, tribal, State, and Federal levels, as well as the roles of private-sector organizations. Emergency management is the coordination and integration of all activities necessary to build, sustain, and improve the capability to prepare for, protect against, respond to, recover from, or mitigate against threatened or actual natural disasters, acts of terrorism, or other manmade disasters.

Local Governments. Resilient communities begin with prepared individuals and depend on the leadership and engagement of local government, NGOs, and the private sector. Individuals, families, and caregivers to those with special needs should enhance their awareness of risk and threats, develop household emergency plans that include care for pets and service animals, and prepare emergency supply kits.[5] Individuals can also volunteer in their communities.

Local police, fire, emergency medical services, public health and medical providers, emergency management, public works, environmental response professionals, and others in the community are often the first to detect a threat or hazard, or respond to an incident. They also are often the last to leave an incident site or otherwise to cope with the effects of an incident. The local senior elected or appointed official (the mayor, city manager, or county manager) is responsible for ensuring the public safety and welfare of residents. In today's world, senior officials and their emergency managers build the foundation for an effective response. They organize and integrate their capabilities and resources with neighboring jurisdictions, the State, NGOs, and the private sector. Increasingly, businesses are vital partners within communities wherever retail locations, service sites, manufacturing facilities, or management offices are located. NGOs and not-for-profit organizations also play a key role in strengthening communities' response efforts through their knowledge of hard-to-reach populations, outreach, and services.

States, Territories, and Tribal Governments. States, territories, and tribal governments have responsibility for the public health and welfare of the people in their jurisdiction. State and local governments are closest to those impacted by incidents, and have always had the lead in response and recovery. During response, States play a key role coordinating resources and capabilities throughout the State and obtaining resources and capabilities from other States. States are sovereign entities, and the Governor has responsibility for public safety and welfare. While U.S. territories, possessions, freely associated states[6], and tribal governments also have sovereign rights, there are unique factors involved in working with these entities. Stafford Act assistance is available to States and to Puerto Rico, the Virgin Islands, Guam, American Samoa, and the Commonwealth of the Northern Mariana Islands, which are included in the definition of "State" in the Stafford Act. [7]

States have significant resources of their own, including State emergency management and homeland security agencies, State police, health agencies, transportation agencies, incident management teams, specialized teams, and the National Guard. The role of the State government in response is to supplement local efforts before, during, and after incidents. **If a State anticipates that its resources may be exceeded, the Governor can request assistance from the Federal Government and/or from other States through mutual aid and assistance agreements such as the Emergency Management Assistance Compact (EMAC).**[8]

The Federal Government. The Federal Government maintains a wide array of capabilities and resources that can be made available upon request of the Governor. When an incident occurs that exceeds or is anticipated to exceed State, tribal, or local resources, the Federal Government may provide resources and capabilities to support the State response. For incidents involving primary Federal jurisdiction or authorities (e.g., on a military base or a Federal facility or lands), Federal departments or agencies may be the first responders and first line of defense, coordinating activities with State, territorial, tribal, and local partners. The Federal Government also maintains working relationships with the private sector and NGOs.

Pursuant to the Homeland Security Act of 2002 and Homeland Security Presidential Directive (HSPD) [6], the Secretary of Homeland Security is the principal Federal official for domestic incident management. Incident management refers to how incidents are managed across all homeland security activities, including prevention, protection, and response and recovery. Other Federal departments and agencies have key responsibilities to support national response activities and carry out those responsibilities within the overarching coordinating mechanisms of this *Framework*. DHS coordinates with other agencies to surge Federal support at the headquarters, regional, and field levels.

The Private Sector and NGOs. The private sector and NGOs contribute to response efforts through partnerships with each level of government. Private-sector organizations and NGOs are encouraged to develop contingency plans and to work with State and local planners to ensure that their plans are consistent with pertinent plans, the *NIMS*, and this *Framework*.

Private-sector organizations play an essential role in protecting critical infrastructure systems and implementing plans for the rapid restoration of normal commercial activities and critical infrastructure operations in the event of disruption.[9] The protection of critical infrastructure and the ability to rapidly restore normal commercial activities can mitigate the impact of an incident, improve the quality of life of individuals, and accelerate the pace of recovery for communities and the Nation. There are not-for-profit owners/operators of critical infrastructure and key resources (CIKR) facilities, notably in healthcare and power generation.

NGOs also serve a vital role at the local, State, and national levels by performing essential service missions in times of need. They provide sheltering, emergency food supplies, and other vital support services. NGOs bolster and support government efforts at all levels.[10]

Response: The What and the How

The *National Response Framework* is always in effect, and elements can be implemented at any level at any time. The *Framework* is capabilities based, which is to say that local governments, tribes, States, and the Federal Government all develop functional capabilities and identify resources that may be required based on hazard identification and risk assessment, threats, and other potential incidents such as those represented by the National Planning Scenarios.

The *Framework* describes *what we do* and *how we respond*. In short, the *National Response Framework* explains how, at all levels, the Nation effectively manages all-hazards response consistent with the *National Strategy for Homeland Security*. The remainder of this Introduction explains the *Framework's* scope, the response doctrine that animates it, and the preparedness strategy of which it is a part. It correlates with an outline of the overall document.

Scope

The *Framework* provides structures for implementing nationwide response policy and operational coordination for all types of domestic incidents. It can be partially or fully implemented in the context of a threat, in anticipation of a significant event, or in response to an incident. Selective implementation allows for a scaled response, delivery of the resources needed, and an appropriate level of coordination.

In this document, incidents include actual or potential emergencies or all-hazards events that range from accidents and natural disasters to actual or potential terrorist attacks. They include events wholly contained within a single jurisdiction and others that are catastrophic in nature and national in their scope or consequences.

It is not always obvious at the outset whether a seemingly minor event might be the initial phase of a larger, rapidly growing threat. The *Framework* incorporates standardized organizational structures that promote on-scene initiative, innovation, and sharing of essential resources drawn from all levels of government, NGOs, and the private sector. Response must be quickly scalable, flexible, and adaptable.

The *Framework* is also intended to accelerate the assessment and response to incidents that may require Federal assistance. In practice, many incidents require virtually reflexive activation of interagency coordination protocols to forestall the incident from becoming worse or to surge more aggressively to contain it. A Federal department or agency acting on independent authority may be the initial and the primary Federal responder, but incidents that require more systematic Federal response efforts are now actively coordinated through the appropriate *Framework* mechanisms described in this document and in its supporting annexes. This initial coordination of Federal incident assessment and response efforts is intended to occur seamlessly, without the need for any formal trigger mechanism.

This *Framework*, therefore, eliminates the Incident of National Significance declaration. The *Framework* neither requires nor makes such declaration. The authorities of the Secretary of Homeland Security to coordinate large-scale national responses are unaltered by this change. Elimination of this declaration will, however, support a more nimble, scalable, and coordinated response by the entire national emergency management community.

Response Doctrine

Response doctrine defines basic roles, responsibilities, and operational concepts for response across all levels of government and with NGOs and the private sector. The overarching objective of response activities centers upon saving lives and protecting property and the environment. Five key principles of operations define response actions in support of the Nation's response mission. Taken together, these five principles of operation constitute **national response doctrine**.

Response Doctrine: Five Key Principles

1. Engaged partnership

2. Tiered response

3. Scalable, flexible, and adaptable operational capabilities

4. Unity of effort through unified command

5. Readiness to act

Response doctrine is rooted in America's Federal system and the Constitution's division of responsibilities between Federal and State governments. Because this doctrine reflects the history of emergency management and the distilled wisdom of responders and leaders at all levels, it gives elemental form to the *Framework*.

This doctrine "evolves in response to changes in the political and strategic landscape, lessons learned from operations, and the introduction of new technologies. Doctrine influences the way in which policy and plans are developed, forces are organized and trained, and equipment is procured. It promotes unity of purpose, guides professional judgment, and enables responders to best fulfill their responsibilities."[11]

Response doctrine is comprised of five key principles: (1) engaged partnership, (2) tiered response, (3) scalable, flexible, and adaptable operational capabilities, (4) unity of effort through unified command, and (5) readiness to act. An introductory word about each follows.

Engaged Partnership

Leaders at all levels must communicate and actively support engaged partnerships by developing shared goals and aligning capabilities so that no one is overwhelmed in times of crisis. Layered, mutually supporting capabilities at Federal, State, tribal, and local levels allow for planning together in times of calm and responding together effectively in times of need. Engaged partnership includes ongoing communication of incident activity among all partners to the *Framework*, and shared situational awareness for a more rapid response. In particular, the potential for terrorist incidents requires *a heightened state of readiness* and nimble, practiced capabilities baked into the heart of our preparedness and response planning.

Engaged partnerships are essential to preparedness. Effective response activities begin with a host of preparedness activities conducted well in advance of an incident.

Preparedness involves a combination of planning, resources, training, exercising, and organizing to build, sustain, and improve operational capabilities. Preparedness is the process of identifying the personnel, training, and equipment needed for a wide range of potential incidents, and developing jurisdiction-specific plans for delivering capabilities when needed for an incident.

Preparedness activities should be coordinated among all involved agencies within the jurisdiction, as well as across jurisdictions. Integrated planning, described later in this *Framework*, will assist in identifying gaps in capability and developing strategies to fill those gaps.

Nationwide preparedness is described in the *National Preparedness Guidelines* and the *National Exercise Program*.[12] These documents lay out 15 National Planning Scenarios that form the basis of the newly coordinated national exercise schedule and priorities, and identify 37 core capabilities that are needed to support response across the Nation. The *Guidelines* identify core local, tribal, community, and State capabilities that will be supported by the DHS homeland security grant programs.

Tiered Response

Incidents must be managed at the lowest possible jurisdictional level and supported by additional capabilities when needed. It is not necessary that each level be overwhelmed prior to requesting resources from another level. Incidents begin and end locally, and most are wholly managed at the local level. Many incidents require unified response from local agencies, NGOs, and the private sector, and some require additional support from neighboring jurisdictions or the State. A small number require Federal support. National response protocols recognize this and are structured to provide additional, tiered levels of support when there is a need for more resources or capabilities to support and sustain the response and initial recovery. All levels should be prepared to respond, anticipating resources that may be required.

A basic premise of the Framework is that incidents are generally handled at the lowest jurisdictional level possible.

Scalable, Flexible, and Adaptable Operational Capabilities

As incidents change in size, scope, and complexity, the response must adapt to meet requirements. The number, type, and sources of resources must be able to expand rapidly to meet needs associated with a given incident. The *Framework*'s disciplined and coordinated process can provide for a rapid surge of resources from all levels of government, appropriately scaled to need. Execution must be flexible and adapted to fit each individual incident. Responders must remain nimble and adaptable for the duration of a response and as needs grow and change. Equally, the overall response should be flexible as it transitions from the response effort to recovery.

This *Framework* is grounded in doctrine that demands a tested inventory of common organizational structures and capabilities that are scalable, flexible, and adaptable for diverse operations. Adoption of the *Framework* across all levels of government and with businesses and NGOs will facilitate interoperability and improve operational coordination.

Unity of Effort through Unified Command

Effective *unified command* is indispensable to response activities and requires a clear understanding of the roles and responsibilities of each participating organization. Success requires *unity of effort,* which respects the chain of command of each participating organization while harnessing seamless coordination across jurisdictions in support of common objectives.

Use of the Incident Command System (ICS) is an important element across multi-jurisdictional or multiagency incident management activities. It provides a structure to enable agencies with different legal, jurisdictional, and functional responsibilities to coordinate, plan, and interact effectively on scene. As a team effort, unified command allows all agencies with jurisdictional authority and/or functional responsibility for the incident to provide joint support through mutually developed incident objectives and strategies established at the command level. Each participating agency maintains its own authority, responsibility, and accountability. This *Framework* employs the *NIMS* standardized structures and tools that enable a unified approach to be effective both on scene and at the emergency operations centers.

The Department of Defense (DOD) is a full partner in the Federal response to domestic incidents, and its response is fully coordinated through the mechanisms of this *Framework*.[13] Concepts of "command" and "unity of command" have distinct legal and cultural meanings for military forces and military operations. For Federal military forces, command runs from the President to the Secretary of Defense to the Commander of the combatant command to the DOD on-scene commander. Military forces will always remain under the operational and administrative control of the military chain of command, and these forces are subject to redirection or recall at any time. The ICS "unified command" concept is distinct from the military chain of command use of this term. And, as such, military forces do not operate under the command of the Incident Commander or under the unified command structure.

The *NIMS*[14] supports response through the following elements of unified command: (1) developing a single set of objectives; (2) using a collective, strategic approach; (3) improving information flow and coordination; (4) creating common understanding of joint priorities and restrictions; (5) ensuring that no agency's legal authorities are compromised or neglected; and (6) optimizing the combined efforts of all agencies under a single plan.

Readiness to Act

Effective response requires readiness to act balanced with an understanding of risk. From individuals, households, and communities to local, tribal, State, and Federal governments, national response depends on the instinct and ability to act. A forward- leaning posture is imperative for incidents that have the potential to expand rapidly in size, scope, or complexity, and for no-notice incidents.

Once response activities have begun, on-scene actions are based on *NIMS* principles. To save lives and protect property and the environment, decisive action on scene is often required of responders. Although some risk may be unavoidable, first responders can effectively anticipate and manage risk through proper training and planning.

Command, single or unified, is responsible for establishing immediate priorities for the safety of not only the public, but the responders and other emergency workers involved in the response, and for ensuring that adequate health and safety measures are in place. The Incident Commander should ensure that each incident has a designated safety officer who has been trained and equipped to assess the operation, identify hazardous and unsafe situations, and implement effective safety plans.

Acting swiftly and effectively requires clear, focused communication and the processes to support it. Without effective communication, a bias toward action will be ineffectual at best, likely perilous. An effective national response relies on disciplined processes, procedures, and systems to communicate timely, accurate, and accessible information on the incident's cause, size, and current situation to the public, responders, and others. Well-developed public information, education strategies, and communication plans help to ensure that lifesaving measures, evacuation routes, threat and alert systems, and other public safety information are coordinated and communicated to numerous diverse audiences in a consistent, accessible, and timely manner.

Part of a Broader Strategy

The *National Response Framework* is required by, and integrates under, a larger *National Strategy for Homeland Security (Strategy)* that serves to guide, organize, and unify our Nation's homeland security efforts. The *Strategy* reflects our increased understanding of the threats confronting the United States, incorporates lessons learned from exercises and real-world catastrophes, and articulates how we should ensure our long-term success by strengthening the homeland security foundation we have built. It provides a common framework by which our entire Nation should focus its homeland security efforts on achieving the following four goals:

1. Prevent and disrupt terrorist attacks.

2. Protect the American people and our critical infrastructure and key resources.

3. Respond to and recover from incidents that do occur.

4. Continue to strengthen the foundation to ensure our long-term success.

While the first three goals help to organize our national efforts, the last goal entails creating and transforming our homeland security principles, systems, structures, and institutions. This includes applying a comprehensive approach to risk management, building a culture of preparedness, developing a comprehensive Homeland Security Management System, improving incident management, better utilizing science and technology, and leveraging all instruments of national power and influence.

The *Framework* primarily focuses on the third goal: respond to and recover from incidents that do occur. The *Strategy* also provides the context that given the certainty of catastrophes on our soil – no matter how unprecedented or extraordinary – it is our collective duty to provide the best response possible. It states that, when needed, we will bring to bear the Nation's full capabilities and resources to save lives, mitigate suffering, and protect property. The *Strategy* also reminds us that as the Nation responds to an incident, we must also begin to lay the foundation not only for a strong recovery over the short term but also for the rebuilding and revitalization of affected communities and regions over the long term.

The *Strategy* calls for a *National Response Framework* that helps to strengthen the foundation for an effective national response, rapidly assess emerging incidents, take initial actions, expand operations as needed, and commence recovery actions to stabilize the area. It also calls for the *Framework* to be clearly written, easy to understand, and designed to be truly national in scope, meeting the needs of State, local, and tribal governments and the private sector and NGOs, as well as the Federal Government. In addition, the *Strategy* underscores the need to ensure that those communities devastated or severely affected by a catastrophic incident are set on a sustainable path for long-term rebuilding and revitalization. The *Framework* is designed to respond to and support the *Strategy* and is intended to be informed by and tie seamlessly to national, State, tribal, and local preparedness activities and investments.

The *Strategy* further describes how the other three national goals are supported through other strategies, plans, and ongoing efforts. For example, the national goal to prevent and disrupt terrorist attacks is further supported by the updated *National Strategy for Combating Terrorism,* released in September 2006, which articulates our Nation's strategy for winning the War on Terror. The sections in both on preventing and disrupting terrorist attacks are complementary and mutually reinforcing. In order to prevent and disrupt terrorist attacks in the United States, we are working to deny terrorists and terrorist-related weapons and materials entry into our country and across all international borders, disrupt their ability to operate within our borders, and prevent the emergence of violent Islamic radicalization in order to deny terrorists future recruits and defeat homegrown extremism. Our *National Strategy to Combat Terrorist Travel, National Strategy for Maritime Security*, and *National Strategy for Aviation Security* are helping to guide our efforts in this area.

The national goal to protect the American people and our critical infrastructure and key resources is also supported by existing plans. The *Strategy* sets forth that to protect the lives and livelihoods of the American people, we must undertake measures to deter the threat of terrorism, mitigate the Nation's vulnerability to acts of terror and the full range of manmade and natural catastrophes, and minimize the consequences of an attack or disaster should it occur. Safeguarding the American people also includes the preservation of the Nation's CIKR. Guiding our efforts to protect the Nation's CIKR is the 2006 *National Infrastructure Protection Plan (NIPP)* and its supporting Sector-Specific Plans, which were developed pursuant to HSPD-7, issued on December 17, 2003. The *NIPP* sets forth a comprehensive risk management framework and provides a coordinated approach to CIKR protection roles and responsibilities for Federal, State, local, and private-sector security partners. It sets national priorities, goals, and requirements for the effective distribution of funding and resources that will help ensure that our government, economy, and public services continue to function in the event of a manmade or natural disaster.

The last national goal is to continue to strengthen the foundation to ensure our long-term success. To fulfill these responsibilities over the long term, we will continue to strengthen the principles, systems, structures, and institutions that cut across the homeland security enterprise and support our activities to secure the homeland. Ultimately, this will help ensure the success of our *Strategy* to secure the Nation.

SUMMARY

Catastrophes have been part of the human experience since the beginning, and will continue to be part of our lives in the future. As human populations grow and technology advances, new and too often unforeseen threats will rise to take their tolls in lives and property damage. The need for trained, professional emergency managers is no longer in doubt, and new management strategies and organizational concepts are being developed and tested in the field. Formal training in emergency management is a fairly new practice, but it will become increasingly common in the future.

ADDITIONAL DISCUSSION TOPICS

- How does the text's technical definition of disaster differ from the vernacular, or layman's understanding of the word? Why does there need to be a set of "technical" definitions for certain words in emergency management?

- Can you think of any examples of human encroachment creating exposure to hazards? Why do people chose to live or work in places that experience disasters frequently?

- How is the planning needed for disasters caused by natural events, technological accidents or terrorist attacks different between the three causes?

Endnotes

[1] The following material was taken from Catastrophic Event Prevention Planning by Irmak Renda-Tanali and Claire B. Rubin, pp. 1-7, 0-536-94155-6, which was derived from the FEMA-EMI course textbook, Introduction to Emergency Management (working draft) Chapter 1, "Introduction to Emergency Management," Wayne Blanchard, 2004. Located at http://training.fema.gov/EMIWeb/edu/introtoEM.asp

2 To support users of the *Framework,* the Department of Homeland Security has created an online **NRF Resource Center,** available at http://www.fema.gov/NRF. This online resource will routinely grow and evolve in support of the *Framework* and those who work with it. The initial postings contain multiple supporting documents, operational plans, standard forms, and other tools that are commonly used by the incident management community. The site will further explain technical aspects of the *Framework,* and will routinely post supporting documents as they are newly generated or improved.

3 Note that within this document, use of the term "agency" when referring to Federal entities is inclusive of executive agencies, departments, and Government corporations.

4 The set of scenarios, while not exhaustive, is representative of a broad range of terrorist attacks ant natural disasters that would stretch the Nation's preventions and response capabilities. Collectively, they yield core prevention and response requirements that can help direct comprehensive planning efforts.

5 More information on preparing a household emergency plan is available at http://www.ready.gov

6 The *Framework* is applicable to U.S possessions and insular areas, as well as the Federated States of Micronesia and the Republic of the Marshal Islands. The U.S. Government does not provide disaster assistance to the Republic of Palau, in accordance with the Compact of Free Association. Insular areas include Guam, the Commonwealth of the Northern Mariana Islands, American Samoa, and the U.S. Virgin Islands.

7 Often throughout this *Framework,* discussion of authorities and roles of States is also intended to incorporate those of U.S. territories and possessions and tribal nations.

8 A reference paper on EMAC is available at the NRF Resource Center, http://www.fema.gov/NRF

9 Additional information on protection of critical infrastructure and key resources (CIKR) can be found in the CIKR Support Annex available at the NRF Resource Center, http://www.fema.gov/NRF.

10 The American Red Cross is a federally chartered instrumentality of the U.S. Government, but it is not a Federal agency under this *Framework.*

11 *United States Coast Guard: America's Maritime Guardian,* Coast Guard Publication 1 (Washington, DC: January2002, second printing), p. 3. The term "doctrine" has clear and rich meaning as a guide to action within the military services. See also U.S. Department of Defense's Joint Operations Planning and Execution System, an overview of which is available at http://www.dtic.mil/doctrine/jel/other_pubs/jopes.pdf.

12 Information on the *National Preparedness Guidelines* can be found at the **NRF Resource Center,** http://www.fema.gov/NRF.

[13] The Secretary of Defense retains command of DOD military forces providing Defense Support of Civil Authorities. National Guard forces under the command and control of a Governor are not DOD military forces. Nothing in this Framework impairs or otherwise affects the authority of the Secretary of Defense over the DOD.

[14] The *National Incident Management System* is available at the **NRF Resource Center,** http://www.fema.gov/NRF.

CHAPTER NINE

DISASTER MANAGEMENT

Always plan ahead. It wasn't raining when Noah built the ark.
—Richard C. Cushing

When planning for a year, plant corn. When planning for a decade, plant trees. When planning for life, train and educate people.
—Chinese Proverb

I will act as if what I do makes a difference.
—William James

KEY TERMS

"All Hazards" concept
Comprehensive Emergency Management (CEM)
Vulnerability
HAZUS-MH
Non-Governmental Organizations (NGOs)

OBJECTIVES

- Describe the history of the U.S. federal emergency management organizations.

- Describe the "all-hazards" approach to emergency management.

- Identify pre-impact conditions and various physical and social vulnerabilities.

- Define the elements of a response protocol.

- Describe how multiple responding agencies are coordinated.

DISCUSSION TOPICS

- How did the 1978 restructure of emergency management services at the Federal level lead to the creation of FEMA? What agencies were involved?

- When FEMA became a subordinate agency under the umbrella of the Department of Homeland Security, do you feel that the capabilities for disaster response were improved or diminished?

- Write your own definition for a catastrophe, disaster, and an emergency and compare and contrast your definition with your classmates and with definitions found in FEMA documents.

- Why do you believe the myth persists that people are dazed and disoriented in times of disaster?

- What do you think demands the most focus from the Federal Government during a disaster? Address the physical impact or the societal impact of the disaster.

9

INTRODUCTION

Since the beginning of time mankind has struggled to survive through emergencies and disasters, both natural and manmade. Anthropologists tell us that the need for protection from natural disasters and against predation from other people drove the development of human civilization and technology, and our recent experiences with the 2004 tsunami in Indonesia, hurricane Katrina in New Orleans and the 9/11 attacks show that these events are still central to our experience.

In this chapter we'll be discussing some of the organizations created to improve planning for, response to, and recovery from catastrophic events, as well as the concepts used to develop response and preparation protocols. Vulnerability assessment will be explained, as will the considerations necessary to predict a disaster's impact. Finally, the interdisciplinary and multi-jurisdictional nature of planning and responding to disasters and methods of coordination will be explored.

A BRIEF HISTORY OF FEDERAL EMERGENCY ORGANIZATIONS

Since the founding of the United States, the responsibility for and the locus of emergency and disaster management has moved throughout the federal government (as well as state and local governments). Except for two pieces of legislation, however, very little systematic work was done that resembles modern emergency management until the 1930s. Drabek (1991b: 6) reports that the first national disaster management or response effort lies in the 1803 Fire Disaster Relief Act which made funds available to the city of Portsmouth and the state of New Hampshire to help with recovery from extensive fires that same year. The other piece of legislation came 125 years later. Platt (1998:38) has reported that the Lower Mississippi Flood Control Act of 1928 was passed as a means of responding to the lower Mississippi River flooding in 1927. It is interesting to note that both of these pieces of early legislation *followed* a disaster and were aimed at supporting *recovery*. The strategy that is embodied by these actions, after the fact rebuilding, took firm hold and guided emergency response efforts at the federal level well into the 1990s. Disaster management—if we characterize it is as concerted attempts to manipulate the consequences of natural forces—at the federal level really began with President Franklin Roosevelt's first administration in 1933.

At the federal level, permanent government agencies concerned with domestic and defense emergencies have existed since President Roosevelt created the Reconstruction Finance Corporation in 1933 and authorized it to make loans to repair public buildings damaged by earthquakes (Drabek 1991b). In addition, many New Deal social programs provided services and various types of aid to natural disaster victims. Aside from individual programs, the National Emergency Council (NEC) operated within the White House between 1933 and 1939 primarily to cope with the Great Depression, but also to oversee natural disaster relief. The Flood Control Act of 1936 established the Army Corps of Engineers as an important agency in the management of American waterways. In 1939, when the economic crisis had begun to subside, the NEC was moved to the Executive Office of the President and renamed the Office for Emergency Management (OEM). Natural disaster relief continued to be centered in the OEM, and the agency functioned as a "crisis management" team for national scale threats of various types.

The beginning of World War II demanded the full attention of the Roosevelt administration in much the same way as the Depression had previously. In addition to natural hazard responsibilities, OEM became the President's agency for civil defense plans and addressing war-related emergencies on the home front. Many programs devised by OEM were based in the Department of War, under the Office of Civil Defense (directed by Fiorello La Guardia). This office was abolished in 1945 (Yoshpe 1981:72), leaving OEM again as the principal federal emergency agency.

Following the war, President Harry Truman initially resisted pressures to establish another civil defense agency, believing that civil defense should be the responsibility of the states (Perry 1982). An Office of Civil Defense Planning was created in 1948 under the then year-old Defense Department, and OEM was again left to concentrate on natural disasters and other domestic emergencies. This separation of planning for civil defense versus natural and domestic disasters continued for nearly two years, but has reappeared over the decades with subsequent reorganizations of federal efforts. After the Soviet Union tested their first atomic bomb in the summer of 1949, Truman relented and created the Federal Civil Defense Administration (FCDA) within the Executive Office of the President in December of that year (replacing the OEM). Responsibility for federal assistance in the case of major natural disasters became the responsibility of the Housing and Home Finance Administration. Legislation quickly followed with the passage of the Federal Civil Defense Act of 1950 and the Disaster Relief Act of 1950 (Blanchard 1986: 2). It is interesting that the legislation continued to assign responsibility for civil defense and disasters to the states, and attempted to spell out specific federal obligations. At the end of President Truman's administration on January 16, 1953, Executive Order 10427 was signed which added natural disaster relief responsibility to FCDA, removing it from Housing and Home Finance (Yoshpe 1981:166).

This arrangement of functions and agencies persisted through both Eisenhower administrations, though the primary agency name changed first to the Office of Defense and Civilian Mobilization and then to the Office of Civil Defense Mobilization (OCDM). The OCDM was the first emergency organization to be given independent agency status (in 1958), rather than being under another cabinet department or the White House. On the policy side, also in 1958 the Federal Civil Defense Act was amended to make civil defense a joint responsibility of the federal government and state and local governments. The amendment also provided for federal matching of state and local government civil defense expenditures, which were actually funded under the administration of President John F. Kennedy in 1961. Thus, the Kennedy era saw the first rapid expansion of civil defense agencies at the state and local level. President Kennedy again separated federal responsibility for domestic disasters and civil defense in 1961 when he created the Office of Emergency Planning (in the White House) and the Office of Civil Defense (in the Defense Department). President Johnson moved the OCD to the Department of the Army in 1964, signaling a reduction in importance (and funding) for this function. This general separation of functions was maintained until 1978, although the OCD became the Defense Civil Preparedness Agency in 1972. Beginning with the creation of the Office of Emergency Preparedness under the Executive Office of the President in 1968, programs to deal with natural and technological hazards began a process of being reconstituted and parceled out among a variety of federal agencies. In 1973, President Nixon dismantled the OEP. Concern with post-disaster relief and reconstruction was moved to the Department of Housing and Urban Development to become the charge of the Federal Disaster Assistance Administration. General management and oversight of federal programs was assigned to the Office of Preparedness and moved to the General Services Administration. In 1975, this office became the Federal Preparedness Agency.

Throughout the 1970s, as new federal legislation or executive orders mandated federal government concern with different aspects of natural and man-made hazards, new programs were created within a variety of federal offices and agencies. These were included in the Department of Commerce establishment of the National Weather Service Community Preparedness Program (1973) and the National Fire Prevention and Control Administration (1974). The Federal Insurance Administration had been established in 1968 as part of the Department of Housing and Urban Development. Following the 1972 havoc wreaked by Hurricane Agnes, the Disaster Relief Act of 1974 was passed, granting individual and family assistance to disaster victims (administered through FDAA). In the late 1970s, four major programs were established within the Executive Office of the President: Dam Safety Coordination, Earthquake Hazard Reduction Program, Warning and Emergency Broadcast System, and Consequences Management in Terrorism. Technological hazards programs involved such agencies as the Environmental Protection Agency, Nuclear Regulatory Commission, and the Departments of Energy and Transportation.

The general collection of federal agencies addressing disaster concerns in the U.S. did persist through the late 1970s however, and in one sense set the stage for the restructuring of federal emergency management in the 1980s. As time passed though, there was a growing concern both in the executive branch and the congress that federal programs for disaster management were too fragmented. In the late 1970s, the National Governor's Association (NGA) "Disaster Project" in the late 1970s that began to trace many of the states' problems in emergency management back to federal arrangements. It was argued that federal fragmentation hampered effective preparedness planning and response, masked duplicate efforts, and made national preparedness a very expensive enterprise.

Responding to these concerns, in 1978 President Carter initiated a process of reorganizing federal agencies charged with emergency planning, response, and recovery. This reorganization resulted in the creation in 1979 of the Federal Emergency Management Agency (FEMA), whose director reported directly to the President of the United States. In practice, FEMA was a consolidation of the major federal disaster agencies and programs. Most of the new organization's administrative apparatus came from combining the three largest disaster agencies: the Federal Preparedness Agency, Defense Civil Preparedness Agency, and Federal Disaster Assistance Administration. A total of 13 separate hazard-relevant programs were then moved to FEMA, including most of the programs and offices created in the 1970s (Drabek 1991b). These moves gave FEMA responsibility for nearly all federal emergency programs of any size, including civil defense, warning dissemination for severe weather threats, hazard insurance, fire prevention and control, dam safety coordination, an emergency broadcast and warning system, earthquake hazard reduction, terrorism, and the planning and response to technological hazards. Where FEMA did not absorb a program in its entirety, interagency agreements were developed giving FEMA coordinating responsibility; these agreements included such agencies as the Environmental Protection Agency, the National Oceanic and Atmospheric Administration, the Nuclear Regulatory Agency, and the Department of Transportation.

At least on paper, the Executive Order made FEMA the focal point for all federal efforts at disaster management. While FEMA was the designated "federal lead agency" in most cases, there are other independent agencies with disaster responsibilities. The Environmental Protection Agency, the Federal Energy Regulatory Commission, the National Transportation Safety Board, Nuclear Regulatory Commission, Small Business Administration, and the Tennessee Valley Authority all have their own authorities and missions. The creation of FEMA moved federal emergency management to a much more central position than it had ever been given previously, but it was not possible to completely consolidate all federal programs and offices within the new agency.

When FEMA was an independent agency, the FEMA Director was appointed by the President of the United States. During the term of James Lee Witt, the last director to head the independent agency, he was given cabinet status by President Clinton. The organization has a regional structure composed of 10 offices throughout the United States, and two larger "area" offices. Although by far the most comprehensive effort, the establishment of FEMA represented the third time that all federal disaster efforts and functions were combined; the first was the National Emergency Council (1933-1939), followed by the Office of Civil Defense Mobilization (1958-1961). The early history of FEMA was devoted primarily to attempts to get a hold on its own bureaucracy and mission. John Macy, the agency's first director, was faced with organizational consolidation as a most pressing task: converting 30 separate nationwide offices to 16 and eight Washington, D.C. offices to five (Macy 1980). Ultimately, creating a single bureaucracy (with a $630 million budget) from 13 entrenched organizations proved to be a Herculean task.

The efforts to obtain an optimal structure for FEMA have continued; major reorganizations of headquarters were subsequently undertaken and FEMA's mission, like its structure, continued to evolve. The early years of FEMA saw much significant legislation and activity. In 1979, Hillary Whittaker (1979), working on the National Governor's Association (NGA) Disaster Project, published the first statement of Comprehensive Emergency Management (CEM; the notion that authorities should develop a capacity to manage all phases of all types of disasters), and the concept was subsequently adopted by both the NGA and FEMA. In 1980, the Federal Civil Defense Action of 1950 was amended to emphasize crisis relocation of population (evacuation of people from cities to areas less likely to be Soviet nuclear targets), signaling a fundamental change in U.S. civil defense strategy. Also in 1980, the Comprehensive Environmental Response, Compensation, and Liability Act (called The Superfund Law) passed, precipitated by the 1978 dioxin contamination of Love Canal, New York (Rubin and Renda-Tanali 2004). In 1983, FEMA adopted the concept of Integrated Emergency Management Systems (IEMS) as part of the strategy for achieving CEM (Drabek 1985; Blanchard 1986). The basic notion was to identify generic emergency functions—applicable across a variety of disaster events—and develop these in a modular sense to be used where and when appropriate. For example, population evacuation is a useful protective technique in the case of hurricanes, floods, nuclear power plant accidents, or a wartime attack (Perry 1985). Similar generic utility exists for warning systems, communication systems, victim sheltering systems, and others. Thus, in the early 1980s, FEMA was formed, shaped by organizational growing pains, and also shaped through the adoption of new philosophies of emergency management. While FEMA's basic charge of developing a strategy and capability to manage all phases of all types of environmental hazards remains, the precise definitions of hazards, the basic concept of emergency management, and the organizational arrangements through which its mission will be accomplished continued to evolve through the end of the 20th century.

The end of the 1980s saw passage of The Superfund Amendments and Reauthorization Act (SARA) in 1986 (Lindell and Perry 2001) and President Reagan's Presidential Policy Guidance (1987) that became the last gasp of nuclear attack related civil defense programs in the United States (Blanchard 1986). Passage of the Robert Stafford Disaster Relief and Emergency Assistance Act of 1988 again boosted state and local emergency management efforts. The Stafford Act established federal cost sharing for planning and public assistance (family grants and housing).

The 1990s brought public controversy for FEMA. In 1989 FEMA's response to Hurricane Hugo was criticized as inept; a charge repeated in 1992 when Hurricane Andrew struck Florida. As a consequence of the many problems at every level of government, Congress mandated FEMA to commission a study from the National Academy of Public Administration. The final report of that group, *Coping with Catastrophe: Building an Emergency Management System to Meet People's*

Needs in Natural and Manmade Disasters (February 1993), was an important base-line assessment of FEMA. Additionally, it had both immediate and far-reaching effects on the Congress and on FEMA's organization and mission.

In 1993, flooding in the midwestern U.S. resulted in six states receiving federal disaster declarations and caused more than $15 billion dollars damage. President Clinton appointed James Lee Witt Director of FEMA in 1993, marking the first time an experienced state emergency manager held the post. Witt (1995) aggressively changed the emphasis in federal emergency management to focus on mitigation and began a reorganization effort. Prior to this time, the federal emphasis had been largely on recovery issues and "after the disaster" concerns; Witt began the first real change in federal strategy since emergency management efforts had begun. As the 21st century began, the overall emphasis of FEMA remained mitigation, and both comprehensive emergency management and integrated emergency management systems remained concepts in force.

The most recent epoch in American emergency management began on September 11, 2001. The attack on the World Trade Centers shocked Americans and challenged government capabilities to respond to disasters. The attack initiated a comprehensive rethinking of "security," "emergencies," and the appropriate role of the federal government. During October, 2001 President Bush used Executive Orders to create the Office of Homeland Security (appointing Governor Tom Ridge, Director) and the Office of Combating Terrorism (General Wayne Downing, Director). On October 29th, President Bush issued Homeland Security Presidential Directive Number 1, which established the Homeland Security Council, Chaired by the President. In June of 2002, President Bush submitted his proposal to Congress to establish a cabinet-level Department of Homeland Security, which was passed later that year.

As of this writing the Department of Homeland Security continues to work to accommodate the 22 agencies and nearly 180,000 employees that it inherited upon its formation. It continues to adjust its mission, scope, strategies, and organizational arrangements. In fact, such adjustments are expected to go on for years and probably decades. Among the most important changes in 2005 relevant to the practice of emergency management are (a) the adjustment of the department to its second Secretary, Mr. Michael Chertoff; (b) the implementation of the new National Response Plan and the related National Incident Management Systems; and (c) the creation of new national strategy statements regarding vulnerability and other aspects of homeland security.

VISIONS OF EMERGENCY MANAGEMENT

This brief examination of emergency management in the United States has included a discussion of the kinds of organizations that operate within the system, the different patterns of responsibility and interaction among the components of the system, and the general time phases of emergency management. The development of a perspective on emergency management requires consideration of at least two additional topics: The first of which deals with the evolution of prevailing federal conceptions of how hazards are managed—especially the underlying assumptions that define what goals are important and that determine the creation and structure of emergency organizations; the second topic concerns the way in which hazards are conceptualized—whether one focuses upon the event itself, or upon the demands that events place upon social systems.

In the late 1970s, driven by economic need and also the need for a more stream-lined intergovernmental process, the National Governors Association (NGA) became a strong advocate for an "all hazards" approach to emergency manage-ment. Based on some seminal research and four major research reports from its disaster research project team, the NGA called for a new system, which they termed "comprehensive emergency management." Their work drew intellectual strength from the comparative research at the Disaster Research Center (formerly housed at Ohio State University, and now located at the University of Delaware).

These forces gave rise to Comprehensive Emergency Management (CEM) as a basic conceptual approach to disasters and to managing emergencies. In 1979, the NGA issued a *Governor's Guide to Comprehensive Emergency Management* (Whit-taker 1979) that provided an articulate statement of the philosophy and practice of CEM. The approach was further legitimized through its adoption and promo-tion by FEMA in 1981. In 1993, when the U.S. Congress repealed the Federal Civil Defense Act of 1950, a provision (Title VI) was added to the Stafford Act to require the federal government to utilize the all hazards approach inherent in comprehensive emergency preparedness. Comprehensive emergency manage-ment refers to the development of a capacity for handling emergency tasks in all phases—mitigation, preparedness, response, and recovery—in connection with all types of disaster agents by coordinating the efforts and resources of a variety of organizations or agencies. Comprehensive emergency management is distin-guished from previous conceptualizations—particularly dual use—by two impor-tant characteristics: First, CEM emphasizes comprehensiveness with respect to the performance of *all disaster relevant activities* by dictating a concern with mitiga-tion, preparedness, response, and recovery; the second distinguishing feature of CEM is its concern with the management of *all types of emergencies* whether tech-nological, natural, or attack related. This characteristic is an outgrowth of the idea that an emergency may be seen as a disruption of the normal operation of a social system. To the extent possible, one would like to minimize the likelihood and magnitude of system disruptions in the first place, and minimize their duration by creating the potential for quickly stabilizing the system and subsequently restoring it to its normal activities following an unpreventable disruption. In this context, the "cause" of the disruption is less important than the nature and mag-nitude of its effects upon the social system. The only reason to distinguish among disrupting agents rests on the extent to which different agents impose distinctive demands on the system. For example, floods can be distinguished as events that afford long periods of forewarning when compared with explosions.

In developing a framework for managing all phases of all types of disasters, CEM may be seen as an attempt to integrate emergency management techniques and problems by developing a body of management techniques effective for cop-ing with multiple disaster agents. CEM represents an extremely significant departure from historical views of emergency management that partition agents and claim that a unique strategy must be developed for managing each of them.

Furthermore, aside from the intuitive appeal of a more parsimonious theoretical approach, cost-conscious officials at all levels of government are attracted to the more efficient use of resources promised by a comprehensive approach to emergency management (Quarantelli 1992).

Over the years, most state and local governments have adopted some variant on comprehensive emergency management. FEMA introduced the concept of Integrated Emergency Management Systems (IEMS) in 1983. The goal of IEMS was to facilitate the development of disaster management functions and (at the time it was introduced) to increase congressional support for a larger civil defense budget (Perry 1985: 130). The attempt to enhance the civil defense budget failed, but IEMS persisted. When pressed to distinguish IEMS from CEM, the principal reply was: "CEM is the long-term objective; IEMS is the current implementation strategy" (Drabek 1985: 85). It appears that the meaning of IEMS on a practical level derives from the term integrated: identifying the goal of addressing all hazards and consolidating emergency actions into a single office or organization within a jurisdiction. It remains, however, that comprehensive emergency management is the primary vision of disaster management in the United States.

Since 9/11 and also since the formation of the Department of Homeland Security, emergency management now operates in the context of homeland security. There are many dimensions to these changes, and documenting them will take many years. Given the volume and pace of the changes in the fields of emergency management and homeland security, there are not yet many textbooks on the subject. In the short term, many special reports—such as those of the 9/11 Commission and those of the Council on Foreign Relations—help to describe and interpret recent and current events, as well as programs and outcomes. Additionally, existing as well as new professional journals publish articles by scholars and practitioners, who want to share their research and insights on the changes. Two such examples are the *Journal of Homeland Security and Emergency Management* (http://www.bepress.com/jhsem/) and the *Journal of Emergency Management* (http://www.pnpco.com/pn06001.html).

TYPES OF HAZARDS/THREATS/DISASTERS — UNDERSTANDING RISKS[1]

An emergency management vision that addresses "all hazards" must by necessity focus upon the concept of generic functions, while acknowledging that special functions will be needed in the case of disaster agents that present unique or singular challenges. Comprehensive emergency management (CEM) implies a basic comparability across types of disasters. Moving from emergency management to the academic study of disasters, one implication of comparability is that one should be able to group disaster agents in terms of common characteristics. A typology (of disasters) is a system for classifying disaster agents into categories within which social management demands are similar. On a practical level, implementing CEM involves identifying generic emergency response functions, and then specifying circumstances (tied to the impact of different disaster agents) under which they will need to be employed. If one could use such functions as key characteristics of disasters, then one could begin to develop meaningful taxonomies.

Classifying or Grouping Disasters

To date there have been only a few attempts to make systematic comparisons (typologies) of human response to different disaster agents. Indeed, there has been a tendency among academics to avoid examining relationships among different disaster agents, partly on the assumption that each "type" of event was simply unique. For example, the matter of comparing natural with technological threats rarely appeared in the professional literature at all until the 1970s. In part this condition reflects the state of disaster research. For many years disaster studies were journalistic and descriptive in nature (Gillespie and Perry 1976). Hence, attention has often focused upon the event itself—the hurricane or the earthquake—and upon descriptions of specific consequences for disaster victims. Therefore the literature provided illustrative accounts of earthquake victims crushed under rubble, fire victims plucked from rooftops, and hurricane victims drowned in the storm surge. In this context, researchers argued that different agents have different characteristics and impose different demands on the social system and as a result probably must be explained using different theories. A typology is actually a form of theory created through taxonomy or reasoning (Perry 1989). Thus, human reactions to different disaster events were expected to be different.

In one sense, it is entirely correct to consider each disaster agent, as well as each impact of each agent, to be different. Floods present obvious differences from hurricanes, and the March 27, 1980 eruption of Mt. St. Helens Volcano in Washington was very different from its eruption on May 18, 1980. Such comments reflect an essentially phenotypic classification system, focusing upon the surface or visible properties of each event. Emergency managers and disaster researchers are not so much interested in classifying disasters in these terms, however, because their goals are associated primarily with *human and organizational behavior*. It is human action relative to the natural environment, our own technology, or relative to other humans that produce the disasters of flooding, tornadoes, nuclear power plants, or war. Thus, the goal is to distinguish among social causes, reactions, and consequences, not necessarily to distinguish hurricanes from nuclear power plants. There has been an increased concern with the development of conceptual schemes for explaining human behavior in disasters. This theoretical concern directs one to answer the question of "what features of disaster events seem to control the nature and types of disaster-generated and response-generated demands imposed upon stricken communities?" In answer to this question, one can create a classification system that characterizes disasters, not in phenotypic terms, but in terms of features that will have an impact on the kinds of assessment, corrective, protective, or management actions that might be used in disaster management. To pursue such a goal, one might begin by choosing a given function—population warning for example—and examine the ways in which performance of that activity varies across disaster events as a function of differing *agent characteristics* such as the amount of forewarning provided by prediction and detection systems.

There has been much discussion and only limited consensus among academic disaster researchers regarding either definitions of the concept of disaster or classification schemes for disasters. However, as Perry (1998) has pointed out, most definitions of disaster contain many common elements—disagreements among definers tend to lie in minor aspects of definition or in the logic that is used to develop a definition. From the standpoint of practicing emergency management, such minor variations do not often pose operational difficulties. Most events that are characterized as disasters, whether they arise from natural forces, technology, or even wartime attacks, fit most of the academic definitions of the term. As defined by Fritz (1961: 652), a disaster is any event:

> concentrated in time and space, in which a society or a relatively self-sufficient subdivision of society, undergoes severe danger and incurs such losses to its members and physical appurtenances that the social structure is disrupted and the fulfillment of all or some of the essential functions of the society is prevented.

From this classic definition (as well as from the definitions discussed in the previous chapter) one can surmise that disasters occur at a distinguishable time, they are geographically circumscribed, and that they disrupt social activity. Barton has proposed a similar definition, but chose to focus upon the social system itself, arguing that disasters exist "when many members of a social system fail to receive expected conditions of life from the system." (1969: 38) Both Fritz and Barton agree that any event that produces a significant change in the pattern of inputs and outputs for a given social system may be reasonably characterized as a disaster. The important point to be derived from these definitions is that events precipitated by a variety of agents—floods, chemical spills, volcanoes, nuclear power plant accidents, terrorist attacks—all fit equally well into these definitions as disasters. At this level of abstraction, there is no compelling reason to differentiate between natural, technological, or other agents. Given the breadth of most definitions of disasters, the *analytical problem* becomes one of determining the characteristics by which to distinguish among the events that do satisfy the definition. As noted earlier, such dimensions should not be restricted to physical characteristics of the hazard agent and its impact, but should also include attributes relevant to the effects of the event upon the social system and its consequences for management.

There has been some discussion among researchers regarding the lines along which natural and technological and wartime disasters might be meaningfully distinguished. While there remains much disagreement in the research community about *which* dimensions are meaningful, it is possible to begin to identify dimensions from the research literature. Much of this work can be traced to the staff of the Disaster Research Center who have attempted to draw parallels between natural disaster response and possible response to nuclear attack (particularly between 1963 and 1972; see Kreps 1981). Barton (1969) developed a scheme for identifying distinguishing features of disasters that characterize the nature of social system stress. In his system Barton, identified four basic dimensions: scope of impact, speed of onset, duration of impact, and social preparedness of the threatened community. These dimensions have been used by a number of researchers in developing classification schemes (Lindell and Perry

1992), and can be briefly explained here. *Scope of impact* is a geographic reference categorizing impact as involving a small area or number of people (more narrow impact) or as encompassing a larger area or population (more widespread impact). Aside from sheer size, this dimension has implications for resource mobilization within the affected social system, and for the availability of supporting resources which might be drawn from nearby or more distant social systems. *Speed of onset* refers to the suddenness of impact or to the time between first detection of a threat and its impact on a social system. Speed of onset varies both by the inherent nature of the threat and by the level of technological sophistication of the social system. For example, the technology to forecast meteorological hazards such as hurricanes has developed considerably over the course of the past 50 years. Consequently events that could at one time occur with little or no forewarning are now routinely monitored and forecast days in advance. Speed of onset is usually conceived as a continuum ranging from sudden through gradual onset. *Duration of the impact* refers to the time that elapses between initial onset and the point at which the threat to life and property has been stabilized. This can be a few minutes (short) in the case of a tornado, a few hours or days (moderate) in the case of riverine floods, or intermittent for years (long) in the case of volcanoes. Finally, *social preparedness* is a dimension that attempts to capture the ability of the social system both to anticipate the onset of an event, to control its impact, or to cope with its negative consequences.

Anderson (1969) contributed another comparative dimension from his research on the functioning of civil defense offices (now more commonly called emergency management departments) during natural disasters and attempted to extrapolate to the nuclear attack environment. In developing his analysis, Anderson (1969: 55) concluded that in spite of obvious differences between nuclear threats and natural disasters:

> [these differences] can be visualized as primarily ones of degree. With the exception of the specific form of secondary threat, i.e. radiation, and the probability that a wider geographic area will be involved, a nuclear [threat] would not create essentially different problems for community response.

Anderson's analysis introduced the issue of secondary impacts of disaster agents as an important defining feature. It should be remembered that virtually all hazards, whether natural, or technological, accidentally or deliberately caused, entail some secondary impacts. Indeed, the secondary threat can be more devastating than the initial threat. Riverine floods tend to deposit debris and silt that persists long after the water has receded. Earthquakes often produce urban fires, and volcanic eruptions can melt glaciers or ignite forest fires.

By assembling lists of distinguishing characteristics such as those discussed above, one can compare or classify an apparently widely differing (in terms of surface features) range of disaster events. As an example of how such comparisons might work, Table 9.1 compares three disaster agents—riverine floods, volcanic eruptions, and nuclear power plant accidents—in terms of the five distinguishing characteristics. It is interesting to note that, at this analytic level, volcanic eruptions and nuclear power plant accidents are similarly classified. Both threats involve variable scopes of impact that are potentially widespread. Usually the threats of a volcanic eruption to human safety are limited to within a

Table 9.1. Classification of Selected Disaster Agents

Defining Characteristics	Riverine flood	Volcanic eruption	Nuclear power plant accident
Scope of impact	Highly variable long, and narrow	Highly variable broad area	Highly variable broad area
Speed of onset	Rapid: flash flood Slow: main stem	Rapid	Variable
Duration of impact	Short	Long	Long
Health threat	Water inhalation	Blast, burns, ash inhalation	Ingestion, inhalation, direct radiation
Property threat	Destruction	Destruction	Contamination
Secondary threats	Public health danger from water/sewer inundation	Forest fires, glacial snowmelt	Secondary contamination
Predictability	High	Poor	Variable ability to predict releases after accident onset

Source: FEMA-EMI course textbook, *Introduction to Emergency Management* (working draft), 2004, Wayne Blanchard, Chapter 1, "Introduction to Emergency Management."

few miles of the crater. Life threatening levels of radiation exposure from a nuclear power plant accident is likely to be confined to the plant site or a few miles downwind from it (U.S. Nuclear Regulatory Commission 1978). Under special conditions, however, either type of event may involve a considerably greater scope of impact.

The May 18, 1980 eruption of Mt. St. Helens volcano spread a heavy layer of volcanic ash over a three-state area and a "worst case" reactor accident like the Chernobyl incident (involving a core melt) can spread radioactive material over an entire region. The speed of onset for volcanic eruptions and nuclear power plant accidents is likely to be rapid, although each of them has the potential for a significant degree of forewarning prior to the onset of a major event. These two events are also similar with respect to the duration of impact of the primary threat to human safety. In both cases, a volcanic eruption and a release of radioactive materials, the event could last from hours to days. Persistence of secondary impacts could, in each case, last for years, although the long-term health effects of volcanic ash are less significant than radiation. To the extent that volcanic eruptions are clustered over time in an eruptive sequence that may last for years, the duration of impact can be said to be long. A nuclear power plant accident would be expected to be of moderate length; although since few actual accidents have occurred, the empirical data are extremely limited. The accident at the Three Mile Island nuclear power plant, which is more accurately labeled as an emergency than a disaster, involved a danger period of about six days.

Both volcanic eruptions and power plant accidents generate secondary threats. The sheer number of secondary threats associated with volcanoes is quite large; ultimately they involve long-term threats to public health, to the stability of man-made structures, and to plants and animals in land and water ecosystems. The most probable secondary threat of a nuclear power plant accident is associated with the effects of residual radiation exposure arising from ground deposition and water contamination by radioactive materials. In addition to the potential exposure by way of external gamma radiation and inhalation of radioactive materials, there is the threat of exposure by means of ingestion of contaminated vegetation or animal products (meat or milk).

Finally, the state of technology is such that neither volcanic eruptions nor nuclear accidents may be forecast accurately much in advance. There is in both cases, however, a technology for detecting and monitoring events once they are in progress. In the case of some volcanoes, once an eruptive sequence has begun either seismic or geochemical clues may be used to make approximate forecasts of eruptive events. With nuclear power plants, monitoring instruments are designed to detect even minor aberrations early in order to facilitate the implementation of corrective action before more serious difficulties arise. Thus, while one might not be able to predict a power plant accident, instruments are designed to detect problems in their early stages before they can escalate to an atmospheric release of radioactive material.

Riverine floods differ from the other two hazard agents primarily in terms of two defining characteristics: floods are frequently predictable, often hours or days in advance, and speed of onset typically is gradual (by definition requiring a minimum of six hours to reach a flood crest, although more rapid onset can occur during flash floods in mountainous areas). Another general point of distinction is the frequency with which floods occur; they are the most common geophysical hazard in the United States (Perry, Lindell & Greene 1981). Thus, from the standpoint of both emergency managers and the public, riverine floods are a familiar threat. The duration of the primary flood impact is much shorter than a volcanic eruptive sequence and generally more comparable to that of a nuclear power plant accident. Secondary impacts of floods include both public health threats and dangers to man-made structures, but in general the extent and duration of the effects of their secondary threats are less than either of the other two disaster agents. Finally, like a volcanic eruptive sequence or a nuclear power plant accident, the scope of impact of riverine floods is highly variable. Usually the scope of flood impacts is narrower than either of the other hazards, but there is a potential for widespread scope.

The preceding discussion demonstrates that it is possible to classify diverse disaster agents in terms of an underlying set of dimensions and then to discuss the agents in terms of functional emergency management activities. Such dimensions may include the physical characteristics of the hazard agent and its impact, as well as attributes relevant to the effects of the event upon the social system and its consequences for management. The characteristics derived from the disaster research literature have provided a systematic set of attributes that could be used to examine and compare riverine floods, volcanic eruptions and nuclear power plant accidents. As indicated above, the differences among classification schemes in the academic literature tend to rest on differences among researchers regarding exactly which dimensions and how many dimensions are optimal in creating the typology. The 21st century has seen no more agreement than the 20th century did, although there are two discernable trends in the literature. One trend, followed by only a few, involves attempts to elaborate on the analytic approach described here, adding or subtracting dimensions or otherwise changing the complexity of the approach (Kreps 1989; Tobin and Montz 1997). By far most disaster researchers have continued to ignore the issue of analytic typology and remained with some sort of phenotypic classification, most commonly with the classic categories of "natural disasters," "technological disasters," and "wartime attacks" (cf. Cutter 2001; Drabek 1986).

Without regard to the low level of consensus among researchers, analytic classification systems are more than an abstract intellectual exercise. They provide an opportunity to demonstrate how, by means of careful examination, one may begin to identify differences among disaster agents with respect to their demands upon the emergency response system. From the information listed in Table 1, an emergency manager may observe that two protective measures might be used in all three events: population evacuation and the imposition of access controls to the threatened area. Because a volcanic eruption or a nuclear power plant accident could present a health threat resulting from inhalation of airborne materials (volcanic ash or radioactive gases and particulates, respectively), taking shelter indoors and using respiratory protection is feasible. Ad hoc measures for respiratory protection could be as simple as folding a wet towel and breathing through it.

The importance of developing a comparative perspective structured by disaster agent characteristics lies in the prospect for identifying a profile of disaster demands that, in turn, define the functions that the emergency response organization must perform. By adopting this type of approach, one is better able to identify emergency management strategies that may be appropriately used across a range of disaster events. Hence, one is able to better identify "generic functions" that comprehensive emergency management demands to achieve its "all hazards" orientation. However, this approach does not ignore distinctive aspects of disaster events. While the focus is upon defining characteristics, individual events are described along these dimensions in considerable detail; enough detail should be provided to capture any special features. These special features may then be taken into account by the emergency manager in the process of specifying exactly how a given generic function must be addressed in managing the event. The role of distinctive aspects of hazards is not to define the event as "unique," but rather to highlight those ways in which generic emergency management techniques must be adapted to the needs of a particular type of emergency. For example, evacuation was listed as one protective measure in nuclear power plant accidents and it was noted that the primary health threat to citizens in such events was radiation exposure. Research indicates that radiation hazard is feared as much or more than other natural and technological hazards

(Lindell and Earle 1983). Assuming the conditions were appropriate for an evacuation warning, the emergency manager would be well advised of the possibility for an evacuation shadow (more people are inclined to evacuate than are advised to do so). In turn, this alerts the manager to a need for timely dissemination of information to the public about the characteristics of the impact and the potential personal consequences of exposure, thereby reassuring those who are not at risk that they are indeed safe.

A Model of Disaster Impacts

A disaster occurs when an extreme event exceeds a community's capability to cope with that event. Understanding the process by which natural disasters produce community impacts is important for four reasons.

- First, information for this process is needed to identify the pre-impact conditions that make communities vulnerable to disaster impacts.

- Second, information about the disaster impact process can be used to identify specific segments of each community that will be affected disproportionately (e.g., low-income households, ethnic minorities, or specific types of businesses).

- Third, information about the disaster impact process can be used to identify the event-specific conditions that determine the level of disaster impact.

- Fourth, an understanding of disaster impact process allows planners to identify suitable emergency management interventions.

The process by which disasters produce community impacts can be explained in terms of models proposed by Cutter (1996), Lindell and Prater (2003), and Prater, Peacock, Lindell, Zhang and Lu (2004). Specifically, Figure 9.1 indicates the effects of a disaster are determined by three pre-impact conditions—*hazard exposure, physical vulnerability,* and *social vulnerability*. There also are three event-specific conditions, *hazard event characteristics, improvised disaster responses,* and *ad hoc disaster recovery*. Two of the event-specific conditions, *hazard event characteristics* and *improvised disaster responses,* combine with the pre-impact conditions to produce a disaster's *physical impacts*. The *physical impacts,* in turn, combine with *ad hoc disaster recovery* to produce the disaster's *social impacts*. Communities can engage in three types of emergency management interventions to ameliorate disaster impacts. Physical impacts can be reduced by *hazard mitigation practices* and *emergency preparedness practices,* whereas social impacts can be reduced by *recovery preparedness practices*.

The following sections describe the components of the model in greater detail. Specifically, the next section will describe the three pre-impact conditions *hazard exposure, physical vulnerability,* and *social vulnerability*. This section will be followed by sections discussing *hazard event characteristics* and *improvised disaster responses*. The fifth section will discuss disasters' *physical impacts, social impacts* and *ad hoc disaster recovery*. The last section of the chapter will discuss three types of strategic interventions, *hazard mitigation practices, emergency preparedness practices,* and *recovery preparedness practices*.

Figure 9.1. Conceptual Model of Disaster Impacts

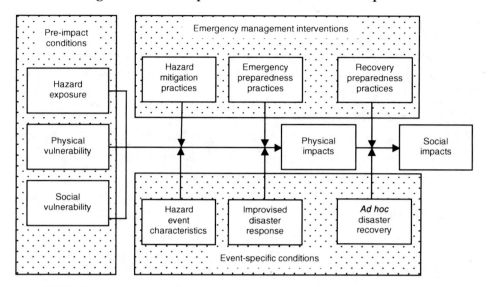

Source: FEMA-EMI course textbook, *Introduction to Emergency Management* (working draft), Chapter 6, "Hazard and Vulnerability Analysis," Wayne Blanchard, 2004.

Pre-Impact Conditions

Hazard Exposure

Hazard exposure arises from people's occupancy of geographical areas where they could be affected by specific types of events that threaten their lives or property. For natural hazards, this exposure is caused by living in geographical areas as specific as low-lying margins of the Atlantic and Gulf coasts where hurricanes make landfall or as broad as the Great Plains of the Midwest where tornadoes frequently strike. For technological hazards, exposure can arise if people move into areas where they could be exposed to explosions or hazardous materials releases. In principle, hazard exposure can be measured by the probability of occurrence of a given event magnitude, but these exceeding probabilities can be difficult to obtain for hazards about which the historical data are insufficient to reliably estimate the probability of very unusual events. For example, many areas of the U.S. have meteorological and hydrological data that are limited to the past 100 years, so the estimation of extreme floods requires extrapolation from a limited data series. Moreover, urbanization of the watersheds causes the boundaries of the 100-year floodplains to change in ways that may be difficult for local emergency managers to anticipate. Even more difficult to estimate are the probabilities of events, such as chemical and nuclear reactor accidents, for which data are limited because each facility is essentially unique. In such cases, techniques of probabilistic safety analysis are used to model these systems, attach probabilities to the failure of system components, and synthesize probabilities of overall system failure by mathematically combining the probabilities of individual component failure.

The greatest difficulties are encountered in attempting to estimate the probabilities of social hazards such as terrorist attacks because the occurrence of these events is defined by social system dynamics that cannot presently be modeled in the same way as physical systems—that is, the elements of social systems are difficult to define and measure. Moreover, the interactions of the system elements have multiple determinants and involve complex lag and feedback effects that are not well understood, let alone precisely measured. Indeed, there are significant social and political constraints that limit the collection of data on individuals and groups—further inhibiting the ability of scientists to make specific predictions of social system behavior.

Physical Vulnerability

Human vulnerability. Humans are vulnerable to environmental extremes of temperature, pressure, and chemical exposures. As noted in the previous chapter, extreme environmental conditions can cause death, injury, and illness. For any hazard agent—water, wind, ionizing radiation, toxic chemicals, infectious agents—there often is variability among in the physiological response of the affected population—that is, given the same level of exposure, some people will die, others will be severely injured, still others slightly injured, and the rest will survive unscathed. Typically, the most susceptible to any environmental stressor will be the very young, the very old, and those with weakened immune systems.

Agricultural vulnerability. Like humans, agricultural plants and animals are also vulnerable to environmental extremes of temperature, pressure, chemicals, radiation, and infectious agents. Like humans, there are differences among individuals within each plant and animal population. However, agricultural vulnerability is more complex than human vulnerability because there is a greater number of species to be assessed—each of which has its own characteristic response to each environmental stressor.

Structural vulnerability. Structural vulnerability arises when buildings are constructed using designs and materials that are incapable of resisting extreme stresses (e.g., high wind, hydrodynamic pressures of water, seismic shaking) or that allow hazardous materials to infiltrate into the building. The construction of most buildings is governed by building codes intended to protect the life/safety of building occupants from structural collapse—primarily from the dead load of the building material themselves and the live load of the occupants and furnishings—but do not necessarily provide protection from extreme wind, seismic, or hydrostatic loads. Nor do they provide an impermeable barrier to the infiltration of toxic air pollutants.

Social Vulnerability

The social vulnerability perspective (e.g., Cannon, Twigg, and Rowell 2003; Cutter, Boruff and Shirley 2003) represents an important extension of previous theories of hazard vulnerability (Burton, Kates and White 1978). As a concept, social vulnerability has been defined as "characteristics of a person or group in terms of their capacity to anticipate, cope with, resist, and recover from the impacts of a natural hazard" (Blakie, Canon, Davis and Wisner 1994). Whereas people's physical vulnerability refers to their susceptibility to biological changes (i.e., impacts on anatomical structures and physiological functioning), their social vulnerability refers their susceptibility to behavioral changes. As will be discussed in greater detail below, these consist of psychological, demographic, economic, and political impacts.

The central point of the social vulnerability perspective is that, just as people's occupancy of hazard prone areas and the physical vulnerability of the structures in which they live and work are not randomly distributed, neither is social vulnerability randomly distributed—either geographically or demographically. Thus, just as structural vulnerability can increase or decrease the effect of hazard exposure on physical impacts (property damage and casualties), so too can social vulnerability. Social vulnerability varies across communities and, especially, across households within communities.

Event-Specific Conditions

Hazard Agent Characteristics

Hazard impacts often are difficult to characterize because a given hazard agent may initiate a number of different threats. For example, tropical cyclones (also known as hurricanes or typhoons) can cause casualties and damage through wind, rain, storm surge, and inland flooding (Bryant 1991). Volcanoes can impact human settlements through ash fall, explosive eruptions, lava flows, mudflows and floods, and forest fires (Perry and Lindell 1990; Saarinen and Sell 1985; Warrick, Anderson, Downing, Lyons, Ressler, Warrick, and Warrick 1981). However, once these distinct threats have been distinguished from each other, each can be characterized in terms of six significant characteristics. These are the *speed of onset, availability of perceptual cues* (such as wind, rain, or ground movement), the *intensity, scope*, and *duration of impact*, and the *probability of occurrence*. The speed of onset and availability of perceptual cues affect the amount of forewarning that affected populations will have to complete emergency response actions (Lindell 1994). In turn, these attributes determine the extent of casualties among the population and the degree of damage to structures in the affected area.

The impact intensity of a natural hazard generally can be defined in terms of the physical materials involved and the energy these materials impart. The physical materials involved in disasters differ in terms of their physical state—gas (or vapor), liquid, or solid (or particulate). In most cases, the hazard from a gas arises from its temperature or pressure. Examples include hurricane or tornado wind (recall that the atmosphere is a mixture of gases), which is hazardous because of overpressures that can inflict traumatic injuries directly on people. High wind also is hazardous because they can destroy structures and accelerate debris that can itself cause traumatic injuries. Alternatively, the hazard from a gas might arise from its toxicity, as is the case in some volcanic eruptions. Liquids also can be hazardous because of their toxicity but the most common liquid hazard is water, which is hazardous to structures because of the pressure it can exert and it is hazardous to living things when it fills the lungs and prevents respiration. Lava is solid rock that has been liquefied by extreme heat and therefore is hazardous to people and structures because of its thermal energy. Solids also can be hazardous if they take the form of particulates such as airborne volcanic ash or flood-borne mud. These are particularly significant because they can leave deposits that have impacts of long duration.

The scope of impact defines the number of affected social units (e.g., individuals, households, and businesses). The probability of occurrence (per unit of time) is another important characteristic of natural hazards, but this affects disaster impacts indirectly because more probable hazards are likely to mobilize communities to engage in hazard mitigation and emergency preparedness measures to reduce their vulnerability (Prater and Lindell 2000).

Improvised Disaster Response

Disaster myths commonly portray disaster victims as dazed, panicked, or disorganized, but people actually respond in a generally adaptive manner when disasters strike. Adaptive response is often delayed because *normalcy bias* delays people's realization that an improbable event is, in fact, occurring to them. Further delays occur because people have limited information about the situation and, therefore, seek confirmation of any initial indications of an emergency before initiating protective action. In addition, the vast majority of people respond in terms of their customary social units—especially their households and neighborhoods—which usually consumes time in developing social organizations that can cope with the disaster's demands. Contrary to the stereotype of selfish protection of one's self and one's property, disaster victims often devote considerable effort to protecting others' persons and property. Accordingly, there is considerable convergence on the disaster impact area, as those in areas nearby move in to offer assistance. When existing organizations seem incapable of meeting the needs of the emergency response, they expand to take on new members, extend to take on new tasks, or new organizations emerge (Dynes 1974).

Ad Hoc Disaster Recovery

Once the situation has stabilized to the point that the imminent threat to life and property has abated, disaster-stricken communities must begin the long process of disaster recovery. Immediate tasks in this process are damage assessment, debris clearance, reconstruction of infrastructure (electric power, fuel, water, wastewater, telecommunications, and transportation networks), and reconstruction of buildings in the residential, commercial, and industrial sectors. Ad hoc disaster assistance is derived primarily from resources that are provided by individuals and organizations within the community. The victims themselves might have financial (e.g., savings and insurance) as well as tangible assets (e.g., property) that are undamaged by hazard impact. As one might expect, low-income victims tend to have lower levels of savings, but they also are more likely to be victims of insurance redlining and, thus, have been forced into contracts with insurance companies that go bankrupt after the disaster. Thus, even those who plan ahead for disaster recovery can find themselves without the financial resources they need (Peacock and Girard 1997). Alternatively, the victims can promote their recovery by bringing in additional funds through overtime employment or by freeing up the needed funds by reducing their consumption below pre-impact levels. Friends, relatives, neighbors, and coworkers can assist recovery through financial and in-kind contributions, as can community-based organizations (CBOs) and local government. In addition, the latter also can provide assistance by means of tax deductions or deferrals.

Disaster Impacts
Physical Impacts

The physical impacts of disasters include casualties (deaths and injuries) and property damage, and both vary substantially across hazard agents. According to Noji (1997), hurricanes produced 16 of the 65 greatest disasters of the 20th Century (in terms of deaths) and the greatest number of deaths from 1947-1980 (499,000). Earthquakes produced 28 of the greatest disasters and 450,000 deaths, whereas floods produced four of the greatest disasters and 194,000 deaths. Other significant natural hazards include volcanic eruptions with nine of the greatest disasters and 9,000 deaths, landslides with four of the greatest disasters and 5,000 deaths, and tsunamis with three of the greatest disasters and 5,000 deaths. There is significant variation by country, with developing countries in Asia, Africa, and South America accounting for the top 20 positions in terms of number of deaths from 1966-1990. Low-income countries suffer approximately 3,000 deaths per disaster whereas the corresponding figure for high-income countries is approximately 500 deaths per disaster. Moreover, these disparities appear to be increasing because the average annual death toll in developed countries declined by at least 75% between 1960 and 1990, but the same time period saw increases of over 400% in developing countries (Berke 1995).

There often are difficulties in determining how many of the deaths and injuries are "due to" a disaster. In some cases it is impossible to determine how many persons are missing and, if so, whether this is due to death or unrecorded relocation. The size of the error in estimates of disaster death tolls can be seen in the fact that for many of the most catastrophic events the number of deaths is rounded to the nearest thousand and some even are rounded to the nearest ten thousand (Noji 1997). Estimates of injuries are similarly problematic (see Langness 1994; Peek-Asa, Kraus, Bourque, Vimalachandra, Yu and Abrams 1998; Shoaf, Sareen, Nguyen and Bourque 1998, regarding conflicting estimates of deaths and injuries attributable to the Northridge earthquake). Even when bodies can be counted, there are problems because disaster impact may be only a contributing factor to casualties with pre-existing health conditions. Moreover, some casualties are indirect consequences of the hazard agent as, for example, with casualties caused by structural fires following earthquakes (e.g., burns) and destruction of infrastructure (e.g., illnesses from contaminated water supplies).

Losses of structures, animals, and crops also are important measures of physical impacts, and these are rising exponentially in the United States (Mileti 1999), but the rate of increase is even greater in developing countries such as India and Kenya (Berke 1995). Such losses usually result from physical damage or destruction, but they also can be caused by other losses of use such as chemical or radiological contamination, or loss of the land itself to subsidence or erosion. Damage to the built environment can be classified broadly as affecting residential, commercial, industrial, infrastructure, or community services sectors. Moreover, damage within each of these sectors can be divided into damage to structures and damage to contents. It usually is the case that damage to contents results from collapsing structures (e.g., hurricane winds failing the building envelope and allowing rain to destroy the contents). Because collapsing buildings are a major cause of casualties as well, this suggests that strengthening the structure will protect the contents and occupants. However, some hazard agents can damage building contents without affecting the structure itself (e.g., earthquakes striking seismically-resistant buildings whose contents are not securely fastened). Thus, risk area residents may need to adopt additional hazard adjustments to protect contents and occupants even if they already have structural protection.

Other important physical impacts include damage or contamination to cropland, rangeland, and woodlands. Such impacts may be well understood for some hazard agents but not others. For example, ash fall from the 1980 Mt. St. Helens eruption was initially expected to devastate crops and livestock in downwind areas but no significant losses materialized (Warrick, et al. 1981). There also is concern about damage or contamination to the natural environment (wild lands) because these areas serve valuable functions such as damping the extremes of river discharge and providing habitat for wildlife. In part, concern arises from the potential for indirect consequences such as increased runoff and silting of downstream river beds, but many people also are concerned about the natural environment simply because they value it for its own sake.

Societal Impacts

Social impacts, which include psychological, demographic, economic, and political impacts, can develop over a long period of time and can be difficult to assess when they occur. Despite the difficulty in measuring these social impacts, it is nonetheless important to monitor them, and even to predict them if possible, because they can cause significant problems for the long-term functioning of specific types of households and businesses in an affected community. A better understanding of disasters' social impacts can provide a basis for pre-impact prediction and the development of contingency plans to prevent adverse consequences from occurring.

For many years, research on the social impacts of disasters consisted of an accumulation of case studies, but two research teams conducted comprehensive statistical analyses of extensive databases to assess the long-term effects of disasters on stricken communities (Friesma, Caporaso, Goldstein, Lineberry and McCleary 1979; Wright, Rossi, Wright and Weber-Burdin 1979). The more comprehensive Wright et al. (1979) study used census data from the 1960 (pre-impact) and 1970 (post-impact) censuses to assess the effects of all recorded disasters in the United States. The authors concurred with earlier findings by Friesma, et al. (1979) in concluding that no long-term social impact of disasters could be detected at the community level. In discussing their findings, the authors acknowledged that their results were dominated by the types of disasters that occur most frequently in the United States—tornadoes, floods, and hurricanes. Moreover, most of the disasters they studied had a relatively small scope of impact and thus caused only minimal disruption to their communities even in the short term. Finally, they noted that their findings did not preclude the possibility of significant long-term impacts upon lower levels such as the neighborhood, business, and household.

Nonetheless, their findings called attention to the importance of the *impact ratio*—the amount of damage divided by the amount of community resources—in understanding disaster impacts. They hypothesized that long-term social impacts tend to be minimal because most hazard agents have a relatively small scope of impact and tend to strike undeveloped areas more frequently than intensely developed areas simply because there are more of the former than the latter. Thus, the numerator of the impact ratio tends to be low and local resources are sufficient to prevent long-term effects from occurring. Even when a hazard agent has a large scope of impact and strikes a large developed area (causing a large impact ratio in the short term), state and federal agencies, and non-governmental organizations (e.g., American Red Cross) direct recovery resources to the affected area, thus preventing long-term impacts from occurring. For example, Hurricane Andrew inflicted $26.5 billion in losses to the Miami area, but this was only 0.4% of the U.S. GDP (Charvériat 2000). The recovery problems described studies reported in Peacock, Morrow and Gladwin (1997) were determined more by organizational impediments than by the unavailability of resources.

Psychological impacts. Research reviews conducted over a period of 25 years have concluded that disasters can cause a wide range of negative psychological responses (Bolin 1985; Gerrity and Flynn 1997; Houts, Cleary and Hu 1988; Perry and Lindell 1978). These include psycho-physiological effects such as fatigue, gastrointestinal upset, and tics, as well as cognitive signs such as confusion, impaired concentration, and attention deficits. Psychological impacts include emotional signs such as anxiety, depression and grief, as well as behavioral effects such as sleep and appetite changes, ritualistic behavior, and substance abuse. In most cases, the effects that are observed are mild and transitory—the result of "normal people, responding normally, to a very abnormal situation" (Gerrity and Flynn 1997, p. 108). Few disaster victims require psychiatric diagnosis and most benefit more from a "crisis counseling" orientation than from a "mental health treatment" orientation, especially if their normal social support networks of friends, relatives, neighbors, and coworkers remain largely intact. However, there are population segments that require special attention and active outreach. These include children, frail elderly, people with pre-existing mental illness, racial and ethnic minorities, and families of those who have died in the disaster. Emergency workers also need special attention because they often work long hours without rest, have witnessed horrific sights, and are members of organizations in which discussion of emotional issues may be regarded as a sign of weakness (Rubin 1991).

The negative psychological impacts described above, which Lazarus and Folkman (1984) call "emotion-focused coping" responses, generally disrupt the social functioning of only a very small portion of the victim population. Instead, the majority of disaster victims engage in adaptive "problem-focused coping" activities to save their own lives and those of their closest associates. Further, there is an increased incidence in pro-social behaviors such as donating material aid and a decreased incidence of anti-social behaviors such as crime (Drabek 1986; Mileti, Drabek and Haas 1975; Siegel, Bourque and Shoaf 1999). In some cases, people even engage in altruistic behaviors that risk their own lives to save the lives of others (Tierney, Lindell and Perry 2001).

There also are psychological impacts with long-term adaptive consequences, such as changes in risk perception (beliefs in the likelihood of the occurrence a disaster and its personal consequences for the individual) and increased hazard intrusiveness (frequency of thought, discussion, and information receipt about a hazard). In turn, these beliefs can affect risk area residents' adoption of household hazard adjustments that reduce their vulnerability to future disasters. However, these cognitive impacts of disaster experience do not appear to be large in aggregate—resulting in modest effects on household hazard adjustment (see Lindell and Perry 2000 for a review of the literature on seismic hazard adjustment, and Lindell and Prater 2000 and Lindell and Whitney 2000 for more recent empirical research).

Demographic impacts. Perhaps the most significant demographic impact of a disaster on a stricken community is the destruction of household dwellings. The loss of one's home affects the household in many ways. First, severe damage to the structure often requires many hours of evaluating bids from contractors and supervising their progress. Second, structural damage is often associated with loss of contents, ranging from cooking appliances to clothing that must be replaced. Thus, household members must take the time to shop for replacement items. Third, few households have enough savings or credit to replace items immediately; most spend hours filing paperwork for insurance payoffs and disaster loans. All of these disruptions are compounded when the home is uninhabitable and household members must move to temporary quarters—often in another neighborhood and frequently in another town. In such cases, parents must travel new routes to work, children must attend different schools, and all must find alternative locations for shopping, recreation, and other activities of daily living. Such adjustments are likely to disrupt normal patterns of interaction with relatives, neighbors, friends, and coworkers. Indeed, the increased time devoted to commuting and other recovery tasks can severely reduce the amount of time spent with other members of the immediate family.

Economic impacts. The property damage caused by disaster impact causes direct economic losses that can be thought of as a loss in asset value that can be measured by the cost of repair or replacement (Committee on Assessing the Costs of Natural Disasters, 1989). Disaster losses in United States are initially borne by the affected households, businesses, and local government agencies whose property is damaged or destroyed but some of these losses are redistributed during the disaster recovery process. There have been many attempts to estimate the magnitude of direct losses from individual disasters and the annual average losses from particular types of hazards (e.g., Mileti 1999). Unfortunately, these losses are difficult to determine precisely because there is no organization that tracks all of the relevant data and some data are not recorded at all (Charvériat 2000; Committee on Assessing the Costs of Natural Disasters 1999). For insured property, the insurers record the amount of the deductible and the reimbursed loss, but uninsured losses are not recorded so they must be estimated—often with questionable accuracy.

The ultimate economic impact of a disaster depends upon the disposition of the damaged assets. Some of these assets are not replaced and so their loss causes a reduction in consumption (and, thus, a decrease in the quality of life), or a reduction in investment (and, thus, a decrease in economic productivity). Other assets are replaced—either through in-kind donations (e.g., food and clothing) or commercial purchases. In the latter case, the cost of replacement must come from some source of recovery funding, which generally can be characterized as either inter-temporal transfers (to the present time from past savings or future loan payments) or interpersonal transfers (from one group to another at a given time). Some of the specific mechanisms for financing recovery include obtaining tax deductions or deferrals, unemployment benefits, loans (paying back the principal at low- or no-interest), grants (requiring no return of principal), insurance pay-offs, or additional employment. Other sources include depleting cash financial assets (e.g., savings accounts), selling tangible assets, or migrating to area with available housing, employment, or less risk (in some cases this is done by the principal wage earner only).

In addition to direct economic losses, there are indirect losses that arise from the interdependence of community subunits. Research on the economic impacts of disasters (Alesch, Taylor, Ghanty and Nagy 1993; Dacy and Kunreuther 1969; Dalhamer and D'Sousa 1997; Durkin 1984; Gordon, Richardson, Davis, Steins and Vasishth 1995; Kroll, Landis, Shen and Stryker 1991; Lindell and Perry 1998; Nigg 1995; Tierney 1997) suggests that the relationships among the social units within a community can be described as a state of dynamic equilibrium involving a steady flow of resources, especially money. Specifically, a household's linkages with the community are defined by the money that it must pay for products, services, and infrastructure support. This money is obtained from the wages that employers pay for the household's labor. Similarly, the linkages that a business has with the community are defined by the money it provides to its employees, suppliers, and infrastructure in exchange for inputs such as labor, materials and services, and electric power, fuel, water/wastewater, telecommunications, and transportation. Conversely, it provides products or services to customers in exchange for the money it uses to pay its inputs.

It also is important to recognize the financial impacts of recovery (in addition to the financial impacts of emergency response) on local government. Costs must be incurred for damage assessment, emergency demolition, debris removal, infrastructure restoration, and re-planning stricken areas. In addition to these additional costs, there are decreased revenues due to loss or deferral of sales taxes, business taxes, property taxes, personal income taxes, and user fees.

Political impacts. There is substantial evidence that disaster impacts can cause social activism resulting in political disruption, especially during the seemingly interminable period of disaster recovery. The disaster recovery period is the source of many victim grievances and this creates many opportunities for community conflict, both in the U.S. (Bolin 1982, 1993) and abroad (Bates and Peacock 1988). Victims usually attempt to recreate pre-impact housing patterns, but it can be problematic for their neighbors if victims attempt to site mobile homes on their own lots while awaiting the reconstruction of permanent housing. Conflicts arise because such housing usually is considered to be a blight on the neighborhood, and neighbors are afraid that the "temporary" housing will become permanent. Neighbors also are pitted against each other when developers attempt to buy up damaged or destroyed properties and build multi-family units on lots previously zoned for single family dwellings. Such rezoning attempts are a major threat to the market value of owner-occupied homes but tend to have less impact on renters because they have less incentive to remain in the neighborhood. There are exceptions to this generalization because some ethnic groups have very close ties to their neighborhoods, even if they rent rather than own.

Attempts to change prevailing patterns of civil governance can arise when individuals sharing a grievance about the handling of the recovery process seek to redress that grievance through collective action. Consistent with Dynes's (1974) typology of organizations, existing community groups with an explicit political agenda may *expand* their membership to increase their strength, whereas community groups without an explicit political agenda may *extend* their domains to include disaster-related grievances. Alternatively, new groups can *emerge* to influence local, state, or federal government agencies and legislators to take actions that they support and to terminate actions that they disapprove. Indeed, such was the case for Latinos in Watsonville following the Loma Prieta earthquake (Tierney, et al. 2001). Usually, community action groups pressure government to provide additional resources for recovering from disaster impact, but may oppose candidates' re-elections or even seek to recall some politicians from office (Olson and Drury 1997; Prater and Lindell 2000; Shefner 1999). The point here is not that disasters produce political behavior that is different from that encountered in normal life. Rather, disaster impacts might only produce a different set of victims and grievances and, therefore, a minor variation on the prevailing political agenda (Morrow and Peacock 1997).

EMERGENCY MANAGEMENT INTERVENTIONS

As indicated, there are three types of pre-impact interventions that can effect reductions in disaster impacts. Hazard mitigation and emergency preparedness practices directly reduce a disaster's physical impacts (casualties and damage) and indirectly reduce its social impacts, whereas recovery preparedness practices directly reduce a disaster's social impacts. Improvised disaster response actions also directly affect disasters' physical impacts but, by their very nature, are likely to be much less effective than planned interventions. Similarly, ad hoc recovery assistance directly affects disasters' social impacts but is likely to be less effective than systematic recovery preparedness practices. [above] includes the four "phases" of emergency management—mitigation, preparedness, response, and recovery—originally introduced by the National Governor's Association (1978), but makes it clear there is a complex relationship among them. In reality, these "phases" might better be called "functions," since they are neither discrete nor temporally sequential.

Hazard Mitigation Practices

One way to reduce the physical impacts of disasters is to adopt hazard mitigation practices, which can be defined as pre-impact actions that protect passively against casualties and damage at the time of hazard impact (as opposed to an active emergency response). Hazard mitigation includes community protection works, land-use practices, and building construction practices (Lindell and Perry 2000). Community protection works, which limit the impact of a hazard agent on the entire community, include dams and levees that protect against floodwater and sea walls that protect against storm surge. Land use practices reduce hazard vulnerability by avoiding construction in areas that are susceptible to hazard impact. The use of the term land-use *practices* instead of land-use *regulations* is deliberate. Landowners can adopt sustainable practices whether or not they are required to do so. Moreover, government agencies can encourage the adoption of appropriate land-use practices by establishing regulations that prevent development in hazardous locations, providing incentives that encourage development in safe locations, or informing landowners about the risks and benefits of development in locations throughout the community. Finally, hazard mitigation can be achieved through building construction practices that make individual structures less vulnerable to natural hazards. Here also, the use of the term building construction *practices* rather than building *codes* is deliberate because building owners can adopt hazard resistant designs and construction materials in the absence of government intervention. Disaster resistant construction practices include elevating structures out of flood plains, designing structures to respond more effectively to lateral stresses, and providing window shutters to protect against wind pressure and debris impacts. Nonetheless, government agencies can encourage the adoption of appropriate building construction practices by establishing code provisions that require hazard resistant building designs and materials, providing incentives that encourage appropriate designs and materials, or informing building owners about the risks and benefits of different building designs and materials.

Emergency Preparedness Practices

Another way to reduce a disaster's physical impacts is to adopt emergency preparedness practices, which can be defined as pre-impact actions that provide the human and material resources needed to support active responses at the time of hazard impact (Lindell and Perry 2000). The first step in emergency preparedness is to use the community hazard/vulnerability analysis to identify the emergency response demands that must be met by performing four basic emergency response functions—emergency assessment, expedient hazard mitigation, population protection, and incident management (Lindell and Perry 1992, 1996). Emergency assessment consists of those actions that define the potential scope of the disaster impacts (e.g., projecting hurricane wind speed), expedient hazard mitigation consists of short-term actions that protect property (e.g., sandbagging around structures), population protection actions protect people from impact (e.g., warning and evacuation), and incident management actions activate and coordinate the emergency response (e.g., communication among responding agencies). The next step is to determine which community organization will be responsible for accomplishing each function (Federal Emergency Management Agency, 1996). Once functional responsibilities have been assigned, each organization must develop procedures for accomplishing those functions. Finally, the organizations must acquire response resources (personnel, facilities, and equipment) to implement their plans and they need to maintain preparedness for emergency response through continued planning, training, drills, and exercises (Daines 1991).

Disaster Recovery Practices

Disaster recovery practices consist of pre-impact recovery preparedness and post-impact recovery actions that are intended to restore a community to its normal patterns of functioning. Important actions include impact assessment, debris management, infrastructure restoration, housing recovery, economic recovery, and linkage to hazard mitigation. It seems to be commonly thought that the development of disaster recovery plans can be delayed until after disaster strikes, but practitioners and researchers agree that community disaster recovery is faster and more effective when it is based on a plan has been developed prior to disaster impact (Geis 1996; Olson, Olson & Gawronski 1998; Schwab, et al. 1998; Wilson 1991; Wu & Lindell 2004).

There are six important features of a pre-impact recovery plan. First, it should define a disaster recovery organization. Second, it should identify the location of temporary housing because resolving this issue can cause conflicts that can delay consideration of longer-term issues of permanent housing and distract policy makers altogether from hazard mitigation (Bolin and Trainer 1978; Bolin 1982). Third, the plan should indicate how to accomplish essential tasks such as damage assessment, condemnation, debris removal and disposal, rezoning, infrastructure restoration, temporary repair permits, development moratoria, and permit processing because all of these tasks must be addressed before the reconstruction of permanent housing can begin (Schwab, et al. 1998).

Fourth, pre-impact recovery plans also should address the licensing and monitoring of contractors and retail price controls to ensure that victims are not exploited and also should address the jurisdiction's administrative powers and resources, especially the level of staffing that is available. It is almost inevitable that local government will not have sufficient staff to perform critical recovery tasks such as damage assessment and building permit processing, so arrangements can be made to borrow staff from other jurisdictions (via pre-existing Memoranda of Agreement) and to use trained volunteers such as local engineers, architects, and planners. Fifth, these plans also need to address the ways in which recovery tasks will be implemented at historical sites (Spennemann & Look 1998). Finally, pre-impact recovery plans should recognize the recovery period is a unique time to enact policies for hazard mitigation and make provision for incorporating this objective into the recovery planning process.

Assessing Hazard Exposure
Mapping Natural Hazard Exposure

States and local jurisdictions across the country vary in their exposure to the hazards. Consequently, an important objective for a local emergency manager is to identify the hazards that his or her community should set as priorities for its emergency management program. There are a number of useful sources of information about the regional incidence of these hazards, one of which is the set of maps contained in the Federal Emergency Management Agency's (1997) *Multi Hazard Identification and Risk Assessment*.[2]

Mapping Hazardous Materials Vulnerable Zones

The U.S. Environmental Protection Agency, the Federal Emergency Management Agency, and the U.S. Department of Transportation have developed guidance for assessing the size of the Vulnerable Zones for fixed-site facilities and transportation of hazardous materials. Emergency managers should work with their Local Emergency Planning Committees to ensure that the locations of all facilities are recorded that have quantities of Extremely Hazardous Substances in excess of Threshold Planning Quantities.[3] The locations of the facilities should be mapped and the radius of the Vulnerable Zone around each facility should be computed. The areas within these Vulnerable Zones should be examined to identify the types of residential, commercial, and industrial land uses within them. It is particularly important to determine if there are any sensitive facilities within each Vulnerable Zone. A reference list of such facilities is listed in Table 9.2 and important characteristics of the facility users are listed Table 9.3.

Emergency managers also should work with their Local Emergency Planning Committees (LEPCs) to identify the highway, rail, water, and air routes though which hazardous materials are transported. Once these routes have been identified, the number of tank trucks, railroad tank cars, and barges carrying each of the different types of hazardous materials can be counted during a commodity flow study to determine what are the types of hazards facing the community.[4] As is the case with the fixed-site facilities, the areas within these Vulnerable Zones should be examined to identify residential, commercial, and industrial land uses and, especially, the presence of any sensitive facilities.

Identifying and Mapping Secondary Hazards

Emergency managers should be aware that some disaster impacts can initiate others. For example, earthquakes can initiate landslides, fires, dam failures, and hazardous materials can release in addition to the expected structural failures caused by ground shaking. One method of identifying areas exposed to multiple hazards is to use a geographic information system (GIS) to overlay the areas subject to these different hazards. This is accomplished by entering all of the data on primary and secondary hazard exposures and special facilities into a GIS so fault lines, areas prone to the highest levels of ground shaking, subsidence, and landsliding; hazardous facility Vulnerable Zones, and locations of sensitive facilities are located in separate layers. Next, these layers are intersected to produce composite maps that display the areas subject to multiple hazards. Finally, the layers identifying the locations of residential, commercial, and industrial areas, and sensitive facilities are overlaid to produce the final maps.

Assessing Physical Vulnerability

Assessing Human Vulnerability

Some risk areas are defined in terms of event magnitude, which is a physical measure of the amount of energy or hazardous material. For example, U.S. Geological Survey earthquake hazard maps plot the peak ground acceleration (PGA) with a 2% probability of exceedance in 50 years. PGA provides a measure of the

Table 9.2. Reference List of Special Facilities

HEALTH RELATED
Hospitals
Nursing homes
Halfway houses (drug, alcohol, mental retardation)
Mental institutions

PENAL
Jails
Prisons
Detention camps
Reformatories

ASSEMBLY & ATHLETIC
Auditoriums
Theaters
Exhibition halls
Gymnasiums
Athletic stadiums or fields

AMUSEMENT & RECREATION
Beaches
Camp/conference centers
Amusement parks/fairgrounds/race courses
Campgrounds/Recreational Vehicle parks
Parks/lakes/rivers
Golf courses
Ski resorts
Community recreation centers

RELIGIOUS
Churches/synagogues
Evangelical group centers

HIGH DENSITY RESIDENTIAL
Hotels/motels
Apartment/condominium complexes
Mobile home parks
Dormitories (college, military)
Convents/monasteries

TRANSPORTATION
Rivers/lakes
Dam locks/toll booths
Ferry/railroad/bus terminals

COMMERCIAL
Shopping centers
Central business districts
Commercial/industrial parks

EDUCATIONAL
Day care centers
Preschools/kindergartens
Elementary/secondary schools
Vocational/business/specialty schools
Colleges/universities

Source: FEMI-EMI course textbook, *Introduction to Emergency Management* (working draft), Chapter 6, "Hazard and Vulnerability Analysis," Wayne Blanchard, 2004.

rate at which the ground moves, so emergency managers can use these maps to identify areas where buildings are more likely to collapse. However, only trained engineers will be able to use the quantitative information to assess the probability of building failure. Even with such information, the expected number of casualties that would result from each level of PGA is extremely difficult to project. Wind maps are similarly limited in their immediate utility to emergency managers because the likelihood of human death or injury is minimal for anything but the highest wind speeds (e.g., at least a Category 3 hurricane or an F2 tornado). By contrast, the maps of some hazards have more direct implications for human safety. For example, areas that are within the 100-year flood plain are clearly hazardous because even shallow depths of moving water can cause fatalities.

Table 9.3. Characteristics of Sensitive Facilities

CHARACTERISTICS OF USERS	SPECIAL CONSIDERATIONS
Mobility of users	Ambulatory Require close supervision Non-ambulatory Require life support
Permanent residence of users	Facility residents Residents of hazard impact area, but *not* of the facility (e.g., prison guards) Transients
Periods of use	Days of week/hours of day Special events
User density	Concentrated Dispersed
Sheltering in place	Highly effective Moderately effective Minimally or not effective
Transportation support	Would use own vehicles Require buses or other high occupancy vehicles Require ambulances

Source: FEMI-EMI course textbook, *Introduction to Emergency Management* (working draft), Chapter 6, "Hazard and Vulnerability Analysis," Wayne Blanchard, 2004.

There are some hazards that are mapped directly in terms of human health consequences. For example, maps of Vulnerable Zones for hazardous materials have very direct relevance for emergency managers because the contours on these maps are defined in terms of gas or vapor concentrations that are imminent health threats. Perhaps the most extreme case of a map with direct relevance to human safety would be one that identifies areas of lava flow because direct contact with flowing lava is sure to produce injuries if not fatalities.

Assessing Agricultural and Livestock Vulnerability

Assessing the physical vulnerability of crops and livestock is a task that is rarely considered to be the responsibility of emergency managers. One reason for giving minimal emphasis to the agricultural sector is that it accounts for a relatively small part of the total vulnerability in many jurisdictions. In those cases where the agricultural sector is a significant part of the local vulnerability, emergency managers should consult agricultural experts such as those from the U.S. Department of Agriculture because, as noted earlier, there is substantial variation among animal and plant species in their susceptibility to extreme environmental conditions. For example, fruit orchards can be devastated by wind speeds that have no impact whatsoever on rangeland. Moreover, the damage to many crops depends on the stage in growth cycle—with some crops having minimal susceptibility to wind damage until just before harvest.

Assessing Structural Vulnerability

There are three major issues in assessing structural vulnerability. First is the question of whether the structure has the strength or resilience to withstand environmental forces such as wind, seismicity, or water. In this case, the concern is about the impact on the structure itself and, consequently, the cost of repair or reconstruction. The second issue concerns the ability of the structure to protect the contents. This issue is distinct from the first one because in earthquakes, for example, buildings that survive ground shaking without damage can transmit the motion to light fixtures, cabinets, and furniture—possibly damaging these items. The third issue concerns the ability of the structure to protect the occupants. This is especially important in connection with hazardous materials because they can infiltrate into a structure and kill the occupants without damaging the building. Of course, the assessment of structural vulnerability usually involves all three issues. For riverine flooding and hurricane storm surge, structures—especially concrete structures with well-anchored foundations—resist battering waves to protect the structure and provide the height to escape the rising water that could threaten contents and occupants. In other cases, it is the strength of construction in resisting wind loads (tornadoes and hurricanes), blast forces (explosions and volcanic eruptions) and ground shaking (earthquakes) that protects the structure, contents, and occupants. For chemical, radiological, and volcanic ash threats, it is the tightness of construction in preventing the infiltration of outside (contaminated) air into the structure that is the important protective feature. Finally, in the case of exposure to a cloud of radioactive material, the construction material can provide shielding from penetrating radiation and from surface contamination.

In summary, it is important for emergency managers to assess structural vulnerability for two reasons. First structural vulnerability assessment enables them to project the likely level of damage from disaster impact and, thus, the priorities for their hazard mitigation and disaster recovery preparedness programs. Second, it enables them to project the likely level of damage from disaster impact and, thus, the need for hazard mitigation. That is, assessing structural vulnerability also allows emergency managers to determine if local structures are sufficient to make in-place sheltering a viable alternative to evacuation as a means of protecting residents in a wide variety of emergencies.

Assessing and Mapping Social Vulnerability

In contrast to physical vulnerability, which arises from the potential for environmental extremes to create adverse anatomical and physiological changes, social vulnerability arises from the potential for these extreme events to cause changes in people's behavior. People can vary in their potential for injury to themselves, their family, and their peers, and in the potential for destruction of their homes and workplaces, as well as the transportation systems and locations for shopping and recreation that they rely upon.

Assessing Psychological Vulnerability

One important component of psychological vulnerability is personal fragility—that is, a lack of emotion-focused coping skills. Another component of psychological vulnerability is rigidity—that is, a lack of problem-focused coping skills defined by an inability to develop adaptive strategies for responding to altered conditions. Ozer and Weiss's (2004) summary of research on post-traumatic stress disorder (PTSD) concluded the four categories of PTSD predictors were 1) a person's pre-existing characteristics (e.g., intelligence, previous psychological trauma), 2) the severity of the personal impact of the disaster, 3) psychological processes immediately after the impact, and 4) life stress and social support after the traumatic event. Quite obviously, only the first of these categories can measure psychological vulnerability that exists before a disaster strikes and none of the variables in this category is routinely available through secondary sources such as Census data. Because direct measures of the incidence of PTSD predictors (e.g., through community surveys) are prohibitively expensive, psychological vulnerability must be measured indirectly, as discussed in a later section.

Assessing Demographic Vulnerability

The hallmark of demographic vulnerability is social isolation. Thus, demographic vulnerability is measured by the infrequency and superficiality of social contacts with peers such as kin (extended family), neighbors, and co-workers. Like psychological vulnerability, routine measures of demographic vulnerability are rarely available through surveys conducted using representative samples of community members. However, there are proxy variables that have statistically significant—although admittedly small—correlations with social isolation. Suitable proxy variables that are routinely available through Census files include age, and ethnicity. Specifically, increasing age is associated with reduced levels of community participation (involvement in voluntary associations) and immersion in kin and friendship networks (Perry 1985; Perry, Lindell & Greene 1981). By contrast, socioeconomic status is positively associated with participation in community organizations (Alvirez & Bean 1976; Tomeh 1973) and minority ethnicity is positively associated with immersion in kin and friendship networks (Bianchi & Farley 1979; Staples 1976; Staples & Mirande 1976; Wilkinson 1999). Accordingly, the use of age, socioeconomic status, and ethnicity as proxy measures of demographic vulnerability will also be discussed below.

Assessing Economic Vulnerability

It is obvious that wealth is a major component of economic vulnerability, but the assets comprising wealth vary in their vulnerability to disasters. Tangible assets such as buildings, equipment, furniture, and vehicles that are located in the disaster impact area are more vulnerable than financial assets such as bank accounts, stocks and bonds that are recorded electronically. Households and businesses both have tangible and financial assets, so both of them are vulnerable to the loss of their tangible assets and both have financial assets that can be used to support disaster recovery. Of course, there are substantial variations among households in their assets and the same is true for businesses.

One noteworthy difference between households and businesses is that the latter also have operational vulnerability arising from dependency upon those who supply its inputs (suppliers and labor) as well as those who purchase its outputs (distributors and customers). Evidence of businesses' operational vulnerability to input disruptions can be seen in data provided by Nigg (1995), who reported that business managers' median estimate of the amount of time that they could continue to operate without infrastructure was 0 hours for electric power, 4 hours for telephones, 48 hours for water/sewer, and 120 hours for fuel. If this infrastructure support is unavailable for time periods longer than these, the businesses must suspend operations even if they have suffered no damage to their structures or contents.

Measures of household wealth are not available, but data on household income are available in Census files. Available census data on businesses are more limited in their relevance to economic vulnerability.[5]

Assessing Political Vulnerability

As will be discussed later, the political impacts of disasters arise from conflicts over the management of the emergency response and disaster recovery. Accordingly, political vulnerability arises from inadequate emergency management interventions—which create situations that pit one group of stakeholders against another—and inadequate mechanisms for managing this conflict when it does arise. The adequacy of mechanisms for managing conflict is a crucial part of civil governance. In particular, government agencies that are believed to lack legitimacy, expertise, and adequate information for making decisions about the allocation of public resources will prove vulnerable in the aftermath of disaster. As is the case with psychological, demographic, and economic vulnerability, there currently are no direct measures of political vulnerability that are readily available for use by emergency managers. Consequently, the use of age, socioeconomic status, and ethnicity as proxy measures of demographic vulnerability will also be discussed in the next section.

Predicting Household Vulnerability

As noted earlier in this chapter, it is important to recognize social vulnerability is not randomly distributed—either demographically or geographically. In particular, psychological resilience, social network immersion, economic assets, and political power vary across demographic groups. Some of these components of social vulnerability can be predicted by demographic characteristics such as gender, age, education, income, and ethnicity. Moreover, these demographic groups tend to be distributed quite systematically within each community. Even though there might not be sharp geographic lines of demarcation between the locations of different demographic groups within a community, there are variations in the concentration of these groups in different neighborhoods. Thus, GISs can be used to conduct disaggregated (e.g., census tract-level) spatial analyses that identify demographic segments that are likely to be the most vulnerable to disaster impacts. In some cases, the demographic predictors of social vulnerability (e.g., gender, age, education, income, and ethnicity) are associated with hazard exposure because the population segments with the fewest psychological, social, economic, and political resources disproportionately occupy the most hazardous geographical areas. Similarly, demographic predictors of social vulnerability are often associated with structural vulnerability because those same population segments disproportionately occupy the oldest, most poorly maintained buildings. Thus, those who are most socially vulnerable are likely to experience the greatest physical impacts such as casualties and property loss. Ultimately, however, these demographic groups are expected to be most socially vulnerable because they are the ones that are most likely to experience the greatest social impacts because they tend to have the fewest household resources and also tend to have limited access to public resources to support their recovery from a disaster. In practice, the analysis of social vulnerability is conducted on Census data, preferably at the lowest possible level of aggregation (e.g., block-group or tract). Recent research has shown that these aggregated indicators of social vulnerability are strongly correlated, so it is advisable to use either a composite measure of social vulnerability or subset of these indicators. Table 9.4 lists a sample set of social vulnerability indicators recently used in analyses of social vulnerability in Shelby County, Tennessee (Prater, et al. 2004).

Table 9.4. Indicators of Social Vulnerability

VULNERABLE GROUPS	VULNERABILITY INDICATORS
Female Headed Households	Percent female headed households
Elderly	Percent individuals over 65 Percent of elderly households
Low income/high poverty	Percent of households below poverty level Percent of households below HUD standards
Renters	Percent of households residing in rental housing Percent of households residing in rental housing by type of dwelling units
Ethnic/racial/language minorities	Percent of individual from Black, Hispanic, and other minorities Percent of non-English speakers
Children/youth	Percent of population in selected age groupings Percent of households with dependency ratios above a specified level
Social vulnerability hot spot analysis	Areas with combined social vulnerabilities.

Source: FEMA-EMI course textbook, *Introduction to Emergency Management*, Chapter 6, "Hazard and Vulnerability Analysis," Wayne Blanchard, 2004.

Based on the recognition, described above, that hazard exposure, structural vulnerability, and social vulnerability tend to be related, Prater and her colleagues advocated identifying vulnerability "hotspots," which can be identified by using a GIS to either overlay or mathematically combine data on hazard exposure (e.g., ground motion and ground failure from earthquakes), structural vulnerability (e.g., due to dilapidated housing), and lifeline vulnerability (e.g., due to dilapidated housing), to identify the geographic areas occupied by the demographic segments that are most vulnerable to disaster impacts. This concept of vulnerability hotspot analysis is illustrated in Figure 9.2 below.

Vulnerability Dynamics

A major challenge for emergency managers is to understand the processes by which communities increase or decrease their hazard exposure, physical vulnerability, and social vulnerability. According to economic theory, excessive hazard exposure and structural vulnerability arise from systemic complexities that can be characterized as *market failures* such as inadequate information, barriers to market entry and exit, and capital flow restrictions (Kunreuther 1998; Lindell, et al. 1997). An ideal pattern of economic development would be one in which risk area occupants purchase property on the basis of adequate information about hazard exposure and structural vulnerability. Moreover, they would locate only where it was economically advantageous in the long term as well as in the short term, and would diversify their assets over other locations and other forms of financial (e.g., savings accounts, insurance, stocks/bonds) and social (e.g., extended family) recovery assistance. Finally, risk area occupants would adopt hazard adjustments to limit their losses if a disaster were to strike. These adjustments would include hazard mitigation (e.g., land use practices and building construction practices), emergency preparedness practices (e.g., detection and warning systems), and recovery preparedness practices (e.g., diversified investments and hazard insurance) to avoid casualties and property damage.

Figure 9.2. Disaster Impact Vulnerability Assessment Model

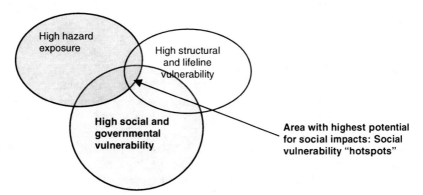

Source: FEMA-EMI course textbook, *Introduction to Emergency Management*, Chapter 6, "Hazard and Vulnerability Analysis," Wayne Blanchard, 2004.

Actual patterns of development are significantly different from the ideal. In many cases, there is migration to hazard-prone areas because of beneficial land uses for agriculture, transportation, and recreation (i.e., people are "pulled in," Bolin and Bolton 1986). This is compounded by a lack of accountability for investment decisions. Developers are at risk for only a short period of time before they pass an investment on to others (homeowners, insurers, mortgage holders) who ultimately will experience hazard impact. Such transactions can occur because many risk area residents are new arrivals who are unaware of the hazard. Even long-term residents of risk areas sometimes have little or no information about hazards and adjustments to those hazards because such information is suppressed by those with a major stake in the community's economic development (Meltsner 1979). Even when there is local knowledge about hazards, there often is a lack of hazard intrusiveness because events that are not recent or frequent tend not to be thought about or discussed (Lindell and Prater 2000). Moreover, people have an "optimistic bias" and tend to ignore low probability events or think of them as occurring far in the future. In particular, politicians tend to ignore consequences that they expect to occur only after their term of office is over, so only frequent, recent, or major impacts lead to increased adoption of community-wide hazard adjustments such as land use controls or more stringent building codes. Even then, the "window of opportunity" for the adoption of these adjustments is open only temporarily (Birkland 1998; Prater and Lindell 2000).

Increased hazard exposure also is caused by displacement from safer areas due to population pressures (i.e., people are "pushed in"). When this occurs, the demographic distribution of risk tends to be inequitable because geographical locations often are systematically related to their residents' demographic characteristics—especially their (lack of) economic and political power to decrease hazard vulnerability. This pattern is very common in developing countries such as Brazil, where *favelas* are located in flood plains and on landslide-prone slopes because the residents cannot afford to purchase homes in safer areas.

There also are problems in the adoption of effective hazard adjustments. One of these arises from households' and businesses' concentration of hazard exposure (i.e., having physical and financial assets located *only* in the risk area). Diversification is an effective way of avoiding concentration of hazard vulnerability, but low-income households and small businesses often have so few physical or financial assets that they cannot afford to locate some of them in safer areas. Hazard insurance is problematic because it tends to suffer from *adverse selection*, which means that only those who are at the greatest risk are likely to purchase it (Kunreuther 1998). Moreover, externalities arise when system dynamics cause the actions of one party to increase the vulnerability of another. In floodplains, upstream deforestation and urbanization increase the speed of rainfall runoff and, thus, increase downstream flood risk. Technological protection works such as dams and levees can offset such increases in hazard exposure, but many risk area occupants overestimate the effectiveness of such hazard adjustments (Harding and Parker 1974). This can cause further development of floodplains and, thus, increased hazard exposure that exceeds the risk reduction provided by the adjustment that was adopted.

Conducting Hazard/Vulnerability Analysis with HAZUS-MH

HAZUS-MH (Hazards US-Multi Hazard) is a software program that models potential losses from earthquakes, floods, and hurricane winds. HAZUS-MH uses GIS software to analyze and display data on estimated structural damage and economic loss estimates for buildings and infrastructure. It also provides estimates of the casualties resulting from earthquakes. HAZUS-MH can be used to conduct analyses in support of hazard mitigation, emergency preparedness, and recovery preparedness planning. In addition, HAZUS-MH can be used to conduct rapid analyses in support of post-impact emergency response and disaster recovery operations.

HAZUS-MH supports three levels of analysis. A Level 1 analysis uses national average data to produce approximate results. Accordingly, a Level 1 analysis is best considered to be an initial screening analysis that can be used to identify communities at highest risk. A Level 2 analysis takes refined data and hazard maps provided by the user to produce more accurate estimates. Input for a Level 2 analysis is obtained from local emergency managers, urban and regional planners, and GIS professionals. A Level 3 analysis uses community-specific loss parameters to produce the most accurate estimate of loss. Input for a Level 3 analysis is obtained from structural and geotechnical engineers, as well as other technical experts to examine threats such as dam breaks and tsunamis.

Data input to HAZUS-MH is supported by the Inventory Collection Tool (InCAST), a Building Inventory Tool (BIT), and Flood Information Tool (FIT). InCAST is a database that is designed to support the management of local building data needed for Level 2 and Level 3 analyses. BIT supports the importation of building data from large files (e.g., over 100,000 records from a tax assessor data file). FIT allows users to transform flood data to the HAZUS flood model's required format.

HAZUS-MH has separate models for earthquakes, floods, and hurricane winds. The earthquake model accounts for ground motion and ground failure; the flood model accounts for flood frequency, depth, and discharge velocity. The hurricane model accounts for wind pressure, missile damage, and rain.

Direct damage can be calculated for the general building stock, essential facilities, high potential loss facilities, transportation facilities, lifelines. Induced damage can be estimated for fire, hazmat release, and debris generation. Direct losses can be estimated for cost of repair/replacement, income loss, crop damage, casualties, shelter, and recovery needs. Indirect losses include supply shortages, sales declines, opportunity costs, and economic losses. These impact modules are most complete for earthquake (only the crop loss module is unavailable), and floods (only the fire following and casualties modules are unavailable). The hurricane model has the fewest features (direct damage to the general building stock, essential facilities and high potential loss facilities; induced damage from hazmat release, and debris generation; direct losses from cost of repair/replacement and shelter and recovery needs).

HAZUS-MH can be used in multi-hazard analyses that provide average annualized loss and probabilistic results from the three hazard models (earthquake, flood, and wind). HAZUS-MH can also link to external models for blast, radiological, chemical, and biological) hazards.[6]

ANALYZING AND DISSEMINATING HAZARD/VULNERABILITY DATA

The widespread availability of powerful desktop computers provides an important method for conducting hazard/vulnerability analyses in identifying areas at risk (Dash 1997; Griffith 1986; Berke, Larsen and Ruch 1984) and projecting the damages resulting from a major incident (French 1986; Haney 1986; Scawthorne 1986). To accomplish these tasks, emergency managers can use software such as GIS (Environmental Systems Research Institute 2000), CAMEO (National Safety Council 1995), ALOHA (FEMA no date), and HAZUS (National Institute for Building Sciences 1998).

In addition, desktop computers also provide emergency managers with a powerful tool for obtaining hazard/vulnerability data from the Web sites of a wide range of government agencies, university research centers, private sector organizations, and non-governmental organizations such as the American Red Cross. In particular, the Internet has become an important method for obtaining the data that are needed for conducting hazard/vulnerability analyses and disseminating the results of these analyses—a technological development that is important for three reasons. First, federal and state agencies have generated many hazard analysis documents, maps, and databases that already are in digital form and are available to put onto Web sites. Second, SEMA Web sites can be linked electronically to other organizations' Web sites, thus allowing users to immediately access additional hazard analysis information that might otherwise take them months to obtain if they were to request it in paper copy. Third, hazard analyses disseminated over the Internet can be updated frequently and, by avoiding the printing costs associated with hundreds of paper copies, can be disseminated less expensively.

Analyzing Hazard/Vulnerability Data

Despite the great promise of computers in analyzing and disseminating hazard/vulnerability data, there is little documentation of the extent to which these tools are actually being used. Some indication of the degree to which progress remains to be made can be seen in Lindell and Perry's (2001) data from Local Emergency Planning Committee (LEPC) Chairs in Illinois, Indiana, and Michigan indicating that only 59% of the LEPCs had calculated Vulnerability Zones around their communities' hazmat facilities. Of those who had calculated Vulnerability Zones, only 36% had used computer models such as CAMEO (National Safety Council 1995) or ARCHIE (Federal Emergency Management Agency, no date) to perform the analyses. Thus, only a small fraction of the LEPCs used computer-based methods to calculate Vulnerability Zones. In addition, there were differences among types of computer use, with some LEPCs using computerized databases more extensively for the management of data on chemical hazards (i.e., chemical inventories at local plants) and community emergency response resources than did other jurisdictions. Thus, these data, though very limited in scope, indicate local emergency management agencies have a long way to go in using emergency management information technology to its fullest advantage.

[PREVENTATIVE MEASURES] OVERVIEW

Realistically preventative measures cannot eliminate the possibility of every disaster. Should there be the occurrence of a catastrophic event, a response scenario will be generated which may require the allocation of many resources, assets, skills, and capabilities. Frequently the very nature of a catastrophic incident will demand a response effort that is comprised of multiple agencies and segments of the community. This requires a high level of planning, coordination, and control that we will begin to discuss in this chapter.

To Define...

Before discussing the elements of a response protocol it may be useful to the student to understand some of the key differences in commonly used terms.

Response: The reaction triggered by an event or occurrence. In regards to emergency response, this term is generally applied to mean a community or organization's initial actions employed to mitigate, stabilize, and contain a disaster. Although simplistic and incomplete, the image that often characterizes this phrase is one of "first responders" such as police, fire, and ambulance services racing to a scene.

Rescue: The actual effort of locating injured victims and initiating emergency treatment and care. In some circumstances this may also be known as a "search" phase.

Relief: Involves latter stage operation after the primary stages of response and rescue. Relief is typically thought of as such things as furnishing, needed food, water, shelter and logistics, medicines, convalescence, communications with family, and psychological and spiritual counseling.

Recovery: Can be thought of as the "clean-up" and return to normalization stage. Recovery is when long-term rebuilding and reconstruction begins. Recovery also has a sadder connotation as well. When a search operation moves from "rescue" to "recovery," it generally means that the assessment of professional rescuers is that they feel there is no longer much hope of rescuing a living victim, but are now more focused on recovering bodies.

Key Elements

The nature of a catastrophic event is that it is likely to overwhelm local resources. The capability of any one agency or community to sustain response, rescue, relief, and recovery operations on its own will be exceeded. Certain factors will have to be considered when preparing a large-scale response, rescue, relief, and recovery effort appropriate for a catastrophe level event. The following pages will begin an examination of these elements.

Multiple Agencies

Catastrophic events typically trigger the need for various different responding agencies. Some commonly involved agencies and organizations are as follows:

Law Enforcement: Such as local police, county sheriffs, state police, and highway patrols; law enforcement agencies may provide such services as scene security, assisting with evacuation, communications, tactical response, air support, search resources, explosives disposal, and traffic and crowd control.

Fire Department: Fire suppression, emergency medical services, evacuation, hazardous material containment, communications, and urban search and rescue.

Emergency Medical Services: Paramedics, emergency medical technicians, disaster medical teams, emergency room personnel—doctors, nurses, surgeons, physician's assistants; EMS can triage, evacuate, treat and mitigate injuries, diagnose symptoms, and identification of possible presence of chemical, biological, or radiological contaminants.

Private and Facility Security: Contract and private security functions employed by corporate, private, residential, and public facilities; assist with evacuation, communications, scene security, first-aid and medical assistance, and crowd and traffic control. In community-wide catastrophic events, public safety agencies will be heavily taxes, if not completely overwhelmed. Corporate facilities, shopping centers, school and college campuses, and other private properties will most likely have to provide for their own emergency response, evacuation, first aid, shelter, logistics, and communications without assistance from local public safety agencies, thus relying on their own internal, private security, and disaster relief functions.

Public Utilities: Power, lights and electricity, civil engineering, public works, telecommunications, water treatment; utilities and public works personnel are as much as part of a community-wide disaster response and recovery effort as are fire, police, and other more commonly-identified emergency responders. Public utilities will often furnish the specialized training and equipment required to secure hazards such as downed power-lines, ruptured gas lines and broken water mains; flood control; hazardous materials containment and clean-up; building safety assessment; and removing debris, downed trees and vegetation.

Construction, Engineering, and Technical Specialists: Private construction and engineering firms may be called upon to play a key role in catastrophic event response. Iron and steel workers, welders, heavy equipment operators, truck drivers, crane operators may be needed to move heavy debris, clear paths blocked to rescuers; assist in search and rescue—particularly where there is widespread structural damage and collapse. Other tradespersons, such as electricians, plumbers, and carpenters may be needed to secure damaged systems and construct ramps, temporary roads, and structures for rescue crews. Finally, engineers and investigators from private contractors also may be required at the scene of a catastrophic event. In the case of a transportation accident for example, engineers involved in the design and manufacture of the vehicle involved may be called upon to consult, help determine root causes, and determine best response options.

Government Agencies and Non-Governmental Organization (NCOs): Such as FEMA and National Guard; federal investigators from the FBI, BATFE, NTSB, DOT, EPA, and USCG, for example; international organizations from the UN or non-governmental disaster relief specialists such as International Red Cross/Red Crescent; Salvation Army; Doctors without Borders, for example. These varying agencies all bring considerable talents and resources to disaster relief and recovery—everything from establishing temporary hospitals and shelters to distribution of relief supplies, logistics, immunizations, food, water treatment, and communications.

Convergent Volunteers: Disasters, particularly community-level catastrophes can evoke a powerful outpouring from community members wishing to help, as well as activating skilled volunteers specifically trained and equipped for such response. Volunteer organizations may include corporate or community emergency response teams, local shortwave radio clubs, Civil Air Patrol, U.S. Coast Guard Auxiliary, and Sheriff's Search and Rescue Teams. A rush of volunteers can lend badly needed manpower and equipment to relief and recovery efforts, but also may sometimes represent a challenge to on-scene commanders who may find a rush of spontaneous volunteers overwhelming.

Coordination

As we have determined, a catastrophic event will usually require a diverse number of responders, equipment, skills, and resources. Organizing, coordinating, and communicating these various elements is a substantial undertaking. ... For this rudimentary discussion, however, we will just touch upon the topic of multi-agency and event coordination. The following are some key elements you should consider including in any large-scale catastrophic response plan.

- *Logistics*: What equipment is required? Logistical coordination may constitute a broad range of equipment ranging from blankets, medicines, communications equipment, potable water, and portable generators up to earth moving equipment, heavy-life cranes and helicopters. In a multi-agency response, coordinating the resources of multiple agencies under the aegis of a single unified command structure, and ensuring that resources are properly utilized and accounted becomes the primary logistical challenge.

- *Delegation and Decision Making*: Unified command concepts such as SEMS and ICS (Incident Command System) were born out of multi-agency catastrophic events responses in which unclear command or jurisdictional authority surfaced as a factor prohibiting an effective and coordinated response effort. The function of an incident commander (IC) and command staff is to establish a centralized response coordinator who will be recognized by all responders as the delegating and decision-making authority. Typically the selection

- *Communications*: Responders must be able to talk to one another; while this would seem to be a fairly obvious point, its importance cannot be understated. On 9/11 over 340 first responders were lost largely because radio equipment used by police, fire, and port authority personnel was not sufficiently interoperable. Critical observations from police helicopters were not able to be passed along to NYFD ICs; the command to evacuate the towers in advance of a collapse was not received by rescuers still in the buildings; even something as minor as the failure to correctly activate a high rise repeater station meant that NYFD chiefs were unable to talk to each other. As much as possible, communications systems need to be compatible, interoperable, and durable in order to meet the particular demands of a catastrophic event response.

- *Planning*: Any effective response protocol has to involve prior planning. First responders, community members, and local, state, and Federal authorities must conduct prior planning in order to determine and reinforce initial actions and response priorities. Building, hospital, and school evacuation drills; tabletop simulations; computer modeling; and large-scale disaster response exercises involving multiple agencies are valuable methods of identifying catastrophic event priorities. In a high rise building first, for example, a building population that has been properly trained on, and able to self-initiate correct evacuation procedures is perhaps the best tool for minimizing injuries and fatalities in such an event. Prior planning will also cut down on confusion among responding agencies. If general ideas already have been established regarding response priorities and agency responsibilities, this can save valuable time and effort during the initial response and rescue phases of an event.

- *Public Information*: ...[I]t is important to note that a key element of response protocol preparation is keeping the media, various authorities, and the general public adequately informed. Good control and coordination of public information helps reduce anxiety and panic, ensures that accurate information and instructions are presented to those who are potentially affected, and can even be useful in enlisting the public's help in avoiding certain areas, not tying up telecommunications networks, or enlisting volunteers. Effective communications with local, state, and Federal authorities can help facilitate the allocation of additional resources and good governmental cooperation.

- *Administration and Finance*: Lastly, a large-scale response effort is going to be an administrative and accounting nightmare if tight and effective controls are not employed early and implemented consistently throughout the event. Resources and logistics must be tracked and accounted for; usage and burn rates predicted and run to ensure that adequate supply chains are maintained—and the money supply cannot be allowed to run out! While not always the most exciting aspect of event response and recovery, effective administration and finance is integral to managing operations, ensuring adequate resource allocation, proper return of logistics to contributing agencies, accounting of finances, and the overall well being of ongoing recovery efforts. Post 9/11 many unfortunate, disappointing, and wasteful revelations came to light about relief funds mismanagement. This provides an excellent example of how significant the role of administration and finance is.

SUMMARY

Until recently, disaster planning was done at various levels and for every type of likely emergency situation. This made coordination of the required logistical and communications support especially impossible and left responders and communities unprepared and slow to respond as each scenario had its own structured response. The value of the "all hazards" concept is in its flexibility and the ease of training those responsible in its use, and improved multi-jurisdictional cooperation will help responders to transfer resources where they are needed and have them ready for utilization when they arrive.

As populations increase and more of the world's surface is built on, natural disasters that endanger people's lives and destroy property will only become more common. Because of modern communications, news of catastrophic events from around the world can travel quickly, and aid resources sourced, pooled and transported faster than ever before, but being able to take advantage of these advantages requires prior study and planning. Vulnerability assessment and impact modeling makes prior planning by FEMA and other allied agencies more effective and helps speed resources to responders and aid to victims. Catastrophe will always be part of the human experience, so we must continue to learn from each experience in hopes of saving lives and mitigating the losses from future emergencies.

ADDITIONAL DISCUSSION TOPICS

- FEMA used to be an independent agency before it was folded into the Department of Homeland Security after 9/11. Do you think this change should have been made? How well do you think the "All Hazards" approach actually prepares for diverse hazards?

- Are there any areas in your city, town or county where the geography encourages flooding, fires or other hazards? Why do people live there and keep rebuilding there after these events?

- Considering the main industries in your area, what secondary effects would be caused if they were damaged by flooding? Tornado/ Hurricane? Terrorist attack?

- Identify three "at risk" populations in your area that would be particularly badly affected by a catastrophic event. What could be done pre-impact to mitigate that affect?

- Do you know your agency's, company's or department's responsibilities and protocols for cooperation with others during an emergency? What are they? Do you have any responsibilities in the relief or recovery phases?

REFERENCES

Anderson, W. A. (1969). *Local civil defense in natural disaster*. Columbus, OH: The Ohio State University Disaster Research Center.

Barrett, C.B. (1986). "Local flood warning systems." pp. 79-91 in U.S. Army Corps of Engineers Hydrologic Engineering Center (Ed.). *Proceedings of a Seminar on Local Flood Warning-Response Systems*. Davis, CA: U.S. Army Corps of Engineers Hydrologic Engineering Center.

Birkland, T.A. (1997). *After disaster: agenda setting, public policy and focusing events*. Washington, DC: Georgetown University Press.

Blanchard, B.W. (1986). *American civil defense 1945-1984*. Emmitsburg, MD: National Emergency Training Center (FEMA 107).

Brunacini, A.V. (2001). *Fire command*, Second Edition. Quincy, MA: National Fire Protection Association.

Brunacini, A.V. (2002). *Command safety: saving our own*. Quincy, MA: National Fire Protection Association.

Buck, G. (1998). *Preparing for terrorism*. Albany, NY: Del Mar Publishers.

Burton, I., Kates, R. & White, G. (1993). *The environment as hazard*. Second Edition. NY: Guilford Press.

Bush, G.W. (2002). *The Department of Homeland Security*. Washington, DC: The White House.

Carr, L. (1932). "Disaster and the sequence-pattern concept of social change." *American Journal of Sociology* 38 (August): 209-215.

Disaster Research Group. (1961). *A review of disaster studies*. Washington, DC: National Academy of Sciences—National Research Council.

Drabek, T.E. (1985). "Managing the emergency response." *Public Administration Review 45* (January): 85-92.

Drabek, T.E. (1991a). "Introduction." pp. xvii-xxxiv in Drabek, T.E. and Hoetmer, G.J. (Eds.). *Emergency Management Principles and Practice for Local Government*. Washington, DC: International City Management Association.

Drabek, T.E. (1991b). "The evolution of emergency management." pp. 3-29 in Drabek, T.E. & Hoetmer, G.J. (Eds.). *Emergency Management Principles and Practice for Local Government*. Washington, DC: International City Management Association.

Drabek, T.E. (1997). *The social dimensions of disaster* (FEMA Higher Education Project College Course). Emmitsburg, MD: Emergency Management Institute.

Federal Emergency Management Agency. (1998). *Principles of emergency management* (Student Manual and Instructor Guide G230). Emmitsburg, MD: Emergency Management Institute.

Federal Emergency Management Agency. (1995). *Introduction to emergency management*. Student Manual 230. Emmitsburg, MD: Emergency Management Institute.

Greenway, A.R. (1998). *Risk management planning handbook*. Rockville, MD: GovernmentInstitutes Press.

Harris, M. (1975). *Significant events in United States civil defense history*. Washington, DC: Defense Civil Preparedness Agency.

Joint Committee on Defense Production. (1976). "Federal, state and local emergency preparedness." *Hearings, 94th Congress, Second session.* Washington, DC: U.S. Senate.

Ketchum, J. & Whittaker, H. (1982). "Hazards analysis." *Comprehensive Emergency Management Bulletin* 2 (1): 1-17.

Kramer, W. & Bahme, C. (1992). *Fire officer's guide to disaster control.* Saddlebrook, NJ: Pennwell Publishing Company.

Kreps, G.A. (1989). *Symposium on social structure and disaster.* Newark, DE: University of Delaware Press.

Lindell, M.K. & Perry, R.W. (1992). *Behavioral foundations of community emergency planning.* Washington, DC: Hemisphere Publishers.

Lindell, M.K. & Perry, R.W. (1997). "Hazardous materials releases in the Northridge Earthquake." *Risk Analysis* 17 (April): 147-156.

Lindell, M.K. & Perry, R.W. (1998). "Earthquake impacts and hazard adjustment by acutely hazardous materials facilities following the Northridge Earthquake." *Earthquake Spectra* 14(May): 285-299.

Lindell, M.K. & Perry, R.W. (2000). "Household adjustment to earthquake hazard." *Environment and Behavior* 32: 590-630.

Lindell, M.K. & Perry, R.W. (2001). "Community innovation in hazardous material management." *Journal of Hazardous Materials* 88 (December): 169-194.

Lindell, M.K. & Perry, R.W. (2003). *Risk communication in multicultural communities.* Thousand Oaks, CA: Sage Publications.

Lowrance, W.W. (1975). *Of acceptable risk.* Los Altos, CA: William Kaufmann, Inc.

Mileti, D.S. (1999). *Disasters by Design.* Washington, DC: Joseph Henry Press.

Pine, J.C. (1991). "Liability issues." pp. 289-310 in Drabek, T.E. & Hoetmer, G.J. (Eds.). *Emergency Management Principles and Practice for Local Government.* Washington, DC: International City Management Association.

Platt, R. B. (1998). "Planning and land use adjustments in historical perspective." pp. 31-46 in R. Burby (Ed.) *Cooperating with Nature.* Washington, DC: Joseph Henry Press.

Perry, R.W. (1979). "Evacuation decision making in natural disaster." *Mass Emergencies* 4 (1): 25-38.

Perry, R.W. (1982). *The social psychology of civil defense.* Lexington, MA: D.C. Heath.

Perry, R. W. (1985). *Comprehensive emergency management.* Greenwich, CT: JAI Press.

Perry, R. W. (1989). "Taxonomy and model building for emergency warning response." *International Journal of Mass Emergencies and Disasters* 9 (November): 305-328.

Perry, R.W. (1991). "Managing disaster response operations." pp. 201-223 in Drabek, T.E. & Hoetmer, G.J. (Eds.). *Emergency Management Principles and Practice for Local Government.* Washington, DC: International City Management Association.

Perry, R.W. (1998). "Definitions and the development of a theoretical superstructure for disaster research." pp. 197-215 in Quarantelli, E.L. (Ed.). *What is a Disaster?* London: Routledge.

Perry, R.W. & Hirose, H. (1991). *Volcano management in Japan and the United States.* Greenwich, CT: JAI Press.

Perry, R.W. & Lindell, M.K. (1990). *Living with Mt. St. Helens: human adjustment to volcano hazards.* Pullman, WA: Washington State University Press.

Perry, R.W. & Lindell, M.K. (1997). "Principles for managing community relocation as a hazard mitigation measure." *Journal of Contingencies and Crisis Management* 5 (March): 49-60.

Perry, R.W. & Lindell, M.K. (2003a). "Understanding citizen response to disasters with implications for terrorism." *Journal of Contingencies and Crisis Management* 11 (2): in press.

Perry, R.W. & Lindell, M.K. (2003b). *Risk communication in multi-cultural communities.* Thousand Oaks, CA: Sage Publications.

Prater, C.S. & Lindell, M.K. (2000). "The politics of hazard mitigation." *Natural Hazards Review* 1, 73-82.

Prince, S.H. (1920). *Catastrophe and social change.* New York: Columbia University Faculty of Political Science.

Quarantelli, E.L. (1984). *Organizational behavior in disasters and implications for disaster planning.* Emmitsburg, MD: FEMA, National Emergency Training Center.

Quarantelli, E.L. (1987). "What should we study?" *International Journal of Mass Emergencies and Disasters,* 5 (March): 7-32.

Quarantelli, E.L. (1992). "The case for a generic rather than agent specific approach to disasters." *Disaster Management* 2 (3): 191-196.

Quarantelli, E.L. (1998). *What is a disaster?* London: Routledge.

Reader, I. (2000). *Religious violence in Japan: The case of Aum Shinrikyo.* London: Curzon Press.

Rubin, C. B., Renda-Tanali, I., & Cumming, W. (2004). *Disaster time line: selected milestone events and U.S Outcomes, 1965-2003.* URL: http://www.disaster-timeline.com.

Tierney, K.J., Lindell, M.K. & Perry, R.W. (2001). *Facing the unexpected: disaster preparedness and response in the United States.* Washington, DC: Joseph Henry Press.

Tobin, G.A. & Montz, B.E. (1997). *Natural hazards: explanation and integration.* New York: Guildford Press.

Whittaker, H. (1979). *Comprehensive emergency management.* Washington, DC: National Governors Association.

Witt, J.L. (1995). Keynote Address, National Mitigation Conference. Arlington, VA: Federal Emergency Management Agency.

Witt, J.L. (1997). *Strategic plan: planning for a safer future.* Washington, DC: Federal Emergency Management Agency.

Yoshpe, H.B. (19981). *Our missing shield: The U.S. civil defense program in historical perspective.* Washington, DC: Defense Civil Preparedness Agency.

Endnotes

[1] Section 2.1. of this chapter was derived from the FEMA-EMI course textbook, *Introduction to Emergency Management* (working draft) Chapter 1, "Introduction to Emergency Management," Wayne Blanchard, 2004. Located at http://training.fema.gov/EMIWeb/edu/introtoEM.asp.

Sections 2.2. through 2.13 were derived from "Chapter 6, "Hazard and Vulnerability Analysis" of FEMA-EMI course textbook, *Introduction to Emergency Management* (working draft), Wayne Blanchard 2004, found at http://training.fema.gov/EMIWeb/edu/introtoEM.asp

[2] This source has an extensive set of maps describing exposure to natural hazards and it also addresses some technological hazards. The maps of natural hazard exposures contained in *Multi Hazard Identification and Risk Assessment* can be supplemented by visiting the web sites of FEMA <www.fema.gov>, the US Geological Survey <www.usgs.gov>, and the National Weather Service <www.nws.noaa.gov>.

[3] U.S. Environmental Protection Agency guidance for conducting this activity can be found at the Chemical Preparedness and Prevention Office's web site <yosemite.epa.gov/oswer/ceppoweb.nsf/content/index.html>.

[4] Information about hazardous materials transportation can be found on the U.S. Department of Transportation (DOT) Web site <hazmat.dot.gov> and specific guidance for conducting commodity flow studies is found at <hazmat.dot.gov/hmep/guide_flow_surveys.pdf>. *The North American Emergency Response Guidebook*, available at <hazmat.dot.gov/ohmform.htm#erg>, can be used to approximate the Vulnerable Zones around these transportation routes. However, use of the procedures in the *Technical Guidance for Hazards Analysis* or more advanced methods identified in the *Handbook of Chemical Hazard Analysis Procedures* is preferred.

[5] The Census Bureau's Web site at <censtats.census.gov> provides ZIP code-level data on the number of businesses in each economic sector, broken down by number of employees. These data can be overlaid onto risk areas for different hazards such as 500-year floodplains, hurricane surge zones, or earthquake seismic zones to develop estimates of the community's economic vulnerability to disaster impact.

[6] Further information about HAZUS-MH is available at the HAZUS Resource Center <www.fema.gov/hazus>. This source includes data on HAZUS-MH hardware and software requirements, manuals, case studies, and contacts for membership in Users Groups.

CHAPTER TEN

INCIDENT COMMAND SYSTEM (ICS)

He who fails to plan, plans to fail.
—Proverb

KEY TERMS

Incident Command Center (ICS)
Incident Management
Emergency Operations
Chemical Agent
Biological Agent
Nuclear/Radiological Agent
Improvised Nuclear Device (IND)
Radiological Dispersal Device (RDD)
Weapons of Mass Destruction (WMD)

OBJECTIVES

- Define Incident Command System (ICS).

- Explain the rationale for the ICS and the benefits it provides.

- Explain the relationship between the Standardized Emergency Management System (SEMS) and the ICS.

- Identify the role of the Incident Commander (IC).

- Describe the significance of resource management in emergency management.

DISCUSSION TOPICS

- Why is a standardized command system important in emergency response?

- What are the benefits of unified command to incident commanders and to the front line responders?

- How does the private sector enhance disaster response?

10

INTRODUCTION

The Incident Command System (ICS) is a well-defined yet dynamic system that provides a "blueprint" for emergency and disaster response. ICS makes possible the efficient coordination of responding agencies, whether or not they have trained or worked together before, so that emergencies of any size and level of complexity can be handled effectively and safely.

The intent is to provide a coordinated response at the local level flexible enough to be adaptable to the potential threats in any particular geographical area, but structured enough that responding agencies that have adopted the principles of ICS can easily work together.

This chapter will examine two distinct concepts in modern catastrophic event planning by contrasting incident management principles with emergency operations planning. In the simplest terms, incident management—a concept we have already discussed at great lengths in this text—involves preparation, planning, and steps for tactical execution during the rescue and response phase of a catastrophic event. Emergency operations planning on the other hand advocates what is called an "all-hazards" approach which uses a comprehensive planning strategy to address an overall prevention and mitigation posture for a broad variety of potential threat scenarios.

In this chapter, we will briefly examine the Department of Homeland Security's National Incident Management System as a refresher of ICS concepts, which have already been discussed in this text. The remainder of the chapter will be allocated to FEMA's Emergency Operations Plan for a Weapons of Mass Destruction (WMD) incident. Throughout your reading, compare and contrast what you have already learned about the ICS system with the layout, detail, and structure of an all-hazards EOPapproach. In particular, notice the emphasis on pre-event planning and preparation and identification of resources for a variety of different possibilities evident in an EOP plan.

NATIONAL INCIDENT MANAGEMENT SYSTEM[1]

Developed by the Secretary of Homeland Security at the request of the President, the National Incident Management System (NIMS) integrates effective practices in emergency preparedness and response into a comprehensive national framework for incident management. The NIMS will enable responders at all levels to work together more effectively to manage domestic incidents no matter what the cause, size or complexity.

The benefits of the NIMS system will be significant:

- Standardized organizational structures, processes and procedures;

- Standards for planning, training and exercising, and personnel qualification standards;

- Equipment acquisition and certification standards;

- Interoperable communications processes, procedures and systems;

- Information management systems; and

- Supporting technologies—voice and data communications systems, information systems, data display systems and specialized technologies.

EMERGENCY OPERATIONS PLANNING[2]

Guide for All-Hazard Emergency Operations Planning
State and Local Guide (101)
Chapter 6
Attachment G — Terrorism
Federal Emergency Management Agency
April 2001
TABLE OF CONTENTS

CHAPTER 6
HAZARD-UNIQUE PLANNING CONSIDERATIONS
ATTACHMENT G — TERRORISM

A. Purpose

The purpose of Attachment G is to aid State and local emergency planners in developing and maintaining a Terrorist Incident Appendix (TIA) to an Emergency Operations Plan (EOP) for incidents involving terrorist-initiated weapons of mass destruction (WMD).[3] The planning guidance in this Attachment was prepared with the assistance of the Departments of Defense, Energy, Agriculture, Health and Human Services, Justice, and Veterans Affairs; the Environmental Protection Agency; the Nuclear Regulatory Commission; the National Emergency Management Association; and the International Association of Emergency Managers.

State and local governments have primary responsibility in planning for and managing the consequences of a terrorist incident using available resources in the critical hours before Federal assistance can arrive. The information presented in this Attachment should help planners develop a TIA that integrates the Federal, State, and local responses. The TIA resulting from this guidance should supplement existing State and local EOPs. A suggested format for a TIA is shown in Tab A.

Federal departments and agencies have developed plans and capabilities for an integrated Federal response to a WMD incident. This Attachment summarizes that response for State and local planners. The Federal Response Plan (FRP), including its Terrorism Incident Annex, provides additional information.

While primarily intended for the use of planners, this Attachment contains information that may be of value to first responders. Planners should consider whether, and how best, to incorporate such information into their plans, procedures, and training materials for first responders.

B. The Hazard

The TIA should identify and discuss the nature of the WMD hazard(s), the hazard agents, potential targets, and release areas, as described below.

1. **Nature of the Hazard.** The hazard may be chemical, biological, nuclear/radiological, and/or explosive.

   a. **Initial Warning.** While specific events may vary, the emergency response and the protocol followed should remain consistent. When an overt WMD incident has occurred, the initial call for help will likely come through the local 911 center. This caller probably will not identify the incident as a terrorist incident, but rather state that there was an explosion, a major "accident," or a mass casualty event. Information relayed through the dispatcher prior to arrival of first responders on scene, as well as the initial assessment, will provide first responders with the basic data to begin responding to the incident. With increased awareness and training about WMD incidents, first responders should recognize that a WMD incident has occurred. The information provided in this Attachment applies where it becomes obvious or strongly suspected that an incident has been intentionally perpetrated to harm people, compromise the public's safety and well-being, disrupt essential government services, or damage the area's economy or environment.

b. **Initial Detection.** The initial detection of a WMD terrorist attack will likely occur at the local level by either first responders or private entities (e.g., hospitals, corporations, etc.). Consequently, first responders and members of the medical community—both public and private—should be trained to identify hazardous agents and take appropriate actions. State and local health departments, as well as local emergency first responders, will be relied upon to identify unusual symptoms, patterns of symptom occurrence, and any additional cases of symptoms as the effects spread throughout the community and beyond. First responders must be protected from the hazard prior to treating victims. Tab D contains an overview of first responder concerns and indicators related to chemical, biological, and nuclear/radiological WMDs.

The detection of a terrorism incident involving covert biological agents (as well as some chemical agents) will most likely occur through the recognition of similar symptoms or syndromes by clinicians in hospital or clinical settings. Detection of biological agents could occur days or weeks after exposed individuals have left the site of the release. Instead, the "scene" will shift to public health facilities receiving unusual numbers of patients, the majority of whom will self-transport.

c. **Investigation and Containment of Hazards.** Local first responders will provide initial assessment or scene surveillance of a hazard caused by an act of WMD terrorism. The proper local, State, and Federal authorities capable of dealing with and containing the hazard should be alerted to a suspected WMD attack after State/local health departments recognize the occurrence of symptoms that are highly unusual or of an unknown cause. Consequently, State and local emergency responders must be able to assess the situation and request assistance as quickly as possible. For a list of Federal departments and agencies with counterterrorism-specific roles, see Tab B; for telephone and online resources from selected organizations, see Tab C.

2. Hazard Agents

a. **Chemical.** Chemical agents are intended to kill, seriously injure, or incapacitate people through physiological effects. A terrorist incident involving a chemical agent will demand immediate reaction from emergency responders—fire departments, police, hazardous materials (HazMat) teams, emergency medical services (EMS), and emergency room staff—who will need adequate training and equipment. Hazardous chemicals, including industrial chemicals and agents, can be introduced via aerosol devices (e.g., munitions, sprayers, or aerosol generators), breaking containers, or covert dissemination. Such an attack might involve the release of a chemical warfare agent, such as a nerve or blister agent or an industrial chemical, which may have serious consequences. Some indicators of the possible use of chemical agents are listed in Table1. Early in an investigation, it may not be

Table 1. General Indicators of Possible Chemical Agent Use

Stated Threat to Release a Chemical Agent

Unusual Occurrence of Dead or Dying Animals
- For example, lack of insects, dead birds

Unexplained Casualties
- Multiple victims
- Surge of similar 911 calls
- Serious illnesses
- Nausea, disorientation, difficulty breathing, or convulsions
- Definite casualty patterns

Unusual Liquid, Spray, or Vapor
- Droplets, oily film
- Unexplained odor
- Low-lying clouds/fog unrelated to weather

Suspicious Devices or Packages
- Unusual metal debris
- Abandoned spray devices
- Unexplained munitions

obvious whether an outbreak was caused by an infectious agent or a hazardous chemical; however, most chemical attacks will be localized, and their effects will be evident within a few minutes. There are both persistent and non-persistent chemical agents. Persistent agents remain in the affected area for hours, days, or weeks. Non-persistent agents have high evaporation rates, are lighter than air, and disperse rapidly, thereby losing their ability to cause casualties after 10 to 15 minutes, although they may be more persistent in small, unventilated areas.

b. **Biological.** Recognition of a biological hazard can occur through several methods, including identification of a credible threat, discovery of bioterrorism evidence (devices, agent, clandestine lab), diagnosis (identification of a disease caused by an agent identified as a possible bioterrorism agent), and detection (gathering and interpretation of public health surveillance data).

When people are exposed to a pathogen such as anthrax or smallpox, they may not know that they have been exposed, and those who are infected, or subsequently become infected, may not feel sick for some time. This delay between exposure and onset of illness, or incubation period, is characteristic of infectious diseases. The incubation period may range from several hours to a few weeks, depending on the exposure and pathogen. Unlike acute incidents involving explosives or some hazardous chemicals, the initial response to a biological attack on civilians is likely to be made by direct patient care providers and the public health community.

Table 2. General Indicators of Possible Biological Agent Use

Stated Threat to Release a Biological Agent
Unusual Occurrence of Dead or Dying Animals

Unusual Casualties
- Unusual illness for region/area
- Definite pattern inconsistent with natural disease

Unusual Liquid, Spray, or Vapor
- Spraying and suspicious devices or packages

Terrorists could also employ a biological agent that would affect agricultural commodities over a large area (e.g., wheat rust or a virus affecting livestock), potentially devastating the local or even national economy. The response to agricultural bioterrorism should also be considered during the planning process.

Responders should be familiar with the characteristics of the biological agents of greatest concern for use in a bioterrorism event (see Tab C for resources). Unlike victims of exposure to chemical or radiological agents, victims of biological agent attack may serve as carriers of the disease with the capability of infecting others (e.g., smallpox, plague). Some indicators of biological attack are given in Table2.

c. **Nuclear/Radiological.** The difficulty of responding to a nuclear or radiological incident is compounded by the nature of radiation itself. In an explosion, the fact that radioactive material was involved may or may not be obvious, depending upon the nature of the explosive device used. Unless confirmed by radiological detection equipment, the presence of a radiation hazard is difficult to ascertain. Although many detection devices exist, most are designed to detect specific types and levels of radiation and may not be appropriate for measuring or ruling out the presence of radiological hazards. Table 3 lists some indicators of a radiological release.

Table 3. General Indicators of Possible Nuclear Weapon/Radiological Agent Use

- A stated threat to deploy a nuclear or radiological device
- The presence of nuclear or radiological equipment (e.g., spent fuel canisters or nuclear transport vehicles)
- Nuclear placards or warning materials along with otherwise unexplained casualties

The scenarios constituting an intentional nuclear/radiological emergency include the following:

(1) Use of an **Improvised Nuclear Device (IND)** includes any explosive device designed to cause a nuclear yield. Depending on the type of trigger device used, either uranium or plutonium isotopes can fuel these devices. While "weapons-grade" material increases the efficiency of a given device, materials of less than weapons grade can still be used.

(2) Use of a **Radiological Dispersal Device (RDD)** includes any explosive device utilized to spread radioactive material upon detonation. Any improvised explosive device could be used by placing it in close proximity to radioactive material.

(3) Use of a **Simple RDD** that spreads radiological material without the use of an explosive. Any nuclear material (including medical isotopes or waste) can be used in this manner.

    d. **Conventional Explosive Devices.** The easiest to obtain and use of all weapons is still a conventional explosive device, or improvised bomb, which may be used to cause massive local destruction or to disperse chemical, biological, or radiological agents. The components are readily available, as are detailed instructions to construct such a device. Improvised explosive devices are categorized as being explosive or incendiary, employing high or low filler explosive materials to explode and/or cause fires. Bombs and firebombs are cheap and easily constructed, involve low technology, and are the terrorist weapon most likely to be encountered. Large, powerful devices can be outfitted with timed or remotely triggered detonators and can be designed to be activated by light, pressure, movement, or radio transmission. The potential exists for single or multiple bombing incidents in single or multiple municipalities. Historically, less than five percent of actual or attempted bombings were preceded by a threat. Explosive materials can be employed covertly with little signature, and are not readily detectable. Secondary devices may be targeted against responders.

    e. **Combined Hazards.** WMD agents can be combined to achieve a synergistic effect—greater in total effect than the sum of their individual effects. They may be combined to achieve both immediate and delayed consequences. Mixed infections or intoxications may occur, thereby complicating or delaying diagnosis. Casualties of multiple agents may exist; casualties may also suffer from multiple effects, such as trauma and burns from an explosion, which exacerbate the likelihood of agent contamination. Attacks may be planned and executed so as to take advantage of the reduced effectiveness of protective measures produced by employment of an initial WMD agent. Finally, the potential exists for multiple incidents in single or multiple municipalities.

3. **Potential Targets.** In determining the risk areas within a jurisdiction (and in multiple jurisdiction areas participating in an emergency response), the vulnerabilities of potential targets should be identified, and the targets themselves should be prepared to respond to a WMD incident. In-depth

vulnerability assessments are needed for determining a response to such an incident. For examples of vulnerability areas to be considered, see Tab E. In addition, reference Risk Management Plans and Emergency Planning and Community Right-to-Know Act (EPCRA) Plans, which include potential target areas and information on industrial chemical facilities, can be obtained from the Local Emergency Planning Committee (LEPC) in your area.

4. **Release Area.** Standard models are available for estimating the effects of a nuclear, chemical, or biological release, including the area affected and consequences to population, resources, and infrastructure. Some of these models include databases on infrastructure that can be useful in preparing the TIA. A good source of information on available Federal government models is the *Directory of Atmospheric Transport and Diffusion Consequence Assessment Models*, published by the Office of the Federal Coordinator for Meteorology (OFCM). The directory is available both in print and online on OFCM's web page, http://www.ofcm.gov (select "Publications," then "Publications Available Online," then the directory). The directory includes information on the capabilities and limitations of each model, technical requirements, and points of contact.

C. Situations and Assumptions

1. **Situation.** The situation section of a TIA should discuss what constitutes a potential or actual WMD incident. It should present a concise, clear, and accurate overview of potential events and discuss a general concept of operations for response. Any information already included in the EOP need not be duplicated in the TIA. The situation overview should include as much information as possible that is unique to WMD response actions, including the suggested elements listed in Table 4.

   WMD situation planning should include provisions for working with Federal crisis and consequence management agencies. The key to successful emergency response involves smooth coordination with multiple agencies and officials from various jurisdictions regarding all aspects of the response.

2. **Assumptions.** Although situations may vary, planning assumptions remain the same.
   a. The first responder (e.g., local emergency or law enforcement personnel) or health and medical personnel will in most cases initially detect and evaluate the potential or actual incident, assess casualties (if any), and determine whether assistance is required. If so, State support will be requested and provided. This assessment will be based on warning or notification of a WMD incident that may be received from law enforcement, emergency response agencies, or the public.
   b. The incident may require Federal support. To ensure that there is one overall Lead Federal Agency (LFA), the Federal Emergency Management Agency (FEMA) is authorized to support the Department of Justice (DOJ) (as delegated to the Federal Bureau of Investigation [FBI]) until the Attorney General transfers the overall LFA role to FEMA. (Source: FRP, Terrorism Incident Annex) In addition, FEMA is designated as the lead agency for consequence management within the

Table 4. Suggested Emergency Operations Plan Elements

- **Maps**   Use detailed, current maps and charts.
- Include demographic information.
- Use natural and manmade boundaries and structures to identify risk areas.
- Annotate evacuation routes and alternatives.
- Annotate in-place sheltering locations.

- **Environment**[a]   Determine response routes and times.
- Include bodies of water with dams or levees (these could become contaminated).
- Specify special weather and climate features that could alter the effects of a WMD (e.g., strong winds, heavy rains, etc.).

- **Population**[b]   Identify those most susceptible to WMD effects or otherwise hindered or unable to care for themselves.
- Identify areas where large concentrations of the population might be located, such as sports arenas and major transportation centers.
- List areas that may include retirement communities.
- Note location of correctional facilities.
- Note locations of hospitals/medical centers/schools/day care centers where multiple evacuees may need assistance.
- Identify non-English-speaking populations.

- **Metropolitan**   Identify multi-jurisdictional perimeters and boundaries.
- Identify potentially overlapping areas for response.
- Identify rural, urban, suburban, and city (e.g., city-sprawl/surroundings) mutual risk areas.
- Identify specific or unique characteristics such as interchanges, choke points, traffic lights, traffic schemes and patterns, access roads, tunnels, bridges, railroad crossings, and overpasses and/or cloverleafs.

---

[a] The environmental Protection Agency (EPA) will work with local and State officials on environmental planning issues.
[b] The Department of Veterans Affairs (VA), in close cooperation with the Department of Health and Human Services (HHS), will work with State and local officials on these issues.

United States and its territories. FEMA retains authority and responsibility to act as the lead agency for consequence management throughout the Federal response. In this capacity, FEMA will coordinate Federal assistance requested through State authorities using normal FRP mechanisms.

    c. Federal response will include experts in the identification, containment, and recovery of WMD (chemical, biological, or nuclear/radiological).

    d. Federal consequence management response will entail the involvement of FEMA, additional FRP departments and agencies, and the American Red Cross as required.

e. **Jurisdictional areas** of responsibility and working perimeters defined by local, State, and Federal departments and agencies may overlap. Perimeters may be used to control access to the affected area, target public information messages, assign operational sectors among responding organizations, and assess potential effects on the population and the environment. Control of these perimeters may be enforced by different authorities, which will impede the overall response if adequate coordination is not established.

D. Concept of Operations

The TIA should include a concept of operations section to explain the jurisdiction's overall concept for responding to a WMD incident. Topics should include division of local, State, Federal, and any intermediate interjurisdictional responsibilities; activation of the EOP; and the other elements set forth in Chapter 4 (Basic Plan Content) of State and Local Guide (SLG) 101. A suggested format for a TIA is given in Tab A.

1. **Direction and Control.** Local government emergency response organizations will respond to the incident scene(s) and make appropriate and rapid notifications to local and State authorities (Table 5).[4] Control of the incident scene(s) most likely will be established by local first responders from either fire or police. The Incident Command System (ICS) that was initially established likely will transition into a Unified Command System (UCS) as mutual-aid partners and State and Federal responders arrive to augment the local responders. It is recommended that local, State, and Federal regional law enforcement officials develop consensus "rules of engagement" early in the planning process to smooth the transition from ICS to UCS. This UC structure will facilitate both crisis management and consequence management activities. The UC structure used at the scene will expand as support units and agency representatives arrive to support crisis and consequence management operations. The site of a terrorist incident is a crime scene as well as a disaster scene, although the protection of lives, health, and safety remains the top priority.

   Table 1 summarizes the coordination relationships between the UC and other response entities. It is assumed that normal disaster coordination accomplished at State and local emergency operations centers (EOCs) and other locations away from the scene would be addressed in the basic EOP. Any special concerns relating to State and local coordination with Federal organizations should be addressed in the TIA.

   Local, State, and Federal interface with the FBI On-Scene Commander (OSC) is coordinated through the Joint Operations Center (JOC). FEMA (represented in the command group) will recommend joint operational priorities to the FBI based on consultation with the FEMA-led consequence management group in the JOC. The FBI, working with local and State officials in the command group at the JOC, will establish operational priorities.

   Response to any terrorist event requires direction and control. The planner must consider the unique characteristics of the event, identify the likely stage at which coordinated resources will be required, and tailor the direction and control process to merge into the ongoing public health response.

Table 5. Responses to a WMD Incident and the Participants Involved

Events	
1. Incident occurs.	
2. 911 center receives calls, elicits information, dispatches first relays information to first responders prior to their arrival on scene, makes notifications, and consults existing databases of chemical hazards in the community, as required.	911 Center, as required. First responders.
3. First responders arrive on scene and make initial assessment. Establish Incident Command. Determine potential weapon of mass destruction (WMD) incident and possible terrorist involvement; warn additional responders to scene of potential secondary hazards/devices. Perform any obvious rescues as incident permits. Establish security perimeter. Determine needs for additional assistance. Begin triage and treatment of victims. Begin hazard agent identification.	Incident Command: Fire, Law Enforcement, Emergency Medical Services (EMS), and HazMat unit(s).
4. Incident Command manages incident response; notifies medical facility, emergency management (EM), and other local organizations outlined in Emergency Operations Plan; requests notification of Federal Bureau of Investigation (FBI) Field Office.	Incident Command.
5. Special Agent in Charge (SAC) assesses information, supports local law enforcement, and determines WMD terrorist incident has occurred. Notifies Strategic Information and Operations Center (SIOC), activates Joint Operations Center (JOC), coordinates the crisis management aspects of WMD incident, and acts as the Federal on-scene manager for the U.S. government while FBI is Lead Federal Agency (LFA).	FBI Field Office: SAC

6. Local Emergency Operations Center (EOC) activated. Support Incident Command, as required by Incident Commander (IC). Coordinates consequence management activities (e.g., mass care). Local authorities declare state of emergency. Coordinates with State EOC and State and Federal agencies, as required. Requests State and Federal assistance, as necessary.	Local EOC: Local agencies, as identified in basic Emergency Operations Plan (EOP).
7. Strategic local coordination of crisis management activities. Brief President, National Security Council (NSC), and Attorney General. Provide Headquarters support to JOCC. Domestic Emergency Support Team (DEST) may be deployed. Notification of FEMA by FBI/SIOC triggers FEMA actions.[a]	SIOC: FBI, Department of Justice (DOJ), Department of Energy (DOE), Federal Emergency Management Agency (FEMA), Department of Defense (DoD), Department of Health and Human Services (HHS), and Environmental Protection Agency (EPA).
8. Manage criminal investigation. Establish Joint Information Center (JIC). State and local agencies and FEMA ensure coordination of consequence management activities.	FBI: other Federal, Sate, and local law enforcement agencies. Local Emergency Management (EM) representatives. FEMA, DoD, DOE, HHS, EPA, and other Federal Response Plan (FRP) agencies, as required.
9. State EMS support local consequence management. Brief Governor. Declare state of emergency. Develop/coordinate requests for Federal assistance through FEMA Regional Operations Center (ROC). Coordinate State request for Federal consequence management assistance.	State EOC: State EMS and State agencies, as outlined in EOP.
10. DEST provides assistance to FBI SAC. Merges into JOC, as appropriate.	DEST: DoD, DOJ, HHS, FEMA, EPA, and DOE.
11. FEMA representative coordinates Consequence Management Group. Expedites Federal consequences management activities and monitors crisis management response to advise on areas of decision that could impact consequence management response.	FBI, FEMA, EPA, DoD, DOE, HHS, and other FRP agencies.

12. Crisis management response activities to incident may continue. Operations, Hazardous Materials Response Unit (HMRU), Joint Technical Operations Team, Joint Inter-Agency Intelligence Support, and additional authorities, as needed.	FBI, Incident Command System (ICS), Special ROC and regional-level agencies.
13. Federal response efforts coordinated and mission assignments determined. A consequence management support team deploys to incident site. All EOCs coordinate.	
14. An Emergency Response Team—Advance Element (ERT-A) deploys to State EOC and incident site, as needed. Base installation sites identified for mobilization centers. Liaisons from WMD-related agencies required for Emergency Support Team (EST) and ROC. Disaster Field Office (DFO) liaisons as needed (may be after extended response phase.	ERT-A: Regional-level FEMA and FRP primary support agencies, as needed.
15. A consequence management support team provides operational technical assistance to Unified Command.	FEMA, DOE, DoD, HHS, EPA, and FBI.
16. Recovery operations. Transition of LFA from FBI to FEMA.	

ª FEMA may initiate FRP response prior to any FBI/SIOC notification.

Operations, Hazardous Materials Response Unit

2. **Communications.** In the event of a WMD incident, rapid and secure communication is crucial to ensure a prompt and coordinated response. Strengthening communications among first responders, clinicians, emergency rooms, hospitals, mass care providers, and emergency management personnel must be given top priority in planning.

3. **Warning.** Every incident is different. There may or may not be warning of a potential WMD incident. Factors involved range from intelligence gathered from various law enforcement or intelligence agency sources to an actual notification from the terrorist organization or individual. The EOP should have HazMat facilities and transportation routes already mapped, along with emergency procedures necessary to respond.
   a. **The warning or notification** of a potential WMD terrorist incident could come from many sources; therefore, open communication

among local, State, and Federal law enforcement agencies and emergency response officials is critical. The local FBI Field Office must be notified of any suspected terrorist threats or incidents.

b. **Threat Level.** The FBI operates with a four-tier threat level system:

(1) **Level Four (Minimal Threat).** Received threats do not warrant actions beyond normal liaison notifications or placing assets or resources on a heightened alert.

(2) **Level Three (Potential Threat).** Intelligence or an articulated threat indicates the potential for a terrorist incident; however, this threat has not yet been assessed as credible.

(3) **Level Two (Credible Threat).** A threat assessment indicates that a potential threat is credible and confirms the involvement of WMD in a developing terrorist incident. The threat increases in significance when the presence of an explosive device or WMD capable of causing a significant destructive event, prior or actual injury or loss is confirmed or when intelligence and circumstances indicate a high probability that a device exists.

(4) **Level One (WMD Incident).** AWMD terrorism incident has occurred resulting in mass casualties that requires immediate Federal planning and preparation to provide support to State and local authorities. The Federal response is primarily directed toward the safety and welfare of the public and the preservation of human life.

4. **Emergency Public Information.** Accurate and expedited dissemination of information is critical when a WMD incident has occurred. Preservation of life and property may hinge on instructions and directions given by authorized officials. In the event of a terrorist attack, the public and the media must be provided with accurate and timely information on emergency operations. Establishing and maintaining an effective rumor control mechanism will help clarify emergency information for the public. Initial interaction with the media is likely to be implemented by an information officer, as directed by the Incident Commander. To facilitate the release of information, the FBI may establish a Joint Information Center (JIC) comprised of representatives from Federal, State, and local authorities for the purpose of managing the dissemination of information to the public, media, and businesses potentially affected by the incident. An act of terrorism is likely to cause widespread panic, and ongoing communication of accurate and up-to-date information will help calm fears and limit collateral effects of the attack.

5. **Protective Actions.** Evacuation may be required from inside the perimeter of the scene to guard against further casualties, either from contamination by an agent released or the possibility that additional WMD or secondary devices targeting emergency responders are present. "In-place sheltering" may be required if the area must be contained because of the need for quarantine or if it is determined to be safer for individuals to remain in place. The TIA should be flexible enough to accommodate either contingency. As with any

emergency, State and local officials must be involved in making protective action decisions. Multi-jurisdictional issues regarding mass care, sheltering, and evacuation should be pre-coordinated and included in the TIA.

6. **Mass Care.** The location of mass care facilities will be based partly on the hazard agent involved. Decontamination, if it is necessary, may need to precede sheltering and other needs of the victims to prevent further damage from the hazard agent, either to the victims themselves or to the care providers. The American Red Cross (the primary agency for mass care), the Department of Health and Human Services, and the Department of Veterans Affairs should be actively involved with the planning process to determine both in-place and mobile mass care systems for the TIA. A "mid-point" or intermediary station may be needed to move victims out of the way of immediate harm. This would allow responders to provide critical attention (e.g., decontamination and medical services) and general lifesaving support, then evacuate victims to a mass care location for further attention. General issues to consider for inclusion in the TIA are [as follows]:
   a. Location, setup, and equipment for decontamination stations, if any.
   b. Mobile triage support and qualified personnel.
   c. Supplies and personnel to support in-place sheltering.
   d. Evacuation to an intermediary location to provide decontamination and medical attention.
   e. Determination of safety perimeters (based on agent).

7. **Health and Medical.** The basic EOP should already contain a Health and Medical Annex. Issues that may be different during a WMD incident and that should be addressed in the TIA include decontamination, safety of victims and responders, in-place sheltering versus evacuation, and multihazard/multiagent triage. Planning should anticipate the need to handle large numbers of people who may or may not be contaminated but who are fearful about their medical well-being.

   The response to a bioterrorism incident will require the active collaboration of the clinicians and local public health authorities responsible for disease monitoring and outbreak investigation. Their activities should be factored into the overall response process.

8. **Resources Management.** The following considerations are highly relevant to WMD incidents and should be addressed, if appropriate, in one or more appendixes to a resource management annex:
   a. Nuclear, biological, and chemical response resources that are available through interjurisdictional agreements (e.g., interstate pacts).
   b. Unique resources that are available through State authorities (e.g., National Guard units).
   c. Unique resources that are available to State and local jurisdictions through Federal authorities (e.g., the National Pharmaceutical Stockpile, a national asset providing delivery of antibiotics, antidotes, and medical supplies to the scene of a WMD incident).
   d. Unique expertise that may be available through academic, research, or private organizations.

E. Organization and Assignment of Responsibilities

As with any hazard-specific emergency, the organization for management of local response may vary for a WMD incident and should therefore be defined in the TIA. The effects of a terrorist act involving a WMD have the potential to overwhelm local resources, which may require assistance from State or Federal governments. The following response roles and responsibilities should be articulated in the TIA.

1. **Local Emergency Responders.** Local fire departments, law enforcement personnel, HazMat teams, and EMS will be among the first to respond to a WMD incident. As response efforts escalate, the local emergency management agency and health department will help coordinate needed services. *Primary Duties.* The duties of local departments, such as fire, law enforcement, and EMS, along with those of the local emergency management agency and health department should be addressed in their respective EOPs. Any special duties necessary to respond to a suspected terrorist WMD incident should be set forth in the local TIA.

2. **Interjurisdictional Responsibilities.** The formal arrangements and agreements for emergency response to a WMD incident among neighboring jurisdictions, State, Tribal, local, and neighboring States (and those jurisdictions physically located in those States) should be made **prior** to an incident. When coordinating and planning, the Risk Assessment and Risk Area sections of the TIA(areas where potential multiple jurisdictions could overlap and interplay) will be readily identifiable. Federal response is already predisposed for interagency and interdepartmental coordination.

3. **State Emergency Responders.** If requested by local officials, the State emergency management agency has capabilities to support local emergency management authorities and the Incident Commander (IC). *Primary Duties.* The duties of all responding State agencies should be addressed in the State EOP. Any special duties necessary to respond to a WMD incident should be set forth in the State's TIA.

4. **Local Emergency Planning Committees (LEPCs), State Emergency Response Commissions (SERCs), and Tribal Emergency Response Commissions (TERCs).** These entities are established under the Superfund Amendments and Reauthorization Act of 1986 (SARA) Title III and the implementing regulations of the Environmental Protection Agency (EPA). LEPCs develop and maintain local hazardous material emergency plans and receive notifications of releases of hazardous substances. SERCs and TERCs supervise the operation of the LEPCs and administer the community right-to-know provisions of SARA Title III, including collection and distribution of information about facility inventories of hazardous substances, chemicals, and toxins. LEPCs will have detailed information about industrial chemicals within the community. It may be advisable for LEPCs, SERCs, and TERCs to establish Memoranda of Agreement (MOAs) with agencies and organizations to provide specialized resources and capabilities for response to WMD incidents.

Primary Duties. Any responsibilities germane to terrorism preparedness or response should be outlined in local, State and Tribal hazardous materials emergency response plans or the hazardous materials annex to the local emergency plan.

5. **Federal Emergency Responders.** Upon determination of a credible WMD threat, or if such an incident actually occurs, the Federal government may respond through the appropriate departments and agencies. These departments and agencies may include FEMA, the Department of Justice (DOJ) and FBI, the Department of Defense (DoD), the Department of Energy (DOE), the Department of Health and Human Services (HHS), the EPA, the Department of Agriculture (USDA), the Nuclear Regulatory Commission (NRC), and possibly the American Red Cross and Department of Veterans Affairs. The roles and responsibilities for Federal departments and agencies participating in both crisis management and consequence management are discussed in more detail in Tab B. See the United States Government Interagency Domestic Terrorism Concept of Operations Plan and the Terrorism Incident Annex to the Federal Response Plan for information on the roles and responsibilities of Federal departments and agencies responding to terrorism incidents involving WMD.

Primary Duties. Upon determining that a WMD terrorist incident is credible, the FBI Special Agent in Charge (SAC), through the FBI Headquarters, will initiate liaison with other Federal agencies to activate their operations centers. The responsible FEMA region(s) may activate a Regional Operations Center (ROC) and deploy a representative(s) to the affected State(s). When the responsible FEMA region(s) activates a ROC, the region(s) will notify the responsible FBI Field Office(s) to request a liaison. If the FBI activates the Strategic Information and Operations Center (SIOC) at FBI Headquarters, then other Federal agencies, including FEMA, will deploy a representative(s) to the SIOC, as required. Once the FBI has determined the need to activate a Joint Operations Center (JOC) to support the incident site, Federal, State, and local agencies may be requested by FEMA to support the Consequence Management Group located at the JOC.

F. Administration and Logistics

There are many factors that make response to a WMD terrorist incident unique. Unlike some natural disasters (e.g., hurricanes, floods, winter storms, drought, etc.), the administration and logistics for response to a WMD incident require special considerations. For example, there may be little or no forewarning, immediately obvious indicators, or WMD knowledge (lead time) available to officials and citizens. Because the release of a WMD may not be immediately apparent, caregivers, emergency response personnel, and first responders are in imminent danger themselves of becoming casualties before the actual identification of the crime can be made. Incidents could escalate quickly from one scene to multiple locations and jurisdictions.

TAB A

SUGGESTED FORMAT FOR A TERRORIST INCIDENT APPENDIX
TO A BASIC ALL-HAZARDS EMERGENCY PLAN
Supplement to a State or Local Basic Emergency Operations Plan

A. PROMULGATION DOCUMENT

B. SIGNATURE PAGE

C. AUTHORITIES AND REFERENCES

D. TABLE OF CONTENTS

E. PURPOSE

The purpose of the Terrorist Incident Appendix (TIA) is to develop a consequence management plan for responding to and recovering from a terrorist-initiated weapon of mass destruction (WMD) incident. The TIA supplements the Emergency Operations Plan (EOP) already in effect.

F. The Hazard

1. **Nature of the Hazard** {Identify WMD hazards that could potentially affect the jurisdiction.}

2. **Incident** {Statement of the situations that would cause the consequence management plan for a WMD incident to go into operation.}

3. **Hazard Agents** {Separate sections for each of the following hazards may be used, as risk area, treatment, etc., are unique to each incident. The plan for identification of the hazard agent may be included here, as well as an assessment of the risk and definition of the risk area.}
   a. **Chemical** {Statement on chemical terrorism. A Tab with the names of chemicals, composition, reference materials (activation, lethality, treatment, handling, mixture, etc.) may be created and included in the TIA.}
      (1) Assessment of risk
      (2) Risk area
   b. **Biological** {Statement on biological terrorism. Reference material (identification, handling, treatment, lethality, etc.,) may be created and included in the TIA in a Tab.}
      (1) Assessment of risk
      (2) Risk area
   c. **Nuclear/Radiological** {Statement on nuclear terrorism. Reference material can be listed in a Tab and may include lethality, handling, treatment, etc.}
      (1) Assessment of risk
      (2) Risk area
   d. **Explosives** {Statement on explosives terrorism. A Tab with the names of explosives, composition, reference materials (activation, lethality, treatment, handling, mixture, etc.) may be created and included in the TIA.}
      (1)　Assessment of risk
      (2)　Risk area

G. Situation and Assumptions

1. **Situation:** Basic information on the terrorist incident threat or potential threat. A description of the locale for which the plan is being written. Any information listed below that is already included in the EOP need not be duplicated here. A general description of the area may be given, with the following information in a Tab. Consideration should be given to maintaining information in a secure place.

    a. **Environment**
       (1) Geographic conditions (terrain).
       (2) Weather (climate).
    b. **Population:** General and special needs individuals, retirement communities and nursing homes, schools, day care centers, correctional facilities, non-English-speaking communities, etc.
    c. **Metropolitan:** Rural/urban/suburban/city (city-sprawl/surroundings).
    d. **Critical Infrastructure/Transportation:** Major highways, secondary roads, tertiary roadways, dirt/gravel roads. Details may include interchanges, choke points, traffic lights, traffic schemes and patterns, access roads, tunnels, bridges, railroad crossings, overpasses/cloverleafs.
    e. **Trucking/Transport Activity:** Cargo loading/unloading facilities (type of cargo), waterways (ports, docks, harbors, rivers, streams, lakes, ocean, bays, reservoirs, pipelines, process/treatment facilities, dams, international roll-on/roll-off container shipments, HazMat [oil] flagged registry).
    f. **Airports:** Carriers, flight paths, airport layout (air traffic control tower, runways, passenger terminal, parking).
    g. **Trains/Subways:** Physical rails, interchanges, terminals, tunnels, cargo/passengers.
    h. **Government Facilities:** Post office, law enforcement, fire/rescue, town/city hall, local mayor/governor's residences, Federal buildings, judicial personnel (i.e., judges, prosecutors, residences, offices).
    i. **Recreation Facilities:** Sports arenas, theaters, malls, theme parks.
    j. **Other Facilities:** Financial institutions (banking facilities/loan institutions), universities, colleges, hospitals, and research institutes (nuclear, biological, chemical, medical clinics).
    k. **Military Installations**
    l. **HazMat Facilities:** Emergency Planning and Community Right-to-Know Act (EPCRA) sites with Risk Management Plan requirements, Comprehensive Environmental Response, Compensation, and Liability Act (CERCLA) sites, nonreporting Resource Conservation and Recovery Act (RCRA) facilities (i.e., combustion sites, generating sites, and treatment, storage, and disposal [TSD] sites), facilities inventoried by the Toxic Release Inventory System (TRIS), utilities and nuclear facilities, chemical stockpile and/or manufacturing sites.

2. **Assumptions:** This plan will go into effect when a WMD incident has occurred or a credible threat has been identified.

H. Concept of Operations

1. **Direction and Control** {Based on the above assessments, provide wiring diagram/flow chart showing the chain of command and control. These diagrams/charts may be specific to WMD or more generally pertinent to any incident.}

2. **Communications** {May elaborate on communications described in the basic EOP.}
   a. Security of communications among responding organizations.
   b. Coordination of communications with Federal responders.

3. **Warning**

4. **Emergency Public Information** {The plan should identify specific methods (channels) to notify the public that an incident has occurred, direct their actions, and keep them informed as the situation progresses. Evacuation and sheltering in place are key actions that may need to be communicated to the public, and continuous updating will be required.}

5. **Protective Actions**
   a. In-place sheltering.
   b. Evacuation routes/means of conveyance should be predetermined based on area and type of agent.
   c. Evacuation support.

6. **Mass Care**
   a. Safe location of mass care facilities
   b. Structural safety
   c. Health and medical services
   d. Provisions for food and water
   e. Policy and procedures for pet care

7. **Health and Medical**

8. **Resources Management**

9. **Recovery Operations**

I. Organization and Assignment of Responsibilities

In concert with guidance already in existence, supplementing the EOP, the roles and responsibilities are outlined here for all jurisdictions and entities.

1. Local

2. Interjurisdictional Responsibilities

3. State

4. Tribal

5. Federal

J. Administration and Logistics

The administrative framework for WMD response operations is outlined here.

1. General support requirements

2. Availability of services

3. Mutual aid agreements

4. Emergency Management Assistance Compacts

5. Administrative policies and procedures (e.g., financial record keeping)

K. Tabs

1. Acronyms

2. Key definitions

3. Points of contact

4. Each of the WMD hazard agents may have a separate Tab with subcategories and subsets of information specific to each, including the identification of departments and agencies that have authority and expertise relevant to incidents involving specific agents.
   a. Index of chemical agents.
   b. Index of biological agents.
   c. Index of nuclear/radiological materials.

TAB B

FEDERAL DEPARTMENTS AND AGENCIES: COUNTERTERRORISM-SPECIFIC ROLES

A. FEDERAL EMERGENCY MANAGEMENT AGENCY

FEMA is the lead agency for consequence management and acts in support of the FBI in Washington, DC, and on the scene of the crisis until the U.S. Attorney General transfers the Lead Federal Agency (LFA) role to FEMA. Though State and local officials bear primary responsibility for consequence management, FEMA coordinates the Federal aspects of consequence management in the event of a terrorist act. Under Presidential Decision Directive 39, FEMA supports the overall LFA by operating as the lead agency for consequence management until the overall LFA role is transferred to FEMA and in this capacity determines when consequences are "imminent" for purposes of the Stafford Act. (Source: Federal Response Plan Terrorism Incident Annex, April 1999) Consequence management includes protecting the public health and safety and providing emergency relief to State governments, businesses, and individuals. Additional information on Federal response is given in the United States Government Interagency Domestic Terrorism Concept of Operations Plan (http://www.fema.gov/r-n-r/conplan/). Web site: **www.fema.gov**

1. **Office of the Director/Senior Advisor to the Director for Terrorism Preparedness.** The Senior Advisor (1) keeps the FEMA Director informed of terrorism-related activities, (2) develops and implements strategies for

FEMA involvement in terrorism-related activities, and (3) coordinates overall relationships with other Federal departments and agencies involved in the consequence management of terrorism-related activities.

2. **Preparedness, Training, and Exercises Directorate (PT).** This office provides planning guidance for State and local government. It also trains emergency managers, firefighters, and elected officials in consequence management through the Emergency Management Institute (EMI), National Fire Academy (NFA), and the National Emergency Training Center (NETC) in Emmitsburg, Maryland. EMI offers courses for first responders dealing with the consequences of a terrorist incident. PT conducts exercises in WMD terrorism consequence management through the Comprehensive Exercise Program. These exercises provide the opportunity to investigate the effectiveness of the Federal Response Plan (FRP) to deal with consequence management and test the ability of different levels of response to interact. PT also manages FEMA's Terrorism Consequence Management Preparedness Assistance used by State and local governments for terrorism preparedness planning, training, and exercising.

3. **Mitigation Directorate.** This office has been assigned the responsibility of providing the verified and validated airborne and waterborne hazardous material models. The office also is responsible for developing new, technologically advanced, remote sensing capabilities needed to assess the release and dispersion of hazardous materials, both in air and water, for guiding consequence management response activities.

4. **Response and Recovery Directorate.** This office manages Federal consequence management operations in response to terrorist events. In addition, it manages the Rapid Response Information System, which inventories physical assets and equipment available to State and local officials, and provides a database of chemical and biological agents and safety precautions.

5. **U.S. Fire Administration (USFA).** This administration provides training to firefighters and other first responders through the NFA in conjunction with the Preparedness, Training, and Exercises Directorate. The NFA offers courses pertaining to preparedness and response to terrorist events.

B. DEPARTMENT OF JUSTICE (DOJ)
Web site: **www.usdoj.gov**
Federal Bureau of Investigation. The FBI is the lead agency for crisis management and investigation of all terrorism-related matters, including incidents involving a WMD. Within FBI's role as LFA, the FBI Federal On-Scene Commander (OSC) coordinates the overall Federal response until the Attorney General transfers the LFA role to FEMA. Web site: **www.fbi.gov**

1. **FBI Domestic Terrorism/Counterterrorism Planning Section (DTCTPS).** Within the FBI Counter Terrorism Division is a specialized section containing the Domestic Terrorism Operations Unit, the Weapons of Mass Destruction Operations Unit, the Weapons of Mass Destruction Countermeasures Unit, and the Special Event Management Unit. Each of these units has specific responsibilities in investigations of crimes or allegations of crimes com-

mitted by individuals or groups in violation of the Federal terrorism and/or Weapons of Mass Destruction statutes. The DTCTPS serves as the point of contact (POC) to the FBI field offices and command structure as well as other Federal agencies in incidences of terrorism, the use or suspected use of WMD and/or the evaluation of threat credibility. If the FBI's Strategic Information and Operations Center (SIOC) is operational for exercises or actual incidents, the DTCTPS will provide staff personnel to facilitate the operation of SIOC.

During an incident, the FBI DTCTPS will coordinate the determination of the composition of the Domestic Emergency Support Teams (DEST) and/or the Foreign Emergency Support Teams (FEST). All incidents wherein a WMD is used will be coordinated by the DTCTPS WMD Operations Unit.

2. **FBI Laboratory Division.** Within the FBI's Laboratory Division reside numerous assets, which can deploy to provide assistance in a terrorism/WMD incident. The Hazardous Materials Response Unit (HMRU) personnel are highly trained and knowledgeable and are equipped to direct and assist in the collection of hazardous and/or toxic evidence in a contaminated environment. Similarly, the Evidence Response Team Unit (ERTU) is available to augment the local assets and have been trained in the collection of contaminated evidence. The Crisis Response Unit (CRU) is able to deploy to provide communications support to an incident. The Bomb Data Center (BDC) provides the baseline training to public safety bomb disposal technicians in the United States. BDC is the certification and accreditation authority for public safety agencies operating bomb squads and is in possession of equipment and staff that can be deployed to assist in the resolution of a crisis involving suspected or identified explosive devices. The Explosives Unit (EU) has experts who can assist in analyzing the construction of suspected or identified devices and recommend procedures to neutralize those items.

3. **FBI Critical Incident Response Group (CIRG).** CIRG has developed assets that are designed to facilitate the resolution of crisis incidents of any type. Notably, the Crisis Management Unit (CMU), which conducts training and exercises for the FBI and has developed the concept of the Joint Operations Center (JOC), is available to provide on-scene assistance to the incident and integrate the concept of the JOC and the Incident Command System (ICS) to create efficient management of the situation. CIRG coordinates a highly trained group of skilled negotiators who are adroit in techniques to de-escalate volatile situations. The Hostage Rescue Team (HRT) is a tactical asset, trained to function in contaminated or toxic hazard environments, that is available to assist in the management of the incident.

4. **National Domestic Preparedness Office (NDPO).** NDPO is to coordinate and facilitate all Federal WMD efforts to assist State and local emergency responders with planning, training, equipment, exercise, and health and medical issues necessary to respond to a WMD event. The NDPO's program areas encompass the six broad areas of domestic preparedness requiring coordination and assistance: Planning, Training, Exercises, Equipment, Information Sharing, and Public Health and Medical Services.

Office for State and Local Domestic Preparedness Support (OSLDPS). This office, within the Office of Justice Programs (OJP), has a State and Local Domestic Preparedness Technical Assistance Program that provides technical assistance in three areas: (1) general technical assistance; (2) State strategy technical assistance, and (3) equipment technical assistance. The purpose of this program is to provide direct assistance to State and local jurisdictions in enhancing their capacity and preparedness to respond to WMD terrorist incidents. The program goals are to

- Enhance the ability of State and local jurisdictions to develop, plan, and implement a program for WMD preparedness; and

- Enhance the ability of State and local jurisdictions to sustain and maintain specialized equipment.

Technical assistance available from OSLDPS is provided without charge to requesting State or local jurisdiction. The following organizations are eligible for the State and Local Domestic Preparedness Technical Assistance Program:

- General technical assistance: units and agencies of State and local governments.

- State strategy technical assistance: State administrative agencies, designated by the governor, under the Fiscal Year 1999 State Domestic Preparedness Equipment Program.

- Equipment technical assistance: units and agencies of State and local governments that have received OSLDPS funding to acquire specialized equipment.

Web site: **www.ojp.usdoj.gov/osldps/**

1. **General Technical Assistance.** OSLDPS provides general overall assistance to State and local jurisdictions for preparedness to respond to WMD terrorist incidents. This technical assistance includes [the following]:
   - Assistance in developing and enhancing WMD response plans.
   - Assistance with exercise scenario development and evaluation.
   - Provision of WMD experts to facilitate jurisdictional working groups.
   - Provision of specialized training.

2. **State Strategy Technical Assistance.** OSLDPS provides assistance to States in meeting the needs assessment and comprehensive planning requirements under OSLDPS' Fiscal Year 1999 State Domestic Preparedness Equipment Support Program. Specifically, OSLDPS
   - Assists States in developing their three-year statewide domestic preparedness strategy.
   - Assists States in utilizing the assessment tools for completion of the required needs and threat assessments.

3. **Equipment Technical Assistance.** OSLDPS provides training by mobile training teams on the use and maintenance of specialized WMD response equipment under OSLDPS' Domestic Preparedness Equipment Support Program. This assistance will be delivered on site in eligible jurisdictions. Specifically, OSLDPS

- Provides training on using, sustaining, and maintaining specialized equipment.
- Provides training to technicians on maintenance and calibration of test equipment.
- Provides maintenance and/or calibration of equipment.
- Assists in refurbishing used or damaged equipment.

C. DEPARTMENT OF DEFENSE (DoD)
Web site: **www.defenselink.mil**

In the event of a terrorist attack or act of nature on American soil resulting in the release of chemical, biological, radiological, nuclear material or high-yield explosive (CBRNE) devices, the local law enforcement, fire, and emergency medical personnel who are first to respond may become quickly overwhelmed by the magnitude of the attack. The Department of Defense (DoD) has many unique warfighting support capabilities, both technical and operational, that could be used in support of State and local authorities, if requested by FEMA, as the Lead Federal Agency, to support and manage the consequences of such a domestic event.

Due to the increasing volatility of the threat and the time sensitivity associated with providing effective support to FEMA in domestic CBRNE incident, the Secretary of Defense appointed an Assistant to the Secretary of Defense for Civil Support (ATSD[CS]). The ATSD(CS) serves as the principal staff assistant and civilian advisor to the Secretary of Defense and Deputy Secretary of Defense for the oversight of policy, requirements, priorities, resources, and programs related to the DoD role in managing the consequences of a domestic incident involving the naturally occurring, accidental, or deliberate release of chemical, biological, radiological, nuclear material or high-yield explosives.

When requested, the DoD will provide its unique and extensive resources in accordance with the following principles. First, DoD will ensure an unequivocal chain of responsibility, authority, and accountability for its actions to ensure the American people that the military will follow the basic constructs of lawful action when an emergency occurs. Second, in the event of a catastrophic CBRNE event, DoD will always play a supporting role to the LFA in accordance with all applicable law and plans. Third, DoD support will emphasize its natural role, skills, and structures to mass mobilize and provide logistical support. Fourth, DoD will purchase equipment and provide support in areas that are largely related to its warfighting mission. Fifth, reserve component forces are DoD's forward-deployed forces for domestic consequence management.

All official requests for DoD support to CBRNE consequence management (CM) incidents are made by the LFA to the Executive Secretary of the Department of Defense. While the LFA may submit the requests for DoD assistance through other DoD channels, immediately upon receipt, any request that comes to any DoD element shall be forwarded to the Executive Secretary. In each instance the Executive Secretary will take the necessary action so that the Deputy Secretary can determine whether the incident warrants special operational management. In such instances, upon issuance of Secretary of Defense guidance to the Chairman of the Joint Chiefs of Staff (CJCS), the Joint Staff will translate the Secretary's decisions into military orders for these CBRNE-CM events, under the policy oversight of the ATSD(CS). If the Deputy Secretary of Defense determines that DoD support for a particular CBRNE-CM incident does not require special consequence management procedures, the Secretary of the Army will exercise authority as the DoD Executive Agent through normal Director of Military Support, Military Support to Civil Authorities (MSCA) procedures, with policy oversight by the ATSD(CS).

As noted above, DoD assets are tailored primarily for the larger warfighting mission overseas. But in recognition of the unique challenges of responding to a domestic CBRNE incident, the Department established a standing Joint Task Force for Civil Support (JTF-CS) headquarters at the United States Joint Forces Command, to plan for and integrate DoD's consequence management support to the LFA for events in the continental United States. The United States Pacific Command and United States Southern Command have parallel responsibilities for providing military assistance to civil authorities for States, territories, and possessions outside the continental United States. Specific units with skills applicable to a domestic consequence management role can be found in the Rapid Response Information System (RRIS) database maintained by FEMA. Capabilities include detection, decontamination, medical, and logistics.

Additionally, DoD has established 10 Weapons of Mass Destruction Civil Support Teams (WMD-CST), each composed of 22 well-trained and equipped full-time National Guard personnel. Upon Secretary of Defense certification, one WMD-CST will be stationed in each of the 10 FEMA regions around the country, ready to provide support when directed by their respective governors. Their mission is to deploy rapidly, assist local responders in determining the precise nature of an attack, provide expert technical advice, and help pave the way for the identification and arrival of follow-on military assets. By Congressional direction, DoD is in the process of establishing and training an additional 17WMD-CSTs to support the U.S. population. Interstate agreements provide a process for the WMD-CST and other National Guard assets to be used by neighboring states. If national security requirements dictate, these units may be transferred to Federal service.

D. DEPARTMENT OF ENERGY (DOE)

Through its Office of Emergency Response, the DOE manages radiological emergency response assets that support both crisis and consequence management response in the event of an incident involving a WMD. The DOE is prepared to respond immediately to any type of radiological accident or incident with its radiological emergency response assets. Through its Office of Nonproliferation and National Security, the DOE coordinates activities in non-proliferation, international nuclear safety, and communicated threat assessment. DOE maintains the following capabilities that support domestic terrorism preparedness and response.

Web site: **www.dp.doe.gov/emergencyresponse/**

1. **Aerial Measuring System (AMS).** Radiological assistance operations may require the use of aerial monitoring to quickly determine the extent and degree of the dispersal of airborne or deposited radioactivity or the location of lost or diverted radioactive materials. The AMS is an aircraft-operated

radiation detection system that uses fixed-wing aircraft and helicopters equipped with state-of-the-art technology instrumentation to track, monitor, and sample airborne radioactive plumes and/or detect and measure radioactive material deposited on the ground. The AMS capabilities reside at both Nellis Air Force Base near Las Vegas, Nevada, and Andrews Air Force Base near Washington, D.C. The fixed-wing aircraft provide a rapid assessment of the contaminated area, whereas the helicopters provide a slower, more detailed and accurate analysis of the contamination.

2. **Atmospheric Release Advisory Capability (ARAC).** Radiological assistance operations may require the use of computer models to assist in estimating early phase radiological consequences of radioactive material accidentally released into the atmosphere. The ARAC is a computer-based atmospheric dispersion and deposition modeling capability operated by Lawrence Livermore National Laboratory (LLNL). The ARAC's role in an emergency begins when a nuclear, chemical, or other hazardous material is, or has the potential of being, released into the atmosphere. The ARAC's capability consists of meteorologists and other technical staff using three-dimensional computer models and real-time weather data to project the dispersion and deposition of radioactive material in the environment. The ARAC's computer output consists of graphical contour plots showing predicted estimates for instantaneous air and ground contamination levels, air immersion and ground-level exposure rates, and integrated effective dose equivalents for individuals or critical populations. The plots can be overlaid on local maps to assist emergency response officials in deciding what protective actions are needed to effectively protect people and the environment. Protective actions could impact distribution of food and water sources and include sheltering and evacuating critical population groups. The ARAC's response time is typically 30 minutes to 2 hours after notification of an incident.

3. **Accident Response Group (ARG).** ARG is DOE's primary emergency response capability for responding to emergencies involving United States nuclear weapons. The ARG, which is managed by the DOE Albuquerque Operations Office, is composed of a cadre of approximately 300 technical and scientific experts, including senior scientific advisors, weapons engineers and technicians, experts in nuclear safety and high-explosive safety, health physicists, radiation control technicians, industrial hygienists, physical scientists, packaging and transportation specialists, and other specialists from the DOE weapons complex. ARG members will deploy with highly specialized, state-of-the-art equipment for weapons recovery and monitoring operations. The ARG deploys on military or commercial aircraft using a time-phased approach. The ARG advance elements are ready to deploy within four hours of notification. ARG advance elements focus on initial assessment and provide preliminary advice to decision makers. When the follow-on elements arrive at the emergency scene, detailed health and safety evaluations and operations are performed and weapon recovery operations are initiated.

4. **Federal Radiological Monitoring and Assessment Center (FRMAC).** For major radiological emergencies impacting the United States, the DOE establishes a FRMAC. The center is the control point for all Federal assets involved in the monitoring and assessment of offsite radiological conditions. The FRMAC provides support to the affected states, coordinates Federal offsite radiological environmental monitoring and assessment activities, maintains a technical liaison with Tribal nations and State and local governments, responds to the assessment needs of the LFA, and meets the statutory responsibilities of the participating Federal agency.

5. **Nuclear Emergency Search Team (NEST).** NEST is DOE's program for dealing with the technical aspects of nuclear or radiological terrorism. ANEST consists of engineers, scientists, and other technical specialists from the DOE national laboratories and other contractors. NEST resources are configured to be quickly transported by military or commercial aircraft to worldwide locations and prepared to respond 24hours a day using a phased and flexible approach to deploying personnel and equipment. The NEST is deployable within four hours of notification with specially trained teams and equipment to assist the FBI in handling nuclear or radiological threats. Response teams vary in size from a five person technical advisory team to a tailored deployment of dozens of searchers and scientists who can locate and then conduct or support technical operations on a suspected nuclear device. The NEST capabilities include intelligence, communications, search, assessment, access, diagnostics, render-safe operations, operations containment/damage mitigation, logistics, and health physics.

6. **Radiological Assistance Program (RAP).** Under the RAP, the DOE provides, upon request, radiological assistance to DOE program elements, other Federal agencies, State, Tribal, and local governments, private groups, and individuals. RAP provides resources (trained personnel and equipment) to evaluate, assess, advise, and assist in the mitigation of actual or perceived radiation hazards and risks to workers, the public, and the environment. RAP is implemented on a regional basis, with regional coordination between the emergency response elements of the States, Tribes, other Federal agencies, and DOE. Each RAP Region maintains a minimum of three RAP teams, which are comprised of DOE and DOE contractor personnel, to provide radiological assistance within their region of responsibility. RAP teams consist of volunteer members who perform radiological assistance duties as part of their formal employment or as part of the terms of the contract between their employer and DOE. A fully configured team consists of seven members, to include one Team Leader, one Team Captain, four health physics survey/support personnel, and one Public Information Officer. ARAP team may deploy with two or more members depending on the potential hazards, risks, or the emergency or incident scenario. Multiple RAP teams may also be deployed to an accident if warranted by the situation.

7. **Radiation Emergency Assistance Center/Training Site (REAC/TS).** The REAC/TS is managed by DOE's Oak Ridge Institute for Science and Education in Oak Ridge, Tennessee. The REAC/TS maintains a 24-hour response center staffed with personnel and equipment to support medical aspects of

radiological emergencies. The staff consists of physicians, nurses, para-medics, and health physicists who provide medical consultation and advice and/or direct medical support at the accident scene. The REAC/TS capabil-ities include assessment and treatment of internal and external contamina-tion, whole-body counting, radiation dose estimation, and medical and radiological triage.

8. **Communicated Threat Credibility Assessment.** DOE is the program man-ager for the Nuclear Assessment Program (NAP) at LLNL. The NAP is a DOE-funded asset specifically designed to provide technical, operational, and behavioral assessments of the credibility of communicated threats directed against the U.S. Government and its interests. The assessment process includes one-hour initial and four-hour final products which, when integrated by the FBI as part of its threat assessment process, can lead to a "go/no go" decision for response to a nuclear threat.

E. DEPARTMENT OF HEALTH AND HUMAN SERVICES (HHS)

The Department of Health and Human Services (HHS), as the lead Federal agency for Emergency Support Function (ESF) #8 (health and medical services), provides coordinated Federal assistance to supplement State and local resources in response to public health and medical care needs following a major disaster or emergency. Additionally, HHS provides support during developing or potential medical situations and has the responsibility for Federal support of food, drug, and sanitation issues. Resources are furnished when State and local resources are overwhelmed and public health and/or medical assistance is requested from the Federal government.

HHS, in its primary agency role for ESF #8, coordinates the provision of Federal health and medical assistance to fulfill the requirements identified by the affected State/local authorities having jurisdiction. Included in ESF #8 is overall public health response; triage, treatment, and transportation of victims of the disaster; and evacuation of patients out of the disaster area, as needed, into a network of Military Services, Veterans Affairs, and pre-enrolled non-Federal hospitals located in the major metropolitan areas of the United States. ESF #8 utilizes resources primarily available from (1) within HHS, (2) ESF #8 support agencies, (3) the National Disaster Medical System, and (4) specific non-Federal sources (major pharmaceutical suppliers, hospital supply vendors, international disaster response organizations, and international health organizations).

Web site: **www.hhs.gov**

1. **Office of Emergency Preparedness (OEP).** OEP manages and coordinates Federal health, medical, and health-related social service response and recovery to Federally declared disasters under the Federal Response Plan. The major functions of OEP include [the following]:
   a. Coordination and delivery of Department-wide emergency prepared-ness activities, including continuity of government, continuity of oper-ations, and emergency assistance during disasters and other emergencies;

    b. Coordination of the health and medical response of the Federal government, in support of State and local governments, in the aftermath of terrorist acts involving WMD; and

    c. Direction and maintenance of the medical response component of the National Disaster Medical System, including development and operational readiness capability of Disaster Medical Assistance Teams and other special teams that can be deployed as the primary medical response teams in case of disasters.

2. **Centers for Disease Control and Prevention (CDC).** CDC is the Federal agency responsible for protecting the public health of the country through prevention and control of diseases and for response to public health emergencies. CDC works with national and international agencies to eradicate or control communicable diseases and other preventable conditions. The CDC Bioterrorism Preparedness and Response Program oversees the agency's effort to prepare State and local governments to respond to acts of bioterrorism. In addition, CDC has designated emergency response personnel throughout the agency who are responsible for responding to biological, chemical, and radiological terrorism. CDC has epidemiologists trained to investigate and control outbreaks or illnesses, as well as laboratories capable of quantifying an individual's exposure to biological or chemical agents. CDC maintains the National Pharmaceutical Stockpile to respond to terrorist incidents within the United States.

Web site: **www.cdc.gov**

3. **National Disaster Medical System (NDMS).** NDMS is a cooperative asset-sharing partnership between HHS, DoD, the Department of Veterans Affairs (VA), FEMA, State and local governments, and the private sector. The System has three components: direct medical care, patient evacuation, and the non-Federal hospital bed system. NDMS was created as a nationwide medical response system to supplement State and local medical resources during disasters and emergencies, provide backup medical support to the military and VA health care systems during an overseas conventional conflict, and to promote development of community-based disaster medical service systems. This partnership includes DoD and VA Federal Coordinating Centers, which provide patient beds, as well as 1,990 civilian hospitals. NDMS is also comprised of over 7,000 private-sector medical and support personnel organized into many teams across the nation. These teams and other special medical teams are deployed to provide immediate medical attention to the sick and injured during disasters, when local emergency response systems become overloaded.

    a. **Disaster Medical Assistance Team (DMAT).**ADMAT is a group of professional and paraprofessional medical personnel (supported by a cadre of logistical and administrative staff) designed to provide emergency medical care during a disaster or other event. During a WMD incident, the DMAT provides clean area medical care in the form of medical triage and patient stabilization for transport to tertiary care.

b. **National Medical Response Team–Weapons of Mass Destruction (NMRT-WMD).** The NMRT-WMD is a specialized response force designed to provide medical care following a nuclear, biological, and/or chemical incident. This unit is capable of providing mass casualty decontamination, medical triage, and primary and secondary medical care to stabilize victims for transportation to tertiary care facilities in a hazardous material environment. There are four such teams geographically dispersed throughout the United States.

c. **Disaster Mortuary Operational Response Team (DMORT).** The DMORT is a mobile team of mortuary care specialists who have the capability to respond to incidents involving fatalities from transportation accidents, natural disasters, and/or terrorist events. The team provides technical assistance and supports mortuary operations as needed for mass fatality incidents.

F. ENVIRONMENTAL PROTECTION AGENCY (EPA)

EPA is chartered to respond to WMD releases under the National Oil and Hazardous Substances Pollution Contingency Plan (NCP) regardless of the cause of the release. EPA is authorized by the Comprehensive Environmental Response, Compensation, and Liability Act (CERCLA); the Oil Pollution Act; and the Emergency Planning and Community-Right-to Know Act to support Federal, State, and local responders in counterterrorism. EPA will provide support to the FBI during crisis management in response to a terrorist incident. In its crisis management role, the EPA On-Scene Commander (OSC) may provide the FBI Special Agent in Charge (SAC) with technical advice and recommendations, scientific and technical assessments, and assistance (as needed) to State and local responders. The EPAOSC will support FEMA during consequence management for the incident. EPA carries out its response according to the FRP, ESF #10, Hazardous Materials. The OSC may request an Environmental Response Team that is funded by EPA if the terrorist incident exceeds available local and regional resources. EPA is the chair for the National Response Team (NRT).

The following EPA reference material and planning guidance is recommended for State, Tribal, and local planners:

- Thinking About Deliberate Releases: Steps Your Community Can Take, 1995 (EPA550-F-95-001).

- Environmental Protection Agency's Role in Counterterrorism Activities, 1998 (EPA550-F-98-014).

Web site: **www.epa.gov**

G. DEPARTMENT OF AGRICULTURE

It is the policy of the U.S. Department of Agriculture (USDA) to be prepared to respond swiftly in the event of national security, natural disaster, technological, and other emergencies at the national, regional, State, and county levels to provide support and comfort to the people of the United States. USDA has a major role in ensuring the safety of food for all Americans. One concern is bio-terrorism and its effect on agriculture in rural America, namely crops in the field, animals on the hoof, and food safety issues related to food in the food chain between the slaughterhouse and/or processing facilities and the consumer.

Web site: **www.usda.gov**

1. **The Office of Crisis Planning and Management (OCPM).** This USDA office coordinates the emergency planning, preparedness, and crisis management functions and the suitability for employment investigations of the Department. It also maintains the USDA Continuity of Operations Plan (COOP).

2. **USDA State Emergency Boards (SEBs).** The SEBs have responsibility for coordinating USDA emergency activities at the State level.

3. **The Farm Service Agency.** This USDA agency develops and administers emergency plans and controls covering food processing, storage, and wholesale distribution; distribution and use of seed; and manufacture, distribution, and use of livestock and poultry feed.

4. **The Food and Nutrition Service (FNS).** This USDA agency provides food assistance in officially designated disaster areas upon request by the designated State agency. Generally, the food assistance response from FNS includes authorization of Emergency Food Stamp Program benefits and use of USDA-donated foods for emergency mass feeding and household distribution, as necessary. FNS also maintains a current inventory of USDA-donated food held in Federal, State, and commercial warehouses and provides leadership to the FRP under ESF #11, Food.

5. **Food Safety and Inspection Service.** This USD Aagency inspects meat/meat products, poultry/poultry products, and egg products in slaughtering and processing plants; assists the Food and Drug Administration in the inspection of other food products; develops plans and procedures for radiological emergency response in accordance with the Federal Radiological Emergency Response Plan (FRERP); and provides support, as required, to the FRP at the national and regional levels.

6. **Natural Resources Conservation Service.** This USDA agency provides technical assistance to individuals, communities, and governments relating to proper use of land for agricultural production; provides assistance in determining the extent of damage to agricultural land and water; and provides support to the FRP under ESF#3, Public Works and Engineering.

7. **Agricultural Research Service (ARS).** This USDA agency develops and carries out all necessary research programs related to crop or livestock diseases; provides technical support for emergency programs and activities in the areas of planning, prevention, detection, treatment, and management of consequences; provides technical support for the development of guidance information on the effects of radiation, biological, and chemical agents on agriculture; develops and maintains a current inventory of ARS controlled laboratories that can be mobilized on short notice for emergency testing of food, feed, and water safety; and provides biological, chemical, and radiological safety support for USDA.

8. **Economic Research Service.** This USDA agency, in cooperation with other departmental agencies, analyzes the impacts of the emergency on the U.S. agricultural system, as well as on rural communities, as part of the process of developing strategies to respond to the effects of an emergency.

9. **Rural Business-Cooperative Service.** This USDA agency, in cooperation with other government agencies at all levels, promotes economic development in affected rural areas by developing strategies that respond to the conditions created by an emergency.

10. **Animal and Plant Health Inspection Service.** This USDA agency protects livestock, poultry, crops, biological resources, and products thereof, from diseases, pests, and hazardous agents (biological, chemical, and radiological); assesses the damage to agriculture of any such introduction; and coordinates the utilization and disposal of livestock and poultry exposed to hazardous agents.

11. **Cooperative State Research, Education and Extension Service (CSREES).** This USDA agency coordinates use of land-grant and other cooperating State college, and university services and other relevant research institutions in carrying out all responsibilities for emergency programs. CSREES administers information and education services covering (a) farmers, other rural residents, and the food and agricultural industries on emergency needs and conditions; (b) vulnerability of crops and livestock to the effects of hazardous agents (biological, chemical, and radiological); and (c) technology for emergency agricultural production. This agency maintains a close working relationship with the news media. CSREES will provide guidance on the most efficient procedures to assure continuity and restoration of an agricultural technical information system under emergency conditions.

12. **Rural Housing Service.** This USDA agency will assist the Department of Housing and Urban Development by providing living quarters in unoccupied rural housing in an emergency situation.

13. **Rural Utilities Service.** This USDA agency will provide support to the FRP under ESF #12, Energy, at the national level.

14. **Office of Inspector General (OIG).** This USDA office is the Department's principal law enforcement component and liaison with the FBI. OIG, in concert with appropriate Federal, State, and local agencies, is prepared to investigate any terrorist attacks relating to the nation's agriculture sector, to identify subjects, interview witnesses, and secure evidence in preparation for Federal prosecution. As necessary, OIG will examine USDA programs regarding counterterrorism-related matters.

15. **Forest Service (FS).** This USDA agency will prevent and control fires in rural areas in cooperation with State, local, and Tribal governments, and appropriate Federal departments and agencies. They will determine and report requirements for equipment, personnel, fuels, chemicals, and other materials needed for carrying out assigned duties. The FS will furnish personnel and equipment for search and rescue work and other emergency measures in national forests and on other lands where a temporary lead

role will reduce suffering or loss of life. The FS will provide leadership to the FRP under ESF #4, Firefighting, and support to the Emergency Support Functions, as required, at the national and regional levels. FS will allocate and assign radio frequencies for use by agencies and staff offices of USDA. FS will also operate emergency radio communications systems in support of local, regional, and national firefighting teams. Lastly, the FS law enforcement officers can serve as support to OIG in major investigations of acts of terrorism against agricultural lands and products.

H. NUCLEAR REGULATORY COMMISSION

The Nuclear Regulatory Commission (NRC) is the Lead Federal Agency (in accordance with the Federal Radiological Emergency Response Plan) for facilities or materials regulated by the NRC or by an NRC Agreement State. The NRC's counterterrorism-specific role, at these facilities or material sites, is to exercise the Federal lead for radiological safety while supporting other Federal, State and local agencies in Crisis and Consequence Management.

Web site: **www.nrc.gov**

1. **Radiological Safety Assessment.** The NRC will provide the facility (or for materials, the user) technical advice to ensure onsite measures are taken to mitigate offsite consequences. The NRC will serve as the primary Federal source of information regarding on-site radiological conditions and off-site radiological effects. The NRC will support the technical needs of other agencies by providing descriptions of devices or facilities containing radiological materials and assessing the safety impact of terrorist actions and of proposed tactical operations of any responders. Safety assessments will be coordinated through NRC liaison at the Domestic Emergency Support Team (DEST), Strategic Information and Operations Center (SIOC), Command Post (CP), and Joint Operations Center (JOC).

2. **Protective Action Recommendations.** The licensee and State have the primary responsibility for recommending and implementing, respectively, actions to protect the public. They will, if necessary, act, without prior consultation with Federal officials, to initiate protective actions for the public and responders. The NRC will contact State and local authorities and offer advice and assistance on the technical assessment of the radiological hazard and, if requested, provide advice on protective actions for the public. The NRC will coordinate any recommendations for protective actions through NRC liaison at the CP or JOC.

3. **Responder Radiation Protection.** The NRC will assess the potential radiological hazards to any responders and coordinate with the facility radiation protection staff to ensure that personnel responding to the scene are observing the appropriate precautions.

4. **Information Coordination.** The NRC will supply other responders and government officials with timely information concerning the radiological aspects of the event. The NRC will liaison with the Joint Information Center to coordinate information concerning the Federal response.

TAB C

HOTLINES AND ONLINE RESOURCES

Note: The Internet sites listed here are current as of April 2001. Users of this Tab should be aware that the Internet is a changing environment. New sites are added frequently. Sites also may be relocated or discontinued. Updated information on online resources will be provided through the FEMA web site, http://www.fema.gov.

A. TELEPHONE HOTLINES

Domestic Preparedness Chemical/Biological HelpLine (phone: 800-368-6498, fax: 410-612-0715, Web: http://www.nbc-prepare.org or http://dp.sbccom.army.mil, e-mail: cbhelp@sbccom.apgea.army.mil) This service provides technical assistance during business hours to eligible State and local emergency responders and their organizations. National Response Center Hotline (800-424-8802) A service that receives reports of oil, chemical, biological, and radiological releases and actual or potential domestic terrorism; provides technical assistance to emergency responders; and connects callers with appropriate Federal resources. The hotline operates 24 hours a day, 365 days a year. Nuclear Regulatory Commission Operations Center (301-816-5100, collect calls accepted) Accepts reports of accidents involving radiological materials.

B. INTERNET REFERENCE ADDRESSES

Army Training Support Center (http://www.atsc.army.mil)
Provides a digital library with approved training and doctrine information. Files include Field Manuals, Mission Training Plans, Soldier Training Pubs, and more.
Centers for Disease Control and Prevention (CDC) (http://www.bt.cdc.gov) Information regarding infectious diseases.
Soldier and Biological Chemical Command (SBCCOM) (http://www.apgea.army.mil) Information on chemical/biological defense equipment and chemical agents.
CBIAC: Chemical and Biological Defense Information and Analysis Center (http://www.cbiac.apgea.army.mil) Collects, reviews, analyzes, and summarizes chemical warfare/contraband detection (CW/CBD) information.
Chemical and Biological Warfare – Health and Safety (http://www.ntis.gov/health/health.html) Department of Commerce National Technical Information Service (NTIS) site has information on chemical and biological agents, Government research, detoxification and decontamination studies, developing immunizations, and drug theories.
Chemical Emergency Preparedness and Prevention Office (CEPPO) (http://www.epa.gov/ceppo/) Information on the CEPPO office, upcoming events, publications, legislation and regulations, and links to outside resources. Also contains information on accident prevention and risk management planning.
Chemical Transportation Emergency Center (CHEMTREC) (http://www.cmahq.com). Source of technical assistance from chemical product safety specialists, emergency response coordinators, toxicologists and other hazardous materials (HazMat) specialists.

Disaster Management Central Resource (DMCR) (http://206.39.77.2/DMCR/dmrhome.html) Lackland Air Force Base (AFB) site with information on civilian support resources, triage of mass casualty situations, medicine and terrorism, terrorism injuries, and WMD medical library.

FEMA– Bio, Toxic Agents, and Epidemic Hazards Reference (www.fema.gov/emi/edu/biblol1.html) Emergency management-related bibliography on biological, toxic agents, and epidemic hazards.

FEMA– Emergency Management – Related Bibliography (http://www.fema.gov/emi/edu/biblo12.htm) Currently 35 links to various emergency management-related bibliographies. At least 10 of these relate to WMD.

Federal Radiological Emergency Response Plan (http://www.nrc.gov/NRC/AEOD/FRERP/ downld.html)

U.S. Army Center for Health Promotion and Preventive Medicine (CHPPM) (http://chppm-www.apgea.army.mil) Home Page providing links especially requests for CHPPM services. Links connect to Directorates of Environmental Health Engineering, Health Promotion and Wellness, Laboratory Sciences, Occupational Health, and Toxicology.

U.S. Army Medical Research and Development (R&D) Command (http://MRMC-www.army.mil) Links include military infectious disease, chemical and biological links, scientific and technical reports, and Web site links.

U.S. Army Medical Research Institute of Chemical Defense (http://chemdef.apgea.army.mil) Provides data links to open literature for medical management of chemical casualties and assay techniques for chemical agents.

U.S. Army Medical Research Institute of Infectious Diseases (http://www.usamriid.army.mil) Provides links to Medical Command (MEDCOM), Ebola site, outbreak reporting site, CDC, Defense Technical Information Center (DTIC), U.S. Army, and more.

C. CROSS-REFERENCE WEB SITES

1. Federal Departments/Agencies

   a. **Environmental Protection Agency (EPA)**

   (1) EPA's Chemical Emergency and Prevention Office (CEPPO). CEPPO provides leadership, advocacy, and assistance to prevent and prepare for chemical emergencies, respond to environmental crises, and inform the public about chemical hazards in their community.
   http://www.epa.gov/ceppo/

   (2) EPA's Environmental Response Team (ERT). The ERT is a group of skilled experts in environmental emergencies who provide on-scene assistance on a "round-the-clock" basis to deal with environmental disasters.
   http://www.ert.org/

   (3) EPA's Role in Counterterrorism. This Web site describes EPA's counterterrorism efforts and shares relevant counterterrorism information and resources.
   http://www.epa.gov/ceppo/cntr-ter.html

b. **Department of Defense (DoD)**

  (1) DoD's Chemical and Biological Defense Information Analysis Center. This Web site is DoD's focal point for chemical and biological warfare information.
  http://www.cbiac.apgea.army.mil

  (2) DoD's Counterproliferation: Chem Bio Defense. This is a DoD "webnetwork" on nuclear, biological, and chemical (NBC) defense.
  http://www.acq.osd.mil/cp/

  (3) DoD's Hazardous Technical Information Services (HTIS). HTIS is a service of the Defense Logistics Agency, located in Richmond, Virginia.
  http://www.dscr.dla.mil/htis/htis.htm

  (4) DoD's Medical (Army Surgeon General). This Web site contains extensive medical documents, training materials, audiovisual clips, a search engine, and links to other sites.
  http://www.nbc-med.org

c. **Department of Justice (DOJ)**

  (1) Federal Bureau of Investigation (FBI)

    (a) Awareness of National Security Issues and Response Program (ANSIR). The ANSIR is the "public voice" of the FBI for espionage, cyber and physical infra- structure protection.
    http://www.fbi.gov/hq/nsd/ansir/ansir.htm

    (b) National Domestic Preparedness Office (NDPO). The NDPO Web site provides a location for information regarding the available Federal training and programs intended to enhance the capabilities of the public safety community in dealing with weapons of mass destruction (WMD). The NDPO mission, members, services, newsletter, and recommended links are contained on this site.
    http://www.ndpo.gov

  (2) Office for State and Local Domestic Preparedness Support (OSLDPS). OSLDPS provides technical assistance to States and local jurisdictions to enhance their ability to develop, plan, and implement a program for WMD preparedness.
  http://www.ojp.usdoj.gov/osldps/

d. **Federal Emergency Management Agency (FEMA)**

  (1) Backgrounder: Terrorism. This FEMAWeb site provides basic background information on terrorism-related issues.
  http://www.fema.gov/library/terror.htm

  (2) Terrorism Annex to the Federal Response Plan. The site includes the full text of the Annex in PDF format that can be downloaded and reproduced.
  http://www.fema.gov/r-n-r/frp/frpterr.pdf

  (3) United States Government Interagency Domestic Terrorism Concept of Operations Plan. The link provides the full text of the plan, which is designed to provide information to Federal, State, and local agencies on how the Federal government will respond to

        potential or actual terrorism threats. The document is in PDF format and can be downloaded and reproduced.
http://www.fema.gov/r-n-r/conplan/

    (4) FEMA's Rapid Response Information System (RRIS). This Web site provides descriptions and links to eight major chemical and biological agent resources.
http://www.fema.gov/rris/reflib2.htm#chembio

    (5) National Fire Academy. The National Fire Academy homepage provides links to the course catalog and to specific courses and job aids relating to terrorism preparedness.
http://www.usfa.fema.gov/nfa/

    (6) FEMA's Emergency Response to Terrorism Self-Study Course. This Web site provides a link to a self-study course designed to provide basic awareness training to prepare first responders to respond safely and effectively to incidents of terrorism.
http://www.usfa.fema.gov/nfa/tr_ertss1.htm

e. **Department of Health and Human Services**

    (1) Office of Emergency Preparedness / National Disaster Medical System – The website provides information on current and previous disaster responses, counter terrorism programs and links to other Federal sites.
http://www.oep-ndms.dhhs.gov

    (2) Centers for Disease Control and Prevention, Bioterrorism Preparedness and Response Program – The website provides information on bioterrorism preparedness issues, response planning and recent publications related to bioterrorism.
http://www.bt.cdc.gov
The Centers for Disease Control and Prevention (CDC) also provide helpful (though not comprehensive) lists of chemical and biological agents that might be used by terrorists. These lists are included in "Biological and Chemical Terrorism: Strategic Plan for Preparedness and Response," in CDC's *Morbidity and Mortality Weekly Report*, April 21, 2000 (Vol. 49, No. RR-4), available at http://www.cdc.gov/mmwr/mmwr_rr.html.

    (3) Metropolitan Medical Response System (MMRS) – Although the MMRS program is locally controlled, this website provides information which will assist any local, State or Federal planner or responder working with domestic preparedness issues.
http://www.mmrs.hhs.gov

2. Other Resources

a. Critical Infrastructure Assurance Office. This Web site provides information on the Administration's current initiatives in critical infrastructure protection.
http://www.ciao.gov

b. DOE's Radiation-Related Web sites. This Web site is maintained by DOE's Office of Civilian Radiation Waste Management.
http://www.rw.doe.gov/

c. National Response Team (NRT). The NRT Web site contains information about standing NRT committees, the Regional Response Teams (RRTs), upcoming events, and NRT publications. *http://www.nrt.org/*

TAB D

INCIDENT INDICATIONS AND FIRST RESPONDER CONCERNS

NOTE: Extensive additional information on weapons of mass destruction (WMD) hazards and response, including information addressing first responder concerns, is available from various commercial publishers.

A. BIOLOGICAL

1. **Indications.** Indicators that a WMD incident involving biological agents has taken place may take days or weeks to manifest themselves, depending on the biological toxin or pathogen involved. The Centers for Disease Control and Prevention (CDC) recently developed the following list of epidemiologic clues that may signal a bioterrorist event:
   a. Large number of ill persons with a similar disease or syndrome.
   b. Large numbers of unexplained disease, syndrome, or deaths.
   c. Unusual illness in a population.
   d. Higher morbidity and mortality than expected with a common disease or syndrome.
   e. Failure of a common disease to respond to usual therapy.
   f. Single case of disease caused by an uncommon agent.
   g. Multiple unusual or unexplained disease entities coexisting in the same patient without other explanation.
   h. Disease with an unusual geographic or seasonal distribution.
   i. Multiple atypical presentations of disease agents.
   j. Similar genetic type among agents isolated from temporally or spatially distinct sources.
   k. Unusual, atypical, genetically engineered, or antiquated strain of agent.
   l. Endemic disease with unexplained increase in incidence.
   m. Simultaneous clusters of similar illness in noncontiguous areas, domestic or foreign.
   n. A typical aerosol, food, or water transmission.
   o. Ill people presenting near the same time.
   p. Deaths or illness among animals that precedes or accompanies illness or death in humans.
   q. No illness in people not exposed to common ventilation systems, but illness among those people in proximity to the systems.

2. **First Responder Concerns**
   a. The most practical method of initiating widespread infection using biological agents is through aerosolization, where fine particles are sprayed over or upwind of a target where the particles may be inhaled. An aerosol may be effective for some time after delivery, since

it will be deposited on clothing, equipment, and soil. When the clothing is used later, or dust is stirred up, responding personnel may be subject to "secondary" contamination.

   b. Biological agents may be able to use portals of entry into the body other than the respiratory tract. Individuals may be infected by ingestion of contaminated food and water, or even by direct contact with the skin or mucous membranes through abraded or broken skin. Use protective clothing or commercially available Level C clothing. Protect the respiratory tract through the use of a mask with biological high-efficiency particulate air (HEPA) filters.

   Exposure to biological agents, as noted above, may not be immediately apparent. Casualties may occur minutes, hours, days, or weeks after an exposure has occurred. The time required before signs and symptoms are observed is dependent on the agent used. While symptoms will be evident, often the first confirmation will come from blood tests or by other diagnostic means used by medical personnel.

B. CHEMICAL

   1. **Indications.** The following may indicate a potential chemical WMD has been released. There may be one or more of these indicators present.
      a. An unusually large or noticeable number of sick or dead wildlife. These may range from pigeons in parks to rodents near trash containers.
      b. Lack of insect life. Shorelines, puddles, and any standing water should be checked for the presence of dead insects.
      c. Considerable number of persons experiencing water-like blisters, weals (like bee-stings), and/or rashes.
      d. Numbers of individuals exhibiting serious heath problems, ranging from nausea, excessive secretions (saliva, diarrhea, vomiting), disorientation, and difficulty breathing to convulsions and death.
      e. Discernable pattern to the casualties. This may be "aligned" with the wind direction or related to where the weapon was released (indoors/outdoors).
      f. Presence of unusual liquid droplets, e.g., surfaces exhibit oily droplets or film or water surfaces have an oily film (with no recent rain).
      g. Unscheduled spraying or unusual application of spray.
      h. Abandoned spray devices, such as chemical sprayers used by landscaping crews.
      i. Presence of unexplained or unusual odors (where that particular scent or smell is not normally noted).
      j. Presence of low-lying clouds or fog-like condition not compatible with the weather.
      k. Presence of unusual metal debris—unexplained bomb/munitions material, particularly if it contains a liquid.
      l. Explosions that disperse or dispense liquids, mists, vapors, or gas.
      m. Explosions that seem to destroy only a package or bomb device.
      n. Civilian panic in potential high-profile target areas (e.g., government buildings, mass transit systems, sports arenas, etc.).
      o. Mass casualties without obvious trauma.

2. **First Responder Concerns.** The first concern must be to recognize a chemical event and protect the first responders. Unless first responders recognize the danger, they will very possibly become casualties in a chemical environment. It may not be possible to determine from the symptoms experienced by affected personnel which chemical agent has been used. Chemical agents may be combined and therefore recognition of agents involved becomes more difficult.

C. NUCLEAR/RADIOLOGICAL

1. **Indications.** Radiation is an invisible hazard. There are no initial characteristics or properties of radiation itself that are noticeable. Unless the nuclear/radiological material is marked to identify it as such, it may be some time before the hazard has been identified as radiological.

2. **First Responder Concerns.** While there is no single piece of equipment that is capable of detecting all forms of radiation, there are several different detectors for each type of radiation. Availability of this equipment, in addition to protective clothing and respiratory equipment, is of great concern to first responders.

TAB E

POTENTIAL AREAS OF VULNERABILITY

Areas at risk may be determined by several points: population, accessibility, criticality (to everyday life), economic impact, and symbolic value. The identification of such vulnerable areas should be coordinated with the Federal Bureau of Investigation (FBI).

Traffic: Determine which roads/tunnels/bridges carry large volumes of traffic.

Identify points of congestion that could impede response or place citizens in a vulnerable area.

Note time of day and day of week this activity occurs.

Trucking and Transport Activity: Note location of hazardous materials (HazMat) cargo loading/unloading facilities.

Note vulnerable areas such as weigh stations and rest areas this cargo may transit.

Waterways: Map pipelines and process/treatment facilities (in addition to dams already mentioned).

Note berths and ports for cruise ships, roll-on/roll-off cargo vessels, and container ships.

Note any international (foreign) flagged vessels (and cargo they carry) that conduct business in the area.

NOTE: The Harbor and Port Authorities, normally involved in emergency planning, should be able to facilitate obtaining information on the type of vessels and the containers they carry.

Airports: Note information on carriers, flight paths, and airport layout.

Annotate location of air traffic control (ATC) tower, runways, passenger terminal, and parking areas.

Trains/Subways: Note location of rails and lines, interchanges, terminals, tunnels, and cargo/passenger terminals.

Note any HazMat material that may be transported via rail.

Government Facilities: Note location of Federal/State/local government offices.

Include locations of post office, law enforcement stations, fire/rescue, town/city hall, and local mayor/governor's residences.

Note judicial offices and courts as well.

Recreation Facilities: Map sports arenas, theaters, malls, and special interest group facilities.

Other Facilities: Map location of financial institutions and the business district.

Make any notes on the schedule business/financial district may follow.

Determine if shopping centers are congested at certain periods.

Military Installations: Note location and type of military installations.

HazMat Facilities, Utilities, and Nuclear Facilities: Map location of these facilities.

NOTE: Security and emergency personnel representing all of the above facilities should work closely with local and State personnel for planning and response.

TAB F

DEFINITIONS

Aerosol – Fine liquid or solid particles suspended in a gas, for example, fog or smoke.

Biological Agents – Living organisms or the materials derived from them that cause disease in or harm to humans, animals, or plants or cause deterioration of material. Biological agents maybe used as liquid droplets, aerosols, or dry powders.

Chemical Agent – A chemical substance that is intended to kill, seriously injure, or incapacitate people through physiological effects. Generally separated by severity of effect: lethal, blister, and incapacitating.

Consequence Management – Measures to protect public health and safety, restore essential government services, and provide emergency relief to governments, businesses, and individuals affected by the consequences of terrorism. State and local governments exercise primary authority to respond to the consequences of terrorism. (Source: FRP Terrorism Incident Annex, page TI-2, April 1999). The Federal Emergency Management Agency (FEMA) has been designated the Lead Federal Agency (LFA) for consequence management to ensure that the Federal Response Plan is adequate to respond to terrorism. Additionally, FEMA supports the Federal Bureau of Investigation (FBI) in crisis management.

Crisis Management – This is the law enforcement aspect of an incident that involves measures to identify, acquire, and plan the resources needed to anticipate, prevent, and/or resolve a threat of terrorism. The FBI is the LFA for crisis management for such an incident. (Source: FBI) During crisis management, the FBI coordinates closely with local law enforcement authorities to provide successful law enforcement resolution to the incident. The FBI also coordinates with other Federal authorities, including FEMA. (Source: FRP Terrorism Incident Annex, April 1999)

Decontamination – The process of making people, objects, or areas safe by absorbing, destroying, neutralizing, making harmless, or removing the HazMat.

Federal Response Plan (FRP) – The FRP establishes a process and structure for the systematic, coordinated, and effective delivery of Federal assistance to address the consequences of any major disaster or emergency declared under the Robert T. Stafford Disaster Relief and Emergency Assistance Act, as amended (42 U.S. Code [USC], et seq.). The FRPTerrorism Incident Annex defines the organizational structures used to coordinate crisis management with consequence management. (Source: FRPTerrorism Incident Annex, April 1999)

1. **Lead Agency –** The Federal department or agency assigned lead responsibility under U.S. law to manage and coordinate the Federal response in a specific functional area. The FBI is the lead agency for crisis management and FEMA is the lead agency for consequence management. Lead agencies support the overall Lead Federal Agency (LFA) during all phases of the response.

2. **Lead Federal Agency (LFA) –** The agency designated by the President to lead and coordinate the overall Federal response is referred to as the LFA and is determined by the type of emergency. In general, an LFA establishes operational structures and procedures to assemble and work with agencies providing direct support to the LFA in order to provide an initial assessment of the situation, develop an action plan, monitor and update operational priorities, and ensure each agency exercises its concurrent and distinct authorities under U.S. law and supports the LFA in carrying out the President's relevant policy. Specific responsibilities of an LFA vary according to the agency's unique statutory authorities.

Mitigation – Those actions (including threat and vulnerability assessments) taken to reduce the exposure to and detrimental effects of a WMD incident.

Nonpersistent Agent – An agent that, upon release, loses its ability to cause casualties after 10 to 15 minutes. It has a high evaporation rate, is lighter than air, and will disperse rapidly. It is considered to be a short-term hazard; however, in small, unventilated areas, the agent will be more persistent.

Persistent Agent – An agent that, upon release, retains its casualty-producing effects for an extended period of time, usually anywhere from 30 minutes to several days. A persistent agent usually has a low evaporation rate and its vapor is heavier than air; therefore, its vapor cloud tends to hug the ground. It is considered to be a long-term hazard. Although inhalation hazards are still a concern, extreme caution should be taken to avoid skin contact as well.

Plume – Airborne material spreading from a particular source; the dispersal of particles, gases, vapors, and aerosols into the atmosphere.

Preparedness – Establishing the plans, training, exercises, and resources necessary to achieve readiness for all hazards, including WMD incidents.

Radiation – High-energy particles or gamma rays that are emitted by an atom as the substance undergoes radioactive decay. Particles can be either charged alpha or beta particles or neutral neutron or gamma rays.

Recovery – Recovery, in this document, includes all types of emergency actions dedicated to the continued protection of the public or promoting the resumption of normal activities in the affected area.

Response – Executing the plan and resources identified to perform those duties and services to preserve and protect life and property as well as provide services to the surviving population.

Terrorism – The unlawful use of force or violence against persons or property to intimidate or coerce a government, the civilian population, or any segment thereof, in furtherance of political or social objectives. Domestic terrorism involves groups or individuals who are based and operate entirely within the United States and U.S. territories without foreign direction and whose acts are directed at elements of the U.S. government or population.

Toxicity – A measure of the harmful effects produced by a given amount of a toxin on a living organism.

Weapons-Grade Material – Nuclear material considered most suitable for a nuclear weapon. It usually connotes uranium enriched to above 90 percent uranium-235 or plutonium with greater than about 90 percent plutonium-239.

Weapons of Mass Destruction – Any explosive, incendiary, or poison gas, bomb, grenade, rocket having a propellant charge of more than 4ounces, or a missile having an explosive incendiary charge of more than 0.25 ounce, or mine or device similar to the above; poison gas; weapon involving a disease organism; or weapon that is designed to release radiation or radioactivity at a level dangerous to human life. (Source: 18 USC 2332a as referenced in 18 USC 921)

TAB G

ACRONYMS

AFB Air Force Base
AMS Aerial Measuring System
ANSIR Awareness of National Security Issues and Response Program
ARAC Atmospheric Release Advisory Capability
ARG Accident Response Group
ARS Agriculture/Research Service
ATC Air Traffic Control
ATSD(CS) Assistant to the Secretary of Defense for Civil Support
BDC Bomb Data Center
CBIAC Chemical and Biological Defense Information and Analysis Center

CBRNE Chemical, Biological, Radiological, Nuclear Material, or High-Yield Explosive
CDC Centers for Disease Control and Prevention
CDRG Catastrophic Disaster Response Group
CEPPO Chemical Emergency Preparedness and Prevention Office
CERCLA Comprehensive Environmental Response, Compensation, and Liability Act
CHEMTREC Chemical Transportation Emergency Center
CHPPM Center for Health Promotion and Preventive Medicine
CIRG Crisis Incident Response Group
CJCS Chairman of the Joint Chiefs of Staff
CM Consequence Management
CMU Crisis Management Unit (CIRG)
CRU Crisis Response Unit
CSREES Cooperative State Research, Education and Extension Service
CST Civil Support Teams
CW/CBD Chemical Warfare/Contraband Detection
DEST Domestic Emergency Support Team
DFO Disaster Field Office
DMAT Disaster Medical Assistance Team
DMCR Disaster Management Central Resource
DMORT Disaster Mortuary Operational Response Team
DoD Department of Defense
DOE Department of Energy
DOJ Department of Justice
DPP Domestic Preparedness Program
DTCTPS Domestic Terrorism/Counter Terrorism Planning Section (FBI HQ)
DTIC Defense Technical Information Center
EM Emergency Management
EMI Emergency Management Institute
EMS Emergency Medical Services
EOC Emergency Operations Center
EOP Emergency Operations Plan
EPA Environmental Protection Agency
EPCRA Emergency Planning and Community Right-to Know Act
ERT Emergency Response Team (FBI)
ERT-A Emergency Response Team – Advance Element
ERTU Evidence Response Team Unit
ESF Emergency Support Function
EST Emergency Support Team
EU Explosives Unit
FBI Federal Bureau of Investigation
FEMA Federal Emergency Management Agency
FEST Foreign Emergency Support Team
FNS Food and Nutrition Service
FRERP Federal Radiological Emergency Response Plan
FRMAC Federal Radiological Monitoring and Assessment Center
FRP Federal Response Plan

FS Forest Service
HazMat Hazardous Materials
HHS Department of Health and Human Services
HMRU Hazardous Materials Response Unit
HQ Headquarters
HRT Hostage Rescue Team (CIRG)
HTIS Hazardous Technical Information Services (DoD)
IC Incident Commander
ICS Incident Command System
IND Improvised Nuclear Device
JIC Joint Information Center
JOC Joint Operations Center
JTF-CS Joint Task Force for Civil Support
LEPC Local Emergency Planning Committee
LFA Lead Federal Agency
LLNL Lawrence Livermore National Laboratory
MEDCOM Medical Command
MMRS Metropolitan Medical Response System
MOA Memorandum of Agreement
MSCA Military Support to Civil Authorities
NAP Nuclear Assessment Program
NBC Nuclear, Biological, and Chemical
NCP National Oil and Hazardous Substances Pollution Contingency Plan
NDMS National Disaster Medical System
NDPO National Domestic Preparedness Office
NEST Nuclear Emergency Search Team
NETC National Emergency Training Center
NFA National Fire Academy
NMRT National Medical Response Team
NRC Nuclear Regulatory Commission
NRT National Response Team
NSC National Security Council
NTIS National Technical Information Service
OEP Office of Emergency Preparedness
OFCM Office of the Federal Coordinator for Meteorology
OIG Office of the Inspector General (USDA)
OSC On-Scene Commander
OSLDPS Office for State and Local Domestic Preparedness Support
PDD Presidential Decision Directive
PHS Public Health Service
POC Point of Contact
PT Preparedness, Training, and Exercises Directorate (FEMA)
R&D Research and Development
RAP Radiological Assistance Program
RCRA Research Conservation and Recovery Act
RDD Radiological Dispersal Device
REAC/TS Radiation Emergency Assistance Center/Training Site
ROC Regional Operations Center

RRIS Rapid Response Information System (FEMA)
RRT Regional Response Team
SAC Special Agent in Charge (FBI)
SARA Superfund Amendments and Reauthorization Act
SBCCOM Soldier and Biological Chemical Command (U.S. Army)
SCBA Self-Contained Breathing Apparatus
SEB State Emergency Board
SERC State Emergency Response Commission
SIOC Strategic Information and Operations Center (FBI HQ)
SLG State and Local Guide
TERC Tribal Emergency Response Commission
TIA Terrorist Incident Appendix
TRIS Toxic Release Inventory System
UC Unified Command
UCS Unified Command System
USC U.S. Code
USDA U.S. Department of Agriculture
USFA U.S. Fire Administration
VA Department of Veterans Affairs
WMD Weapons of Mass Destruction
WMD-CST WMD Civil Support Team

SUMMARY

ICS is rapidly becoming the standard concept in emergency management through-out the US. The flexible response allowed by ICS based emergency management easily scales upward or downward as the event changes, and allows geographi-cally diverse agencies to work together when needed. The unified command and comprehensive resource management concepts provide for accountability in both personnel and equipment, and enhance safety by reducing the chances that any responder could be lost or left without needed supplies and support.

The private sector has a role to play in emergency preparedness as well, and the Department of Homeland Safety has established the Private Sector Office in order to provide preparedness advice and education. As was seen at the World Trade Center after the 9-11 attack, the private sector was often able to provide goods and services more quickly or more cheaply than government sources could.

ADDITIONAL DISCUSSION TOPICS

- What are the advantages to standardizing emergency response with a sys-tem like ICS?

- Are there any reasons why an agency might prefer to use its own non-ICS based response plans?

- California required its responding agencies to adopt SEMS by law. Should there be a federal law requiring adoption of NIMS, the ICS based National Incident Management System?

Endnotes

[1] http://www.fem.gov/nims/

[2] http://www.fema.gov/doc/rrr/allhzpln.doc

[3] Definitions of terms and acronyms used in this documents are given in Tabs F and G, respectively.

[4] Table 5 provides an overview of events likely to occur in a WMD incident. It is designed to help planners better understand the interface that State and local response will likely have the Federal response organizations. The table includes both crisis management and consequence management activities that would be operating in parallel and is intended to illustrate the complex constellation of responses that would be involved in a WMD incident.

CHAPTER ELEVEN

ALL-HAZARDS APPROACH

It's not either terrorism or natural hazards.
Both are important and both need to be addressed.
—Michael Armstrong,
associate director of FEMA's Mitigation Directorate

KEY TERMS

Emergency Management
Mitigation
Preparedness
Response
Recovery
Emergency Operations Plan (EOP)
Emergency Operations Center (EOC)
Emergency Program Manager
Federal Emergency Management Agency (REMA)

OBJECTIVES

- Identify the role of the National Disaster Medical System (NDMS) in disaster management.

- Identify areas in which the NYPD's response to the 9/11 attacks indicated good prior planning or showed the need for more thorough planning for future events.

- Describe the purpose and function of the National Incident Management System (NIMS).

DISCUSSION TOPICS

- What is the National Disaster Medical System?

- Who is responsible for evacuating medical patients from disaster sites?

- How are medical response teams organized and utilized?

- What lessons were learned from the NYPD's post-9/11 audit?

- How does NIMS relate to ICS?

11

INTRODUCTION

The 2008 earthquake in China might have a death toll approaching 50,000 people. In Myanmar, the cyclone of 2008 might have killed up to 78,000 people by some estimates. No one expected these catastrophic events, but nevertheless the consequences must be dealt with.

Disasters are fluid and unpredictable events that effect enormous numbers of lives. Having plans in place and procedures to follow begins to help deal with the chaos at the disaster's beginning and ensures the best possible outcome in the long term. Conducting honest and detailed after action reviews of the response gives the best chance to learn from the experience to improve the responses to future disasters.

CHARACTERIZING EMERGENCY MANAGEMENT ACTIVITIES[1]

Before talking about the tasks that constitute emergency management, it is important to briefly ground the discussion in the process of accomplishing emergency management. There is an ongoing dialogue in the U.S. about the functions and processes entailed in emergency management, both for planning and implementation. Although the history just reviewed focuses largely on federal efforts, in actuality emergency management begins as a local endeavor, and often ends there too. It is essential to remember that the majority of disaster events are dealt with effectively at the local level. A relatively small proportion of disaster events require state assistance, and an even smaller number require federal assistance in any given year. Since the events that do get federal disaster declaration also get national media coverage, the public gets the impression the federal government is involved in the majority of disaster responses.

Disasters always have local consequences, both short-term and long-term. Emergency management can be done optimally only with intergovernmental communication and cooperation that links local, state, and federal efforts. In some instances, such as chemical or biological threats, the special resources of the federal government are needed to even begin the management process. In any significant event, external support or resources—state, federal, non-profit and commercial—may be requested by the local jurisdictions impacted. The chart that follows shows some of the wide array of key components and major actors in the emergency management system, but is not exhaustive. In the case of major damaging disasters in an urban area, the processes and tasks described here take place at every level of government.

The process of emergency management begins with a careful vulnerability assessment that identifies the hazards to which the locality is subject and determines probabilities for impacts and projects consequences (Ketchum and Whittaker 1982; Greenway 1998). Vulnerability assessment is not a static activity because hazards are not static. Vulnerability assessment is probably best conceptualized as

Figure 11.1. Local Emergency Management System.

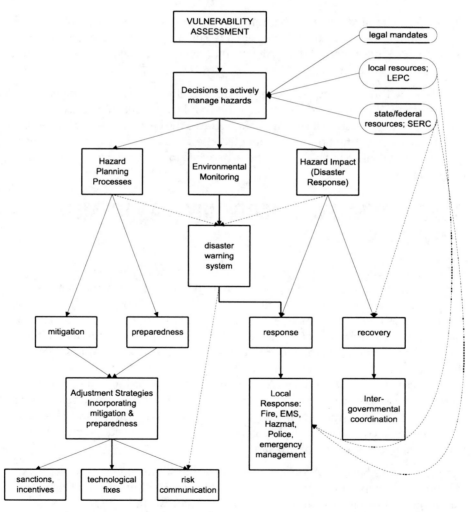

Source: FEMA-EMI course textbook, *Introduction to Emergency Management* (working draft), Chapter 1, "Introduction to Emergency Management," Wayne Blanchard (2004).

a system that periodically reassesses the hazard environment. The assessment comes from the challenging process of deciding which hazards are significant enough to require active management. This is a complex process that involves myriad considerations and input from a variety of actors, and detailed descriptions are available in the work of Prater and Lindell (2000) and Birkland (1997).

Hazard management decisions are influenced by multiply considerations. For example, certain hazards/threats have legal, administrative or statutory mandates connected to their management. Technical hazard data (such as those provided by Local Emergency Planning Committees [LEPC] and State Emergency Response Commissions [SECR] are a critical component of the decision process. In addition, decisions to manage hazards are subject to the local political process, local resources (including the budget), and state and federal resources and policies.

Once a decision to actively manage one or more hazards is made, three processes are simultaneously initiated:

(1) A hazard planning process that directly stimulates consideration of mitigation and preparedness issues. That is, one must consider whether there is a means to completely remove the hazard or adjust to it through some policy. At a local level, these deliberations involve not just emergency managers, but planning departments, departments administering building codes, and political officials because mitigation and preparedness actions are designed for the long term as ways of increasing community resilience.

(2) The process of judging hazard impact begins, using much the same technical hazard data to allow local creation (and coordination) of response strategies when a disaster strikes, and to devise recovery actions. The local response usually centers on preparations for the mobilization of local emergency services (fire department, emergency medical services, hazardous materials teams, police, transportation and public works departments, and emergency managers) under an agreed upon incident management system (Brunacini 2001; Kramer and Bahme 1992). Both response and recovery activities are organized in conjunction with support from external sources, particularly State and national government. Again, the emphasis is to institutionalize response to the greatest extent possible, while looking at recovery as another (in addition to mitigation) path to sustainability or disaster resilience.

(3) Environmental monitoring of the hazards to be managed. Typically, such monitoring is coupled with or produces a warning system, to be activated as a means of initiating response actions when an agent impact is imminent. The quality of the warning systems depends upon the state of technology associated with given hazards and may produce genuine forecasts (in the case of tornadoes). The nature of the warning system is affected by jurisdictional mitigation, preparedness and response plans. In many cases, actual hazard monitoring is beyond the technical and financial and technological capability of most communities and assumed by federal agencies and programs. In such cases, the results of monitoring are relayed to local jurisdictions. Furthermore, information regarding the state of the warning system (its ability to accurately forecast and detect hazards) is shared with hazard planning systems as a means of informing longer term risk management plans.

To review, mitigation and preparedness planning processes generate adjustment strategies that incorporate knowledge about hazards derived from many sources, including the scientific community and state and federal agencies. The scope of adjustment strategy plans must encompass households, public sector organizations and private sector organizations. Adjustment strategies tend to fall into three categories, including sanctions and incentives, technological fixes and risk communication. The imposition of sanctions and incentives and their enforcement involves political processes and may support either mitigation or preparedness measures or both (Lindell and Perry 2003b). Technological fixes usually form mitigation measures, also may involve political processes and intergovernmental support because of cost or complexity, and may be paired with sanctions and incentives. Risk communication represents efforts to induce households and organizations to adopt adjustments which may address either mitigation or preparedness measures.

The four principal functions or phases associated with the conduct of emergency management are mitigation, preparedness, response, and recovery. The origin of these comprehensive emergency management concepts is a research done by the National Governor's Association Emergency management Project led by Hilary Whittaker in 1978. As this group grappled with what is meant to manage emergencies, they generated considerable discussion and some controversy within both the disaster research community and the hazards policy community. Since being adopted and practiced by FEMA for many years, it is now widely acknowledged as an appropriate model for understanding the activities of emergency management. This concise scheme consolidates emergency activities into four discrete but interconnected categories distinguished by time phase relative to disaster impact. Thus, mitigation and preparedness activities are generally seen as taking place before the impact of any given disaster, while response and recovery activities are seen as post-impact measures. The four phases of emergency management are:

1. MITIGATION: Deciding what to do where a risk to the health, safety, and welfare of a society has been determined to exist; and implementing a risk reduction program. It involves minimizing the potential adverse effects of hazard agents. It may also be any cost-effective measure that will reduce the potential for damage to a facility from a disaster event.

2. PREPAREDNESS: Developing a response plan and training first responders to save lives and reduce disaster damage, including the identification of critical resources and the development of necessary agreements among responding agencies, both within the jurisdiction and with other jurisdictions.

3. RESPONSE: Providing emergency aid and assistance, reducing the probability of secondary damage, and minimizing problems for recovery operations.

4. RECOVERY: Providing immediate support during the early recovery period necessary to return vital life support systems to minimize operational levels, and continuing to provide support until the community returns to normal (Petak 1985, p. 3).

Mitigation activities are directed toward eliminating the causes of a disaster, reducing the likelihood of its occurrence of limiting the magnitude of its impacts if it does occur. Officially, FEMA defines mitigation as "any action of a long-term, permanent nature that reduces the actual or potential risk of loss of life or property from a hazardous event" (FEMA 1998: 9). Since 1995, FEMA has emphasized mitigation as the most effective and cost-efficient strategy for dealing with hazards. The focus here is upon prevention; so to speak, stopping disasters before they happen. Although the amount of control that can be exercised over natural event systems is generally limited, technological hazards are more susceptible to such controls. Explosives, toxic chemicals, and radioactive materials can all be produced, stored, and transported in ways that avoid adverse effects jupon plant workers, local residents, and the public at large. However, this control can be lost, resulting in releases to the air, or to surface or ground water. Thus, the choice of whether to mitigate technological hazards by controlling the hazard agent or by controlling the human-use system depends upon political and economic decisions about the relative costs and benefits of exercising these two types of control. Specific questions include who has control over the hazards, what degree of control is maintained, and what incentives there are for the maintenance of control.

The same issues arise in connection with control of the human-use system that is vulnerable to the technological hazard: who can control the human-use system, what degree of control can be maintained, and what incentives are there for the maintenance of control over the human-use system? For example, one can reduce the likelihood of a release of toxic chemicals from a fixed site facility by means of diverse and redundant systems design, by reliable and efficient operations and maintenance procedures, and by effective worker selection, training, and supervision. Alternatively, potential human exposures can be controlled by prohibiting the construction of schools, hospitals, and other facilities with high occupant density in areas close to the plant. Another mitigation measure would be to simply require that a less toxic or nontoxic chemical be substituted in the processes used in the fixed facility.

Attempts to mitigate natural hazards, or events over which there is little human control, involves assessing the geographical extent of the hazard and trying to control human activities in a way that minimizes exposure to the hazard. Thus, land-use management strategies to restrict residential construction in floodplains are important mitigation measures against riverine floods. The Hazard Mitigation and Relocation Act of 1993, for example, allows FEMA to purchase homes and businesses in floodplains and remove this property from harm's way. Although moving entire communities involves considerable stress for all concerned, an intense and systematic management process—characterized especially by close federal-state-local communications—can produce successful protection of large numbers of citizens and break the chain of "flooding-rebuilding-flooding-rebuilding" that is so costly (Perry and Lindell 1997). Likewise, building code requirements are used to restrict construction to those designs that can better withstand the stresses of hurricane force winds or earthquake shocks. The mitigation-related recent federal action includes the Disaster Mitigation Act of 2000 and the issuance of mitigation planning regulations.

Mitigation Planning Regulations were issued by FEMA in February 2002, and also state and local governments were required to submit mitigation plans to FEMA. These requirements were driven by the Disaster Mitigation Act of 2000, codified as part of the Robert T. Stafford Act, 42 US Code sections 5121-5206. Another outcome of the Disaster Mitigation Act of 2000 was the FEMA-issued State and Local Plan Guidance, issues in July 2002....

The Disaster Mitigation Act of 2000. PL 106-390, October 20, 2000 According to FEMA, this act provides an impetus for state and local governments to undertake mitigation planning. The Act does not mandate that terrorism or technological disasters be addressed in hazard mitigation planning; however, it does encourage and reward state and local pre-disaster planning and promote sustainability as a strategy for reducing the effects of disasters. Naturally, this objective can only be fully achieved through incorporating not only natural hazards but also the full spectrum of human-caused disasters. Interim final regulations on hazard mitigation planning were published in the Federal Register on Feb 26, 2002 (see 44 CFR Parts 201 and 206). FEMA extended the original due date of November 2003 for state and local governments to submit mitigation plans to November 2004.

Preparedness activities are those that are undertaken to protect human lives and property in conjunction with threats that cannot be controlled by means of mitigation measures, or from which only partial protection may be achieved. Thus, preparedness activities are based upon the premise that disaster impact will occur and that plans, procedures, and resources need to be prepared in advance support a timely and effective response to the threat. Planning is not a sole component of preparedness—exercising plans, building a resource base, and training personnel are also key features. One may think of preparedness measures as falling into a least three general categories. The first category involves establishing the basis for preparedness. For government jurisdictions this involves creating an emergency management organization, staffing it, and ensuring its basis in statute and regulation. This also usually involves developing a jurisdictional emergency plan to guide e management process and establishing an emergency operations center.

The second category includes activities related to alerting members of response organizations and the affected population about the timing and extent of hazard impact. These types of preparedness measures relate to the development (or use) of detection and prediction technologies that allow authorities to monitor the hazard to assure ample forewarning of the location and magnitude of the disaster impact. Such technologies are evidence in detection and monitoring systems such as rainfall and river gages, radar detection and tracking of severe storms, and sensors and computers designed to assess the magnitude of releases of toxic or radioactive materials (Barrett 1986). Warning dissemination systems that convey information about threats from the authorities to the general public—regarding tornadoes, dam failures, hurricanes, and such—also fall into this category.

The third category of preparedness measures aims at enhancing emergency response operations. Such measures encompass a variety of activities, including developing plans for the activation and coordination of emergency response organizations, and devising standard operating procedures to guide organizations in the performance of their emergency functions. These functions are the generic functions described above such as population evacuation, feeding and sheltering, decontamination, medical management, and the like. Training and education of both emergency personnel and the public, and drills and exercises to test process, personnel, and equipment fall under the rubric of enhancing response operations. Other preparedness activities include stockpiling of resources such as protective equipment for emergency workers and medical supplies for the injured, as well as assembling lists of community resources and their location for use as needed in an emergency.

Emergency response activities are conducted during the time period that begins with detection of the event and ends with the stabilization of the situation following impact. FEMA (1998: 12) indicates that the goal is "to save lives and victims; providing food, water, shelter, and medical are to those in need; and restoring critical public services." Detection varies and can be made by citizens, although an effective hazard monitoring system should ensure that authorities have first knowledge, either through systematic prediction (floods) or technology (seismic evidence) of an earthquake. In some cases, where the state of technology is very sophisticated, advance prediction or early detection allows considerable forewarning and consequently a long period of time for response. In other cases, such as tornadoes or terrorist events, where prediction and detection in advance are difficult or impossible, the time before impact may be extremely short. Stabilization of the situation means that he risk of loss of life and property has de-escalated back to pre-crisis levels. Emergency response activities focus upon protecting the affected population, as well as attempting to limit damage from the initial impact, and minimizing damage from secondary or repeated impact. Second impacts are "disasters caused by he disaster" and include such events as haaczardous materials accidents linked to earthquakes (Lindell and Perry 1997). Repeated impacts of the same disaster agent commonly occur in connection with earthquakes (aftershocks) and volcanic eruptions (Perry and Lindell 1997).

Some of the more visible response activities undertaken to limit the primary impact include securing the impact area, evacuating threatened areas, conducting search and rescue for the injured, providing emergency medical care, and sheltering evacuees and other victims. Operations mounted to counter secondary threats include fighting urban fires after earthquakes, identifying contaminated water supplies or other public health threats following folding, identifying contaminated wildlife or fish in connection with a toxic chemical spill, or preparing for flooding following glacier melt during a volcanic eruption. During the response stage, emergency managers must also continually assess damages and coordinate the arrival of converging equipment and supplies so they may be deployed to those areas in most need.

Emergency response activities are usually accomplished through the coordinated efforts of diverse groups—some formally constituted, other volunteer—and managed via an emergency operations center (EOC). Usually, local first responders dominate the response period: police, firefighters, EMS personnel, public works, and transportation employees. Time pressures and a sense of urgency—less prevalent in mitigation, preparedness and recovery—are important features of the response period. In the world of disaster response, minutes of delay can cost lives and property. Although it must be balanced with good planning and intelligent assessment, speed is typically of the essence in the response period. Finally, emergency response actions need to anticipate the recovery phase. That is, life and property are priorities, but response actions foreshadow recovery actions; for example, damage assessments are preserved for use in requesting Presidential Disaster Declarations, and debris removal might be concentrated on critically need roadways for later operations.

Recovery activities begin after disaster impact has been stabilized and extends until the community has been returned to its normal activities. In some cases, the recovery period may extend for long period of time. FEMA (1995) officially prescribes that "[r]ecovery refers to those non-emergency measures following disaster whose purpose is to return all systems, both formal and informal, to as normal as possible." The immediate objective of recovery measures is to restore the physical infrastructure of the community. More generally, it is to return the quality of life to at least the same levels as before the disaster. Recovery has been defined in terms of short-range (relief and rehabilitation) measures versus long-range (reconstruction) measures. Relief and rehabilitation activities usually include clearance of debris and restoration of access to the impact area, reestablishment of economic (commercial and industrial) activities, restoration of essential government or community services, and provision of an interim system for caring for victims—especially housing, clothing, and food. Reconstruction activities tend to be dominated by the rebuilding of major structures—buildings, roads, bridges, dams and such—and by efforts to revitalize the area's economic system. In some communities, leaders may view the reconstruction phase as an opportunity to institute the community plans for change that existed before the disaster or to introduce mitigating measures into the rebuilding that would constitute an improvement upon the pre-disaster state. Such an approach to reconstruction has been documented after the great Alaska earthquake of 1964 (Anderson 1969). Finally, it should be pointed out that the bulk of the resources used in the recovery phase (particularly on reconstruction) are derived from extra-community sources. In the United States, these sources include private organizations and state governments, but for the most part they come from the federal government. Most of the money and resources for emergency management are consumed in the recovery phase. This is consistent with a cycle, well known to disaster researchers and emergency management professionals, of citizen and governmental interest in disasters. Immediately after impact, the attention of both the public and community officials is riveted upon the physical devastation and social disruption. Although considerable resources are made available, the compelling needs at the time are helter, food, clothing, and financial aid to victims and debris clearance and the physical restoration of critical facilities within the community. Unfortunately, mitigation and preparedness activities, because they lack a large and visible constituency, tend to remain lacking in support.

There is, consequently, a paradox with respect to mitigation and preparedness support that is difficult to overcome. Most mitigation activities have in common the characteristics of being long-range measures. They are taken well in advance of disaster impact, either in response to a previous disaster or after a hazard has been identified and the vulnerability of the community assessed. Interestingly, in the history of attempts of emergency management in the United States, the smallest proportion of resources seems to be devoted to mitigation activities. Like mitigation measures, preparedness activities are conducted or undertaken in advance of a particular disaster event. They provide capabilities for protecting life and property when disasters do strike. Preparedness activities too, have historically received significantly less support than response and recovery activities. There is a general cycle characterized by a sudden outpouring of public interest in hazard mitigation and emergency preparedness immediately following a major disaster: "This should not happen again!" However, public attention declines significantly as time passes. Because considerable time is required to translate such concern into budget allocations and coherent programs, many preparedness measures have simply failed to be implemented. In developing the concept of comprehensive emergency management, a concerted effort has been made to establish the importance of both mitigation and preparedness activities. Particularly since the 1990s, FEMA has argued that it is far more desirable to prevent damage in the first place than it is to try and deal with it after the fact.

In summary, two points should be reiterated here. First, although the distinctions among them are not sharp (transitions from one phase to the next is gradual rather than sharp), the four activities are distinctly time phased. Mitigation and preparedness measures take place in advance of any specific disaster impact, while response takes place during and recovery occurs following disaster impact. Therefore, practical problems accompany the development of mitigation and preparedness strategies because they must usually be accomplished during period of normal activity, when an environmental threat is not imminent. Historical evidence indicates that it has been difficult to mount efforts to engage in these sorts of activities. Response and recovery take place within the context of a disaster impact—clearly unusual times—and benefit from the operation of an emergency social system as well as from the high level of community cohesiveness that usually emerges in the short-range aftermath (Lindell and Perry 1992).

The second point is that in the past, far more resources and emphasis have been given to response and recovery activities than to mitigation and preparedness. To a certain extent this differential emphasis has been a function of the difficulty citizens and political officials have in maintaining a high level of concern about disasters during times when they seem so remote. To do so requires that both citizens and leaders dwell on negative events that may or may not occur sometime in the future—a task that is almost universally regarded as unpleasant and thus elicits procrastination. Terrorism forms one test of this long established mindset. Perhaps equally important in the resource disparity, however, are the limitations posed by the technical state of knowledge regarding various hazards. The state of technology itself imposes limits on the types of mitigation and preparedness activities that may be undertaken. If a potential disaster event cannot be detected in advance or if the technology for doing so is crude (as in the cased of predicting earthquakes and volcanic eruptions), the feasible set of mitigation actions may be severely limited. Furthermore, in the absence of a technology of detection and highly accurate impact predictions, many preparedness measures are not possible. Thus, in the past, it may have not been possible to devote resources anywhere other than to response and recovery. In the future, as more comprehensive forms of emergency management are implemented, the emphasis must shift toward the development of mitigation and preparedness measures within the limits of existing technology, while pursuing research and development designed to advance the state of that technology.

THE FUNDAMENTALS OF EMERGENCY MANAGEMENT[2]

The United States has an ongoing system intended to guide the governmental response to all natural disasters. Under the American system, the process works from the bottom up. It begins at the local level and follows a series of pre-specified steps up through the State and, ultimately, to the National government. Local, state, and national governments are supposed to share their emergency management responsibilities. The higher levels of government are not intended to supersede or replace the activities of the lower levels. All three levels of government are supposed to develop coordinated, integrated emergency management procedures, and they should all participate in the process of implementing disaster-relief policies.

Many other countries (e.g., Great Britain, Sweden, France, and Japan) also rely on local governments in emergencies and disasters, but primary authority for disaster management in those countries flows through a "top down" approach under which the local governmental authority is often routinely superseded or replaced by national government authorities or organizations.

There are many functional demands that emergency managers need to consider in crafting effective emergency management policies and programs and in responding to potential disasters. Among key functional demands that emergency managers need to understand are issue salience, fragmented government responsibility, and technical expertise. How these demands and considerations are met has profound implications.

Issue salience is a perennial political problem of emergency management. Disasters are by their very nature high-risk, low probability events. Their infrequency makes it difficult to justify pre-disaster expenditures of public money in view of seemingly more pressing, on-going public needs and issues. In the aftermath of a major disaster, emergency managers, for a time, enjoy a high political profile and may be able to influence the public and their political representatives to undertake certain essential emergency preparedness or disaster mitigation efforts and projects.

Fragmented Government Responsibility is another political challenge for disaster managers in implementing emergency management programs. The United States is a highly decentralized, federal system of government, which, under the U.S. Constitution, affords the national government a range of authority, with some powers reserved for the States under the 10th Amendment. Similarly, local governments, although legally vestiges of their respective state governments, in some States, are afforded certain powers under home rule provisions approved by their states, by their state constitution, or through enabling statutes. This fragmentation of policymaking vertically between national, state, and local governments is further complicated by horizontal fragmentation among a multitude of competing agencies with overlapping jurisdictional prerogatives. Effective decision-making and program coordination is difficult in this instance. This underlines the need for multi-agency and multi-jurisdictional *coordination concerning emergency and disaster issues.*

Lack of Technical Expertise is another major impediment to effective emergency management policies and programs for emergency managers. Technical expertise to identify and assess hazards adequately, to predict the occurrence of disasters, and to provide the requisite technical information for the design and implementation of effective programs is crucial to effective emergency management. Moreover, even when possible hazards have been identified, it is unclear just how much risk is involved. In by-gone eras, emergency management required little technical knowledge or expertise when compared with many other occupational specialties. Today, emergency managers need to master a specialized body of knowledge, often involving multiple disciplines. Accounting and budgeting skills are important. Public relations expertise and political savvy are necessary. Computing ability, in terms of information management, decision support, and geographic information systems, et cetera, is becoming more a part of routine emergency management work. A working knowledge of disaster-related laws and programs is vital.

Overall, emergency management exists within a complex political, economic, and social environment. In part, this explains why emergency management has so long lacked a coherent, coordinated policy framework. Designing and implementing comprehensive emergency management procedures is easier said than done, principally because of the obstacles to effective action created by problems stemming from political salience, fragmented government responsibility, and a lack of technical expertise. In addition, it is only since about 1950 that federal sand state authorities have cooperated in the development of sound emergency management procedures and have begun to furnish local governments with sufficient resources to design, implement, and maintain effective emergency management programs. Vertical fragmentation results when federal state, and local authorities fail to coordinate their emergency management responsibilities, when they act independent of one another, when they duplicate their efforts or work at cross-purposes, or when one level of government fails to carry out its obligations.

Because disasters are usually geographically localized, county, and municipal authorities most often assume primary responsibility for emergency management. However, the policy-making, administrative, and fiscal capacities of many local governments is often questionable. They are often reluctant, unwilling, or unable to design, implement, and support effective programs.

As noted earlier, horizontal fragmentation often stems from the multiplicity of state and local jurisdictions impacted by a disaster or emergency. Mutual assistance agreements may alleviate some of the jurisdictional confusion, but emergency responses regularly create unanticipated intra- and inter-jurisdictional conflicts that interfere with emergency management. Vertical and horizontal fragmentation is something with which emergency managers must learn to deal. Such fragmentation will not disappear even though "shared governance" holds some potential for achieving effective emergency management. Vertical and horizontal fragmentation often contributes to the problems of sufficient technical expertise, adequate fiscal resources, and unclear legislative mandates.

In this manner, the problem of multi-agency and multi-jurisdictional coordination challenges emergency managers. Disasters and emergencies often change the division of labor and resources in an organization. They compel a sharing of tasks and resources between organizations. They involve the crossing of jurisdictional boundaries, both in terms of geography and responsibility. They require the completion of non-routine tasks under abnormal circumstances. They damage, make unavailable, or overwhelm normal emergency response tools and facilities. Finally, they necessitate new organizational arrangements to meet the problems posed.

Emergency management is also challenged by a fundamental public distrust of governmental planning efforts, strong resistance to land-use and construction regulation, and a tendency, especially at state and local levels, to focus only on recent disasters. Levels of risk are also difficult to measure, and cause and effect relationships are elusive as well. Sadly, it is often politically easier for government officials to wait for emergencies to happen and then deal with them, than it is for them to attempt to prepare for and mitigate their effects. Relief assistance is politically popular and desired, while mitigation and preparedness efforts usually are not politically popular.

In large measure, the federal system of the division of powers accords state governments, and the localities within them, the lead role in responding to most types of hazards and disasters. A facilitating role has been assumed by the federal government through the Federal Emergency Management Agency (FEMA). FEMA leaves it up to state and local governments to actually develop emergency management procedures. America has a highly decentralized and elaborate array of emergency management procedures with local emergency management at its base. There are some qualifiers. For some types—such as civil defense and nuclear accidents—the federal role in policymaking and administration is dominant. Lack of clarity in law, regulations, and historical practice, along with differences in perceptions and interpretations of risk have long complicated the job of emergency management.

DIMENSIONS OF EMERGENCY MANAGEMENT

Decentralization is not necessarily all bad. In fact, decentralization, with sound coordination, is an essential component of successful emergency management. In addition, because most emergency management procedures are implemented by local governments to meet local needs, it is not reasonable to assume that common "all hazard" sets of procedures are applicable to all localities regardless of geography or other factors. The literature that exists on emergency management points out the primary dimensions and factors essential to successful emergency management. The extent to which one dimension is stressed over another depends upon the need of the locality and the types of vulnerabilities that locality faces.

The first dimension of emergency management stressed in the relevant literature is the need for strong cooperation and coordination among and within local, state, and federal governments. Experience has demonstrated that local government is usually the first responder, and its agencies are the primary responders to the emergency, although the federal government may furnish most of the resources and much technical expertise. All citizens expect their local governments to prevent, respond to, and manage emergencies. But, without inter- and intra-governmental cooperation and coordination, local governmental officials cannot implement emergency management as well as they might.

The second dimension found in the literature is the need for strong cooperation and coordination among the public, nonprofit, and private sectors. Since emergency management is normally conducted in a very fluid and often chaotic-filled environment, the government, particularly the local government, faces difficulties in meeting its obligations while at the same time interacting with other governmental jurisdictions and private or nonprofit organizations. For instance, construction companies implement building codes and chemical companies help detoxify hazardous products. Charitable organizations often service human needs that governments cannot. Help from private and non-profit sectors often augments successful emergency management, sometimes meeting needs or filling gaps that the government is unable to fully address.

The third dimension recognizes the need to consider the type of disaster. This dimension may be the most complex....

POLITICAL FACTORS

Disasters also possess several significant political components that emergency managers should be well aware of in their interaction with public officials. In effect, natural disasters and emergencies provide excellent windows of opportunity for public officials. They often use such circumstances to demonstrate their leadership capabilities and willingness to tackle difficult problems. Their actions will almost always receive media publicity and instant public notice. Moreover, it is extremely difficult to oppose or criticize an official who steps in and gives the appearance of taking charge in order to help disaster victims.

Natural disasters also produce conditions that allow political leaders to show their concern for citizens' needs and demands. Disaster victims often encounter problems that they have never before experienced and which they may be unprepared or unequipped to handle on their own. Public officials are in a apposition to highlight the needs and channel the resources to help those who are in distress. Disasters give them a perfect opportunity to demonstrate their responsiveness to the needs of the people. Political leaders who successfully address disaster-related problems are rewarded while those who are unwilling or unable to act can suffer negative political repercussions.

EMERGENCY MANAGEMENT PRESCRIPTIONS

In light of the many factors involved, the literature suggests that the formulation of emergency management follow several prescriptions:

1. Since it is a continuous process, emergency management should not be formulated on the basis of a single emergency, but on several. At the same time, it should allow for the constant incorporation of new findings.

2. It should attempt to reduce uncertainty in crises by anticipating problems and projecting possible solutions. Thus, the appropriateness of response is more important than the speed of response.

3. It needs to be based on what will probably happen; procedures need to address what people are likely to do in emergencies and not be based on myths or common pre-conceptions about human behavior.

4. It must be educational in that involved persons must be aware that such emergency procedures exist, and they must understand and follow them. Consequently, emergency management needs to be "sold" effectively to communities in order to be taken seriously.

5. Finally, it needs to be practiced because the absence of exercises and practice will largely negate even the best plans.

EMERGENCY MANAGEMENT CYCLE[3]

An emergency management program examines potential emergencies and disasters based on the risks posed by likely hazards; develops and implements programs aimed toward reducing the impact of these events on the community, prepares for those risks that cannot be eliminated; and prescribes the actions required to deal with the consequences of actual events and to recover from those events.

If we simplify the emergency management activities into four phases that form a cycle, the phases of the cycle can be summarized as follows:

■ Mitigation — Taking sustained actions to reduce or eliminate long-term risk to people and property from hazards and their effects.

■ Preparedness — Building the emergency management function to respond effectively to, and recover from, any hazards.

■ Response — Conducting emergency operations o save lives and property by taking action to reduce the hazard to acceptable levels (or eliminate it entirely); evacuating potential victims; providing food, water, shelter, and medical care to those in need; and restoring critical public services.

■ Recovery — Rebuilding communities so that individuals, businesses, and governments can function on their own, return to normal life, and protect against future hazards.

The illustration below provides a simplified picture of the emergency management cycle. Phases often overlap to fit individual situations and events.

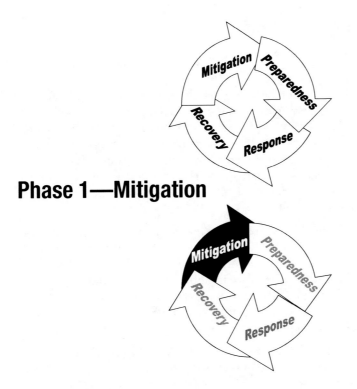

Phase 1—Mitigation

As the costs of disasters continue to rise, it is necessary to take sustained action to reduce or eliminate the long-term risk to people and property from hazards and their effects. These sustained actions are also known as mitigation.

Mitigation is the initial phase of emergency management and should be considered before a disaster or emergency occurs. Mitigation, however, should also be a continuing activity that is integrated with each of the other phases of emergency management to employ a long-range, community-based approach to mitigation.

The goals of mitigation activities are to:

- Protect people and structures.

- Reduce the costs of response and recovery.

Mitigation is accomplished in conjunction with a hazard. A hazard analysis helps to identify:

- What events can occur in and around the community.

- The likelihood that an event will occur.

- The consequences of the event in terms of casualties, destruction, disruption to critical services, and costs of recovery.

To be successful, mitigation measures must be developed into an overall mitigation strategy that considers ways to reduce hazard losses together with the overall risk from specific hazards and other community goals.

Developing a Mitigation Strategy

A sound mitigation strategy is one that is based on several factors:

- *Prevention measures* are intended to prevent existing risks from becoming worse based on new developments or other changes within the community (e.g., road construction, zoning or building code changes). Prevention measures can be very effective in areas that have not been developed or are in an early phase of development. By implementing prevention measures, such as open space preservation and storm water management, future development can be directed in such a way as to minimize the risk from known hazards while maintaining other community goals and the overall quality of life in the community.

- *Property protection measures* are used to modify buildings or their surroundings to reduce the risk of damage from a known hazard. Property protection measures directly protect people and property at risk and may be simple and relatively low cost (e.g., raising utilities or strapping water heaters) or they may be more elaborate and expensive (e.g., acquiring land and using that land for recreational purposes or building earthquake-resistant structures in earthquake zones).

- *Natural resource protection measures* are used to reduce the consequences of a known hazard and to improve the overall quality of the environment. Natural resource protection measures can range from erosion and sediment control to wetlands protection to controlling runoff from farmland sediment into downstream waterways.

- *Emergency services measures* protect people before and after an event occurs and may include warning, response, protective measures for critical facilities; and maintenance of health and safety.

To be effective, emergency protective measures should be built into the emergency planning process, exercised, and revised to incorporate lessons learned from both exercises and actual emergencies.

- *Structural projects* directly protect people and property that are at risk from a known hazard. Structural projects involve the construction of man-made structures (e.g., dikes, levees, elevated roadways) to control the damage from a known hazard. These projects can be very expensive, and over the long-term, may actually disrupt the environment in such a way as to increase the overall risk from other hazards. Additionally, some structural mitigation measures may provide the public with a false since of security, especially in the case of an extreme event, such as the Midwest floods, during which many levees were breached by the floodwaters.

- *Public information* serves to inform and remain people about the hazards they face and measures they should take to avoid damage or injury. Public information measures may include outreach projects, real estate disclosure requirement, technical assistance, and education programs.

The mitigation strategy developed must consider the hazards faced, the potential for damage from those hazards, and the overall needs of the community. Mitigation measures must be consistent with the strategy but can be effective only if considered as part of the larger emergency management cycle.

Mitigation measures can be developed and implemented at the local or state level. Two examples of mitigation measures that have been cited for their effectiveness are included below.

Hazard Mitigation Program: State of Massachusetts

The Hazard Minimization Program was institute in November 1991, as a way to reduce repetitive losses from disasters. The program funds mitigation measures, such as basement window replacement and installation of interior floodwalls as a way of reducing repetitive losses from flooding. To be eligible for the minimization program, individuals or families must have suffered a loss that can be minimized through a one-time mitigation measure.

Following a major storm in December 1992, the State conducted a survey to measure the program's success. Of the 71 homeowners who responded to the survey, 49 (69 percent) indicated that they had homes exposed to floodwaters from the storm, but only 3 (less than 1 percent) were affected by the floodwaters.

Of the three homes affected by the floodwaters, only one case related to a failed minimization project. During a follow-up survey, most participants stated that they would have been affected by the storm had minimization measures not been undertaken. These survey results indicated that the program could have a major impact on reducing future store losses, both in terms of human suffering and in taxpayer dollars saved.

Hazard Mitigation Program: Borough of Avalon, Cape May County, New Jersey

The Borough of Avalon, Cape May County, New Jersey developed a mitigation strategy designed to minimize the impact of storm damage through the implementation of structural and nonstructural mitigation projects. Projects completed under the program included:

- Developing flood-level maps and installing flood-level indicators at specific points in the borough. These maps were then mass-mailed, together with a letter of explanation, to all borough residents.

- Preparing and distributing a quarterly newsletter to inform residents of emergency management proposals, such as evaluation routes, dredging and beach-fill projects, and shelter locations.

- Preparing a hazard mitigation plan for the borough, including goals and objectives, proposed measures, programs, and actions to avoid vulnerability to hazards and overall beach protection strategies.

- Conducting educational seminars in the borough on measures, procedures, and problems related to severe weather emergencies; distributing informational material; and creating an instructional videotape.

- Adopting land-use and development ordinances and funding appropriations for property development restrictions; maintaining beaches, including stalling sand fencing, planting dune grass, and implementing beach renourishment projects. Elevating the municipal building, police headquarters, and public works garage above the base flood elevation. Installing a borough-wide public address warning system that includes television access through the local cable television company.

The strategy was awarded First Place for municipalities by the 1993 National Coordinating Council on Emergency Management.

Source: *Partnership in Preparedness: A Compendium of Exemplary Practices in Emergency Management*, Federal Emergency Management Agency, December 1995.

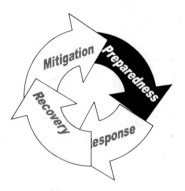

Because it is not possible to mitigate completely against every hazard that poses a risk, preparedness measures can help to reduce the impact of the remaining hazards by taking certain actions before an emergency event occurs. Preparedness includes plans or other preparations made to save lives and facilitate response and recovery operations.

Preparedness measures involve all of the players in the integrated emergency management system—local, state, and federal agencies and citizens—and, at the local level, may including activities, such as:

- *Developing an Emergency Operation Plan (EOP)* that addresses identified hazards, risks, and response measures.

- *Recruiting, assigning, and training staff* who can assist in key areas of response operations.

- *Identifying resources and supplies* that may be required in an emergency.

- *Designating facilities* for emergency use.

The EOP

Generally, the EOP describes how the community (or State) will do business in an emergency. The EOP:

■ Assigns responsibility to organizations and individuals for carrying out specific actions that exceed the capability or responsibility of any single agency.

■ Establishes lines of authority and organizational relationships, and shows how all actions will be coordinated.

■ Describes how people and property will be protected in emergencies and disasters.

■ Identifies personnel, equipment, facilities, supplies, and other resources that can be made available—within the jurisdiction or by agreement with other jurisdictions—for use during response and recovery operations.

■ Identifies steps to address mitigation concerns during response and recovery operations.

Local government is responsible for attending to the public's emergency needs. Therefore, the local EOP focuses on measures that are essential for protecting the public, including:

■ *Warning and communications*: How the local government will warn the public of an existing or impending emergency and communicate internally before, during, and after an event occurs.

■ *Emergency public information*: How government will communicate with the public before, during, and after an emergency occurs. Emergency public information is especially critical in light of the recent terrorism threat. Decisions about what to tell the public and when are critical to gaining a reasoned response from the public, providing confidence that the government is doing all it can to protect the public and control the situation, and—perhaps most importantly—making the public into a response asset will be crucial.

■ *Mass care*: Where and for how long the public's emergency needs, such as shelter and food distribution, will be accomplished. What facilities will be available, what supplies will be stocked, and how the supplies will be distributed are all covered under mass care in the EOP.

■ *Health and medical care*: How victims will be cared for, where, and by whom are addressed in the health and medical portion of the EOP. Special issues, such as decontamination, must also be addressed for hazardous materials and terrorist events.

■ *Evacuation*: What routes will be used if evacuation becomes necessary, special transportation or routing requirements (e.g., evacuating the disabled or making evacuation routes one way to accommodate increased traffic flow), and other issues dealing with emergency egress are all part of the evacuation portion of the EOP.

States also have EOPs. State EOPs serve three main purposes:

- To facilitate a State first response to certain emergencies.

- To assist local jurisdictions during emergencies in which local response capabilities are overwhelmed.

- To serve as a liaison with the Federal government in cases where Federal assistance is necessary and authorized.

The State EOP establishes the framework within which local EOPs are created and through which the federal government becomes involved in response and recovery operations. As such, the state government acts as the coordinating entity to ensure that all levels of government are able to respond to safeguard the well being of its citizens.

The federal EOP is called the Federal Response Plan (FRP). When activated following a Presidentially declared emergency or disaster, the FRP enables FEMA to coordinate the efforts of 27 federal agencies (including the American Red Cross) to assist state and local response and recovery efforts. The FRP is similar to local and state EOPs in terms of its overall goals, but the federal government also can bring highly specialized resources to bear (e.g., Nuclear Emergency Support Teams (NEST), Metropolitan Medical Response Teams, and Urban Search and Rescue Task Force) on emergencies and disasters that are outside the response capabilities of local and state governments. In 2003 for the first time, as a result of Homeland Security Policy Directive [No.] 5, a new name was given to the plan for federal response, and a National Response Plan (NRP) was mandated.

Recruiting, Assigning, and Training Staff

During an emergency or disaster response, it may be necessary to assign personnel to jobs other than those that they normally perform. Some personnel may already be employed within the community, but others may be recruited specifically for service in emergencies. Regardless of employment status, these personnel must be recruited, assigned, and trained for their jobs before an emergency event occurs. Whenever possible, these persons should be included in exercises that enable them to practice the job under simulated emergency conditions so that, when an actual emergency occurs, they are ready to perform in their new capacities with little or no time lost in learning the job.

Identifying Resources and Supplies

Identifying the resources and supplies that will be available for an emergency response is a crucial part of preparedness. Virtually all jurisdictions take an inventory of their personnel and equipment resources to determine what they have and compare it with what they may need in an emergency. Those gaps between on-hand resources and probable requirements can be filled in a number of ways. Among the most common are:

- *Mutual aid agreements with neighboring jurisdictions.* Mutual aid agreements are formal, written agreements between jurisdictions that provide the conditions under which resource sharing can take place during an emergency. Mutual aid agreements are most common among fire departments and law enforcement agencies but may be developed to cover other resources and equipment (e.g., construction equipment) as well.

■ *Standby contracts with suppliers of critical equipment and supplies.* Standby contracts typically are made for equipment, such as dump trucks or other construction equipment, but are also used for supplies, such as plastic sheeting. Under a typical standby contract, the supplier agrees to provide an established quantity of an item at the unit cost in effect on the day before the emergency occurs. Standby contracts are a good way for local governments to meet their resource supply requirements without incurring the costs of stockpiling and without paying the rapidly increasing prices that often follow an emergency.

In some large emergencies, state and federal resources are deployed. For example, the National Guard may be activated following an extremely heavy snow, in the case of wildfire, or following a terrorist incident. Federal resources, including Disaster Medical Assistance Teams (DMATs) and Disaster Mortuary Teams (DMORTs) may be activated following a mass-casualty incident. All requests for state and federal resources must be processed through the state.

Designating Facilities for Emergency Use

To ensure an effective and efficient response, certain facilities are designated as part of the emergency planning process. Typically, these facilities include:

■ *The Emergency Operations Center (EOC),* which is the central location from which all off-scene activities are coordinated. Senior elected and appointed officials are located at the EOC, as well as personnel supporting critical functions, such as operations, planning, logistics, and finance and administration. The key function of EOC personnel is to ensure that those who are located at the scene have the resources (i.e., personnel, tools, and equipment) they need for the response. In large emergencies and disasters, the EOC also acts as a liaison between local responders and the State.[4]

■ *Shelters, which are used to house victims and first responders who are displaced by the even.* Shelters should be designated before an event occurs, and the public should be aware of shelter locations and transportation routes from their neighborhoods or workplaces to the shelters. In most areas, The American Red Cross operates shelters and coordinates with the local volunteer program manager to ensure that sheltering needs are met.

■ *Distribution centers, from which food and emergency supplies are made available to the public.* In most areas, The American Red Cross, together with other local voluntary agencies, coordinate distribution centers.

■ *Storage areas for specific types of equipment.* Warehouses, supply yards, and other facilities that will be used as providers of the equipment necessary for a response should be designated as part of the planning process.

Other facilities may also be designated in advance, based on the jurisdiction's resources and the areas of the community that are likely to be affected. On-scene facilities, such as the Incident Command Post (ICP) and staging areas, typically are not designated in advance because of the requirement for close proximity to the incident site.

Text Telephone (TTY) Alert: Lee County Division of Public Safety, Fort Myers, Florida

TTY Alert is an emergency warning system for deaf and hard-of-hearing residents in northwest Florida. It is the first system of its kind in the Unite States. When an emergency occurs, the Lee County EOP sends out an alert to the TTY machines with information about the emergency and information about what to do to every registered TTY user in the county. If necessary, the system can target a specific area. TTY Alert also allows TTY users to access the system to obtain headline news, weather bulletins, and family disaster preparedness information.

TTY Alert has been well received by the hearing-impaired community and has been recognized by the National Institute on Disabilities Rehabilitation Research.

Local Emergency Management/Industry Partnership: St. Charles Parish, Louisiana

The local emergency management/industry partnership program offers a telephone hotline system to coordinate response to disasters and emergencies. The program was established by the St. Charles Parish EOC in cooperation with 26 petrochemical companies. The system serves as a 24-hour warning system, an emergency information exchange, and a link between the companies and the parish Department of Emergency Preparedness for support during emergencies.

The system has been recognized by the Chemical Manufacturers Association as a model of government-industry cooperation.

Source: *Partnerships in Preparedness: A Compendium of Exemplary Practices in Emergency Management,* Federal Emergency Management Agency, December 1995.

Citizen Preparedness

Private citizens can and should also prepare for emergencies. There are several simple steps that you, as a citizen, can take to prepare yourself for an emergency. Personal preparedness activities cannot only keep you and your family safe but can help you become a response asset rather than a response burden.

- *Complete your own hazard analysis.* If you have lived in the community for any period of time, you are probably aware of the hazards that are high risk for your area. If you are new to the area, talk to some long-time residents to determine what events have occurred historically in your area. Don't forget the "small" emergencies, such as fire or an extended electrical outage.

- *Develop our own emergency plan.* Play the "what if" game with each of the hazards you selected. What would you do if _____ occurs?

Then ask yourself what supplies you would need to take the action(s) you identify, and gather the supplies together.

■ *Practice your plan.* Even simple tasks can become difficult during an emergency. Practice your plan before an emergency occurs until you are thoroughly familiar with the procedures you need to follow if the event occurs.

Response

Response begins when an emergency event is imminent or immediately after an event occurs. Response encompasses *all activities taken to save lives and reduce damage* from the event and includes:

■ Providing emergency assistance to victims.

■ Restoring critical infrastructure (e.g., utilities).

■ Ensuring continuity of critical services (e.g., law enforcement, public works).

In other words, response involves putting preparedness plans into action.

One of the first response tasks is to conduct a situation assessment. Local government is responsible for emergency response and for continued assessment of its ability to protect its citizens and the property within the community. To fulfill this responsibility, responders and local government officials must conduct an immediate *rapid assessment* of the local situation.

Rapid assessment includes all immediate response activities that are directly linked to determining initial lifesaving and life-sustaining needs and to identifying imminent hazards. The ability of local governments to perform a rapid assessment within the first few hours after an event is crucial to providing an adequate response for life-threatening situations and imminent hazards. Coordinated and timely assessments enable local governments to:

■ Prioritize response activities.

■ Allocate scarce resources.

■ Request additional assistance from mutual aid partners, as well as the State, quickly and accurately.

Obtaining accurate information quickly through rapid assessment is key to initiating response activities and needs to be collected in an organized fashion. Critical information, also called *essential elements of information* (EEI), includes information about:

- Lifesaving needs, such as evacuation and search and rescue.

- The status of critical infrastructure, such as transportation, utilities, communication systems, and fuel and water supplies.

- The status of critical facilities, such as police and fire stations, medical providers, water and sewage treatment facilities, and media outlets.

- The risk of damage to the community (e.g., dams and levees, facilities producing or storing hazardous material) from imminent hazards.

- The number of citizens who have been displaced as a result of the event and the estimated extent of damage to their dwellings.

Essential elements of information also include information about the potential for cascading events. Cascading events are events that occur as a direct or indirect result of an initial event. For example, if a flash flood disrupts electricity to an area and, as a result of the electrical failure, a serious traffic accident involving a hazardous material spill occurs, the traffic accident is a cascading event. If, as a result of the hazardous materials spill, a neighborhood must be evacuated and a local stream is contaminated, these are also cascading events. Taken together, the effect of cascading events can be crippling to a community.

Good planning, training, and exercising before an event occurs can help reduce cascading events and their effects. Maintaining the discipline to follow the plan during response operations also reduces the effects of cascading events.

Citizens and Response Operations

What can private citizens do to facilitate an emergency response? Surprisingly, there is much that citizens can do, and many of the actions that will help the response most are relatively simple.

- *Follow your own emergency plan.* Assuming that you developed a plan and practiced what you would do during the preparedness phase, this is the time to implement it. Follow your plan unless something related to the event makes it unworkable or unsafe.

- *Pay attention to and follow emergency directions provided by local officials.* List to emergency broadcasts on the local media and follow the directions provide in the broadcasts. Emergency announcements are prepared by those who are most familiar with what is actually happening at the incident site and will provide you with the information you need to remain safe during the emergency.

- *Don't make unnecessary phone calls*, either by cellular pone or land line. Keep critical lines of communication open for emergency use.

Very importantly, if you think you want to help during an emergency, don't just show up at the scene to help. Volunteer with an established voluntary agency now. Volunteering before an emergency occurs will enable you to receive the training you need so that, when an emergency occurs and your services are needed, you know where you need to go and what you will do. Volunteering before an emergency also helps the agency and local authorities identify their resources and plan their needs.

Recovery

The goal of recovery is to return the community's systems and activities to normal. Recovery begins right after the emergency. Some recovery activities may be concurrent with response efforts.

Long-term recovery includes restoring economic activity and rebuilding community facilities and housing. Long-term recovery (stabilizing all systems) can sometimes take years.

Although recovery is primarily a responsibility of local government, if the emergency or disaster received a Presidential Declaration, a number of assistance programs may be available under the Stafford Act. There are two major categories of Federal aid: public assistance and individual assistance. Public assistance is for repair of infrastructure, public facilities and debris removal, and may include:

■ Repair or replacement of non-federal roads, public buildings, and bridges.

■ Implementation of mitigation measures.

Individual assistance is for damage to residences and businesses or for personal property losses and may include:

■ Grants to individuals and families for temporary housing, repairs, replacement of possessions, and medical and funeral expenses.

■ The Small Business Administration (SBA) loans to individuals and businesses.

■ Crisis counseling for victims and responders; legal services; and disaster unemployment benefits.

Recovery from disaster is unique to each community depending on the amount and kind of damage caused by the disaster and the resources that the community has ready or can get. In the short term, recovery is an extension of the response phase in which basic services and functions are restored. In the long term, recovery is a restoration of both the personal lives of individuals and the livelihood of the community.

After the short-term recovery when roads have been opened, debris removed, supplies and shelters secured, communication channels, water and power, life safety and other basic services and functions are restored. In the long term, recovery is a restoration of both the personal lives of individuals and the livelihood of the community.

Once the early stage of recovery has brought the community back to a safe and operational level of functioning, the long-term state can build on that.

Long-term recovery may take several months of even extend into years because it is a complex process of revitalizing not just homes but also businesses, public infrastructure, and the community's economy and quality of life.

There are many long-term leadership and planning considerations. Applying for assistance programs available from the federal government, as mentioned previously, is important to consider for obtaining financial and other resources in the case of a Presidential Disaster Declaration. Other considerations include:

- Keeping citizens informed and preventing unrealistic expectations.

- Mitigation measures to ensure against future disaster damage.

- Donations.

- Partnerships with business and industry for resources.

- Competing interests of groups involved in the planning process.

- Environmental issues.

- Public health measures to take against the risks of diseases, contamination, and other cascading effects from a disaster.

- The unmet needs of victims.

- Rebuilding bridges, roads, public works, and other expensive parts of the infrastructure.

THE ROLE OF THE LOCAL EMERGENCY PROGRAM MANAGER

The local Emergency Program Manager has the day-to-day responsibility of overseeing emergency management programs and activities. And most emergencies are handled at the local level without state or federal assistance. This role entails coordinating all aspects of a jurisdiction's mitigation, preparedness, response, and recovery capabilities. The Emergency Program Manager:

- Coordinates resources from all sectors before, during, and after an emergency.

- Manages activities relating to mitigation, preparedness, response, and recovery.

- Ensures that all players of the process:
    - Are aware of potential threats to the community.
    - Participate in mitigation and prevention activities.
    - Plan for emergencies using an all-hazards approach.
    - Operate effectively in emergency situations.
    - Conduct effective recovery operations after a disaster.

The Emergency Program Manager coordinates all components of the emergency management system for the community, including:

- Fire and police services.

- Emergency medical programs.

- Public works.

- Volunteers and voluntary organizations.

- Other groups involved in emergency activities.

Other duties of the local Emergency Program Manager might include the following:

- Coordinating the planning process and working cooperatively with organizations and government agencies.

- Advising and information the Chief Elected official about emergency management activities.

- Identifying and analyzing the potential effects of hazards that threaten the jurisdiction.

- Taking inventory of personnel and material resources from private sector sources that would be available in an emergency.

- Identifying resource deficiencies and working with appropriate officials on measures to resolve them.

- Developing and carrying out public awareness and education programs.

- Establishing a system to alert officials and the public in an emergency.

- Establishing and maintaining networks of expert advisors and damage assessors for all hazards.

- Coordinating a review of all local emergency-related authorities and recommending amendments, when necessary.

Based on the community's organization strategy, the Emergency Program Manager may service as:

- Part of the fire/rescue department staff.

- Part of a law enforcement agency staff, located in a police department or sheriff's office.

- Head of a separate organization that reports directly to a governing or executive body.

Regardless of location, the person in this position obviously must devote significant time and energy coordinating with a variety of people and organizations within and outside the community.

STATE EMERGENCY MANAGEMENT ROLE

The role of state government in emergency management in many ways parallels the role of the local emergency management function.

- Legislative and executive authorities exist for state emergency programs, with a range of programs usually operating in a variety of state agencies.

- The state has a responsibility to develop and maintain a comprehensive program for mitigation, preparedness, response, and recovery activities.

The state's role is to supplement and facilitate local efforts before, during, and after emergencies. The state must be prepared to maintain or accelerate services and to provide new services to local governments when local capabilities fall short of demands.

A state government is in the unique position to serve as a link between those who need assistance and those who can assist. It is able to:

- Coordinate with local governments to meet their emergency needs.

- Assess available state and federal resources.

- Help the local government apply for, acquire, and use those resources effectively.

The state also provides direct guidance and assistance to its local jurisdictions through program development, and it channels federal guidance and assistance to the local level. In a disaster, the state office helps coordinate and integrate resources and apply them to local needs. The state's role might best be described as "pivotal."

The governor of a state, who is responsible for the general welfare of the citizens of that state, has certain legislated powers and resources that can be applied to all-hazards emergency management.

All state governors have authority and responsibility for:

- Issuing state or area emergency declarations.

- Initiating state response actions (personnel, materials).

- Activating emergency contingency funds and/or reallocating regular budgets for emergency activities.

- Overseeing emergency management for all four phases.

- Applying for and monitoring federal assistance.

The State Emergency Management Agency:

- Carries out statewide emergency management activities.

- Helps coordinate emergency management activities involving more than one community.

- Assists individual communities when they need help.

- Provides financial assistance on a supplemental basis through a process of application and review.

(The governor reviews the application, studies the damage estimates and, if appropriate, declares a state of emergency.)

If the local community's resources are not adequate, the first place to turn for additional assistance is to the county of state Emergency Management Agency.

Drawing on these resources occurs during restoration, which involves actions that repair critical infrastructure. This may include restoring utility services, conducting radiological decontamination, and removing debris.

Acting on the information provided, the county or state office will dispatch personnel to the scene to assist in the response and recovery effort. Only the governor, however, can request the Federal aid that comes with a Presidential Declaration.

State laws require that all states have a State Emergency Management Agency and an EOP coordinated by that agency.

HOW THE PRIVATE SECTOR AND VOLUNTARY ORGANIZATIONS ASSIST EMERGENCY MANAGERS

The private sector, including private citizens and voluntary organizations, plays a major role in assisting emergency managers before, during, and after an emergency.

- *Private industry* contributes by:
  - Developing and exercising emergency plans before an emergency occurs.
  - Working with emergency management personnel before an emergency occurs to ascertain what assistance may be necessary and how they can help.
  - Providing assistance (including volunteers) to support emergency management during an emergency and throughout the recovery process.

- *Citizens* contribute by:
  - Taking the time necessary to understand the types of emergencies that are likely to occur and preparing a personal disaster kit and emergency plans for those events.

- Volunteering with an established organization and receiving training before an emergency occurs.
- Taking direction and responding reasonably to alerts, warnings, and other emergency public information.

- *Voluntary organizations* contribute by:
  - Training and managing volunteer resources.
  - Identifying shelter locations and needed supplies.
  - Providing critical emergency services, such as the provision of cleaning supplies, clothing, food, and shelter or assisting with post-emergency cleanup to those in need.
  - Identifying those whose needs have not been met and coordinating the provision of assistance.

Each of these players is critical to ensuring an appropriate and efficient response. However, each must become involved during the preparedness phase of the integrated emergency management system to ensure that, when an emergency occurs, all players understand their roles and are ready to contribute without delay.

FEDERAL EMERGENCY MANAGEMENT ROLE[5]

The Federal government's involvement in emergency management often pertains to all four phases of emergency management. Assistance may take the form of fiscal support, technical assistance, or information about materials, personnel resources, and research.... The roles and functions of the federal agencies and departments are spelled out in legislations, executive directives, and regulations. Also, the federal government has the greatest amount of financial resources that may be applied to emergency response and recovery.

The Federal Emergency Management Agency (FEMA) takes a lead role in national preparedness for major crises. It also plays coordinating and supportive/assistance roles for integrated emergency management in partnership with state and local emergency management entities. As necessary, FEMA provides funding, technical assistance, services, supplies, equipment, and direct federal support.

FEMA provides technical and financial assistance to state and local governments to upgrade their communications and warning systems, and it operates an emergency information and coordination center that provides a central location for the collection and management of disaster and emergency information.

FEMA provides information to the President concerning matters of national interest to help with decisions about disaster declarations. The President of the United States is responsible for:

- Protecting the public.

- Making a disaster declaration before federal funds are released to aid disaster victims.

When activated following a Presidential declared emergency or disaster, the FRP enables FEMA to coordinate the efforts of 27 federal agencies (including The

American Red Cross) to assist State and local response and recovery efforts. The FRP is similar to local and state EOPs in terms of its overall goals, but the federal government also can bring highly specialized resources to bear (e.g., Nuclear Emergency Support Teams (NEST), Metropolitan Medical Response Teams, and Urban Search and Rescue Task Force) on emergencies and disasters that are outside the response capabilities of local and state governments. In 2003 for the first time, as a result of Homeland Security Policy Directive [No.] 5, a new name was given to the plan for federal response, and a National Plan (NRP) as mandated.

The new National Response Plan (NRP) was issued in final form in January 2005, and is expected to result in major changes in the way that the federal government, as well as other sector organizations, manages the response to major disasters of all types in the U.S. Many of the changes are based on the perceived needs resulting from the 9/11 attacks. Since the 9/11 terrorist attacks, greater awareness and concern with both national security and homeland security have extended to the nation as a while as well as to many other countries. The NRP specifies how the resources of the federal government will work in concert with state, local, and tribal governments and the private sector to respond to Incidents of National Significance. The NRP is predicated on the National Incident Management System, or NIMS. Together the NRP and the NIMS provide a nationwide template for working together to prevent or respond to threats and incidents regardless of cause, size, or complexity.

In its final form (expected to be issued in August 2004), the NRP will supersede five predecessor plans, namely the Federal Response Plan, National Oil and Hazardous Substances Pollution Contingency Plan, Federal Radiological Emergency Response Plan, Interagency Domestic Terrorism (CONPLAN), and National Plan for Response to Catastrophic Events.[6]

SUMMARY

NDMS and NIMS are important features of the nation's disaster planning and will be a part of every first responder's training for the foreseeable future. Getting the right resources and personnel to the scene of an emergency and having those resources able to seamlessly integrate to scale any response up to the necessary level is the concept behind the Federal NDMS and NIMS campaigns, as well as being a large part of the recommended immediate improvements made to NYPD's response plans. We must be prepared to learn from the past to save lives in future.

ADDITIONAL DISCUSSION TOPICS

- How are Disaster Medical Teams (DMAT) organized to be ready for service throughout the country?

- Definitive patient care changes based on the patient's needs. What would be definitive care for a patient who needs dialysis every other day? How would you make evacuation plans keeping this patient's chronic medical problem in mind?

■ Would NYPD adoption of an ICS based response system like NIMS answer many of the improvements identified in the post 9-11 audit of NYPD response? What problems would you expect when changing the procedures in an organization the size of NYPD?

REFERENCES

Anderson, W.A. (1969). *Local civil defense in natural disaster*. Columbus, OH: The Ohio State University Disaster Research Center.

Barrett, C.B. (1986). "Local flood warning systems." pp. 79–91 in U.S. Army Corps of Engineers Hydrologic Engineering Center (Ed.), *Proceedings of a Seminar on Local Flood Warning-Response Systems*. Davis, CA: U.S. Army Corps of Engineers Hydrologic Engineering Center.

Birkland, T.A. (1997). *After Disaster: agenda setting, public policy and focusing events*. Washington, DC: Georgetown University Press.

Blanchard, W. (2004). *Introduction to emergency management* (working draft). FEMA. Emmitsburg, MD: Emergency Management Institute. URL: http://training.fema.gov/EMIWeb/edu/introtoEM.asp

Brunacini, A.V. (2002). *Command safety: saving our own*. Quincy, MA: National Fire Protection Association.

Drabek, T. (1996). *Social dimensions of disaster: Instructor Guide*. Emmitsburg, MD: Federal Emergency Management Agency.

Federal Emergency Management Agency. (1995). *Introduction to emergency management*, Student Manual 230. Emmitsburg, MD: Emergency Management Institute.

Federal Emergency Management Agency. (1998). *Principles of emergency management* (Student Manual and Instructor Guide G230). Emmitsburg: MD: Emergency Management Institute.

Greenway, A.R. (1998). *Risk management planning handbook*. Rockville, MD: Government Institute Press.

Ketchum, J. and Whittaker, H. (1982). "Hazards analysis," *Comprehensive Emergency Management Bulletin* 2 (number 1): 1-17.

Kramer, W. and Bahme, C. (1992). *Fire officer's guide to disaster control*. Saddlebrook, NJ: Pennwell Publishing Company.

Lindell, M.K. and Perry, R.W. (1992). *Behavioral foundations of community emergency planning*. Washington, DC: Hemisphere Publishers.

Lindell, M.K. and Perry, R.W. (1997). "Hazardous materials releases in the Northridge earthquake." *Risk Analysis* 17 (April): 147-156.

Lindell, M.K. and Perry, R.W. (2003). *Risk communication in multicultural communities*. Thousand Oaks, CA: Sage Publications.

Perry, R.W. and Lindell, M.K. (1990). *Living with Mt. St. Helens: human adjustment to volcano hazards*. Pullman, WA: Washington State University Press.

Perry, R.W. and Lindell, M.K. (1997). "Principles for managing community relocation as a hazard mitigation measure," *Journal of Contingencies and Crisis Management* 5 (March): 49-60.

Petak, W.J. (1985). "Emergency Management: a challenge to public administration," *Public Administration Review*, Vol. 45, Special Issue (January 1985):3.

Prater, C.S. and Lindell, M.K. (2000). "The politics of hazard mitigation," *Natural Hazards Review* 1, 73-82.

Endnotes

[1] This section was derived from the FEMA-EMI course textbook, *Introduction to Emergency Management* (working draft), Chapter 1, "Introduction to Emergency Management," Wayne Blanchard (2004).

[2] This section through "Emergency Management Prescriptions" were derived from Richard Sylves' FEMA-EMI course *Political and Policy Basis of Emergency Management*, 1998.

[3] This section was derived from FEMA-EMI, U.S. Fire Administration Course IS230 - Principles of Emergency Management. March 2003. URL: http://www.training.fema.gov/cmiweb/IS/is2301st.asp

[4] Note that States operate EOCs as well and can activate them as necessary to support local operations. State EOC personnel report to the Governor and act as a liaison between local and Federal personnel.

[5] Editor's note: Since the advent of the DHS, FEMA is now a part of that department. Presently, DHS has the lead role in some instances, rather than FEMA. For the latest information, check the DHS website (www.dhs.gov).

[6] The related links are as follows:

Federal Response Plan - http://www.dtra.mil/news/deskbook/ Full%20text%20documents/Federal%Plans/Interim%20FRP%202003.pdf

National Oil and Hazardous Substances Pollution Contingency Plan - http://www.dtra.mil/news/deskbook/Full%20text%20documents/ Federal%@)Plans/National%20Contingency%20Plan.doc

Federal Radiological Emergency Response Plan (FRERP) - http://www.dtra.mil/news/deskbook/Full%20text%20Plans/FRERP.doc

Interagency Domestic Terrorism CONPLAN - http://www.dtra.mil/news/ deskbook/Full%20text%20documents/Federal%20Plans/ Interagency%20Domestic%20Terrorism$%20CONPLAN.pdf

CHAPTER TWELVE

ICS ROLES AND PROCEDURES

I will study and get ready, and perhaps my chance will come.
—Abraham Lincoln

KEY TERMS

Command
Operations
Planning
Logistics
Finance/Administration
Incident Commander
Command Staff
Predefined Hierarchy
Uniform Terminology
Modular Organizational Structure
Incident Action Plan
Manageable Span of Control

OBJECTIVES

■ Identify the organizational structure for an Incident Command System (ICS) disaster response.

■ Identify the purpose of an Incident Action Plan (IAP).

■ Describe the difference between the National Incident Management System (NIMS) and the ICS.

■ Write an emergency plan and response.

DISCUSSION TOPICS

■ How are responsibilities divided in ICS?

■ What is meant by Unified Command?

■ Originally adopted by firefighters 30 years ago, what agencies are following its guidelines now?

■ How does ICS fit into the NIMS guidelines?

12

INTRODUCTION

In the 1970s the Incident Command System, ICS, was developed after a series of devastating wildfires caused massive damage and took several lives. When the event was studied afterwards it was determined that the responders had all done their work well, but that management had been the weak point of the response. Cooperation between agencies had been limited through a lack of equipment interoperability, and a lack of pre-event integration planning or training. Using management concepts derived from business practice, ICS was developed to improve the ability of emergency managers to efficiently and safely utilize responding agencies.

While the military may have a different view of the Incident Command System (ICS) as a relatively recent innovation in emergency response, the Cole Report that follows sets out to do a 25-year evaluation of ICS by California practitioners. The principal investigator links the inception of ICS to the response of seven agencies to the "disastrous 1970 wildfire season in California." (Cole 207) It is a standard academic research project and should enable professionals in the field to participate in a post-facto evaluation of their own. The ICS questionnaire in Appendix A used to gather the data and the rationale for her findings are included. Students should read the document carefully, complete the items in Appendix A and do a class compilation to determine agreement or disagreement with the list of strengths and weaknesses.

Before reading the Cole Report, a copy of the self-paced ICS orientation provides an understanding of terminology and procedure. The document is one in a series developed by the National Wildfire Coordinating Group (NWCG). Other modules available from NWCG include *Principles and Features of ICS, Incident Facilities, Incident Resources* and *ICS Common Responsibilities.*

Sustained ICS emerged as a post-9/11 issue for FDNY. While extraordinarily well trained and prepared for the "ordinary" emergency in New York City, maintaining command over a sustained period of time is truly "extraordinary. Typically a fire or a street response begins and ends before the next tour comes on duty. Even multiple-alarms rarely extend beyond 8 or 12 hours. Firefighters perform their function, assure that the fire is out of that victims receive appropriate medical service and turn the "clean-up" over to policy and other emergency medical personnel. With increased terrorism on the horizon, expertise of the agencies accustomed to sustained incidents such as forest fire, earthquake and other natural disasters led to increased ICS training.

Format changes have been made to facilitate reproduction. While these research projects have been selected as outstanding, other NFA EFOP and APA format, style, and procedural issues may exist.

Incident Command System National Training Curriculum ICS Orientation Certification Statement on Behalf of the National Wildfire Coordinating Group

The following training material attains the standards prescribed for courses developed under the interagency curriculum established and coordinated by the National Wildfire Coordinating Group. The instruction is certified for interagency use and is known as **ICS Orientation**.

Description of the Performance Based System

The Wildfire Fire Qualifications Systems is a "performance-based" qualifications system. In this system, the primary criteria for qualification is individual performance as observed by an evaluator using approved standards. This system differs from previous wildland fire qualifications systems which have been "training based." Training based systems use the completion of training courses or a passing score on an examination as primary criteria for qualification.

A performance based systems has two advantages over a training based system:

- Qualification is based upon real performance, as measured on the job, versus perceived performance, as measured by an examination or classroom activities.

- Personnel who have learned skills from sources outside wildfire suppression, such as agency specific training programs or training and work in prescribed fire, structural fire, law enforcement, search and rescue, etc., may not be required to complete specific courses in order to qualify in a wildfire position.

1. The components if the wildland fire qualifications system are as follows:
   a. *Position Task Books (PTB)* contain all critical tasks, which are required to perform the job. PTBs have been designed in a format, which will allow documentation of a trainee's ability to perform each task. Successful completion of all tasks required of the position, as determined by an evaluator, will be the basis for recommending certification.

   IMPORTANT NOTE: Training requirements include completion of all required training courses prior to obtaining a PTB. Use of the suggested training course or job aids is recommended to prepare the employee to perform in the position.

b. *Training courses and job aids* provide the specific skills and knowledge required to perform tasks as prescribed in the P113.

c. *Agency Certification* is issued in the form of an incident qualification card certifying that the individual is qualified to perform in a specified position.

2. Responsibilities

The local office is responsible for selecting trainees, proper use of task books, and certification of trainees, see the Task Book Administrator's Guide 330-1 for further information.

Preface

This module is one of seventeen modules, which comprise the Incident Command System (ICS) National Training Curriculum. The entire curriculum has been developed by an interagency steering group and a contract consultant. The curriculum was sponsored by the National Wildfire Coordinating Group, and development was directed and supported by the National Interagency Fire Center, Division of Training. The Steering Group was represented by several application areas (Search & Rescue, Law Enforcement, Structural Fire, Wildfire, etc.) which guided the work of the contractor in the development of this package.

The Steering Group was

David P. Anderson — USDA, Forest Service
Mike Colgan — Orange County Fire Department
Dave Engle — USDI, Bureau of Land Management
Dan Francis — California Department of Forestry
Ken Mallette — New Jersey State Police
Mike Munkres — USDI, Bureau of Land Management
Gary Nelson — Los Angeles County Fire Department
Bill Vargas — State of New Mexico Department of Public Safety

The Contract Consultant was The Terence Haney Company, Woodland Hills, California.

Table of Contents

PREFACE

CONTENTS

STUDENT INFORMATION
  Introduction to Reference Text
  Course Description
  Target Audience
  Suggested Prerequisite Modules
  Instructional Objectives
  Delivery Method

Student Information

INTRODUCTION TO REFERENCE TEXT

ICS Orientation is designed to help you learn the principles of the Incident Command System and to briefly acquaint you with the basic ICS structure and terminology.

The majority of the reference text is to be used as a note-taking guide, but other practical information and exercises are included that replicate situations you may encounter in any incident. Many are applicable in planning and conducting planned events as well.

To measure how well you received and retained this information, there will be a final examination covering all the course material.

We hope you will have a good learning experience, which helps you accomplish your job more effectively.

COURSE DESCRIPTION

ICS Orientation is intended for personnel assigned to an incident or event who have a minimum requirement for understanding ICS. This module reviews the ICS organization, basic terminology, and common responsibilities. It will provide enough information about the Incident Command System to enable you to work in a support role at an incident or event, or to support an incident from an off-site location.

This module may also be used as a pre-course study program by personnel who will be continuing their training with additional modules.

TARGET AUDIENCE

This is an orientation for entry-level personnel assisting at an incident or event, persons working in support roles, and off-incident personnel who require a minimum of ICS orientation.

SUGGESTED PREREQUISITE MODULES

This is the first of seventeen modules of the ICS National Training Curriculum. No prerequisites are necessary.

There are other ICS National Training Curriculum materials that will help you understand tis course material more easily. You may wish to obtain copies of the following documents:

ICS Development Paper

ICS Glossary

ICS Forms Manual

ICS Position Descriptions & Responsibilities

Contact the person assigned to administer and assist you with completing this self-paced instruction for help in acquiring copies of the documents listed above.

Instructional Objectives

At the conclusion of this self-study module, you should be able to do the following:

1. List the five major organizational activities within the Incident Command System and explain their primary functions.

2. Give the titles, and explain the duties of Command and General Staff members.

3. Match organizational units to appropriate Operations, Planning, Logistics, or Finance Sections.

4. Match supervisory titles with appropriate levels within the organization.

5. Describe the terms used to name major incident facilities, and state the function of each.

6. Describe what an Incident Action Plan is and how it is used at an incident.

7. Describe how span of control functions within the incident organization and in the use of resources.

8. Describe the common responsibilities (general instructions) associated with incident or event assignments.

9. Describe several applications for the use of ICS.

DELIVERY METHOD

This module is self-paced.

For successful completion of this course, you must receive a minimum of 70% average score on the final exam.

A self-study examination is located at the [end] of this [chapter].

Duration

This module can be completed in two-to-four hours of self-paced study time.

Evaluation

An evaluation summary questionnaire is included in Appendix A. It is to be completed and returned to the person assigned to administer and assist you with the completion of the course.

Figure 12.1. Incident Command System Organization

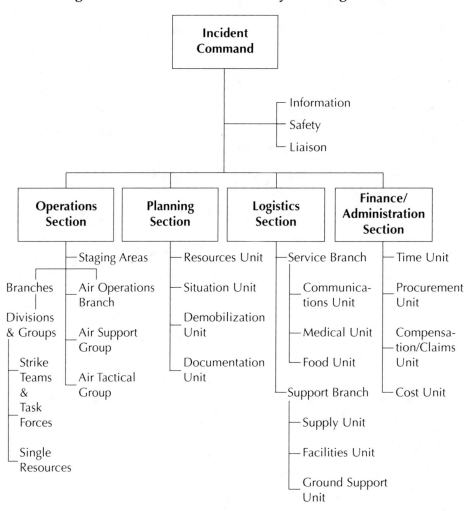

ICS Orientation

I. Introduction

The Incident Command System is used to manage an emergency incident or a non-emergency event. It can be used equally well for both small and large situation.

The system has considerable internal flexibility. It can grow or shrink to meet differing needs. This makes it a very cost-effective and efficient management system. The system can be applied to a wide variety of emergency and non-emergency situations. Listed below are some examples of the kinds of incidents and events that can use the ICS:

Figure 12.2. Application for the Use of The Incident Command System

- Fires, HAZMAT, and multicasualty incidents
- Multijurisdiction and multi-agency disasters
- Wide-area search and rescue missions
- Pest eradication programs
- Oil spill response and recovery incidents
- Single and multi-agency law enforcement incidents
- Air, rail, water, or ground transportation accidents
- Planned events; e.g., celebrations, parades, concerts
- Private sector emergency management programs
- State or local major natural hazards management

ICS has a number of features, which will be covered in this module. Major areas to be covered include:

- ICS Organization
- Incident Facilities
- The Incident Action Plan
- Span of Control
- Common Responsibilities
- Applications

II. ICS Organization

Every incident or event has certain major management activities or actions that must be performed. Even if the event is very small, and only one or two people are involved, these activities will still always apply to some degree.

The organization of the Incident Command System is built around five major management activities. These are depicted in Figure 12.3.

Figure 12.3. Incident Command System Major Activities

COMMAND
SETS OBJECTIVES AND PRIORITIES, HAS OVERALL RESPONSIBILITY AT THE INCIDENT OR EVENT.

OPERATIONS
CONDUCTS TACTICAL OPERATIONS TO CARRY OUT THE PLAN, DEVELOPS THE TACTICAL OBJECTIVES, ORGANIZATION, AND DIRECTS ALL RESOURCES.

PLANNING
DEVELOPS THE ACTION PLAN TO ACCOMPLISH THE OBJECTIVES, COLLECTS AND EVALUATES INFORMATION, MAINTAINS RESOURCE STATUS

LOGISTICS
PROVIDES SUPPORT TO MEET INCIDENT NEEDS, PROVIDES RESOURCES AND ALL OTHER SERVICES NEEDED TO SUPPORT THE INCIDENT

FINANCE/ADMINISTRATION
MONITORS COSTS RELATED TO INCIDENT, PROVIDES ACCOUNTING, PROCUREMENT, TIME RECORDING AND COST ANALYSIS

These five major management activities are the foundation upon which the ICS organization develops. They apply whether you are handling a routine emergency, organizing for a major event, or managing a major response to a disaster.

On small incidents, these major activities may all be managed by one person, the Incident Commander (IC). Large incidents usually require that they be set up as separate Sections within the organization as shown in Figure 12.4 below.

Figure 12.4. ICS Sections

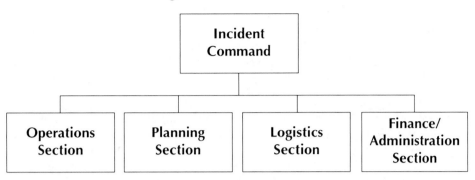

Each of the primary ICS Sections may be sub-divided as needed. The ICS organization has the capability to expand or contract to meet the needs of the incident.

A basic ICS operating guidelines is that the person at the top of the organization is responsible until the authority is delegated to another person. Thus, on smaller situations where additional persons are not required, the Incident Commander will directly manage all aspects of the incident organization.

Now we will look at each of the major functional entities of the ICS organization starting with the Incident Commander and the Command Staff.

A. Incident Commander and the Command Staff

Incident Commander

The Incident Commander is the person is charge at the incident, and must be fully qualified to manage the incident. As incidents grow in size or become more complex, a more highly qualified Incident Commander may be assigned by the responsible jurisdiction or agency. The Incident Commander may have one or more deputies from the same agency or from other agencies or jurisdictions. Deputies must always be as qualified as the person for whom they work.

The Incident Commander may assign personnel for both a Command Staff and a General Staff. The Command Staff provides Information, Safety, and Liaison services for the entire organization. The General Staff are assigned major functional authority for Operations, Planning, Logistics, and Finance/Administration.

Initially, assigning tactical resources and overseeing operations will be under the direct supervision of the Incident Commander. As incidents grow, the Incident Commander may delegate authority for performance of certain activities to others as required.

Taking over command at an incident always requires that there be a full briefing for the incoming Incident Commander, and notification that a change in command is taking place.

Command Staff

In addition to the primary incident response activities of Operations, Planning, Logistics, and Finance/Adminstration, the Incident Commander has responsibility for several other important services. Depending on the size and type of incident or event, it may be necessary to designate personnel to handle these additional activities.

Persons filling these positions are designated as the Command Staff and are called Officers. The Command Staff is shown in Figure 12.5. There is only one Command Staff position for each of these functions. The Command Staff does not have deputies. However, each of these positions may have one or more assistants if necessary. On large incidents or events, it is not uncommon to see several assistants working under Command Staff Officers.

Figure 12.5. ICS Command Staff

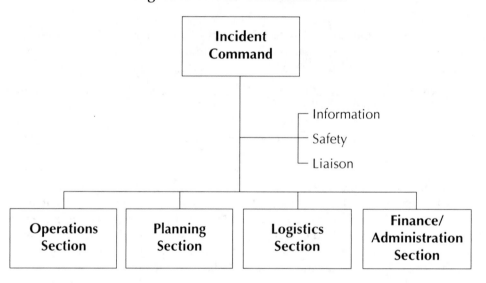

- Information Officer—The information officer will be the point of contact for the media, or other organizations seeking information directly from the incident or event. Although several agencies may assign personnel to an incident or event as Information Officers, there will only be one Incident Information Officer. Others will serve as assistants.

- Safety Officer—This individual monitors safety conditions and develops measures for assuring the safety of all assigned personnel.

- Liaison Officer—On large incidents or events, representatives from other agencies (usually called Agency Representatives) may be assigned to the incident to coordinate their agency's involvement. The Liaison Officer will be their primary contact.

Figure 12.6. ICS General Staff

THE INCIDENT COMMAND SYSTEM GENERAL STAFF

- Operations Sections Chief

- Planning Section Chief

- Logistics Section Chief

- Finance/Administration Section Chief

B. The General Staff

The people who perform the four major activities of Operations, Logistics, Planning, and Finance/Administration are designated as the General Staff.

Each of the General Staff may have a deputy or more than one if necessary. The role of the deputy position is flexible. The deputy can work with the primary position, work in a relief capacity, or be assigned specific tasks. Deputies should always be as qualified as the person for whom they work.

In large events, especially where multiple agencies or jurisdictions are involved, the use of deputies from other agencies can greatly increase interagency coordination.

At the section level, the person in charge will be designated as a Chief. For example, in the Logistics Section, the person in charge will always be called the Logistics Section Chief.

Within the ICS organization, there are a number of organizational elements that can be activated as necessary. Each of the major Sections has the ability to expand internally to meet the needs of the situation.

Let's start with the Operations Section of the ICS organization.

1. Operations Section

   The Incident Commander will determine the need for a separate Operations Section at an incident or event. Until Operations is established as a separate Section, the IC will have direct control of tactical resources.

   When activating an Operations Section, the IC will assign an individual as the Operations Section Chief. The Operations Section Chief will develop and manage the Operations Section to accomplish the incident objectives.

   There is only one Operations Section Chief for each operational period. That person is normally (nut not always) from the jurisdiction or agency which ahs the greatest involvement either in terms of resources assigned or area of concern. The Operations Section Chief may have deputies from the same agency, or from other agencies or jurisdictions. Using deputies from other agencies often helps in the coordination of actions.

Within the Operations Section, two additional levels or organization can be used as necessary. These are Divisions and/or Groups, and Branches.

Divisions

The Operations organization usually develops from the bottom up. This is due to the need to expand supervision as more and more resources are applied. For example, the Incident Commander or the Operations Section Chief on an incident may initially work with only a few single resources. This is shown in Figure 12.7.

Figure 12.7. Single Resources in Operations

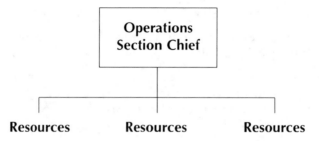

As more resources are added to the incident, another layer of organization may be needed within the Operations Section to maintain proper span of control. Normally, this will be done at the Division or Group level as shown in Figure 12.8.

The goal is to keep the organization as simple and as streamlined as possible, and not to overextend the span of control.

A Division is established to divide an incident geographically. How that will be done will be determined by the needs of the incident. Divisions covering an area on the ground are usually labeled by letters of the alphabet.

Figure 12.8. Example of Two Divisions within Operations Section

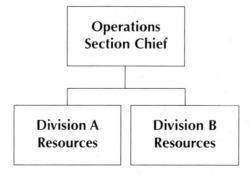

Within a building, divisions are often designated by floor numbers. The important thing to remember about ICS divisions is that they describe some geographical area related to the incident.

Groups

Groups are established to describe functional areas of operation. The kind of group to be established will be determined by the needs of an incident. For example, in an earthquake incident with widespread structural damage, search and rescue activity would be organized geographically using divisions.

A specialized resource team using dogs or electronic equipment in an earthquake, or a salvage group in a maritime incident may be designated as functional groups. Groups will work wherever they are needed, and will not be assigned to any single division.

Divisions and Groups can be used together on an incident. Divisions and Groups are at an equal level in the organization. One does not supervise the other. When a functional group is working within a division on a special assignment, division and group supervisors must always report to the Incident Commander unless the Operations Section Chief and/or Branch Director have been established. Deputies are not used at the Division and Group level.

Branches

On some incidents, it may be necessary to establish another level of organization within the Operations Section called Branches.

There are generally three reasons to use Branches on an incident or an event.

- Span of Control—If the number of Divisions and Groups exceed the recommended Span of Control, another level of management is necessary. Span of Control will be discussed in more detail later in this module.

- Need for a Functional Branch Structure—Some kinds of incidents have multiple disciplines involved, e.g., police, fire, search and rescue, and medical, that may create the need to set up incident operations around a functional branch structure.

- Multijurisdictional Incidents—In some incidents it may be better to organize the incident around jurisdictional lines. In these situations, Branches may be set up to reflect differences in the agencies involved. For example, in flooding, earthquake, or wildfire incidents, federal, county, and city property all could be simultaneously affected. One way of organizing operations in these kinds of incidents is to designate a separate Branch for each of the agencies involved.

Various kinds of Branch alignments are shown in Figure 12.9 below:

Figure 12.9. Options for Establishing Branches Within ICS

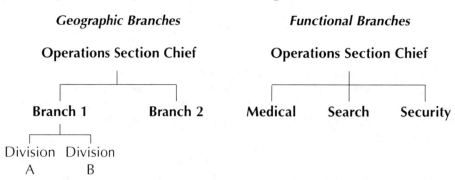

Each branch that is activated will have a Branch Director. Deputies may be used at the Branch level.

There are two other parts of the Operations Section that you may need to understand.

Air Operations

If established separately at an incident, Air Operations will be activated at the Branch level within the Operations Section. Usually this is done on incidents which may have complex needs for the use of aircraft in both tactical and logistical operations.

Staging Areas

Staging Areas may be established wherever necessary to temporarily locate resources awaiting assignment. Staging Areas and the resources within them will always be under the control of the Operations Section Chief. Staging Areas will be discussed later under incident facilities.

Summary

There is no one "best" way to organize an incident. The organization should develop to meet the functions required. The characteristics of the incident and the management needs of the Incident Commander will determine what organization may change over time to reflect the various phases of the incident.

2. Planning Section

Briefly stated, the major activities of the Planning Section are to:

- Collect, evaluate, and display information about the incident.

- Develop Incident Action Plans for each operational period, conduct long-range planning, and develop plans for demobilization at the end of the incident.

■ Maintain resource status on all equipment and personnel assigned to the incident.

■ Maintain incident documentation.

The Planning Section is also the initial place of check-in for any Technical Specialists assigned to the incident. Depending on their assignment, Technical Specialists may work within the Planning Section, or be reassigned to other incident areas.

Several Planning Section Units may be established. Duties of each Unit are covered in other modules. Not all of the Units may be required, and they will be activated based upon need. Planning Section Units are shown in Figure 12.10.

Figure 12.10. Planning Section

3. Logistics Section

The Logistics Section is responsible for all of the services and support needs of an incident, including obtaining and maintaining essential personnel, facilities, equipment, and supplies.

The Incident Commander will determine the need to establish a Logistics Section on the incident. This is usually determined by the size of the incident, complexity of support, and how long the incident may last. Once the IC determines that there is a need to establish a separate Logistics function, an individual will be assigned as the Logistic Section Chief.

Six functional units can be established within the Logistics Section. If necessary, a two-branch structure can be used to facilitate span of control.

The titles of the units are sefl-descriptive. Detailed duties of each unit are covered in other modules. Not all of the units may be required, and they will be established based upon need. Branches and Units in the Logistics Section are shown in Figure 12.11.

Figure 12.11. Branches and Units in the Logistics Section

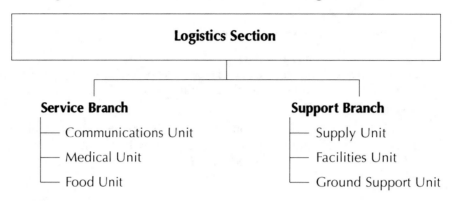

4. Finance/Administration Section

The IC will determine if there is a need for a Finance/Administration Section, and designate an individual to perform that role. If no Finance Section is established, the IC will perform all finance functions.

The Finance/Administration Section is set up for any incident that may require on-site financial management. More and more, larger incidents are using a Finance/Administration Section to monitor costs.

Smaller incidents may also require certain Finance/Administration functions. For example, the Incident Commander may establish one or more units of the Finance/Administration Section for such tings as procuring special equipment, contracting with a vendor, or for making cost estimates of alternative strategies.

The Finance Sectrion may establish four units as necessary. Duties of each unit are covered in other modules. Not all of the units may be required, and they will be established based upon need.

Finance/Administration Section Units are shown in Figure 12.12.

Figure 12.12. Finance/Administration Section Units

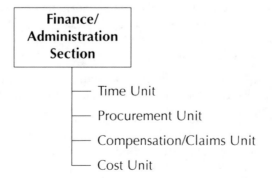

C. Organization Terminology

At each level in the ICS organization, individuals with primary responsibility positions have distinctive titles, as shown in Figure 12.13

Figure 12.13. ICS Organizational Terminology

PRIMARY POSITION	TITLE	SUPPORT POSITION
Incident Commander	Incident Commander	Deputy
Command Staff	Officer	Assistant
Section	Chief	Deputy
Branch	Director	Deputy
Division/Group	Supervisor	N/A
Strike Team/Task Force	Leader	N/A
Unit	Leader	Manager
Single Resource	Use Unit Designation	N/A

D. Incident Facilities

Facilities will be established depending on the kind and complexity of the incident or event. It is important to know and understand the names and functions of the principal ICS facilities. Not all of those listed below will necessarily be used.

Figure 12.14. ICS Facilities

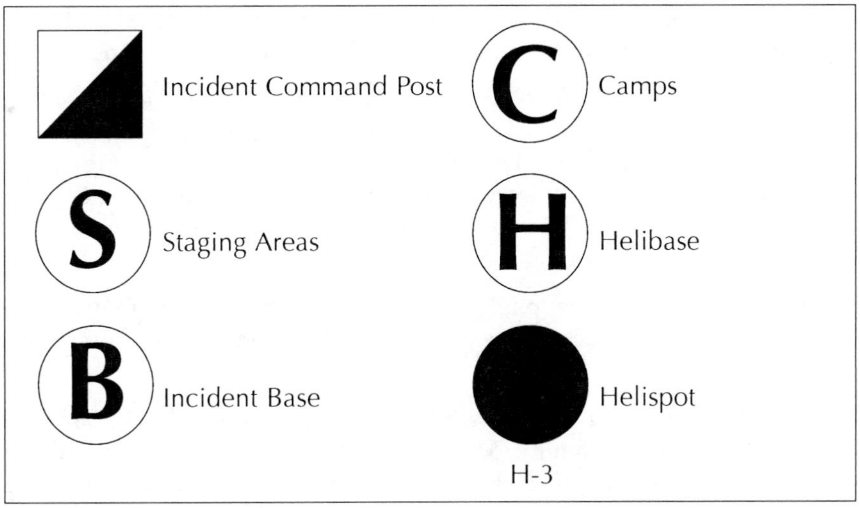

Each of the facilities is briefly described below:

- **Incident Command Post (ICP)**—The location from which the Incident Commander oversees all incident operations. There is only one ICP for each incident or event. Every incident or event must have some form of an Incident Command Post.

- **Staging Areas**—Locations at which resources are kept while awaiting incident assignment. Most large incidents will have a Staging Area, and some incidents may have several. Staging Areas will be managed by a Staging Area Manager who reports to the Operations Section Chief or to the Incident Commander if an Operations Section has not been established.

- **Base**—The location at the incident at which primary service and support activities are performed. Not all incidents will have a Base. There will only be one Base for each incident.

- **Camps**—Incident locations where resources may be kept to support incident operations. Camps differ from Staging Areas in that essential support operations are done at Camps, and resources at Camps are not always immediately available for use. Not all incidents will have Camps.

- **Helibase**—A location in and around an incident area atr which helicopters may be pared, maintained, fueled, and equipped for incident operations. Very large incidents may requie more than one Helibase.

- **Helispots**—Helispots are temporary locations where helicopters can land and load and off-load personnel, equipment, and supplies. Large incidents may have several Helispots.

E. Incident Action Plan

Every incident must have an oral or written action plan. The purpose of the plan is to provide all incident supervisory personnel with direction for future actions. Action plans which include the measurable tactical operations to be achieved are always prepared around a timeframe called an Operational Period.

Operational Periods can be of various lengths, but should be no longer than twenty-four hours. Twelve-hour Operational Periods are common on many large incidents. It is not unusual, however, to have much shorter Operational Periods covering, for example, two- or four-hour time periods. The length of an Operational Period will be based on the neds of the incident, and these can change over the course of the incident.

The planning for an Operational Period must be done far enough in advance to ensure that requested resources are available when the Operational Period begins.

Large incidents, which involve a partial or full activation of the ICS organization, should have a written Incident Action Plan. Incidents extending through an Operational Period should also have a written Incident Action Plan to

Figure 12.15. Forms Commonly Used in Incident Action Plan

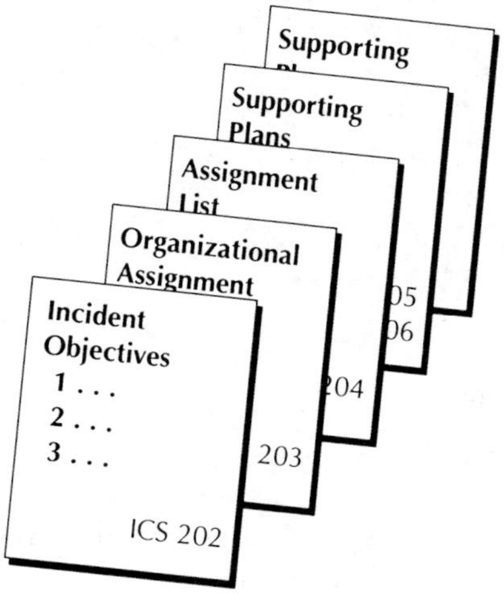

ensure continuity due to personnel changes. The decision to have a written action plan will be made by the Incident Commander.

Several forms have been developed to help in preparing the Incident Action Plan.... They will be discussed in other modules.

Essential elements in any written or oral Incident Action Plan are:

Statement of Objectives—Appropriate to the overall incident.

- Organization—Describes what parts of the ICS organization will be in place for each Operational Period.

- Assignments to Accomplish the Objectives—These are normally prepared for each Division or Group and include the strategy, tactics, and resources to be used.

- Supporting Material—Examples can include a map of the incident, communications plan, medical plan, traffic plan, etc.

The Incident Action Plan must be made known to all incident supervisory personnel. This can be done through briefings, by distributing a written plan prior to the start of the Operational Period, or by both methods.

F. Span of Control

Span of Control means how many organizational elements may be directly managed by another person. Maintaining adequate Span of Control throughout the ICS organization is very important. Effective Span of Control may vary from three to seven, and a ratio of one to five reporting elements is recommended. If the number of reporting elements falls outside of these ranges, expansion or consolidation of the organization may be necessary. There will be exceptions, for example in some applications specially trained hand crews may utilize a larger span of control.

Figure 12.16. Recommended ICS Span of Control Guideline

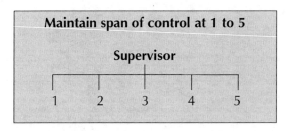

G. Common Responsibilities

There are certain common responsibilities or instructions associated with an incident assignment that everyone assigned to an incident should follow. Following these simple guidelines will make your job easier and result in a more effective operation.

1. Receive your incident assignment from your organization. This should include, at a minimum, a reporting location and time, likely length of assignment, brief description of assignment, route information, and a designated communications link if necessary. Different agencies may have additional requirements.

2. Bring any specialized supplies or equipment required for your job. Be sure you have adequate personal supplies to last you for the expected stay.

3. Upon arrival, follow the Check-in procedure for the incident. Check-in location smay be found at:

   ■ Incident Command Post (at the Resources Unit)

   ■ Staging Areas

   ■ Base or Camps

   ■ Helibases

   ■ Division or Group Supervisors (for direct assignments)

4. Radio communications on an incident should use clear text, that is, no radio codes. Refer to incident facilities by the incident name, for example, Rossmoor Command Post, or 42nd Street Staging Area. Refer to personnel by ICS title, for example, Division C not numeric code or name.

5. Obtain a briefing from your immediate supervisor. Be sure you understand your assignment.

6. Acquire necessary work materials, locate, and set up your work station.

7. Organize and brief any subordinates assigned to you.

8. Brief your relief at the end of each Operational Period and, as necessary, at the time you are demobilized from the incident.

9. Complete required forms and reports and give them to your supervisor or to the Documentation Unit before you leave.

10. Demobilze according to plan.

III. Conclusion

The information you have learned through this short self-study module will provide you with enough general background to understand the principles and primary organizational elements of ICS.

You are encouraged to expand your understanding of the ICS by taking other modules or courses.

Please complete the self-study examination [below].

Module 1—ICS Orientation Test

After you have completed your self-paced study of this module, answer the following questions.

1. Name the five major activities around which the ICS is organized.

2. The General Staff consists of:

3. Name the three major activities of the Command Staff.

4. The Incident Commander may have one or more deputies from the same agency or from other agencies or jurisdictions.

   _____ True

   _____ False

5. Deputies must always be as qualified as the person for whom they work.

   _____ True

   _____ False

6. Deputies may be used at which of the following levels of the ICS organization? Check all that apply.

   _____ Unit

   _____ Section

   _____ Command Staff

   _____ Divisions/Groups

   _____ Branch

7. For each of the organizational elements listed below on the left, designate the number for the appropriate ICS title.

Branch_____   1. Leader

Section_____   2. Officer

Division_____   3. Supervisor

Command Staff_____   4. Chief

Group_____   5. Director

                             6. Manager

8. Groups and Division are at the same organizational level.

_____ True

_____ False

9. List the principal facilities which may be located at an incident.

10. Groups have _____responsibility. Divisions have _____ responsibility.

11. The decision to have a written Incident Action Plan is made by [whom]?

_____ Operations Section Chief

_____ Incident Commander

_____ Planning Section Chief

_____ Safety Officer

12. Select four essential elements of any written Incident Action Plan.

_____ List of total resources assigned to the incident

_____ Objectives

_____ List of agencies involved

_____ Assignments

_____ Supporting plans and material

_____ Organization

_____ Technical Specialist locations

13. Check-in at an incident takes place [where] (check all that apply):

_____ Staging Areas

_____ Base or Camps

_____ Safety Officer

_____ Procurement Unit

_____ Helibases

_____ Division of Group Supervisors (for direct assignments)

14. Operational Periods are how long?

_____ One hour

_____ Two hours

_____ Not over twenty-four hours

_____ Twelve hours

_____ No fixed length

15. Air operations if activated at an incident will be at what organizational level?

_____ Division

_____ Unit

_____ Section

_____ Branch

_____ Group

16. Span of Control at an incident may vary within what range?

_____ One to five

_____ Three to seven

_____ One to three

17. Listed below are the names of various organizational elements found within the ICS organization. Please the letter of the element on the row adjacent to the appropriate ICS Section.

Operations Section = O

Planning Section = P

Finance/Admin. Section = F

a. _____ Cost Unit

b. _____ Branch

c. _____ Food Unit

d. _____ Resources Unit

e. _____ Communications Unit

f. _____ Technical Specialists

g. _____ Division

h. _____ Documentation Unit

i. _____ Facilities Unit

j. _____ Compensation/Claims Unit

k. _____ Air Operations

l. _____ Ground Support Unit

m. _____ Staging Areas

n. _____ Situation Unit

o. _____ Time Unit

p. _____ Medical Unit

q. _____ Procurement Unit

r. _____ Demobilization Unit

s. _____ Group

t. _____ Supply

18. Name five applications for the use of ICS.

19. Which of the following are general responsibilities associated with an assignment to an incident (check all that apply)?

_____ Use clear text in all radio communications at an incident.

_____ Know the names of all Command and General Staff.

_____ Bring any specialized supplies or equipment required for your job.

_____ Organize and brief any subordinates assigned to you.

_____ Prepare an information release for your agency.

_____ Upon arrival, follow the Check-in procedure for the incident.

_____ Report directly to a Staging Area.

_____ Obtain a briefing from your immediate supervisor.

_____ Ensure that all personnel assigned to you are from the same agency/jurisdiction.

_____ Demobilize according to plan.

_____ Attend all planning meetings.

_____ Brief your relief at the end of each Operational Period.

_____ Hold a strategy meeting with personnel from your agency.

_____ Complete required forms and reports and give them to your supervisor or to the Documentation Unit before you leave.

_____ Acquire necessary work materials, locate, and set up your work station.

20. Name the appropriate ICS organizational element that if activated directs the activities below.

_____ Responsible for Staging Areas.

_____ Provide support and services to meet incident needs.

_____ Set objectives and priorities.

_____ Collects and evaluates information, maintain status.

_____ Prepares information releases.

_____ Monitor costs, provides accounting, procurement, and time-recording devices.

_____ Develops measures for assuring safety of all personnel.

_____ Conduct tactical operations, develop tactical objectives, and direct all tactical resources.

Appendix A   Evaluation Summary Questionnaire

Course Name and Title_____

Date and Location_____

Lead Instructor_____

Telephone Number_____

Instructors_____

_____

_____

1. Did instructors meet the required instructor prerequisites? Were course instructional and performance objectives achieved?

   _____

   _____

2. Were any modifications made to the published course package? If so, describe modifications and why they were needed.

   _____

   _____

3. List any specific problems with course materials identified by the students related to content, exercises, visual aids, tests, delivery methods, etc., during their evaluation of the course.

   _____

   _____

4. List any specific problems with course materials identified by the instructor or cadre related to the content, exercises, visual aids, delivery methods, etc., of the course.

   _____

   _____

5. What recommendations can you offer that would improve the ability to learn and/or teach the objectives of this course.

   _____

   _____

Please use additional pages as needed to complete your comments, then return to

National Interagency Fire Center
Division of Fire and Aviation Training
Branch of Training Standards and Technology
3833 S. Development Avenue
Boise, Idaho 83705

The Incident Command System: A 25-Year Evaluation by California Practitioners Executive Planning

By: Dana Cole, Assistant Chief California Department of Forestry and Fire Protection St. Helena, California

Format changes have been made to facilitate reproduction. While these research projects have been selected as outstanding, other NFA EFOP and APA format, style, and procedural issues may exist.

An applied research project submitted to the National Fire Academy as part of the Executive Fire Officer Program.

February 2000

ABSTRACT

Few innovations in recent years have had more impact on emergency services than the introduction and widespread adoption of the Incident Command System (ICS) for managing emergencies of all types. The problem addressed by this research is that, despite the emergence of ICS as the world's leading management system for the command, control, and coordination of emergency scenes, there has never been a comprehensive performance evaluation of the system.

The purpose of this research project was to provide the beginnings of such an evaluation of ICS at the end of its first quarter-century of use in California. To accomplish this a system performance audit was conducted using information provided by Command and General Staff members of California's 17 standing major incident teams, most of whom have used ICS since its very inception in California in the 1970s.

An evaluative research methodology was applied using an approach called a "SWOT" analysis (the acronym standing for strengths, weaknesses, opportunities, and threats) to answer the following questions:

1. What are the primary strengths of the ICS?

2. What are the primary weaknesses of ICS?

3. What strategic opportunities and threats are suggested by the analysis of ICS strengths and weaknesses?

To conduct the evaluation of a 21-item survey instrument was distributed via electronic mail to 206 current and past Command and General Staff members of California's major incident teams, which consist of representatives from local, state, and federal government agencies. Respondents rated 16 attributes of ICS on a 10-point scale. A 60 percent response rate allowed for rigorous statistical analysis of the results. A rank order listing of the attribute ratings is presented in Table 2, but perhaps the most significant result was that none of the ICS attributes received a mean rating in the lower half of the 10-point scale. Thus, statistically speaking, none of the ICS attributes was considered an absolute weakness by the sample population. Even the lowest-rated attribute, with a mean rating of 6.23, was rated significantly greater (at the 95 percent confidence level) than the statistical midpoint of the 10-point scale used.

Using statistical confidence intervals, the author stratified the 16 attributes into three mutually exclusive tiers of statistical confidence. The highest rated of these, or "first tier strengths" represent the essence of what California's veteran ICS practitioners most value about the system, which the author describes as predetermined internal alignment. The second and third tier attributes were also evaluated, and "opportunity targets" for improving ICS were identified, primarily in the area of improving the system's external alignment with non-ICS users.

Based on the performance evaluation by California's veteran ICS practitioners, the author offers three recommendations for improving the Incident Command System. The first of these is to establish a formalized national systems management process. Second, develop a strategy for promoting ICS as the standardized model for emergency management. And third, institutionalize an ongoing national systems evaluation process.

TABLE OF CONTENTS

Abstract

Table of Contents

List of Tables

Introduction

Background and Significance

Literature Review

Procedures

Results

Discussion

Recommendations

References

Appendix A   ICS Questionnaire

LIST OF TABLES

Introduction

One of the most significant trends to occur in the emergency service field during the last quarter of the twentieth century has been the widespread adoption of the Incident Command System (ICS) as "the model tool for the command, control, and coordination of resources and personnel at the scene of emergencies" (Federal Emergency Management Agency [FEMA], 1992).

The ICS was initially developed by a group of seven fire agencies[1] who came together in the aftermath of the disastrous 1970 wildfire season in California. This coalition took the name Firefighting Resources of Southern California Organized for Potential Emergencies, or FIRESCOPE.[2] Chartered by the U.S. Congress in 1972, the FIRESCOPE coalition was charged with a national mandate to develop a system for multi-agency coordination of complex emergencies that exceeded the capabilities of any single jurisdiction (FEMA, 1987).

As one of the original seven FIRESCOPE cooperators, the California Department of Forestry and Fire Protection (CDF) has participated in the development of ICS since the very beginning. CDF was among the first agencies to test the earliest versions of ICS, and to adopt ICS as the standard system for managing emergencies of all types.

Since 1987 CDF has continuously staffed a cadre of on-call Major Incident Command Teams. These teams, which also include representatives from local government, are available year-round to respond to the most complex and difficult incidents—typically those that exceed the management capability of single jurisdictions. Over the past 12 years these teams have managed hundreds of major incidents, including not only large wildfires but also high-rise fires, floods, earthquakes, multi-casualty incidents, hazardous materials accidents, search and rescue operations, and more. They have been sent to dozens of states across the U.S., as well as to other countries.

From the birthplace of ICS in California to the National Fire Academy (NFA) and FEMA, the consensus among long-time practitioners seems to be that "ICS works." In all my years as a member of a Major Incident Command Team, and in all my research and review of the literature, I have not yet heard a single suggestion that ICS should be abandoned. But neither have I heard anyone claim that ICS is perfect.

The specific problem that this research is meant to address is that, despite the widespread adoption of ICS, there has never been a comprehensive strategic evaluation of the system. The purpose of this research project is to provide the beginnings of such an evaluation of the Incident Command System at the end of its first quarter-century of use in California. To accomplish this a system performance audit was conducted using information provided by some of the most experienced practitioners of ICS: current command and general staff members of California's 17 standing Major Incident Teams.[3] The target sample population represents some of California's most seasoned fire and emergency professionals, many of whom have used ICS since its very inception, and in some cases, participated in the system's design and development.

An evaluative research methodology was used to answer the following questions:

1. What are the primary strengths of ICS?

2. What are the primary weaknesses of ICS?

3. What strategic opportunities and threats are suggested by the analysis of ICS strengths and weaknesses?

Background and Significance

California's wildfire problem has grown steadily throughout the twentieth century. By 1970 the problems had grown so severe that a series of devastating wildfires in late September completely overwhelmed the state's wildfire protection system. Several weeks of unrelenting Santa Ana winds had resulted in wildfires that ranged from the Oakland Hills in the northern part of the state to the Mexican border, 400 miles to the south. Never before had so many fires, affecting so many communities, ignited in such a short period of time. And never before had the state's firefighting resources at all levels of government been spread so thin for such a sustained period. One fire alone, the Laguna Fire in San Diego County, had personnel and equipment committed from more than 70 fire departments.

By late September dozens of uncontrolled fires were simultaneously spreading across the Los Angeles Basin with no regard to jurisdiction—from national forests to unincorporated state watershed lands and regional parks, across county boundaries, and into the City of Los Angeles. Wildfires jumped freeways and roared through suburban housing developments. In the bedroom community of Chatsworth, for example, dozens of homes burned to the ground, none of them more than 5 years old. In all, 885 homes were destroyed and 16 people killed. The economic loss was approximately $233 million (FEMA, 1987).

But the numbers do not tell the story of the total chaos that enveloped the dozens of emergency services agencies that responded to these fast moving, erratic wildfires. A primary reason for the confusion was the sheer number of agencies involved, each with its own jurisdictional mandate. This resulted in a "stovepipe" management mentality in which each jurisdictional unit had its own vertical structure of policies and protocols, communications and feedback. In hindsight, responding departments recognized that the emphasis on vertical flow inhibited the sharing and coordination of information between jurisdictions. This meant that as fires burned across and out of one jurisdiction to another, individual jurisdictions were often "flying blind" and forced to improvise management response with no clear organization of authority between departments, no prede-termined rules for collective decision-making, and no coordination of even the most basic communications.

The lack of unifying concepts and systems thinking resulted in unprecedented operational problems. Fire engines from the north part of the state would pass engines from the south on Interstate 5, each dispatched to fires hundreds of miles away when they could have been dispatched closer to home. Confusion reigned over the nomenclature for equipment, lack of compatibility of communication frequencies and "ten-codes," and disparate command and span-of-control man-agement approaches used by dozens of responding agencies. At times even the most experienced firefighters were forced to throw up their hands in the spiral-ing chaos that crashed the public fire protection system in California during Sep-tember of 1970. While there were plenty of examples of heroic and effective firefighting, these were accomplished mostly on a freelance or ad hoc basis. Coordination was often impossible (FEMA, 1987).

The FIRESCOPE program rose out of the ashes of this multi-jurisdiction debacle when representatives from the initial seven cooperating fire agencies came together in mutual frustration. Working with consultants from the Rand Corpo-ration and the aerospace industry, who brought with them the latest concepts in the burgeoning field of "systems theory" (Lilienfeld, 1978), the FIRESCOPE part-ners began to develop improved procedures for utilizing and coordinating fire-fighting resources. This included the development of a new systems approach to overcoming the complexities of emergency management. In the early 1970s this new "Incident Command System" represented one of the first practical applica-tions of modern systems thinking to the organizational management of complex and dynamic operational problems. The key to this systems approach was the recognition that "the first problem and potential solutions must be addressed as a single entity consisting of the sum of all subsystems and their interrelation-ships" (Maloney and Potter, 1974).

By 1980 this evolving standardized emergency management system had taken root in California, and in 1982 it became a cornerstone of the National Intera-gency Incident Management System. A year later FEMA's NFA adopted and began teaching ICS, which it recognizes as "the model tool" for emergency man-agement (FEMA, 1992).

But ICS is far from perfect. As is the case with any rapidly growing technology, the adoaption of ICS by new user groups is rarely painless or seamless. For exam-ple, few fire departments have escaped the "growing pains" that inevitably accompany the initial integration of ICS into traditional operational environments (Wenger, et al., 1990). For non-fire agencies, the transition to ICS has proven even more difficult. Law enforcement agencies, for ex ample, have often been reluctant to "play by ICS rules" *Ullman, 1998). And when it comes to integrating non-government agencies and the private sector into incident operations and manage-ment, the challenges to using ICS can be even greater (Kincaid, 1997).

One of the problems often encountered when introducing ICS to new users is the difficulty in communicating key concepts and procedures that were developed primarily for emergency fire response to cooperators who may not have a fire background, or who may not even be emergency responders at all. This can necessitate a virtual translation of terminology, principles, and working relationships to those cooperators who have little or no experience with ICS.

Adopting ICS represents a monumental change to many potential users. Before they will undertake such a substantial effort they must be convinced that the effort is warranted. Certainly one major incentive for fire agencies is the adoption of iCS by the NFA as the national emergency management standard, but other potential users may require a more thorough assessment of the pros and cons of ICS before embracing it. The intent of this research paper is to provide the beginnings of such an assessment based on the experience CDF and its partner fire agencies in California.

The approach taken in this research has been influenced by both the *Strategic Management of Change* (SMOC) and the *Executive Planning* courses at the NFA. With respect to SMOC, there has been perhaps no more significant strategic change in the California fire service over the past 25 years than the universal adoption of ICS. And yet according to the NFA's "Change Management Model," which is the cornerstone for the SMOC course, if change is to be strategically managed it must not merely be planned and implemented, but also formally evaluated (FEMA, 1996). This research is an attempt to begin just such a systematic evaluation of ICS from the point of view of some of California's most experienced practitioner.

The evaluation approach taken in this research is specifically linked to the Applied Strategic Planning Model presented in the *Executive Planning* course (Goodstein, et al., 1992). This model calls for organizations to identify and evaluate the strategic lines of business used to fulfill their missions. In the private sector, for example, a *strategic line of business* for a bank might be real estate loans. For this research I treated incident management as a strategic line of business for my department.

In the Applied Strategic Planning Model a performance audit is conducted using employees to evaluate the lines of business in which they work. The activity is accomplished through a tool called "SWOT" analysis (the acronym standing for strengths, weaknesses, opportunities, and threats). The three research questions presented in the "Introduction" of this paper are designed to collectively comprise a SWOT analysis of California's experience with the Incident Command System.

Literature Review

In the Fifth Discipline, the required text for the Executive Planning course, author Peter Senge (1990) describes five "component technologies that are converging to innovate learning organizations" (p. 6). It is the fifth of these that ties them all together into an "ensemble of technologies that are critical to each others' success" (p. 6). The fifth discipline of Senge's title is **systems thinking**. According to Senge:

> Systems thinking is a discipline for seeing wholes. It is a framework for seeing interrelationships rather than things, for seeing patterns of change rather than static "snapshots." It is a set of general principles—distilled over the course of the twentieth century, spanning fields as diverse of the physical and social sciences, engineering, and management...for seeing the "structures" that underlie complex situations (Senge, 1990, p. 68).

The Incident Command System may well be considered one of the longest-running experiments in applied systems thinking. It is a systems design-in-progress that has been applied to literally thousands of "complex situations" worldwide during the last quarter of the twentieth century. It is a framework not just for "seeing" the interrelationships and structures that underlie crises, but also for managing them.

ICS allows management of the underlying structures of crisis at two primary levels: conceptual and operational. At the conceptual level it represents an acknowledgment that complex crises usually transcend jurisdictional and functional boundaries, and thus can best be addressed systematically. At the operational level this translates to a coordinated approach to crisis by all responding entities utilizing a prearranged system of constituent principles that are consistent from one incident to another, regardless of type, geography, or jurisdictional involvement.

Before strengths and weaknesses could be identified it was necessary to identify the most important constituent parts of the whole system. Perhaps the most valuable resource in this regard was a unique monograph published in 1987, in which FEMA cited the Incident Command System as an "exemplary practice in emergency management" due largely to a set of "unifying operational principles" (FEMA, 1987, p. 20).

Several authors subsequently suggested additional management principles that are built into ˆCS. Ted Goldfarb, a 33-year veteran of the New York City Fire Department, noted the importance of a clear chain of command and unity of command (i.e., each person reports to and receives orders from only one boss). Another principle he describes is "parity of authority and responsibility," by which he means "each person receivers the necessary authority to fulfill given responsibilities to accomplish goals" (Goldbarb, 1997).

Flexibility and adaptability are CIS strengths that are frequently mentioned in the literature. For example, FEMA training materials point out that while the ICS concept wsa originally devised to address complex wildfire scenarios in California, it has subsequently proven flexible enough for managing any type of emergency, including floods, hurricanes, earthquakes, hazardous material releases, riots, and other natural and human-caused emergency incidents (FEMA, 1992). Lois McCoy, President of the National Institute for Urban Search and Rescue, describes how ICS became the "preferred choice" for rescue operations, especially in multi-agency and long-term emergencies. In the 1989 double-deck freeway collapse in Oakland during the Loma Prieta Earthquake, she points out, the Oakland Fire Department (which had not used ICS previously) "asked the State of California for assistance in its command and control operation. A CDF overhead team...was successfully integrated into a tired and extended local command, without friction and with satisfactory operations continuing under ICS Unified Command" (McCoy, 1990, p. 11).

The adaptability of ICS means that the system can accommodate not only a variety of incident types, but also a variety of incident sizes and operational environments. Since specific functions and organizational elements are activated only at the time and to the extent dictated by the operational requirements of a particular incident, the system can be custom-scaled to the needs at hand (Chase, 1980; Goldfarb, 1997). And because of its flexible design CIS "may be used in a variety of organizational structures, including single jurisdiction/single agency involvement, single jurisdiction with multi-agency involvement, and multi-jurisdiction/multi-agency involvement" (FEMA, 1992).

Kincaid (1997) documents the successful use of ICS in cooperation with the Walt Disney World Company in Buena Vista, Florida. Brewster (1990) touts ICS as a model of implementing broad community-wide planning efforts by providing a system for incorporating not just emergency responders, but "all community assets and missions into an on-scene management structure" (p. 9). Irwin (1990) echoes this sentiment, calling ICS an effective vehicle for "integrating different disciplines, agencies, and government levels" (p. 9).

But ICS has also been criticized for its failure to accommodate non-fire entities into its management structure. For example, one article makes the claim that the fire department orientation of ICS inhibits the interaction with other "relevant local and outside organization" and that "the system is particularly weak in integrating the activities of relief and welfare agencies as well as being not receptive to the use of volunteers" (Wenger et al., 1990, p. 12). Other authors address some of the difficulties of integrating law enforcement into a multi-disciplinary approach to incident management (Rubin, 1997; Ullman, 1998).

Another attribute of ICS that is mentioned as a weakness by more than one author is the process for transferring command to more senior staff as incidents escalate, and vice-versa as they de-escalate. One author recounts an instance where a fire chief was issuing orders as an "advisor" on an incident for an hour and a half before taking over as Incident Commander (Goldfarb, 1997). Others describe command transitions as "blueprints for the loss of information and effective management" (Wenger et al., 1990, p. 12).

Another common criticism of ICS is that there are considerable differences in how the system is implemented from one agency to another, and from one region to another. According to one article, "For some departments the ICS simply means someone is 'in charge' of the disaster site" (Wenger, et al., 1990, p. 9). McCoy (1990) suggests that FIRESCOPE funding for the development of ICS expired before protocols could be completed for a "top level of the ICS system" that presumably could coordinate implementation nationally and reconcile agency and geographical inconsistencies (p. 11).

A final criticism of ICS noted in the literature is what is sometimes referred to as "mobilization overkill." One article suggests that because ICS was developed originally to manage diffuse and spreading disaster impacts such as wildfires, it is not well designed to deal with incidents where impacts occur in limited areas. Without offering specific examples, the authors state that ICS can create "serious problems of convergence and congestion at the disaster site" (Wenger, et al., 1990, p. 9).

Procedures

As a first step in evaluating the Incident Command System, a preliminary online literature review was conducted during the months of May through July of 1999. This was followed by an exhaustive onsite literature search at the National Emergency Training Center's (NETC's) Learning Resource Center (LRC) and at the publication center of the Emergency Management Institute (EMI) during two weeks in August of 1999. More than 50 published articles, monographs, and EFOP research papers were reviewed. Many of these documented the successful application of ICS principles, quite often in non-fire contexts, while a smaller number directed criticisms at ICS. Collectively, these writings provided a draft list of attributes to be evaluated as perceived strengths and/or weaknesses of ICS.

This draft list was distributed to a test group of 10 veteran ICS practitioners. Based on progressive input and discussions with this test group, the list was revised three times before it was finalized. Following a final draft review and discussion with this group, a comprehensive questionnaire was prepared for distribution (Appendix A). Questions 1 through 5 were designed to characterize the experience of the sample population. Question 6 was designed to evaluate a total of 16 attributes of the Incident Command System. Respondents were asked to rate these 16 attributes on a scale of 1 to 10 to indicate the relative weakness or strength of the attribute as a feature of ICS. To remove any order bias from the statistical analysis 16 versions of the questionnaire were distributed, each presenting the 16 items in a different order. Finally, respondents were invited to add their own comments about ICS.

The questionnaire was distributed by electronic mail to current and recent Command and General Staff members of the 17 major incident teams in California. These include 12 statewide Major Incident Command Teams comprised of representatives from state and local government, and the first federal Type 1 Major Incident Management Teams assigned to California. Questionnaires were sent to each Team's Incident Commander, Command Staff (Information Officer, Liaison Officer, and Safety Office), and General Staff (Operations Section Chief, Planning Section Chief, Logistics Section Chief, and Finance/Administration Section Chief). Questionnaires were sent to about 50 veteran ICS practitioners who have "rotated off" team assignments, but who are still active and available for overhead assignments as needed. In total, 206 questionnaires were distributed.

This sample population were selected for its knowledge and expertise, and represents some of the most experienced practitioners of ICS anywhere. It is only after years of training, certification, and successful completion of ICS assignments at progressively higher levels of incident management responsibility that one can qualify for appointment to these teams at the Command and General Staff Level. In CDF, for example, fewer than two percent of the department's emergency response personnel are assigned to Major Incident Command Teams.

Electronic mail via the Internet (and CDF intranet) provided to be a convenient vehicle for the distribution of the questionnaire, as respondents merely had to type their answer into the body of the message and use the "Reply to Sender" feature to return the completed questionnaire. In this manner, 40 completed questionnaires were returned on the first day alone. In all, 122 completed questionnaires were returned between November 15 and December 31, 1999. This presents a 60 percent response rate, and except for three questionnaires returned by Fax and one by postal mail, the entire sampling procedure was conducted online.

Limitations

A generic comment that is sometimes made regarding ICS is that it is "the California system," probably because ICS originated in California in the 1970s, and has been applied in California longer than anywhere else. One limitation of this study is that only California practitioners were surveyed. A benefit in using such a sample population lies in the sheer amount of ICS experience it represents: It's not probably that a sample population this large, with this much experience using ICS during the system's first 25 years, could be found anywhere else. And yet a limitation of using this sample population is that the results may be seen to exhibit a "California bias" or a "wildland bias." As such, it is important to emphasize that this study does not purport to be a comprehensive analysis of ICS, but rather an evaluation from the point of view of the first generation of California practitioners.

A second limitation of this study pertains to the use of email for sampling purposes. A handful of the target sample population could not be reached by email, either because they had not email address or because a correct one could not be located.

Definitions of Some Selected Terms

CDF: California Department of Forestry and Fire Protection

Command and General Staff: The Command Staff consists of the Information Officer, Safety Officer, and Liaison Officer; the General Staff consists of the Operations Section Chief(s), Planning Section Chief, Logistics Section Chief, and Finance Section Chief. All of these incident management personnel report to the Incident Commander.

FIRESCOPE: Firefighting Resources of California Organized for Potential Emergencies.

ICS: Incident Command System

Line of business: Major category of activity pursued by an organization to fulfill its mission.

SWOT Analysis: A strategic analysis of an organization's line of business based on an assessment of strengths, weaknesses, opportunities, and threats.

Results

As illustrated in Table 1 the sample population represents a high level of career experience, both in the fire service (average 26.6 years) and using the Incident Command System (average 17.7 years). The 122 respondents to this research stusdy also exhibit a great deal of executive-level ICS experience as indicated by the averagte of 6.5 yars of Command/General Stuff assignment on one of California's major incident teams. In this capacity respondents have been assigned to an average of 14.5 major incidents, or just over two per year on average. For the purpose of this stusdy "major incidents" were defined as those lasting for three or more consecutive operational periods. Major wildfires, floods, and earthquakes accounted for the majority of such incidents.

Table 1 Sample Population Characteristics

Experience	Years
Fire Service	26.6
Using ICS	17.7
Member of Major Incident Team Staff	6.5

Evaluation of ICS by Practitioners

To address the first two questions posed by this evaluative research study, the questionnaire directed the veteran practitioners to evaluate 16 attributes of ICS and rate them on a 10-point scale, with "1" indicating maximum weakness and "10" indicating maximum strength (see Question 6 in Appendix A). The results of this evaluation are summarized in Table 2, in which the 16 attributes are listed in rank order from highest to lowest mean rating.

Each ICS attribute was analyzed using mean, mode, standard deviation, coefficient of variance, and 95 percent confidence intervals (Wonnacott and Wonnacott), 1985). Modal tendency and coefficient of variance provided minimally useful information. The employment of confidence intervals, on the other hand, provided a useful measure of the range of actual population norms, which are illustrated by the letters in the last column of Table 2. Only those attributes with no matching letters in this column can be considered to have statistically different strength ratings at the 95 percent confidence level (indicated by "P=95 percent"). Thus, for example, the data shows with 95 percent confidence that the highest rated attribute (Predefined hierarchy) has a significantly higher strength rating than attributes 5 through 16. On the other hand, it cannot be said with 95 percent confidence that the differences in mean rating scores of attributes 1 through 4 are due to anything other than sampling error, as indicated by the "A" accompanying these attributes in column 4. All attributes denoted with an "A" can therefore be considered co-equal strengths at the 95 percent confidence level; likewise for each letter B through G.

Table 2. Rating of ICS Attributes (10-Point Scale)

ATTRIBUTE BY RANK ORDER n = 122	Mean Rating	Standard Error	Statistical Significance (95% confidence)*
1. Predefined hierarchy	8.80	0.105	A
2. Uniform terminology	8.73	0.115	A, B
3. Modular organizational structure	8.70	0.113	A, B
4. Incident Action Plans	8.68	0.126	A, B
5. Span of Control	8.42	0.140	B
6. Standardized forms	8.17	0.152	C
7. Delegation of authority	8.06	0.131	C
8. Cross-jurisdictional relationships	7.78	0.154	C. D
9. Communications plan	7.73	0.158	D
10. Decision-making process	7.67	0.145	D
11. Transition of authority	7.50	0.196	D
12. Resource mobilization	7.27	0.183	E
13. Integration of non-fire agencies	6.84	0.189	F
14. Consistency of implementation	6.61	0.175	F, G
15. Integration of non-government	6.27	0.205	G
16. Agreement on system modifications	6.23	0.231	G

* Those attributes with the matching letters in Column 4 are not statistically different at the 95 percent confidence level. All others are. For example, Items 1-4 are not statistically different from one another (all have A's) nor are Items 2-5 (all have B's). But Item 1 is statistically different from Item 5.

Comparison of confidence intervals with the rank order of attributes allows for a more realistic interpretation of the data than by using rank order along to evaluate strengths and weaknesses. Viewing the data in this manner suggests that ICS attributes should be placed in tiered groupings of roughly equal levels of significance rather than on an absolute scale of 1 through 16. These groupings are presented in the "Discussion" section of this paper.

Perhaps the most significant result is that none of the ICS attributes received a mean rating in the lower half of the 10-point scale, and thus the data does not support stratification of attributes as absolute strengths or weaknesses. In fact, statistically speaking, none of the ICS attributes is considered a weakness by the sample population. Even the lowest-rated attribute (Agreement of system modifications) with a mean rating of 6.23 is significantly greater (P=95 percent) than the presumed neutral value of 5.5, which is the statistical midpoint of the 10-point scale used.

An interesting observation can be made regarding the standard error (SE) values presented in Table 2. The highest rated attribute, Predefined hierarchy, also exhibits the lowest SE value (0.105), indicating a strong tendency toward una-nimity in rating this attribute highly. Conversely, the lowest rated attribute, Agreement on system modifications, exhibits the highest SE value (0.231), which indicates a great deal of disparity in how this attribute was rated.

Finally, the third question posed by this evaluative research project pertains to the "opportunities and threats" suggested by the SWOT analysis approach described earlier (Goodstein, et al., 1992). Due to the interpretive nature of this aspect of the analysis, "opportunities and threats" are presented in the "Discussion" section that follows.

Discussion

The evident reluctance of assign "weakness" values to any of the 16 attributes indicates that even those attributes receiving the lowest mean ratings are not considered by the veteran ICS practitioners to be system "weaknesses" so much as the "weakest of the strengths." By using the confidence interval codes from Table 2, the attributes can be clearly stratified into three tiers of statistical significance: the "AB" tier, the "CD" tier, and the "EFG" tier. The three tiers are mutually exclusive in that the attributes in each have significantly different ratings than attributes in the other two tiers (P=95 percent). The terms assigned to these categories are first tier strengths, second tier strengths, and third tier strengths. The three tiers are summarized in Table 3, and will be discussed in turn.

Table 3. Tiered Groupings of ICS Attributes

CATEGORY	ICS ATTRIBUTE
First Tier Strengths (A, B)*	Predefined hierarchy, uniform terminology, modular organization structure, Incident Action Plans, span of control
Second Tier Strengths (C,D)*	Standardized forms, delegation of authority, cross-jurisdictional relationships, communications plans, decision-making process, transition of authority
Third Tier Strengths (E, F, G)*	Resource mobilization, integration of non-fire agencies, consistency of implementation, integration of non-government agreement on system modifications

* Letter codes indicate statistical significance at the 95 percent confidence level. They are taken from Table 2.

First Tier Strengths of ICS

These five highest-rated attributes constitute the essence of what makes ICS an effective management system in the eyes of California's veteran practitioners. Using the specific wording from the questionnaire (attached as Appendix A), the five major strengths of ICS, in rank order, are

1. Predefined hierarchy, including chain-of-command and delineated responsibilities for every position.

2. Uniform terminology for identifying resources and organizational functions.

3. Modular organizational structure that is expanded and contracted as needed.

4. Incident Action Plans that are updated for each operational period.

5. Manageable span-of-control.

Taken together, these five attributes constitute something that can be termed predetermined internal alignment: It is predetermined because due to these attributes the workers know the rules by which the system functions even before the incident begins. In CDF, this is true not just for Command and General Staff, but for all personnel on an incident. Since ICS is incorporated into the most basic training, even the rookie firefighter knows the rules and operates in "ICS mode" on a routine basis. These rules seem to work best internally; that is, within the system, where all the workers know the termino0logy and roles. They know where their own specific responsibilities begin and end, and they have an understanding where they fit within the system's span of control. And they are in alignment, which, according to Peter Senge, is a phenomenon that occurs "when a group of people function as a whole so that a commonality of direction emerges, and individuals' energies harmonize" (Senge, 1990, p. 234).

The predetermined features of the system ensure that workers can "hit the ground running" because they use common terminology and function within a common organizational structure and planning process; time and energy need not be wasted negotiating "who does what" and "who reports to whom." Since everyone within the system "speaks the same language and works from the same script" they are able to get immediately to the most important business at hand: managing the problem.

It is remarkable how rare this approach is outside the field of emergency services. ICS may in fact be one of the most advanced and well-practice examples of applied systems thinking anywhere. Peter F. Drucker, who has been writing about management issues for more than 60 years and is considered by many to be the most important management thinker of the 20th century (Stone, 1998), recently proposed a set of principles he calls "Management's New Paradigms for the 21st Century" (Drucker, 1999). Among the very first of these is the seemingly obvious principle that "Organizational Structure is Needed." But he explains, there are hundreds of versions of organizational structure; the key is to identify the specific one "that fits the task" (p. 16).

ICS is an excellent example of Drucker's principle: The average practitioner represented by this research study—27 years in the first service, 18 years using ICS—is someone who has spent most of a career helping to define and refine a specific organizational structure "that fits the task" of managing complex emergency incidents. Drucker has never written about ICS, but he may as well be referring to the system's major strengths when he writes:

> One hears a great deal today about "the end of hierarchy." This is blatant nonsense....In a situation of common peril—and every institution is likely to encounter it sooner or later—survival of all depends on clear command. If the ship goes down, the captain does not call a meeting, the captain gives an order. And if the ship is to be saved, everyone must obey the order, must know exactly where to go and what to do... "Hierarchy," and the unquestioning acceptance of it by everyone in the organization, is the only hope in a crisis (Drucker, 1999, p. 11).

Second Tier Strengths of ICS

The second tier of ICS strengths consists of six attributes that are rated significantly lower (P=95 percent) than those in the first tier strengths. Even so, it should be noted that these are still rated in the supper quartile of the 10-point scale, which can be interpreted as favorable endorsement by the sample population. Again, using the specific wording from the questionnaire and rankings from Table 2, the second tier strengths, in rank order, are

6. Standardized forms are used for all incidents.

7. Ample flexibility and authority are given to staff for accomplishing objectives.

8. Cross-jurisdictional and cross-functional working relationships when ICS is used.

9. Communications plan that is coordinated among responding agencies.

10. Clear decision-making process.

11. Process for transitioning command authority from one level of government to another as incident complexity changes.

Whereas ICS is characterized by internal alignment as indicated by the first tier strengths, the system is not quite as strong in effecting external alignment; that is, alignment with forces outside the system structure itself. External forces include organizations that do not use ICS, as well as political, economic, social, environmental, legal, and cost implications that are not entirely within the system's ability to manage (FEMA, 1999). It stands to reason that ICS may not be quite as effective in the external arena for the simple reason that external forces differ from incident to incident. And while these entities may be directly impacted by the incident is cannot be assumed they "know exactly where to go and what to do" (Drucker, 1990, p. 11). Some of the biggest challenges occur with cooperators who may be unfamiliar with ICS or who may not be receptive to "playing by ICS rules," a point that often appears in the literature. (See, for example, Wenger, et al., 1990; Kincaid, 1997; Ullman, 1998).

And yet ICS does provide means for addressing these potentially problematic external issues, as evidenced by the favorable rating given to the attributes in this tier. While none of the second tier strengths deals exclusively with external forces, each has an external dimension. For example, the use of Standardized forms assures that all internal users are "on the same page." But these same forms can have an external function as well, as when the ICS-204 ("Division Assignment List") depicts assignments for law enforcement or relief agencies, or when an ICS-209 ("Incident Status Summary") is provided to the media to show cost and loss information.

Other second tier strengths that are predominantly external alignment issues include Cross-jurisdictional working relationships and the Process for transitioning of authority as incident complexity changes. These can become major external issues, especially in the politically charged atmosphere of a rapidly escalating major disaster, where numerous jurisdictions can have overlapping authorities. Two other attributes in this tier, the Coordinated communications plan and the Clear decision-making process, must be aligned both internally and externally. The latter, for example, must be aligned internally through the operational planning process and documented in the Incident Action Plan, but the process must also be accessible to external forces, usually through a unified command structure.

In summary, the second tier strengths clearly contribute to the effectiveness of ICS, though there may be an unavoidable price to pay in the form of additional complications and workload over and above internal incident commands. It is likely that this somewhat reduced level of system control over these attributes resulted in the slightly lower ratings given by practitioners.

Third Tier Strengths

It is tempting to refer to this lowest-rated tier of attributes as "relative weaknesses," or more accurately from a statistical point of view, as "the weakest of the strengths." But neither of these terms captures the double-edged nature of these attributes. Each of them has positive aspects, as indicated by ratings that are statistically well above the 5.5 midpoint value. And yet there must be valid reasons these five attributes were rated significantly lower than the others. For this reason the author believes that the attributes below offer the best targets for improvement of ICS:

12. Resource mobilization effectiveness.

13. Effectiveness of integrating non-fire government agencies (e.g., law enforcement, public works) into the ICS structure.

14. Consistency of implementation among various agencies.

15. Effectiveness of integrating non-government organizations (e.g., relief agencies, businesses, citizens) into ICS structure.

16. Agreement among agencies about who has authority to modify the ICS "rules of the game."

All five of these attributes are mentioned prominently in the literature as potential problems with ICS. For example, if Resource mobilization is not handled effectively, then "overkill mobilization" can cause problems of "convergence and congestion" at the incident site (Wenger, et al., 1990, p. 9). Such a situation can result in further external problems if it is viewed by the public as a bureaucratic boondoggle and waste of tax dollars. But as an Oregon Emergency Management Coordinator points out, "Over mobilization is an implementation issue, and not one directly related to the ICS model itself" (Dimmick, 1990, p. 10). By this view resource mobilization under ICS may be considered a strength: admittedly not perfect, but better than the free-for-all alternative that led to the formation of FIRESCOPE.

Two related attributes that are weakly endorsed by the sample population are Effectiveness of integration into ICS of both non-fire agencies and non-government organizations. But while ICS has been criticized because "the fire department is in 'charge' and there is little place for others" (Wenger, et al., 1990, p. 9), the sample population had very different reasons for withholding strong endorsement for the effectiveness of integrating others into the ICS structure. A number of comments were offered by respondents that echoed the observation by a representative of the Pennsylvania Emergency Management Agency that most "multi-organizational" coordination problems are "caused by inadequate training rather than flows in the system," and that regardless of its shortcomings, ICS is "better suited to the task than any of the other variations of command and control systems previously used" (Long, 1990, p. 9). Few would disagree, however, that the effective integration of non-fire agencies and non-government organizations is a major target for improvement.

Somewhat related to this is the attribute pertaining to Consistency of implementation among agencies, which can be a source of frustration for even the most experienced ICS practitioners. And while this can be a problematic external issue for ICS, practitioners muster lukewarm endorsement of this attribute, probably because they believe that, when it occurs, inconsistent implementation "is a result of inadequate jurisdictional attention to planning, training, and the procedural aspects of incident management" and not the fault of ICS itself (Irwin, 1990, p. 10).

Finally, the lowest-rated of the 16 ICS attributes is the Agreement among agencies who has authority to modify the "rules of the game." This is a longstanding issue, and one that has been exacerbated by the rapid spread of ICS throughout and beyond the U.S. over the past three decades. The Incident Command System is a work in progress, and as adaptations and changes are made to suit local or agency-specific needs, there is no universally accepted governing authority or clearing house to offer resolution to conflicts and confusions that can arise. Terence Haney, a FIRESCOPE consultant who was involved in the original development of ICS, and later, in the transition of ICS into the National Interagency Incident Management System, focused on this issue in 1990 when he suggested the need for a "national system manager [to] oversee ICS multi-hazard applications, new developments, training, and orientation" (Haney, 1990, p. 12). This represents possibly the most significant improvement target for ICS, and will be discussed further in the "Recommendations" section.

"Opportunities and Threats"

The final research question pertains to identifying the primary opportunities and threats suggested by the practitioners' evaluation of ICS, thus completing the "SWOT analysis" approach presented in the Executive Planning course (Goodstein, et al., 1992).

It is the author's opinion that the primary opportunity suggested by this research is to leverage the system's predetermined internal alignment features to provide organizational structure for managing much more than emergency incidents. To illustrate why this may be a natural evolution for ICS, consider how far this system's model has come since it was initially developed for the very specific purpose of managing complex wildfires. Certainly California wildfires provided plenty of opportunities to practice with early versions of the ICS model, but it soon became apparent that the system could work equally well for non-fire disasters, including earthquakes, floods, riots, and hazardous material incidents (FEMA, 1992). Meanwhile, departments like CDF found that it made sense to use this management tool not just for major disasters, but for everyday emergencies as well. Thanks to the system's scalability—that is, its ability to be expanded or contracted as needed to fit the operational requirements of a particular incident—users found that virtually any incident, regardless of size, could be managed using ICS. In some fire departments ICS became more than a tool for managing extraordinary events; it became an everyday "line of business" (Goodstein, et al., 1992). For a department like CDF, ICS is used from the moment of initial dispatch to an incident. So, for example, if a fire is not controlled during initial attack and requires additional resources, ICS allows the system response to "scale up" and keep pace with the changing needs of an expanding incident without having to switch operational modes.

Peter Senge (1990) writes that one of the most common threats to systems thinking is "The almost total lack of meaningful 'practice' or 'rehearsal'" (p. 258). He writes

> Imagine trying to build a great theater ensemble or a great symphony orchestra without rehearsal. Imagine a championship sports team without practice. In fact, the process by which such teams learn is through continual movement between practice and performance (Senge, 1990, p. 238).

Few systems models have undergone more "practice and performance" than ICS during the past 25 years. The system has been used thousands upon thousands of times; it has been tested, refined, and literally forged in the heat of repeated "trials by fire." While not perfect, ICS is a proven structure for making people productive in working together to accomplish critical tasks during times of crisis.

But remove the crisis nature of the task, and the basic advantages of predetermined internal alignment still apply. The same principles that make this systems model so effective for managing emergencies can also be applied as a system for managing planned non-emergency events and complex projects. For example, ICS has been used successfully by CDF and others to implement numerous major conferences and training exercises, and to assist in managing such planned events as the 1984 Olympics in Los Angeles and the opening of the Ronald Reagan Presidential Library in 1992.

One of the primary reasons that the ICS model works so well is that it is continually "practiced and performed," in the words of Peter Senge (1990, p. 238), and as such, has become an effective, systematic way of operating for departments like CDF. It has evolved from being a management tool for merely responding to disaster, to one that also offers great opportunity as a proactive management tools for strategic planning and project implementation. This is consistent with Drucker's (1999) recommendation to focus on opportunities by "exploiting success" (p. 82). In this view, if an organization develops a management structure that "fits" the key task of the organization, it may make sense to expand the use of that structure so that it becomes the organization's predominant management paradigm.

Given organizations' natural resistance to change, such as approach is not likely to be free of problems. But as Drucker (1999) writes, the key to exploiting success is "to starve the problems and feed the opportunities" (p. 82). The results of this research point to the problems that collectively pose the single biggest threat to the effective use of ICS: external misalignment.

The potential problems that can lead to external misalignment are suggested by the third tier strengths. Specifically, implementation failures of these attributes can result in "ICS horror stories" that can damage the system's credibility among entire communities or user groups. Such failures can occur on incidents characterized by inefficient or wasteful resource mobilization, insensitivity or inadequate attention to the integration of non-fire or non-government entities, uncoordinated decision making processes, confusion regarding agency responsibilities, or anything else that might give the impression of a "bureaucracy run amok." Any of these problems have the potential to threaten the system's integrity whenever ICS is used with uninitiated external entities.

In the author's experience, however, most often such entities become "ICS converts" when they experience how well the system works for managing even the most complex and chaotic incidents. The key at such times is to "starve" the threat of external misalignment by "feeding the opportunity" to build trust among the various entities that are thrust together in times of crisis. When chaos proliferates in times of emergency there is great incentive to put aside differences and pull together. ICS offers the structure within which to do that.

Recommendations

Based on the performance evaluation by California's veteran ICS practitioners, the author offers three recommendations for improving the Incident Command System:

1. **Establish a multi-disciplinary national systems management process to ensure the integrity and consistency of implementation of ICS.**

The adoption of ICS has spread rapidly and extensively. It is no longer used solely by the fire service, but also by agencies in law enforcement, health care, and public works, among others. The U.S. Coast Guard now uses ICS for environmental responses and search and rescue operations, and the U.S. Department of Energy is adopting ICS for use in responding to nuclear emergencies. As the use of ICS expands throughout the fire service and beyond, to a wide range of disciplines, new users often "customize" ICS to fit their particular needs. While ICS is designed to be adaptable, unilateral changes can potentially compromise the general set of principles that underlie the system. This can lead to conflict and confusion when disparate entities are brought together on major incidents.

A proposed systems management process would most appropriately be coordinated by FEMA and include an oversight board with representation from the various geographical regions and ICS user groups. These should include representatives from a full spectrum of disciplines, including the fire service, law enforcement, medical and health services, public and private utilities, environmental protection, relief organizations, and National Guard, and others as deemed appropriate. One model for this approach is provided by California's Standardized Emergency Management System (State of California, 1995).

A multi-disciplinary national oversight board is long overdue and necessary for providing ongoing policy guidance and direction if ICS is to be an effective national system standard for managing emergencies. A primary function of this board would be to act as a clearinghouse for reviewing and arbitrating any unresolved issues of system standards, compliance, implementation, operation, and training.

2. Develop a strategy for promoting ICS as the standardized model for emergency incident management.

Whereas the preceding recommendation pertains to the quality control of the system itself, the second recommendation pertains to the alignment between the system and "the rest of the world." Whenever ICS is deployed there is an inevitable systems interface between those who are indoctrinated to function within the parameters of the system (ICS users) and those who are not. It is simply a given that the system will have to interact with non-system users, including the myriad agencies, volunteer, and relief organizations that are not indoctrinated to ICS, as well as the general public, the media, and others. This issue of external alignment is further complicated by the fact that it is often impossible to anticipate In advance who these non-system users will be. Major incidents vary widely in their scope and impacts, and it is not always possible to know beforehand what agencies and which personnel will be thrust together, nor the nature of the crises they will confront.

FEMA has begun to address this through its disaster planning and response process. The challenge—and the opportunity—is to do a better job of promoting the general function-based ICS organization model as the national standard implementation tool for FEMA's function-oriented disaster planning and response process. This will require coordination and leadership at the federal level to ensure standardized national guidelines and cross-disciplinary training, a role that would seem to fall most logically to FEMA, which is already providing ICS curriculum and training for fire management through its National Fire Academy. Alignment with non-fire disciplines will not occur easily, however, unless an expanded multi-disciplinary training curriculum is developed to promote ICS as the universal inter-entity management model.

3. Institutionalize an ongoing systems evaluation process.

Earlier in this paper the observation was made that the overwhelming sentiment among veteran practitioners is that "ICS works." Perhaps the best evidence of this is the system's rapid and widespread adoption over the past 25 years.

And yet how do we know what works and what doesn't, and what improvements need to be made? As new disciplines adopt the ICS approach, how do we know what adaptations need to be made to make ICS a truly universal system for emergency management? Is such a universal system even practical? And how do we know which problems encountered by ICS users are system problems, and thus need to be addressed through further refinement or redesign, and which of these problems are inherent in the chaotic nature of emergency management?

These and other questions have no easy answers, but one things seems evident: They need to be addressed systematically by those familiar with the system. ICS has been developed and applied methodically over the years, but a missing ingredient to this methodology has been a systematic evaluation. Such an evaluation is long overdue.

The Incident Command System cannot afford to "fly blind" into a new century to emergency management. It is not a perfect system and it is not a panacea. But in the author's opinion, too much progress has been made to even consider starting over. In fact, the biggest problem confronting ICS at the dawn of the twenty-first century may be a "surfeit of success," which has resulted in so many adaptations and innovations that the system threatens to take on an unwieldy life of its own. Without systematic, ongoing evaluation in conjunction with the other recommendations for managing and promoting ICS as a universal model, the opportunity may be missed to institutionalize positive changes and necessary modifications that will ensure the continuance of ICS as "the model tool" for emergency management.

References

Brewster, P. (1990, May). Clearer understanding of ICS proves value for emergency management. *Hazard Monthly*, pp. 7-9.

Chase, R.A. (1980). *FIRESCOPE: A new concept in multiagency fire suppression coordination*. General Technical Report PSW-40. Berkeley, CA: USDA Forest Service Pacific Southwest Experiment Station.

Dimmick, M. (1990, May). ICS: Making criticism constructive. *Hazard Monthly*, pp. 7-10.

Drucker, P.F. (1999). *Management challenges for the 21st century*. New York: Harper-Collins.

Federal Emergency Management Agency (FEMA). National Emergency Training Center, Emergency Management Institute (1987). *Exemplary practices in emergency management: the California FIRESCOPE program*. Monograph Series No. 1. Emmitsburg, MD: Federal Emergency Management Agency, National Emergency Training Center, Emergency Management Institute.

Federal Emergency Management Agency (FEMA), National Emergency Training Center, Emergency Management Institute, (1992, May). *Overview of the Incident Command System.* Student Manual SM 305-7. Emmitsburg, MD: Federal Emergency Management Agency, U.S. Fire Administration, National Fire Academy.

Federal Emergency Management Agency (FEMA), U.S. Fire Administration. (1996, May). *Strategic management of change.* Student Manual NFA-SMOC-SM. Emmitsburg, MD: Federal Emergency Management Agency. U.S. Fire Administration, National Fire Academy.

Federal Emergency Management Agency (FEMA), National Emergency Training Center, Emergency Management Institute. (1999, February). *Incident Command System curriculum.* [CD-ROM]. Student Manual G196. Emmitsburg, MD: Federal Emergency Management Agency, National Emergency Training Center, Emergency Management Institute.

Goldfarb, T. (1997, January). Putting the Incident Command System into perspective. *Fire Engineering,* pp. 64-72.

Goodstein, L.D., Nolan, T.M., & Pfeiffer, J.W. (1992). *Applied strategic planning: An overview.* San Francisco, CA: Jossey-Bass.

Haney, T. (1990, May). ICS: A question of implementation. *Hazard Monthly,* pp. 7-12.

Irwin, R.L. (1990, June). Challenging the critics of ICS. *Hazard Monthly,* pp. 9-10.

Kincaid, K. (1997). *Partnering with business in incident management.* Executive Fire Officer Program Research Paper, Emmitsburg, MD: National Fire Academy.

Lilienfeld, R. (1978). *The rise of systems theory.* New York: John Wiley & Sons.

Long, C.R. (1990, June). [Letter to the Editor, untitled]. *Hazards Monthly,* p. 8.

Maloney, J.E., & Potter, M.O. (1974). *The fire management system: Preliminary results and design concepts.* Ottawa, Ontario: Forest Fire Research Institute.

McCoy, L.C. (1990, June). ICS works when used correctly. *Hazard Monthly,* pp. 9-11.

Rubin, D.L. (1997). The Incident Command System: Myths, rumors and unnatural acts. *Fire Chief,* 41, pp. 63-68.

Senge, P.M. (1990). *The fifth discipline.* New York: Doubleday.

State of California (1995). *SEMS guidelines: Standardized emergency management system.* Sacramento, CA: Governor's Office of Emergency Services.

Stone, N. (Ed.) (1998). *Peter Drucker on the profession of management.* Boston: Harvard Business Review Books.

Ullman, M.L. (1998). *Integration of the Incident Management System between the police and fire departments of the city of Goodyear, Arizona.* Executive Fire Officer Program Resaerch Paper, Emmitsburg, MD: National Fire Academy.

Wenger, D., Quatrantelli, E.L., and Dynes, R.R. (1990, May). Is the Incident Command System a plan for all seasons and emergency situations? *Hazard Monthly,* pp. 8-12.

Wonnacott R.J. & Wonnacott, T.H. (1985). *Introductory statistics.* New York: John Wiley & Sons.

Appendix A

ICS Questionnaire (should take no more than 10 minutes)

I am doing a research project for the National Fire Academy that evaluates the Incident Command System from the point of view of veteran ICS practitioners. If you would like your input included in this research, please complete the survey below.

Just type in your answer after each question. When you're done, REPLLY to dana_cole@fire.ca.gov.

Thanks in advance for your participation.

Dana Cole, CDF.

(707) 963-3601 ext. 108

email: dana_cole@fire.ca.gov

Directions:

Type the appropriation number after each question.

1. How many years of experience do you have in the fire service?

2. How many years of experience do you have using the Incident Command System? (approximate if you're not sure)

3. How many years of experience do you have as a member of a major incident command/management team? (if none, enter "0")

4. In your career, approximately how many incidents with duration of 3 or more consecutive operational periods have you been assigned to as a team member at the Command & General Staff level?

5. How many of these incidents were non-emergencies (conference, project, etc.)?

6. Please read the following scenario and then rate the listed features of ICS.

SCENARIO: Imagine that you are contacted by a heath care administrator with whom you have worked on a major disaster. She saw ICS applied and is considering adopting an ICS approach for managing major medical emergencies at her company's hospitals. She knows you have years of experience working with ICS, and she wants to discuss your perception of its weaknesses and strengths.

Directions:

Rate each of items A-P below on a scale of 1 to10 to indicate its relative WEAK-NESS or STRENGTH as a feature of ICS. (For example, a score of 2 is a more significant weakness than a score of 3; an 8 indicates a more significant strength than a 7)

Remember there are no right or wrong answers. I am just looking for your honest opinion.

1	2	3	4	5	6	7	8	9	10

WEAKNESS   STRENGTH

A. Uniform terminology for identifying resources and organizational functions.

B. Resource mobilization effectiveness.

C. Modular organization structure that is expanded or contracted as needed.

D. Consistency of implementation among various agencies.

E. Communications plan that is coordinated among responding agencies.

F. Incident Action Plans that are updated for each operational period.

G. Agreement among agencies about who has authority to modify the ICS "rules of the game."

H. Manageable span-of-control.

I. Clear decision-making process.

J. Cross-jurisdictional and cross-functional working relationships when ICS is used.

K. Standardized forms used for all incidents.

L. Predefined hierarchy, including chain-of-command and delineated responsibilities for every position.

M. Ample flexibility and authority are given to staff for accomplishing incident objectives.

N. Process for transitioning command authority from one level of government to another as incident objectives.

O. Effectiveness of integrating non-fire government agencies (e.g., law enforcement, public works) into ICS structure.

P. Effectiveness of integrating non-government organizations (e.g., relief organizations, private citizens, and businesses) into ICS structure.

Both the ICS Orientation and the 25-Year Evaluation detail the ICS construct. Obviously it is not a perfect system but becomes more significant as future threats involve interagency cooperation. Anyone in the field knows full well that the history of relationships when more than one service responds has not been a rosy one in this country. Popular literature draws plot lines around local police distrusting federal agencies; fire and police rescue companies competing for control and other emergency responders shut out of the inner circles. The romantic harmony of the televised *Third Watch* is much more fiction than fact.

SUMMARY

Major incidents such as terrorist attacks or natural disasters happen unexpectedly and can lead to disorganization, tragedy, and chaos if the response is not structured and planned well. The Incident Command System is intended to provide a set of guidelines that enable such a structured, planned approach and minimize the impact of an incident. A major part of ICS is aimed at organizing the command structure when responding to an incident so that appropriate tasks at an incident scene can be assigned and completed in an orderly and efficient manner.

ICS is the tactical on-scene level of a larger National Incident Management System (NIMS) that focuses on the entire incident management process, including strategic planning activities, resource management, and communications as well as ICS. Both are part of the National Response Framework (NRF), which ensures that all emergency response personnel understand the domestic incident response roles, responsibilities, and relationships to respond more effectively to any type of incident. With more agencies becoming NIMS complaint all the time, NIMS and ICS are going to be tools every emergency manager will be expected to use for the foreseeable future.

ADDITIONAL DISCUSSION TOPICS

- Review the five incident complexity levels. Describe disaster events likely in your area that might require a type 2 or greater response.

- How are ICS and NIMS related? Why isn't ICS enough by itself?

- During the aftermath of hurricane Katrina, police, fire and EMS agencies from as far away as California and Minnesota sent units to help out in New Orleans and other affected areas. What strategies could you suggest for training exercises to simulate and prepare for working with agencies so far from their jurisdictions?

Endnotes

[1] The original seven "partner agencies" are the California Department of Forestry and Fire Protection, California Office of Emergency Services, Los Angeles City Fire Department, Los Angeles County First Department, Santa Barbara County Fire Department, Ventura County Fire Department and the U.S. Forest Service.

[2] In 1982, the word "Southern" was dropped from the acronym when FIRESCOPE was formally established as a statewide program.

[3] In California, teams comprised of representatives from state and local government go by the name Major Incident Command Teams. Federal teams are termed Major Incident Management Teams. For purposes of this paper, the generic term Major Incident Teams is used.

CHAPTER THIRTEEN

ETHICS & THE ART OF WAR

Art, like morality, consists of drawing the line somewhere.
—G.K. Chesterton, English Essayist and Poet (1874-1936)

Morality is the best of all devices for leading mankind by the nose.
—Friedrich Nietzsche, German philosopher (1844-1900)

We talk on principle but we act on interest.
—William Savage Landor, English author (1775-1864)

KEY TERMS

Confirmation process
War crimes
Torture
Conflict of interest
Norms
Looting

OBJECTIVES

■ Assess ethical elements of the critical points of the war on terror and assess the balance between survival and ethics.

■ Identify and evaluate the concept of torture, and whether or not there are cases where it should be condoned.

■ Discuss the selection process for leaders in the war on terror, and evaluate as to whether our best interests are the focal point of the process.

■ Understand the influence of norms on human behavior.

■ Discuss looting behavior.

DISCUSSION TOPICS

■ If you were the president of the United States, are there situations as to whether or not you would condone torture?

■ Can a war against terror be fought by ethical means and have a successful conclusion?

■ Can you imagine a better process for selecting national leaders? How would your process differ from the political process now used?

■ Are there situations when you believe it is right not to volunteer assistance during a disaster? What would they be?

■ Do you believe the likelihood of looting is high or low in the place you live? Would it be different at your place of work?

13

INTRODUCTION

In this chapter we will discuss ethics from two perspectives, the global war on terror and the role of the responder community. Our ethics discussion will include how to critically assess the issue of prisoner and torture, how the behavior of looting occurs at disaster scenes, and ethically assessing the operational aspects of disaster scenes. Articles, scenarios, and case studies are provided as an evaluative platform for the reader.

In this chapter we hope to initiate critical assessment of different perspectives and enable the reader to enhance their perceptions of ethics as applied to war and disaster response.

FIGHTING AN ETHICAL WAR AGAINST TERROR

Ethical issues are discussed throughout this text but there are several philosophical perspectives that weigh heavily on the collective consciousness of the American people regarding the war on terror. What is the right thing to do? What must we do to protect ourselves? Should the American people condone torture? What means is appropriate to stop terrorists from killing us?

The question to be answered is how do we balance our ethical and moral belief system with the reality of our situation—that is, "us versus them" in a struggle to the death?

The benefits of critical thinking are never more important than when determining an ethical course of action. Without an objective view of events on which to base decisions, it is impossible to determine an ethical course of action.

We are at war with a ruthless enemy who thinks nothing of committing grisly murders of innocent civilians and broadcasting it over the Internet. Are ethics best left for after-dinner discussions during times of peace? Is there an ethical way to conduct war?

The first article addresses the outsourcing of torture and is critical of the U.S. government—that is, the Central Intelligence Agency policy of deporting terrorists to countries where they can be subject to extraordinary means of interrogation, or torture.

Many nations around the world, including Egypt and Saudi Arabia, have experienced far more terrorist activity that has the US and are valuable allies delivering intelligence and other aid to American forces in the War on Terror. Their laws are not the same as those in the US, and their citizens do not enjoy many of the rights that Americans do. Due process and protection against unreasonable search and seizure are two guarantees not available within these countries, and their security forces routinely use methods that would be illegal in the US but are perfectly legal there. How much assistance should American security forces give to regimes like these? If the US is not willing to deliver captured suspected terrorists wanted in Egypt, how much assistance will the Egyptians be willing to give the US when asked? Al Qaeda is most active within Saudi Arabia, and a large percentage of captured Al Qaeda fighters are Saudi citizens. Should the US not repatriate them for fear of the treatment they will likely receive legally in Saudi Arabia?

Balance this concern with the fact that we have always had a policy of deporting immigrants and other temporary residents of the US who commit crimes in the US to their countries of origin. The question that the article begs: Should people who leave a country which practices human rights violations to come the United States to commit acts of terror be protected with political asylum?

Torture by Proxy[1]

One of the biggest non-secrets in Washington these days is the Central Intelligence Agency's top-secret program for sending terrorism suspects to countries where concern for human rights and the rule of law don't pose obstacles to torturing prisoners. For months, the Bush administration has refused to comment on these operations, which make the United States the partner of some of the world's most repressive regimes.

But a senior official talked about it to The *Times*'s Douglas Jehl and David Johnston, saying he wanted to rebut assertions that the United States was putting prisoners in the hands of outlaw regimes for the specific purpose of having someone else torture them. Sadly, his explanation, reported on Sunday, simply confirmed that the Bush administration has been outsourcing torture and intends to keep doing it.

For years before the 9/11 terrorist attacks, the CIA had occasionally engaged in the practice known in bureaucratese by the creepy euphemism "extraordinary rendition." But after the attacks in New York and Washington, President Bush gave the agency broad authority to export prisoners without getting permission from the White House or the Justice Department. Rendition has become central to antiterrorism operations at the CIA, which also operates clandestine camps around the world for prisoners it doesn't want the International Red Cross or the American public to know about.

According to the *Times* article, the CIA has flown 100 to 150 suspected terrorists to countries like Egypt, Syria, Saudi Arabia, Jordan and Pakistan—each a habitual offender when it comes to torture. It's against American law and international convention to send prisoners to any nation where they are likely to be tortured, so the official said no prisoner is sent to another country without assurances from that government that they will be treated humanely. He said that CIA officials "check on those assurances, and we double-check." Those assurances are worthless, and the Bush administration surely knows it. In normal times, the governments of these countries have abysmal standards for human rights and humane treatment, and would have no problem promising that a prisoner won't be tortured—right before he's tortured. And these are not normal times. The Bush administration has long since made it clear that it will tolerate torture, even by men and women in American uniforms. And why send prisoners to places like Syria and Saudi Arabia, if not for the brutal treatment Americans are supposed to abhor? The senior official said it saved manpower and money, compared with keeping them in the United States or at American-run prisons abroad. The idea that this is a productivity initiative would be comical if the issue were not so tragically serious.

No rational person would deny the need to hunt down terrorists, to try to extract lifesaving information from them and to punish them, legally. But the CIA has sent prisoners to countries where they were tortured for months and then either disappeared or were released because they knew nothing. The guilty ones can never be brought to justice—not after they have been illegally imprisoned and even tortured.

American officials have offered pretzel logic to defend these practices. Attorney General Alberto Gonzales has said that if the United States sends a prisoner abroad, then our nation's Constitution no longer applies.

This is just the sort of thinking that led to the horrible abuses at prisons in Iraq, where the Army is now holding more Iraqi prisoners than ever: nearly 9,000. The military says it's doing a better job of screening these prisoners than in the days when a vast majority of Iraqi prisoners were, in fact, innocent of any wrongdoing. But there is still a shortage of translators to question prisoners, the jails are dangerously overcrowded, and there's never been a full and honest public accounting of the rules the American prison guards now follow.

Let's be clear about this: Any prisoner of the United States is protected by American values. That cannot be changed by sending him to another country and pretending not to notice that he's being tortured.

What Is Torture?

Defining torture can be as difficult as defining terrorism. The way both words are used often tells more about the speaker than about the person or activity to which they are referring. Since few Americans have personal experience with torture, our beliefs about torture and what constitutes torture are often based more on how torture is depicted in novels and movies than on the true reality of torture as it is used around the world.

One commonly cited definition of torture comes from the United Nations Convention Against Torture,[2] which defines it as

> "any act by which severe pain or suffering, whether physical or mental, is intentionally inflicted on a person for such purposes as obtaining from him or a third person information or a confession, punishing him for an act he or a third person has committed or is suspected of having committed, or intimidating or coercing him or a third person, or for any reason based on discrimination of any kind, when such pain or suffering is inflicted by or at the instigation of or with the consent or acquiescence of a public official or other person acting in an official capacity. It does not include pain or suffering arising only from, inherent in or incidental to lawful sanctions."

One obvious problem with this definition is that it does not allow for torture by non-official actors, which is very unsatisfying during a War on Terror in which only one side is represented by a national government.

International Humanitarian Law (IHL) is made up of customary and case law as well as several treaties, the best known of which include the Geneva Conventions and the Hague Conventions. Its definition does not require the torturer to be acting in an official capacity, but does require that the pain or mistreatment be inflicted for a purpose, such as gaining information, before it becomes torture.[3]

The European Union bans torture in its Convention on Human Rights, but does not closely define it. Torture is described as "inhuman treatment, which has a purpose, such as the obtaining of information or confessions, or the infliction of punishment, and it is generally an aggravated form of inhuman treatment."[4]

There are several reasons that international agencies have difficulty defining torture. The most common is political: Nations do not want to limit their options more than necessary in pursuing their national security, so leave some room for argument in the definition. Also, it is impossible to draw a clear line between practices that are degrading, uncomfortable, or cruel, and those that cross the threshold into torture. Certainly, the nature and severity of the act must be taken into account, but it cannot be reduced to a set of proscribed practices.

Charges of torture must be taken within the context of the accuser as well as of the situation itself because it is frequently leveled for some sort of gain. Al Qaeda training manuals teach operatives to claim torture whenever they are detained or arrested because they know that such charges against Western governments and their allies carry great weight, even while they themselves videotape torture sessions against their enemies for Internet distribution.

Ethical Considerations...

You have a family member being held by extremists. They are threatening to behead your family member and broadcast the murder over the Internet. Your family member is a truck driver who was delivering supplies to civilians and not involved in any military operations. You have discovered that a member of the extremist group is in custody in the United States. This extremist has asked for legal counsel and refuses to answer questions. The extremist knows the location of your family member. There is time for a rescue team to respond and rescue them. To what lengths would you go in order to find the location of your family member?

Your country has been invaded and the government overthrown. You do not have public support within your country for the former government or the military means to repel the invaders. Your only weapon is to kill civilians and create chaos. The press refers to you as a "fighter" or "insurgent" and your acts of chaos get world attention. Are these acts justifiable? Are you a freedom fighter or terrorist? What is the difference?

The next article is from a speech to a victim's advocate group. I found this to be a moving speech that demonstrates, at least to your author, a solid foundation of critical assessment of the events to be discussed. The victims and potential victims of terror—the citizens of the United States homeland—should be our primary concern. War is an ugly business, and it is only exceeded in its ugliness by terrorism.

Lies Terrorists Tell[5]

It is a privilege and honor to address this conference. By focusing on the victims of terrorism you are acting in exactly the opposite fashion of the terrorists. They turn individual human beings into instruments of propaganda. You remind the world that terrorists' victims are, before all else, individual human beings. By doing this you expose the evil core of terrorism and proclaim the truth, the truth which is the constant companion of justice.

I first encountered terrorism close-up as a junior diplomat assigned to the U.S. Embassy in Tel Aviv. It was there that I first understood the terrible reach of terrorists, the way in which their depredations damaged so many more lives than those reached by their blasts and bullets. At the time Israel's population was about the same as my home state of Oklahoma— less than three million. Yet almost every Israeli I met knew someone killed or injured by terrorists. I had no frame of reference. Not even the Vietnam War, which at that time continued with diminished U.S. participation, affected so many individuals at home.

In the bare 18 months I spent in Israel there were 14 terrorist attacks. One of them, at Ma'alot on May 15, 1974 was clearly intended to disrupt the then-current disengagement negotiations between Israel and Syria; 20 school children died in that attack. I still recall the Israeli government's statement that it would negotiate with the Popular Front for the Liberation of Palestine terrorists holding the children. The government said it was negotiating because "it would not make war on the backs of children." The negotiations broke down and the children died. I remember Golda Meir's cracking voice as she announced the deaths of the children. Those of you who think of Middle Eastern terrorism as an exclusively Muslim activity should note that the PFLP was founded by George Habash, a Christian physician.

In the three decades since my tour in Israel ended I have seen far too much terrorism; terrorists have killed personal friends in Peru, El Salvador, Italy, and the United Kingdom.

Across these decades, things have changed.

In a few fortunate areas, terrorism has diminished, but overall terrorism claims more lives than ever. Western Europe may be free of the Red Brigades style terrorism, but may be more threatened than ever. Many of the countries of the former Soviet Union, whose totalitarianism protected them 30 years ago, now face serious terrorism; terrorism is up in Southeast Asia and the Philippines. I need not tell this audience what has happened in the Andes, especially here in Colombia.

But for all the changes, for all the blood that has flowed, for all the victims lost, for all shattered lives of the friends and families and survivors, one thing has not changed.

Terrorists lie.

To justify their actions they lie to their enemies; they lie to their friends; they lie to themselves.

Today, I ask you to join me in examining some of those lies. I do so because understanding those lies, rejecting their lies, strengthens us, helps us resist the terrorists and helps save the lives of victims yet unknown.

Lie Number One: "We must eradicate the 'root causes' of terrorism."

September 6, 1986 was the Jewish Sabbath, Saturday. It was also Yom Kippur, the holiest day on the Jewish calendar.

On that Yom Kippur, two operatives of the Abu Nidal Organization entered Istanbul's main synagogue and machine-gunned the worshipers. They then poured gasoline on the dead and wounded and set them afire. They killed 22 and wounded three others.

Although accounts vary, it seems that two of the men killed themselves with hand grenades, holding the grenades against their faces so that their fingerprints would be blown off and their teeth destroyed so that they could never be identified.

Some months after that, when I was working in the counterterrorism office of the State Department, I met with a small group of private citizens who had asked the State Department to brief them on U.S. counterterrorism policy. I ticked off the main policy points and asked if there were questions. One of the members of the group, a protestant clergyman (I have forgotten his denomination) brought up the Istanbul synagogue murders. He described the terrorists who had killed themselves, noting that one was probably no more than a teenager.

"What had happened to that young man," he asked, "to make him do such a horrible thing? To destroy himself in such a terrible manner?"

Even with over a decade's experience of diplomacy, it was hard to contain my fury. I managed not to shout, but cannot say that the tone of my voice was smooth or that my words were diplomatic:

"That young man murdered 22 people while they were praying, *praying*; he burned some of them alive! You want me to worry about what happened to him? I don't give a damn about what happened to him and neither should you! Pray for his victims! Let him go to hell!"

That ended the meeting.

I later wondered what had happened to that pastor. What had so disoriented him morally that he would focus on the murderer and not the victims?

I came to understand the pastor's error. He had come to believe the "root cause" lie, the lie that holds that terrorism is the "effect" of some "cause."

Neither God nor man creates a terrorist. Terrorists create terrorism. They create terrorism by choosing terror as the means to advance their political goals.

The terrorist has decided that the shortest path to his political goal is terrorism. He has passed over democratic elections, passive resistance, and armed struggle against others in arms. He has chosen to target the defenseless and the innocent.

And then he encourages us to believe that his terrorism has a "root cause."

Those born to comfortable circumstances are particularly susceptible to this lie. That is why the "root cause" lie enjoys such currency amongst well-to-do Western intellectuals.

In few places have muddled thinking and thinly veiled support for terrorists come together to more infamous result as in the title of this document prepared by the Sixth Committee of the UN Secretariat over 30 years ago:

> *Measures to Prevent International Terrorism Which Endangers Human Lives Or Jeopardizes Fundamental Freedoms, And Study of the Underlying Causes Of Those Forms of Terrorism And Acts of Violence Which Lie in Misery, Frustration, Grievances And Despair And Which Cause Some People to Sacrifice Human Lives, Including Their Own, In an Attempt to Effect Radical Changes."*
>
> United Nations Document A/C 6/418 (1972)

Note the reference to "underlying causes" and "misery, frustration, grievances and despair."

Academics who rigorously study terrorism and political violence know this lie has no basis in fact. They have examined the backgrounds of terrorists and they have discovered that most terrorists, at least those who are in charge, come from solid, middle-class backgrounds:

- Ilich Ramirez Sanchez, better known to the world as "Carlos the Jackal," was born into a Venezuelan family so rich that his father was known as the "Marxist Millionaire."

- Osama Bin Laden's wealth is well-known.

- Abimael Guzman, who led the blood-thirsty Sendero Luminoso as "Presidente Gonzalo," came from a nice, middle-class family in Arequipa, Peru.

Those who spread the "root cause" lie hardly recognize the class snobbery inherent in their analysis. They cannot imagine, from the vantage point of their privilege, that poor people living under despotic governments cannot recognize that it is wrong to murder innocent people. They deny the poor the dignity of moral understanding. Their logic would lead us to believe that poverty causes theft. By this logic rich people would not steal.

But terrorists love this analysis because if you believe it, you are prepared for:

Lie Number 2: Terrorists are soldiers in a revolution

I have spoken on terrorism many times and, having spent most of my adult life living in Latin America, I have spoken to many Latinos about terrorism. Inevitably, in a region where so much history and so much mythology are devoted the revolutionary, the question always presents itself:

> "But isn't terrorism what tyrants call revolutionaries? Isn't one man's terrorist another man's freedom fighter?"

No.

One man's terrorist is another man's terrorist.

Terrorists are different from revolutionaries and freedom fighters because terrorists target the innocent. Terrorists select women, children, airline passengers, office workers, worshipers and others uninvolved in combat and, generally speaking, incapable of defending themselves.

There are many definitions of terrorism, some of which are extremely convoluted, but there is a single question, the answer to which can separate terrorists from guerrilla fighters: *Would the act, if undertaken by a uniformed soldier in time of war, constitute a war crime?*

Some cases are hard to judge, but nine times out of 10, answering this question clears away intellectual fog. It makes you realize that terrorism is a war crime committed by someone not a soldier.

This intellectual clarity is important, important not just to those of us who have lost family members or friends. Intellectual clarity is important to civilization itself.

When we fail to recognize the distinction between warfare and terrorism, we strip soldierly dignity from those who protect us from barbarism and award it to murderers.

This injustice doubly punishes terrorism's victims.

First, the terrorist turns the victim into an instrument of his armed propaganda. He transforms a human being into a bloody wall poster. Then, the terrorist or his intellectual apologist converts the victim into a legitimate target for military action, telling us there is no difference between an airliner and a military base, that a religious procession is no different from a column of soldiers.

He forces us to suffer the intellectual insult of being told that Carlos the Jackal is the legitimate heir of Simon Bolivar, that President Lincoln and Presidente Gonzalo were politically and morally equivalent.

We are not children. We know soldiers sometimes kill innocents. I recently spent a year in Iraq and I know innocent people have been killed by soldiers. Consider the following example: A driver does not see a signal to stop. When the driver does not slow, a soldier opens fire and an innocent family is killed. This is tragedy. It is tragedy and an error, but it is not terrorism and it is not murder.

Every person here knows the difference between the grim accidents of warfare and the seizure of the Dominican Embassy or Supreme Court of Colombia.

It is the difference between a soldier and a terrorist.

Lie Number 3: "Terrorism is a word made up by oppressive regimes"

Nonsense.

To deny the legitimacy of armed rebellion is to deny the heritage of all the Americas.

But rebellion can take many forms without becoming terrorism. Some successful rebellions have been non-violent-note recent events in the Ukraine.

When Gandhi took up non-violent protest against the British in India others practiced violent revolution in the same cause. We know who triumphed.

Martin Luther King, who studied Gandhi, did more than any other individual to end a pernicious, centuries-old system of racial oppression in the United States.

It is fair to say that Gandhi and King would not have succeeded against Hitler or even Trujillo. True enough, but it is still possible to wage violent revolution without attacking innocents.

I find Fidel Castro a tyrant. He has spilled rivers of blood to stay in power. Most recently, he sent three before a firing squad for the bloodless hijacking of a ferry boat last April.

But Fidel, tyrant that he is, won his revolution, to the best of my knowledge, without resorting to terrorism.

The Greatest Lie of All

There is one great and final lie that terrorists tell. It is a lie they tell themselves and others, the lie that has propitiated great evil for centuries uncounted.

What is this great lie?

"Nothing is more important than this!"

It is the lie of the Nazis.

"Nothing is more important than racial purity!"

It is the lie of Robespierre, and Stalin and Mao and Pol Pot.

"Nothing is more important than the revolution!"

It is the lie of ETA.

"Nothing is more important than a Basque Homeland!"

It is the lie of both the Inquisition and of al Qaida.

"Nothing is more important than doing God's will!"

The greatest lie, which all terrorists tell the world and themselves, is that some political outcome is more important than recognizing and honoring the humanity of each and every person.

I ask your forgiveness for speaking so much about terrorists at a conference about victims.

I did this because thought it important that we focus, for a few moments, on the lies that make terrorism possible; on the lies that strip terrorist victims of their humanity, the lies that scar so many people in this room.

I urge you to recognize the lies terrorists tell. For when you recognize their lies, when you refute them, you have begun to disarm the terrorists. You have begun to disarm them because they need their lies more than they need their bullets or guns or bombs.

Thank you.

HOW DO WE SELECT OUR LEADERSHIP IN THE WAR ON TERROR?

The process of Senate confirmation for critical positions in any White House administration is grueling and detailed. Every aspect of a nominee's background is scrutinized. Often, political goals of the confirmation panels come in to play, resulting in press leaks and exploitation of events. The following article addresses some of the concerns about the National Intelligence Director nominee.

Intelligence Nominee Vows to Sell Stock[6]

WASHINGTON – John Negroponte, President Bush's choice for intelligence chief, is a multimillionaire who promised last year to sell stock in companies that have business stakes in Iraq's reconstruction, according to his financial disclosure reports.

It is unclear from two April reports, Negroponte's most recent filings, whether he followed through on sales of General Electric and other companies helping to rebuild Iraq, where he is U.S. ambassador. The White House did not immediately comment Monday.

Less than two weeks ago, Bush asked Negroponte to take on the new job of national intelligence director, bringing together 15 independent intelligence agencies.

That assignment may force Negroponte to take a fresh look at whether any financial holdings present conflicts of interest — a process he went through last spring when he was nominated ambassador to Iraq.

Then, Negroponte agreed not to participate in decisions that would effect his personal holdings. To minimize problems, he agreed to sell his interests in Citigroup, General Electric and GE Capital. The three companies are providing postwar Iraq with everything from power generators to help in restructuring the claims of private commercial creditors against the country.

Negroponte has not had to file another disclosure report since then to confirm the transactions took place.

In a letter to a State Department ethics official on April 23, Negroponte said he would "remain alert" on the possible need to remove himself from certain decisions or to request a written waiver to qualify for an exemption.

Government officials must file financial disclosure reports annually or when they receive a new appointment. That helps ensure that they are complying with federal laws and regulations that bar officials from making government decisions that lead to personal profit. The forms list the officials' holdings, but give the values only in broad ranges.

According to Negroponte's April reports, which cover 2003 and the first part of 2004, his portfolio contained investments in a number of banks and investment funds, retail stores such as Family Dollar and global technology and information companies.

Last spring, Negroponte's investments were worth at least $2.7 million, and possibly over $9 million. His largest single investment was between $1 million and $5 million in a trust called the Federated Investors' tax-free obligations fund.

Because many national security-related contracts are classified, it is impossible to pinpoint all conflicts of interest that might arise should the Senate confirm him as national intelligence director, as expected. Yet some seem apparent.

Negroponte, for instance, owns $15,000 to $50,000 in California-based Hewlett-Packard, an information-technology company active in government work. The company has worked with Lockheed Martin on defense and intelligence programs, particularly in areas of information sharing, security and systems management.

It also participates in the Computer Science and Telecommunications Board, a federal advisory panel that is studying the application of biometric technologies for counterterrorism purposes. The work is sponsored by the CIA and the Defense Advanced Research Projects Agency.

In September 2003, Negroponte sold $100,000 to $250,0000 of stock with his employer from 1997 to 2001, McGraw-Hill, a global information-services provider. The company has a homeland security division that offers search engines and databases aiding in infrastructure and border security.

According to the disclosures, Negroponte has continued to receive installments on a bonus deferred from 1999. One of the filings indicated that he received $208,000 in the 12 months ending last April. As ambassador, Negroponte promised not to participate in matters that would affect the company's ability to pay him.

Also in his disclosure reports:

- In February 2003, while U.S. ambassador to the United Nations, Negroponte invested $15,000 to $50,000 in AIG, which has insured people and companies doing business in Iraq. He sold the stock a month later.

- In December 2003, he purchased $15,000 to $50,000 of Kaydon Corp., which makes shock absorbers, bearings and filtration products. The company is a supplier of the U.S. military and its stock value has increased since the March 2003 Iraq invasion.

- In June 2003, Negroponte invested $15,000 to $50,000 in Avery Dennison, a maker of adhesives and office supplies. Avery Dennison was the victim in a case involving the U.S. government's first criminal prosecution over economic espionage, in 2002. Prosecutors said the company's adhesive formula was stolen by a Taiwanese businessman.

We need people in critical positions who are of the highest character. All questions should be addressed and resolved before nomination. In the case of the initial nominee for the Secretary of the Department of Homeland Security, Bernie Kerick, he was a very capable "outsider," who probably had the grit and skills to move the department out of the quagmire of politics that has slowed the development of our security systems to a near grinding halt; however, Mr. Kerrick had background issues that resulted in his withdrawal from nomination.

The candidates for these key positions must have a sense of daring, commitment, and a track record of business expertise and a history of excellence in their management skills—but how many candidates that fit that mold are interested in going through the scrutiny of the nomination microscope? How many are interested in having every aspect of their personal and business life brought under the public eye?

Most of the concerns about Mr. Negroponte, which were addressed in the preceding article, are common to successful executives and officials. Although he was confirmed, the ethical question to be addressed is, "was he the most capable, or the least offensive?"

NORMS AND ETHICS DURING DISASTERS

Ethical issues related to post-disaster situations cut across a broad spectrum of disciplines. There is a myriad of research dealing with ethical issues in post-disaster situations. This chapter will explore some important areas of concern using training materials and news articles. The first section, written by Rottman (2000), illustrates the importance of ethical behavior in terms of interpersonal responsibility and explains the theory about volunteer behavior. The second section, written by Drabek (1996), looks at "looting behavior" from a sociologic point of view and he also discussed the discrepancy between myths or false public expectations regarding in the aftermath of major disasters. Drabek helps link the research and practice of emergency management, in an effort to help emergency managers manage response effectively. The rest of the chapter is devoted to additional readings:

- The Emergency Medical Technician Code of Ethics (Gillespie, 2001);

- An article on Disaster Relief Ethics in general and experiences during post September 11th by the Markkula Center for Applied Ethics of Santa Clara University (2002);

- A short paper on the challenges observed by disaster responders in 2004 Tsunamis that devastated the Indian Ocean shorelines (Potter, 2005);

- The 14 general principles of ethics for government workers of the U.S.; and

- Five case studies from FEMA are provided to illustrate situations posing ethical questions for government employees during disaster.

Norms[7]

This section illustrates the importance of interpersonal responsibility and ethical behavior in emergency settings. It includes discussions of why our obligations to assist others in a disaster situation not only have value to the lives and well being of our families, but through efforts on behalf of total strangers, to our society as a whole.

People generally behave in social situations based on what they perceive to be the norms, or rules, of the community. Norms are learned and they set a standard of what individuals should or shouldn't do in a given setting. These expectations tend to lend order and predictability to human behavior (getting in line to use an automated teller machine at the bank, rather than pacing around the machine and pushing others out of the way so you can use it; not shouting "fire" in a crowded movie theater so you can see the effect; helping an elderly lady with her packages find a seat on the bus).

Norms are powerful influences over human behavior. People follow norms because they are either pressured or permitted by them to act the way most other people would in a similar situation. Furthermore, acting differently would risk disapproval by the rest of the group. This could produce anything from a psychologically uncomfortable consequence at the most mild end of the continuum to, in the case of criminal violation of a norm, imprisonment.

Helping Behavior

Family norms to societal norms
Psychologists tell us that helping behavior begins as early as 2 years old, following examples of those around them—their family norms. As children grow older, the expectation that being helpful is a good thing and being selfish is not begins to reflect the norm of the society as a whole.

Religious responsibilities
Some theorize that people find a religious basis for altruism as a reciprocal form of behavior (do unto others as we would have them do unto us).

Give and take theory
Others believe people only do good deeds because they'll receive something of equal benefit in return. But by young adulthood, many people help others when there is virtually no likelihood that they will be rewarded by others for their actions.

Action of helping is a reward in itself
One explanation for this is that the action is its own reward; that is, the doer enjoys (perhaps selfishly) the uplifting feeling elicited by their helpful behavior.

Empathy
Another theory suggests that people help others because they empathize with them or their situation, not because they will get some personal gain from their actions. In fact, studies have shown that when people identify with the circumstances of others, they are likely to continue their helpful efforts even when doing so might be personally unpleasant.

Cultural norms
Finally, and perhaps most relevant to our discussions, is the theory that people perform altruistic behaviors simply because they fulfill the expected norms of the culture, and these norms have developed to provide adaptive behavior for society. If helping is normative, then all who are parts of the community will be likely to receive assistance should they ever need it.

Four Determinants of Volunteer Assistance

Four characteristics of a situation help to determine whether or not helping behavior is likely.

1. Do people recognize the need for help?
If there is absolutely clear evidence that someone needs assistance (especially a direct request for help), virtually 100% of people will respond. If the situation is perceived to be at all ambiguous, the majority will watch but take no personal action.

Preparedness education tip: Since most people will respond to a direct request for help by a stranger, teach bystanders to ask if people need help.

2. How attractive is the person in need?
Studies have shown that people will help others whom they like or find attractive (physically attractive, well dressed).

It's hard to ask people to groom themselves and dress nicely in the event of a disaster! Educate your community to the concept that these events may occur at unpredictable times, and have little regard for the appearance or background of their victims. Stress the importance of reaching out to all who have been impacted by the disaster. Remind them of the "rules of behavior" which guide our society. Helping others is an important social norm.

3. How familiar is the setting?
Familiarity with the setting fosters more assistance. People tend to offer assistance more when they are in a setting in which they have been many times before, and less so when the situation is relatively novel. Perhaps this has to do with a level of comfort of the surroundings, knowledge of where other resources are and how to access them, or a perceived sense of safety just because the landmarks of the setting are familiar.

Most uninjured survivors of a disaster find themselves in familiar surroundings (at home, school, work). They either personally know or have seen others who have survived or who are victims. In a disaster situation, there is likely to be familiarity with the setting, and this should be less of a constraint on helping behavior.

4. How many other people are around?
Having more people at site seems to discourage individual action. While you might think that having lots of other people around would encourage an individual to help, the opposite is actually the case. The more people who are at the site, the more inhibiting this is on any one individual's helping behavior. Each person thinks that another in the crowd will take action.

Perhaps people feel that because of the presence of others, it is no longer their responsibility to help. This sense is exaggerated if the others present are strangers. But if the others in the group know each other, there is a greater tendency to take a helpful course of action.

Again, since in a disaster the surroundings are likely to be familiar, many of the people also are likely to be familiar. We know that individuals who may be inhibited from helping by the very presence of others are less inhibited if they know others in the group. Stress this point in disaster preparedness education.

Why Some People Do Not Help in Emergency Situations

Why doesn't everybody help in an emergency?

If all of these "helping behaviors" or hypotheses concerning them are true, then everybody ought to conduct himself in a helpful, altruistic fashion in a crisis. But not everybody does. Think of the dozen onlookers who waited for someone else to act and help that 16 year old trapped in the burning car. Why didn't they do anything? How can we maximize the chances that people will help each other in time of need?

Some reasons why people may not help out in emergency situations:

- Fear of
  - *Lawsuits/liability*
  - *Getting hurt*

- Someone else will take care of the situation, or "passing the buck."
  - *It is the responsibility of someone else.*
  - There are others around who will/can help out.

- Unable to help.
  - *Physically incapable of performing the required helping actions demanded by the circumstances.*

- Don't know what to do.
  - *Many people either don't know which emergency actions are appropriate, or how to perform them.*

There are many reasons why people help each other, but most would agree that altruistic behavior is a powerful social norm. Yet, despite these behavioral expectations, there are specific circumstances that affect whether or not people ultimately will take action to help each other. By learning about what helps or inhibits individuals from coming to the aid of others, people can change their willingness to act in an emergency situation. For example, people were almost twice as likely to offer assistance once they learned about how the presence of others on the scene might inhibit them from engaging in helping behavior. By incorporating these concepts into individual and community disaster preparedness education, program planners will increase the likelihood of developing a cadre of involved, action-oriented disaster responders.

Disaster preparedness experts need to be cognizant not only of the general principles outlined here, but they also must be attuned to the unique characteristics of various groups, which may be identified within their community. Thus, just as individuals tend to offer assistance based on predictable normative standards of behavior, disaster preparedness educators must be certain that in their efforts to prepare the community, they do so in an ethical, equitable fashion.

Understanding Looting Behavior[8]

This section pinpoints the discrepancy between the false public expectations regarding looting and behavioral research findings. It also introduces a specific example of detailed findings that indicate significant variations among disasters with different analytic criteria. It provides an example of how science can inform emergency managers about a topic that is misunderstood. When they inform personnel in other agencies that looting rarely occurs after disasters, many will confront them with reports of looting after civil disturbances and Hurricane Hugo, especially on the island of St. Croix. They must be aware of the empirical research base and distinctions among events regarding looting behavior. Note that under the right social conditions, looting behavior will occur. Typically, disasters do not occur when these special conditions are present. Hence, while rare, there are documented instances of looting.

Looting Myth

Looting is defined as the taking of goods by theft. Acts of looting have been observed throughout history during wars. The term looting is used interchangeably with plunder. Following a violent event, either natural, technological, or conflict-based, many people assume that lots of individuals will steal from stores or houses that are left unprotected. (Quarantelli & Dynes, 1972, 69). The public expects and fears looting behavior, even though it rarely occurs.

Research base: In a review of over 300 field studies, the Disaster Research Center staff uncovered extremely few verified cases of looting. Reports are widespread in the media, but not verified.

Public fears: Quarantelli and Dynes (1972, 69) refer to a study conducted by the research team at the National Opinion Research Center (NORC). "...58 percent of the persons questioned said they had heard of others' property being stolen. In fact, nine percent claimed that they had even seen looting in progress or had seen looters being arrested. The study team that was on the scene, however, could verify the theft of only two major items—a cash register and a piano."

Public fears during evacuation: Researchers have documented that over one-half (57%) of the people considering evacuation indicate that they fear looting (Lindell & Perry, 1992, 266).

Individual explanations of looting: Quarantelli and Dynes (1970, 169-173) describe several explanations of looting behavior that reflect an individual perspective. They conclude that these are totally inadequate. "All of the preceding explanations of looting rest basically on the notion of shallow, incomplete or faulty socialization. Given the opportunity, the animal in man comes forth. Given enough stress, the frustrated creature strikes out." (170). "Popular as the individual approach to looting behavior may be, it does not square with a number of empirical observations and studies. The Jekyll and Hyde image of man implied in some of the previous discussions is not supported by facts." (172).

Event Differences

There are three differences in the pattern of looting found in consensus and dissensus crises. Natural disasters are consensus events whereas civil disorders are events reflecting dissensus. The professor should ask students to describe the three pattern differences documented by Quarantelli and Dynes (1970, 173-175), i.e., (1) widespread vs. rare; (2) collective vs. individual; and (3) public vs. private acts.

"In civil disorders looting is very widespread whereas in natural disasters actual looting incidents are quite rare." (Quarantelli & Dynes, 1970, 173).

In the 1965 civil disorder in the Watts area of Los Angeles, California, an estimated $40 million in damage was caused by individuals who participated in this looting rampage. Less severe incidents occurred in many other urban areas during this same summer.

Following the acquittal of police officers (April, 1992) who were tried for the beating of Rodney King, riots persisted in south Los Angeles for a four day period.

In civil disturbances "...looters often work together in pairs, family units, or in small groups. This is a marked contrast to looting in natural disasters, where it is carried out by solitary individuals" (Quarantelli & Dynes, 1970, 174).

In civil disturbances looting is very public, whereas in natural disasters it is private. "Goods are taken openly and in full view of others, bystanders as well as co-participants, and often even policemen. In natural disasters, such looting as occurs is covert and secret, with looters taking care not to be observed by others" (Quarantelli & Dynes, 1970, 125).

Likelihood of Looting

Looting is most likely during civil disturbances. Following a few natural disasters, incidents of looting have been documented. Three social factors impact the probability of looting. These are based on Quarantelli's research in St. Croix after Hurricane Hugo (1994).

In a highly stratified society there is a collective sense of disenfranchisement, which increases the likelihood of looting after a disaster. Poor people do not feel that they are able to influence political and social decisions that impact their lives.

In St. Croix there was a continuity of petty theft which occurred daily. This normative acceptance of certain forms of theft carried over to the post-disaster environment. Looting was simply an escalation, albeit short-term, of an existing pattern whereby the poor took from the middle class or wealthy.

After Hurricane Hugo there was a temporary loss of social control by legitimate authority for a few days. Law enforcement and military personnel were overwhelmed by the enormity of the disaster demands. Large areas were not protected. Escalating a prior pattern of petty theft and reflecting an acute sense of disenfranchisement from the government and ruling class, large numbers of poor seized the opportunity to carry away goods of various types.

Emergent Norm Theory

To explain the widespread looting during civil disorders, Quarantelli and Dynes (1970, 176-177) use emergent norm theory. This theory proposes that in crisis events, people behave generally in accordance with the same norms (shared expectations) they use in everyday life. There is continuity in much disaster behavior between pre-disaster and post-disaster periods. In certain crisis circumstances, however, new norms are required.

In natural disasters all property rights are suspended temporarily for the common good. "Thus, warehouses can be broken into without the owner's permission to obtain generators necessary to keep hospitals functioning; and the act is seen as legitimate if undertaken for this purpose even though the participants might agree that it was technically an act of burglary" (Quarantelli & Dynes, 1970, 176).

Looting behavior reflects a specialized instance of this process. There is a redefinition of property rights. "The looting undertaken is likewise a temporary manifestation of a new group norm, in which the right to use available resources becomes problematical. If property is thought of as the shared understanding of who can do what with the valued resources within a community, in civil disorders we see a breakdown in that understanding. What was previously taken for granted and widely shared becomes a matter of dispute among certain segments of the general population.

Viewed in this way, much of the pattern of looting in civil disturbances discussed earlier also makes sense. At the height of such situations, plundering becomes the normative, the socially accepted thing to do. Far from being deviant, it becomes the conforming behavior in the situation. As in natural disasters, the legal right does not change; but there is local group consensus on the massive use and appropriation of certain public and private goods, be these police cars or items on grocery store shelves. In many ways, a new property norm has emerged." (Quarantelli & Dynes, 1970, 177).

Anderson and Dynes (1976) have proposed that civil disturbances are best viewed as expressions of political discontent. As with natural disasters, mitigation rather than emergency response, is a preferred course of action. After completing field work in several U.S.A. communities during 1968, 1969, and 1972, they examined civil disturbances in Curacao during the spring of 1969. They documented that many of the changes desired by the protesters were implemented rather quickly in Curacao, whereas more modest change was forthcoming in the U.S.A. At the height of the Curacao incident, 300 Dutch marines were called in to bolster the local security forces. The toll of the "May Movement" as it came to be called, was two deaths, 79 injuries and damages estimated in the $35-40 million range.

"...the Curacao protest produced two genuine reform parties, the Liberation Front and MAN, and both won legislative seats and championed the rights of the poor and the working masses. Labor acquired more political influence in Curacao as a result of the May protest. Furthermore, blacks were appointed to the highest government offices following the disturbance. It does not seem that the recent disturbances in the United States had this type of immediate political impact" (Anderson & Dynes, 1976, 46-47).

"...when disturbances occur, some segments of society become involved in countermovements and control activities, rather than support movements. White segregationist groups were formed in the United States in the wake of the disturbances and in Curacao some established political groups took actions to combat the growing strength of the new labor party that had evolved from the disturbance. The countermovement as one aspect of a society's response to civil disturbance is perhaps best exemplified in the case of the United States. In the United States during the 1960s some white neighborhoods formed self-protection groups. Also, professional law enforcement organizations throughout the country secured massive amounts of riot control equipment, expanded their riot training, developed an antiriot ideology and created a body of knowledge on riot control which was shared through professional publications, conferences, meetings, and informal contact." (Anderson & Dynes, 1976, 53-54).

Four Principles of Crowd Management

Neal and Webb (1994) formulated four principles of crowd management based on their field observations of a Ku Klux Klan rally (December, 1993), a Pearl Jam (rock) concert, and the 1994 Dallas Cowboy SuperBowl Parade.

- Dispell myths about crowd management. "...a number of city officials attempt crowd management practices based upon incorrect perceptions of crowd behavior" (13).

- Recognize that crowds are not anonymous. It is assumed by many that crowd participants believe they are anonymous and hence drop their social inhibitions and engage in behavior they normally would not. "...research shows most crowds are not anonymous" (14).

- Recognize that crowds can be good. In contrast to an image of all crowds being evil, research has documented many acts of helping behavior. "...during the 1994 Dallas SuperBowl parade, a street vendor's cart fell over from strong winds, which blew away his pennants, shirts and other souvenirs. Bystanders in the crowd saw the incident, helped the merchant upright his cart, and chased down the scattered merchandise. An evil crowd would have stolen all the goods." (14).

- Adopt a community policing policy. A strong show of force by officers in riot gear may actually incite a riot. Efforts to make quick arrests can trigger violence. In contrast, community policing requires local officers to work with crowd leaders in advance. Relationships developed early on can thwart violent outbreaks or at least contain those that might. Neal and Webb document an instance at a KKK rally wherein a large young African-American male became acutely agitated over the message of hate coming from speakers. "Instead of arresting the protester, the officer put his arm around him and calmly talked with him while walking away from the site." (14).

William A. Anderson, Russell R. Dynes and E.L. Quarantelli (1974, 11:50-55) reviewed disturbances in six cities during 1968 and 1969 (Columbus, Ohio; Indianapolis, Indiana; Youngstown, Ohio; Louisville, Kentucky, Springfield, Ohio; and Cleveland, Ohio). The first three of these disturbances lasted for several days and precipitated considerable police mobilization.

Counterriot activity, especially after the killing of Dr. Martin Luther King, was documented in each. Counterriot activity is defined as actions taken by blacks to dissuade other blacks from engaging in violence.

While their work was confined to blacks, any ethnic minority could be encouraged to press both formal and informal leaders to engage in such activities. This strategy could be an important component of the community policing approach outlined by Neal and Webb.

Relevance to Emergency Managers

Understanding looting behavior is important to emergency managers for five reasons. To perform effectively, professional emergency managers must be able to

- Debunk mythology. Both in their own images of disaster, and especially those held by personnel in other agencies, emergency managers must debunk the mythology related to looting. Failure to do so will result in disaster planning practices that will fail because they are not consistent with behavioral realities. Resources will be allocated inefficiently and key tasks will remain unmet.

- Recognize event differences. Professional emergency managers are able to discuss the differences between dissensus events like civil disorders and natural disasters with regards to looting behavior. While other responses may be consistent among events that reflect this analytic quality, looting behavior is a documented difference. The three pattern differences can help other agency personnel understand this, i.e., widespread vs. rare; collective vs. individual and public vs. private acts.

- Know when looting is most likely. Hurricane Hugo, on the island of St. Croix, produced a looting response because three key social factors were operative. These are present, more or less, in every American community. When they are maximized, as they were in St. Croix, larger numbers of looting actions must be anticipated.

- Use emergent norm theory. It is not enough to tell agency personnel that looting is rare following natural disasters except when three social factors are present. Professional emergency managers must understand the theory that explains these pattern differences. This theory recasts looting behavior into an understandable response that at times is symptomatic of real social evils. Attention to these structural conditions in the community is as much the job of emergency managers as facilitating a floodplain management program. It is just another form of mitigation that is directed at another type of hazard.

- Press for enlightened crowd management. This means that professional emergency managers must seek to: 1) dispel myths about crowd management; 2) recognize that crowds are not anonymous; 3) understand that crowds can be good; 4) encourage community policing.

"The local emergency manager's role in planning for crowd management and civil disturbances will continue to grow. To be effective, local emergency managers must rely on a state-of-the-art knowledge base regarding crowd behavior. An emergency manager promoting outdated approaches to crowd management is similar to an emergency manager planning for extensive looting, mass panic, and mass hysteria following a disaster.

Emergency managers must encourage and work with local police in promoting a community policing model regarding crowds. Most crowd leaders can be identified in advance. By working with key players in large crowd settings, a community can help people exercise their basic constitutional rights in a safer manner." (Neal & Webb, 1994, 15).

References

Anderson, W. A., Dynes, R. R., & Quarantelli, E. L. (1974). Urban Counterrioters. *Society, 11*, 50-55.

Anderson, W. A., & Dynes, R. R. (1976). Civil Disturbances and Social Change—Comparative Analysis of United States and Curacao. *Urban Affairs Quarterly, 12*, 37-56.

Drabek, T. E. (1996). *Instructor Guide* for the FEMA/EMI Course Social Dimensions of Disaster. Denver, CO: University of Denver.

Lindell, M. K., & Perry, R. W. (1992). *Behavioral Foundations of Community Emergency Planning*. Washington, DC: Hemisphere Publishing Company.

Neal, D. M., & Webb, G. (1994). Rethinking Crowd Management. *Bridges: A Special Edition of the NCCEM Bulletin*, 13-15.

Quarantelli, E. L., & Dynes, R. R. (1970). Property Norms and Looting: Their Patterns in Community Crisis. *Phylon, 31*, 168-182

Quarantelli, E. L., & Dynes, R. R. (1972). When Disaster Strikes (It Isn't Much Like What You've Heard or Read About). *Psychology Today, 5*, 67-70.

Quarantelli, E. L. (1994). *A Disaster Research Agenda for the Future: Theoretical, Empirical, and Methodological Issues*. Paper presented at the XIIIth World Congress of Sociology, Bielefeld, Germany.

Rottman, S. J. (2000). *Instructor Guide* for the FEMA/EMI Course Individual and Community Disaster Education. Los Angeles: University of California, Los Angleles.

SUPPLEMENTAL READINGS ON ETHICAL CONSIDERATIONS IN RELATION TO POST-EVENTS

EMT Code of Ethics[9]

Written by: Charles Gillespie M.D.
Adopted by: The National Association of Emergency Medical Technicians, 1978.

Professional status as an Emergency Medical Technician and Emergency Medical Technician-Paramedic is maintained and enriched by the willingness of the individual practitioner to accept and fulfill obligations to society, other medical professionals, and the profession of Emergency Medical Technician. As an Emergency Medical Technician-Paramedic, I solemnly pledge myself to the following code of professional ethics:

- A fundamental responsibility of the Emergency Medical Technician is to conserve life, to alleviate suffering, to promote health, to do no harm, and to encourage the quality and equal availability of emergency medical care.

- The Emergency Medical Technician provides services based on human need, with respect for human dignity, unrestricted by consideration of nationality, race creed, color, or status.

- The Emergency Medical Technician does not use professional knowledge and skills in any enterprise detrimental to the public well being.

- The Emergency Medical Technician respects and holds in confidence all information of a confidential nature obtained in the course of professional work unless required by law to divulge such information.

- The Emergency Medical Technician, as a citizen, understands and upholds the law and performs the duties of citizenship; as a professional, the Emergency Medical Technician has the never-ending responsibility to work with concerned citizens and other health care professionals in promoting a high standard of emergency medical care to all people.

- The Emergency Medical Technician shall maintain professional competence and demonstrate concern for the competence of other members of the Emergency Medical Services health care team.

- An Emergency Medical Technician assumes responsibility in defining and upholding standards of professional practice and education.

- The Emergency Medical Technician assumes responsibility for individual professional actions and judgment, both in dependent and independent emergency functions, and knows and upholds the laws which affect the practice of the Emergency Medical Technician.

- An Emergency Medical Technician has the responsibility to be aware of and participate in matters of legislation affecting the Emergency Medical Service System.

- The Emergency Medical Technician, or groups of Emergency Medical Technicians, who advertise professional service, do so in conformity with the dignity of the profession.

- The Emergency Medical Technician has an obligation to protect the public by not delegating to a person less qualified, any service which requires the professional competence of an Emergency Medical Technician.

- The Emergency Medical Technician will work harmoniously with and sustain confidence in Emergency Medical Technician associates, the nurses, the physicians, and other members of the Emergency Medical Services health care team.

- The Emergency Medical Technician refuses to participate in unethical procedures, and assumes the responsibility to expose incompetence or unethical conduct of others to the appropriate authority in a proper and professional manner.

The Ethics of Disaster Relief[10]

Markkula Center for Applied Ethics, Santa Clara University
(1/2002)

Issue

How can we ensure that all disaster relief funds for the September 11 tragedy are managed and distributed equitably? What criteria should be used to make decisions on how much aid eligible people will receive?

Context

Donations for September 11 disaster relief efforts totaled more than $1.5 Billion, as of December 14, 2001 (Source: The Foundation Center: http://www.fdncenter.org). The American Red Cross, the major recipient of these contributions, offered humanitarian assistance and other immediate relief in keeping with its core mission.

The United States Congress also established an $11 billion open-ended federal fund to provide relief compensation to all the September 11 victims and their families. Kenneth Feinberg, the special master appointed to dispense damage awards under this fund, created a system for dispersing relief reflecting the victims' economic losses and such hardships as lost companionship and emotional suffering.

Many questions have been raised regarding the allocation of these relief funds. Should private charitable contributions be restricted only to the September 11 victims, or should some funds be set aside for future relief efforts? Should private aid funds be subtracted from any award given by the federal government? What about insurance payments? Pensions for firefighters and police? Are civilian victims' families less 'deserving' of the federal funds than those of public service personnel? Are those who earned more entitled to more in compensation from the government.

This paper analyzes these ethical considerations, which could set a precedent for future decisions by other relief organizations and the federal government. Specifically, this analysis assesses arguments for allocating relief based primarily on four criteria: economic impact/loss, pain and suffering experienced, real need, and role in the community.

Criteria for Ethical Decision-Making

(For more detailed information on this framework, please visit the following web-site: http://www.scu.edu/ethics/thinking.html)

1. Utilitarian Approach

Which option will produce the most good and do the least harm?

ALLOCATION OPTION	BENEFITS	HARM
1. By economic impact (i.e., based on lost earnings)	■ Provides uniform economic measure for allocation of relief aid ■ Compensates families based on probable losses according to established legal precedent	■ Victims with low earning power as well as unemployed victims will receive lesser aid. An extra dollar of aid for a poor person would be worth more than an extra dollar for a wealthy person. ■ Also, high-earnings victims might have employed spouses and insurance plans that could compensate for lost earnings ■ Applies a punitive, tort-based formula to a situation where those at fault are not those paying the compensation
2. By pain and suffering experienced by victims	■ Compensates using a compassionate measure based on duration and severity of suffering	■ It is difficult to quantify and compare suffering accurately leading to errors in judgment ■ There could be frivolous claims of suffering that may have to be supported by taxpayers
3. By need (taking into account the current wealth of victims and their families)	■ Compensates people (especially low-income, unemployed victims) based on their real economic and emotional needs; maximizes good done ■ Increases aid available to the really needy by compensating less, those with other resources	■ Already wealthy victims or their families may receive little or no aid. Does not recognize their "loss" of future income.
4. By role in the community	■ Compensates based on heroism, selfless sacrifice, and life-long community service. Uniformed personnel (such as firefighters) will be compensated for their public sacrifice ■ Provides incentive for public service by assuring public workers that their families will be taken care of	■ Uniformed personnel most likely have government supported pension plans and insurance to help their families, which many civilian victims may not have ■ Civilian victims may have displayed as much courage and patriotism as the uniformed personnel ■ Disproportionate relief to uniformed services makes less funds available for all other victims

2. Rights Approach

Which option protects the rights and dignity of all stakeholders?

RIGHT AFFECTED	SAMPLE ARGUMENTS
1. Right to be treated equally by the government	■ Victims from all sectors of society should receive equal government aid, regardless of income or profession ■ Government aid should equalize total aid given to victims by giving more to those who get less private aid
2. Right of freedom of choice for donors	■ Donors' wishes and sentiments to aid specific victims should be honored fully, even if that means giving disproportionate aid to certain groups ■ However, if the needs of one group of victims have been fully met, donors should be given a chance to redirect aid to other needy groups of their choice

3. Fairness of Justice Approach

Which option treats all people consistently unless there is a morally justifiable reason for treating them differently?

OPTIONS/ACTIONS	SAMPLE ARGUMENTS	
	FOR	AGAINST
1. By economic impact	■ Families of high-income workers have suffered greater economic loss than low-income families did, and should be compensated for it.	■ Low-income and unemployed victims will get less relief, regardless of their need
2. By pain and suffering experienced	■ The suffering experienced is probably as valid as the fact of death itself in determining aid	■ It is impossible to determine how much each victim actually suffered ■ Surviving victims may be compensated disproportionately higher because they can communicate their experiences directly ■ Benefits paid to families of deceased victims do not actually compensate the victims themselves.

3. By need	■ The need for food, clothing, shelter, medical care, and the education of children is the fairest way to distribute aid ■ Aid will not be wasted on those who do not need it, since this approach can take into account total aid received from all other sources, such as life insurance	■ The use of aid as the criterion may lead to a significant lowering of thestandard of living for higher income victims and families, and raising the future standard for lower income victims to levels above 9/11 levels
4. By role in the community	■ It is fairest to reward uniformed personnel for their career of service to others and their specific sacrifice in this case.	■ Civilian victims may not get as much compensation as uniformed victims despite their possibly higher needs and/or their own acts of courage

4. Common-Good Approach

Which option promotes the common good and helps all participate more fully in the goods we share as a society?

Sample Arguments

1. Some relief funds must be reserved for future disasters, as long as the immediate needs of the victims and their families are met. This could help the community as a whole in any future disasters, when fund raising may not be as successful.

2. Some relief funds should be diverted to local charities and other natural disasters, whose fund-raising has been hurt this year, as long as the immediate needs of the Sept. 11 victims and their families are met.

3. The common good and trust in the distribution of aid requires careful tracking, accounting, and oversight of all relief funds. Whatever criteria are selected eventually must be applied diligently to this distribution process with substantial transparency. Trust also requires honoring the donors' wishes.

5. Virtues Approach

Which option would enable the deepening or development of those virtues or character traits that we value as individuals? As a society?

Sample Arguments

1. Donors' wishes should be honored fully to encourage future compassion and philanthropy. Assessments need to be made through comprehensive surveys to evaluate whether all these fund allocation efforts have encouraged more charitable giving from people or not.

2. Aid should be allocated primarily by need to encourage the public to be compassionate towards the poor.

3. Allocating relief aid based on exposure to suffering and pain could increase public awareness and empathy towards those who suffered in these disasters, encouraging more preventive efforts.

***THE FOLLOWING IS An article from the Philanthropy News Digest (News originated from *The New York Times* and *The Wall Street Journal*) reporting on the formation of a coalition of a dozen charities to coordinate relief efforts and eventually track aid to victims.) (12/14/01)

Ethics for Tsunami Recovery[11]

P. Potter[12]
January 10, 2005

The outpouring of concern for the victims and survivors of the Boxing Day Tsunamis that devastated Indian Ocean shorelines has been an inspiring reminder of our shared humanity. The speed with which individuals, communities, non-government organizations, and governments have converted a shared horror over the scale of destruction into offerings of aid and assistance, inspires us to believe in the power of goodness in the midst of a world divided by ideology and belief, power politics, socio-economic inequality, and environmental deterioration. Yet, in the midst of such largesse, we stand to be reminded that the disaster which arose from natural forces of plate tectonics and hydrodynamics was amplified by local social, economic, and political arrangements. The destructive power of the Tsunamis was all the more devastating in areas where poverty had pushed people into fishing villages located at the very edge of usable land. The natural barriers of mangroves and other vegetation that might have cushioned the destruction power of the waves had long ago been displaced to make room for shrimp farms and other aquaculture. Tourism development had cleared vast swaths of shoreline and drawn thousands of people into vulnerable areas where housing and sanitation for local residents were barely adequate. The possibility for establishing Tsunami warning systems in the Indian Ocean had been undermined by budgetary politics. The transportation and power infrastructure that might have speeded the delivery of aid had been weakened by political conflict—particularly in Aceh and Sri Lanka. In order to be truly successful, relief and recovery efforts must address the human dimensions of the tragedy – not simply in terms of assisting victims to rebuild what was lost but instead to create new and improved conditions for human well-being in the affected areas. In this sense, Tsunami aid involves an opportunity to support people in the devastated areas to build new communities where sustainability and human value are paramount. For this to happen, the aid effort must be able to rise above the limitations of parochial political interests, inequitable economic arrangements, and ethnic conflict. For it is by only honoring the needs and aspirations of the people most affected that we can truly measure the effectiveness of our efforts to help. Establishing an ethical review process for the Tsunami aid effort will be an important step toward achieving this goal.

The Challenge

The human toll of the Tsunamis—more than 150,000 dead and millions left homeless – cries out for relief. The immediate disaster assistance efforts by the international community, including Canada's Disaster Assistance Response Team (DART), will likely ease the burdens faced by the worst-hit regions in the near term by providing short-term access to clean drinking water, sanitation facilities, medical care, and temporary housing, clothing, and schools. However, our zeal for a ready solutions and quick responses should not cloud our appreciation of the fact that the communities which bore the brunt of the disaster will require many years to recover. The social and economic devastation of lives and livelihoods dependent on fisheries and subsistence agriculture, both of which were already marginalized and now are bereft of usable land and accessible markets, will require long-term strategies of response and assistance.

Significant efforts will be needed to respond to the destruction of local social and economic systems. The death toll from the Tsunamis has undermined local familial and social networks, which served critical civic functions in the absence of fully effective local institutions of social welfare. The physical destruction has also nearly eliminated what limited infrastructure and production systems had been available to support local economies. But rebuilding should involve more than simply recreating what was lost. For the extent of existing poverty in the region testifies that the social and economic systems which pre-dated the Tsunamis were highly flawed. Therefore, new elements of sustainability must be included in the relief effort. Relief assistance should attend to factors of environmental and resource stewardship, as new economic production and distribution systems are put in place. Recovery efforts should place high priority on participation and empowerment for local people affected by the disaster, so that they become more than mute recipients of aid but instead become active participants in creating new arrangements for living. In short, the relief effort should be directed to do more than simply turn back the clock, but instead should reflect a commitment to supporting the people in the region to reclaim lives of dignity and human value. The aid program also must not be driven by the parochial interests of donor economies. While the extent of death and injury to vacationing tourists helped focus the attention of wealthy economies, the aid effort should not be limited by this particular dimension of the tragedy. Recalling that the many of the conditions, such as tourist beaches and shrimp farms, which made the Indian Ocean littoral particularly vulnerable to the Tsunamis, were created for the benefit of wealthy economies in Asia and the West, the aid effort should accept responsibility for the role that the international political economy has played in creating vulnerability to natural disaster. Once again this means placing the emphasis on the lives and livelihoods of people in the affected areas. However, pursuing these priorities will be difficult. Despite the current levels of funding offered for disaster relief, the attention span of donor countries is notoriously short. Aid dollars often are spent within donor economies to support needs assessments, expert analyses, policy reviews, and the like, rather than in direct assistance to the people in need. Funding commitments often go unmet as new priorities emerge. Donor economies are often tempted to use aid to support local allegiances against perceived terrorist threats or for broader geo-strategic reasons. The Tsunami crisis presents a new opportunity for donor economies to rise above these challenges and to sponsor and complete relief efforts centered on the well being of local people affected by the tragedy. As well, relief efforts must overcome the political divisions existing in the affected areas. Already we have seen efforts by local governments to insulate their political authority from the challenges of accepting and becoming beholden to international aid. As well, the temptation will be strong for local governments to steer aid toward political constituents and away from dissident social movements. The potential has already arisen for abuse of aid contributions by local military and security forces, either through diversion of resources or denial of aid to particular groups. While respect for local sovereignty is essential, this should not undermine relief support for people in need.

An Ethical Response

An ethical review process can help the Tsunami relief effort to stay focused on the imperative of helping those in need. Similarly to ethical review processes in hospitals, human rights audits in aid agencies, and environment audits for infrastructure development projects, an ethical review process for Tsunami relief will help ensure that the aid is generated and delivered in ways that honor both the recipients – and in so doing honor the donors as well. A possible model would involve establishing ethical review boards comprised of members of the local recipient communities, donor representatives, ethics and area specialists, and outside community representatives. These ethical review boards could be established for particular donor countries or organizations, and for specific aid projects. Funding for the ethical review boards should be committed by donor countries from funds not already earmarked for Tsunami relief. The boards would be empowered to review the design, funding, and implementation of Tsunami aid projects to confirm the beneficial impacts for local communities in need. The factors that might be considered by the ethical review boards might include the following:

General Benefits: To what extent do Tsunami relief projects support general goals of public welfare, human rights and social justice, sustainability, peace, and human dignity in the areas affected. Do relief projects include these goals in design and implementation?

Autonomy and Freedom: To what extent do Tsunami relief projects support autonomy and freedom for the people in need? Do relief project proceed on the basis of needs and aspirations articulated by local people themselves?

Double Effect: To what extent do Tsunami relief projects account for and resolve ancillary harmful consequences? Do the design and funding processes account for unintended consequences?

Pragmatism: To what extent do Tsunami relief projects support pragmatic approaches to relieving human suffering? Are relief projects designed and implemented in ways that are efficient and effective in responding to the needs and aspirations of people in the affected areas?

Deontological principles: To what extent are Tsunami relief projects based on the intrinsic worth of human beings, valuing diversity and local culture and putting people first? Are processes for funding, designing, and implementing relief programs aimed at supporting needs and aspirations of people in the affected areas?

Accountability: Are Tsunami relief projects accountable to local communities? Are reporting processes for relief projects include provisions for local accountability?

Summary

The Tsunami tragedy offers important opportunities for the world community to re-imagine how people in the devastated regions can reclaim their lives and livelihoods, in ways that honor our common humanity. An ethical review process can be a useful step toward ensuring that the international relief effort responds to the needs and aspirations of the people most directly affected by the tragedy. Canada can take the lead in this task, by establishing ethical review processes for government sponsored and managed relief efforts. This can set an example for the private and NGO sectors, and help to build long-term support within Canada for sustainable relief efforts in the region. Canada's lead might encourage parallel efforts in other donor economies. In this way, we can move beyond the tragedy of the Tsunamis, to realize the opportunities they present for building new approaches to sustainable development and people-centred communities. This might truly honor the memory of the dead and the hardships of the survivors.

United States Office of Government Ethics[13]
The 14 General Principles—5 CFR 2635.101(b)(1-14)

1. Public service is a public trust requiring employees to place loyalty to the Constitution, the laws and ethical principles above private gain.

2. Employees shall not hold financial interests that conflict with the conscientious performance of duty.

3. Employees shall not engage in financial transactions using nonpublic Government information or allow the improper use of such information.

4. An employee shall not solicit or accept a gift or other item of monetary value from a prohibited source unless authorized to do so.

5. Employees shall put forth honest effort in the performance of their duties.

6. Employees shall not make unauthorized promises binding the Government.

7. Employees shall not use public office for private gain.

8. Employees shall act impartially and not give preferential treatment to any private organization or individual.

9. Employees shall protect and use Federal property for authorized activities.

10. Employees shall not engage in outside employment or activities that conflict with their official Government duties and responsibilities.

11. Employees shall disclose waste, fraud, and abuse to appropriate authorities.

12. Employees shall satisfy in good faith their obligations as citizens, including all just financial obligations that are imposed by law.

13. Employees shall adhere to legal authorities providing equal opportunity for all Americans regardless of race, color, religion, sex, age or handicap.

14. Employees shall endeavor to avoid any actions creating the appearance that they are violating the law or the ethical standards.

CASE STUDIES[14]

Case Study 1

PHOTO OPPORTUNITY

Purpose: The purpose of this activity is to apply the ethics principles and guidelines to specific situations that may be encountered at a Disaster Field Office.

Instructions:

1. Review the situation presented below.

2. After reviewing the situation, work with your team to answer the question that follows the situation.

3. Select a spokesperson. The spokesperson will read the situation aloud and present the group's response.

Situation:

Chris is a member of the Joint Information Center Staff and an excellent photographer. During the past 2 weeks he has been photographing the damage and disaster victims' reactions. Chris is so excited about the quality of the photos, he sent copies of them to a camera manufacturer that he works for as a freelance photographer. The photos were taken during his off hours, using camera equipment and film that the manufacturer gave to Chris. Many of the photos were taken in an area that was closed to the public after the disaster. The photos include close-up shots of disaster victims. The camera manufacturer asked Chris if they could use his photos and a picture of Chris at the disaster site wearing his FEMA hat in their promotional materials. Chris told the manufacturer that it would be fine as long as he did not accept compensation for the photos.

Question:

Are Chris' actions in compliance with Government ethics principles and standards? *Explain why or why not.*

Case Study 2
AN HONEST DAY'S WORK

Purpose: The purpose of this activity is to apply the ethics principles and guidelines to specific situations that may be encountered at a Disaster Field Office.

Instructions:

1. Review the situation presented below.

2. After reviewing the situation, work with your team to answer the question that follows the situation.

3. Select a spokesperson. The spokesperson will read the situation aloud and present the group's response.

Situation:

Rose is a local hire working in Community Relations. People have been complaining bitterly to her about price gouging by local contractors. Rose has heard many stories of contractors taking down payments and failing to show up to do the work when they promised. Rose's brother is a builder who lives in a nearby State. Rose knows that her brother Joe will bring a crew into the State and do the work at a fair price and at high quality levels. However, before Joe goes to the trouble of relocating his crew, he needs to know if there will be enough work to cover his expenses. Rose tells Joe that she cannot solicit work for him but that she will give him a list of names and telephone numbers of people she has visited as part of her community relations activities. Rose knows that the individuals on her list will be very relieved to finally hear from a reputable contractor.

Question:

Are Rose's actions in compliance with Government ethics principles and standards? *Explain why or why not.*

Note: The release of names and telephone numbers of disaster victims is a violation of the Privacy Act. Even though Rose is trying to help the people who are in search of an honest contractor, her actions could be viewed as using access to nonpublic information to promote her brother's firm.

Case Study 3

WHAT'S A FEW HOURS?

Purpose: The purpose of this activity is to apply the ethics principles and guidelines to specific situations that may be encountered at a Disaster Field Office.

Instructions:

1. Review the situation presented below.

2. After reviewing the situation, work with your team to answer the questions that follow the situation.

3. Select a spokesperson. The spokesperson will read the situation aloud and present the group's responses.

Situation:

The Disaster Field Office is open from 8:00 a.m. to 8:00 p.m. Jack comes in every day at 8:00 a.m. and has been working until 8:00 p.m. when the DFO closes. Betty noticed that after 6:00 p.m., Jack never seems busy. Jack sits at his desk during this 2-hour block of time. Each time the supervisor comes by, Jack finds something to make it appear as if he is very busy. As soon as the supervisor is gone, Jack sits with his hands folded across his chest. Betty decides to ask Jack why he stays until 8:00 when his work seems to be done at 6:00 each night. Jack's response is that it would be unfair for him to get less hours than everyone else who is working in the DFO. Betty decides not to push the issue further and ignores the situation.

Questions:

Are Jack's actions in compliance with Government ethics principles and standards? *Explain why or why not.*

Note: Jack's actions are a misuse of official time and constitute a wasteful use of Government resources. His actions are not ethical.

Are Betty's actions in compliance with Government ethics principles and standards? *Explain why or why not.*

Note: Betty has an obligation to report fraud, waste, and abuse. By ignoring the situation, Betty has also violated her ethical obligations.

Case Study 4

THIS ONE'S ON THE HOUSE

Purpose: The purpose of this activity is to apply the ethics principles and guidelines to specific situations that may be encountered at a Disaster Field Office.

Instructions:

1. Review the situation presented below.

2. After reviewing the situation, work with your team to answer the question that follows the situation.

3. Select a spokesperson. The spokesperson will read the situation aloud and present the group's response.

Situation:

The DFO is phasing down. Fifteen staff members go to a favorite after-work spot near the DFO for a farewell celebration. The pub's business has certainly increased since the DFO moved into the neighborhood. Everyone orders full dinners and several rounds of drinks. When it's time to leave, the group asks for the check. The owner of the pub insists that tonight's celebration is on her. She says, "It's the least I can do, FEMA has been wonderful to me. Not only did you help my business, you gave me a place to live when I really needed it." The staff members explain that they appreciate her gesture, but that they need to pay something. They ask her if they can at least leave a big tip.

Question:

Are staff members' actions in compliance with Government ethics principles and standards? *Explain why or why not.*

Note: The acceptance of the food and drinks could be seen as payback for the owner receiving disaster housing assistance. To avoid the appearance of unethical actions, the group should pay for their dinners and drinks, not just for the tip.

Case Study 5
COULD YOU DO ME A FAVOR?

Purpose: The purpose of this activity is to apply the ethics principles and guidelines to specific situations that may be encountered at a Disaster Field Office.

Instructions:

1. Review the situation presented below.

2. After reviewing the situation, work with your team to answer the question that follows the situation.

3. Select a spokesperson. The spokesperson will read the situation aloud and present the group's responses.

Situation:

Mary supervises several Infrastructure Support inspectors who are conducting damage surveys in the field. Mary's daughter is celebrating her thirteenth birthday next week. Mary's daughter has asked that her mom send her some Native American craft items. One of the inspector teams using a FEMA van will be going within 15 miles of the area where the crafts can be purchased. Mary knows that she will not be able to leave the DFO during the next week. Mary asks the team if they would mind going a little out of their way to pick up a gift for her daughter. The team readily agrees to the side trip. Mary tells the team members that they will make one teenager very happy on her birthday.

Question:

Are Mary's actions in compliance with Government ethics principles and standards? *Explain why or why not.*

Mary is asking the team to use Government property (the FEMA van) for personal use. The Government van and team taking a side trip to go shopping could be seen as misuse of Government property and of official time.

SUMMARY

Ethics are a universal element of business and government from the entry-level employee to the chief executive. Sound ethics are critical to our national identity. But how do we separate our desire for ethics from our need to survive? Do we have our greatest heroes at the forefront, or our most palatable politicians? Do we have to choose between fighting a war ethically and fighting a war to win?

What can we learn from studies that explain human behavior under the stress of a disaster, or within a crowd? Is looting really to be dismissed as expected human behavior when social structures collapse, or is it an aberrant behavior? How does this change our security planning and procedures in case of a disaster?

The critical thinker must assess these questions and determine how their answers affect personal and organizational plans. Crisis management must be based on the reality of the crisis, and not on preconceived notions of how the situation is "supposed" to occur. Evidence-based research such as was reviewed in this chapter gives invaluable information for planning the best protection for both life and property.

ADDITIONAL DISCUSSION TOPICS

- Apply the critical thinking skills to Mr. Hamilton's list of lies. Are there any common fallacies in his argument? Even if you agree with what he professes, does his stated case hold water?

- Will your background and character hold up to the scrutiny of a confirmation hearing process? Does that make you a bad person? Who would you rather have in charge of your security, a capable person with some questionable history, or a person with an impeccable background? What factors would you consider important? Should all factors considered be job related or taken in their totality? Remember, the chapter subject is ethics.

RESOURCES

Doing Ethics in Journalism : A Handbook With Case Studies
Jay Black, Bob Steele, and Ralph Barney
1998 / ISBN / Allyn & Bacon.

The Responsible Public Servant
Kenneth Kernaghan and John W. Langford
1990 / ISBN / Institute for Research in Public Policy.

Ethics and the Professions
David Applebaum and Sarah Verone Lawton
1990 / ISBN / Prentice Hall.

Media Ethics: Cases and Moral Reasoning, 5th ed.
Clifford Christians, Mark Fackler, Kim Rotzoll, and Kathy Brittain McKee, eds.
1998 / ISBN / Longman.

Web Links
　　Applied Ethics Resources: http://www.ethicsweb.ca/resources/
　　American Amateur Press Association:
　　　　http://members.aol.com/aapa96/index.html
　　The American Communication Association: http://www.americancomm.org/
　　Canadian Association of Journalists: http://www.eagle.ca/caj/
　　Fairness and Accuracy in Reporting: http://www.fair.org/index.php
　　MIPT terrorism knowledge base: http://www.tkb.org/Links.jsp

Endnotes

[1] Source: The New York Times editorial as found on ans-cbnNEWS.com.

[2] Convention against Torture and Other Cruel, Inhuman or Degrading Treatment or Punishment, United Nations, 10 December 1984.

[3] ICRC FAQ found at http://www.icrc.org/Web/eng/siteeng0.nsf/html/69MJXC

[4] *Yearbook of the European Convention on Human Rights* (1969), p. 186.

[5] Source: Donald R. Hamilton, Deputy Director, National Memorial Institute for the Prevention of Terrorim (MIPT), as prepared for delivery to the Second International Conference on Terrorism, Bogotá, Columbia, February 23, 2005.

[6] Source: Associated Press, Mon Feb 28, 2005, 11:15 PM ET. Whitehouse-AP Cabinet & State, by Katherine Shrader, Associated Press writer and Associated Press writer, Ted Bridis, contributed to this report.

[7] This section was derived from Rottman, S.J. (2000). Instructor Guide for the FEMA/EMI Course Individual and Community Disaster Education. Los Angeles: University of California, Los Angeles.

[8] This section is excerpted from Drabek, T. E. (1996), *Instructor's Guide for the FEMA/EMI Course Social Dimensions of Disaster.* Denver, CO: University of Denver.

[9] Source: <http://www.tdh.state.tx.us/hcqs/ems/sethics.htm>.

[10] Source: <http://www.scu.edu/ethics/publications/briefings/philanthropy.html>.

[11] Source: <http://www.asiapacific.ca/tsunamis/ethics.pdf>.

[12] Professor of Law and Director, Institute of Asian Research, University of British Columbia.

[13] Source: <http://www.training.fema.gov/emiweb/downloads/et2000SM.doc>.

[14] Case studies are derived from Federal Emergency Management Agency - Disaster Field Training Organization. (2001). *Government Ethics-Instructor Guide.*

CHAPTER 14

EMERGENCY COMMUNICATIONS AND TECHNOLOGY

*Planning is bringing the future into the present
so that you can do something about it.*
—Alan Lakein

KEY TERMS

Computer-Aided Dispatch
Broadcast Media
Traffic Management Center
Emergency Alert System
Internet
Alternative Communication Systems

OBJECTIVES

- Understand the evolution of communication technology.

- Become familiar with the common and alternative systems and technologies utilized in emergencies.

- Understand what has been learned from past mistakes.

- Identify how technology can be used for emergency planning, preparation, and response.

DISCUSSION TOPICS

- What mainstream communications systems are used in emergencies?

- What non-emergency communications systems might be pressed into use in an emergency?

- What alternate communications and emerging technologies are available in an emergency?

- How have communications failed in emergencies (9-11, Katrina)?

- How can various technologies be used for planning, preparation, and response?

14

INTRODUCTION

In this chapter, we will discuss the role of communications in Homeland Security/ Disaster Recovery. Our communications discussion will center on the evolution of communications technologies, the common and alternative systems of communication used in emergencies, causes and consequences of communication failure in emergencies, and the uses of technology in emergency planning, preparation, and response.

9/11 TAPE RAISED ADDED QUESTIONS ON RADIO FAILURES[1]

For much of the last year, New York City has said the devastating breakdown in fire communications at the World Trade Center was largely caused by the failure of an electronic device in the complex called a repeater, which was designed to boost radio transmissions in high rise buildings. Now, however, the Port Authority of New York and New Jersey's analysis of its 78-minute tape of firefighter communications from Sept. 11 flatly contradicts the city's version of what went wrong. It also raises questions about the thoroughness of the city's investigations into the worst loss of life any fire department has ever experience—343 men.

If the Port Authority's position is correct, it raises the possibility that different factors—failure of other equipment, design of communications consoles in the lower lobbies, or a simple mistake made at a moment of high stress—might have accounted for the communications breakdowns. Many firefighters believe those breakdowns contributed to the department's staggering losses.

On the tape, which recorded transmissions as they were passed through the repeater, firefighters in the south tower can be heard speaking over their radios until the building collapses. Practically no communications are recorded from firefighters in the north tower, even though the same repeater served both of the towers. Before the voices from the south tower are heard, a series of coded tones are captured on the tape, marking the moment that the radio repeater was turned on, a spokesman for the Port Authority said. In the view of Port Authority officials, those transmissions show beyond any doubt that the repeater worked, contrary to the accounts given in an official study of the emergency response that has been endorsed by Mayor Michael R. Bloomberg and Fire Commissioner Nicholas Scoppetta. Asked, then, what would account for the communications failures, a spokesman for the Port Authority, Greg Trevor, said, "You will have to put those questions to the Fire Department."

The tape is likely to be remembered as far more than a record of what went wrong. It contains the only permanently preserved voices of firefighters from the tower stairwells, including transmissions from the fire chief who climbed highest into the building. As the firefighters raced up the stairs of the south tower, and right until the final seconds, they can be heard calmly organizing help for injured civilians as high as the 78th floor "All right, Tommy," a firefighter from Ladder 15 is heard saying minutes before the collapse," it's imperative that you try to get down to the lobby command post and get some people up to 40. We got injured people up here on 70. If you make it to the lobby command post, see if they can somehow get elevators past the 40th floor. We got injured people all the way up here." A spokesman for the Fire Department, Francis X. Gribbon, said yesterday that the department still believed the machinery had failed in some way. "The system was tested in the lobby by two experienced chiefs who came to the conclusion that it was not functioning," he said, referring to the north tower.

That leaves unanswered one of the most stinging of all the questions about fire operations that day. Even though the north tower stood 29 minutes longer than the south tower, at least 121 firefight3ers did not escape from it. While chiefs in the north tower lobby issued orders to come down, they received no response. The accounts of witnesses and firefighters who survived suggest that most of the men in the building simply did not know how much trouble they were in. Witnesses said that scores of firefighters, unaware of the peril, were resting on the 19th floor of the north tower during its final minutes. Some firefighters who managed to get out said that they had no idea the other building had already fallen, and said that they thought that few of those who perished knew.

In February, even as the department was beginning a study of its September 11 response, fire officials declined invitations to listen to the Port Authority's tape, which was recovered by Port Authority police officers from the rubble. Not until the tape's existence was reported by The New York Times in July did fire officials decide to listen to it. Mr. Scoppetta has said that his aides did not tell him about the tape. By then, the department's study of the Sept. 11 response was all but complete. The consulting firm that was conducting the study, McKinsey & Company, sent one of its associates to listen to the tape and to hear the analysis by the Port Authority, according to Carlos Kirjner, the McKinsey official who lead the study.

In the end, Mr. Kirjner said that, even with the tape, it was not clear that the repeater had worked flawlessly throughout the buildings. No one could prudently ignore the perspective of senior fire chiefs, who had tested the system and believed it was not operating, he said. "We came to the conclusion that arguing about the different versions was not a fruitful exercise," Mr. Kirjner said. So the report from McKinsey addressed the communications failure from the perspective of the fire chiefs, who believed the repeater did not work. Mr. Kirjner, who has a doctorate in electrical engineering and specializes in wireless communication, said his firm did not take a position on the repeater.

At the Port Authority, officials have long felt that the complaint about the failure of the repeater simply shifted the blame. While blame for the catastrophe is the subject of many lawsuits, Port Authority officials have resented the suggestion that their equipment failed. The repeater was installed on the tope floor of 5 World Trade Center after the first terrorist bombing in 1993. "During our radio coverage tests, we concluded that the system worked exceptionally well," Deputy Fire Commissioner Steven Gregory wrote in a 1994 letter to Allen Reiss, the Port Authority official who oversaw the installation.

On September 11, it did not seem to be working well to Battalion Chiefs Joseph Pfeifer and Orio Palmer, two of the first chiefs to respond. They tested their radios but could not hear each other, an effort that was recorded by the repeater tape. One possible explanation, according to a Port Authority radio expert who reviewed the tape, is that the problems originated with the radio console that had been set up in the lobby by the Port Authority at the request of the Fire Department. The console resembled a telephone and served as a fire radio. The official suggested that a broken earpiece could have made it impossible for Chief Pfeifer to hear Chief Palmer. Another possible explanation is that the volume had been turned all the way down before they arrived. In any event, Chief Pfeifer needed to establish communications quickly, so he turned to a backup repeater in his car, the tape makes clear. That repeater also did not appear to work. When the second plane hit, Chief Palmer dispatched into the south tower with a senior chief, Donald Burns. There, both were able to speak over the trade center's repeater channel that had stymied Chief Palmer a few minutes earlier.

Chief Palmer took an elevator to the 40th or 41st floor, and then climbed on foot to the 78th floor within 30 minutes. As he ascended, he radioed reports on the conditions to the chief in the lobby and to other firefighters in the stairwells.

To Port Authority officials, those reports from the core of the building shoed the repeater worked in the most difficult of environments. Despite a public position that the repeater did not work, the city's tope officials now want to replicate the trade center's system in high rises all over the city. Indeed, two weeks ago, Mr. Scoppetta sent a letter to the Port Authority saying that the mayor wanted the technical l plans for the trade center's repeater system. "The City of New York contemplates using the WTC Radio Repeater system as a model for future system development throughout the City," Mr. Scoppetta wrote.

Was there a failure of the radio repeater system, or confusion, or a failure of other communications equipment? Was there a mistake made under stress? Addressing this debate and others like it will further our level of preparedness in homeland security. Answers to these and other questions will bring us closer to refining more efficient tactical communication strategies that we can employ in similar situation in the future.

In this text, we will study the importance of the radio to tactical communications and learn the history and development of its use in emergency operations. We will also investigate the impact of the cellular phone on emergency communications. Chapter Four will explore tactical strategies that we can fall back on if and when our customary communication networks fail.

THE EVOLUTION OF COMMUNICATION TECHNOLOGY[2]

Humans are social animals. Few of us thrive in isolation from our fellows, so the ability to communicate with one another is fundamental. As such, one of our oldest economic problems is that of *information cost*.

Information cost is a simple-enough concept: it costs something to learn something. Schools charge tuition, telephone and cable companies charge service fees, even the simple act of listening takes time. Yet, when the costs of information are considered in a societal context, the implications for property rights, trade, law, war, revolution, etc., are truly astounding. Gutenberg's mechanical printing processes (ca. 1439) lowered information costs from the existing method (hand copying) and fueled the Lutheran Reformation, the Renaissance, and the Scientific Revolution.

Consider some of the revolutions in communication technology, and their ongoing evolutionary development:

- Written language
- Steam engine
- Telegraph
- Telephone
- Aircraft
- Radio
- Television
- Internet

Clearly, much of humankind's scientific inquiry and technical innovation, from clay tablets to the World Wide Web, have been directed at reducing information costs, i.e., solving communication problems.

Common Communication Systems Used in Emergencies
911 Computer Aided Dispatch (CAD)

The idea of a single phone number to contact emergency services can be traced back at least as far as 1937, when England implemented its 999 system after phone calls were delayed reporting a multiple-fatality fire. New Zealand introduced its 111 emergency system in 1958; Canada's first 999 system (converted to 911 in 1972) debuted in Winnipeg, Manitoba in 1959, and Australia rolled out its 000 system in the metropolitan areas in 1961.

Recommendations for a single emergency number had been bandied about in the US since at least 1957. In testimony before the US House of Representatives in 1967, response time was cited as a factor in the high number of fire deaths in the US compared to other countries. The report of President Johnson's Commission on Civil Disturbance, issued March 1, 1968, mentioned the need for a single emergency number nationwide in its investigation of the previous summer's urban riots.

The first 911 call in the United States was placed at 2 pm., Friday, February 16, 1968, by Alabama Speaker of the House Rankin Fite from the Haleyville City Hall to U.S. Representative Tom Bevill (Dem.) at the city's police station. Robert Fitzgerald, Inside Plant Manager for Alabama Telephone Company, designed the circuit and watched as the mechanical switching gear tripped to "9-1-1."

On October 26, 1999, President Clinton signed Senate Bill 800 into law, which made 911 the national emergency response number.

Although a vast improvement over trying to remember the number to the fire department as one's house burns, early 911 systems suffered from many technical limitations such as the need for hard-wired routing rules, poor or no logging capability, lack of Caller ID (number and location) capability, and the need for manual hand-off from the operator to the appropriate responders.

Technological advances enabled the creation of the Enhanced 911 (E911) system. Mechanical switches gave way to computers. Caller line and location information, selective routing, and selective transfer of calls became standard features.

Increases in computing power, and decreases in the cost of that power, have brought us to the age of computer aided dispatch (CAD). CAD systems offer:

- A National Crime Information Center (NCIC) interface that enables automatic queries for warrants, driver's license information, and vehicle registration information

- Mapping interface capabilities that plot the location a call was made from, allowing CAD users to view the location of the unit making the call

- Automatic Vehicle Location (AVL) that utilizes the global positioning system (GPS) to automatically track unit movement on a map

- Messaging that provides silent communications between mobile units and CAD users

- Automatic population of data fields via interfaces with dispatch protocol and fire records software

Properly implemented, a 911 CAD system can reduce redundancy and costs, enhance reliability, and reduce response times of police, fire and EMS personnel.

Broadcast Media

After newspapers and motion pictures, radio (1895) and television (1927) are our oldest mass media technologies. Unlike newspapers and movies, which require substantial lead times to transfer information to physical media which then must be transported to distribution points, radio and television allow for near-instantaneous (live) communication of events as they occur.

Again, as technology grows grows at once smaller, cheaper, and more powerful, the ability of broadcast media to respond quickly and agilely to unfolding events increases. Everything from concerts to wars can now be covered live, on-scene, with minimal advance notice and preparation. Even newspapers have had their lead times reduced by innovations such as electronic typesetting, digital photography, laptop computers, Internet uploads, and World Wide Web distribution.

Emergency messages can be delivered to select audiences based on geographic location through the Emergency Alert System (EAS). The EAS is most commonly used during severe weather, but it is available for response to all emergencies. EAS may be used in conjunction with warning sirens.

Table 14.1 FEDERAL COMMUNICATIONS COMMISSION FACT SHEET

THE EMERGENCY ALERT SYSTEM (EAS)

"This is a test of the Emergency Alert System — this is only a test...."

This is the new test script that you will occasionally hear on your favorite broadcast station or your local cable system. We say that the test script may only be heard occasionally because the new EAS weekly test does not require a test script. Instead the new weekly test consists of an eight-second digital data signal. The signal contains the information necessary to test the EAS. There is also a monthly test that has a test script. The monthly test script is developed locally and usually contains information that is relevant to the local area.

Since **January 1, 1997**, all AM, FM and TV broadcast stations have been using the above test procedures. Also, since **December 31, 1998**, cable systems that have 10,000 or more subscribers are part of the EAS. They are doing the above tests and have the capability to transmit emergency messages on all of their video channels.

There are other important changes as well. The EAS uses digital technology to distribute messages. This allows for a lot of improvements in providing emergency information to the public. The new system provides state and local officials with a new method to quickly send out important local emergency information targeted to a specific area. The information can be sent out through a broadcast station and cable system even if those facilities are unattended. Also, the EAS digital signal is the same signal that the National Weather Service (NWS) uses on NOAA Weather Radio (NWR). This allows NWR signals to be decoded by the EAS equipment at broadcast stations and cable systems. Broadcasters and cable operators can then retransmit NWS weather warning messages almost immediately to their audiences.

Also, specially equipped consumer products, such as televisions, radios, pagers and other devices, can decode EAS messages. The consumer can program these products to "turn themselves on" for the messages they want to receive.

WHY HAVE AN EMERGENCY ALERT SYSTEM?

The EAS is designed to provide the President with a means to address the American people in the event of a national emergency. Through the EAS, the President would have access to thousands of broadcast stations, cable systems and participating satellite programmers to transmit a message to the public. The EAS and its predecessors, CONELRAD and the Emergency Broadcast System (EBS), have never been activated for this purpose. But beginning in 1963, the President permitted state and local level emergency information to be transmitted using the EBS.

WHAT DOES THE NEW EMERGENCY ALERT SYSTEM MEAN FOR YOU?

- **Automatic Operation.** The EAS digital system architecture allows broadcast stations, cable systems, participating satellite companies, and other services to send and receive emergency information quickly and automatically even if those facilities are unattended.

- **Redundancy.** The EAS requires monitoring of at least two independent sources for emergency information. This insures that emergency information is received and delivered to viewers and listeners.

- **Less Intrusive.** EAS tests are shorter and less obtrusive to viewers and listeners. Therefore, when people do hear or see the EAS messages, they will take them more seriously.

- **Second Language.** Do you or someone you know watch Spanish-language programming? EAS digital messages can be automatically converted into any language used by the broadcast station or cable system.

WHO MAKES THE EMERGENCY ALERT SYSTEM WORK?

The FCC designed the new EAS, working in a cooperative arrangement with the broadcast, cable, emergency management, alerting equipment industry, the National Weather Service and the Federal Emergency Management Administration.

WHAT IS THE ROLE OF EACH OF THESE AGENCIES?

FCC. The FCC provides information to broadcasters, cable system operators, and other participants in the EAS regarding the requirements of this emergency system. Additionally, the FCC will ensure that EAS state and local plans developed by industry conform to the FCC EAS rules and regulations and enhance the national level EAS structure.

NWS. NWS provides emergency weather information used to alert the public of dangerous conditions. Over seventy percent of all EAS and EBS activations were a result of natural disasters and were weather related. Linking NOAA Weather Radio digital signaling with the EAS digital signaling will help NWS save lives by reaching more people with timely, site-specific weather warnings.

FEMA. FEMA provides direction for state and local emergency planning officials to plan and implement their roles in the EAS.

WHERE CAN YOU GET MORE INFORMATION?

Consumers, broadcasters, organizations, or other service providers who want to understand the new EAS can contact:

FCC. The FCC provides a toll-free number that provides information on a wide variety of subjects, including the EAS. The number is 1-888-CALL FCC [1-888-225-5322]. The toll-free TTY number is 1-888-TELL FCC [1-888-835-5322].

NWS. Contact Herbert White (301) 713-0090 extension 146.

FEMA. Contact Don Jacks (202) 646 3985

Source: Federal Communications Commission
Source of fact sheet: http://www.fcc.gov/eb/easfact.html Dan

Traffic Management Centers

Large metropolitan areas are becoming more and more equipped with state-of-the-art traffic management facilities. These central command centers are vital in facilitating the most efficient movement of traffic through urban and congested areas.

What Is It?

- The Traffic or Transportation Management Center (TMC) is the hub of a transportation management system, where information about the transportation network is collected and combined with other operational and control data to manage the transportation network and to produce traveler information.

- It is the focal point for communicating transportation-related information to the media and the motoring public, a place where agencies can coordinate their responses to transportation situations and conditions.

- The TMC links various elements of Intelligent Transportation Systems such as variable message signs, closed circuit video equipment, roadside count stations, etc., enabling decision makers to identify and react to an incident in a timely manner based on real-time data.

Key Results

TMCs can help reduce incident response times, lower incident rates (mainly secondary incidents), disseminate traveler information and hence reduce congestion and enhance safety. To date there is little data quantifying the exact benefits resulting from TMCs. One study conducted by MnDOT reported decrease in accident rates by 25 percent, 20-minute reduction in response time, 35% increase in average speeds (34 mph to 46 mph) during rush hours and 22% increase in capacity of freeways, after the implementation of their TMC.

Benefits

TMCs provide a number of potential benefits. The main benefits are:

- Faster incident response and reduction in incident rates.

- By broadcasting traveler information and coordinating their activities with the State Patrol, etc, TMCs have been successful in reducing congestion in freeways and arterials.

- Increases traffic safety by effective incident response and clearance techniques. By providing traveler information regarding incidents it minimizes the likelihood of secondary incidents.

- Enhanced communication in all aspects of transportation management (planning, design, implementation, operation, maintenance).

- Monetary savings by sharing responsibilities between fewer staff, achieved by co-location of participating agencies at the center.

- Agencies working closely together in a TMC typically produce a more consistent, unified response to a situation, increasing the overall effectiveness of the transportation resources.

Costs

The cost of implementing TMCs vary depending upon the size and functions of the TMC. Overall costs involve:

- Conception, design and implementation of TMCs.

- Yearly operational costs including the cost for co-hosting the number of agencies present. (For example, the yearly operation budget for Seattle TMC is in the range of $1.4 million, and that for San Antonio ranges from $700,000 to $1 million. The Houston TranStar is located in a $11.5 million, 52,000 sq. ft. TMC housing transportation and emergency personnel.)

Implementation and Operational Challenges

The challenges that a modern transportation management center face are not confined to implementation alone, equally challenging is its operation and maintenance.

- The TMC planning, design, and implementation involve not only several departments within the implementing agency (or agencies), but also the efforts of a variety of private sector product and service providers. This requires both significant coordination and ongoing effort to build and maintain consensus.

- The TMC may be in planning, design, and implementation several years, requiring it to deal with multiple technology generations.

- The agency owning the TMC faces a daunting challenge of implementing, operating, and maintaining not only a complex transportation environment, but a mass of complex and rapidly evolving technology.

- Often, multiple individuals and organizations are involved in any given transportation situation, with differing (and potentially unclear) roles and responsibilities. These participants may be acting from incomplete understandings of the situation and with differing motivations and priorities. Communication and coordination between the participants is seldom complete.

Where Is It Implemented?

Throughout the United States, Western Europe and South East Asia and on a more limited basis in Latin America.
Author: Indu Sreedevi. Source: Intelligent Transportation Systems

TMCs are complex, expensive, and vital infrastructure facilities. As such, they are inviting targets for terrorist attack.

Telephones

The telephone, in all its forms, remains a most useful communication device. As the price of cellular technology has come down, telephones are more ubiquitous than ever. Pay phones have been removed from many locations, as they have been made unprofitable in a day and age in which nearly everyone has a phone in his or her pocket or purse.

Cellular circuits may become overloaded in a disaster, as may landlines. Cellular towers, however, require electrical power and may be knocked out of service if power is interrupted and their backup generators are damaged or run out of fuel. A conventional, hard-wired phone (not cordless) may continue to function if electrical power is disrupted, as these telephones operate on a separate electrical system from the main power grid: this should be considered by anyone tempted to give up his landline service in favor of cellular.

For disaster responders, telephones are an essential adjunct to the two-way radio. Since only one person at a time can have control of the radio frequency, radio transmissions should be kept brief and reserved for command and control decisions requiring an immediate response. Telephones may be used to relay more detailed information, to pass on and receive less time-sensitive information, and to conduct conference calls.

In 2005, cellular carrier Nextel entered into a $4.8 billion deal with the FCC to buy electromagnetic spectrum it previously had shared with public safety agencies. An estimated $2.5 billion will be used to upgrade and retune public safety radios across the United States. Nextel traffic sometimes interfered with public safety traffic in the 1.9-gigahertz band, and Nextel needs that band for its next-generation high-speed Internet services. The transition is expected to be complete in 2008.

Technology Solutions and Alternative Communication Systems

There are five alternative wireless communication technologies in use today. They are:

- 49 MHz personal communicators
- Family Radio Systems (FRS)
- Citizens Band radio (CB)
- General Mobile Radio Service (GMRS)
- Amateur Radio

For general use, the 49 MHz units may be dismissed out-of-hand. Their range is too limited (less than one-quarter mile) and they are subject to interference from motorcycle intercoms, baby monitors, older cordless phones, and other devices. They do, however, possess the advantages of light weight and compact size, low power drain, and hands-free operation, so may have some utility when operating in close confines where protective equipment and/or ambient noise make voice communications or handheld radio communications difficult. They may also be useful when one member of a household is relaying information about conditions in or around the house to another member of the household who is in radio or telephone contact with the outside world.

GMRS and FRS radios may be considered together. FRS was approved by the FCC in 1996, due to the widespread use of GMRS. Both of these personal communications systems use a simple pairing of frequencies in the 462 MHz range. FRS units are light and compact, low-powered, and have a maximum range of two miles. They are popular with hikers and hunters as a way of maintaining contact with their partners in the backcountry. FRS does not require an FCC license.

GMRS is more powerful than FRS and requires an FCC license for legal operation. GMRS licensing requires only the payment of a fee to the FCC ($85 as of this writing); no examination is required. GMRS has a maximum range of 25 miles, depending on power (50 watts maximum, per FCC regulations), terrain, and antenna position. One GMRS channel is recommended for emergency use and is monitored by REACT (Radio Emergency Associated Communications Teams) volunteers.

CB radio has declined greatly in popularity from its heyday in the mid-1970's. Still, it does bring its own advantages to the table in an emergency situation.

There are no fees, licensing requirements, age limits, or citizenship requirements for CB operators in the United States. CB radios are inexpensive. Most can be powered off a car's 12 volt electrical system or, at home, by a small, inexpensive motorcycle battery.

In a disaster, REACT and other volunteers could be deployed as a mobile repeater chain, to relay information to the outside world. Information could be relayed through parties (long-haul truckers, for example) passing on the fringe of the affected area, or to volunteers assigned to patrol outside the affected area in cars, boats or aircraft.

During periods of peak sunspot activity, even low-powered CBs can be heard for hundreds or thousands of miles. Bouncing signals off the ionosphere ("working skip") is illegal and unpredictable. Still, as a last resort for an individual, family, or community in need of immediate rescue and without other links to the outside world, the possibility should not be ignored.

Amateur Radio (AR) is the most powerful and versatile radio system. It also is the most costly, in terms of equipment, training, and licensing. A nationwide system of repeaters, built and maintained by amateur radio clubs, provide nearly seamless coverage. Small, handheld radios can have a range as great as 50 miles; some are even capable of satellite communication. Home base stations operators communicate with other amateurs around the world.

Licensed amateurs enjoy the greatest leeway in building and modifying transmitting equipment, and in operating on the various frequencies in their bands. In the United States, there are three classes of Amateur license, each allowing greater access to the spectrum and more desirable call signs.

As of 2007, licensees no longer have to demonstrate proficiency in Morse code. Morse remains popular, however, because of its signal-to-noise advantages and because its standardized code groups allow communication between operators who speak different languages.

Amateur Radio clubs frequently participate in government-sponsored disaster drills, and have a long and distinguished record of responding to natural disasters, search and rescue operations, and other emergencies. AR worked when other systems failed in the 9-11 attacks of 2001, the 2003 North America Blackout, and Hurricane Katrina in 2005.

WHEN TRADITIONAL SYSTEMS FAIL

Communications systems fail. Sometimes this is an inadvertent failure; however, sometimes the failure occurs during the worst possible time—during an actual disaster. Pre-planning for communication failures of various types will allow communications to run smoother in the event of an actual disaster or real communications failure. We are do dependent upon our various methods of communication that denying that we will even lose will only create more of a disaster for ourselves when and if these systems fail.

Communications Failures

The chapter's opening case study demonstrated how communications fail in a disaster and the potentially tragic results of that failure. Cell phone lines were jammed. Two way radios were failing for multiple suspected reasons: a major antenna on top of one of the twin towers was down, repeaters were not functional, and buildings and debris were in the way.

A catastrophe like September 11, is not the only scenario where communications may be disputed. When the nation went from December 31, 1999, to January 1, 2000 (Y2K) there were many fears of communication failures due to obsolete computer programs that could not handle the switch to the year 2000. Fortunately, there were few problems encountered in that transition. The fear of computers disrupting communications continues; however, because of worms, viruses, and hackers.

Another threat we have to our communications systems, and actually, any electrical system is the e-bomb. E-bombs are electromagnetic bombs designed to destroy machines that use electricity. All phones, cell phones, radios, generators—EVERYTHING—would be non-functional if an e-bomb was deployed. E-bombs are an electromagnetic pulse (EMP) weapon. It overwhelms electrical circuitry by creating an intense electromagnetic field. Nuclear weapons may create such an EMP. Non-nuclear weapons, such as those employing High Power Microwaves (HPM) can create an EMP to wipe out electrical circuits.

Because of the threats of a true loss of traditional communications in catastrophic disasters with computer problems, or with EMP weapons, we much consider a communications plan that is very basic, and that will work effectively in the events of a partial communications failure, or in the event of a full-scale communications failure.

A Plan

Any plan is better than no plan at all for a communications system failure. The plan must consider if some communications forms, like radios and cell phones, are non-functional, while other forms or communication remain functional. This plan should be taken clear down to the level of what to do if there are no means of communications. Certainly, if communications are destroyed to the point of using emergency runners running handwritten messages back and forth, this system will show much greater function if pre-planning is done, so that runners know where to wait for messages, and other staff knows where to meet the runners.

Absence of Radios and Cell Phones

Radios and cell phones were a problem in New York City on September 11. We will begin with a contingency plan that discusses the absence of radios and cell phones initially. If landline phones are functional, notifications of the communications failure must be made. Notifications will depend upon the cause of the failure and the size of the community and the agencies involved. Examples of notifications include the incident commander, the dispatchers, the Emergency Operations Center (EOC), each precinct, other agencies such as fire, EMS, law enforcement, utility company personnel associated with the communication means that has failed, such as the radio or cell phone company. Communication and utility personnel must immediately begin work to restore some kind of communications.

Telecommunications Failures

The inverse problem may also occur. Radios and cell phones may remain functional, but landline telephones may fail. If landlines fail, faxes and dial-up Internet systems will fail. The 911 system should be checked to see if it can still receive incoming cell phone calls. The same notifications should be made as discussed in the previous section; however, with no telephones, notification must be by radio, cell phone, or in person. In addition, notification should be made to the public via television and AM/FM radio, or by door-to-door notifications if radio and television are non-functional. The notification to the public should explain what is known about the situation, and provide information concerning the status of the 911 system. Even if the 911 system is accepting incoming cell calls, instructions should be given to those persons who do not have cell phones.

Depending upon the size of the community, citizens may be instructed to go to a neighborhood fire station to report an emergency, or different emergency vehicles with functional radios should be stationed at intervals throughout the community. The public should be informed of the vehicles' locations, and should be told to go to one of the emergency vehicles to report an emergency so that the emergency can be radioed to the appropriate agency. The telephone company personnel must be notified so they may restore telecommunications.

Additional Communications Systems Failures

An infinite number of communications systems may fail. Power may fail. Flexibility must be built into any communications emergency plan. Satellite telephones may be a possibility as a backup. Bidirectional satellite Internet may also be a possibility as a backup. Any kind of functioning email may serve as a backup. Ham radio operators may help if their equipment is still functional. AlphaNumeric and Digital pages may help, and handheld wireless devices such as Blackberries may help; however, keep in mind that all systems may fail.

Runners and Messengers

In the event of total (or near total) communications failures, a system of runners and messengers must be set up at pre-determined locations. Depending upon the community, runners may be on foot, on bicycle, on horseback, car, ATV—or any means of travel from one point to another. The runner must be clearly marked as an emergency runner or messenger. These persons must carry paper or 3x5 cards, and pens or pencils. Runners should be located where the citizens can find them easily in an emergency. Runners must know the locations of the runners around them, so that they can go and had off a message to be taken to the appropriate person or agency, so that the runner can quickly return to his or her designated post.

The public must be informed of this runner system so they may find a runner to obtain emergency help when needed. Utility personnel must be notified so that some form of communications can be restored as soon as possible. Because a runner system is slow and cumbersome at best, planning and pre-emergency practice is important to allow this system to run as smoothly as possible when it is actually needed.

Additional Considerations

In the event of a disaster that results in a communications failure, there are many other concurrent considerations. All of these considerations will vary, depending upon the cause of the disaster or reason communications have failed. These concerns include water safety, natural gas safety, downed power lines and electrocution hazards, traffic hazards if traffic signals are out, the dangers to the public in extremes of temperature if heat or air conditioning is out. There is additional risk is buildings have collapsed or there are fires or explosions. If the communications failure is a result of a terrorist attack, there is always the risk of a secondary attack, or a risk that the initial attack was also a checmical, biological, EMP, or nuclear attack. Whatever the intial cause of the communications failure, immediate steps must be taken to mitigate the problem and get computers, power, and communications back online.

In the event of such a communications failure, different emergency agency personnel must have a place to meet where runners can reach them to send them on emergency calls, and thus place will also help to account for emergency personnel after each mission since they cannot be contacted in the field in an emergency. They can also report back to others and the command staff what the conditions are in the affected community.

Mass Casualty and Disaster Communications[3]

Communications may be the single most important aspect of an emergency response system. The best-trained paramedics, driving the newest ambulances with the most sophisticated equipment, are ineffective during an incident if they cannot adequately communicate with each other, their dispatch center and other responding agencies. Despite the critical nature of this system element, significant communications failures continue to occur in systems everywhere during high-impact events.

Communication is widely identified as a weakness in virtually every after-action review of an MCI (Mass Casualty Incident) or disaster.[4] In fact, it is the single largest point of failure noted. Problems like radio frequency incompatibilities, lack of common terminology and the traditional isolation of emergency services agencies have existed for more than 35 years.[5] Despite the historical knowledge about these problems, however, little has been done to correct them.

Routine Versus Incident Communications

In order to correct the problems inherent with communications today, we must first differentiate between routine communications and those that take place during incidents. The same procedures should be followed for all incidents, from the smallest to the largest.

As an incident occurs, the first and most important task is to implement and use the Incident Management System (IMS). Command is established by the first arriving unit and given a unique name based on the location of the incident.[6]

The incident commander then transmits an accurate size-up of the incident as soon as possible, including basic information regarding the type of incident such as a MVA (Motor Vehicle Accident), fire, etc., approximate patient count (is the incident stable or escalating?), location of command, what additional resources will be needed, and where those resources should stage. Giving this information to the dispatcher and other units accurately and early prevents having inadequate resources during the incident or incoming units from staging poorly, which complicates scene management.

Tactical Radio Channels

Local communications systems have many different configurations. Some systems have dedicated EMS channels, some share channels with fire or police operations, and others have special channels for on-scene communications. At times, it is beneficial to share communications with local agencies on small incidents. When fire and EMS agencies are both operating at a small MVA, for example, it may be helpful to have all operations on one channel. However, as incident complexity increases, it becomes necessary to move communications for different types of operations onto tactical or on-scene channels. This prevents incident communications from overloading the primary EMS channel and prevents interference between agencies with different primary functions. However, it is beneficial to have the ability for command officers from different agencies to communicate on a common channel when needed.

Depending on the complexity of the incident, you will need to decide when to move operations onto a tactical or on-scene channel. If you share a channel with other agencies, this point will be reached when you begin to expand the incident management system. Agencies with a dedicated tactical channel should move operations onto tactical channels as soon as an MCI is declared.

All responding units, as well as the units already on scene, should move any further communications for the incident to the secondary channel. This allows units communicating about the incident to speak without interfering with other emergency operations and places all primary incident communications on one channel. It is very important that dispatchers monitor this channel closely and that units are not required to change channels to speak with the dispatcher. There is significant potential for missed messages if units have to change channels back and forth, and it may result in poor operations or compromised responder safety.

Because most on-scene communications take place on portable radios, the tactical radio channel used for incident communications should be repeated.[7] Rebroadcasting transmissions at a higher power used by a repeater system allows the portable radios to reach greater distances and prevents missed messages. However, it is more important to move communications to a secondary channel available in portable radios than to have this channel repeated. On repeated channels, the capability exists for radios to transmit in talk-around, or direct mode, bypassing the repeater. This allows units to communicate if the repeater fails of if a local message is desired but it has drawbacks. Generally, the dispatcher transmits over direct messages, resulting in missed communications. Direct mode is also at lower power and may not reach all points of a widespread incident scene.

There are two important points to remember about portable radios. First, make sure all the frequencies you will need for incident management are available in the portable radios you carry every day. These are the radios that you will use in the initial phases of an incident, and command officers will be using them extensively. Also, be sure to have an adequate supply of spare batteries ready to be deployed, or you may find the radios useless a few hours into the incident.

Staging

In the event of an incident of extremely large magnitude, geographic size, or ongoing time, other channels can be used if available. Incidents separated by distance can be segregated onto secondary channels, as can staging for extremely large numbers of incoming units. In fact, it is essential that all agencies that may respond to an incident have the capability of communicating on the same tactical channels. It may be very difficult to develop the capability for all responding units to communicate on one tactical channel. Different agencies usually have separate channels and sometimes use different frequency bands requiring different radios. However, it is essential to share resources and put aside political differences as regional coordination channels are developed.

Additional channels add complexity to an already unstable situation. Like the Incident Management System toolbox theory, they should only be used when necessary. Ideally, the communications system for an incident should be kept as simple as possible—the dispatcher, the incident commander, IMS officers and ambulances ca n communicate on one channel. When the volume of ambulances required necessitates a Staging Officer and Level II staging area, a staging channel should be considered. Incoming ambulances need only communicate with the Staging Officer, keeping the primary tactical channel clear for on-scene communications.

Hospital Communications

Another channel will be necessary for hospital notification. Most areas already have a dedicated channel for this purpose during everyday operations. During incidents, this channel has two important uses: In the initial phases of an incident, it can be used by the dispatcher to notify potential receiving hospitals of the mass casualty incident and request a capability assessment. Based on the estimated number and condition of patients in the size-up, hospitals can consider activating their disaster plan and take an immediate count of the number of critical, non-critical and ambulatory patients they can accept.

Once disaster notification has been made, hospitals should keep the channel open and monitored at all times. The Transport Officer or EMS Communications

Officer will keep inventory of the receiving hospitals' capabilities and the patients prepared for transportation. Once a patient leaves the scene in an ambulance, the receiving hospital should be notified of the patient's triage color (red, yellow, or green), age, sex, major injury, and estimated time of arrival (ETA). This relieves ambulances of having to notify hospitals of incoming patients, which is especially important when the ambulance may not be familiar with the local hospitals. Having this channel available in the portable radio used by the Transport or EMS ComOfficer saves being restricted to a vehicle.

Command and Control

On an incident scene, communications have the potential to become overwhelming. Radio communications should be kept to a minimum, with only those people authorized to talk using radios. One of the biggest pitfalls in incident management is personnel freelancing, which can be controlled by limiting radio use. Lines of communication should essentially follow the lines of the IMS organization chart, talking upward or downward through branches, divisions or groups to the managers in charge of these areas.[8] Communications should generally not flow between sectors, and people not authorized to transmit should stay off the radio, with the exception of emergency messages. Again, as the incident becomes more complex, it may be necessary to move indicnt functions or geographic divisions onto separate channels.

Field communications (FieldCom) units offer additional capabilities for incident communications. The FieldCom unit can act as the dispatch center on the scene of an incident, allowing dispatchers to concentrate on regular operations and have a single point of contact for the incident. Messages flow between the FieldCom unit and persons on the incident scene. When necessary, the FieldCom unit can contact the agency dispatch center. FieldCom units can also provide a means for all agencies on an incident to communicate through one central point.

One of the most common points noted after major incidents is different agencies' lack of ability to communicate with each other on scene.[9,10] The common expectation of messages to flow to a dispatcher via radio, be relayed by telephone to another agency dispatcher, then back to another unit is unrealistic. The dispatchers will probably be overwhelmed, and the telephone system may not be operational. An interagency coordination channel between EMS, fire and police units is essential for major incidents. Command officers should operate on the command channel while another person (command aide, scribe or communications officer) monitors the tactical channel.

Include your dispatchers in all MCI and incident management training. Dispatchers set the tone for an incident. Those who remain calm have better control over field operations, and field crews will take cues from the tone and mannerisms of dispatchers. While involving communications center personnel in planning for high-impact events, consider using dispatchers to staff the FieldCom unit. Remember that the dispatch center itself will probably be overwhelmed with radio and telephone messages, so additional dispatchers will be needed in that area. Consider how you will recall people who are off duty and how they will integrate into the dispatch center. Are there enough chairs and telephones?

Medical Control Communications

Depending on the structure of your EMS system, online medical control may be necessary before beginning some or all ALS (Advanced Life Support) procedures. If your system operates under a comprehensive set of standing orders, you will rarely need online medical control during an MCI' however, if your system requires physician or nurse contact, someone in the treatment area will have to contact a base station for the required orders. It is strongly recommended that all systems develop a set of protocols for use in mass casualty situations, where radio or telephone contact for orders may be difficult or impossible.

Radio Procedures

Radios are the bread and butter of EMS communications. Because virtually every EMT, paramedic, firefighter, and police officer carries a portable radio, it is very important that everyone practice good radio discipline. First, and most important, think before you speak. Do you really need to transmit this message over the radio? What exactly are you trying to say? Try to eliminate words or phrases that have no meaning, such as "be advised" and "at this time." Remember to key your radio for one second before speaking to ensure the beginning of your message is not missed. If you do this every time you use a radio, the procedure will be ingrained in your behavior during high-stress periods.

Another essential radio procedure is to *use plan English*! Get rid of all radio codes. Radio codes have outlived their original purpose and can cause massive confusion or danger on major events. Neighboring agencies may use codes with vastly different meanings from yours. Every version of the Incident Management System requires the use of plan English radio traffic. The excuse that "We've been doing it this way for 30 years" just doesn't cut it.

When faced with a dangerous situation, transmit the keyword *Emergency*. This message takes precedence over all other actions, and all radio traffic should cease until the emergency condition is corrected. When conducting an MCI drill, make sure that everyone knows the keyword for a real illness or injury on the drill scene. Messages for actual emergencies that occur at an exercise are often confused with those of the drill itself.

One last note on radio traffic: Never say something over the radio that you wouldn't want everyone to hear. A good way to measure a department's professionalism is to monitor its routine radio traffic. What do the dispatchers and field units say, and how do they say it? The media probably monitor everything you say and have tapes of your radio traffic. Would you want your radio traffic played on the network news?

Contingency Planning

Although most agencies have implemented plans for major incidents, most of those plans don't consider what happens during a disaster. Imagine an incident that is so massive it overwhelms all of your resources—not just your jurisdiction's resources, nbiut those of your entire community. What would happen if the incident affected the infrastructure of your community? Consider your department's mass casualty or disaster plan, and try to imagine utilizing that plan without a radio system.

On virtually every disaster, available channels are overwhelmed with radio traffic. During many natural disasters, the infrastructure is damaged, resulting in a loss of transmitter sites, the dispatch center or power. During explosives incidents, devices that transmit RF energy cannot be used within 1,000 feet of the site. These are only some of the ways that your primary radio system can suddenly be rendered inoperable.

It is essential to develop backup radio communications capabilities to prevent losing your primary radio system. Place secondary radio bases independent of the primary system and connect them to a secondary dispatch center. Both of these systems should have independent backup power supplies, and everything should be as hardened and secure as possible. Hold regular drills where communications are shifted to the secondary system so dispatchers and field personnel will become familiar with the process.

Alternative Communications

Even the best contingency plans may not keep you from losing radio communications during a disaster. If you have not already done so, begin to explore some alternative means of communications. Mobile data terminals, one possible secondary communications pathway, have the advantages of allowing two-way communications and decreasing voice communications, and they are difficult to monitor. However, there is a major expense involved in installing them in units, they cannot be used outside a vehicle, and they are vulnerable to loss of radio frequencies in the same way as voice channels.

AlphaNumeric pagers are the poor-man's MDT, and offer some significant advantages. Due to the relatively low cost, they can be issued to every member of your department and carried at all times. They are also difficult to monitor, decrease voice communications, can be used on explosives incidents, and allow personnel recall during major incidents. The pagers can also be configured with most computer-aided dispatch systems to transmit dispatch information and call times to crews, significantly decreasing the amount of voice traffic into the dispatch center. However, pagers do not offer two-way communications, and there is a monthly leasing cost.

Cellular telephone service has expanded significantly over the last several years. Cell phones offer an alternative means of two-way voice communications, but can only be used from one individual to another. They can be mounted in most emergency vehicles and thus provide a secondary means of communication if the radio system fails; however, monthly lease rates can be expensive, and usage costs can be even more so. The media also present several problems with cellular phones. Not only can they monitor your messages, on major incidents, the media will occupy most of the available cells in the area, so you have a difficult time getting service. Work with your local cellular provider to overcome this problem.

Your local cellular or telephone company may be able to provide several other services to you during a disaster. Local telephone providers can set up landlines directly into a command post for long-term operations, but a mechanism for payment should be worked out in advance. Landlines can provide a link between the command post and your community's Emergency Operations Center, reducing the need for radio communication. Cellular phone providers often have mobile cellular sites for use on disasters. They can set up a van with a cellular tower and issue cell phones that are keyed directly to that tower. Both of these alternatives are for long-term incident use, and obtaining access to them should be preplanned.

In the event that all of your communications systems have failed, there is one method that always works—sending runners with messages from one officer to another. Although this method is slow and can only be used over a limited area, there are advantages. The messages are guaranteed delivery, and are absolutely secure. Practice using runners in the event of communications failure so this method can be implemented quickly on an incident scene.

SUMMARY

"Those who cannot remember the past are condemned to repeat it."[11] These are communications guidelines for use in an ideal world. This is not the way to conduct MCI and disaster operations—merely some suggestions learned the ahrd way from past mistakes. Adapt these lessons learned the hard way from past mistakes. Adapt these lessons learned to your system, but make progress in improving the way your communicate. Avoid having to make the same mistakes made by others at the potential expense of people's lives.

Following are key points to remember:

- Preplan! Find a way for police, fire, and EMS units to communicate on scene. Make sure that your can communicate with all of the EMS units near you, and practice doing it. Think about what would happen if your primary radio system died.

- Use alternative channels for incident communications, preferably repeated channels.

- Practice radio discipline. Think before you speak, and key your radio for one second before speaking. Use plain English rather than radio codes, and make sure everyone knows the procedure for emergency radio traffic.

- Buy the right radios. It is preferable to have all the channels you will need in your portable radios, and make sure you have extra radio batteries available. The dispatcher sets the tone for the incident. Dispatchers who remain calm and keep control over system operations will make an incident run smoothly.

- Always remember that everyone is listening to what you way on the radio and how you say it, including the media.

ADDITIONAL DISCUSSION TOPICS

- How might emerging technologies, such as social networking sites, twitter, and text messaging impact emergency communications?

- If you were the commander of a disaster scene, and all traditional communications systems broke down, how might you set up a communications network with your responders and associated response resources? What may be the pitfalls in your plan?

- How might terrorists compromise a communication system at an emergency?

- What steps might you take if you were a public safety official managing a disaster and you discovered that some of your radios had been stolen? What may be the consequences?

- What do you think is the best way to balance security and functional communication, specifically, is it better to use codes so outsiders who may be monitoring emergency communications will be confused, or to use plain English so members of various agencies who have their own codes will know what to do?

Endnotes

[1] Jim Dwyer and Kevin Flynn, New York Times, November 9, 2002.

[2] *Author:* Indu Sreedevi. Source: Intelligent Transportation Systems

[3] By Matthew R. Streger, BA, NREMT-P. From www.emsmagazine.com, Summer Communications, Inc.

[4] Auf der Heide E. *Disaster Response: Principles of Preparation and Coordination.* St. Louis, MO: C.V. Mosby, 1989.

[5] Ibid.

[6] *Incident Command System for Emergency Medical Services.* Federal Emergency Management Agency, U.S. Fire Administration, National Fire Academy.

[7] Steele, S. *Emergency Dispatching: A Medical Communicator's Guide.* Englewood Cliffs, NJ: Brady Publishing, 1998.

[8] Cristen J. Maniscalco P. *The EMS Incident Management System.* Upper Saddle Rive, NJ: Brady Publishing, 1998.

[9] Goldfarb Z, Kuhr S. "EMS response to the explosion," *The World Trade Center Bombing: Report and Analysis.* Provided by Fire Engineering: Manning W., Ed., USFA Technical Report 076.

[10] The EMSA/AMR response to the April 19, 1995 bombing, *Final Report: Alfred P. Murrah Federal Building Bombing,* April 19, 1995. Stillwater, OK: Fire Protection Publications, 1996.

[11] Santayana G. (1863-1952).

CHAPTER FIFTEEN

CAREERS AND THE ROLE OF EDUCATION

The great aim of education is not knowledge, but action.
—Herbert Spencer

KEY TERMS

Security Industry
Physical Security
Information Security
Information Systems Security
Personnel Security
Security Specialties

OBJECTIVES

- Examine security protection and incident response for medical facilities.

- Examine security protection and incident response for businesses.

- Examine security protection and incident response for public utility workers.

- Examine security protection and incident response for emergency responders.

- Examine security protection and incident response for social service providers.

- Describe the role of education in homeland security.

DISCUSSION TOPICS

- What anti-terrorism security measures are used in the healthcare industry? How is security balanced with free access for patients?

- Why is business concerned with security, and what skills must their personnel have to provide it?

- What are the security concerns of social services organizations such as the Red Cross or Salvation Army? What role do their workers play in organizational security?

15

INTRODUCTION

Almost every career field has a homeland security role. Whether it is in medicine, business, government, education, or social services, at some point there is a homeland security responsibility.

With natural disasters and the very real threat of terrorist aggression on any number of domestic targets within the United States, the emergency responses to those realities have been reevaluated on many levels. It's no longer the sole responsibility of the police, fire departments, and the military. The responsibility to be prepared lies with a multitude of organizations and individuals, and the need for education and a professional standard of performance for security workers is finally being widely recognized. In this chapter we'll be exploring the role of the security industry and of the Emergency Medical System (EMS) in homeland security.

WHY IS THERE A "SECURITY INDUSTRY"?

The security industry had been growing by leaps and bounds even before the terrorist attacks of 1993 and 2001. Driven by the day-to-day losses through theft of property and information, and the less common losses that occur due to incidents of workplace violence or terrorist attack, the security industry, in all its facets, has risen to consuming over $100 billion annually.

All business organizations have a need to protect themselves from activities that threaten to disrupt their business operations and, eventually, negatively impact their "bottom line". Security has become an integral business function, and one of the items that investors evaluate for "due diligence" before they invest. Contracts to provide services or goods to both government agencies and other businesses frequently dictate certain business security practices to ensure that those goods and services will be reliably available after a significant event, either natural or manmade, and audits of procedures and training records are made to evaluate the organizations' adherence to the industry's current "best practices understanding.

At one time there was the impression that security managers needed to be former police officials, but while the leadership experience brought by a command level police officer can be valuable, skills in business management and technology now drive the industry. While most of us still think first of a uniformed security officer patrolling the halls and fence lines to deter criminal activity and report any unsafe or suspicious things they see, the industry also provides less obvious services.

The security industry includes both contracted and proprietary services. The uniformed guard is often a contract employee, as are the consultants who install and maintain the physical security measures like alarms, fences and lighting. Larger organizations often use proprietary, or "in house", employees for at least part of the security management team; though they also might hire consultants with specialized knowledge to assess their information security needs, for example, and recommend changes. There is very frequently a mix of contract and proprietary employees providing security services, and each business organization must decide which needs are better met by which class of worker.

For the worker in the security field, the decision whether to work in house or as a contractor is an important one, and there are benefits and drawbacks to each. While it is common that in house security guards are paid more and have better benefits than contract guards, the contract guard usually has more flexibility in work schedule and can change workplaces when other contracts are available. Those who provide consulting services in designing security systems, whether for physical, personnel or information security, can often make a higher wage as a contracted consultant, but job security is lower than that of a corporate security manager's.

PRIVATE SECTOR AND PUBLIC SECTOR

While the use of security guards and services is commonplace in the private sector, many people do not realize that there are many non-police related public sector security functions as well. Public sector security forces exist at all levels of government and, to confuse the distinction even more, a mix of public and private sector companies are often used to provide security manpower to government facilities.

At the Federal level, it is not uncommon for contract employees to be supervised by government employees. Many Federal courts are, for example, secured by armed contractors supervised by employees from the U.S. Marshal's office. The State Department and other organizations use contract officers to guard Top Secret facilities, supervised by members of their own security arms. These contractors often have Federal authority and arrest powers while on duty and undergo training and hold security clearances similar to that of the security forces that other agencies maintain in house.

Similar situations exist in many states, and even down to the local level. Local government offices and public buildings are often protected and patrolled by government employees hired to provide security services. Sometimes the police chief or county Sheriff's offices oversee these protective services agencies, but they are often autonomous. Each level of government has laws and policies that determine how much of their security functions can be contracted to the private sector. A task that may require arrest powers or access to confidential information that only government employees can have in one state, may be legally contracted out in another.

SECURITY'S RELATIONSHIP TO LAW ENFORCEMENT

While security officers are often called "Rent-a-Cops," their responsibilities are very different than those of police officers. Though concerned with different tasks, police and security agencies should work in a spirit of cooperation to enhance the value of both. Mutual understanding of the needs and abilities of both of these complimentary fields will help develop an attitude of trust and respect between police officials and security providers.

Police and Security: Similarities and Differences

Law enforcement and security providers have different roles to play, though they frequently overlap and interact. Briefly stated, law enforcement is reactive in nature, while security providers are proactive. This means that the police focus on enforcing laws that have been broken by identifying and prosecuting the culprits, while security practitioners try to protect their organization from crime and loss before it occurs.

The most visible part of the police and security forces are their uniformed patrol officers. Both provide criminal deterrence through a highly visible presence performing unpredictable patrols, but as police resources are increasingly stretched, crime deterrence has become far less a part of police work in most places. Since both wear uniforms, they are the visible symbols of authority in an emergency, but the police officer is responsible to society at large while the security officer is only responsible to the organization that employs him.

Today there are about three workers in the various security fields for every one employee of a law enforcement agency according to extrapolations from the *Hallcrest Report II, Private Security Trends (1970-2000)*. It seems obvious that the security industry has both the resources and motivation to work closely with law enforcement when appropriate, but this cooperation has not been common until recently.

For many years the private security industry has been stereotyped negatively as poorly trained and underpaid "wannabe" cops who could not get "real" police jobs. There were always enough bad apples to justify this stereotype for many, but progress is being made to change this. Many states require significant training and rigorous background checks for new security officers, and the average age of the workers themselves has been declining while their pay and career opportunities have been rising.

The lack of standards for security providers, coupled with law enforcements' lack of understanding of what the security industry can actually do has led to a lack of respect and communication between the two fields. As the standards for hiring and training of security workers increases, so will the cooperation with law enforcement as they see it is in the public's interest. Consider the following scenarios:

- A uniformed guard contracted to work at a large retail outlet arrests a suspect for shoplifting. When law enforcement arrives, the security officer looks unkempt and cannot give a coherent report. The item he claims the suspect attempted to steal was returned to the shelf, and there is no video evidence as the camera was turned to watch a female checker. The responding officers feel their time has been wasted, as there is not enough usable evidence to prosecute the suspect, and will not hurry to respond next time.

- A uniformed guard contracted to work at a large retail outlet arrests a suspect for shoplifting. When law enforcement arrives, the security officer gives them a report detailing the arrest, explains how the elements of the crime are present, quotes the suspect's own incriminating spontaneous statements and has the video evidence prepared. The professional knowledge and practice of this security officer reflects well on himself, his employer and the retail outlet. Officers responding to this outlet will see the security force there as resources in future and will gladly respond when called.

At the upper ends of the industry, the situation is already somewhat better. For example, public sector cyber crimes investigators have long needed the cooperation of private computer security professionals. They frequently train together and have joined to support the passage of new laws more reflective of the threat posed by modern computer criminals. Professional personal protection and executive protection providers know exactly what evidence is needed for police to enforce a restraining order, or to prosecute a stalker, and so can legally empower law enforcement to arrest a potentially dangerous attacker before the attack occurs.

As training and hiring standards improve throughout the industry, the increased professionalism of security providers throughout the various specialties will encourage better cooperation. In this age of terrorism, where the targets are as likely to be privately held, as they are to be government related, the increasing the capabilities of the security industry is a given, and improving cooperation with law enforcement is a priority.

SECURITY DISCIPLINES[1]

The diversity of the tasks in which the security industry is involved can be daunting. In order to explore the various aspects of the industry, we will break the security function into four disciplines. Some security professionals may work in only one of these disciplines, and others may have positions, which require they be familiar with all four, but all security functions will fall under at least one of these disciplines.

Physical Security

The protection of people, property and facilities makes up the physical security discipline. It is the most visibly practiced discipline as it involves human security forces, security systems and corporate policies and procedures intended to protect employees and company property.

Security forces include the personnel of the guard force, whether contract or proprietary and uniformed or plain clothes. Those with guard force supervisory or training responsibilities are also physical security personnel. The responsibilities of the guard force vary, but generally include crime deterrence through visible presence, observation and reporting of suspicious activity or safety hazards and other service related functions. Other classic duties of the guard force include access control and enforcement of company policies. Some are given training and equipment for emergency medical response, and the guard force should be trained and practiced to be an integral part of emergency evacuation plans.

Security systems include mechanical access control devices, electronic alarm or surveillance devices and physical barriers. Though high tech alarm and surveillance camera systems are the first thing we think of when considering security systems, physical security includes much simpler devices as well. When designing an access control system, simple door locks become far less simple. Access devices might include keys, electronic recognition badges or even biometric sensors: Each has its drawbacks.

Key control becomes a major distraction if more than a few employees are allowed access to an area. A lost key can mean that every door it opens will have to be rekeyed, and the old keys collected and new keys issued. Combination locks do not require keys, but the combinations must be changed periodically, and some employees will write them down for fear they will forget them. Access cards can be lost or stolen like keys, but reprogramming the system to ignore lost cards is easier than replacing all the keys. If they are printed with an employee's name and picture, they provide a way to quickly identify whether the holder is allowed in a specific area. Biometric sensors are expensive to install and maintain, and many feel that they are needlessly intrusive.

Alarms systems and surveillance cameras are best placed by trained specialists. Modern alarms can run under very sophisticated rule sets that change under any programmed conditions including by time of day, day of the week or area of the intrusion. They may employ motion detectors, door or window sensors or sound detectors, and they can be tied into a fire or chemical hazard alarm system as well. Cameras may be movable or fixed, and there will likely be a number of each within the system. Even access control barriers are more complex than it seems to a layman. Fences canalize movement and prevent easy access to restricted areas, but landscaping, lighting and seemingly decorative features can do the same. Corporate clients do not want their buildings to look like prisons, but a skilled access control designer can create a secure space that does not look intimidating.

Physical security enhancing policies and procedures are commonplace in companies large and small. If employees must wear issued ID badges, or are trained not to allow others to follow them in a secured door without using their own ID badge, then both writing and enforcing these policies are aspects of physical security.

Information Security

The phrase "information security" conjures images of government secrets and espionage, but all organizations have sensitive information that must be safeguarded. Whether the information is related to a secret manufacturing process, an upcoming product, personnel information or lists of clients and orders, a competitor could easily benefit from stealing it. Holding some information actually presents a legal responsibility to safeguard it. Medical records, for example, must be positively protected by those medical organizations that use them.

Information security also defines who should be able to access specific information, even within the organization, how that information should be stored and how it should be destroyed once it is no longer needed. The information could be stored in any medium, electronic, magnetic, paper etc. and the information security specialist will have to understand the risks of each.

Security policies and employee education efforts are especially important to safeguard information as it can be released accidentally and without intending to damage the owner. Misaddressed emails, manuals left at the coffee shop and magnetic storage tape thrown away without being thoroughly erased can all create inadvertent information losses.

Information System Security

Information system security refers to the protection of information storage and transmission systems from hackers, viruses, unauthorized usage or accidental damage. Information systems security providers are responsible for developing and maintaining hardware and software safeguards, as well as for security awareness procedures and training for authorized users. An organization's Information Security Officer needs to be educated in computer science and in the security specialty. In a large organization such as a university or corporate environment, the security specialist will need to understand the network's architecture and the application servers used. They may need to have varying degrees of expertise in several operating systems and applications in order to spot potential risks, and they are responsible for planning for system upgrades and additions. All information stored in an organization's computers, or transmitted across the organization's networks must be protected, and any application run is a potential weakness. Often, they are also responsible for developing procedures and plans for data backup and safe storage to minimize the impact of an accident or natural disaster that destroys part of the organizations networks or servers.

Security is always a compromise allowing an adequate level of security while impacting legitimate users as little as possible. Information systems may have thousands of users with varying levels of access, hundreds of computers and other specialized equipment types linked through dozens of departments and outside the organization to the unsecured internet. Even careful users can unknowingly install malicious software such as viruses or programs that open doors for hackers.

In the event of an intrusion, the security specialist must know how to minimize the data lost or damage caused, and should understand the legal rules of computer evidence in order to liaison with cyber crime investigators should prosecution be pursued. Law enforcement does not have the resources to investigate computer crimes in corporate information systems, so the security expert becomes the primary source delivering this information to the authorities.

Personnel Security

Every organization is, when broken down to its core, made up of its human members. Personnel security is the discipline responsible for safeguarding the organization's employees and ensuring their integrity. Because it is employees who have access and inside knowledge, it should not be surprising to find that less than 10% of losses through theft, fraud or sabotage come from people without a connection to the victim organization. Put another way, employees cause greater losses to their employers than burglars and robbers do. When accidental damage through human error or failure is included, the percentage of employee caused loss goes even higher.

The tools of personnel security are brought to bear even before hiring. An organization can be held accountable for damages resulting from negligent hiring of personnel, and can be held vicariously liable for their employees' actions, so more and more are finding legal ways to verify a prospective employee's integrity and ethical outlook. Background investigations and other pre-employment screening methods attempt to establish patterns of past behavior in order to determine what a prospective employee's future actions might be. There are legal limits to the extent of the background investigation that can be done that vary from state to state and even from industry to industry: A prospective police officer may be investigated more thoroughly than a prospective florist because the danger posed by a police officer who misuses his position is greater.

Personnel security also comes into play when an employee leaves the organization, even if under good terms. An exit interview is needed in which the employee is reminded of the terms of their original employment. Because an employee who leaves may gain proprietary knowledge valuable to competitors through the course of their daily work activities, non-compete clauses and non-disclosure warnings are commonly agreed to at hire.

Emergency Medical Responders and Physical Security

No emergency management plan is complete without consideration of the abilities and availability of emergency medical responders. We tend to think of EMS as being a government responsibility, and most do not realize that there is more to the system than ambulance response.

Current EMS practice has evolved with the rest of the emergency management field, both private and public, in the light of modern concerns over terrorism.

Just as there are both private and public security providers, many organizations are learning the need for private medical responders as well. Many of the same personality traits that draw an individual into the security industry are present in EMT's and paramedics, and the emergency management skills taught in each specialty can be useful as the practitioner advances through their careers.

Medical response can be thought of as a specialty within the physical security discipline, and many organizations require even their entry level security guards to have, at least, first aid certification. Organizations with large campuses, that use toxic substances routinely, and that have far flung or hard to access facilities often have on duty EMT's as part of their security forces. The specialized knowledge of a trained medical responder can be invaluable when creating emergency response plans, and when evaluating the various risks to an organizations workers and visitors. Safety from accidental or purposeful release of toxic chemicals, and even from accidental injury in construction or when conducting daily work tasks is an appropriate field of responsibility for a security department.

Medical responders who pursue careers in emergency management can easily follow one of two different paths, though there are also others. Should they want to stay with medical response, they can go from Emergency Medical Technician (EMT) to paramedic, and as a paramedic they can pursue specialized education and certification in, for example, trauma care or rescue. An experienced medic might chose to travel further in the medical field and enter clinical practice as a nurse, physician's assistant or physician, or might pursue a career as a specialist in HAZMAT or catastrophe rescue operations. Either career path can create, with the needed education, an effective emergency manager.

One aspect of the physical security of EMS that we have not, yet, seen much of in the US is the targeting of medical responders in secondary terrorist attacks. In a secondary attack, those responding to a first attack are themselves attacked. The reason for this is two fold: one is to reduce the population's confidence in the authorities' ability to protect them be demonstrating that they cannot protect themselves, and the other is to reduce the number of people willing to respond to an attack and thereby to increase the number of casualties. Secondary attacks on medical personnel, both on scene and at the hospital are not uncommon in other parts of the world, and should be expected as a preferred terrorist tactic.

HIGHER EDUCATION IN EMERGENCY MANAGEMENT

A web search conducted by the author in June 2008 showed over 100 college and university degree programs with security application available across the United States. The degrees ranged from the Associates level all the way to the Master's, and all four of the major disciplines described above were represented. Each discipline is represented by one or more professional organizations, which provide training and certification in security related topics. Unlike the security industry, the EMS field has national licensing requirements and a well-established set of credentials and certification requirements. Because of this, and because some of the requirements change based on local or state laws, we will be focusing on more specifically security related education and certification here.

Because it is now understood that security and protection are business functions rather than law enforcement responsibilities, those with ambition to become professional security providers should pursue the advanced education available. Course work in personnel, business and information management are as appropriate to the aspiring professional as security management. Computer science and information technology are as useful as law and emergency management to today's security industry.

Degrees and Certification

College and university degrees from accredited schools are universally accepted, and many career level security positions, especially in the Federal government, require applicants to have a bachelor degree. Certainly, degrees give employers in the more technical portions of the security industry confidence that a prospective employee will be successful in the field. Further, the improved written and verbal communication skills honed in years of college report writing and presenting will be useful throughout an entire career, and the value of the peer network developed during the school years cannot be overlooked.

For all the benefits of college education in security, investing two to six years in gaining it can be difficult for some. Non-traditional schools that do their courses online or in other formats can be very helpful, though care must be taken to ensure the school is accredited and that the program is appropriate to the student. Some students need the structure or personal interaction which is given at a regular school, and will not be successful when allowed to attend school on their own schedules, as is the norm for online programs while other students thrive in the relative isolation of online classes.

Certification programs are also an important part of a professional security worker's career development. Certification is usually granted by a professional organization with an interest in a specific specialty, and may require demonstration of a specified minimum years of experience coupled with completion of a self study course and test, or a series of live classes or seminars. If it can be said, in general, that a college education is intended to produce a well rounded individual capable of learning whatever skills are necessary for success, then certifications can be described as recognizing the already existing expertise in specific topics of those who earn them. They are not competing forms of recognition as much as they are complimentary forms.

Not all certificates are the same, however. Any organization can award certificates so it is incumbent on the student to find out which are the respected ones in their desired field. It must be remembered that no certificate that is respected is a trivial accomplishment, and that the student should be prepared to put in the required work. Since certificate granting organizations can be more difficult for a student to evaluate on their own than a university, a short list of respected certificate granting organizations will be included at the end of this section.

Both degrees and legitimate certification earn their bearers professional credibility and demonstrate a level of knowledge and skill that an employer will respect.

The significant investments in both money and time required to earn them not only increases the earnings potential of their bearers, but also increase the number of professional opportunities afforded them throughout their careers.

Examples of Respected Certifying Bodies

This list is not exhaustive, and is not intended to recommend or disapprove any program. It is provided to give the student a starting point for their own research into certification that suits their career needs.

- American Society for Industrial Security
  CPP Certified Protection Professional
  PCI Professional Certified Investigator
  PSP Physical Security Professional

- International Foundation for Protection Officers
  CPO Certified Protection Officer
  CSS Certified Security Supervisor

- Academy of Security educators and Trainers
  CST Certified Security Trainer

- Executive Protection Institute
  PPS Personal Protection Specialist

- International Association for Healthcare Security and Safety
  CHPA Certified Healthcare Protection Administrator

- Disaster Recovery Institute
  CDRP Certified Disaster Recovery Professional

Triumph Through Training

The following article explains how an experienced immigration investigator, though untrained in its formal application, used the technique of behavioral profiling to deny entry into the U.S. of an individual now believed to have been entering the country to participate in the 9/11 hijackings. Behavioral profiling is sometimes called "street smarts" and it was once assumed that only through years of experience could someone learn to develop this "inexplicable" insight. We now know that the technique is teachable and is used successfully throughout the world to thwart criminals and terrorists.

Fighting Terrorism Requires Training[2]

Jose Melendez-Perez saved untold lives and possibly the Capitol or the White House by turning away a Saudi visitor at the Orlando airport immigration check point in August 2001.

We hope homeland security officials draw the obvious lesson from Melendez-Perez's experience: behavior profiling, rather than bomb and weapons screening, is the best way to protect commercial aircraft from terrorist attack.

Melendez-Perez, an immigration inspector, told the national Sept. 11 Commission at a recent hearing that something about Mohamed al-Kahtani gave him "the creeps." While al-Kahtani's documents seemed genuine, his "arrogant and military" manner was suspicious. Beyond that, al-Kahtani had a one-way ticket, no hotel reservation and no credit cards - all of which made him appear even more suspect. Melendez-Perez went with his "gut" and denied al-Kahtani entry.

Officials now believe al-Kahtani was meant to serve as the fifth hijacker aboard United Airlines Flight 93, which crashed in a Pennsylvania field after a passenger uprising. The fact that only four hijackers were aboard might have helped the uprising succeed.

Without calling it that, Melendez-Perez was using a form of Behavior Pattern Recognition, albeit in this case a somewhat primitive version of an Israeli-style passenger observance and screening technique now formally in use at only one airport in the nation - Boston's Logan International.

Massport officials just announced an expansion of the plan, instituted by former Ben Gurion Airport security head Rafi Ron, to include the training of federal air marshals, supplementing the state police and airport employees who now use BPR.

Other recent revelations from the ongoing Sept. 11 Commission inquiry underscore the weakness of an aviation security system that still relies on weapons screening. The hijackers apparently had knives and mace, not just small box cutters, to subdue — and kill — passengers and crew. Routinely, knives, mace and even guns still are getting through airport security checkpoints.

And, nine of the 19 hijackers actually were flagged by a Federal Aviation Administration computer profiling system known as CAPPS, which triggered further scrutiny. The flagged hijackers' luggage was checked for bombs and cleared, but apparently the hijackers themselves walked right through checkpoints armed with knives.

It wasn't the discovery of a knife or bomb that caused this one astute immigration inspector to bar a potential hijacker from entering the country. It was something far more intangible. Adopting Behavior Pattern Recognition at every airport will ensure good training replicates Melendez-Perez's good instincts.

Much like behavioral profiling, it was often assumed that emergency management was only learned "on the job," and that years of experience in a public agency was the only way to gain that knowledge. We now know that this is also untrue, and that the techniques and strategies of emergency management are available to anyone motivated to learn them.

SECURITY SPECIALTIES

Many people would never consider a career in the security industry, as the only part of it to which they have been exposed is the uniformed guard performing access control duties. Few really understand the variety and complexity of functions and responsibilities that a professional security provider or EMS responder can be tasked with through the course of a career.

Earlier, we described the security industry and the security functions found throughout business as diverse. Here we will explore several specialties within the security and emergency response fields. As you read them, think about how each is represented within the security disciplines or EMS skill sets. Neither the list of specialties nor the duties and tasks given for each are intended to be comprehensive, but rather an introduction and thought provoking exercise for those beginning their security careers.

Medical Facility Security

Medical facilities have many and diverse security needs which must be met before effective and safe medical care can be given. The patients in hospital are an at risk population for many reasons: physical weakness, impaired mobility and impaired psychological coping skills are common traits. The facility must remain open and accessible at all hours, and no one requiring medical care may be turned away, but the safety of the patients and staff requires some security control. It can be a very complex system.

Imagine a public hospital system in a large, urban area. There are thousands of employees throughout the system, and tens of thousands of patients, visitors and other guests daily. Uniformed security officers, who may be armed or not depending on the perceived need, must be almost chameleon like in their ability to adapt their behavior and communication style, as the situation requires. Patients may act out due to adverse drug effects, disease or injury processes or psychological impairment, and visiting family members are under significant stress. There is a very fine line between normal stress reactions and activities that negatively impact health care operations, and the security officers are expected to demonstrate sensitivity and understanding in determining that line unique in the industry. This is especially important in the both the medical and psychological emergency departments, where patients are so frequently under the influence of alcohol or street drugs when they first arrive. The ability to communicate with physicians and nurses one moment, with distraught family members the next and with injured or ill patients of any cultural background is not easily trained or learned, but is absolutely necessary in the health care environment,

Technical security measures play a major part in a large medical system, and impact nearly every employee's work performance. Confidentiality is a legal requirement, so information security is planned into the procedures that are then taught and enforced. Large facilities cannot employ enough security officers to be everywhere, so very large surveillance systems involving cameras and emergency communications devices are required. On floors where infants and newborns are cared for, systems are in place to prevent the rare but tragic instances of infant abduction. These systems often involve high tech sensors that command doors to close and elevators to stop when an infant is taken past specific programmed areas. The planning, installation, maintenance and use of these systems can be a major undertaking for specialists in this security area.

Hospitals will become centers of activity after any terrorist attack, with both victims and the "worried well" clamoring for limited resources. Part of the preparation for this event is training all employees in their roles and even training non-security staff to assist in security duties as necessary. This could mean something as simple as having the facilities crew prepared to use their forklift to move a large barricade for traffic control, or to set up prefabricated chemical decontamination stations.

Supervisory officers and especially those in positions of management must be prepared to wear many hats. They are responsible for training both their security forces and all other employees in security procedures. They will need to be able to explain the facility's security needs in terms of both safety and business sense, and must be able to operate and communicate on equal terms with other heads of departments in order to gain their respect and cooperation. They will need to keep current with legal requirements unique to medical care givers, as well as with the industry's understanding of "best practices" through active participation in professional organizations such as ASIS and IAHSS.

The career opportunities in health care system security are enormous for individuals with the right combination of education and sensitivity.

Security in Business and Industry

Opportunities for security in business and industry are as varied as the environments in which people work to sell or produce goods and services. Protection of people and assets is the priority when working for a business organization, whether it is a small auto parts store or a multinational bank. These environments are where most people notice the efforts of the security provider as they go through their daily lives, The uniformed guard called to unlock a door or checking employee's access badges is often a part of our daily lives, but it barely begins to describe the depth of work done in corporate security.

A company's assets may be physical, and so loss prevention specialists are used to reduce theft from employees and "shoplifting," but their assets may be information and so the skills of information and information systems security specialists would be in more need. Corporate security, however, mitigates far more than simple theft.

In case of a natural disaster or terrorist attack business continuity is insured by, for example, preplanned off site storage of the proprietary information and records needed to get the company back up and running quickly. The corporate information technology (IT) department will manage this recovery plan, but in doing so they are fulfilling a security function and will require the services of specialists in information systems security. Companies that perform sensitive work for the government are required by the terms of their contracts to hire trustworthy employees and to protect any classified information from theft by employees or outsiders. Personnel security specialists will be required to provide the background checks and other investigations as allowed by law to show that adequate steps to protect the information have been taken.

One aspect of corporate security often overlooked is the physical security specialists who design building features, decorations and landscaping to enhance security. After the Oklahoma City bombing, decorative flower planters made of concrete filled with earth and attractive plants became common features. While attractive, their true purpose is to provide "stand off" distance between the building and where a vehicle borne bomb might be parked. Landscaping with hedges and lighting can enhance physical security through canalizing legitimate visitor and employee traffic while making approach by bad actors more difficult. Specialists skilled in designing these passive and cost effective techniques are in great demand.

Large corporations often have their own intelligence gathering risk management departments attempting to determine what the most likely threats to a business's interests around the world are and how to mitigate them. Security providers at this level require education and training in international affairs, current events, counter terrorism and, often, executive protection.

From the loss prevention "store detective" checking that the door is locked after the business day is over, to the risk management specialist evaluating threats to business interests and personnel on a different continent, there will always be a need for professional corporate security providers. Contracted, consultants or in house employees, talented generalists and skillful specialists will always be an integral part of business plans.

Public Utilities

Utilities are a part of the nation's critical infrastructure that we seldom give much thought to. Like the air we breathe, uninterrupted supplies of power and water are taken for granted and, indeed, our cities would quickly become uninhabitable without them. It does not require much imagination to picture the pandemonium that would break out if the water supply to a large city was interrupted, or if telephone communications was suddenly lost. We have experience with large scale power outages, but those have been relatively short term. With thousands of miles of transmission wires and pipelines, far flung and unguarded power switching stations, cell phone towers and water reservoirs make securing the entire system almost impossible.

An attack on our utilities might not be recognized immediately as there are many reasons parts of the systems fail occasionally. Repair crews may be the first to

585 CAREERS AND THE ROLE OF EDUCATION

realize that the damage was purposeful when they survey the damage for repair, so they should be trained to recognize signs of tampering or destruction. Because of the large area covered, and the numerous points it is possible to attack, uniformed security officers usually have limited roles to play.

Security in the increasingly automated utilities industry starts as an engineering problem. Water quality is tested for adulterants as it flows to customers; patterns of electrical outages are monitored to ensure an attack would be quickly identified and routed around. The computers that control and monitor the utility delivery are themselves targets for attack, so information systems security is a priority. Employees throughout the system are taught physical security awareness because they know how the area for which they have responsibility should work and how it should look.

One area where uniformed guard forces are evident is in securing the nation's nuclear power plants. The uniformed guards are armed and trained like police SWAT teams with military grade body armor and automatic weapons, but they are only part of the security team. All the disciplines are represented as information systems security specialists protect the computers that control the plant, information security specialists protect the sensitive and classified information that necessarily goes with nuclear technology and personnel security is a major priority with very strict rules from the Department of Energy dictating the standards for background checks and security clearances.

Security and Social Services

Social services agencies operate in a fashion that is difficult to secure. Government and private organizations like the Red Cross and Salvation Army provides social services during emergencies and on an ongoing basis to populations that are considered "at risk" in one way or another.

In an emergency such as a major natural disaster, thousands of people can be left homeless and without adequate supplies for survival. Though looting and other similar behavior is, as we've discussed in a previous chapter, not common, there is always a risk involved in bringing supplies into a disaster area. The stress of the experience and fear of the unknown can create a volatile mixture if those who are coming for aid get the impression there is not enough for them to get "their fair share." Added to the potential threats from disgruntled clients are the general safety concerns for anyone in a disaster area. These considerations together make the job of providing a secure environment very challenging.

The population served by social services agencies on a day to day basis is similarly potentially volatile. They are, at a much higher percentage than the total population, afflicted with mental health problems, including abuse of street drugs and alcohol, and have been known to attack social workers and other care givers.

Security providers in these organizations walk a fine line between access and security. Because some of the organization's clients have had trouble with the criminal justice system, seeing uniforms may dissuade some who need help from asking for it. The population served is usually found in the worst parts of a city, or in the hardest hit portions of a disaster scene, so the resources cannot be sited in the safest areas without reducing their ability to provide assistance.

Security providers in this environment must be sensitive to the needs of the community served, but also to the safety needs of the rest of the organizations' members. If employees are injured, or supplies stolen, the agency cannot perform its function, yet they must operate in high risk and high stress environments. Much like security providers in the health care field, social services security is more than just a physical security problem and requires a specialist that understands the legal and practical aspects of information security and confidentiality as well as the physical threats.

Security in Public Safety

While the concept that the security industry and law enforcement have different tasks has been stressed in this chapter, there are aspects of security practice that are necessary for the safety of emergency response personnel. We have explored the reactive nature of law enforcement, and it seems fire and EMS response would also be reactive since they are called to incidents that are already in process, but even in the public safety field prevention is considered better than reaction. Because of the constant pressure to cut costs in government and the rising demands placed on the smaller departments by an increasing population, for example, police crime prevention patrols and other tactics have largely fallen by the wayside, and fire or EMS safety programs are funded by local businesses or civic organizations, if they exist at all.

In the case of response to a major emergency, we have seen that scene safety and security is a function and responsibility defined and assigned in the ICS framework. An obvious example of physical security concerns is the security of the equipment and material gathered. Comprehensive resource management requires accountability for resource availability, which cannot be guaranteed if it is left unprotected. Is this really best done with police forces, or could their resources and skills be better utilized elsewhere?

Safety is also a security concern. The safety of responding personnel must be a paramount concern: injured responders cannot rescue anyone else and take resources from the incident's other victims. Fire departments, especially, have experience in gauging the safety of a damaged structure or disaster scene, and part of their security function would include identifying unsafe areas and developing procedures to ensure a maximum of safety for those who must enter them. NIMS compliant agencies were not common in 2005, NIMS having been released by FEMA in 2004, but the ICS concept was already accepted and trained by most police departments and nearly all fire departments and rescue squads. Agencies responded from all across the country and had to be integrated into a unified command structure to be of service. The potential for injury due to inadequate communication interoperability was high, and became a driving force nation-wide in NIMS compliance.

Private security companies have a supporting role to play in a disaster. When hurricane Katrina struck the New Orleans area in 2005, a small army of private security workers were mobilized by corporations to protect their properties and reduce the damage caused. The presence of these security agents enhanced the abilities of the public safety responders in several ways. They searched and secured large hotel complexes and flushed out stragglers hiding within them. An armed, sometimes heavily, and visible security presence created a calm area within the city that allowed responders to concentrate their response to other hard hit areas and provided a safe area for material storage. The security industry also provided hundreds of extra eyes and ears to monitor the changing status of their areas of responsibility, which provided intelligence to the emergency responders allowing them to more effectively manage their resources. In at least one instance, local police and fire responders were housed during the worst of the storm and afterwards, in an unofficial effort for mutual support, in a large hotel that was being secured by private security forces. This allowed the public responders to stay where they were needed rather than commuting each day to the official billeting area over two hours away. The larger corporate security teams even brought their own EMS medics prepared to render aid to their responding employees, contractors and anyone else who needed the assistance.

In the case of a major terrorist attack, the model for response would likely be the same. Security and emergency response forces, both public and private, will work together to perform their different tasks and the private sector, having been trained in public sector protocols, will integrate seamlessly. With most of the nation's critical infrastructure in private ownership, it makes sense both financially and practically, for the private sector to be heavily involved in the protection of its assets.

SUMMARY

The private security industry is a diverse and expanding one. The opportunities for professional security providers are almost limitless for those with the energy and ability to find a niche for themselves. Education and certification enhance the quality and professionalism of the industry, and is available for any of the disciplines in modern security practice. Professional security providers no longer have to be embarrassed or ashamed by the industry in which they work, and can take pride in their contributions to the national economy and to homeland security.

No matter what the organization, business, or function, anyone or anything can be a potential target for terrorism. It has become incumbent on us all to be more vigilant and more aware of our surroundings than ever before and we must all be aware that safety does not come from policemen, and that news does not always happen to someone else. It will take each of us in a combined, concerted, and continuous effort to safeguard lives and property in this new security era.

ADDITIONAL DISCUSSION TOPICS

- What are some medical and health measures that would be necessary after a large scale disaster that are not normally encountered by hospital clinical workers? How can they be prepared to provide those measures?

- You are a police officer responding to a bomb threat in a large, four storey office building. You have decided to use office workers for the first bomb sweep since they know what should and should not be there. Write brief instructions to the workers explaining what to look for, where to look and what they should do if they find something unusual or out of place.

- What information do you think you could get from an experienced "Department of Water and Power" worker that would help identify potential terrorist targets in his area?

- Why would social services organizations' operations make good terrorist targets for secondary attacks?

Endnotes

[1] The following is from Career Opportunities in Security, ASIS International, 2005.

[2] The following is from Career Opportunities in Security, ASIS International, 2005.

[3] Boston Herald Editorial Staff, Sunday, February 1, 2004. Found on the Web at http://news.bostonherald.com/opinion/view.bg?articleid=4118&format=

[4] Boston Herald Editorial Staff, Sunday, February 1, 2004. Found on the Web at http://news.bostonherald.com/opinion/view.bg?articleid=4118&format=

[5] Boston Herald Editorial Staff, Sunday, February 1, 2004. Found on the Web at http://news.bostonherald.com/opinion/view.bg?articleid=4118&format=